'collects a rich supply of testimony [which] confirms the consistent picture of an advancing northward tide of clash and resistance'
The Australian

'...[a] detailed, authoritative study of the deadly 80-year conflict between Aborigines and white settlers in 19th-century Queensland.'
Sydney Morning Herald

'lays out noisy piece of evidence after noisy piece of evidence that the movement of indigenous people from their lands in Queensland was nasty, brutal and murderous'
Canberra Times

'Bottoms' comprehensive delineation of the Queensland massacres clearly demonstrates that the reality of violence can no longer be denied. It is a story that needs to be told.'
Journal of the Royal Australian Historical Society

'*Conspiracy of Silence* reminds us that local events that took place a century ago have the power to resonate nationally well into the twenty-first century.'
Australian Historical Studies

CONSPIRACY OF SILENCE

Queensland's Frontier Killing-Times

TIMOTHY BOTTOMS

ALLEN&UNWIN
SYDNEY•MELBOURNE•AUCKLAND•LONDON

First published in 2013

Copyright © Timothy Bottoms 2013

Allen & Unwin
Sydney, Melbourne, Auckland, London

83 Alexander Street
Crows Nest NSW 2065
Australia
Phone: (61 2) 8425 0100
Email: info@allenandunwin.com
Web: www.allenandunwin.com

Cataloguing-in-Publication details are available
from the National Library of Australia
www.trove.nla.gov.au

ISBN 978 1 74331 382 4

Maps by Ian Faulkner
Index by Puddingburn
Set in 11/15 pt Granjon by Midland Typesetters, Australia
Printed by Griffin Press

10 9 8 7 6 5 4

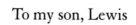

To my son, Lewis

Contents

Acknowledgements

This book came out of researching and writing *A History of Cairns—City of the South Pacific 1770–1995* (PhD 2002). This was a time of incredible violence between Aboriginals and white settlers on the local frontier and I began to check other regions to see how Cairns and district compared. During this process, I caught up with Ernie Grant, a Jirrbal/Girramay Elder from Tully, and discovered that he had been researching massacres in the Tully district and elsewhere for about 45 years. Ernie's faith in me led him to use my historical research skills at what was then the Indigenous Education & Training Alliance, where I worked on material covering the whole of Queensland. Ever since, Dr Ernie Grant has been a staunch supporter and friend. It is him that I wish to thank for his encouragement and backing.

Similarly, Professor Raymond Evans' response to my work gave me inspiration and confirmed the quality of my research, and I am extremely grateful to him not just for this, but for his continued encouragement and comment over the years. I also thank the National Museum of Australia and Dr Peter Stanley from the Centre for Historical Research, whose award of a Visiting Fellowship in early 2009, gave me the necessary impetus to take on the book full-time. Also Matthew Coxhill, whose faith in my work and strenuous efforts at promotion enabled publication to come to fruition.

Many others have been a great source of strength in unearthing the truth about how Queensland was acquired by Europeans, including: Howard Thomas, Viv Sinnamon, Ray Rex, Nick Heym, Jasse Walton, Ross Verevis,

Steve Swayne, Michael Watt, Alan Williams, Giselle Sheehy, Allen and Mark Chapman, Greg McKeown, Ken Hossen, David Williams, Steve O'Hallorahan, Charles Silver, Tony Kloss, Richard Lee Long, Barry and Carolla Hunter, Darrin Lee Long and Theo and Francis Utzinger. On a professional and collegial level: Helen Tolcher, Robert Ørsted-Jensen, Steve Mullins, Ros Kidd, John Taylor, Bruce Rigsby, Cathie Clements, Sally Babidge, Jane Lydon, Patrick Collins, Hilary Kuhn, Carolyn Nolan, Paul Gorecki, Peter Bell and Iain Davidson. Also The Royal Historical Society of Queensland, and Pearl Eatts who kindly shared her photographs of Skull Hole at Bladensburg National Park, south of Winton; John Dymock whose original research was extremely helpful in covering the Gulf Country; the staff of James Cook University Library (Cairns campus), particularly Kathy Fowler, and the John Oxley Library staff who have gone beyond the call of duty. The National Library of Australia, particularly the Petherick Room, as well as the staff at the Australian Institute of Aboriginal and Torres Strait Islander Studies, whose interest and help was greatly appreciated; they're a great mob. To the Rockhampton, Clermont, Emerald and Goondiwindi Libraries and their staff, I found them most helpful and cooperative in digging for local information; also Robynne Hayward at the Mitchell Library (State Library of NSW). Rick Wigglesworth of Sofala, for allowing me to photograph his notched 1873 Alexander Henry Carbine; Jonathan Richards for his sharing and assistance in chasing primary sources; similarly, members of the Professional Historians Association (Qld) for their positive feedback; Liz Hatte from Northern Archaeology Consultants and Col McLennan from the Jangga Aboriginal Corporation, who showed not just wonderful hospitality, but also passionate support for the project. Lastly, to all the many and varied authors whose writing has enabled me to follow the trails of our colonial history, both primary and secondary— I thank you.

The author acknowledges the generous assistance of the National Museum of Australia through its National Museum of Australia Visiting Fellowship Program.

List of Maps

Map 1.1 Some Massacres on the Australian Colonial Frontier

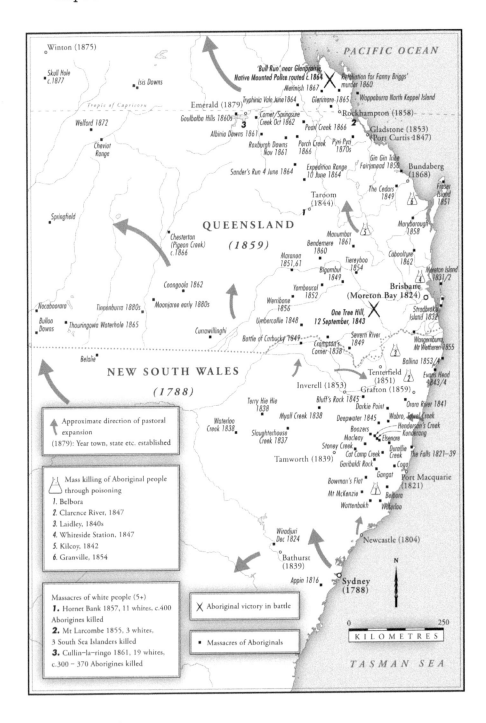

Map 1.2 Some Massacres on the Frontier——North Queensland

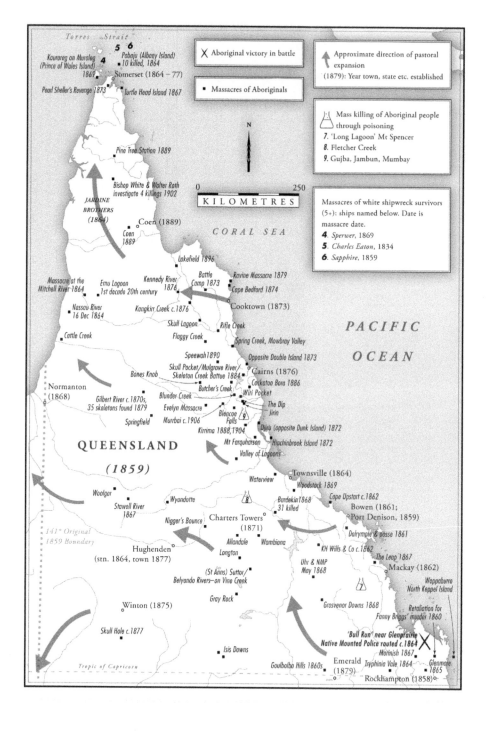

Map 1.3 Some Massacres on the Frontier——Gulf Country

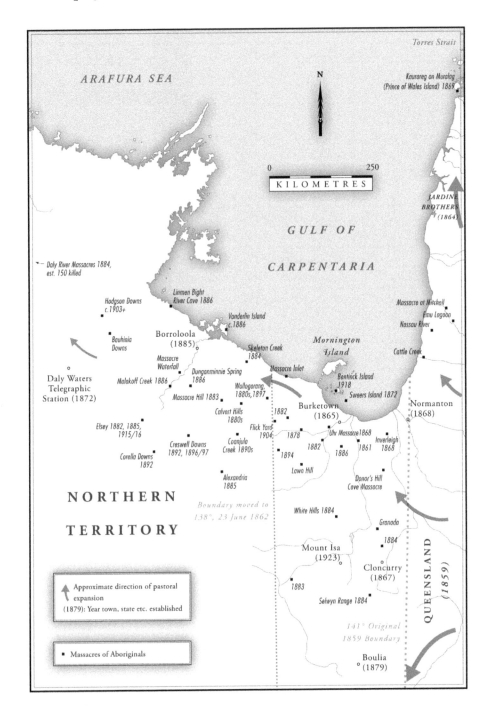

Map 1.4 Some Massacres on the Frontier——Channel Country

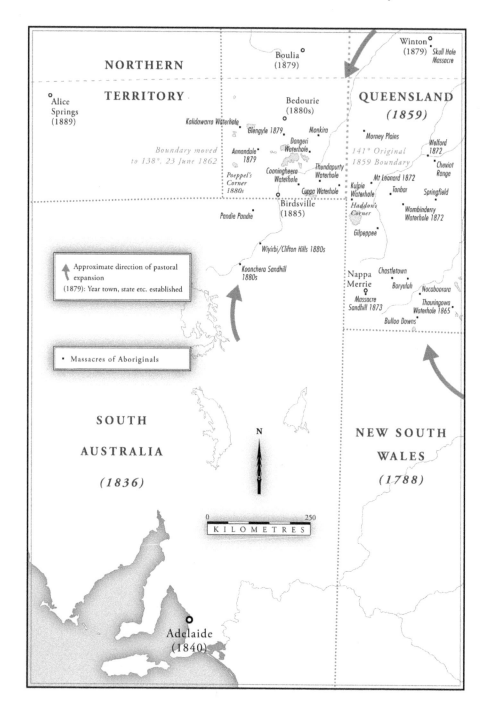

NORTHERN

Winton ○
(1879) *Skull Hole
Massacre*

Boulia ○
(1879)

Bedourie
(1880s)

○ Alice
Springs
(1889)

TERRITORY

QUEENSLAND
(1859)

Kalidawarra Waterhole

Glengyle 1879

Monkira

Morney Plains

*Welford
1872*

*Dangeri
Waterhole*

*Boundary moved
to 138°, 23 June 1862*

*Annandale
1879*

*141° Original
1859 Boundary*

*Cheviot
Range*

*Cooningheera
Waterhole*

*Thundapurty
Waterhole*

Mt Leonard 1872

*Poeppel's
Corner
1880s*

Cuppa Waterhole

*Kulpie
Waterhole*

Tanbar

Springfield

Birdsville
(1885)

*Haddon's
Corner*

*Wombinderry
Waterhole 1872*

Pandie Pandie

Gilpeppee

Wiyirbi/Clifton Hills 1880s

Approximate direction of pastoral
expansion
(1879): Year town, state etc. established

*Koonchera Sandhill
1880s*

Nappa
Merrie ○

Chastletown

Baryulah

Nocaboorara

*Massacre
Sandhill 1873*

*Thauringowa
Waterhole 1865*

Bulloo Downs

• Massacres of Aboriginals

SOUTH

AUSTRALIA

(1836)

N

NEW SOUTH

WALES

(1788)

0   250
KILOMETRES

○ Adelaide
(1840)

Map 2 Pastoral Expansion and Settlement in Queensland

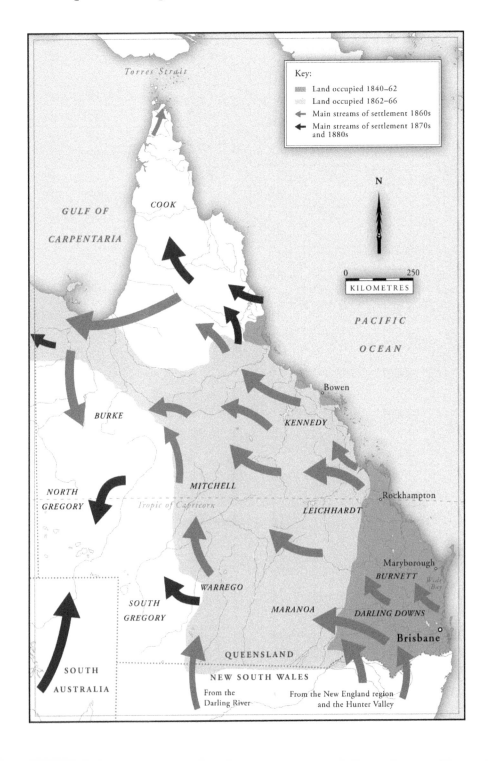

Key:

▨ Land occupied 1840–62
▨ Land occupied 1862–66
← Main streams of settlement 1860s
← Main streams of settlement 1870s
and 1880s

N

0   250
KILOMETRES

Torres Strait

GULF OF
CARPENTARIA

COOK

PACIFIC

OCEAN

Bowen

BURKE

KENNEDY

NORTH
GREGORY

MITCHELL

Tropic of Capricorn

LEICHHARDT

Rockhampton

Maryborough

BURNETT   Wide Bay

WARREGO

SOUTH
GREGORY

MARANOA

DARLING DOWNS

Brisbane

SOUTH
AUSTRALIA

QUEENSLAND

NEW SOUTH WALES

From the
Darling River

From the New England region
and the Hunter Valley

Foreword

The cruellest lies are often told in silence.

Robert Louis Stevenson

As an expression of national soul-searching, the word 'blemish' gained wide currency in Australian political life around the turn of the Millennium. Prime Minister Kevin Rudd used it in his National Apology to the Stolen Generation in 2008, while Prime Minister John Howard before him had employed it many times during the late 1990s and early 2000s to dispel what he considered to be undue historical emphases on acts of wrong-doing in Australia's past.

Yet, as a term of self-criticism, 'blemish' is a curiously comforting word. *The Concise Oxford Dictionary* defines it as a 'physical or moral flaw' that sullies 'the beauty or perfection' of something—in this case, the Australian nation. The political message, therefore, implies the existence of a few isolated blemishes, like sun spots, on an otherwise faultless complexion. In John Howard's and my own adolescence, the word had currency mainly in relation to our generation's spotty teenage pimples that we camouflaged and abolished with a product called *Clearasil*.

'Blemish', however, is clearly an insufficient term and, indeed, an insultingly inappropriate one when used to describe the forceful dispossession of many hundreds of small Aboriginal 'First Nations' by incoming settler colonists over a period of more than a century. Though it may be a word that many white Australians can happily live with today, most Aboriginal people would find it both risible and illusory. A blemish, after all, is only skin-deep. In summary, the description hardly approaches meeting the deeper historical case.

As Tim Bottoms' massacre maps of Queensland in this volume alone reveal, we are not looking here so much at a historical 'blemish' but more at a protracted case of flaming acne. For the average reader, this may in itself be more than enough to digest in one gulp; but it needs to be emphasised that this is only an impressionistic example of the frontier violence that actually occurred. There is a general consensus today among researchers that a massacre constitutes the killing of five or more non-combatants in a single, violent attack. This, of course, immediately omits all of the random single or group murders of less than five, which were probably legion.

Furthermore, it has now become clearer that the killing incidents occasioned by the State-financed, equipped and run Native Police squads, which operated in Queensland for more than half a century between 1849 and the 1900s, would have numbered in the thousands. The historian, Robert Ørsted-Jensen has recently calculated that the average number of people killed in any one of these so-called 'dispersals' was in the vicinity of eleven. If this is correct, we may be potentially looking at several thousand *officially* organised and sanctioned Aboriginal massacres alone, before we even begin to take into account the havoc wreaked by private settlers with their guns and poison.

Of course, it has been known for some considerable time that the Queensland frontier was a particularly vicious one. It was widely reported as such in the nineteenth century, while, in the mid to late twentieth century, professional historians, such as Noel Loos, Henry Reynolds and myself, revisited the issue in some detail. On the one hand, there did exist a powerfully sustained conspiracy of silence, shielding perpetrators from social censure and legal prosecution as well as protecting the ongoing communal reputation of the colony and State; but, on the other, there was also a considerable stream of minority reportage, in the colonial press, in official documentation, in private or public letters, in diaries, pioneer memoirs and confessionals, in illustrations and even occasional photographs, compiled and preserved by whistle-blowers, activists, eye-witnesses, bystanders and even perpetrators that pointed to the contours of a desperate and bloody struggle.

Aboriginal survivors and their descendants knew so much of it too, and far more intimately and painfully, passing the stories down orally over the generations, as Ernie Grant's arresting chapter on the Cardwell district attests. Yet, during the recent Howard years, and in the wake of the Mabo decision and Prime Minister Keating's forthright Redfern Address, a campaign of rebuttal was mounted by the political Right to deny the accuracy of such claims. This misguided and vindictive crusade, dubbed a 'history war' against 'black arm-band' historians, which gained substantial trajectory from support in the Australian mass media, particularly the Murdoch press, has presently served to debunk the concept of intensely violent colonial origins in many white Australian minds.

Conspiracy of Silence, therefore, operates as a roadmap back into what seems, from a modern perspective, to be a barely conceivable past. Bottoms' careful and wide-reaching research takes us all over Queensland and revisits reported massacre sites, both historically and geographically. The places are visually and spatially identified and the recorded details retold. It is a harrowing trip. Reading through these chapters, I could not help but think of how Queensland's Aboriginal–European contact history is rather like a strange amalgam of two well-known television science fiction series, *Dr Who* and *Star Trek*. First, we hear the raspy, blood-chilling cry of the Daleks: 'Exterminate! Exterminate!'; and then, in the post-frontier phase, the flat, monotonal command from *Star Trek*: 'We are Borg. You will be assimilated. Resistance is useless'. Not pretty images to be sure, but then this is not a very nice story.

It is, however, clearly one that needs to be known and retold, both for the sake of the victims and in the name of honesty and reconciliation. The colonial conquest of Queensland involved the taking of a land-mass around two-thirds the size of Europe. This territory contained considerably more than 35 per cent of Australia's Aboriginal population, as compared with, say, around 19 per cent in New South Wales and less than one per cent in Tasmania. Queensland's Aboriginal population probably numbered around

250,000 (and possibly as many as 300,000). During the nineteenth century, around 4–500,000 incomers utterly dispossessed them. And, by the years of World War One, Aboriginal numbers were seemingly less than 20,000—an attrition rate well above 90 per cent. Up to 1500 of the invading population had also perished in the process. Queensland, therefore, is the pre-eminent region where the historical problem of dispossession in Australia is to be best and most comprehensively understood. This volume, *Conspiracy of Silence*, unfolds, at ground-level and in stark outline, how it all happened.

Raymond Evans
July 2012

Prologue—The Reason

I fell in love with the Australian people and landscape as I grew up. I remember playing in the ruins of a white settler's stone house on the other side of the creek that divided the sparsely populated outer suburb of the South Australian township of Naracoorte (established 1845), where my family initially lived. The house had been a relatively substantial structure, which as a child made me wonder why it had been abandoned. Similarly, the historic colonial settlement of Robe (1846) in the late 1950s, near the majestic cliffs and swelling, pounding southern seas of the Great Australian Bight, intrigued but never quite answered how the land was acquired. The sunburnt plains of northern Victoria and the blue-brown hills of southern NSW dissected by the mighty upper reaches of the Murray River, all permeated my youthful soul, but left a nagging silence about our colonial period.

Like so many other white Anglo-Saxon Protestant Australians I grew up blithely unaware of Aboriginal Australia. Throughout my youth, despite my love of the Australian countryside, there seemed to be something missing and I couldn't put my finger on it. As a schoolboy I often felt there was a hazy confusion about our colonial history, for some strange reason one could not really get a core understanding of early white settlement. The story was always brief and swept over rather too quickly. As an undergraduate I found Australian history predictable and boring, so I studied American, South Asian, Ancient and Medieval history. In the rural highlands of Armidale, New England (in northern NSW), my intellect was stimulated, not by my nation's history, but that of Medieval Europe, and by political scientist, Colin Tatz. It was his lectures that identified the disparity in treatment of indigenous Australians, particularly in Queensland. In this rural university town I also noticed Aboriginal Australians for the first time. There had been few or none where I grew up down south in Albury.

However, it was not until my return from travelling overland to Europe in 1979, when I took a job teaching Aranda children on the edge of the Simpson Desert, that I started to see another side of our country's history, not only of our colonial period, but of Australian history in general. Interpretations that were being propounded did not quite gel. Some Aranda Elders told of being whipped by squatters twenty to 30 years before, and there were ominous hints of other nefarious acts having been committed. On several occasions I saw incidents of racism against my Aboriginal pupils and was indignantly horrified. Yes, they were different from children I had come across in my background and upbringing, but they were lovely kids. During my time at Ltyentye Apurte (Santa Teresa) I had to take several days off school because of illness. Late one afternoon during my recovery I heard a murmur of Aranda words followed by a tentative knock on the door. Upon opening the door I was presented with all my boys from school asking after my well-being, and not far away on a rise in the ground stood the girls. Their concern for me was truly humbling. On trips out from the settlement with my class, I learnt much about the Aranda perspective of the landscape and a hint of their traditional cosmology. Their intimate knowledge of the fauna and flora made me realise that there was far more to Australia than I had previously understood. It was the start of an awakening which was to take several more years, for I moved to Sydney to chase a career in acting, radio announcing and producing; skills which would later prove advantageous in far north Queensland.

In 1984 I started teaching at the isolated Aboriginal community of Kowanyama on the west coast of Cape York Peninsula. It was on the traditional lands of the Kunjen, Kokoberra and Yir Yoront that I truly began to learn about the other side of the frontier from the Aboriginal perspective. Inspired by Henry Reynolds and Noel Loos' work and frustrated by

Bjelke-Petersen's Education Department and the Department of Aboriginal and Islander Affairs, I moved to Cairns. Here I discovered, despite a noticeable indigenous population, that there was little readily available information about the local rainforest people, the Djabugay–Yidinydji. This stimulated me to begin research with the local university's Cairns campus. Surprisingly, no one had bothered before. It was a revelation to me that there was a people with such a rich human history and culture, yet it was virtually unknown to local white Australians. I discovered a completely different way of looking at the landscape—and a more fascinating one than that portrayed in the 'Pioneering Myth'.

Upon completing my MA(Qual), 'Djarrugan—the Last of the Nesting' (James Cook University), which looked at the Djabugay–Yidinydji culture and history, I was invited to help a local clan group, the Malanbarra Yidinydji at Gordonvale, to the south of Cairns. Again I found warm and friendly people who had incredible stories to tell, many of which were not very edifying with regards to white settlement. At the same time I was employed as a visiting lecturer for the TAFE Aboriginal Ranger Training Program on the west coast of Cape York. This involved flying out to Aurukun, Kowanyama, Burketown and Doomadgee as well as Mornington Island and Thursday Island in the Torres Strait. Living and socialising with the rangers and their families and friends brought an increased understanding of their humanity and the difficulties they faced in dealing with the various levels of government and the broader white community. The acceptance of me by my Aboriginal friends and their wonderful humour brought into focus the need to be more honest in understanding our shared history.

I then gained employment as the Wet Tropics Ranger Trainer Coordinator, which involved adults from the Djabugay, Malanbarra Yidinydji and Yirrganydji in the Cairns district. Our mob attained an inspiring esprit de corps, only to be disappointed by the State and Federal governments' short-term funding approach; a problem that still permeates government funding programs and contributes to the failure of many promising projects.

Working and socialising with the rangers, as well as meeting other family members, made me realise that to write history one has to be more inclusive of all peoples who have contributed to the past life of a region. Thus, when I began researching and writing *A History of Cairns—City of the South Pacific (1770–1995)* I attempted to give as honest an interpretation from the primary sources as I possibly could. The resulting work was greeted by assessors and professional historians in a most positive way. My passion for writing balanced history encouraged my acceptance of research work from Ernie Grant, a Jirrbal/Girramay Elder, who asked me to join the team (at the Indigenous Education & Training Alliance, now the Indigenous Schooling Support Unit). I was then awarded a Visiting Fellowship at the National Museum of Australia in Canberra, where I began working full-time on this book.

The more I dug, the more appalled I was, not only by the violence and disregard for Aboriginal humanity, but also by what had been concealed. Australian historians had failed their fellow Australians dismally. They re-affirmed a form of 'spin' as being acceptable in their attempt to 'heroify' our history.

I drove the 2500 kilometres to Canberra photographing massacre sites, checking out the 'lie of the land', talking with people and digging for information in local libraries. From this research it was possible to gain a clearer insight into the difficulties faced by Europeans as they expanded their land-grab and dispossessed the original owners. The trip impressed on me the vastness and diversity of the terrain that comprises the State of Queensland. Much of the primary source writings were made more explicable because of this. It was also possible to garner some understanding of the respective Aboriginal cosmological perspectives (Dreamings). Patently the country that I had been brought up to think of as new was in fact seething with an ancient rhythm. Modern white Australia had tried to extirpate this; but despite the violent expropriation of the land, there was still a presence. In this book, I want to recapture that presence and give, or at least attempt to give, from primary source evidence, recognition of the murdered original inhabitants. The ramifications of this acknowledgement profoundly affects how we look at and portray Australian history. Our national story will require gracious attribution as it pervades and influences almost every aspect of previous historical interpretations and alters how we perceive ourselves as a nation: the good, the bad and the ugly.

My approach has been to address the thinking reader who wants to come to terms with and develop an awareness of the elements that comprise Australian history. This is a journey that involves facing the awful truth and becoming familiar with who the characters are, and where and why the action took place. Simplistically labelling these actions as 'racist' is not enough, as they need to be seen in the context of the period. Greed and frustration in the effort to make profits is part of the reason for the callous disregard for the humanity of indigenous Queenslanders. It is still a component motivator today, but without the killing and violence. The political machinations of the past and the subsequent consequences have relevance for contemporary Australia. I hope the reader will gain enough of an insight by journeying through this work to enable an effective contemplation of where we have been as a nation and what we can learn from this for the twenty-first century.

Introduction

It is the fashion usually, to speak of these poor people as 'aborigines': the idea meant to be conveyed being that they are a relic, so to speak, of the past, intruders in the path of the white man, and to be improved from the face of the earth accordingly. The argument seems to be, that God never intended them to live long in the land in which He had placed them. Therefore, says the white man, in his superiority of strength and knowledge, away with them, disperse them, shoot and poison them, until there be none remaining; we will utterly destroy them, their wives and their little ones, and all that they have, and we will go in and possess the land. This is no rhapsody or overstatement, but represents, in words, the actual policy which has been pursued towards the natives of the Australian colonies, and which is being acted upon vigorously in Queensland to-day.

George Carrington, Colonial Adventures and Experiences,
Bell and Daldy, London 1871, pp.143–44.

The Queensland frontier had been expanding for 40 years when George Carrington wrote about the treatment of Aboriginal people, and it was to last another 40-odd years after his publication in 1871. Carrington was not alone in recognising the mistreatment of Aboriginals, nor was his almost 'Jekyll and Hyde' approach to 'teaching the Blacks a lesson' unusual, for he too had been involved in frontier violence.[1] This apparent contradiction is prevalent in other works and suggests that initially certain frontiersmen (but not all) adopted the violent response, but then the continuing nature of the brutality impinged upon their conscience and caused them to acknowledge the events and decry them.[2]

Thus it appears that there are two distinct patterns of censorship and disclosure throughout the period covered in this book. Initially, while the killing was proceeding, perpetrators were trying to shut down the debate and conceal evidence, and whistle-blowers—who were far fewer on the ground but often quite determined, despite community censure—were continually trying to open it up. A see-saw interpretive struggle was going on, with the State very determinedly on the side of suppression of information. In fact, members of the Executive and wealthy landowners were largely orchestrating the suppression, while elements of the liberal press were trying 'to get at the truth', as good journalists should. Later, with the frontier winding down and closing around the 1890s and Federation, however, the denialism became far more hegemonic, pervading education, literature, media, religion and politics.[3] In short, a new total paradigm of 'good and peaceful Australia' was rapidly forged to shore up a new nationalism, and opposition became extremely muted and marginalised. The original smaller conspiracy in effect kept getting bigger and bigger.[4]

This attitude initially might seem quite perverse, but it can be seen as an Australian trait. Up to the 1970s, silence regarding the convict era and European–Aboriginal history pervaded Australia's understanding of its past.[5] It was only in the 1980s that there was a popular change in attitude regarding Australia's convict heritage, with the lead-up to the Bi-Centenary (1988). What had for over 150 years been hidden or 'swept under the carpet', started to be claimed by convict descendants. Australians began to not only acknowledge convict ancestors, but to be proud of them. At the end of the first decade of the twenty-first century, some 30 years on, one might be forgiven for thinking that a convict ancestor had never been considered a 'birthstain'. Just as previous generations had selective amnesia in relation to their convict history, so too has this approach been applied to violence and harsh treatment of Aboriginal Australians on the frontier, as it continually moved north and inland in Queensland for over 80 years.

Ross Johnston, in his 1982 volume, *The Call of the Land—A History of Queensland*, observes:

... with misunderstanding on both sides, and with determination
and conviction on the part of the Europeans that the land was theirs
for the taking, it was inevitable that conditions would deteriorate
on the frontier, virtually to a situation of a war. But it was a moving
frontier as new regions were being opened up, so that, while a more
established region would settle down to peace, the frontier, moving
further north or inland, would set the scene for a further bout of
fighting and killings.[6]

Other researchers have also confirmed this was the situation for Queenslanders, who 'inherited the harsh racist attitudes which had developed on
the expanding frontiers during the 1820s and 1830s'.[7]

Although we do have quantitative evidence of killings, we do not have
definitive evidence of the whole picture quantitatively. As the squatters
expanded their land-grab and the frontier continued to move, it becomes
extremely difficult to identify numbers because they were concealed. This is
particularly the case in inland Queensland, west of the area between Rockhampton and Townsville. Today only archaeological evidence hints at the
large numbers of people who once lived in the region. This is not because
there were no killings, but because the conspiracy of silence came into play.
Tony Roberts' research has identified that many of the squatters in the Gulf
and the Northern Territory border region came from central Queensland.
Some 140 years later, only half a dozen Aboriginal families lay claim to
their traditional lands in central Queensland.

In the Australian context, because of European technological developments, British settlers considered themselves at the apex of human evolution.
This affected the mindset of colonial Queenslanders who were influenced
by ideas and concepts developed in the late eighteenth and early nineteenth
centuries. The Great Chain of Being was one such concept, which 'ranked
all organic matter in hierarchical order, from the lowest to the highest. When
it came to mankind, Europeans were ranked pre-eminent'.[8] Aboriginal
Australians scraped in on the lowest human rung on this hierarchy. The
Great Chain of Being is about *all* creation not just humanity. This theory
was replaced by the new sciences from the eighteenth century in the form of

polygenism, which saw 'the descent of a [*Homo sapien*] species or race from more than one ancestral species'.[9] Historian Raymond Evans notes what a profound effect this functional theory had on Queensland:

> For its key effect, in suggesting that white genealogies proceed from a different act of creation to that of non-whites, when translated into social interaction, was to provide 'a rationale for treating some human groups like animals of another species'. Its British, European and American heyday covers the time-span from the 1830s to the 1850s, the period when, in the Queensland region, a convict frontier was ceding to a pastoral one. Of course, polygenism provided a powerful rationale for treating blacks both as vermin and as chattel labour, and for warning against European sexual intermixture and especially inter-marriage with Aborigines, Melanesians or Chinese. But its functional role, in popular or folk racism, extended in Queensland society well into the twentieth century.[10]

The development of the European 'science' of phrenology, which was 'the theory that one's mental powers are indicated by the shape of the skull',[11] played a prominent role 'in fostering the notions that Aboriginal mental powers were limited and their prospects for improvement slight'.[12] This nineteenth-century racial belief became a material force in a colony like Queensland, which was unusually a tropical white settler colony dependent on non-white labour.

Charles Darwin's *The Origin of Species* was published in 1859[13] and particularly influenced European thought. By the late 1860s and early 1870s Queenslanders were generally aware of his ideas on evolution, and in particular the Spencerian concept of 'the strong exterminating the weak'.[14] Some colonial frontiersmen used this concept to justify the fate of indigenous Australians. The 'doomed race' theory appears to have grown out of a mixture of these racial 'scientific' theories, and 'was a manifestation of ultimate pessimism in Aboriginal abilities'.[15] So much so that 'regarding the law and its duty towards Aborigines', a prominent colonial lawyer and parliamentarian in 1883 wrote that Aborigines were 'in the same position as those lower animals in whose behalf the law in certain circumstances thinks fit to interpose'.[16] In 1875, part-time journalist and then lawyer (and later judge), Charles Heydon, who was on the ship *Governor Blackall* sent from Sydney to search for the survivors of the wreck *Maria* off the far north Queensland coast near Cardwell, claimed that:

> . . . private persons go out to kill blacks, and call it 'snipe shooting'. Awkward words are always avoided, you will notice 'Shooting a snipe' sounds better than 'murdering a man'. But the blacks were never called men and women and children; 'myalls', and 'niggers', and 'gins', and 'piccaninnies' seem further removed from humanity.[17]

The Queensland colonial government organised the Native Police force, which operated from before the colony was established, from 1848 to around 1910, an extensive period of 62 years.[18] Similarly, white revenge posses were privately organised, together with (on occasions) the Native Police, but more generally, independently. Jonathan Richards' research into the operation of this para-military organisation concludes that it: 'operated under the direct control of the colony's most senior administrators—the Executive Council. The governor, in concert with the colonial secretary and other ministers, decided where to deploy the Native Police, who to appoint and which officers to dismiss.'[19] The pivotal role played by the Queensland Native Mounted Police was far more prominent and lethal than in other Australian colonies. They were used as death squads to remove the Aboriginal inhabitants who were considered an impediment to the squatters and settlers' land-grabs.

The Executive Council knew what was happening and they endorsed it. One only has to read the Parliamentary Debates in 1861, along with the Select Committee on the Native Police Force of the same year to see this. In particular, as historian Robert Ørsted-Jensen has noted, the interviews conducted on 16 June 1861 and the resulting Select Committee 'paper represents the first government of this state taking full responsibility for the force'.[20] The President of the Upper House, Sir M C Connell, who to his credit opposed the Native Police, responded to questioning from the Select Committee:

> I think that, if the Native Police are left to pursue a wholesale system of extermination, and keep the blacks from all contact with the whites, that you may protect the lives of the white population, but at a great sacrifice—and I believe an unjust sacrifice—of the lives of the aborigines.[21]

It was openly acknowledged during this parliamentary 'investigation' that the term 'dispersing' meant 'shooting to kill'.[22] The Committee was also made aware of Lieutenant Bligh's dispersal in the streets of Maryborough and his execution of a black standing up in a boat in the Mary River; Lieutenant Wheeler's killing of a group of middle-aged to old men at Logan and Fassifern (Dugandan Scrub); and young Morisset's killing of at least ten Aboriginals near Manumbar Station in the Burnett area. All incidents were thoroughly described. Ørsted-Jensen observed:

> None of these dispersals was in response to killing of whites, and there were no documented killings of livestock in either case.
>
> They knew alright and the Select Committee of 1861 represents the takeover of responsibility and the manner in which it was conducted was virtually a Government licence to the Native Police to kill at their own discretion (discretion was the word used and it simply meant—make sure you are not caught red-handed)![23]

In Queensland, reports from individuals and newspaper correspondents about massacres and violence received responses attempting to refute allegations of wholesale slaughter. The arrogant, authoritarian nature of the men in power enabled them to ignore and dismiss these allegations. Ostracism and intimidation appear to have been far more prevalent in the small white population of Queensland. Whistle-blowers were often sidelined and forced out of the colony.[24] For example, the death of Alfred Davidson, who campaigned from 1861 to 1881 to identify the brutal treatment of

Aboriginal Queenslanders and oppose the importation of South Sea Islanders for labour, was ignored by the *Brisbane Courier*. There was no obituary for Davidson, even though he had been involved in public life for decades as (and probably because he was) the local representative of the London-based Aborigines Protection Society.[25]

Similarly, the Reverend Duncan McNab, who lobbied both the Papacy in Rome and the Colonial Office in London regarding the treatment of Aboriginal Australians, failed in his attempts to seek justice and died in relative obscurity in Melbourne. There was also Arthur James Vogan who travelled widely around Queensland as a correspondent for the *Illustrated London News*. After publishing *The Black Police* in 1890, which was a thorough indictment of the Native Police, he found that his public life was ruined. This Vogan acknowledged on several occasions when asking for help from the Aborigines Protection Society to find a position outside Australia:

> My book 'Black Police' has virtually closed my newspaper life in Australia, I wrote upon the unpleasant subject, out of a sense of duty owed to my fellow countrymen ... But it has done me such harm here—this meddling with the pet national sin of Australia that I am forced to seek fresh pastures.[26]

The creation of the Pioneering Myth during the 1890s began the blurring of the truth about the frontier, so much so that during the twentieth century the myth about the peaceful settlement of Australia came to be readily accepted. It was historian John Hirst who identified 'The Pioneer Legend' which has come to be called the 'Pioneering Myth'. By calling it this, any confusion with the *Australian Legend* can be avoided, which Hirst acknowledges: 'is very different from the one devised by Russel Ward.'[27] Hirst's legend or 'Pioneering Myth' celebrates:

> ... courage, enterprise, hard work, and perseverance; it usually applies to the [white] people who first settled the land, whether as pastoralists or farmers, and not to those employed, although these

were never specifically excluded. It is a nationalist legend which deals in an heroic way with the central experience of European settlement in Australia: the taming of the new environment to man's use.[28]

There is no mention of Aboriginals and their inextricable link to their traditional lands, their violent treatment on the frontier or their incarceration under authoritarian control on reserves and missions. This control really only came to an end with the departure (1986) of the last mandarin director of the Department of Community Services, formerly the Department of Aboriginal and Islander Advancement, and earlier the Department of Native Affairs. It is one of the reasons why Aboriginals today do not like to use the word 'native'—it has connotations of suppression and control that dehumanised them.[29]

Aboriginal people fought very hard to defend their lands and on numerous occasions had the incomers on the back foot. There were massacres of whites and occasionally Native Police groups, though these are dwarfed by the hugely violent responses of the dispossessors. This was a very uneven war.

The conspiracy of silence prevails contemporaneously, sanitised by denying the independent and corroborated research done by so many.[30] Anyone reading primary source documents will find a completely different account of our frontier history, as one will also find with Aboriginal and white oral history recollections, for:

> ... the validity of oral testimony lies in the sheer magnitude and persistence of the 'massacre' narrative in Aboriginal oral tradition relating to country. That such an overwhelming and near-universal history is some kind of invention defies logic.[31]

It is important to acknowledge that our nation has been built on a violent foundation, and that the 'Pioneering Myth' national-story has been knowingly or unknowingly perpetrating the falsehood of a peaceful settlement of the Australian continent.

This form of selective forgetfulness or outright disinformation, amnesia or a conspiracy of silence, still pervades our national character. What is more, it continues to deny Aboriginal Australians their rightful place in the nation's identity. Other countries proudly tout their indigenous people and their cultures, but not so Australia. Why? Could it be that there are things that we as a nation have yet to come to terms with—a stolen land, a decimated people and a series of government systems that controlled every aspect of Aboriginal life for nearly 90 years,[32] (including stealing wages honestly earned)?[33] It is likely from this sense of shame, guilt and denial (or for that matter, pure ignorance) about what was perpetrated on the colonial frontier that a good part of Australia's 'cultural cringe' emanates. Given this, the other part, not surprisingly, seems to come from a sense of cultural inferiority to England. Even in 1890, Archibald Meston was readily acknowledging in the *Queenslander* that:

> The records of those unhappy years are unspeakably ghastly in their accounts of murders of white men and slaughter of the blacks. The whites were killed in dozens, the blacks in hundreds. The history of the early blacks can advantageously be consigned to the same speedy and merciful oblivion that ought to hide for ever the convict period of this colony.[34]

This was a man whom a political adversary alleged, had 'on more than one occasion boasted of the number of blacks who had fallen to his rifle'.[35] How many others experienced this and then realised the horror of the reality, and went on to acknowledge and protest at the continuing slaughter on the moving frontier? From each era there were letters to the newspapers and protests to the government about the massacres or mistreatment of the First Australians.[36] Their protests were ignored. Political stonewalling seems to have become a Queensland government trait, regardless of political persuasion.

The generally accepted number for a massacre in other parts of Australia appears to be a tally of five or six,[37] and I have mapped those clashes that rated this and more Aboriginal deaths and for which there is some form of corroborative evidence. It is a very conservative approach but, visually, the maps demonstrate emphatically that large-scale killings were numerous. Surely the invaders could have achieved their ends without such a scale of mass killings. The point about my choice is that one cannot argue about the numbers—they are overwhelming, particularly when realised diagram-matically. This is not to trivialise the tragic sporadic killings of individuals and small groups, but to give an indication of the veracity of what was at the time referred to as the 'Black Wars' of Queensland which lasted for over 80 years.[38] The unfortunate aspect about this current coverage is that it can in no way claim to be definitive; there are many more tragic tales to tell than are covered here, elements of which may never be known. While it is imperative to scour the official records as Jonathan Richards has done with regard to the Queensland Native Police, one also has to balance these with oral history accounts, letters, diaries, correspondence, folklore and other information gained from other disciplines such as archaeology, anthro-pology, linguistics and genetics. Winston Churchill corresponded with historian Lewis Namier regarding chapters he had written for his book, *Marlborough, His Life and Times*. He felt that:

> One of the most misleading factors in history is the practice of histo-rians to build a story exclusively out of the records which have come down to them. These records are in many cases a very small part of what took place, and to fill in the picture one has to visualize the daily life—the constant discussions between ministers, the friendly dinners, the many days when nothing happened worthy of record, but during which events were nevertheless proceeding.[39]

This perspective is particularly pertinent when studying the frontier of nineteenth-century Queensland. Unfortunately, the official records only tell a fraction of the story, while diaries, private letters and newspaper reports, along with Aboriginal and white oral histories, tell a much more fulsome tale. Admittedly, many histories and published works written in the nine-teenth century do provide a more realistic portrayal of events, but they have been glossed over and ignored during the twentieth century.[40] Nevertheless, they still avoid the true nature of frontier violence. Jonathan Richards has concluded that:

> The omission of frontier violence in published histories is inextricably linked to the denial of prior Aboriginal occupancy and ownership of the land. Much of the frontier history written relies too heavily on the works of a small group of men with an interest in perpetrating the stereotyped perceptions ... Many later historians quote their works as if they were accurate accounts based on official records and reliable witnesses. They were not.[41]

This then, is an attempt to record what actually happened on the frontier and dispel the conspiracy of silence which has obscured and denied the brutal treatment of Aboriginal Queenslanders. *Conspiracy of Silence* traces European expansion on Queensland's nineteenth-century frontier as it moves from region to region, and identifies a range of the many numerous violent incidents that occurred. My approach has erred towards conservative numbers. The mapping of the Queensland massacres are labelled 'Some massacres on the Queensland frontier' to indicate that I've documented only those sites where at least five Aboriginal deaths can be corroborated. There are almost certainly more sites of Aboriginal deaths throughout the state. The book is a comprehensive, but not definitive, coverage of what Aboriginal Queenslanders experienced. It puts paid to the furphy that Queensland, and Australia in general, was peacefully settled and challenges us to come to terms with this reality. It is particularly pertinent in the context of what we as a nation portray as being a part of our national character—being honest or straightforward. If we are to have any integrity as a nation, let alone as individuals, it is appropriate for us to recognise the unvarnished truth about our past.

Chapter 1

Post-Convict Era and the Future South-East Queensland 1842—1859

We are a generous Christian people—we take a continent from its first possessors, and pay them with the curses of our civilization (without its attendant alleviation) with an annual blanket and with what is, perhaps, under such circumstances a real boon—the annihilation of their race.

Moreton Bay Courier, *Saturday 3 April 1858.*

In the early part of the nineteenth century, the Australian colony of NSW had four mainland penal settlements and one offshore settlement: Port Jackson/Sydney (1788), Port Hunter/Newcastle (1804), Port Macquarie (1821) and Norfolk Island which was re-opened in 1825.[1] In 1824, the penal settlement of Moreton Bay was established, and moved the following year to the site that became Brisbane. It was the most isolated northern NSW settlement and specifically located to discourage convict runaways. Between 1826 and 1832, however, there were over 60 convict escapees who were returned from Port Macquarie to Moreton Bay. The Commandant of Moreton Bay, Captain Patrick Logan, established a military post at 'Point Danger' (actually Fingal Head, 5 kilometres to the south, in what is now NSW), in order to recapture 'bolters'.[2] This initially stopped absconders, but the outpost was closed in 1832.[3]

By 1819, the British population of greater NSW had reached about 25,000, of whom 9940 were convicts (8100 males and 1840 females) plus 850 children of convicts.[4] Between 1824 and 1842, 2300 convicts were sent to Moreton Bay. From these there were over 700 separate escapes with 98 whose fate is completely unknown.[5] Logan's stewardship was stern— convicts suffered the lash frequently (from 75 to 300 lashes) and did fourteen-hour shifts operating a grinding treadmill on Windmill Hill (1828–29). This explains why so many convicts 'ran'. The indigenous inhabitants had little to do with the settlement, although they did aid in the recapture of many runaways and were rewarded for doing so. The only large-scale killings as far as the records show were at Moreton and Stradbroke Islands.

The Amity (Point) Pilot Station and Store was established on Stradbroke Island in 1825 to enable ships to trans-ship to the Store, so river craft could then take the goods up to Brisbane, as well as supplying pilots for those ships that wanted to traverse the dangerous south entrance to Moreton Bay. Six years later, in mid-1831, following the deaths of two whites, a Noonuccal Elder was killed and decapitated in response. Two separate attacks on the Pilot Station resulted in injuries being sustained by two soldiers and one convict. Captain Clunie of the 17th Regiment, whose soldiers had been wounded, warned the Noonuccal 'of the severe measures which would follow any acts of aggression on their part'. Another assault occurred with the result that one tribesman was killed and another wounded.[6] Clunie responded with a number of sorties which ended with several Aboriginal deaths. In one dawn attack by the military, they surrounded a camp of Ngugi on the edge of a freshwater lagoon close to the southern extremity of Moreton Island, killing up to twenty of them. George Watkins recorded:

> ... nearly all were shot down. My informant, a young boy at the time, escaped with a few others by hiding in a clump of bushes. Affairs of a similar kind took place on Stradbrooke [*sic*], one in the neighbourhood of Point Lookout, and another farther to the south. A genuine stand-up fight came off west of the Big Hill on Stradbrooke, where the blacks were badly beaten.[7]

The violence continued and in late November 1832, the Noonuccal waddied the convict hutkeeper, William Reardon, to death in payback for decapitating one of their elders. More clashes followed, but no one was killed. However, when a landing party returning from Port Macquarie by ship was set upon and Chief Constable McIntosh was wounded and two convicts taken prisoner by the Noonuccal, Clunie responded with another reprisal. Reinforced with more soldiers and constables after the convicts were found murdered in late December 1832, another clash ensued, this time with Aboriginal deaths. Raymond Evans has demonstrated that:

> ... between July 1831 and December 1832, in a zig-zagging escalation of conflict, embodying a possible ten or more violent incidents, five Europeans had been killed and at least four others wounded. Probably between thirty and forty Ngugu and Nunukul people had similarly been slain or hurt in these military engagements. The scale of violence can best be appreciated when it is remembered that normally only a dozen or so whites were stationed on the island ... These island clashes of 1831–32, along with the killing of Captain Logan in October 1830, mark the highest point of racial conflict during the convict era. Significantly, they also accord with the years in which European numbers peaked at Moreton Bay—that is, a total of 1,241 men, women and children in 1831—and when the acreage devoted to cultivation and outstations reached its greatest geographical spread.[8]

The shrinkage of the cultivation area of the Moreton Bay penal settlement, from 500 acres (202 hectares) in 1835 to 50 (20 hectares) in 1838 was, as Evans points out, an indication to the Aboriginals 'that the "mogwi" [white people] were at last gradually leaving as mysteriously as they had come. Doubtless it would have seemed to the Aboriginals as if their policing of the peripheries, their return of runaways and their intermittent assaults on the strangers were at last being crowned with success.'[9] A similar false sense of 'successfully driving out the white interlopers' was experienced by the Gulf tribes, after a four-year hiatus from 1866 to 1870.[10]

By 1834, colonial pastoralists wielded considerable political clout, due to the importance to the colonial economy of their wool exports. Ross Fitzgerald notes that:

> As the overlanding settlers, the 'land-grabbers', spread like ripples in a pond, the centre of which was Sydney, the occupation of the fertile grazing lands of the Moreton Bay region became inevitable . . . [Despite the introduction of a £10 p.a. 'squatter's licence'] . . . The rush continued; frontiers were extended even more rapidly . . . It wasn't long before graziers were overlanding sheep north from the Liverpool Plains and New England towards the Darling Downs. The first squatters in what is now Queensland owed little to Brisbane Town: they emanated from distant southern settlements.[11]

The Myall Creek massacre on 10 June 1838 at Henry Dangar's outstation in what is now northern NSW, and the subsequent hanging of seven white perpetrators for shooting and sabring 28 Ngarabal people (old men, women and children), set in motion the white settlers/squatters' approach to violence on the frontier: *they kept quiet about it*.[12] So began white Australia's 'conspiracy of silence'. If one looks at the twenty-year period from 1839 to 1859, it is possible to see that what was espoused officially had little to do with what was actually going on in the wilds of the moving frontier. It set the pattern for colonial behaviour after the separation of Queensland from NSW in December 1859 for the remainder of the nineteenth and early twentieth centuries.

May 1839 saw the closure of the Moreton Bay penal settlement and three years later the NSW colonial government proclaimed the area open to free settlement, 'which the squatters greeted . . . like the sound of a starter's pistol. So quickly was the Darling Downs occupied that, in the same year [1842], the bolder spirits hungered to learn what riches might lie to the north'.[13] In 1843 Moreton Bay was given representation in the NSW Legislative Council.

The turning point for the Aboriginals came with the opening up of the traditional lands of the Yuggera, in the gateway area to the Darling Downs, west of Ipswich (1842) from the foothills in the Lockyer Creek valley up the Great Dividing Range to where Toowoomba was proclaimed in 1849. Led first by 'Moppy' and then his son, 'Multuggerah', the Yuggera and their allies instituted a guerilla campaign to stop supplies getting through to the new runs on the Downs. Their offensive actions culminated in the ambush of three loaded bullock drays in the shadows of Mt Davidson (south of the current Warrego Highway).

> Multuggerah had organized and planned a masterful retreat. Jacky Jacky, Peter and the Limestone men, plus Multuggerah's own warriors—their Yuggera cousins—sought the shelter of a ledge some fifty or so feet above the road on Mount Davidson and took a defensive position . . . [The Commissioner of Crown Lands, Stephen] Simpson, with his four Bush Constables saw . . . [the warriors] moving toward the top of the range and went for the retreating Aboriginals. The twenty squatters discovered the men on Mount Davidson and completely ignoring a side spur to the ledge which would have taken them and their horses straight to the Aborigines on an easy path, they dismounted and starting a frontal attack, on foot, up the face of the mountain. Both attacks, Simpson's and the squatters', were disasters.[14]

Simpson withdrew before another ambush and the squatters retreated from the hillside attack after several of their men were injured by rocks and stones rolled down on them. This became known as the Battle of One Tree Hill, and is important as an example of a successful Aboriginal attack against the invading white pastoralists. However, the repercussions were profound with many of those involved later being chased, harried and shot.

The actions of James Rogers, the manager of George Mocatta's station at Grantham, in stealing hundreds of sheets of ironbark from a local Yuggera village for use on his employers' run caused serious trouble. From late September 1841, nearly 500 warriors from across the Lockyer and Brisbane River valleys began attacking the newly established stations and driving off thousands of sheep. To the north, shepherds on Evan McKenzies' Kilcoy run were wounded, while at Mocatta's outstations and neighbouring Tent Hill Station, operated by George Somerville, shepherds were killed.[15] The response was a heavily armed posse led by Rogers and Somerville in a punitive raid in late October 1841, where at dawn a surprise attack on a Yuggera village caused panic among their victims. This was later portrayed as a battle in which only a dozen shots were fired with two whites speared and several Aboriginals wounded, but we have, unusually, another coverage of events from 'a literate Sri Lankan ex-convict from Moreton Bay, George "Black" Brown', who was an ally of the clan. Historian Raymond Evans notes that Brown 'recorded a markedly different version of events from the white account . . . What eventuated was more of a massacre than a fight'.[16] Brown records that Rogers carried a double-barrelled rifle, a brace of pistols and a sword, and that as:

> . . . the young natives were making their escape to the scrub; the Horsemen were riding after them; the natives were jabbing their spears at them . . . The firing was continued about half an hour. I cannot say the numbers that were killed.[17]

Between 1842 and 1844, on the Darling Downs, Aboriginal warriors killed thirteen white people.[18] Hostile collisions with Europeans by 1846 resulted in an estimate by the NSW Select Committee on the Aborigines that at least 300 Aboriginals had lost their lives on the Moreton Bay frontier, and 50 Europeans had been killed,[19] a ratio of six Aboriginals for every European.

The establishment of the NSW Native Police in 1848, and their operations on the Darling Downs, led to an escalation in the number of Aboriginals killed on this northern frontier. In the twelve months to August 1849, Aboriginal resistance was estimated to have cost the Darling Downs, Moreton Bay and Wide Bay districts £10,000, and made labour 'scarce & dear'.[20] This acute labour shortage was also affected by the abolition of the transportation of convicts to NSW in 1840, and by rushes to the Californian (1849–50), Victorian and NSW goldfields (1851). These factors saw a marked change in contact between the convict era and pastoralism. In the convict period we do not see massacres on the scale that comes with the pastoral era. There does not even seem to have been a big reprisal raid mounted when Captain Logan was killed, the only Penal Commandant to perish from violence in office in Australian history. The attack would not be allowed to go unanswered in the pastoral era.

A series of factors marks the distinction between the two eras. In the convict period, the Europeans were not trying to take large tracts of land for pastoral use, but with the new era that is precisely what the newcomers did, and they stocked the land with large numbers of introduced exotic animals (cattle and sheep). Major waterholes were commandeered and the clans whose traditional lands the pastoralists had usurped were prevented from using them. Similarly, many of the newcomers saw their capital investment in cattle and sheep as more important than the lives of the original inhabitants. Any infringement on white expansion, be it spearing of their introduced animals, or one of their own kind, met with overwhelmingly bloody responses. Hence the 'keeping the Blacks out' policy, which only changed when the whites' fear of the Aboriginal threat of retaliation subsided and they needed to use them for cheap labour.

The Native Police force became the legitimate instrument of government policy, first in NSW and later in the newly formed colony of Queensland.[21] The Native Police comprised of out-of-area Aboriginals had three duties: to break up—'disperse'—large assemblages of Blacks, and at the same time to intimidate them by constant patrolling; to apprehend Aboriginal 'criminals'; and to act as a punitive force for the local settlers.[22] Officers 'were forbidden to report in detail'.[23] An officer who served with Queensland's 'Black Police' during the 1860s commented:

'AUSTRALIA has been won by a hundred years of bloodshed.' So I have heard more than one old squatter aver, and there is truth in the statement . . . we organised a force of Native Mounted Police in the new colony of Queensland, for the purpose of protecting outside settlers from the raids of the blacks . . . They were commanded by white officers and distributed in small squads in various outlying parts of the country . . . [and] . . . these half-civilised natives, now turned into troopers, were enlisted from different tribes . . . [24]

Official attitudes towards the operation of the Native Police were formed while NSW still 'governed' what became Queensland, and as Evans and Walker note:

> Although the Native Police acted as a para-military body engaged in border warfare while in the field, no legal recognition of this role could be given, for, officially, the territory of others was not being conquered. It was merely seen as 'Crown Land' being 'settled'. Resisting natives were therefore held to be British subjects, behaving criminally, rather than being accorded status as the legitimate force of a warring people, opposing the invasion of their lands.[25]

The colonists' sense of fear on the frontier can be gauged from letters to the editor of the *Sydney Morning Herald*. 'A Squatter' wrote from Moreton Bay in July 1842, that:

> The state of the district with respect to the aborigines [*sic*], appears now to have arrived at such a crisis that the necessity of some means being immediately adopted to suppress outrage on their part, and unwarranted retribution on the part of the settlers, is obvious. [26]

It might have been, but the British system of justice found Aboriginal evidence legally inadmissible. Also any court hearings were held in Sydney, not Moreton Bay, which required lengthy and expensive trips down south, where the courts were not so sympathetic towards the squatters and their actions. In the north, 'justice', as Rod Fisher has observed:

> . . . was often dispensed on the spot, particularly from the barrel of a gun. These reprisals were rarely recorded in any detail. Yet the savage murders, ruthless raids, government neglect, legal

inadequacies, court leniency, misguided philanthropy and northern sense of grievance were fully aired in the newspapers for all to see.

The picture conveyed by these sources is one of fierce but diffuse Aboriginal resistance to European intrusion, its timing, location and extent being determined by the spread of pastoralism and the degree of force. In 1842–45 the main arena was Ipswich to the Darling Downs, followed by the upper Brisbane valley 1842–46, the Logan district 1844–53, Pine River 1845–58, Wide Bay–Burnett 1850–59 and Sandgate 1853–59.[27]

Effectively, it was not until the *Moreton Bay Supreme Court Act of 1857* that a resident Judge (Alfred James Lutwyche) began operating in Moreton Bay.[28] Aboriginal evidence in court became acceptable in 1884. This is very important because massacres could be committed with virtual impunity throughout the main frontier period. Historian Robert Ørsted-Jensen observes that:

> . . . the Governments of Queensland was [*sic*] from day one deeply involved in attempting to legalise and secure continuation of the Native Police, and in various ways protect the force against outside criticism. Not the least was the first government under Governor Bowen and his first secretary Robert Herbert. Herbert stepped in when the position of Magistrate on two occasions proved to be a danger to Native Police work at the frontier (then at Ipswich and later Rockhampton), thereafter ensuring that retired Native Police officers were allowed first choice to the semi-retirement positions of Magistrates and similar key positions at the frontier. From this point former Native Police officers were the ones to investigate complaints about active Native Police officers. That is why you have Magistrate Murray to investigate the murder allegation against Lt. Frederick Wheeler in 1876, and it is the same throughout Queensland . . . this was deliberate. If you had any complaint about the Native Police you would have to go to a semi-retired former Native Police officer with it—there were no others to go to.[29]

The poisoning of 60 Giggabarah at Kilcoy Station in 1842, along with the arsenic poisoning deaths of 50 to 60 Gubbi Gubbi (Kabi-Kabi) at White-side Station in mid-April 1847, caused uproar among the Aboriginal people of the region and beyond.[30] Both of these disparate groups were partici-pants in the triennial Bunya-Bunya Festival, where clan groups travelled, not just from the surrounding districts, but from far and wide: from the Richmond River in what is now north-coast NSW, from the Burnett River valley and many other coastal regions. The massive fruiting of the bunya nut enabled large inter-tribal gatherings to feast on the surplus. It was a time which enabled great social interaction: family reunions of distant rela-tives, trade, negotiations and ceremony, as well as sharing of dances, Stories, gossip and information, and on occasions the settling of quarrels. It was a pivotal point on the calendar of the Aboriginal people who lived in the area that became south-eastern Queensland and the adjacent districts in northern NSW. Naturally, the horrifying stories of the poisonings of large numbers, horrified the visiting tribal groups.

At first European writings considered the Bunya gatherings with interest and concern for preservation of the trees; this transformed into viewing the large gatherings as a threat to white settlement. It was believed that any gathering of the 'natives' would be to plan raids or attacks on whites. While no doubt the whites might be an irritant, it is more than likely that the 'Festival' had priority in Aboriginal eyes as it was more than just a gathering —it had a spiritual role to play. It was known as *Boobarran Ngummin*—'our Mother's breast'—as Djerripiwalli of the Jarowair identified:

> We invited all these people from north, northwest, Kabi Kabi people
> on the coast, Rockhampton, even further. It was every three to four
> years, with harvests. The Jarowair sent out messages, when Mother's
> milk will be ready to be drunk. Messengers, runners went out, they
> had message sticks. For thousands of years they were welcome, to
> come to *Boobarran Ngummin* ... and go back, completely healed
> and full of spirituality from our Mother. [31]

In 1845, Europeans who coveted these resources, had difficulty in obtaining them, for, as pastoralist John Macarthur noted, the NSW Government 'has expressly reserved the Bunya-Bunya country for the aborigines, no white person being allowed to occupy pastures in the vicinity . . . [and] . . . the Natives live upon the seeds'.[32] Christopher Rolleston, Commissioner for Crown Lands for the Darling Downs, recognised the importance of the Bunya Mountains to the Aboriginal people of the future southern Queensland, and recommended that the area be set aside for an Aboriginal reserve.[33] The *New South Wales Government Gazette* of 1842 granted that,[34] but Rolleston also noted that some white settlers were deliberately destroying bunya-bunya trees in order to try to clear the region of Aboriginal people.[35]

Three years later the NSW Select Committee heard testimony by the Roman Catholic Archbishop of Sydney, John Bede Polding, that many northern frontier squatters thought 'there was no more harm in shooting a native than in shooting a wild dog'. The Archbishop observed:

> Very recently in the presence of two clergymen, a man of education narrated, as a good thing, that he had been one of a party who had pursued the blacks in consequence of the cattle having been rushed . . . and he was sure they shot upward of a hundred. When postulated with, he maintained that there was nothing wrong in it, that it was preposterous to suppose they had souls. In this he was joined by another educated person present . . . [36]

Although, as Evans has noted: 'Notwithstanding the fact that there were considerate and largely conciliatory squatters on the northern frontier, such as the Archer brothers of Durundur or Joshua Bell of Jimbour Station [established in close vicinity to the Bunya Mountains], the overall European impact was a prolonged saga of cruelty and devastation.'[37] The actions of the Native Police demonstrated that they were targeting groups going to, and coming from, the Bunya Festival gatherings, which effectively contributed to declining attendances.[38]

On the coastal Blackall Ranges, where there had been a profusion of bunya trees, saw-millers decimated the surviving stands, so that today there are hardly any at all, while the capitalist politicians of the time exploited on the timber stands in the region. Men such as Queensland Premier Thomas McIlwraith, and Post Master General Boyd Morehead, and other government members as well as squatters and others trying to make a 'fast buck', formed the Darling Downs and Western Land Company, which built the Great Bunya Sawmills late in 1883 at the foot of the range.[39] The last sizeable Bunya gathering was in 1875 at Mt Mowbullan in the Bunya Mountains, although it seems to have petered out before 1880.

Between Ipswich and the NSW border are the traditional lands of the Ugarapul (the most southerly of the Yuggera-speaking people). Although whites began their incursion into these lands in the 1840s, it was not until December 1860 that the heavy hand of the Native Police descended on the Aboriginals of the Dugandan scrub. After tobacco and blankets had been stolen from an outlying hut, John Hardie, a local white settler, wrote to the Native Police for help.

Lieutenant Frederick Wheeler joined the force in 1857 under the jurisdiction of the NSW government, and went on openly killing Aboriginal people for another nineteen years despite myriad complaints about his behaviour which authorities ignored. Eventually, even his police colleagues soured of his actions, and upon his murdering of an Aboriginal in 1876, he was charged and dismissed from the force. Wheeler absconded overseas and died six years later in Java. However, at the start of 1861, it was due to Wheeler's attitude as expressed in his reports that: 'The Government viewed with strong disapproval Wheeler's intention of killing innocent Aborigines as punishment for the crimes of others.'[40] He was reprimanded and transferred to Sandgate, where he received Hardie's letter. Wheeler and his detachment rode from Sandgate, on the coast some 18 kilometres north of Brisbane, to the Dugandan scrub. They arrived at Hardie's station on 2 January 1861. Local Aboriginal Cyclone Jack told Bill Rosser how his grandfather saved his five-year-old father by climbing a tall tree and hiding with the child among the foliage high in the canopy.

> When they shot my uncle in the thigh—my father's uncle—they
> went up to him and shot him in the head. The mongrels were

laughing all this time . . . They all got killed except my grandfather.
When the shooting started, they jumped into the water. I think it
must [have] been Christmas Creek. But my grandfather took off for
the bush on his own. He reckon he could see the water go red when
they were hit.[41]

Later, after the 'dispersal', Jack's grandfather climbed down with his son
and when he 'got close to the camp he said he could smell some funny smell.
When he looked he saw all these people had been put on a fire. That was
where the smell was coming from'. Jack's grandfather went looking for the
rest of his tribe as some had managed to escape and 'they had just scattered.
Some went down towards the coast and some went down to Mt Lindsay'
(right on the border not far north of Woodenbong). Wheeler also led a
dispersal at Fassifern.[42] One aspect of this recollection, which is incredibly
poignant, is that Rosser's informant was about 85 years old, driven to live
some 1800 kilometres from his father's verdant traditional lands, at Uran-
dangie (on the Northern Territory border) in dry country not his own, and
although the massacre happened 129 years before, he was still having night-
mares about it. It was, as Rosser put it, 'somewhat tragic to watch this frail
old man, this grimy, unkempt, lovable and neglected little man whose stoop
and frailty suggested . . . that soon he would return to his Dreaming'.[43] He
did, several days later, but his memory of the past did not, hence the story's
inclusion here.

Following the 1842 decree throwing open the Moreton Bay region to
settlement, there was a rush by land-hungry squatters. The *Moreton Bay
Courier* reported in July 1846, that 'thirteen stations have already been
taken up [not 'from', if you happened to be a local Aboriginal] on the Boyne
[Mary River] . . . it is more than likely that in the course of another year
upwards of forty stations will be formed there'.[44] In 1843:

... the headstation at Tiaro, and the outstations at Gigoomgan,
Girkum, and Owanyilla were abandoned. Persistent attacks by Mary
River Aborigines were so successful in delaying white settlement,

that those settlers who moved into the area in the late 1840's were taking up country abandoned two, and even three times before.[45]

To the traditional owners, the Badtjala and surrounding Gubbi Gubbi, this pastoral invasion was met with fierce resistance, so that over the six years from 1847 to 1853, some 28 squatters and shepherds were killed.[46] Two squatting partners, Gregory Blaxland (youngest son of the explorer) and William Forster, overlanded from the Clarence River droving 30,000 sheep and 800 cattle, with the help of three teenage brothers by the name of Pegg. They arrived and set up their run at Tirroan Station on Gin Gin Creek in 1848. The following June, two of the young Pegg brothers were speared while out shepherding, with half their flock driven off. Word was sent to the nearest station, Walla, 14 miles (22 kilometres) to the south on the Burnett River, which had been established earlier the previous year. Blaxland led over 50 station-hands and squatters who rallied to seek revenge. They moved downstream and located a large Aboriginal camp in dense scrub, in an area that has since become known as 'The Cedars', a sugar plantation, at Bingera. Clem Lack tells how:

> The white man attacked at picanniny dawn. More than a 100 myalls [wild blacks] were asleep, gorged with roast mutton, in groups around the ashes of burnt out fires, half a mile away from the waters of the Burnett. The affray was one of the bloodiest in Queensland frontier history, although no white man was killed. Many of the Aboriginals escaped by plunging into the Burnett and swimming to the other side. Some were picked off by marksmen and sank beneath the surface. More than half a century later, ploughmen at The Cedars ... brought to light grim relics. Skulls, bones, stone tomahawks, boomerangs, and other weapons ...[47]

Within twelve months of this event, after the remnants of the 'Gin Gin Tribe' had returned to their traditional lands where Blaxland and Forster had established their Tirroan Station, revenge by members of the Gurang led to their killing Gregory Blaxland in 1850.[48] This led to another large punitive expedition where:

> Squatters and station hands [once again] rallied from stations near and far. Walla, Tenningering, Yenda, Wetheron, Monduran, Kolonga, Eureka, Ideraway, Barambah, Boonara and Boubyjan all sent strong contingents of armed resolute horsemen; more than 100 men set out on the vengeance trail . . . along the banks of the Burnett . . . [The Gurang] were discovered camped on Paddy's Island in the region of what afterwards became Fairymead sugar plantation [some 9 kilometres north-east of the future Bundaberg (1868)]. The horsemen hurtled through the shallows in a headlong charge . . . Showers of spears greeted the attackers as they galloped up a muddy slope . . . the resistless fury of the charge cowed the Aboriginals, who fled back into the shelter of the scrub. The riders dismounted and crawled into the scrub after them, aiming at the black shadows that flitted among the trees. Hundreds were shot down with ceaseless cracking fire of rifles; the thudding of bullets drumming among the leaves in a storm of raining death. Hundreds of Aboriginals raced for the river bank. As they streamed into the open, riders ran to their horses and rode many of them down before they could reach the water's edge. But scores [40 plus?] of them got away to safety . . . [in the] Woongarra scrub.[49]

There can be no doubt that both The Cedar and Paddy's Island massacres happened. Precise casualties are difficult to gauge, but it seems clear that they were sizeable.

The next year, Blaxland's 30-year-old business partner William Forster, sold Tirroan to the Brown brothers who renamed it Gin Gin. Forster, however, continued to amass runs of 25,900 hectares (64,000 acres), but returned to Sydney in 1854, retired from active country life and went into politics in 1856. He became Premier of NSW in October 1859, just as the colony of Queensland came into existence on 10 December.[50]

Throughout this period the white residents of Maryborough were in a perpetual state of anxiety and apprehension at the threat of Aboriginal aggression, which was prompting white settlers to leave the district and hampering European development. The town's second Magistrate, A E Halloran, in November 1853 reported: 'It is almost impossible for me to describe the constant state of alarm in which the Townspeople are kept from a dread of the aggressions of the blacks, whose treachery and audacity are almost incredible.' Twenty months later his concern had increased when he informed the Colonial Secretary in Sydney: 'More than one family who has recently arrived here are about leaving immediately from fear of the blacks . . . [This] dread . . . prevents many people settling in Wide Bay and materially retards the advancement of the place.'[51]

Meanwhile, Commandant Frederick Walker of the Native Police finally made his way from the Macintyre River to Maryborough. Between Christmas Eve 1851 and 3 January 1852 he led a large party comprising 24 troopers, Lieutenant Marshall and Sergeant Major Dolan, as well as local squatters 'Messrs. James Leith Hay, Norman Leith Hay and Wilmot', backed up by Captain Currie of the schooner *Margaret and Mary* and his crew. 'All armed and sworn in as special constables' they proceeded to Fraser Island to apprehend 'sundry felons'. On 5 January 1852, Frederick Walker wrote a very vague and guardedly condensed report, which discussed the difficulties his party experienced regarding rain, heat, mosquitoes and sandflies, and rough terrain, but kept an 'extraordinary secrecy of the result of that jaunt, and much surprise [was] expressed at the profound silence maintained concerning their exploits, by this most heterogeneous body of black hunters'.[52] R Evans and J Walker in their assessment of events conclude that:

> Walker's report, however, strains credulity to the utmost when he admitted to the rather suspect measure of allowing his troopers to move out alone 'to pursue the hostile blacks . . . from the 31st to the 2nd January', simply because he felt too footsore to accompany them. His account continues ambiguously, 'they followed them . . . never getting up to them UNTIL they reached the east side of the island, when the blacks took to the scrub.'[53] He fails here to explain

how the low lying coastal scrub could so utterly frustrate the persistent trackers who had managed to negotiate the mountainous jungle
regions of the central island without losing the trail of their prey.[54]

One cannot help but agree with Evans and Walker that 'Perhaps some
credence should be paid to the *Moreton Bay Courier* correspondent who . . .
disclosed the information that "rumours are afloat that the natives were
driven into the sea, and there kept as long as daylight or life lasted . . . "'[55]
Similarly, the correspondent noted the alteration in the way the 'natives' of
Fraser Island dealt with ship-wrecked survivors. Prior to the Native Police
efforts, the Badtjala showed kindness and gave assistance to the crews
of the wrecked ships *Countess of Minto* and *Rokeby Castle*, 'so opposite to
their behaviour *since*, that [it] is difficult to find reasons for the change,
except from a spirit of revenge'.[56] Five months later, Vox ['Voice'], from the
Burnett River, wrote to the editor of the *Sydney Morning Herald*, published
in the capital of the colony:

> GENTLEMEN,—It is about time that something transpired
> relative to the doings of the black police in December last, at
> Frazer's [*sic*] Island. I have been anxiously waiting to hear; because,
> although a new resident, and one of the oldest [white] inhabitants
> in these parts, I cannot for the life of me discover for what purpose
> they were sent or went there. I know great preparations were made
> for the jaunt—squatters and storekeepers swelled the party—moist
> and dry provisions were abundantly laid in, &c., but still nothing
> is made known of the trip, and so much secrecy really makes the
> whole matter look bad.[57]

Considering the normal hullabaloo made by colonials in marking occasions
such as departures and arrivals of expeditions, the silence surrounding
the expedition and minimal coverage in Walker's report, along with
nary an official word of the events seeping out, suggests very dark deeds
indeed, which Vox probably knew about and possibly wanted to prick the

conscience of the governing authorities with, as well as bringing it to the attention of the public.

After finishing with the Ugarapul in early 1861, the infamous Lieutenant Wheeler continued carrying out reprisal raids from his barracks at Sandgate (c.18 kilometres north-east of Brisbane). Ray Kirkhove has recorded some of Wheeler's adventures:

> On . . . 11 April 1861 he 'dispersed' the 'bunya bunya natives' (presumably the Nalbo and Dallabarra of the Nambour-Maleny-Kenilworth region). On 10 June . . . he patrolled; up into Kilcoy and the bunya lands. In 1862, he patrolled to Caboolture and then, on 31 July . . . he was met by a grand force of Obi Obi (Maleny–Mapleton), Brisbane and Caboolture warriors at Cressbrook. He managed to 'disperse' these too . . . Wheeler boasted that he had driven most of the inhabitants either out to the Moreton Bay islands, down into New South Wales, across the Divide or into northern rainforests.[58]

In 1913, the Chief Protector of Aborigines, J W Bleakley, included in his annual report a coverage of the Wangerriburra, whose traditional lands were to the south of Brisbane and:

> . . . occupied the country in the basin of the middle Albert River and the headwaters of the Coomera River. Their territory stretched from Cedar Creek on the north to the Macpherson ranges on the south; and from the Birnam Range on the west to the Upper Coomera and Nerang watershed on the east. It contained the well-known Tambourine Mountain. Its greatest length from north to south was 33 miles [53 kilometres], its greatest breadth 15 miles [24 kilometres] . . . [And comprised] . . . ever-running creeks and rivers, the mountain scrubs and forests, the river flats and rich plains were the haunts of abounding animal life . . . [59]

In the report, a Wangerriburra descendant, Bullumm (John Allen), recalled:

... many a mournful day when the cruel hand of civilisation pressed harshly upon them; when the black troopers raided their camps, murder and rapine being the fate of the victims, and wretched hiding in swamps and scrub the luck of the survivors.

About his earliest impression of things was when a party of his tribe was surprised by troopers at Mt Weatheren. The blacks—men, women, and children—were in a dell at the base of a cliff. Suddenly a body of troopers appeared on the top of the cliff and without warning opened fire on the defenceless party below. Bullumm remembers the horror of the time, of being seized by a gin [sic] and carried to cover, of cowering under the cliff and hearing the shots ringing overhead, of the rush through the scrub to get away from the sound of the death-dealing guns. [60]

Another story that Bullumm told was about the murder of a German woman and her son by 'Nelson' at Sandy Creek, Jimboomba in 1855. The Native Police knew that the murderer was a Coomera black who visited the Albert and Nerang tribes, and after he had escaped upon being captured: 'They had no scruples in shooting any blacks in the hope that the victim might be the escaped murderer. From 30 to 40 blacks were killed by troopers in this way, but "Nelson" died a natural death in spite of it all, some years after in Beenleigh.'

The interesting thing about the 1913 report was how openly the violence was acknowledged in an official government publication, thirteen years into the twentieth century. A decade earlier, in 1903, in response to Dr Walter Roth's (the Northern Protector of Aborigines) report to Parliament on the establishment of the west Cape York Reserves, Protector Galbraith was also frank in stating: 'It will act as a deterrent in preventing some white men ... from rounding up small mobs of wild natives and despoiling their women. The practice is more common than many people imagine.'[61] Such open acknowledgements confirm that the frontier violence—now it was largely over— had become an officially accepted position. It shows too that the curtain of denial about frontier mayhem and massacre, although closing by this time, had not yet swept completely across the public stage.

Chapter 2

European Invasion of the Future Southern Queensland [1]

In our Wide Bay and Burnett district blackfellows were shot down at sight
by some of the settlers, and many scores of men and women were poisoned by
strychnine being placed in the flour that was distributed to them, or that had been
left in places handy for the blacks to themselves take possession of.

Daily News and Mail, *29 July 1933.* [2]

Between 1848 and 1849, the Colonial Office in London ordered that pastoral
leases should allow for dual usage of territory: that Aboriginal occupancy
must be a legal requirement of the lease. [3] By driving Aboriginals out pastoralists were actually acting contrary to the legal requirements of their lease.
This was just another illegality that accompanied the takeover of Aboriginal lands and enormously increased the possibility and actuality of violence.
There is some evidence that Frederick Walker was outraged that pastoralists
were flouting the law in this way and using the Native Police to enforce the
wrongful usage of their leaseholds. It is one of the reasons he was dismissed
and became such an outspoken critic of the Native Police system. [4]

A war of resistance by the indigenous people of the Moonie, Macintyre
and Barwon Rivers in the area now bounded by St George, Goondiwindi
and Moree, led to seventeen stations on the Macintyre being abandoned in

1843, and only thirteen were re-established after 1846.[5] By 1843, sixteen settlers had been killed on the Macintyre, while in the Moreton Bay region it was alleged that there were more than a dozen fatalities.[6] The Aboriginal campaign to rid the district of white settlers led them to target settlers' horses and cattle and seriously endanger the newcomers' economic viability.[7] The leaseholder of Carbucky Station, D Lanarch, had within a year lost over 50 per cent of the 1600 head of cattle he had brought to his run in 1847.[8]

Matters were not helped by the violent vigilante actions of some of the settlers, such as James Marks, at Goodar (40 kilometres north-west of Goondiwindi) who, in September 1847 shot a 'native boy' sent by the neighbouring Callandoon Station to share meat from a recently killed beast.[9] This outraged the Bigambul, one of whom, in retaliation, killed Marks' son and dismembered his body.[10] A year-long reign of terror by Marks and his fellow landowners and stockmen against the local Aboriginal people resulted.[11] At least 47 Aborigines died in a series of attacks from October 1847.[12] Within a year attacks had been made on indigenous people camped on Carbucky, Broomfield, Callandoon and Umbercollie Stations surrounding the future Goondiwindi.

William Telford recounts how he heard from:

> ... the late Constable Duane of Tamworth who was formerly stationed at Surat in [the future] Queensland in 1848 [that] they had a fight with the Blacks at tallavera [*sic*] on the Ballone [River, where] one blackfellow was very conspicuous with a plume of Eagles feathers in his hair leading and encouraging the rest to battle ... the blacks called him Willari ... [and] ... made a good stand but were put to rout losing the Cheif [*sic*] who was shot with about fifty others.[13]

Almost a decade to the day of the Myall Creek massacre (10 June 1838, south-west of Inverell), on 11 June 1848, and bearing an eerie similarity to the earlier horror 200 kilometres to the north-west, an attack at Jonathan

Young's Umbercollie Station got underway. Led by James Marks in the early morning, one of the participants described how:

> We all came up to the rails we could see the place where the blacks were lying—we fired upon them—We were close to the sheep-yard—We fired two or three times loading and firing as fast as we could with cartridge—After firing two or three shots Mark Steebie and Reardon and Martin and Jones and the Blackfellow jumped over the rails and rushed the camp.[14]

The station-owners, Margaret and Jonathan Young, witnessed the attack and later discovered several mutilated Aboriginal female bodies. After the event, Mrs Young observed the continuing violence, when: 'Some weeks later the police came back shooting still more natives whether guilty or not; we lost twelve more of our station blacks.' It appears that the police came from the Warialda (NSW) Police District.

Two months later, in August 1848, an investigation was begun by the Gwydir Crown Lands Commissioner, Richard Bligh. Statements were taken from the Youngs and three Aboriginal people, who identified the men involved in the attack the previous June. Several of the Umbercollie killers were arrested in February 1849 and committed to stand trial at Maitland. Despite the evidence against them no conviction was recorded, as the Attorney General ignored Bligh's belief that a hutkeeper, George Harris, had perjured himself in saying that he had not seen an armed party heading for Umbercollie in June 1848. This flimsy defence enabled the Attorney General to conclude that: 'The contradiction of the approver by Harris is important . . . and weakens very considerably the case against them.'[15]

Calls continued for government help in the campaign against the Aboriginals until the arrival of the first contingent of NSW Native Police in 1849 on the Macintyre River. On 10 May 1849 Frederick Walker and his fourteen Native Police troopers (from southern NSW) arrived and ambushed Aboriginals on the Severn (Dumeresq) River. A squatter on the Severn, John Watts, reported that the troopers attacked 'a large tribe' and 'were so excited that Captain Walker could not control them, this being the first time they had been in action' and hinted sinisterly that 'the number they killed no one but their commander and themselves knew'.[16]

Walker's Native Police next went into action at Carbucky Station, which had only recently been bought by W B Tooth, a member of the NSW Legislative Assembly, 'at a sacrifice' from Lanarch, the previous owner. Lanarch had written in November 1848 complaining that if protection from the Aboriginals was not forthcoming he would have to abandon his run.[17] Walker's detachment found some Gambuwal killing cattle near the new owner's camp. Tooth wrote that: 'The blacks were so completely put down on that occasion, and terrified at the power of the police, that they never committed any more depredations near there.'[18]

Augustus Morris, a Member of the NSW Legislative Council and a friend of Walker's, directly credited the peace to the 'Battle of Carbucky', observing: 'A very favourable change has come over the hitherto hostile Aborigines. Since the engagement near Carbucky they appear to think that they cannot carry on their former depredations with impunity.'[19] Squatters such as Morris and Tooth not only saw the value of their runs increase, but also a decline in wages expended on employees, as it was now not as dangerous on the frontier properties as it had previously been.

Over the ensuing months of May and June 1849, Bigambul resistance was overwhelmed by the NSW Native Police as they criss-crossed the district.[20] Frederick Walker reported: 'On 24th June I arrived with ten troopers on the Condamine. I found the country in a most disturbed state; several of the stations had been abandoned; twelve white men had been murdered and the loss in cattle and sheep was immense . . .'[21] According to William Telfer, Walker tried to prevent the 'Sable warriors from Surat' joining up with the 'Macintyre [River] blacks':

> . . . he meant to fight them separately not giving them any time to join their forces so he travelled in the night getting within a short distance of their camp [possibly Blacks Camp Creek, c.50 kilometres south-east of Surat]. Just at daybreak they made an attack on the sleeping camp some of them fled hearing the horses coming. Making for the scrub but were met by the native police who drew their

swords cutting and slashing the fugitives a great number were slain also a lot shot dead . . . thus was broken up this large tribe nearly one hundred perished under the sword and bullet of the white man.[22]

In July, believing he was being misled by Aboriginal peace overtures, Walker followed their trails and found slaughtered beasts at each of the camps he visited. Long before dusk on Monday 9 July his detachment came across a group of Bigambul cutting up a beast that belonged to Mr R Pringle. They tried to escape across the plain, but were driven back by Corporal Logan and his detachment, while two troopers blocked access to the river. Local squatters Marshall, Rens and Morris, along with Walker and four troopers, were cut off by a party of 30 or more Bigambul. The Aboriginal defenders were rushed by the Native Police on foot, and at twelve paces were fired on by muzzle-loading carbines. Without serious injuries to their attackers, the Bigambul were driven from their cover and took their 'final stand'.[23] The encounter was described by the *Maitland Mercury* (1 August 1849):

> Spears and boomerangs were flying in every direction, the flashing of fire arms shewing the blacks the position of their assailants; the yells of the savages, answered by the war cry of the police, and the ring of carbines must have had a most exciting effect . . . It is surprising that the government does not declare the disturbed districts in a state of siege, and thus relieve the Commandant from his great responsibility. Why does the government not at once acknowledge there is a war, when it is so notorious?

Interestingly, Walker was cautioned by the NSW Colonial Secretary seven days later 'not to commit acts of aggressive warfare against the Aboriginal Natives, and that the Command of the Native Police had been entrusted to him for the maintenance of peace and order and not for the purpose of carrying warfare to an enemy country'.[24] Walker's deputy, Richard P Marshall, was also warned by the Governor that 'proceedings

against the Aborigines have been characterized by too harsh and belliger-
ent a spirit'.[25]

Nevertheless, Walker felt vindicated when he later wrote (on 7 November
1850) to the NSW Colonial Secretary, that:

> In the Macintyre country I used my own discretion, and although
> the Honourable the Attorney General told me he feared I had not
> acted legally throughout, yet the result shows that I was morally
> right for I affirm that the Country of Cumberland is now more
> secure from the aggressions of the aboriginal natives.[26]

Two years later Walker was boasting that his actions on the Macintyre
had resulted in 'A run which could not have fetched £100 in May 1849,
was disposed of in January [1850] for £500'.[27] William Telfer recalled that
'it was not unusual in the Sixties [1860s] to find their ['the Blacks'] skelletons
[*sic*] in the bends of the river where they had been shot down and destroyed'.[28]
Within four years (by January 1854) only 100 Bigambul were left.[29]

Further north on the junction of Cooranga Creek and the Condamine
River (25 kilometres south-west of the future Chinchilla), Thomas Davis
(Steele Rudd's father) told how his surveying party camped and:

> On the afternoon of the fifth day we heard distant but frequent
> gunshots. 'Bang! . . . Bang!' and the 'boo-oom' came nearer and
> nearer . . . Suddenly a disordered army of affrighted blackfellows
> burst through the brushwood into the open where we were camped.
> Like a lot of hunted emus they made for the big scrub on the edge
> of which was a large waterhole. In twos and threes they dashed
> in and disappeared—but not all. Three of four before reaching it
> fell—dead! While two in the rear, disabled, painfully limped along.
> These just reached the scrub when hot in pursuit came several white
> men armed and mounted.[30]

Upon being asked why they were shooting them like that, the station-owner
proclaimed they were shooting the wretches as they had been spearing his

cattle. The way Davis tells it, one gains the impression that this was not an uncommon approach by squatters. At one stage in Davis' travels, in about 1850, his horse got away from him on the upper reaches of the Moonie River and several days later he arrived at Greenbank, a few miles from Dalby, and overtook a stockman leading the lost horse.

> No doubt many will regard it as strange that I was not molested by blacks during this time. It wasn't strange at all. The blacks, even this far back, were quiet on the Darling Downs. Hodgson, the Leslies and others by many conflicts had taken the go out of them. To this day the bones of many an aboriginal still lie bleaching on well-known parts of some Downs stations.[31]

In 1854, having left surveying, Davis was offered a job by Harry Whitty, the Commissioner of Crown Lands, as Postmaster and Clerk of Petty Sessions at Surat, and he and his new wife caught a lift with a dray returning with stores to the settlement from Drayton (just south of Toowoomba, established in 1858). All went well until nearing Chinchilla, when the bullock driver, 'Hell-fire George', had a fight with his black off-sider, Tommy, who was winning until Davis intervened and then 'Hell-fire George' fired a gun loaded with shot at his adversary's head. Not surprisingly the mauled Tommy:

> ... turned sulky and his manner from day to day was anything but assuring. When about thirty miles [48 kilometres] from Surat he slipped away one night—we were in his native part of the country ... A couple of days later, while we were camped on the [Balonne] river, our off-sider accompanied by half-a-hundred of his [Mandandanji] tribe, armed to the teeth, returned. Their meaning was plain. Halting when about sixty or seventy yards [55 to 64 metres] from us, they held a council of war. I saw my wife safely under the dray ... Then the wild yells of them! And a shower of spears and boomerangs rattled round the dray. We were well supplied with firearms and ammunition, and opened fire on them

under cover of the dray. Some fell—the rest immediately made off, for which we felt thankful . . . Meanwhile a black trooper was sent on ahead to acquaint Whitty of [the] dangerous situation. Next morning a sergeant at the head of eighteen black police met us. He followed the blacks and—shot down the lot of them.[32]

Davis felt that 'Such fearful slaughter was unnecessary and unjustified'. Even though he then goes on to mention the murder of a station-hand 'by blacks just a few miles north of us' and the plundering of his rations, the Native Police were unable to find them. One gains an insight into the white population's insecurity when Davis comments, that 'The country around was alive with blacks and one never knew when the place might be surprised'.

At Burgurrah Station on the Balonne River, north-east of St George (1864),[33] Davis recalled that:

. . . some blackfellows called for their gins and were refused posses-sion. No force was attempted, but the blacks in strong numbers rounded up and drove away every working horse that was on the place . . . [The Native Police at Surat were informed and went in pursuit, and] At Waggor [Warroo?] they came upon the blacks numbering between two and three hundred shepherding the Bingera [Burgurrah?] horses . . . The Lieutenant gave the word to fire and a fearful conflict began. The blacks stood their ground and fought bravely—fought until the dead lay thick about them— and only retreated when darkness set in. When morning broke upon the scene they had all disappeared and nothing but the dead remained.[34]

In 1854, north-west of the future township of Miles (1869) at Wallen Station (on Wallan Creek), a shepherd named Kettle refused to return 'his' gin [sic] to her husband. She made her way to the hut of the other shepherd, Mick Burns, and the supposed safety of his wife. Both shepherds were later found naked and speared, and the two women dead on the floor of Burns' hut. The retribution party split up in order to evade the Native Police, however, at Tiryboo (Tiereyboo) Station, some 15 kilometres north to north-west of Bonner Knob (Condamine, 1859), on the northern bank of the Balonne River, the Native Police came:

> ... upon a large number of blacks there, comprised chiefly of old men, women and children, and without taking the least case to discover if these were the guilty people, poured lead into them indiscriminately. Afterwards it was proved beyond doubt that two men only out of this mob so unmercifully butchered had had a hand in the murders [of the whites]. This abominable piece of work was reported to the Government by [Lands Commissioner] Whitty and an enquiry was held. I regret to say it ended in smoke.[35]

Thomas Davis assessed the Aboriginal people as:

> A happy and contented people—independent, respectful, with noble traits in their character, yielding submission to none and with dignity proclaiming—not in words but by gesture—their hereditary rights and independence. And when at times viewing hundreds of men of this stamp, I could no other than wish, and anxiously wish, that some effort be made to save at least a remnant of this interesting race from total annihilation.[36]

Nevertheless, he also participated in the killing-times, which he acknowledged in his recollections. He recalled that word was received that 'the blacks were gathering on Donga Creek [c.30 kilometres east of the station] with the object of attacking Wirabone Station (today's Werribone, c.30 kilometres south-west of Surat, several kilometres east of the Balonne River). They had already slaughtered a number of [Matthew] Gogg's cattle'. With a feeling of a 'boys-own adventure' Davis describes how:

> With little delay a well-equipped party, consisting of Sergeant [David] Graham and black police, Dick Walker—once an officer

in the English army—James Norman, Matthew Goggs, Harry Whitty and myself, was soon riding hard through sand and mulga towards . . . Donga Creek. There camped on both sides of the stream, was a mob of fully four-hundred blacks . . . With our firearms resting on our thighs we rode up . . . Though confused, they stubbornly held their ground. Into the thick of them we emptied our pieces. Their tactics became warlike. In a short time we were almost surrounded. Compelled to fall back we separated and from behind trees cut gaps in their numbers with our rifles. Still their determination never lessened. Some of our party were wounded—myself among the number. A spear pierced my thigh and pinned me to the saddle . . . Fair in the face of powder and ball rushed two or three daring fellows making for Dick Walker. Only one reached him . . . They fell, rolled, struggled in the grass . . . Walker dropped his revolver. His hand went quickly to his side, and the next instant the naked man was ripped from the lower part of his abdomen to his brisket. The shades of night came down and we rode some miles and camped. Rest or sleep we could not.[37]

This event appears to have taken place in 1856, as that was when the mercenary-like Richard Walker was superintendent at Yamboucal Station near Surat.[38] Once again one cannot gauge the numbers of Mandandanji who were wiped out in this melee, but it appears to have been quite significant, or why else would Davis mention it, as well as the numbers involved. The attitudes, approaches and violence in taking the land from the Mandandanji in the Condamine and Maranoa regions has been comprehensively covered by Patrick Collins.[39]

Amazingly, Davis, despite his involvement in shooting blacks on the frontier, also goes to great lengths to try to record information about the people he has been helping to kill. Perhaps it was because of his own sense of guilt that he could write:

Out where the grinning skulls bleach whitely
Under the saltbush sparkling brightly;

Out where the wild dogs chorus nightly—
That's where the dead men lie.[40]

Certainly, the massacre of eleven whites at Hornet Bank in 1857 led to horrendous retaliation, as did the massacre of nineteen whites four years later in 1861 at Cullin-la-Ringo, 300 kilometres to the north-west (near the future Emerald). There were reasons for these attacks by the local Aboriginals. The Hornet Bank murders were in part the result of the older Fraser sons repeatedly raping local Jiman women, the same reason for the murders of shepherds on the Upper Dawson stations. Queensland Parliamentarian J D Wood was told by Sub-Lieutenant Nicholl of the Native Police that in 1857 Mrs Martha Fraser had 'repeatedly told him to reprove her sons for "forcibly taking the young maidens" and that, in consequence, she "expected harm would come of it" . . . Several other informants told Wood that the Frasers were "famous for the young gins" and all agreed "that those acts were the cause of the atrocity".'[41]

Historian Gordon Reid has analysed the Hornet Bank massacre, and identified possible causes for the attack. The Jiman resented being kept out of the station which had been built on their land, particularly as foreign blacks were allowed in, who behaved in a superior fashion towards them (especially the Native Police). The previous Christmas of 1856 saw a pudding laced with strychnine given to a clan group with devastating results. Then a group of squatters on the upper Dawson got together to discuss the spearing of cattle bogged by heavy rains and decided to teach the 'niggers a lesson'. While they failed to find the marauders, they did manage to kill twelve innocent station blacks. Compounding this were the rapacious sexual appetites of some squatters (including the Fraser boys, already mentioned) who raped local Jiman women. Lastly, he notes the false accusation by an overseer, of a Jiman who had whiteman's rations in his gunyah, which he explained had been given as payment for prostituting his wife. The overseer claimed the Aboriginal had stolen them and then shot him dead.[42] A combination of these factors was the deciding point for the Jiman and their allies to throw out the invading whites. For justice to be done, 'the punishment must fit the crime' and the main crime was that of rape; hence the approach taken at Hornet Bank. Four years later at Cullin-la-Ringo the Aboriginals did not rape white women as this was not the crime for which the whites were thought to be guilty.

After the Fraser killings, it appears that some upper Dawson River people fled as refugees from the retribution for Hornet Bank, to the Darling Downs. Second Lieutenant Frederick Carr of the Native Police reported clashes on the Condamine River at Bendemere:

> Following on the tracks I came on the blacks (a mob of upwards of 100) all of the Upper Dawson tribe encamped within ¼ of a mile of the huts on the station. On my approaching the camp the blacks gathered in a body and commenced a most determined assault on the police ... During the affray fifteen blacks were shot amongst others one Baulie a notorious black who is believed to have been the leader of the Hornet Bank murders.[43]

There were also white posses operating independently of the Native Police. One of these was called 'The Browns', which operated as a 'death squad' for months after the Hornet Bank massacre, and tried to kill every Aboriginal they came across. Ernest Davies, a relative new chum, was working at Hawkwood Station (about 70 kilometres south-west of Mundubbera) and recalled a party consisting 'of McArthur, Serrocold [sic], Piggot, Olton, Prior, Thomas and myself and two Brisbane blackboys for tracking', setting out for six weeks of 'hunting'.[44] Later, George Serocold, who had a partnership in Cockatoo Station, roughly halfway between Hawkewood [sic] and Hornet Bank, wrote to his brother Charles in England, declaring 'Whatever you do be careful as I do not wish anybody to be able to read what I have written'. He confirmed his involvement with Davies' posse when he wrote: 'Twelve of us turned out and taking rations with us we patrolled the country for 100 miles [161 kilometres] round for three weeks and spared none of the grownup blacks which we could find.'[45] George D Lang, the eldest son of Presbyterian clergyman J D Lang, wrote to his uncle noting he had learned 'from various sources that a party of twelve—squatters and their confidential overseers—went out mounted and armed to the teeth and scoured the country for blacks . . . and shot upwards of eighty men, women and children'.[46] The posse went on to shoot twelve station blacks working for white squatters; while the Native Police, according to George Lang, also shot over 70 blacks.

Just weeks before the Fraser murders in 1857 came news of the Indian Mutiny, which as Denis Cryle observed 'fed the biblical wrath of the indignant white community by providing it with a global interpretation of the Hornet Bank events'. The 'diabolical outrages', which had been met with crushing revenge by the British and hyped by the local press, appear to have influenced how the white settlers reacted to the local situation.[47]

Immigrant Cooranga station-worker, Konrad Nahrung, travelled to Bendemere Station on Yuleba Creek (about 65 kilometres west of Roma, 1867) to bring his sister back to Wallon, an outstation of Cooranga. On his trip there he had been harassed and told his sister: 'We were nearly murdered by the blacks.' Nahrung recorded:

A mob of myalls were camped about a mile from the station, but they had shown no aggressiveness and were expected to shift shortly. A few of them were employed on the station. One day Mr Sim [the Manager] was riding home and a little picaninny [sic], who was sitting under a tree near the road jumped up and frightened Mr Sim's horse and he was almost thrown off. Sim, in anger, got off his horse, picked up a stone and hit the little boy. The station blacks made a great noise about it and the Myalls heard of it and war was declared. At night the mob came nearer and the station hands saw the necessity of preparing for the attack. They barricaded the door and bored auger holes to fire through. A few of them [that is, Aboriginals] came close with firebrands, but it is well known blacks don't like fighting at night. This was no exception for they settled down a little distance off. In their own mind they were sure of their game for they were 50 to 1 [so this is a very large group]. A native police camp was about 20 miles [32 kilometres] away and a smart young stockman got out of the hut unobserved, caught a good horse and galloped for the police. It did not take him long to tell his story and twelve troopers and their officer started for Bendermere. Allowing no grass to grow under the horses' feet, they arrived at daybreak, in time to save the whites. But what about the blacks [?] They were surprised, and had no mercy shown them. Some were shot trying to escape in the water, others before they got that far. The police pursued them till late in the day, killing all they could. And what had caused this? The one rash act of Mr Sim.[48]

This appears to be the Bendemere massacre of 1860. From this it is apparent that the whites made assumptions about Aboriginal intentions to attack, without understanding their language or customs. The carrying of firebrands suggests that they were going about their normal affairs, for if they were planning an attack they would not have drawn attention to their location. This seems to be a common misinterpretation by Europeans on the frontier.

The *Brisbane Courier* (1 September 1862), under the heading 'The Blacks at the Cabulture [*sic*]', identified that the Native Police, 'some two or three weeks since', and led by 'Lieutenant Wheeler [had] visited the locality with his troopers and shot some eight or ten of the supposed depredators'. The paper made further enquiries into the massacre at 'Cabulture' (50 kilometres north of Brisbane), and confirmed the total as eight, because 'it was insinuated in certain quarters that our statements were exaggerated' and found 'confirmation of the impression that the attack on the blacks was most wanton and unprovoked'.[49] Members of the Waka Waka (from the Burnett, Gayndah, Eidsvold towards Murgon area) were 'holding a corroboree, and that, while they were so engaged, the Native Police surprised their camp, fired upon them, and killed seven men and one gin, besides wounding others'. The newspaper's informant stated 'positively that they had been very peaceably and quietly disposed of late, and done nothing to justify the attack made by the Native Police'. Lieutenant Frederick Wheeler was in charge of the detachment and defended 'his conduct on the ground that his instructions compel him to disperse the blacks wherever they may have congregated', although the *Courier* seriously questioned whether 'those instructions warrant such an act'.[50] It was another four years before the government gazetted the regulations for the operation of the Native Police, and Regulation 31 initially substantiated Wheeler's assertion when it stated: 'It is the duty of the officers, at all times and opportunities, to disperse any large assembly of blacks,' but qualifies this by stating: 'without unnecessary violence.'

The true impact of white retribution, particularly for the Hornet Bank killings, is seen when considering Thomas Davis' observation that:

> In the fifties and sixties my occupation frequently took me over the Dawson country, necessitating my traveling via Hornet Bank Booroonda and Mount Hutton. Often I have ridden over the very ground where the police came up with the murderers of the Fraser family and saw the bleaching bones of the dead blacks strewn here and there—a gruesome sight!—full-ribbed bodies, fleshless arms, disjointed leg-bones and ghastly grinning skulls peeping out of the grass. And I have passed the place in the dead of night with yet twenty miles before me, through wilderness without a soft side— Nature in, what always seemed to me, her worst aspect—but never without a shudder ... To have wended one's way through the Dawson scrub leaving the bones of the slaughtered blacks far behind was joy indeed.[51]

There was still some 40 more years of bloody terror ahead on the moving frontier for the original inhabitants of Queensland. It is interesting to see as one reads about these incidents how often the massacre is prompted not by any killing of whites but simply by disturbing or killing cattle and sheep. It shows the fallacy of trying to construct the Aboriginal death rate by referring to numbers of Europeans killed and then multiplying by ten or whatever. Aboriginals were killed for being there and being in the way of the great land theft.

Chapter 3

European Invasion of the Future Central Queensland [1]

Extermination is then the word—wholesale massacres of men, women and children . . . These terrible *razzias* [plundering raids] occurring in the remote back settlements and pastures, are for the most part ignored by the local authorities—crown land commissioners, police magistrates, and others, or else considered a justified negrocide.

'Residence and Rambles in Australia', Blackwoods Magazine,
September 1852 (Vol.72), p.304. [2]

Between 1843 and 1845, Ludwig Leichhardt journeyed from Jimbour Station (27 kilometres north of Dalby) through to Cape York Peninsula and around the Gulf of Carpentaria to Port Essington in the Northern Territory. Thomas Mitchell found good grazing land around the Barcoo River system in 1846, in what was to become central Queensland, and Edmund Besley Kennedy also explored the areas of the Barcoo and Maranoa Rivers in 1847, and died of spear wounds while exploring Cape York Peninsula in 1848. There were further explorations by William Landsborough, Augustus Gregory and surveyor James Charles Burnett. In 1847, a short-lived settlement under Lieutenant Colonel George Barney was founded at Port Curtis (known as 'Gladstone colony', this is the same site that the present town of Gladstone was founded on, in 1853). Victoria's separation from NSW in 1851 re-activated the growing separation movement in the north, where the squatters had only remote contact with the government in Sydney. In 1857, gold was discovered at Canoona, 160 kilometres north of Gladstone (56 kilometres from the 1853 village that became the town of Rockhampton in 1858), and caused the first rush to the north before separation, involving as many as 16,000 gold seekers at its peak. Unfortunately for the miners it was a disaster and many had great difficulty in returning to the southern colonies.

A newspaper correspondent, Frederick Sinnett, commented on frontier race relations at the new gold-rush settlement, two years after the first white settler, William Thomas Elliott, had established his run there in 1856, on the traditional lands of the Darumbal:

> The ordinary relation between the black and white races is that of war to the knife. The atrocities on both sides are perfectly horrible, and I do not believe the Government makes any effort to stop the slaughter of the aborigines. A native police force is indeed actively engaged, but exclusively against the blacks who are shot down . . . I believe the blacks retaliate whenever they can . . . [3]

On 10 December 1859, the British colony of Queensland came into being with a white population of 28,000, 'of whom only six thousand lived in Brisbane'.[4] During May to July 1861 the Queensland Report of the Select Committee on the Native Police considered the treatment of Aboriginal Queenslanders on the frontier. One witness, Captain John Coley, a resident of Brisbane since 1842, estimated that 250 white people had been killed over the nineteen-year period 1842–61.[5]

In late October 1860, a 'pretty young girl' named Fanny Briggs disappeared from her residence just outside the fledgling northern township of Rockhampton. A search was begun when the owner of the run she was living on returned to find her missing. In early November her decomposed body was found and 'the double crime of ravishment and murder had been perpetrated'.[6] By late January 1861, two of the culprits involved from the local Native Police detachment, Gulliver and Alma, had been arrested. Alma drowned trying to escape while wearing leg-irons and Gulliver was also shot trying to escape.[7] The startling aspect of these deaths, as historian Robert Ørsted-Jensen has uncovered, was that the troopers were in fact killed on the orders of Governor Bowen and the Executive Council. Apparently this was because they feared the troopers might be acquitted before a judge and jury.[8] The previous month the correspondent for the *Moreton Bay Courier* identified that 'the late atrocity has embittered the at no time friendly feeling of the white population'.[9] This caused a lot of unwanted publicity and criticism of the Native Police.[10] Had the colonists known the truth about the 'escaped troopers' and the role of the Executive Council:

> It would probably have led some people to call for the resignation of the Governor and the Executives, and the later biographical accounts of Governor Bowen and his ministers would have had a very different appearance.[11]

Some time later Konrad Nahrung, a German immigrant who worked inland at Cooranga Station for the Ferguson brothers, was involved in taking bales of wool into Rockhampton, where:

> On this trip we saw a gruesome sight. It appears the blacks had murdered a girl not far from Rockhampton [Fanny Briggs?], and the native police and volunteers had caught the murderers up and avenged the girl's death. The blacks were camped in a patch of scrub, when overtaken, and nearly all were shot. The avengers had not been particular in burying the bodies and corpses were lying everywhere.[12]

The former Native Police Commandant Frederick Walker, now a private citizen, with his business partner Daniel Cameron took up Planet Downs (100 kilometres south-east of Springsure) a little west of the gap through the Expedition Range about 1859; while to the east, near the foot of the range, in 1860, Charles Dutton established Bauhinia Downs Station (148 kilometres south-east of Springsure). Walker found his Wadjingu landlords friendly and cooperative in running his station, as did Dutton. Walker had, since his days in charge of the NSW Border Native Police on the Macintyre River, espoused a policy of encouraging squatters to 'let in' local Aboriginal groups and utilise their labour. However, with separation from NSW and the creation of the new colony of Queensland, squatters and their allies, because of the property qualifications for voting, dominated the first parliament.[13] Known as the Squatting Ministry they increased the funding and recruitment of the Native Police and were unsympathetic towards 'Walker's policy'.[14]

The Native Police Commandant, Edric Morisset, appointed the inexperienced Second-Lieutenant Alfred March Patrick to the district, and peace reigned for the remaining half of the year (1861) as the Wadjingu workers on the stations helped with shearing on Planet Downs, Albinia Downs and Bauhinia Downs. However, after this interlude, Patrick led his troopers in a high-handed removal of black station-workers, particularly at Christopher Rolleston's Albinia Downs, where he ordered members of the Gayiri off and followed them up with his troopers. Patrick claimed he then came across about 70 Aboriginals and was attacked, although Frederick Walker wrote to the Colonial Secretary stating that the 'peace was broken by the Native Police under Mr Patrick, attacking and killing and wounding several of the friendly blacks at Mr Rolleston's station'.[15] This became known as the Planet Creek killings. There is no record of how many were killed or wounded, but the peace had been irretrievably broken.

Patrick, whose Native Police camp was near Bauhinia Station, attempted to drive the Aboriginal workers there from the property, despite remonstrations from Dutton who had recently been appointed as a Magistrate. Walker claimed that Patrick was stopped only when Henry Dutton (Charles' brother) threatened the officer with a revolver.[16] Dutton wrote to Commandant Morisset, but he had resigned by the time the letter arrived in Rockhampton, and his replacement, John Bligh, received it. Dutton quoted Patrick who angrily justified himself 'by saying that other Police officers before they had been in the force a fortnight had sent dispatches (I use his own words) of lots of blacks shot and here has he been in the force six months before he has shot a single black ...'[17] Dutton was horrified by Patrick's outlook and responded: 'Can anything be more repugnant to every feeling of humanity [than] that such a violation of every principle of justice and good faith should commence with us?' Both he and Walker warned of serious trouble ahead. Four years later and 520 kilometres to the north, at Bowen, the editor of the *Port Denison Times* noted that:

> Many of the officers are but young, hot-headed men, who from habit, and perhaps from nature, think no more of shooting a black-fellow than a pigeon. They hold a theory that an offence commit-ted by one portion of a tribe should be wiped out by the wholesale slaughter of as many of the first party they can come across as the troopers can shoot down, and they see nothing wrong in the act.[18]

This attitude was to persist for another 40 years. The obvious question is, why, or how could it continue? Judith Wright succinctly identified the political machinations of the period:

> The new Squatting Ministry was far more concerned with getting the country settled as quickly as possible by rent-paying squatters than with the problem of pacifying Aborigines. It was engaged in passing legislation to that end, for the interest of the Colony demanded that the empty Treasury be filled before the first year's debt's be paid. The new land laws not only provided generous terms to the squatters, but stipulated that the runs must be stocked, within a year of taking up, to a quarter of their supposed capacity. If the great flood of livestock were to be taken out to new country in safety, it would require harsh dealing with its previous occupants; and Morisset's policy of driving the Aborigines off the stations immedi-ately was obviously to the Ministry's taste. The Native Police would be an essential instrument of the new government.
>
> It was openly said that the members of the Squatting Ministry themselves would be the first to benefit from the provision which required quick occupation with livestock, for most of them were stock-owners from the Darling Downs whose sheep had built up

so high on those rich pastures that they urgently needed to lighten the load on the grass. The haste with which the new country was stocked would also ensure high prices.[19]

The Native Police force was receiving bad press and their cold-blooded violence was attracting unwanted censure in the already settled areas of the colony as well as in the southern centres. To diffuse this, the government established its first inquiry into the Native Police.[20] Contemporary commentators viewed it as a 'whitewash'. The *Moreton Bay Courier* ran an editorial damning the make-up of the inquiry, accusing the government that 'a more one-sided selection could not have been made'.[21] The editor felt that 'We shall not be very sanguine in our anticipations of the report emanating from this committee' and went on to predict the inquiry's outcome. Three weeks later the *Courier* published an extremely critical letter by H H H from Port Curtis (Gladstone 1863), noting 'that again the Government have set about stifling an honest inquiry into the misdoings of this disgraceful [Native Police] force, and absolutely "packed" a committee of the house to effect their object'.[22] The correspondent complained about the 'heartless unnecessary murdering of the natives . . . [at] Maryborough, Gladstone, Rockhampton and those places; all of which have been hushed up by the government'.[23] The Gayndah correspondent for the paper in another article was particularly critical of R R Mackenzie.

The Chairman, Robert Ramsey Mackenzie, had his fingers in many pies, and had been co-owner of Cockatoo Station, 85 kilometres east of Hornet Bank, when the Jiman had wrought their unfortunate revenge against the Fraser family. The committee, comprised mainly of squatters, ignored Charles Dutton's complaints and smoothed over a series of embarrassing events. One probable reason for Commander Morisset's resignation, although he said it was because of his wife's ill-health, was because his younger brother, Rudolph Roxburgh Morisset, and his troopers, had shot more than eight Waka Waka near Manumbar (50 kilometres south-east of Murgon, and 160 kilometres north-west of Brisbane). The resulting publicity from an advertisement submitted by J and A Mortimer, whose run Morisset had done his shooting on, put his elder brother and the government in an awkward position.[24] Similarly, the publicity surrounding Lieutenant Wheeler's shooting of four men near Ipswich, one of whom was the 'tame blackboy' of a leading squatter, along with the brutal behaviour of Lieutenant Bligh, who was to take over the position of Commandant, contributed to the negative publicity. At Maryborough, Bligh, although he only had a warrant for one man, had driven a number of Badtjala into the Mary River and shot many within sight of the townsfolk.[25] Despite all the negative publicity, the government and avaricious businessmen and squatters were determined that the 1861 inquiry would avoid asking many of the obvious and challenging questions.

Two months later, the *Courier* trumpeted:

> A more piquant farce was never enacted. It is excruciatingly funny to witness the apparent solicitude of the chairman for the souls of the aborigines, and to see how cleverly each member of the committee extracted as much as he wanted from the doubtful witnesses, and no more.

Then the editor, T P Pugh, identifies (if ever so obliquely) that one gentleman witness felt the committee members:

> . . . were less anxious to hear my evidence, as I would give it, than to twist it into a particular shape. All seemed anxious, by their peculiar questions, some scarcely relevant,—others almost asking me to doubt the evidence of my own senses,—and by their neglect to ask other questions naturally arising,—that my evidence should appear as trifling as possible.[26]

The witness was Dr Henry Challinor, who went on to question why the committee was formed to investigate 'grave charges, and all of them, in sympathy and interest, leaning towards a particular side, without a single counteracting element . . . the committee is rather for *exoneration* than *investigation*'. The editor concluded that having seen 'the material of which the Assembly is composed—we do not hesitate to affirm that the whole proceedings will be regarded by the public as a perfect farce'. Twelve weeks later, on 17 October 1861, the massacre of nineteen whites at Cullin-la-Ringo[27] dramatically changed the political milieu and acted as a welcome distraction and justification for maintaining the Native Police force, despite the public acknowledgement in the *Courier* that Lieutenant Wheeler:

> ... knows well enough that the force is a work of *extermination*; and that, to carry out this object efficiently, it is necessary to avoid operations in the presence of those whose evidence would be admissible in cases of awkward exposure, when a hempen necklace *might* be the reward of the arch-perpetrator. And this is the force that the committee seek to perpetuate ... [28]

The voices of concerned citizens were once again ignored, or more likely diverted, by the insinuated analogy of Queensland's own Sepoy rebellion, or at least the brutal response. Unlike the British with the Indian 'Mutiny', colonial Queenslanders kept quiet or minimised and even distorted accounts of mass killings. It was best forgotten or veiled in a conspiracy of silence.

Frederick Walker, for example, identified an element among the Magistrates, who 'told me notwithstanding the repeated desisions [*sic*] of the Judges of the Supreme Court, that the Aboriginal, were not British subjects & not amenable to British law'.[29] This identification was not welcome, partly because of British capital investment in loans to squatters, and the British government was no longer interested in colonial attitudes to Aboriginals. Frontier settlers and their backers were in a financially precarious position. While gambling on making a success of their property investment, the threat of Aboriginal resistance and accompanying stock losses, meant that the government could count on (land-qualifying) voters' tacit support which synthesised itself in silence.

The prevailing attitude enabled the events of 17 October 1861 to unfold, when nineteen whites were massacred at Cullin-la-Ringo Station (c.80 kilometres south-south-west of the future Emerald).[30] This resulted in a further massive retribution, where at least 370 Aboriginal people were killed. Conservatively, this equates to a ratio of nineteen Aboriginals killed for each of the Cullin-la-Ringo whites killed. Possibly suspecting he wouldn't get published, Charles Dutton wrote not to the Brisbane papers but to the *Sydney Morning Herald* (3 February 1861) stating that:

> Before there were any complaints against the blacks in the district, the conduct of the native police was characterized by the grossest cruelty, the most oppressive and exasperating acts, inspiring a feeling of hatred, and desire of revenge, which the conduct of many whites has rather tended to inflame than to soothe or allay.

The tragedy occurred because the manager of nearby Rainworth Station, Jesse Gregson, had, along with Second-Lieutenant Patrick and his Native Police troopers,[31] shot members of the local Gayiri, and it was a retaliatory response. Cedric Wills was later to recall that his brother Tom told him, 'If the truth is ever known, you will find that it was Gregson through shooting those blacks that was the cause of the murder'. There can be no doubt that Cedric firmly believed this account, as he wrote: 'It makes my blood boil when I start on this subject—that Gregson, just for the sake of a few sheep, committed the act which was to cause the murder of my father and all his party—men, women and children.'[32]

The British Australian squatters' response was a complete overreaction, with some 400 Aboriginals killed because of the massacre of eleven whites at Hornet Bank in 1857, and somewhere between 300 and 370 killed directly in response to the massacre at Cullin-la-Ringo. The new Commandant of the Native Police, John O'Connell Bligh, wrote to the Colonial Secretary in early December 1861 informing him that he had ordered all settlers to 'turn all blacks away' and for all gatherings of natives to be considered as 'large war parties'.[33] Six years later Harry Arlington Creaghe, overseer at Albinia Downs (100 kilometres south-east of Cullin-la-Ringo), described the reaction of the neighbouring squatters: they formed a posse which enacted 'fearful havoc, wreaking a terrible and bloody vengeance' and made a pact to shoot Aboriginals on sight.[34]

Adjoining Cullin-la-Ringo to the north, 13 kilometres south from St Helens Station, is the conical-shaped hill of Mount Gobulba, then known

1. 'One Tree Hill' illustration, *Courier Mail* 16 April 1938.

2. Old bunya tree marked with foot and hand holds, Bunya Mountains, 1953. (Picture Queensland Collection, State Library of Queensland)

3. Woodcut 1854 'An affray of Aboriginal tribes, three miles from Brisbane, New South Wales [sic]' (John Oxley Library, State Library of Queensland)

4. Sketch by Thomas J. Domville Taylor (1843) 'Squatters attack on an Aboriginal camp, One Tree Hill, Queensland' depicting the massacre of Aboriginal men, women and children by white squatters at One Tree Hill near the road from Moreton Bay to Darling Downs. (National Library of Australia, pic-vn4970952-v)

5. 'Cumjam' speared Ferguson, an elderly white stockman, at Mentana Station in March 1894. Later that year when Cumjam went to Lochnagar Station (18 km south-west of the future Kowanyama), Jack Alford seized him and secured him with a neck chain. (Photo by Alphonse Chargois)

6. The late Victor Highbury (in front) and Colin Laurence at Emu Lagoon, east of Kowanyama, between the Mitchell and Alice rivers. It was Victor's father who found the bodies floating in the lagoon after the massacre in the mid 1890s. (Kowanyama Land Office Archive)

7. Hornet Bank Station, west of Taroom, in the 1880s, over twenty years after the massacre of eleven whites.

8. Herbert River Native Police Barracks in the 1870s, located on Waterview Station (centre distance), about 40km south of Ingham, between Mt Spec and Halifax Bay.

as Goulbolba (21 kilometres south-west of Emerald). In 1899, a correspondent for the *Morning Bulletin* in Rockhampton, while travelling in the
district, recalled 'a wholesale slaughter of aborigines took place [here] more
than thirty years ago', probably in the late 1860s. He noted that:

> After the terrible murder of the Wills household by the blacks,
> a shepherd was found speared and mutilated near his hut in an
> outlying part of the run. Summary chastisement had been meted
> out to the aborigines on account of the 'Wills murders' on several
> occasions after that melancholy event; and it was thought the dusky
> denizens of the bush were acquiring civilized tendencies ... the
> whites were determined to organize all the force obtainable in the
> neighbourhood, together with the assistance of the black police, and
> declare war against the aborigines [*sic*].[35]

An eyewitness informed the correspondent how 'a friendly blackfellow'
who used to visit the local stations and heard about the intended war,
warned the Gayiri about the whites' intentions, so they sought refuge with
their wives and children in caves and numerous depressions in the Goulbolba Hills. Inspector Frederick Wheeler was in charge of the Native Police
detachment and organised 'as many white volunteers as possible':

> The party, which numbered nearly a hundred, bivouacked at dusk
> within a mile from the stronghold of the natives. Just at dawn the
> order was given to proceed ... The hill was entirely surrounded.
> Those having the best class of arms were given the longest range,
> from the furtherest shore of the lake which skirted the base of the
> hill. As the party approached the native citadel a storm of yells in
> defiance rent the air as a spear hurled by a blackfellow standing on a
> projecting ledge of rock fell harmlessly short. Although the distance
> was great for the class of firearms in those days, a stalwart stockman
> put his carbine suddenly to his shoulder and sent a bullet through
> the brain of the savage. When the other blacks saw one of their
> number fall dead from the rock and his body roll down the hill into

the lake, they were appalled. Yells of defiance gave place to frantic gesticulation, which increased as the terror-stricken savages realized the destruction of their comrades by the leaden messengers of death that came mysteriously whistling up the hillside. By this time the natives showed no resistance, but concerned themselves chiefly in attempts to escape from their deadly foes. As they rushed over the hill from side to side they were met with bullets. The Native Police, principally New South Wales aborigines, climbed the hill and shot those in ambush [hiding?], sparing neither women nor children . . . Many of the savages in their desperation jumped from great heights into the lake and dived under the water, thinking no doubt to escape by that means the flying bullets of their enemies. But alas! It only gave the besiegers a better opportunity for closer range. Whenever a dusky head appeared above the surface to take breath bullets fired from several carbines scattered the brains of the savage over the waters of the lake. About three hundred of the natives were shot or drowned in the lake. Up till a year ago [in 1898] numerous evidences of the battle could be seen in the shape of skulls and bones strewn about the hill sides. Recent bush fires have, however, destroyed almost all the remnants of the conflict.[36]

It is not surprising that if one travels this country today, one rarely meets an Aboriginal Australian.

In July 1865, at Glenmore Station, 10 kilometres from Rockhampton, the local Darumbal gathered for ceremony. The nervous station-owner, Samuel Birkbeck, watched and worried throughout the night as they moved back and forth through the scrub carrying lighted torches to see their way; the event became something menacing to Birkbeck and so he sent for the Native Police.[37] If it was going to be an ambush party, the Darumbal would not have been carrying lighted torches within sight of their supposed quarry. The cultural ignorance of the colonials no doubt led them to make many such misinterpretations.[38] Lorna McDonald notes:

The officer first breakfasted with the family and then took his troopers out to 'disperse' the blacks, an action witnessed by the three youngest boys of the family. They saw eighteen Aboriginals shot and their bodies burnt in a mass grave. According to the *Bulletin*, 'The troopers, while dispersing the blacks and in self defence shot six of them.' Not even the most gullible of readers would have believed the necessity to shoot eighteen in self defence. After this incident Aboriginals threatened to kill every white man on the station in revenge, and so all employees came in from out-stations.[39]

Birkbeck and his family and workers found refuge in a boat in the middle of the Fitzroy River.

Despite the genuine fear of Aboriginal attacks and the difficulty in obtaining shepherds as the frontier expanded, some horse-play may have compounded the situation. In 1863, William H Corfield picked up some Lancashire workers, two married couples and three single men, from Maryborough. After travelling for 20 kilometres they stopped overnight at a South Doongal Station and were lent an empty hut to stay in. Corfield recalled:

> At dinner that evening I told . . . [the station owner] and the overseer how very frightened the emigrants were of the blacks. 'Is that so,' he said. 'Well, we will try them to-night after the boys have had their evening corroborree.' A number of blacks were camped there at the time, so he sent word to his station boys to come up. When they did so, he told them to surround the hut, and yell out, 'Kill 'em white fella, kill 'em white Mary.' We went down to see what we thought was fun . . . the new chums . . . streamed out of the hut in their night attire, and made for the house. I had the greatest difficulty in pacifying them. They refused to return to the hut, and camped on the verandah, the single men remaining on watch. After their flight from the hut, the pigs appropriated their rations which confirmed their belief in a narrow escape from wholesale slaughter.[40]

Corfield was to rue this practical joke, as 'for the remainder of the journey they would not leave the dray or go for water, unless the black boy went with them'. Not surprisingly the new workers were not a success as shepherds.

The impact of the government policy of using the Native Police to disperse the local Aboriginals was inadvertently identified in an editorial in the *Port Denison Times* at Bowen (8 August 1868), where:

> ... the number of orphans existing among the wild tribes is on the increase, and will be so long as the war of extermination now waged by several is carried on. It is not at all uncommon to try the range of a Terry's breech-loader on a mob of blacks, or to hunt them like kangaroos for sport, or to exterminate them by the score without regard for sex or age. We are glad to hear of the likelihood of a criminal prosecution being instituted against one person not many hundred miles from Cardwell, who has gained an unenviable notoriety in this respect. In some places so great is the alarm excited in the native mind, that they have in some instances ventured in upon the stations and offered to sell their children for a few pounds of flour or sugar, or a few articles of clothing, with the double intention of disencumbering themselves and saving their children from slaughter ...

The Reverend J K Black planned to place Aboriginal orphans with white families in the Bowen region.[41]

A letter writer to the *Port Denison Times* (17 April 1869), noted that, 'Whole hetatombs [large-scale slaughter]' of Aboriginal people at the hands of the Native Police and white volunteers had occurred, 'From the first opening of this port to the present time the severity with which the Aboriginals have been treated has been a subject of universal regret ...' The killing, he considered, had been treated with a degree of secrecy, and Aboriginals who had come into Bowen, were:

> ... a mournful sight—about thirty male survivors out of all that tribe, which not long ago could be numbered by the hundreds, and

dates back to the days of its misfortunes and decimation to the introduction, not of the bottle, but of the rifle (which is the quickest?)
when the Native Police, to use the words of an eye-witness, visited
the public house after their work at the shambles, 'the heels of their
boots covered with brains and blood and hair.'[42]

The fact that this letter was published still did not have any impact
or influence on the government.[43] A saddened George Bridgman wrote
to Edward M Curr, an ethnologist, that in the first decade of European
occupation of the Mackay district (1860s), 'about one half of the aboriginal
population was either shot down or perished from loathsome diseases . . .
the black troopers, however . . . have been the chief destroyers'.[44] This
resulted in a preponderance of Aboriginal females and children in the
region.[45] Seven years earlier when considering whether colonists 'shall
admit the blacks', one author's view expressed in the *Port Denison Times*
traced it to a station:

> . . . not 100 miles from the Burdekin [Woodstock?] . . . That stood
> foremost in slaughtering the blacks and admitting the *gins* there can
> be no doubt. There have long been rumours of cruel doings there,
> but the last is not the least . . . the gins were admitted, whilst the few
> surviving husbands had to *stand* afar off gazing with longing eyes
> from the mangroves at their white tormentors living promiscuously
> with their wives.[46]

The Bowen newspaper also warned:

> We know the storm that was raised in England against Governor
> Eyre about the Jamaican riots, yet . . . the whole sacrifice of life . . .
> did not exceed four hundred. What then will the people of England
> say when they learn that more than this number of natives fall each
> year in Queensland, partly by the hands of the settlers and partly by
> a blood-thirsty Native Police . . . illegally constituted.

Chapter 4

South-West Queensland—the Channel Country

'The whites, far from showing any regard for the lives of the original owners of the country, ignored all their rights as to property, and yet were most brutal in retaliation when their rights were transgressed.'

Northern Star, *28 July 1914.[1]*

The frontier expanded from what is now north-western NSW into south-western Queensland: 'the country at least as far as the Bulloo to the north-west and possibly as far as Cooper's Creek had already been checked out by tight-lipped pastoralists even before Burke and Wills got there.'[2] The disastrous Burke and Wills Expedition of 1861, an attempt to cross Australia from Melbourne to the Gulf of Carpentaria, with the subsequent search expeditions to find the missing adventurers, encouraged others to explore southern and western Queensland. When John Costello took a draft of 200 horses 1376 kilometres to the sale-yards of Adelaide in late 1867, he travelled through four isolated selections, the last being Nockatunga Station on the Wilson River, before heading for the Strzelecki Creek and Adelaide, which he reached in the first week of 1868.[3] This preceded the more famous cattle-duffing exploits of Harry Redford, who two years later stole 1000 head from

Bowen Downs (over 400 kilometres to the north, north-east) and drove them down the same route to Adelaide.[4]

Indigenous oral history recollections have identified that during the 1860s, the Aboriginals of north-western NSW formed relationships with other groups. They:

> Found welcome allies in those formidable warriors from the area of Cooper['s] Creek, known to their white victims as 'Salt Water Blacks'. Some of these Cooper Creek tribes had traditional ties with their southern neighbours in the Flinders Ranges of South Australia, and in the Corner country of New South Wales. They came down annually on pilgrimage to the Flinders Ranges to replenish their store of ochre.[5]

Their ceremonial activities were curtailed as they hunted stock along the way and left the local tribes to cope with the white retribution. The South Australian Protector even went to the trouble of supplying ochre via Kopperamanna mission station.[6] Nevertheless, as their lands were invaded and their annual cycle of activities and ceremonies became more disjointed and numbers thinned through the killing-times, fewer were able to continue their age-old lifestyle.

Mr and Mrs H & P Williams, their five sons and two daughters, had just taken up Coongoola Station in early 1862 (about 53 kilometres north of the future Cunnamulla township, 1868),[7] when:

> ... the young Williamses going out for a muster, never dreaming that their home would be in danger had left only one man, together with a traveller; but as it happened to come on to rain they turned back, and on reaching the station were surprised to find it in a state of siege, surrounded by hundreds of blacks, creeping through the grass, drawing their spears after them between their toes. The inmates of the dwelling, however, had barricaded it, and firing through the loopholes, kept their assailants at bay ... Each stockman being armed with a revolver, and a good pouch of cartridges, the assailants

precipitately [*sic*] raised the siege, and there was an exciting cavalry pursuit wherein the assailants obtained such practice experience of the prowess of their intended victims that it obviated any further attempt on their part [to] exterminate them.[8]

The H & P Williams extract shows how invading squatters perceived their right to take the land and the offensive, in defending their land-grab. Pastoralists from the older southern colonies of NSW and Victoria tried to carve out 'new' territory, and then hopefully sell it for a profit and re-invest in more land, further out. Surveyor G C Watson, who practised his profession throughout this period, observed that: 'The wave of pastoral enterprise having set it upon Western Queensland, there was a large inflow of capital, principally from Victoria, for the taking up and stocking of new country, which I was now surveying.'[9] The surveys proved to the Eurocentric mindset that they were utilising the land, in supposed contrast to the traditional indigenous owners.

In mid-1868 Patrick Durack (1834–98) moved his family into the nine-year-old colony of southern Queensland and 'took up' selection at Thillung-gurra Waterhole, Thylungra to the newcomers. John Costello (1838–1923) and his family settled 40 kilometres downstream on Kyabra Waterhole and Creek, and named their station after the watercourse.[10] Thylungra was officially registered in June 1871 and Kyabra Station the following year.[11] These were early days for the men who were to become Australian cattle barons. Interestingly, Jeremiah or 'Dermot' Durack, youngest son of Patrick, who was born in 1877 and grew up in the shadow of his father's expanding pastoral empire, commented to his niece that:

> I cannot remember that Father had any faults, except perhaps he was somewhat mercenary. Or should I say 'acquisitive'? And is that a fault? It stemmed from his desire to give his family the advantage and security he had missed in his own youth. He reached out after great lands and great wealth and in his time held both. He would have done better to keep a firm grip on somewhat less.[12]

In 1864, Jones, Sullivan and Molesworth Greene established Bulloo Downs Station (c.113 kilometres south-west of the future Thargomindah, and 20 kilometres north of the NSW border). The following year, the owner of Fort Bourke Station on the Darling River, Captain John (Jack) Dowling, formed Ardoch Station and not long afterwards, his brother, Vincent James Dowling, took up Thargomindah Station.[13] Later in 1865, while managing his brother's station, John Dowling was out on the run mustering, and was beaten to death with a waddy while sleeping beside his campfire. His 'tame black boy', 'Pimpilly', had sought revenge for a beating he received from Dowling for not promptly bringing water to his 'master' and his horse when so ordered. A Kooma descendant, Hazel McKellar, recalled: 'As a reprisal . . . [they] found the tribe camped on the eastern side of the river, chased them towards the hills [Grey Range], shooting them down as they ran.'[14] This occurred at Thouringowa Waterhole on the Bulloo River (roughly halfway, south-west, between Thargomindah and Bulloo Downs). E O Hobkirk was in Vincent Dowling's white posse that went in search of the alleged perpetrator. He described how they had corralled a camp of Kullilli, and Dowling had demanded to know who had killed his brother, but the Kullilli confessed that they knew nothing about the murder, to which Dowling responded:

> 'If you do not tell me I will shoot the lot of yous'. Still they remained silent. Mr Dowling and the others then set to work and put an end to many of them, not tuching [sic] the lubras and young fry. This I know to be true as I helped first to burn the bodies and then to bury them. A most unpleasant undertaking! but I was only a 'Jackaroo' on Cheshunt station at the time, I had to do what I was told. Later in the day the party went to another Camp of blacks, about 20 miles down the river and there again shot about the same number.[15]

Dowling continued to terrorise the Aboriginal population to avenge his brother's murder, while employing Aboriginal labour.[16] The bookkeeper at Norley Station (c.30 kilometres north of Thargomindah) recalled that in 1911, there was an old Aboriginal there who:

> . . . claimed to be the sole survivor of the massacre. A piccaninny
> at the time, his mother had hidden him under bark in a hole in
> the floor of the gunyah. The troopers burnt the camp, including the
> gunyahs, over his head, but he stayed there and crawled out later.[17]

It was reported that nearly 300 people were killed in this incident. Although the numbers may well have been an exaggeration, it was nevertheless a sizeable killing spree. Vincent Dowling's former head stockman, John Edward Kelly, also described the atrocities meted out to Aboriginal groups on the upper Darling River, some 300 kilometres to the south-east, before Dowling's move to southern Queensland. Kelly observed that, 'We felt perfectly certain that we have not exaggerated one single statement that we have made' about frontier killings as 'We have seen the bones'.[18] At Thouringowa Waterhole on the Bulloo River, which is only about 100 kilometres south-east of Nocaboorara (today's Nockaburrawarry Waterhole) near the junction of the Wilson River and Cooper's Creek, another 'big mob was also massacred'.[19]

Over the Great Dividing Range, south-west from Springsure and the area where retribution had been meted out to the central Queensland tribes in response to Cullin-la-Ringo (1861), Blagden Chambers tells another story of violence perpetrated by the Native Police near Chesterton Station in 1862,[20] on Hoganthulla Creek (c.92 kilometres north-east of Augathella). Chambers attributes the events described to Pigeon Creek Station, a name that appears to have come from the region where the events took place between 1865 and 1867, although it was named with Chesterton in mind.[21] Judith Wright acknowledges some timeline and age discrepancies regarding Chambers' story, although Robert Ørsted-Jensen considers it was merely his literary style (which was rather typical of other reminiscences) and 'can see no reason to question the actual events Chambers describes, this is no doubt what he once experienced and it obviously made a very powerful impression on him'.[22] Wright considers that: 'There was evidence of massacres which makes the story told in *Black and White* appear a commonplace series of events.'[23] The original Chambers narrative was published when the author was nearing his eighties, between June 1926 and

May 1927 (in serial form in *Country Life*, NSW), when, as Wright notes: 'the great amnesia had already set in.'[24] There can be no doubt that there is a strong dollop of truth to his coverage of a massacre in the vicinity of Chesterton, on 'Top Plain' just north of the Chesterton Range. Here Chambers and his mate observed the results of a Native Police engagement where nine Bidjara men and women were slain. The herding together of women and children hints at darker deeds yet to be perpetrated, and their liberation gives the reader an opportunity to rejoice.[25] Three years later, in 1870, the district was still in such a state of turmoil that the Native Police established a camp on Yo Yo Creek, 20 kilometres south of Augathella. It was to last another nine years.[26]

Meanwhile, John Costello and Patrick Durack were not only settling into their newly created stations, they were also expanding their land appropriations. They were of course not alone. Durack wanted more settlers in the region of south-western Queensland and encouraged his relatives to move there.[27] According to one of their descendants, John Costello and Patrick Durack altogether registered holdings of some 91,000 square kilometres; Costello's land-grab amounted to 4.4 million hectares (44,000 square kilometres) and Durack's 'somewhere near the same area'.[28] While this was going on, Alex Reid formed a new station at Wombinderry (today's Wombunderry Waterhole, 60 kilometres south, south-west of Windorah) on Cooper's Creek. At some time in 1872 his business took him elsewhere and he left in charge a lad of eighteen named Maloney and an older man, Silletor.[29] Maloney managed to enrage members of the Birria by shooting one of their camp dogs and was attacked and killed when he went fishing in one of the tributaries of Cooper's Creek. Alice Duncan-Kemp who was born in 1901 at Mooraberrie Station (60 kilometres north of Betoota), and grew up with local Mithaka people, explained that 'It is a serious matter for a gin to lose her dog, for as she grows old and decrepit the dog noses out game, runs it down, and brings it to her hands. The sturdier dogs accompany the bucks [adult Aboriginal males] on big-game hunts.'[30] The shooting of one of their pet dogs was, as Pamela Lukin Watson identifies, 'an action the cultural equivalent of which would have been killing a squatter's horse'.[31]

It was around 1869 that 'a polished young Englishman . . . [by the name of Richard Welford][32] who had come to Australia in search of fortune and adventure' visited the Duracks at Thylungra. Welford established his station Welford Downs (now a part of Welford National Park on the Barcoo River, 40 kilometres east from the junction with Cooper's Creek). It was here in 1872 at the age of 43 that he met his death at the hands of a newly arrived Aboriginal who he was teaching to use an adze, 'when the boy took up a heavy tool and brought it down on his . . . head'.[33] The remaining stockman, Hall, made a dash for Charleville 500 kilometres away with the news of Welford's death. According to his descendant, Patrick Durack tried to warn the Kungkari to move to Thylungra, where he would protect them from the vengeance of the Native Police, but only a handful accepted while the rest perished in the indiscriminate raids that followed.[34]

John Costello had shown Reid and his partner, Fraser, the site of Wombinderry and also found the dazed and demented Silletor after the killing of Maloney. Costello sent word 200 kilometres to Thargomindah, where Sub-Inspector Gilmour and his Native Police detachment were stationed.[35] Gilmour and his troopers travelled to Wombinderry and found Maloney's body in the waterhole, 'and one still grey dawn the Native Police shot everyone they found in a nearby Aborigines' camp'.[36] It may be that one of the survivors was Minyaling, a prominent man of the Birria, whose son Upperty later recalled his father escaping the massacre of his tribe by 'police and whites at Poolpiree waterhole on Keeroongooloo' Station (c.80 kilometres south of Windorah).[37] Wombinderry and Poolpiree waterholes are very close to one another on Cooper's Creek, which suggests that it may have been the same massacre. Mary Durack observed that:

> There were, however, no questions asked of the blacks as to who had committed the crime or why. No arrests were made and the bodies of those shot around the camp at dawn were left to the ravages of wild dogs and birds of prey.[38]

Bert James Rayment was born in 1883 at Windorah, just to the southwest of Welford Station, and stated in his recollections that:

I have never ceased to feel bitter about the murders of blacks that men whispered about during those years and the slaughter of a whole tribe of men, women and children in a gorge in the Grey [Cheviot] Range in retaliation for the killing of Welford... The Welford killing and retaliation took place about 10 years before my time, but it was fresh in men's memory. The only survivor of the tribe, 'Waddy Mundowie'... [who as] a baby... fell from his mother's arms when she was shot in the slaughter. A burning tree fell across the child's legs, burning them off between the knee and ankle. He was rescued and reared by a stockman who had more humanity than his companions.[39]

Mona Henry, as a young nursing sister at Birdsville, recalled a 90-year-old Aboriginal Elder and rainmaker named Mintulee (Joe), telling her how near Mt Leonard Station (near Betoota):

... his mother had saved his life, during a massacre, when he was a baby. The attackers killed the Aborigines swimming in the river, so Joe's mother hid her baby in the lignum [tall, almost leafless shrubs] growing along the bank. She saved her own life by floating downstream with a piece of buckbush on her head. That night, when all was quiet, she returned to the river and rescued her child.[40]

A Wangkumara man, 'Ngaka' Ebsworth, interviewed in 1981, related stories from his great-grandmother, who had helped to deliver him on the banks of Ngakanuru Waterhole on Cooper's Creek in 1919. He told of the Mt Leonard Station massacre in 1872, which was apparently in response to Welford's murder over 200 kilometres to the east. Ngaka had visited the site and examined 'skulls with lead bullets still embedded in them'.[41]

In May 1873, while on his way to establish a station further out west, John Conrick left his herd, which continued on to Mt Margaret Station (c.32 kilometres south of the future Eromanga), and went to Thargomindah to meet up with Robert Bostock, a fellow new settler. There they met

Sub-Inspector James Merry Gilmour and Acting Sub-Inspector Thomas Herbert and eight Native Mounted Police troopers. According to Conrick the adjacent lands were almost in a state of warfare and 'the wild blacks were afraid for their lives' as he had seen them flee in fear at the approach of his party.[42] This was not surprising as the Native Police were still hunting Aboriginals thought responsible for killing Welford and Maloney. However, the violence had been going on even earlier, as the *Darling Downs Gazette* (31 October 1861) editorialised about the traditional owners: 'They are also, I am sorry to say, very badly treated by the whites on the Bulla [Bulloo] and Wilson [Rivers]. No less than nine were shot the other day for stealing on the Bulla, and such treatment we have every reason to believe, is not infrequent.'[43]

Gilmour, as an Acting Sub-Inspector, had patrolled the roads near Roma during 1865, and was promoted to Sub-Inspector in 1867. Four years later (in 1871) at Cooper's Creek, Gilmour was conducting a search for the remnants of Ludwig Leichhardt's ill-fated expedition of 1848. Thomas Herbert was appointed to the Native Police as an Acting Sub-Inspector in 1872 and became camp-keeper at the Bulloo River and was a relatively inexperienced junior officer, although he had apparently once been the aide-de-camp to a Queensland governor.[44] Whatever the cause, in late 1873 Gilmour and Herbert had a falling-out and brawled publicly in Cunnamulla with the result that the junior officer was dismissed. Although Police Commissioner Seymour noted that Gilmour 'should have been suspended', nothing further seems to have been done and the Sub-Inspector died the following year (1874).[45]

Conrick and Bostock went on to Mt Margaret and collected their cattle and supplies. They made their way to Eurongella Waterhole, where they made arrangements with John Costello for the agistment of their cattle, as this was part of Kyabra Station (now the township of Eromanga). The intrepid duo then set out in search of 'new' lands towards the South Australian border. They reconnoitered the region, including Burke and Wills' Depot 65 at Fort Wills and the 'Dig Tree', and made their choices as to where they wanted to establish their respective runs on lands of the Wangkumara, Yandruwandha and Yawarrawarrka.[46] They then returned and collected their cattle and supplies and several weeks later, on 28 October 1873, they crossed the flooded Cooper at Goondabinna Waterhole and camped on the north bank. As they settled in for the evening they were joined by 29-year-old Acting Sub-Inspector Brabazon Richard Stafford and his eight Native Police troopers who were out on patrol.[47] Conrick noted the scarcity of the usual Aboriginal presence, which was undoubtedly due to the Native Police. Bostock and company (including the dismissed former Acting Sub-Inspector Herbert) went on to Innamincka Waterhole to establish his run, and then rode back to Charleville to register his block as well as Conrick's. Unfortunately, it appears that Bostock had a loose tongue as others, namely Messrs Nutting and Doyle, had already registered Goondabinna, sight unseen. Rather than fight a costly legal battle, Conrick moved 60 kilometres west and chose the site which the local traditional owners called 'Ngapamiri' and Conrick called Nappa Merrie. The new station was on the lower reaches of Cooper's Creek, about 20 kilometres from the Queensland–South Australian border.[48]

Edith McFarlane, who married a station manager and lived for 40 years in the outback region of south-western Queensland, acknowledged that some of the early white settlers had 'made a successful attempt to incorporate the natives into the life of the white man, [but] too many thought only to destroy them'. At Nappa Merrie in 1926 she remembered meeting an old man:

> ... who as a boy, had been the only one to survive such a massacre which had taken place at about the time John Conrick settled there [in 1873]. The child had hidden under a bush, and when Mr. Conrick found him later he took him and cared for him. The massacre was not on Nappa Merri [sic], but ... in the sandridges further south.[49]

It seems likely that it was Sub-Inspector Stafford and his troopers who were responsible for the massacre. Conrick saw few local inhabitants and those he did see fled in fear, by either diving into waterholes or hiding in the lignum.

One of the Goondabinna gazumpers turned out to be John Bligh Nutting, acting Police Magistrate at Cunnamulla (1871–78) and former Inspector of the Native Police (1865–71), who, along with his business partner, Robert Doyle, established Chastleton Station (also referred to as Baryulah). In 1875 Sub-Inspector John McKay Dunne and his unit from Thargomindah were operating in the area. In response to an Aboriginal group of 40 warriors led by Marracoota, who had been spearing cattle and attacking white settlers, one William Olliffe who worked at Barryooloo (Baryulah) was instructed by his employer, Doyle, to act as guide to the police party.[50] Dunne and his troopers tracked Marracoota to Cooper's Creek, and surrounded the war party on three sides with the river at their back on the fourth side. The melee that followed saw Marracoota shot. Olliffe later wrote about his experiences and claimed that the rest of 'the outlaw band surrendered with a chorus of wails', and were then given a stern warning as to what would happen to them if they persisted in their activities.

There are some discrepancies relating to this account: the Native Police were not renowned for their leniency or restraint and although other tribesmen were shot we are not told how many. Was Olliffe actually trying to hide a massacre? Similarly, his claim that as a result of Dunne's warning cattle spearing or attacks on settlers ceased, doesn't explain why Conrick and nine other white settlers wrote complaining to the Colonial Secretary about the lack of protection provided by Dunne and his troops, 'thereby entailing great pecuniary loss to the leaseholders of this district'.[51] Two years later, Dunne died from 'softening of the brain' (*delirium tremens*), at Fort Burke (on the Darling River) in north-western NSW.[52]

The result of the settlers' complaint was that a detachment of Native Police under Sub-Inspector Walter Frederick Cheeke was sent to Chastleton in May 1877. How much Nutting's part-ownership of the run influenced the rapidity of the response is a moot point, but within a month of their arrival, another dispersal had occurred. Cheeke's troopers built a stockade on high ground among the coolibahs near Goondabinna Waterhole and then went into action. South-west of the Chastleton homestead around a big sandhill, 100 people were killed.[53] Conrick was horrified and wrote to Cheeke's superiors which may have influenced the result, for the detachment was withdrawn. The Sub-Inspector was retrenched from the force in 1880 and died in the Dunwich Benevolent Asylum in 1928.[54]

About 30 kilometres west of Cunnamulla in Kunja territory, one of the traditional owners, Granny McKellar, recalled from her childhood, how 'a lot of her people were shot' at Moonjaree Waterhole in the early 1880s. Another indigenous descendant, Tom McKellar, told 'how he found a large number of bones in the sandhills south of Tinnenburra Station'.[55]

By the 1870s the moving frontier had made it to the south-west corner of Queensland and the traditional lands of the Mithaka. In 1881, the tiny settlement of Diamantina Crossing was established and four years later after it had been surveyed by F A Hartnell, it became known as Birdsville.[56] In 1875, while on an exploration trip to the north, close to Thundapurty Waterhole (just east of the future Durrie Station, c.100 kilometres north-east of Birdsville), John Conrick's small party came across among the sandhills, 'the burial place of 42 Aboriginals, killed in a skirmish with the Queensland Native Police some time before; this, Conrick concluded, explained the fear of the Aborigines they had met' on their journey from Nappa Merrie.[57]

In early 1879, Sub-Inspectors Kaye and Gough and their troopers made three patrols out of Bluff Station (c.13 kilometres north-east of Birdsville). On the third patrol, just before Annandale Station, 100-odd kilometres to the north-west: 'Gough and Kaye started after the blacks, found a large camp, and dispersed them ... arrived at Annandale on March 6 [1879].'[58] After failing to find Miller, a stockman who had accompanied them as a guide, Sub-Inspector Kaye: 'patrolled up the Herbert to Glengyle, where he dispersed a large camp of niggers as punishment for the murder of a stockman named Scott, about a month previously.'[59]

A strangely similar tale comes from across the colonial border. South Australian police became concerned when learning of Aboriginal killers escaping into their colony and possibly influencing their own natives. Writing to the Police Commissioner in Adelaide from his station at Cowarie on Wharburton Creek (in South Australia 300 kilometres south, south-west of Birdsville and c.800 kilometres north of Adelaide), William Paull recorded several points of disquiet. He noted the response to the killing of a stockman working for Urquhart and Fraser:

... this being across the Queensland Border, a party from different
Stations made a raid on the blacks killing 27 of them, shortly afterwards the native police made a second raid killing 29 more which
so frightened those remaining in that locality that they came down
the creek into South Australia mixing with the natives on the run,
and Mr Hood writing from the station south of Messrs Urquhart
& Fraser a short time ago states that he had not seen the track of a
black on his run since Jany [sic] 1879.[60]

William Paull later mentioned the response to the killing of a 'white
man' on Campbell's Glengyle Station (37 kilometres south of Bedourie),
where 'the Whites again combined & killed 11 Blacks and a large party
including the actual murderer escaped into South Australia and again
mixed with our natives here'.[61] This was in January 1879 and seems to be a
confirmation of Kaye and Gough's dispersal.

In 1950 George Farwell recorded that at Cooningheera Waterhole (c.100
kilometres north-east of Birdsville), some 25 kilometres west of Durrie
Station (or 80 west of Betoota), on the Diamantina River: 'In the 1870s
when it was an outstation for Urangie, two men were camped there, young
Johnnycake Miller and Maconochie, the cook. They developed a taste for
the women of the tribe.'[62] Miller, on returning to camp, was warned by:

... his mate's lubra [who] ran out, shouting to him to clear for his
life. He saw some black warriors coming for him with spears, leapt
on his horse bareback, and managed to escape. The cook's head was
later found in a camp-oven. The white avengers were even more
brutal, for a whole tribe, including old men, women and children
were hunted like wallabies and put to death. Even today [in 1950]
there is an awful silence about the ruins of Cooninghera [sic].[63]

Two hundred kilometres to the east of Cooningheera Waterhole,
Edith McFarlane, while at Tanbar Station (c.100 kilometres south-west of
Windorah) from 1932–56, recalled that:

Cruelty to the natives in the very early days was evident at times. We once saw a sandhill near the river where bones had been uncovered when a strong wind blew away the sand. It was obvious that this was not a native burial ground, as the area was subject to flooding, and the blacks buried their dead out of reach of flood waters. In addition, the skeletons lay at awkward angles which made it clear that they had been herded together and shot, as it was known [that it] had happened at a spot further down the river, subsequently named 'Massacre Sandhill.'[64]

A relatively contemporary visitor to this area in the late twentieth century described the site he identified as 'Skeleton Sandhill', and linked it to McFarlane's 'Massacre Sandhill', which is:

... roughly forty feet [12 metres] at its highest point and covers approx two acres [0.809ha] ... [where] skeletal forms so old as to crumble at the touch of a finger tip were observed in windswept hollows and elsewhere. However, there were no skulls or parts thereof. This was put down to predators, the scavengers, and to the bone-sucking cattle thought to be suffering from a mineral deficiency.[65]

Farwell, who travelled the region over 60 years ago, identified that: 'A vengeance party was led by Captain Little, [a] policeman at Bedourie barracks. With a posse of black trackers, he chased the whole tribe all over the country, overtaking the first of them six miles from the waterhole, where they were shot out of hand.'[66] He is referring to Robert Kyle Little, previously a captain in the 97th and 22nd Regiments, who became an Acting Sub-Inspector in 1875 at the age of 34 and was based at Eyre Creek Native Police camp at Bedourie (c.200 kilometres north of Birdsville).[67]

From Durack and Duncan-Kemp's writings, Pamela Lukin Watson suggests that a more sinister intention emerged, in the form of 'ethnic-cleansing'.[68] Certainly, within a decade of John Costello and Patrick Durack arriving in the region, Mary Durack claimed that 'many settlers now openly declared that Western Queensland could only be habitable for whites when the last of the blacks had been killed out—"by bullet or by bait".'[69] She concluded that:

> ... it was soon clear to all that the black troopers [Native Police] rode to kill—to shatter the old tribes, the Bootamurra, the Pita-Pita, the Murragoon, the Waker-di, the Ngoa, the Murrawarri and the Kalkadoon, to leave men, women and children dead and dying on the plains, in the gullies and river beds.[70]

There were also killings at Kalidawarra Waterhole (c.100 kilometres south-west of Bedourie), Monkira Station (c.160 kilometres south-east of Bedourie) and Dangrie Waterhole (c.70 kilometres north-east of Birdsville). In early 1876 the man in charge at Morney Plains Station wrote to the owner, Robert Collins (1838–1901):

> I observe what you say about the blacks and your orders shall be obeyed so far as lays in my power, but I consider they did not get more than they deserved. I caught them killing a sheep, and I have since learned that they have killed more than one. You grant that I would be justified in punishing them if they destroyed property. I consider they destroy property when they camp on a waterhole where cattle are running as the animals are scattered all over the face of the earth ... I have known cattle to go 20 miles through the rotten niggers [sic]. You know as well as I that they get shot on other stations, and if they are allowed to camp on this run it will soon get too hot for me ... [71]

The implications of the manager's innuendo and the disappearance of local Aboriginal clan groups suggests that the rifle was used to remove the 'rotten niggers'. Robert Martin Collins had bought Whitula and Morney in 1874 and by '1878 these and additional blocks had been stocked and sold'. He and his brother William in 1877:

... were among the organizers of the North Australian Pastoral Co., of which (Sir) Thomas McIlwraith, William Forrest and Sir William Ingram, proprietor of the *Illustrated London News*, were also members. The company's land included nine thousand sq. miles [23,309 square kilometres] in South Australia, properties in the North Gregory district of Queensland, Alexandria station in the Northern territory and land west of Bowen.[72]

These were pastoral companies operating on a large scale and with prominent members of colonial society, and along with the rapidity of pastoral expansion and stocking of the land, it becomes clear the traditional owners were seen primarily as an impediment to the process. It is interesting to note that A J Vogan was working for the *Illustrated London News* when he collected the material for his book, *The Black Police*.[73] So what did his boss, the owner of his newspaper, Sir William Ingram, and an investor in large pastoral projects, think about Vogan's book?

During the 1880s there were three major massacres in the vicinity of the white settlement of Birdsville. All three occurred while Aboriginal inhabitants were participating in great ceremonial gatherings. Luise Hercus recorded that Mick McLean Irinjili (c.1888–1977), 'the last man to be brought up in the Simpson Desert before white contact':[74]

... knew about the massacre of the Wardamba people near Poeppel's Corner in the eastern Simpson Desert. The Wardamba, a ceremony very much like the Mindiri, was in full swing, when many Midaga, Wanganuru, Nulubulu, Wanggamadla and Yaluyandi people were shot down by police in retribution for the murder of a White man. Ironically the Nulabulu man responsible was aware of the danger; he managed to escape and was subsequently pardoned by the police.

The worst massacre was probably the one at Wiyirbi near Clifton Hills [c.140 kilometres south-west of Birdsville in northeastern SA] where many Yaluyandi, Garanuru and Yawarawarga were killed by Black-trackers over a grudge. Nobody knows exactly what happened, nobody could outwit the Black-trackers: nobody escaped.[75]

Mick McLean Irinjili also told of the demise of the Mindiri people at Koonchera Waterhole, in north-eastern South Australia in August 1971. He had been told by the last survivor, Charlie Ganabidi:

> The police from Andrewilla killed them all, hundreds of men, hundreds of women and many children, all because of a bullock, just a small one, a mere calf, at Koonchera . . . Some of the women had gone to a place close by (over a small sandhill) . . . they kept them guarded there all night, they ranged right round and fired at them. They killed all the women, the blind old men and the young initiates, they killed them all at Koonchera . . . only five got away . . . Charlie Ganabidi, (another) Charlie, Niba, Waya-waya and Guranda 'Sticknest rat'. . . . they just managed to dive into the water like waterhole frogs, they swam in the water, they were really scared . . . they . . . went back to the river, the Diamantina, to the 'Two Waterholes' that is Old Lagoon Station, never to return . . . 'How many, how many are there that we have killed?' (asked the police). They laid them out all around and pulled them and dragged them into one heap . . . to burn them up . . . [76]

The Aboriginal estimate for the massacre at Koonchera was around 500 people, although George Farwell, who first wrote of massacres in this region in 1950, estimated that 200 people were killed.[77] However, one would be wise to take into account Helen Tolcher's cautioning regarding the concept of numbers as, 'To accept as accurate claims of hundreds of victims, coming from informants who were passing on stories told to them by other people whose nineteenth century estimate of the number of victims was probably "a mob" or "big mob", is to risk distorting history'.[78] Perhaps Tolcher is right; but she may also be operating from the contemporary mainstream perspective that killings of 100 or more at one time were not really feasible. Evidence given in this book shows that not only could this happen, but that it did happen over and over again, even when the guns were not repeating rifles. In these distant regions bodies were not so often burned as buried in sandhills or simply just left to rot as there was hardly any traffic in such remote areas and the chance of discovery was very slight indeed.

Hercus interviewed another old man, Ben Murray, when he was 84 years old. Murray was 'nephew' to Ngadu-Dagali ('side-spearing' or 'Rib-bone Billy'), a distinguished Simpson Desert Wangganguru man, and told exactly what Ngadu-Dagali had passed on to him.[79] During the latter part of the nineteenth century, in the vicinity of Clifton Hills Station:

> A whole lot of people from up there killed a bullock and cooked it (they were planning) to take it away ready cooked, and to go a long way off (with the pieces of cooked meat) and to stay away . . . The white-fellows caught sight of those people out in the open plain (near the creek), they saw that there was meat there. Those people hadn't gone far enough, they were still quite close really. The white-fellows killed them all (twenty of them) as many as all my fingers and all my toes. . . . They shot them all, even the pitiful little babies.[80]

During this same event, Ngadu-Dagali's wife was shot dead and, after hiding, he 'left that country altogether'.

An anthropologist specialising in the Channel Country, Paul Gorecki, has told how:

> The oral history of some Mithaka families tells of three locations in country that should be visited with care or should be avoided outright. This is because of massacres of their people by whites, even if the detail and time of these massacres are no longer remembered: Cuppa Waterhole on Farrars Creek [c.15 kilometres west of Durrie Station]; Gilpeppee at the northern edge of Lake Yamma Yamma (which was the location of a Police camp) and Kulpie waterhole very close to Haddon Corner.[81]

Today, where there was once a thriving population of indigenous clan groups, there is but a remnant of Aboriginal descendants and a very small number of whites. Such is the legacy of the white pastoral invasion.

Chapter 5

Poisonings and Sexual Exploitation

'What must the people of England think of Queensland with the foul stain that is upon her ...'

Richard Bird Hall, Alice River, Townsville, 27 July 1872.[1]

'As for arsenic [the] only experience the poor devils had of it was when mixed purposely with station flour.'

Dr Walter Roth, to Director of Queensland Museum, Ronald Hamlyn-Harris, 6 August 1915.[2]

From the 1840s onwards, the white squatters continued their confrontation with the traditional landowners, for whom, as Donald Horne noted, 40 years ago:

> ... the rush to the grasslands was a guerilla war in which the enemy seized the key rivers, creeks, lagoons and waterholes, drove away the native game, despoiled sacred places, set up dissension by pushing one tribe into the territory of another, and killed insidiously by spreading new diseases ... If the blacks killed animals or men, the settlers formed armed patrols which in reprisal might slaughter

whole groups, perhaps quite innocent, in the scrub; when a force of
Native Police was formed it became a new instrument of murder.
It was almost impossible to get court evidence against killers of the
blacks since blacks were not permissible court witnesses; settlers
might shoot blacks in the scrub without anyone knowing, or leave
them gifts of flour mixed with arsenic . . . [3]

This behaviour was openly acknowledged in the Queensland *Daily News
and Mail* (29 July 1933),[4] when there were still men living who had participated in the violence on the frontier:

> In our Wide Bay and Burnett district blackfellows were shot down
> at sight by some of the earlier settlers, and many scores [twenty plus]
> of men and women were poisoned by strychnine being placed in the
> flour that was distributed to them, or that had been left in places
> handy for the blacks to themselves take possession of.[5]

It had been done before—poisoning had been used on the frontier when
colonists were moving into the Richmond and Clarence River regions of
what is now coastal northern NSW. In June 1841, Thomas Coutts took up
a run on Kangaroo Creek which flows into the Clarence River, an area of
53,760 acres (21,756 hectares) on the traditional lands of the Gumbaynggir.[6]
In late November 1847, Coutts paid his Aboriginal workers with 10 lbs
(5 kilos) of flour and tobacco. Shortly afterwards 23 of them were writhing
in agony after vomiting, and then died. Several Gumbaynggir survived
and informed a local shepherd, John Tomkinson, what had occurred.[7]
Subsequently, Commissioner of Crown Lands, Oliver Fry, and the Chief
Constable of Grafton and several troopers, after inspecting the gruesome
remains and taking statements from four European employees, arrested
Thomas Coutts, committed him for trial on 17 January 1848 and sent him
to Sydney. Apparently, local white settlers were not impressed with Coutts'
behaviour; fellow landowner, Charles Tindal, wrote to his father stating
that it was an 'atrocious murder of Blacks' and that 'everybody hopes
he will be hung'.[8] On 23 February, the Chief Justice of NSW, Sir Alfred

Stephen, granted Coutts bail of £1000, of which Coutts put up £500 and two Sydney businessmen £250 each. Two and a half months later, on 10 May, the Attorney General, John Plunkett, determined not to continue with the case, ostensibly because of lack of evidence, even though later he stated: 'I am sorry to say that the suspicion is very strong that the prisoner is not guiltless of the dreadful deed charged against him.' This decision was despite Fry's comments when forwarding the depositions to Sydney, that this event was 'one of the most hideous enormities that has ever taken place, in any age or Country. The atrocity to which I allude, is the murder by poisoning of not fewer (it is believed), than twenty-three Aboriginal natives . . .'[9] Two of Coutts' white workers were subsequently killed by surviving Gumbayng-gir, very likely because of their association with the poisoner, for no stock or goods were taken.[10]

In 1850 Coutts relocated to Tooloom Station on the northern arm of the Clarence River and then moved his family to Balmain in Sydney. Around 1850 he purchased Ellengowan on the Darling Downs and in early 1865 Coutts purchased 23,000 acres (9,308 hectares) called North Toolburra Station, 13 kilometres north of Warwick, southern Queensland.[11] The lengthy coverage that the *Queenslander* gave in its 12 September 1874 issue of a Supreme Court legal battle between descendants of Coutts, suggests that he had achieved some position of note. J V D Coutts in his 1950 coverage of 'The Coutts Family' makes no mention of the Kangaroo Creek poisoning in the Clarence district, but does note that:

> Toolburra has a sad history, and I often wonder whether there is a 'hoodoo' on the place. Besides the tragic death of Thomas Coutts, and Charles Swinburne, there was an accident about 1892 when Coutts Ross, and his friend Reutz, from Brisbane were shooting on the lagoon; both were shot, but the mystery has never been solved.[12]

The *Brisbane Courier* quite ironically, although unintentionally, felt that the Coutts' brothers' 'names live in the remembrance of genuine Queenslanders'.[13]

William Coote (1822–98), in his 1882 *History of the Colony of Queensland*, assesses the validity of reports relating to the poisoning of Aboriginal people and observes that prior to the extension of the frontier into what became southern Queensland:

> ...a similar instance, but on a larger scale (that is, more than seventy of all sexes and ages are said to have been poisoned at once by the admixture of poison in cakes given to the unsuspecting victims), occurred in the Clarence River district [Grafton]. The circumstances provoked such comment, that the presumed principal delinquent was, as I am informed by a member of our Legislature long resident here, with whom I have conversed on the subject, apprehended and sent to Sydney, where after some detention, he was discharged from the want of available evidence against him.[14]

Coote is referring to Robert Ramsey Mackenzie, who chaired the 1861 Select Committee on the Native Police (and later became Premier/Colonial Secretary of Queensland, 1867–68).[15] Previously, MacKenzie had had a lease at Wattenbakh in the Manning River area on the central coast of NSW (south-west of Port Macquarie), but sold up and moved to Moreton Bay in 1840. However, he would have been aware of the Mt McKenzie massacre of 1835 and other ensuing fatalities.[16] Later, as Colonial Secretary, he was in a position to officially ignore frontier violence. Writing in 1964, Douglas Rye records that:

> Early in the 1830s the A[ustralian] A[gricultural] Company established a heifer station at Belbora, between Gloucester and Wingham. The blacks in due course gave considerable trouble in the way of stealing from the huts. To teach them a lesson the Company's servants went to the extreme of leaving damper poisoned with arsenic in the huts, with the result that a number of Aborigines perished. The massacre at Wattenbakh took place in 1835, following the spearing of five of Mackensie's [*sic*] convict shepherds by the blacks.[17]

The NSW Commissioner for Crown Lands in the Clarence River District, Richard Bligh, acknowledged rather cryptically, that the settlers during the 1840s:

> Seem to have restrained the blacks in the way in which you, no doubt, as a bushman, are aware that blacks are restrained in the bush, where no authorised system of protection exists. There are ways of doing that, which, though not strictly legal, are very effective. People, of course, will defend themselves when left to their own resources.[18]

The desperate behaviour of whites on the frontier, and their reaction to their isolated position, was identified during the 1861 Queensland Select Committee on the Native Police Force, where an old settler and Magistrate, John Ker Wilson, acknowledged that:

> These men would be frightened out of their lives by the blacks, and not being strong enough to go out and fight them, and being always in a state of fear, they would pop a gun through the slabs of the hut and fire upon them, and perhaps kill a blackfellow; at other times they would put poison in a damper and give it to the blacks. It was never the case when the stations were strongly manned . . . [19]

In January 1842, the frightened shepherds of Kilcoy Creek,[20] about 100 kilometres to the north-west of Brisbane Town (1824), fled their outstation and left poisoned flour behind, causing around 60 agonising Aboriginal deaths.[21] The former convict, David Bracewell, related how there was:

> . . . a great meeting of the native tribes, 14 or 15 in number, in the vicinity of the great Bunya Scrub, called Booroon, lying N.W. about 2 days journey from the Glass House Mountains. The meeting is called a *Toor* (ring) . . . To this meeting a Party of Blacks from the District of the Bunya Scrubs to the South called the Inwoorah & Tombarah Tribes . . . They described the following symptoms with

much minuteness: swelling of the head, foaming at the mouth, violent retching & thirst, trembling of the limbs & sudden prostration. These Tribes vowed vengeance . . . Nine or ten Tribes suffered more or less and one the Wooganbarah suffered so severely as to be unable to attend the meeting which subsequently took place . . . The White Men's Station lies to the Southward among the mountains; from a watch which [James] Davis obtained from one of the Blacks . . . which is now in my possession & proves to have formerly belonged to a Shepherd of Mr Evan Mackenzie, named Murray, it is difficult not to have suspicion as to the locality alluded to: for the very man Murray with another shepherd of Mr Mackenzie's was barbarously murdered by the Blacks about three months since by way of retaliation, as Davis states, for the loss of their poisoned friends.[22]

William Coote assessed the validity of the Kilcoy poisoning, and observed that the owner of the run, Sir Evan MacKenzie, remembered: 'The overseer saying to me one day, "Don't you think it would be a good thing to give those fellows a dose?" Of course I expressed my abhorrence of the suggestion, and no more was said about it.'[23]

What he failed to mention was that it was his brother, Colin John, who was most likely the authority responsible for instigating this ruthless form of 'dispersal'.[24] Coote concluded that:

The enquiry of the overseer appears to me of great significance. It pointed not to an experiment, but a method—something already tried and found sufficient for the purpose, and intended to be repeated as occasion might seem to require. Taking the whole of the evidence in conjunction with the narratives of Schmidt and Petrie, it would be difficult, in the absence of stronger proof to the contrary, to doubt the truth of the charge brought.[25]

Certainly, 34 years later, Ebenezer Thorne in his book *The Queen of the Colonies* accepted that the poisoning took place and that somewhere between 40 and 80 Aboriginals died as a result of eating the poisoned flour. Thorne noted that:

> Some few escaped death; but nearly all the children of the tribe died, with many of the adults . . . [and] For many years, on offering a present of flour to any blackfellow, one was met with the inquiry, 'Mackenzie sit down?'—the name by which the poison became universally known among them for many miles.[26]

In the Caboolture and Pine River area during the mid-1840s, two murders in 1846 and another two the following year, made settlers particularly nervous, as Erica Long describes:[27]

> . . . fears already apparent were fuelled, disquiet heightened and a siege mentality fostered due to graphic descriptions published in the *Moreton Bay Courier*.[28] One month after the murder of Andrew Gregor it reported the assault of a Whiteside hut keeper who had been horribly disfigured by a waddy blow to the face.[29] [Tom] Petrie related this incident and added that a shepherd had also been killed. He stated that the Aborigines told him later they had murdered the shepherd because he had poisoned them.[30]
>
> They went to his hut and looked in . . . they saw some flour, and feeling hungry went off, and made damper of it. When cooked they commenced to eat, but found it 'barn' (bitter); then some got sick, and three of the number 'very much jump about' and died . . . the blacks swore that they would have revenge for their dead friends.[31]

The *Sydney Morning Herald* reported on the poisoning, followed by a passionate account in the *Moreton Bay Courier* which exonerated the Griffins (owners of Whiteside Station) and held a dismissed employee responsible.[32] The evidence was comprehensive and, as Erica Long has concluded, left 'no doubt that the poisoning had occurred whether deliberate or not'.[33]

Edgar Foreman recalled how, as a little boy in 1867, he 'rode through a small pocket on what was called Rush Creek and saw scores of bleached bones, including a complete skeleton. Mr Griffin afterwards told me what the bones were, and how they came there'.[34] Earlier Foreman had noted that 'fifty or sixty of them lost their lives through being poisoned'.

One can glean an indication of frontier violence on the Inner Darling Downs from the reminiscences of William Stamer who went there during the late 1850s. He observed:

> It was enough to make ones blood run cold to listen to the stories that were told of the diabolical manner in which whole tribes had been 'rubbed out' by unscrupulous squatters. No device by which the race could be exterminated had been left untried. They had been hunted and shot down like wild beasts—treacherously murdered whilst sleeping within the paddock rails, and poisoned wholesale by having arsenic or some other substance mixed with the flour given to them for food. One 'lady' on the Upper Condamine [River] had particularly distinguished herself in the poisoning line, having, if report spoke the truth, disposed of more natives than any squatter by means of arsenic alone . . . [35]

Two kilometres east of the village that was established as Maryborough in 1843, adjoining Hervey Bay and Fraser Island, there was further cause for an escalation of conflict:

> Late in November 1854 . . . when Aborigines ate flour laced with strychnine, among provisions stolen from the store of Henry Palmer, 'There was a great wailing heard in the camp at Granville where they were sent every night,' an old settler recorded, 'and in the morning several of them were found dead, poisoned.' [36]

In response to complaints about his actions in the Marlborough district, Sub-Inspector Frederick Wheeler reported to the Commissioner of Police in August 1872, that the complainant:

McLennan has boasted to me of the way he used to lay *poison* for the Blacks at his out stations, which of course in former times the Blacks took, and caused their enmity towards him—The District well knows that this is the case—none of these things would ever have been mentioned, but when persons bring unnecessary charges—in self-defence the party aggrieved must bring counter-charges . . . [37]

Four years later in 1876 Wheeler was charged with the murder of an Aboriginal at Banchory and dismissed, and despite the charges was allowed to remain free. He then disappeared and six years later died in Java.[38]

North-west of Cooktown following the massacre of Battle Camp in 1873, Jack Harrigan, whose mother was only one of a handful of survivors, told how, in order to seek revenge for the deaths of troopers and others assisting them, the whites left:

. . . poisoned flour near known places where the mob would come for water and poisoned the water in the waterholes itself. Jack said his mother had told him that more Normanby *bama* [Aboriginal people] died this way than actually being shot or killed in the actual battle of Battle Camp.[39]

Thirteen years later and further down the coast, Harold Finch-Hatton, in his 1886 recollections of his eight years on the Queensland frontier, tells of:

A gentleman who shall be nameless, but who once resided at a place well known as the Long Lagoon, in the interior of Queensland, is still famous for the tremendous 'haul' of Blacks which he made in one day. They had been giving him a great deal of trouble, and had lately killed four of his shepherds in succession. This was past a joke, and he decided that the niggers [*sic*] required something really startling to keep them quiet, and he hit upon the following device, which everyone must admit was sufficiently startling. One day, when he knew that a large mob of Blacks were watching his movements, he packed a large dray with rations, and set off with it from the head station, as if he was going the rounds of the shepherds' huts. When he got opposite to the Long Lagoon, one of the wheels came off the dray, and down it went with a crash. This appeared to annoy him considerably; but after looking pensively at it for some time, he seemed to conclude that there was nothing to be done, so he unhitched the horses and led them back to the station. No sooner had he disappeared than, of course, all the Blacks came up to the dray to see what was in it. To their great delight, it contained a vast supply of flour, beef, and sugar. With appetites sharpened by a prolonged abstinence from such delicacies, they lost no time in carrying the rations down to the waterside, and forthwith devoured them as only a Black-fellow can.

Alas for the greediness of the savage! alas for the cruelty of his white brother! The rations contained about as much strychnine as anything else, and not one of the mob escaped. When they awoke in the morning they were all dead corpses. More than a hundred Blacks were stretched out by this ruse of the owner of the Long Lagoon. In a dry season, when the water sinks low, their skulls are occasionally to be found half buried in the mud.[40]

Long Lagoon is part of Mt Spencer Station 50 kilometres inland from Mackay and was owned in various partnerships between the Finch-Hatton brothers individually, their kinsman, Lionel Knight Rice, and the station manager, Charles Walter Toussaint.[41] Oblique as Harold Finch-Hatton is, his intimate knowledge of detail suggests it may well have been his older brother, Henry, who perpetrated the poisoning. The gentlemen were members of the English aristocracy, and it is therefore not surprising that a conspiracy of silence surrounded the event. Henry Stormont Finch-Hatton left Queensland around 1884–85.[42] By the end of the following year (December 1886) the Finch-Hatton brothers were insolvent,[43] and although Henry revisited for a business trip in 1887, he appears to have never returned. In 1898 Henry inherited his title as the Earl of Winchilsea and Nottingham, and would have no doubt been aware of the hypocrisy of his family motto as it applied to him: '*Nils conscire sibi*' ('Conscious of no evil').[44]

Fletcher Creek, about 50 kilometres north-east of Charters Towers, is also remembered as the scene of a toxic encounter with the white settlers.[45] In central Queensland and far north Queensland, including Cape York Peninsula, into the early part of the twentieth century, there were still regular reports of poisonings. Historian Noel Loos notes that, 'In fact it is possible that poison was used as frequently against Aborigines in this twilight situation [of the winding down of the frontier] as it was in the previous period of open conflict'.[46] East of Thornborough on the Hodgkinson Goldfields (c.100 kilometres inland from Cairns), under the frivolous heading, 'Dark Doings with the Sable Savages', a pastoralist was recorded as having come across a big mob of Aborigines around a freshly speared bullock. Unable to take revenge with his rifle before they scattered, he thought:

> . . . it a pity to lose so good an opportunity of poisoning some of the hawks and dingoes with which the country is infested, our pastoral friend literally peppered the carcass of his quondam [former] grass-eater with that violent corrosive venom—arsenic; and (in order that none of the pilfering curs whom the feast was intended should partake of it) labeled the body 'POISON'. His surprise may be imagined when, visiting the spot to see the result of his scheme, he discovered that, disregarding his caution, a large number of the original monarchs of the soil had injudiciously partaken of the insalubrious 'bullocky' and, as a natural consequence most of them had become slightly indisposed.[47]

The familiarity with this approach can also be seen with the construction of the Cairns–Kuranda railway (1886–93), when men were getting hickory logs for the railway, between the second section (of the railway) and Jamieson's (at Buchan Point), they found the Yirrganydji (coastal Djabugay) an 'intolerable nuisance'. They had to leave one man on guard in camp, 'otherwise every scrap of food is taken by the thieving rascals'. The *Cairns Post* suggested that 'a little "Rough on Rats" [arsenic] judiciously disposed amongst some damper would effectually stop these annoyances'.[48] The matter of fact way the editor identifies poisoning by whites as a means of removing so-called human 'pests' and his conclusion that: 'if the Government won't help the people in the North, they will have to help themselves', suggests this was a relatively common approach.[49]

The Shelfo Homestead poison flour incident occurred around 1900–01, near the confluence of the Alice and Mitchell Rivers (c.40 kilometres east of Kowanyama), when Kunjen people were given flour laced with poison. Fortunately, they realised they were being poisoned and scraped rust from fencing wire, mixed it with mussels and ate the concoction raw to make themselves vomit. They also bled their arms and providentially all survived.[50] However, in many other instances indigenous people were not so lucky. It would appear that poisonings were more prevalent in Queensland than down south, possibly because of the larger numbers of Aboriginal people residing over such large areas and the small numbers of white pastoralists and settlers. This no doubt engendered a great deal of fear amongst the whites of the potential for attack and destruction of their stock. Similarly, as the frontier expanded into the more populated Aboriginal inhabited northern regions, these fears seem to have enabled the smaller white populations to resort to poisoning more frequently.

Sexual Exploitation

Another iniquitous activity on the frontier involved the sexual exploitation of women, boys and girls. Arthur J Vogan, author of *The Black Police* (1891) and correspondent for the *Illustrated London News*, travelled widely around Queensland, including South Gregory and the Warrego, and termed the period of the 1870s and 1880s as 'the red shocking years'. As Pamela Lukin Watson notes:

> ... land-greedy pioneers in far western Queensland shot the Aboriginal males and older females but spared the lives of youths and girls 'in order to have the use of them for their more or less illegitimate needs. No words can express the horrors that arose—but the worldly wise can guess and understand.'[51]

The dispirited response by Aboriginal survivors to the impact of health hazards, such as tobacco, venereal disease, poor nutrition and the psychological impact of white 'settlement' was encapsulated by one 'old man' Elder, who commented: 'Before whitefellow come, blackfellow could run like emu; but now, supposing big one run, then big one tired, and plenty heart jump about; not always like that blackfellow.'[52]

In 1899, from Camooweal on the Northern Territory border, the local Constable wrote:

> ... if half the young lubras now being detained (I won't call it *kept*, for I know most of them would clear away if they could) were approached on the subject, they would say that they were run down by station blackguards on horseback, and taken to the stations for licentious purposes, and kept there more like slaves than anything else. I have heard it said that these same lubras have been locked up for weeks at a time ... anyway, whilst their heartless persecutors have been mustering cattle on their respective runs. Some, I have heard, take these lubras with them, but take the precautions to tie them up securely for the night to prevent them escaping.[53]

By the late 1890s, in outback Queensland, other reports were coming into the police at Bedourie (halfway between Dajarra and Birdsville) and from Durham Downs (approximately one-third of the way between Innamincka and Windorah) to the Southern Protector of Aborigines, Archibald Meston, regarding the keeping of Aboriginal women.[54] They tell a similarly repetitive tale:

> Scrub-cutters offered work at Ardoch station [between Quilpie and Thargomindah] were horrified to find eight or nine Aboriginal women fenced in with rabbit-proof netting adjoining the house: this property was owned and regularly inspected by the Queensland National Bank ... Black women were graded: 'stud gins' [who] were reserved for the sole use of the boss; class number two were for the 'colonial experience men' and the third grade for general hands ... the

most feeble toiled continuously in the sun, carting water from the creek to the shed, a distance of about 280 yards [255 metres].[55]

Raymond Evans notes that 'Inter-racial sexual relations of frontier and post-frontier existence fall mainly into the patterns of outright capture and rape, prostitution and concubinage'; which was comprised 'of male aggression and domination, as well as human degradation'.[56]

Sources show that the act of kidnapping children appears to have been a common occurrence in nineteenth-century Queensland. Similar behaviour has also been described in the Northern Territory by Ann McGrath, along with Deborah Bird Rose's research on Victoria River Downs, Humbert River and Wave Hill Stations, which indicates how prevalent sexual exploitation was, well into the twentieth century.[57] The approach and behaviour appears very much akin to slavery.

Thomas Davis, Steele Rudd's father, who lived at Surat during the 1850s, noted that: "'Twas a custom of the whites to keep a few gins on the stations—say, one apiece. The gin's husbands permitted them to stay until they should require them to shift to some other part of the country.'[58] He felt that attacks on outstations which refused to give up their 'gins' were not 'without some justification'. Davis also observed that the:

> Wandaigumbil ['Wondai Gumbal'[59] Native] Police Barracks early in the fifties [1850s] was a perfect harem—young and old gins ranging from twelve to fifty years, could be seen there any time. The cause of the crimes originated with the whites. The white man was to blame.[60]

Running concurrently with the violence was the sexual exploitation of women and children. Ted Egan's song about 'the Drover's Boy' is possibly a more romanticised version of what was actually going on, but that Aboriginal women dressed like men and worked cattle with their white boss, was definitely the case, as was their sexual role when not 'working'.[61]

Little boys and girls were snatched by the Native Police and pastoralists and then given or traded across the outback to fulfil the role of cheap servants. John Swann travelled the Burke district in 1890, having been in the colony for over 40 years, and noted:

> ... from Normanton to Camooweal there is not 50 white men employed you will find one or two whites on stations the remainder are black boys that in reality are gins in trousers. Now Sir how were the boys and gins procured and how is the supply kept up. I will inform you by organised parties going up the Nicholson River and along the coast Point Parker way also Gunpowder river supplies some, these children are brought in and tied up and the slewth hound gin that has found favour in her master sight is put over them to keep them from running away and if they manage to get away and are caught God help them ...

Regarding Frank Hann, Swann recorded that:

> ... when I left Lawn Hill [there were] 13 gins [and] three half caste children ... his Chinese cook has a gin, his fencers has gins his stockman has gins. Hann himself has seven as a sort of bodyguard or small regiment of amazons [sic] ... his next neighbour Shadforth has not whites of any description gins and boy gins predominating ... [62]

Almost a year later, in response, second-class Inspector Alex Douglas wrote from Normanton, confirming:

> ... it is the practice by many Squatters to herd their cattle with Gins and this has been the custom for a great many years. When I first took charge here I made enquiries on the subject and was informed that in the early days of settlement the male aboriginals had been nearly exterminated and that the Gins to prevent them from spearing had been utilized as Stockmen. [63]

This was the same man who, nearly fourteen years earlier when he was a Sub-Inspector, and out on patrol with his troopers and a white man (who by regulations was forbidden to be there), was reported by J Hamilton (in 1880), for allowing a:

> ... captured female, quite a child who after being washed by his troopers in a creek was taken to the camp and ravished by them. My friend hearing her cries and groans during the whole night— That next morning when they saddled up, the child stood dazed and as they moved to leave, staggered towards them apparently not knowing if she were still a prisoner or at liberty; they rode off leaving her in the bush.[64]

Twenty years later, in 1901, Dr Walter Roth visited the Gulf and border country as Queensland's Northern Protector of Aborigines and found that the situation was the same. He was concerned that 'one special abuse' was the taking of children into Queensland and NSW from the Northern Territory.[65] Three years later, the serving Native Police Inspector, Percy Galbraith, who had been the Aboriginal Protector at Normanton for the same period, acknowledged the long-established practice of kidnapping children, and that:

> A number of private families, also stations, have gins. Most of these gins have been given to their owners when about seven or eight years of age. These gins are not allowed to mix with other Aboriginals. After a time, this enforced separation is strengthened by the girl's surroundings. She gets attracted to white men and looks down upon males of her own race ... A large number of individuals have an idea that they can trade an Aboriginal as they would a horse, or a bullock—some of these people are good church-goers. One lady informed me that an Aboriginal had been left to her by will. She did not, however, mention if probate had been granted.[66]

A further tragedy is that this practice also led to a burgeoning of venereal disease among the captured Aboriginal women.[67] In 1897, Police Commissioner Parry-Okedon commented negatively on the impact of white sexual exploitation and the subsequent rapid increase in syphilis and gonorrhoea.[68]

Yet, publicity about the mistreatment of Aboriginal people, including sexual exploitation, had been going on for over 30 years. The *Port Denison Times*, for example, identified in May 1869 that more than 400 Aboriginals were killed each year by settlers and the Native Police. The author also acknowledged that the Queensland government refused to follow the precedents established by every other colonial government (in Australia) and that they were 'taking no measures whatever for the recovery of the Aboriginals, and utterly refusing to listen to any schemes for their benefit'. The author notes that while some squatters would have completely exterminated the original inhabitants (but for limitations of time and material?), even those squatters of a more humane disposition have taken 'the law into their own hands, and in desperation dyed their hands in the blood of the blacks'. If this was not enough, the author traces why the first calls to 'let in' Aboriginals arose: to gain access to the women.[69] The perverse irony is the negative attitude shown towards so-called 'half-castes' who were the result of the activities of white men.

Chapter 6

Early Gulf and Central Queensland

One thing is for sure, they were all squatting on Aboriginal land. There was no question of paying rates or compensation to the original owners. The land was simply confiscated from the Aborigines and very little reference is made in the early history to the plight of Aborigines.

Hazel McKellar. [1]

In 1861, search parties of explorers set out from four different directions to find the missing Burke and Wills Expedition, and in the process reconnoitered the Gulf of Carpentaria and the area east through north Queensland. The Victorian Relief Expedition, led by Alfred Howitt, set out from Melbourne on 4 July 1861 and reached Cooper's Creek on 15 September, where they found the last survivor of Burke's party, John King. However, Howitt had not returned before the other search parties set out. John McKinlay (1819–72) left Adelaide in mid-August, trekking north via Cooper's Creek and the Diamantina River to the Gulf, then to Bowen (Port Denison) on the Queensland coast. William Landsborough (1825–86), who had previously explored the Nogoa and Peak Downs districts in central Queensland, landed by ship at the Albert River in the Gulf on 1 October and made his way south to the Darling Downs and thence to Melbourne.

None of these expeditions mention killing any of the local inhabitants. McKinlay appears to have had quite close and positive interactions with rather large numbers of people, perhaps 100 to 150, while Landsborough had little interaction, and only with very small groups of one to two. The former Commandant of the Queensland Native Police, Frederick Walker, on his exploration expedition, managed to shoot twelve Mbara [?] warriors at Stawell River (c.100 kilometres north-west of the future Hughenden). In his journal entry for 30 October 1861, Walker wrote:

> The mounted party met about thirty men, painted and loaded with arms, and they charged them at once. Now was shown the benefit of Terry's breech-loaders, for such a continued steady fire was kept up by this small party that the enemy never was able to throw one of their formidable spears. Twelve men were killed, and few, if any, escaped unwounded. The hill mob probably got alarmed at the sound of heavy firing, and did not consider it convenient to come to the scratch. The gins and children had been left camped on the river and as there was no water there, our possession of a spring was no doubt the *casus beli* [ground for war].[2]

One month later, near his Camp 55 and close to where Amraynald Station was later established, 50 kilometres south-east of the future Burke-town (1864), on the traditional lands of the Mingin [?], Walker described how the natives' 'appearance looked hostile', and:

> ... they were stretching out in a half moon, in three parties. This move, which my men term stockyarding, is, I believe, peculiar to blacks throwing spears with a woomera, the object being to concentrate a shower of spears. ... Their right wing, which was, I think, the strongest mob, got over the river, and were off; but their centre and left wing suffered a heavy loss.[3]

Interestingly, there was a fifth 'explorer', Duncan McIntyre (1831–66), but his party was looking for the remnants of Ludwig Leichhardt's last expedition (1848). McIntyre's party made their way overland during 1864 from Melbourne, to investigate the 'new' lands of the Gulf of Carpentaria.[4] McIntyre claimed that 'he never on any occasion during his trip to the gulf had any real occasion to fire at a black, and . . . owing to the dry state of the country, he saw more than all the other explorers put together'.[5] One member of his party, George McGillivray, later recorded in January 1865 that: 'The Queensland settlers seem to hunt and shoot the blacks whenever they see them, instead of making friends with them, and afterwards making them useful. I believe there are ways of managing them without shooting and exterminating.'[6] McGillivray demonstrates a far more humane way of interacting with the indigenous inhabitants when he acknowledges:

> . . . that they are capable of being made in a new country the settlers' best friends. They are for a time of course strange, and require a deal of trouble being taken with them; but I believe they are ultimately worth it all. For instance, I have got some of the Paroo blacks shepherding on the run ever since I arrived here—now nearly three years ago, and during that time they have never once left the sheep, and take as much pride in their flocks as any white man, and a great deal more than most . . . they have been my friends on the Darling and on the Paroo . . . [and] If the blacks are shot down, they will, to a certainty, retaliate; they have laws of right and wrong, which ought to be respected as well as those *civilized* men.[7]

Unfortunately for the indigenous people and the colony's history, McGillivray's approach to his runs and Aboriginal inhabitants was not one that the Queensland government and the frontiersmen were going to adopt. Tony Roberts' research in the Gulf and Northern Territory led him to conclude:

> The harsh treatment of Aboriginals by many of the first European settlers was in sharp contrast to the generally benign way in which local [Aboriginal] people treated the explorers and the first over-landers. Leichhardt, Fevenc and others who showed no hostility were given hospitality in the belief they were not there to take over

the land.[8] Abraham Wallace had no need for firearms when travelling the Coast Track [from Queensland into the Northern Territory along the Gulf of Carpentaria] with cattle for Elsey station in 1881. Only when the vast herds began arriving and the [white] visitors started putting down roots, claiming exclusive use of precious waterholes, did the attitude of local [Aboriginal] peoples change to one of spirited resistance.[9]

Following the various Gulf explorations and their reports on the 'lie of the land' and assessments of potential pastoral use, particularly Landsborough's journal, squatters began moving north and north-west towards the supposed 'Plains of Promise' of the Gulf Country. Ernest Henry wrote to his mother in late December 1863, acknowledging that: 'The land law in Queensland is occupation, the first [European] occupier becomes the possessor, so you see I had not a moment to spare.'[10] Henry had already stocked Baroondah (1860), 50 kilometres west of Taroom and Mt McConnell (1861), 75 kilometres due west of Collinsville and then explored and took up country around Hughenden in 1863.[11]

There was a growing distinction between the squatters of the Darling Downs and the squatters who moved into central Queensland:

> The ambitious newcomers were a different breed from the 'Pure Merinos'. Relying more on courage and experience than on breeding or natural right to realize their hopes of prosperity. Many were proven bushmen with squatting experience on southern properties. Others had simply been lucky on [the] Victorian gold-fields. Two dominant features characterised the men of the new pastoral frontier—recklessness and recklessness. In the rush north and west, run after run was taken up and promptly abandoned for new land further out.[12]

Many of these peripatetic squatters also moved on to claim runs in the Gulf and the Northern Territory. Roberts has identified the extent of violence there and that many of the perpetrators were from central Queensland.

This is an area today where archaeological evidence indicates a large indigenous population of thousands, so what happened to them?

It was from the then most northerly Queensland settlement of Port Denison (1859) that southern squatters and pastoralists began their move into the newly proclaimed Kennedy District recently traversed by the explorers. George Elphinstone Dalrymple (1826–76) was sent to Port Denison and established Bowen in 1861. Bruce Breslin has identified that:

> Dalrymple had no intention of avoiding bloodshed and establishing good communications with the Aborigines. What he *said* and what he *did* were often two very different things ... [and] ... historians did not bother to distinguish his rhetoric from reality. Dalrymple showed from the very beginning that he would arm and alarm the frontier.[13]

Noel Loos clearly acknowledged the rapidity of white expansion, for:

> Within six weeks of Dalrymple's arrival, runs had been taken up in an unbroken 350 miles [560 kilometres] inland [from Port Denison/ Bowen] despite the fact that there was intense Aboriginal resistance by the third week of settlement. By the middle of 1862, 454 runs and 31,504 square miles [83,190 square kilometres] had been applied for and, by 1863, almost the whole of the Kennedy District had been settled [by whites].[14]

Teamsters established routes from Bowen inland to the outback stations: to the south-west via Eatonvale to St Ann's to Bowen Downs (over 450 kilometres, 'as the crow flies'); and to the west, north-west, crossing the Burdekin and then (further west) travelling up the river at the back of the coastal ranges. They were following the tracks of those who had set out to establish their runs on Aboriginal lands, and in the process they also followed pathways established by local indigenous inhabitants.[15] Unfortunately, as historian Geoffrey Bolton indicated nearly 50 years ago, 'most settlers came expecting trouble'.[16] No doubt this was inspired by Dalrymple,

and, as Breslin has shown, it became a self-fulfilling prophecy, one requiring a sincere change in perception, as 'Both pioneers and historians have
unswervingly insisted that the Aborigines at Port Denison demonstrated
hostility towards the white invaders from the moment of contact. Close
analysis tends to reveal the contrary'. [17]

Certainly, within days of establishing Bowen, Dalrymple was reporting
an attack within 20 kilometres of the settlement.[18] A small party of white
men who had been exploring Abbot Bay, 80 kilometres north-west of
Bowen, reported that a force of 120 Aboriginals had shown signs of 'hostile
intentions'. Lieutenant Walter Powell of the Native Police had four of
his troopers desert, and Dalrymple reports that 'a number of gentlemen
residing here accompanied him as volunteers'. Nothing seems to have been
said about this by the authorities, but it was in breach of the Native Police
regulations.[19] Needless to say Dalrymple was one of the volunteers and
recorded that, 'Within two miles of the settlement I met a party of armed
natives & at once dispersed them'.[20] Again, numbers are not mentioned.

In early October 1863, on the banks of the Bogie River, some 25 kilometres upstream from its junction with the Burdekin, nearly a hundred
Biri warriors gathered near J G MacDonald's Strathbogie Station (100 kilometres west of Port Denison). The occupants of the station, P Armstrong
and a Brisbane Aboriginal, Charley, had been forewarned of the attack, but
nevertheless had to retreat to their huts amid a hail of spears and missiles.
At least two of the Biri warriors were shot dead and several wounded. The
Brisbane Courier noted: 'The fight lasted two hours. The defenders were
armed with Terry's breech-loading rifles, and they were able to keep up the
fire with little intermission.' However:

> The next day the mob was tracked by a party of people from the
> neighboring [*sic*] stations, and they got another lesson that will
> probably deter them from attacking a station again in a hurry. It has
> been estimated that about twenty-five were killed, and amongst them
> two runaways or discharged men from the Native Police Force. [21]

Prior to this, Ludwig Leichhardt (1813–48) on his 1844 expedition had identified a 'most picturesque landscape' on the upper Burdekin River which he called the Valley of Lagoons. It was to here that Dalrymple and his business partners, the Scott brothers (and silent organising partner, R G W Herbert, Queensland's first Premier 1859–66),[22] came to establish their station of the same name. This also accounts for why Dalrymple was so intent on establishing Cardwell (1864) as a port, as the newly created station was 100 kilometres inland. The districts of Burke and Cook were proclaimed open for white settlement in January 1864.[23]

Similarly, from Westernport Victoria came Joseph Hann and his sons, William and Frank, to invest in north Queensland stations. In partnership with Richard Daintree and some investors from Melbourne, Hann took up Bluff Downs, Maryvale and Lolworth Stations. Joseph Hann was drowned in January 1864, the year that Richard Daintree and his family moved to Maryvale. During this early period of stocking the station, William and his family also lived at Maryvale and Frank formed an outstation at the 'Twelve Mile' on Lolworth Station. The new arrivals were the targets of the local Aboriginal inhabitants, along with dingoes, speargrass and later, falling wool prices.[24] However, 'matters went along a little roughly with the blacks',[25] when they cleaned out the rations from the hut at the 'Twelve Mile'. The station workers tracked the members of the Gudjala to a conical hill and remonstrated with them, to which they received the response of buttock smacking as a form of derision. The whites could do nothing as they were without cartridges for their weapons. Unfortunately for the Gudjala, William and Frank Hann turned up and:

> The two brothers had a Winchester each and a full belt of cartridges. They returned to the hill, and no sooner did they reach there than the younger nigger [sic] commenced the by-play. Some others, now frolicsome with full bellies, commenced the same game with great glee. They'd all jump forward and smack simultaneously, with a shout like a corroboree. William and Frank Hann waited with the Winchesters until the game was in full play, and then they fired.[26]

From that point on, the conical hill was called 'Nigger's Bounce' and is apparently still called that today. Aboriginal oral history recalls massacres at Allandale, Longton and Wambiana Stations;[27] all within a 120-kilometre radius. St Ann's is also mentioned by Sally Babidge's informants. The station adjoins Vine Creek and Yacamunda Stations and seems likely to be where the Fetherstonhaugh Vine Creek massacre occurred. While this appears to be the only reference to William Hann's involvement in these nefarious acts, his younger brother Frank went on to establish a fearsome reputation, particularly after 1875 when he took over the Waanyi site called Ngoomari, renamed Lawn Hill.[28]

From Rockhampton, the Jardine Brothers drove 250 cattle on the first attempt by the new settlers to take cattle up the west coast of Cape York Peninsula, to where their father, ex-Rockhampton Magistrate, John Jardine, had established Somerset in 1863.[29] His two sons, Frank and Alexander Jardine, managed to kill nine 'natives' north of the Nassau River on 16 December 1864. Frederick Byerley records from their journals that:

> ... the natives, having left their gins on the other side, swam over the creek and tried to surround them. Being thus forced into a 'row', the Brothers determined to let them have it, only regretting that some of the party were not with them, so as to make the lesson a more severe one. The assailants spread out ... but seeing eight or nine of their companions drop, made them think better of it, and they were finally hunted back across the river, leaving their friends behind them. [30]

The question here is, who was trespassing on whose land? Surely the Kokoberrin warriors were merely protecting their families and their traditional lands.

Over 31 indigenous people were killed when the Jardines came across a gathering of some 70 to 80 men probably on the Alice River,[31] and quite likely participating in ceremony. 'The natives at first stood up courageously, but ... they got huddled in a heap, in, and at the margin of the water, when ten carbines poured volley after volley into them from all directions, killing and wounding with every shot with very little return . . .' The Jardines believed that they killed or wounded up to 59 Aboriginals.[32]

On 28 December 1864, on Kendall Creek, 'some' may conservatively equate to two men being killed, but it could well have been more. The irony is that they are described as having 'paid for their gratuitious [sic] attack' when the Jardines acknowledge that it was the whites who advanced on the Aboriginal men 'who waited for the whites, close to a mangrove scrub, till they [the whites] got within sixty yards of them, when they began throwing spears. They were answered with Terry's breech-loaders . . .'[33] Historian David Day has suggested that: 'The party shot perhaps as many as 72 Aborigines in 11 separate incidents without incurring a single casualty themselves.'[34] Okunjen Elder, Mrs Alma Wason, of Kowanyama, observed:

> Today there are big gaps in the genealogies of the clans of the top end groups—Okunjen, Uwkangand and Olkol as well as visiting neighbouring clans, including amongst others, the Awbakhn and Oyaan, Kokomenjena, and Kokobera, whose territory it was that the Jardines trespassed upon.[35]

The brothers readily acknowledged that 'We shot our way through',[36] and Frank Jardine having carved 80 notches on his rifle stock was described by a visiting contemporary as having 'the blood of many natives on his soul'.[37]

After 1862 pastoralists began taking up stations in the Gulf following, as John Dymock, who was the first to comprehensively research this area's history, has identified, 'the western and northerly course of the Flinders River which, forming a natural path of [white] settlement, became in effect the highway to the Gulf of Carpentaria'.[38] By November 1864 George Sutherland with eleven men had driven 8000 sheep from near Rockhampton to the head of the Georgina River (then called the Herbert), close to the border with the South-Australian-controlled Northern Territory; a distance of 2080 kilometres (1300 miles). Landsborough had named two lakes on the upper reaches of the river after his nieces: Lake Frances, where Camooweal was later established, and Lake Mary, where Sutherland formed his Rocklands Station. George Sutherland recorded that their thirsty sheep smelt water:

> Then there was a terrible baaing and galloping. On the left bank of the river at the lake, the ground was high and rocky. Fires were burning in scores right down to the water's edge—a sure sign of a large camp of blacks. On rushed the sheep through fires, blacks, and all other impediments to quench their thirst. The unfortunate niggers [sic] had a terrible time of it. To be roused up out of their sleep at midnight by some eight thousand sheep rushing madly and tumbling over them, was chaos, was something demonical to the simple natives, who never saw or heard of jumbucks before. Of course the whole tribe took up their beds quick smart, and ran. To this day [1913] the Georgina blacks have a corroboree indicating 'the rush of sheep to water at night'.[39]

Other pastoralists followed, establishing their runs inside the Northern Territory boundary 130–160 kilometres west of Rocklands.[40]

The Europeans' fear of Aboriginals led to some absurd situations. Sutherland described how:

> The night was dark; one man's watch was up, so he woke up the next, and they walked round the sheep. The other man walked round the opposite side. They met in a broken bushy place very suddenly, and neither expecting the other to be there the revolvers were immediately drawn to shoot the 'blackfellow!' One shot was fired before the mistake was discovered, but fortunately without grave results. This episode caused a good deal of fun in the camp for some time after.[41]

The pastoralist expansion followed in the wake of the explorers and was also given impetus by the American Civil War (1861–65). The Union North blockaded the Confederate South, which led to a shortage of cotton on the world market, especially for Britain's textile industry. This increased the demand for Australian wool and hence the rapid spread of white pastoralists and their flocks.

Beames Brook (south-west of the future Burketown) was established in 1864 and followed the next year by the selection of Graham McDonald on the Gregory and Leichhardt Rivers, where he formed Gregory Downs and Floraville Stations.[42] Other stations were also established during this period, including Cecilia Downs, Myrton Vale, Aspasia and Lawn Hill in 1866.[43] Burketown was established in 1865 and in February the following year the first Police Magistrate for the area, William Landsborough arrived with Acting Sub-Inspector Wentworth D'Arcy Uhr (1845–1901) and eight Native Police. News that three white men had been killed and their supply wagon looted near the McArthur River (over the border in the Northern Territory), led to Uhr and his troopers being sent to punish the offenders. A mate of Uhr's described how:

> Uhr said in one camp the wild blacks showed fight and rushed out towards them with clubs. Uhr had his rifle barrel bent and the hammer knocked straight guarding a blow from a club and would have been done in only one of the trackers shooting the nigger [*sic*] attacking him . . . they nearly shot the whole tribe of bucks, as Uhr called them; it done a lot of good [for whites] for years after.[44]

By April 1868, the correspondent for the *Brisbane Courier* was reporting that Uhr had succeeded in shooting upwards of 30 blacks, within ten miles (16 kilometres) from Burketown:

> No sooner was this done, than a report came in that Mr Cannon had been murdered by blacks, at Liddle [Little] and Hetzer's station near the Norman [river]. Mr Uhr went off immediately in that direction, and his success I hear was complete. One mob of fourteen he rounded up; another mob of nine, and a last mob of eight, he succeeded with his troopers in shooting. In the latter lot there was one black who would not die after receiving eighteen or twenty

bullets, but a trooper speedily put an end to his existence by smashing his skull.[45]

Thirty-one Aboriginals in two separate incidents paid the ultimate price. The Burketown correspondent then proclaimed:

> Everybody in the district is delighted with the wholesale slaughter dealt out by the native police, and thank Mr Uhr for his energy in ridding the district of fifty-nine (59) myalls. Cassidy's station, on the Upper Leichhardt, has also been attacked, and one man speared. Albert Downs station, on the Gregory [river], was also attacked by blacks a short time back, and all the fire-arms, axes, and chisel's taken off.

There is a discrepancy with the correspondent's figures. He gives a total of 59, whereas if one tallies the figures given previously, then the total of 'Myalls' shot equals 61.[46] Whatever the case, Uhr's response was by anyone's standards illegal. It confirms that the Aboriginal Gulf residents were not being treated as British subjects and that they were not taking the invasion of their homelands lightly. Later that year, Uhr was demoted for being 'guilty of conduct unbecoming an officer in the Public Service'. The following year (1869) he resigned, but continued in his wicked ways by stealing Aboriginal children, and maintained running disputes with Sub-Inspector Coward, Police Magistrate Landsborough and Crown Commissioner Scarr. He was charged with crimes including assault, fraud, obscene language and the murder of Aboriginal people.[47] Twice Uhr was charged, once in the Gulf and again when he went on to the Palmer River diggings and conducted more dispersals, but this time as a private citizen. On both occasions he was acquitted. 'It was', as Tony Roberts notes, 'rare indeed for whites to be convicted of murdering Aboriginals on the frontier'.[48]

William H Corfield recalls travelling from Burketown to Floraville Station and onto Donor's Hill Station, which was established in 1865 by Jack and Tom Brodie on the Cloncurry River (c.130 kilometres south-west of Normanton):

> At this place I visited a cave containing many skulls of blacks, who had been dispersed by the whites, after committing a series of depredations in the district. I was told the cave was so dark that matches were lighted to allow of aim being taken at the blacks during the dispersal.[49]

To elements of the local clan group, the Mayi-Yapi, this appears to be the only written record referring to their extermination.

Meanwhile, low wool prices and the cost of haulage to Burketown, plus the high freight to Sydney around Cape York Peninsula, made wool growing uneconomical. Hudson Fysh noted that: ' . . . the tide of settlement was rolled back from the far outposts. About 1868 even the settlement at Burketown was quite deserted . . . following the devastating epidemic that swept the town and district in 1866, when'[50] forty of the 70 people living there died from 'Yellow Jack' fever.[51] A resurgent white pastoral interest in the region had to wait until the next decade, but there was at least a hiatus for the Gulf tribes.

Much further to the south, in 1865, Sub-Inspector Paschen reported on the activities of his own and two other detachments in central Queensland. At Coomoo boolano, 110 kilometres west of Rockhampton, he found that Acting Sub-Inspector Cecil Hill had been killed and Trooper Fred was severely wounded. Paschen reported four major 'dispersals of blacks' between 4 and 10 June near the Expedition and Comet Ranges.[52] Whatever the numbers were, they were never divulged publicly.

During the 1860s, white settlers banking on making their fortune continued to move into what we now call central Queensland, west of between Rockhampton, Bowen and Mackay. Korah Halcomb Wills (1828–96) was one of them. He had arrived as a 21-year-old in Adelaide, went to the Victorian goldfields with his family at the age of 34, and moved from Brisbane to Bowen in 1862. Wills wrote in his 1890s memoir that 'there is very little dispersing going on now in the colonies', however:

> . . . what there is must be done very much on the quiet or you may hap get into trouble, but in my time they were dispersed by

hundreds if not thousands . . . [on] one of my dispersing expeditions I was in company of a few squatters and their friends . . . When the Blacks had been playing up. And killing a shepherd and robbing his Hut . . . we turned out and run them to earth where they got on the top of a big mound and defied us and smacked their buttocks at us and hurled large stones down on us. And hid themselves behind large trees and huge rocks but some of them paid dearly for their bravado. They had no idea that we could reach them to a dead certainty of a mile by our little patent breach [sic] loading 'Terry's'.[53]

Wills then tells us that he kidnapped a little Aboriginal girl who rode on the front of his saddle, the 80 miles (129 kilometres) to Bowen, crying nearly all the way. Incredibly, he follows this up with the following information:

I took it in my head to get a few specimens of certain limbs and head of a Black fellow . . . I first found the subject that I intended to anatomize, when my friends were looking on, and I commenced operations dissecting. I went to work business like to take off the head first, and then the arms, and then the legs, and gathered them together and put them into my Pack saddle[.]

Later Wills stripped the flesh off the limbs in a lagoon, much to the disgust of seasoned fellow dispersers. Korah Wills became the Mayor of Bowen in 1867, and later Mayor of Mackay in 1876–77, before retiring in 1882 and returning to England.

Cuthbert Fetherstonhaugh (pronounced 'Fan-shaw') owned Vine Creek Station west of the Suttor River near the junction with the Belyando River, at the southern end of the Jangga people's territory. He relates an incident at Vine Creek in 1864, where a large flock of sheep was stolen and two shepherds killed.[54] A punitive expedition with the Native Police resulted and after ten days of the chase, a group who were assumed to have been responsible were cornered and twelve men shot. Several women were also captured and Sub-Inspector Reginald Uhr of the Native Police and Fetherstonhaugh shared their dinner among the corpses and the bound and roped women.[55] Within six weeks of this incident, '... twenty-one whites were killed by the Blacks' within a 200-mile (320-kilometres) radius. According to Jangga oral history, this became Murdering Lagoon—east of Mt Hope, north-east of Mt Douglas Station, c.200 kilometres due west of Mackay.

The Jangga recall this event as occurring east north-east of Mt Hope, just off Vine Creek, towards Hanging Rock, 20–30 kilometres west of Yacamunda Station. Nearby, Tom Addo and George McLennan (both stockmen with Col McLennan's father) recalled that a sharp pole was used to skewer or impale local Aboriginal people. The remaining local Jangga people did not like to talk about this as they considered it too awful to remember. Only Col and another older brother who is now deceased remembered this story.[56]

Judith Wright also noted that there had been four years of conflict prior to her grandfather Albert Wright's arrival and ownership of Avon Downs north of Clermont.[57] At Fort Cooper, north of Nebo, in early 1869, he recorded in his diary that 'About sixty Blacks were shot at Grosvenor [Downs] last week'.[58] So inspired was Judith Wright by what she learnt about her forebears' experiences, that she researched and wrote *The Cry for the Dead* (1981). An insightful work, it places in context the rapidly expanding frontier in central Queensland, while acknowledging an unwritten law that made white men keep silent about how it was achieved.[59]

Lorna McDonald makes the relevant point that 'It is significant that in the early years of frontier warfare the Aboriginals attacked only two kinds of people—the squatters and shepherds who threatened their way of life, and the Native Police who indiscriminately shot members of the tribe'.[60]

Some 60 kilometres to the south-west, Oscar de Satgé (1836–1906), in partnership with Gordon Sandeman had established Wolfang Downs in 1861.[61] This initially highly successful wheeler-dealer pastoralist and 'pure merino', readily acknowledged that '... there is a kind of "greed of country" that comes over the pioneer, which spurs him up to great efforts if the reward before him is a good slice of rich sheep country'.[62] He, like other Queensland squatter land-speculators, promoted a vigorous scheme of heavy stocking.[63] With Gordon Sandeman, a wealthy Sydney businessman, they appropriated an immense area they called Peak Downs, to the north of the future township of Emerald (1879). Pamela Lukin Watson equates the:

... seizure of ... tribal territory ... [as being] more like real estate development than home-making. The pastoralists acquired land to which they had no long-term commitment. They developed it by irrevocably changing the environment, the lifestyles of the residents and the identity of those who had access to it. Like contemporary developers, at least some of the speculator-pastoralists worked with insufficient capital and/or large loans, and were under extreme stress to increase their profits in order to avoid bankruptcy. Finally, they merchandised the land to others, using their profit as seed money for the next venture.[64]

De Satgé played a prominent role in representing squatters in the Queensland Legislative Assembly. He made a vast fortune from his pastoral exploits, although when he died 24 years later, after returning to England in 1882, his estate was valued at only £443.

Mining became important in the Clermont/Peak Downs/Moranbah/Nebo area to the west of Mackay from the early 1860s. Gold was found as well as copper and during the 1880s, fourteen copper miners were attacked and killed at Mt Gotthardt by Aboriginal warriors. In response the clan was wiped out on the slopes of the mountain.[65]

It was in the region of central Queensland or as George Carrington referred to it, 'Capricornia', that this university man remembers:

I was travelling on a road where for more than a quarter of a mile the air was tainted with putrefaction of corpses, which lay all along the ridges, just as they had fallen. It was true that the offence was the murder of five shepherds, on one station, in a week, but such wholesale and indiscriminate vengeance seems rather disproportionate, to say the least.[66]

Carrington also recalls seeing 'two large pits covered with branches and brush, secured by a few stones, and the pits themselves were full of dead blackfellows, of all ages and both sexes'. Like many of his contemporaries, Carrington fails to give any firm indication of where the events he records actually took place, although he does identify the region (Capricornia), and implies that the killings were implemented by the Native Police.[67]

In late 1860, several Native Police troopers sexually assaulted and murdered a white woman, Fanny Briggs, near Rockhampton (1857). Denis Cryle points out: 'Significantly, the informants in this case were local Aboriginal women who themselves complained of having been molested by the troopers.'[68] Briggs' murder and the Native Police's involvement was to cause a great deal of unwanted publicity and criticism of the Native Police. At the same time in response, as Cryle noted, the: 'Native Police and squatters carried out a bloody campaign of extermination in [and] around the town.'[69]

Alluvial gold was discovered in 1866 on the head of Louisa Creek, about 56 kilometres north-west of Rockhampton. This became the Morinish Diggings. In mid-June the following year, the Police Commissioner received a telegram from Sub-Inspector George Elliot: 'Some Blacks shot by Native Mounted Police 12th instant, in Morinish Diggings; great excitement and indignation shown by inhabitants—calling for an inquiry. The press has taken the matter up . . .' A newly appointed Acting Sub-Inspector, Myrtil Aubin, heard grievances from whites regarding the blacks pilfering. The 25-year-old subaltern and his troopers made a dawn visit to the local camp and he claimed that he ordered his troopers to fire three blanks, but instead their volley killed four males and a young girl. Aubin was suspended. He wrote an explanation to his superior but despite this, the Executive Council dismissed him from the force.[70] Aubin's gaff was, as Inspector George Murray expressed to the Commissioner: 'It was clearly Mr Aubin's duty to disperse that mob of Blacks and it is very much to be regretted that he did not do so quietly.'[71] 'The finding condemns him', Jonathan Richards observed, 'not for unlawful killing but for indiscretion'.[72] The hypocrisy of the Police Commissioner and Executive Council can be clearly seen with regard to this episode. It was not the killing of Aboriginal people per se, but the doing so close to white settlement with potentially independent witnesses, which could then generate unwanted publicity for the sinister operations of the Native Police, that was Aubin's failing.

Archaeologist Liz Hatte has been working in the central and north Queensland region for over twenty years and makes the following observations:

> The picture that has emerged purely from the archaeological evidence indicates that this region [of the Bowen Basin] was fertile, heavily forested and capable of supporting relatively large popula-tions of people on a long-term basis. Many thousands of sites have been recorded throughout this region, consisting of artefact scatters, hearths and cooking fireplaces, freshwater shell middens, cultur-ally scarred trees, stone arrangements, fish traps, native wells, stone quarries, rock shelters containing Aboriginal artwork and tradi-tional walking tracks through the country. [73]

It is possible to gauge an indication of the Aboriginal population before European invasion of their traditional lands in what became central Queensland. Admittedly, it is difficult to identify actual numbers, but one can justifiably state that there were many thousands living in the region where today, only six families lay claim to parts of this huge area.

Chapter 7

The Frontier Moves to Far North Queensland and Cape York Peninsula

Do we regret the decay and disappearance of the native tribes? Assuredly we ought, for we are the cause of it. We have seized their territory; we occupy their hunting grounds; we destroy the food suited to their physical constitution and their ancestral habits; our horses and cattle and sheep have usurped the lands of the black man's birthright.

John Fraser, The Aborigines of Australia, 1882.[1]

South of Ingham (1864), 8 kilometres from Waterview Station, an ex-Native Police trooper told a newspaper correspondent of dispersing nine blacks whose skeletons could still be seen.[2] The correspondent was also told 'by an officer of police here that he would shoot every black he could find'. Apparently, this was in revenge for the murders of two whites near Strathalbyn Station, over 200 miles from Ingham (c.240 to 320 kilometres to the south-east on the Burdekin River, which, as the report acknowledged, the local blacks had no connection with. Sub-Inspector Robert Arthur Johnstone also told how he had 'shot as many as thirty-five in one camp a few miles [c.40 kilometres north-west] from here, at Mt Farquharson'.[3]

Tasmanian-born Johnstone was appointed Acting Sub-Inspector in 1867 at age 24. He commanded Native Police troopers at the Nebo killings in

1869 but resigned in the same year. Johnstone moved to the Cardwell area (1870–80) and in 1871 managed the Bellenden Plains sugar plantation. Later that year he was re-appointed as an Acting Sub-Inspector and following the wreck of the *Maria* off Cardwell in 1872, when some survivors were killed by local Aboriginals, led punitive killing raids against the Djiru at Dunk Island and at Clump Point.[4] Johnstone reported to the Commissioner of Police on 31 March 1873, stating that he and his detachment had met up with Acting Sub-Inspector Armit while out patrolling Herbert Vale Station (1865) 40 kilometres north-west of Ingham (1875). Johnstone informed Commissioner Seymour how:

> On 14 March [1873] under Mt Leech [Leach] I dispersed a large mob, and returned to camp on 19 March. On 21 February I succeeded in dispersing three mobs on the Seaview Range [c.40-kilometres to the west] where I had the assistance of Acting Sub-Inspector Dumaresq's troopers, who were baled up by floods, and on 27 March on the Lower Herbert I dispersed a large mob who had been at the Stone station, and returned to camp on 31 March.[5]

If Johnstone's earlier skiting is anything to go by, it seems the Acting Sub-Inspector and his troopers over one month had killed quite a few rainforest people. Later in 1873 he was promoted to Sub-Inspector. With his troopers he joined Dalrymple's north-east coast expedition and was involved in killing Yirrganydji opposite Wangal Djungay (Double Island) and then was involved in examining the 'lie of the land' in the Cairns area and marking a road to Thornborough. He resigned in 1880 and went on to serve as Police Magistrate at Ingham, Bundaberg, Howard and Tiaro (1882–87).[6] Johnstone's name has been 'lionised' in the region by naming a river and shire in his honour, despite being a murderer and rapist in the normal course of his policing duties.

Over 100 kilometres inland and west of Cardwell, the Scott brothers (Walter and Arthur) in partnership with G E Dalrymple (and Colonial Secretary Herbert) established the Valley of Lagoons Station on the traditional lands of the Gugu Badhun.[7] Other pastoralists searched for their 'land of opportunity', such as Ezra Firth and family in 1864 who made their way north-west and after scaring a camp of 'over one hundred niggers [*sic*], naked and wild', called their newly acquired land, Mt Surprise.[8] Firth had been 'one of the party that went out and helped disperse the blacks', after the Hornet Bank tragedy.[9] One wonders whether he applied his previously learned skills in 'surprising' members of the Agwamin.

Twenty years later and 40 kilometres north, the Williams brothers at Fossilbrook Station were besieged, quite likely by members of the Agwamin on whose traditional territory the run had been established. The siege was raised when Sub-Inspector Frederick Urquhart and his troopers appeared in the early hours of the morning and galloped in amongst the besiegers. Hudson Fysh recalled that: 'Two days later the chase was taken up, and the natives were finally located in rough country above the Lynd Falls, which drops a clear seventy feet [21 metres] to the rocky river bed below. Again an outrage was avenged.'[10] Notice how oblique Fysh is with this description, but it seems likely that the fleeing Agwamin were driven over the Falls.

West to south-west of here, on the upper reaches of the Gilbert River, a massacre site showing all the signs of a Native Police dispersal was discovered in 1879, where 'Thirty-five skeletons, including those of children, displayed bullet and hatchet wounds, suggesting the slaughter of an entire camp'.[11]

In 1866 there was a small gold rush to the Star River, but a shortage of water made it unfeasible for the numbers of Europeans who had made their way there.[12] It was Richard Daintree's systematic geological surveys of the North Kennedy district which informed a party of prospectors in finding payable gold on the Cape River in July 1867. Within a month there were 250 men on the field who had overlanded from Peak Downs in central Queensland or from Bowen on the coast. Within three months there were 600 men on the new field, and by 1868, there were some 2500 miners.[13] Pastoralists gained by obtaining a ready market for their livestock. Daintree went on to investigate the headwaters of the Gilbert River in 1869 and a new miners' stampede ensued, with further prospecting enabling the establishment of the Etheridge goldfield in 1870, centred on Georgetown.

Gold was discovered at Ravenswood and Charters Tors (Towers) in 1871, giving further impetus for southerners to rush north.

William Hann's 1872 exploration of lower Cape York led to the identification of traces of gold. The following year James Mulligan, acting on the news from Hann's expedition, during which the Palmer River was located and re-named, set out on the first of his own prospecting expeditions with a party of five from the Etheridge River (5 June 1873).[14] Travelling via Mt Surprise, Fossilbrook run, the Lynd, Tate and Walsh Rivers re-named by Hann, Mulligan's party along their northerly route observed numerous 'Darkies' townships' and 'thousands of blacks' tracks'.[15] To the north of Mt Mulgrave, Mulligan declared that they had reached the Palmer (29 June 1873). Regular traces of gold were found and from mid to late August, the party camped on the Palmer where they 'got payable gold'.[16] Following the publication of Mulligan's account of his exploration around the Palmer River, the seeds of encouragement were sown for the hardy and foolhardy to rush to the northern goldfield.

Three years later Mulligan reported eleven Aboriginal townships in four miles (6.4 kilometres) and the paths 'well trodden' for miles. This was southward 'along the scrub' between Tolga and Carrington on what was to become the southern Atherton Tableland.[17] The trickle of Europeans into the traditional lands of Aboriginal far north Queenslanders was about to turn into a flood.

It was gold that brought Europeans to far north Queensland, and in particular to the Palmer River Goldfield nearly 200 kilometres inland from the township of Cooktown, which was established overnight on James Cook's Endeavour River on the Guugu Yimithirr site of Waymburr,[18] on Saturday 25 October 1873. Over 90 miners plus government officials landed as the precursor to some 18,000 new arrivals working the goldfields of the Palmer in the years to follow. All in all, some 110 souls and 31 horses made up this first batch of gold-seekers. One of the official members of the party wrote to a friend in Brisbane from the new diggings, a letter which was then published in the *Brisbane Telegraph*. It was to cause quite a public outcry, which like all previous criticisms of the treatment of the original owners of the land was sidelined and ignored.

The party started out from the Endeavour River on 30 October 1873 and on the fifth day of their journey (3 November),[19] had three clashes, as they:

> Started over the spur of the range running to E[ast]. Came to Normanby River (15 miles). Started a mob of blacks. Shot four and hunted them. Fine river. November 4—Started, 15 miles Surprise Lagoons. Camped 5th for spell. November 6—Blacks surprised us at daybreak, about 150; all were armed. Got close to camp before anyone heard them. Great consternation; shot several. They ran into the waterholes for shelter, where they were shot. Travelled then unmolested for two or three days to Kennedy River . . . Followed river Kennedy up course S[outh], 15 miles; camped. Had an encounter with the blacks; shot a lot.[20]

This matter-of-fact letter suggests a wholesale slaughter, which historian Noreen Kirkman observes: 'seems to imply the entire 150—after trapping them in the lagoon.'[21] Whether that was the case, there can be no doubt that the numbers were sizeable. Interestingly, within three months of the above newspaper report, sixteen members of the party had signed a statement in which they: 'most Emphatically State . . . that in no single instance, did we *see* any of the officers of the Expedition, or any one accompanying the Expedition fire a single shot at the Blacks . . .'[22] However, as Kirkman observes, they do not mention the Native Police. Nearly 50 years later, one of the signatories, William J Webb, contradicted the 1874 statement and confirmed the original newspaper report. He recalled this early morning event:

> . . . while the stars were still shining, a crowd of natives came up yelling out a terrible war cry, and they reached to about 70 yards [64 metres] from where we lay all over the ground. There were about 40 in the first rank and as many more in the reserve some distance behind. Just as day was breaking, Messrs MacMillan and St George advanced towards them. I noticed that they fired over the heads of the blacks, but some of the men fired straight at the blacks, some of

9. Native Police, Rockhampton, 1860s. George 'Black Jack' Murray standing, centre.

10. Sub-inspector Stanhope O'Connor and his Native Police Troopers (from left) Jack, Barney, Jimmy, (O'Connor), Johnny and Hero, at Cooktown in 1879.

11. 'Leaden persuasion: an incident of pioneer life in the north' by Blagden Chambers, published in *The Illustrated Sydney News*, 20 January 1883.

12. Samuel Clemens, known as Mark Twain, included Dan Beard's illustration in his *Mark Twain in Australia and New Zealand*, 1897. The illustration depicts the poisoning of Aboriginals. In his book, Twain wrote about white men's treatment of Aboriginals: 'It is robbery, humiliation, and slow, slow murder, through poverty and the white man's whisky.' The ribbon along the bottom of the illustration reads 'Peace on earth, good will to men'.

13. 'Dina's flogging' Illustration from AJ Vogan, *The Black Police, A Story of Modern Australia*, London, 1890.

14. The Jardine brothers photographed before their 1864 expedition. Sitting: Frank (left), John (right). Standing: Archie Richardson (left), Alex (right). The two Aboriginal men with rifles are not identified.

15. Okunjen elder, Mrs Alma Luke (Wason) of Kowanyama. 'Today there are big gaps in the genealogies of the clans of the top end groups—Okunjen, Uwkangand and Olkol as well as visiting neighbouring clans, including amongst others, the Awbakhn and Oyaan, Kokomenjena, and Kokobera, whose territory it was that the Jardines trespassed upon.' 5 May 1998. (Courtesy of the Kowanyama Land Office Archive)

16. 'Eight Mile [Native Police camp] Patrol' in the Cook District on Cape York Peninsula. Located on Endeavour River and established in 1881, the camp closed in 1899.

17. 'Native troopers dispersing a camp'. Illustration by Frank Mahoney, *Picturesque Atlas of Australia*, p. 36.

whom fell. Thereupon the blacks ran away and were pursued as far as a large lagoon, and all that went there stayed there.[23]

Webb implies that some 80 Gugu-Warra were killed on this occasion, in a place which became known as Battle Camp. Somewhere between 80 and 150 Aboriginal men were killed here. In addition, the losses for the family clan groups from which they came were compounded by the later poisoning of waterholes and leaving of poisoned flour at their favourite campsites. According to the son of one of the survivors, his mother told him that many more died from the poisoning than those killed at Battle Camp.[24] The combined results would have been truly devastating for the local clan groups. The reason for the initial attack by the Gugu-Warra at Battle Camp was divulged seven years later, when it was acknowledged that a woman and child had been abducted by the Native Police, and the woman accidentally shot and killed.[25]

This was probably the only time that members of the Gugu-Warra challenged the interlopers with a traditional 'open display of shouting and gesticulating before an advance', for all recorded cases thereafter were done stealthily.[26] Most of the attacks on whites were on individuals or small parties. Some two months later, in January 1874, Sub-Inspector Douglas found another track branching to the south via the future Laura, and across the Conglomerate Range through a narrow gap that became known as Hell's Gate. Initially this track was heavily used, but as it became a favourite area for ambushing miners by the local Gugu-Yulanji, its use declined until it was rarely used after 1875.[27]

Revenge killings in response to European teamsters' and miners' behaviour led to the brutal murder of the Straher ('Strau') family at a lagoon camping site 26 kilometres from Battle Camp.[28] On the evening of 17 October 1874, John and Bridget Straher and their infant daughter Annie were bludgeoned to death with stone axes and their bodies stripped of clothing (most likely to determine their gender). European reaction was swift and pitiless, and three Native Police detachments led by Inspector Tom Coward, along with Sub-Inspectors Douglas and Townsend, 'followed the murderers across the Normanby River, where they overtook and dispersed them'.[29] The site of the dispersal became Skull Camp.[30] The site where the Straher family was killed became known as Murdering Lagoon.

There were other unhappy encounteres between local Aboriginals and Europeans. On New Year's Day 1876, one of teamster William H Corfield's saddle horses came into camp at Maytown, 'with a portion of a spear in his rump'.[31] He followed up the tracks and found that two of his horses had been butchered, and by coincidence Sub-Inspector Stanhope O'Connor had just received information that two packers had been wounded: 'apparently the same tribe as killed my horses. Six troopers, O'Connor and myself, all fully armed, started.' Along the banks of the Kennedy River they found the remains of a horse feast:

> On the afternoon of the third day, the boys saw a column of smoke about a mile ahead. We immediately left the river, and erected our tents for a camp . . . The moon rose about midnight, and as the rain had ceased, we decided to start about 2 a.m., leaving our horses and belongings there . . . we wended our way along the river. Five naked blacks in single file in the lead, their only dress consisting of a cartridge belt round the waist, and cap in hand. O'Connor, myself, and corporal brought up the rear. After travelling some distance through grass, which in places was over our heads . . . Near daylight we heard shots about a mile down the river. O'Connor, the boy, and I ran in the direction of the shots . . . We eventually reached the place where the blacks had camped, but the boys had previously dispersed most of them.[32]

Corfield gives no further details about numbers, ages or gender of the dispersed victims, but justifies the carnage, for:

> If at any time I felt compunction in using my rifle, I lost it when I thought of the murders of Strau [Straher]. His wife and daughter, and the outrages committed upon them, and again of the murder and eating [although no proof is given] of the two packers so recently. We burnt all the blacks' weapons and several dilly-bags

containing the dead bodies of infants, which they carried about with them [as part of their mortuary practices, of which he doesn't seem to be aware].[33] The stench of burning human flesh was sickening.[34]

He then describes a trooper shooting another two 'black fellows' in a hollow in the river. Why would Corfield have bothered to recall this dispersal, some 45 years after the event, if it had not had such a profound effect upon him—even though he attempts to justify his and the Native Police troopers' behaviour?

Populist historical writer Glenville Pike, who grew up on the Cape, notes that:

> ... [European] reprisals were dreadful. Their Snider rifles took a terrible toll and were used without mercy. Blackfellow Creek, a Palmer tributary, was so named because diggers rushing to the Hodgkinson field in March 1876 came upon 'acres of bones' where a whole tribe had obviously been wiped out—an Australian version of 'the killing fields' that has been hidden or whitewashed for nearly 120 years. The name of the creek was changed to Kangirr Creek [also known as Kangkerr Creek] which name appears on a board where the Mulligan Highway bridges it [some 4 kilometres north of the turnoff to Maitland Downs Station].[35]

Some three years later, across the Endeavour River from Cooktown, Messrs Hartley and Sykes were severely wounded by members of the Guugu Yimithirr when trying to retrieve a cedar log from the beach. Retribution was swift. Several expeditions set out, but it was Sub-Inspector O'Connor with six troopers who crossed the harbour by moonlight and:

> ... made a detour in the direction of Cape Bedford, and by Sunday morning had hemmed the blacks within a narrow gorge, of which both outlets were secured by the troopers. There were twenty-eight men and thirteen gins thus enclosed, of whom none of the former escaped. Twenty-four were shot down on the beach, and four swam

out to sea. The inspector and his men then sat down on the beach, and waited for the swimmers to return, but without success, and as after several hours they were lost sight of, it is conjectured they were drowned.[36]

This is the same O'Connor who was sent with Native Police troopers to hunt Ned Kelly in Victoria.[37] It was his actions that Anglican Bishop Hale complained about to Colonial Secretary Palmer, who then ignored the complaint and the problem.[38]

Over the decade 1873 to 1883, a maximum of 42 whites were killed.[39] Kirkman's conclusion is pertinent:

> Finally there is the aspect of the long list of violent clashes with Aborigines, which popular accounts suggest were attributable to the extraordinary degree of ferocity and hostility on the part of local Aborigines. This interpretation ignores the fact that the outbreak of hostilities can be precisely dated and was invariably the result of acts of deliberate provocation on the part of Europeans. The contrast between the brutality with which Europeans engaged Aborigines, and their apparent restraint both within local European society and in coping with Chinese competition, arose essentially from the policies of the goldfield administration.[40]

Probably because of the isolation, the Europeans felt the need to band together for mutual protection; and their fear was projected as unrestrained violence towards the Aboriginal inhabitants.

In 1876, about 150 kilometres to the south of the Palmer, a new goldfield, the Hodgkinson, was opened. This led to a search for a coastal port and the establishment of Cairns on the southern portion of Trinity Bay.

Mick McNamara from Mt Molloy (1896) recalled that 'when the Palmer was just about finished [c.1883] a fellow from Byerstown, Johnny Byers, was coming up [to the field] with six wagons and he got held up by the Abo's [sic] at [what became] Skull lagoon . . .', located on the upper reaches of the Mitchell River, 6 kilometres south of Mt Carbine and 5 kilometres downstream of the confluence with Mary Creek. These were Muluridji who were camping there and 'they sent over a shower of spears. Of course [Byers and company] got stuck into them with the Snider rifles and the Abo's [sic] backed off... [but] During that time the Abo's would come down every now and then and send over a shower of spears just to keep them in order'. The lagoon was full of water mussels which enabled them to hold off the teamsters for about three days. However:

> A [Native Mounted] Police patrol of about twelve men came down by chance from a station... Johnny Byers told them what was going on and so they went to find the Abo's [sic]. Some of the Abo's dived into the lagoon and came up under big lily leaves [in order to breathe]... Some of them took off up the mountain and as a boy I could still see piles of mussel shells [that] they dropped going up the mountains. Of course the troopers got stuck into them—everywhere a lily pad moved, they fired a Snider bullet into them. They killed quite a few of them. At flood time the skulls used to wash out of it and that's why they call it Skull Lagoon.[41]

Although there were still prospectors traversing Cape York, it was the expansion of pastoralists onto the peninsula, along with the activities of bêche-de-mer and pearl-shellers, that was to impact on the Pama/Bama in the late nineteenth and early twentieth centuries. Certainly, over 200 kilometres north of the Palmer on the homelands of the Kaanju,[42] on the newly established cattle stations, conflict was bound to occur.

The Cape York Telegraph Line was constructed between 1883 and 1887 and the line and telegraph stations or 'forts' and workmen were protected by detachments of the Native Police. Logan Jack identified that:

> One of their camps was on the then deserted Coen diggings and another on Clayhole Creek, near Mein [Telegraph Station]... For some time, the line and stations had to be vigilantly guarded against the DEPREDATIONS OF THE NATIVES.[43]

As a result of the cooperation between the construction parties and the Native Police there had been: 'NO TROUBLE WITH THE NATIVES.'

May 1889 saw an explosion of Native Police and settler activity in response to the murder of Edmund Watson and bashing of James Evans at Patrick Fox's Pine Tree Station (1887), on the upper reaches of the Archer River, near the Mein Telegraph Station (some 100 kilometres north of Coen). Sub-Inspector Frederick Urquhart commanded three detachments along with European volunteers, amounting to more than 40 men, and conducted five dispersals in the Batavia (Wenlock) area.[44] The *Cooktown Courier* naturally gave quite extensive coverage of this,[45] but it was also reported in the *Thargomindah Herald*, at the other end of Queensland in South Gregory. The *Herald*'s brief report concluded: 'Every station on the Peninsula is contributing men to give the blacks a lesson.'[46] In early June, Urquhart, Watson and troopers went to Merlunah (Merluna) Station for rations and left there on 9 June and 'came up with them on the Batavia [Wenlock] River on 11 June, dispersed them and recovered telegraph wire iron pins and insulators in their camp'.[47] Again it is extremely difficult to identify how many Kaanju people perished as a result of these dispersals.

At least another four pastoralists met violent deaths on the Cape York Peninsula frontier: Jones at Koolburra, 60 kilometres north-west of Laura; Donald Mackenzie at Lakefield, c.75 kilometres north of Laura; Ferguson from Mentana, 110 kilometres west of Highbury; and Charles Massey from Lallah Rookh (1882), located on the Stewart River (east, south-east of Coen).[48] What retaliatory response occurred, if any, is not clear and needs further research.

The Palmer and Hodgkinson goldfields petered out during the last twenty years of the nineteenth century while pastoral expansion was still making in-roads onto the lands of the west coast Cape York Aboriginal groups. (Old) Koolatah Station was established on Uw-Oykangand traditional lands, just north of the Alice River and its junction with the Lower Mitchell River. It comprised about 3000 square miles (7700 square kilometres) of country and was taken up by McEacharn and Bell in 1886.[49] During the mid-1890s a family by the name of Adamson took over the run, and following a contretemps with the Uw-Oykangand and the spearing of a horse, the Adamsons whistled up the Native Police from their Lynd Junction Barracks (Highbury from 1896).[50] It seems very likely that Sub-Inspector Lyndon Poingdestre led his band of troopers out on this patrol, and at Emu Lagoon they dispersed a group of men, women and children. It was Victor Highbury's father (an Uw-Oykangand) who discovered the massacre, while the men had been down on the Alice spearing freshwater crocodiles, and that the altercation was caused by a speared horse. An infant was found still suckling on her dead mother's breast. The Adamsons who instigated the Native Police's activities left soon after, never to return.[51]

At Rutland Plains Station, some 19 kilometres south to south-west of the Mitchell River Mission (today's Kowanyama):

> The slaughter of Aborigines had become routine to the extent that [Frank] Bowman's stockman, McIntyre, had taken to cutting off a finger from each Aborigine he killed as evidence of his deeds, a gruesome tally to demonstrate his effectiveness in dealing with 'the blacks'.[52]

Indigenous oral history suggests that Native Police, freed from the moral constraints of their own society, implemented a form of violence that contemporaneously we find unimaginable. One Olgol Elder, Lofty Yam, recalled the violation of a murdered woman:

> One tracker now, young fellow, they been shoot this young girl, he been shoot him [her], he be look, 'Oh, this girl they shoot 'em' . . . You know what him been do? Him been start mucking around with that young girl! Dead Body! Muck Around![53]

In 1770, unknown to the Aboriginal inhabitants on the Australian continent, their traditional lands were theoretically expropriated when Captain James Cook landed on a tiny island off the tip of Kie Daudai (renamed Cape York Peninsula), and took possession of the east coast in the name of King George III. However, the islands of the Torres Strait were to remain under the control of their traditional owners for another 100 years. Not of course that any of the local inhabitants were aware of the impending control of colonial Queensland and their involuntary joining of the British Empire.

Contact with the Melanesian Torres Strait Islanders had been occurring sporadically since the early part of the nineteenth century, most of it not particularly pleasant for the Europeans concerned. First, in 1834, 22 survivors of the wreck of the *Charles Eaton* on two rafts met with a canoe of central Islanders who 'appeared to be friendly, but later they turned on the castaways and killed and decapitated all except four boys'.[54] Two years later two of the boys were rescued from the island of Mer (Murray) and their story was picked up by the colonial press. Twenty-five years later, in 1859, a second massacre of Europeans occurred, where eighteen survivors of the wreck of the *Sapphire* were slaughtered.[55] It was this event that 'triggered the colonial occupation' later suggested by Governor Bowen, and implemented by John Jardine in 1863 with the establishment of Somerset on the north-eastern tip of Cape York Peninsula. Jardine served as Magistrate there until December 1865, then he returned to Rockhampton where he had come from two years earlier. Steve Mullins identifies that 'in the annals of central Queensland he [Jardine] is most often remembered for authorising vigilante action in 1861 after the Aboriginal attack on Cullin-la-Ringo station . . .'[56]

It took less than a month before Jardine had antagonised the local Gudang, on whose territory the settlement had been established. He, falsely as it turned out, accused a twelve-year-old boy of stealing an axe and then publicly caned him,[57] while his son, Johnny, using a 6-metre-long whip, chastised several other Gudang nearby. Obviously, this sort of behaviour by the Magistrate and his son was bound to cause acts of retaliation at Somerset.[58] And it did.

The mindset of the Executive Council (in Brisbane) was such that, when there was divergence in the representation of these events, the newly arrived Lt Pascoe's version was ignored in favour of that of Jardine, who it was considered 'had more practical experience of the Australian Aborigines, or who has dealt with them more successfully'.[59] Nonie Sharp's research led her to conclude, that:

Far from eliciting the slightest government reprimand or caution of the Police Magistrate for his brutal treatment of the youth or his son's vicious demonstration of settler power, Pascoe's criticism of Jardine only had the effect of consolidating support behind the latter. Upholding the Colonial Secretary's assurance to Jardine 'of the entire approval and continued confidence of the Government of Queensland' in him.[60]

This was despite a retaliatory attack on the settlement by the Gudang where two marines were wounded, one of whom died.

A month later the Police Magistrate orchestrated an ambush of four Gudang turtle-hunters on the beach at Pabaju (Albany Island), opposite Kaleebe (Somerset). The surgeon of the settlement, Dr Richard Cannon, twenty-odd years later in his *Savage Scenes from Australia* (1885), recalled what happened when he accompanied the ambush party. Jardine, armed with his long rifle observed '. . . we've got them this time . . . a supper for the sharks my boy', as the Gudang made for their canoe and paddled feverishly out to sea:

'Now for it' gasped old Jardine as he cocked his rifle. The others followed suit . . . the Marines' boat gains on them, gains and gains whilst fast and faster in this race for life . . . Wilson let fly and we saw one of the natives topple over, grasp frantically at his paddle and bound into the air. The blue waters closed over him and the sharks rejoiced. Now, flash, flash, flash, from the [Marines'] boat and three black figures are only to be seen, delving furiously into the sea with frantic paddles. See the boat is on them. Now into the sea go the dark forms . . . When will they come up, never, they are shot or drowned. No! see a black head far away . . . bang, bang, bang from the boat, but the head is down again. 'Duck shooting by Jove', cries Johnny. Again and again, hither and thither pulls the boat whilst flash, flash, flash comes from our crew and . . . far away on the tide drifts the tenantless canoe a melancholy wreck.[61]

Later that day, the party landed on Albany Island and a further six Gudang were chased in their canoe and shot.[62]

By March 1865 the Police Magistrate's other sons, Frank and Alex, finally arrived after their violent ten-month journey up the west coast of Cape York Peninsula. They boasted of their exploits. Between April and August 1866 Yadhaigana (pronounced: 'Yud high gana') warriors speared 51 head of Frank Jardine's cattle which led to further shootings. On the evening of 7 July 1866, at Point Vallack Station, the Yadhaigana made a daring attempt to spear Frank Jardine. The following year (1867), while Frank was away, his Aboriginal stockmen killed ten Yadhaigana at Turtle Head Island, some 20 kilometres south of Somerset.[63]

Simultaneously, the role and influence of the two missionaries, Reverend FC Jagg and William Kennett, and the negative attitude of the Jardines towards them, has enabled their non-proselytising Christian work as teachers and mediators to be sabotaged and diminished. Sharp concludes that 'their successes suggest that with even the slightest cooperation between officials and missionaries, the lives of many local people may have been spared'. C F Pascoe, writing at the turn of the last century, notes how Kennett 'exhibited the degree of Christian spirit which won the confidence of the natives thus proving that if they are treated kindly they are capable of much more good than is generally thought possible'.[64]

Nonie Sharp describes Frank Jardine as 'a man of violence, of this there is no doubt'.[65] In 1867, Frank lied to the Colonial Secretary in refuting Constable Ginivan's assertion that he had shot Barnie and Sambo, two of his 'native police' who had been involved in raiding his brother, Johnny's, station run, Point Vallack.[66] Kennett's confirmation of Ginivan's assertion confirms Jardine's duplicity. As Police Magistrate, Jardine undoubtedly abused his position and treated Ginivan in a most despicable manner, by refusing to allow Ginivan to resign and not paying him his wages, which he desperately needed to pay for medicine for his extremely ill wife.

The massacre of the eight crew members of the *Sperwer* by the Kaurareg in mid-April 1869 was to have very serious repercussions for the indigenous inhabitants of Muralag (Prince of Wales Island). Two separate retribution parties were launched from Somerset; the first by Police Magistrate Frank

Jardine in conjunction with Captain McAusland and his crew from the *Melanie*, and the second by acting Police Magistrate Henry Chester, who temporarily replaced Jardine while he was on leave. Frank's son, Bootles Jardine, recalled that:

> The village was in a bit of a valley, high at one end. The kanakas [South Sea Islander crew of the *Melanie*] burned it all out, once they got going nobody could stop them. They had rifles and no one [amongst the Kaurareg] was prepared. It was too sudden. There was a terrible killing. No one knows how many were killed . . . I know my father shot one of the kanakas. He was trying to stop the killing. The village killing, when they all attacked, when the kanakas ran amok. He never liked to talk about that day. Not to me.[67]

Chester relieved Jardine from 1 August 1869 and made two sorties, the first to reconnoitre and the second to take hostages for the return of the wife of Gascoigne (from the *Sperwer*), but she had not been aboard her husband's trading vessel in the first place; she was still in Melbourne. It was in April the following year that Chester led a party of 25 bluejackets and nineteen Aboriginals, eight of whom were Native Police (of which five had just been released from St Helena's prison for armed robbery and rape), and sailed to Muraleg on HM frigate *Blanche*. On the say-so of members of the Gudang, three Kaurareg were identified as having taken part in the *Sperwer* killings and immediately shot. Chester attempted to justify his actions by claiming that: 'Every care was taken to explain the reason of their punishment and I am convinced they understood it. Without unnecessary bloodshed a moral effect has I trust been produced . . .'[68]

Sharp makes the salient point that:

> The police magistrates were well aware of the illegality of shooting local people; such practices they knew to be frowned upon in official circles. In the light of the continuing criticisms of Police Magistrate, Frank Jardine, which we have documented, it seems that the two had very good reason to conceal their reprisals from their superiors.[69]

Jardine resumed his role as Police Magistrate and Customs House Officer and developed the only pearl-shell base at Somerset. The *Brisbane Telegraph* (28 July 1873) accused him of running a monopoly, and again an investigation in Brisbane dismissed the charges brought. Following this Jardine resigned on 7 November 1873. However, prior to this James Atkins, one of Jardine's sea captains who supervised Frank's three pearling boats, went missing from the pearlers' camp eight miles (c.13 kilometres) from Somerset. It was presumed that Atkins had been killed by the Yadhaigana in their war of resistance, and Jardine then led a retributive party comprising the crew of two pearl-shelling boats and Native Police against them. Some 30 miles (48 kilometres) from Somerset a large force of Yadhaiganas 'showed a most determined resistance', but were 'properly dispersed'.[70] Again no figures are given.

Once the government moved from Somerset to Nurupai (Thursday Island) in 1878, Jardine bought out the government assets and became a law unto himself. Oral history from Injinoo and along the tip of Cape York still refers to Jardine's wholesale slaughter of Aboriginal camps. By 1875 the Gudang were considered extinct and by 1896 there were maybe 100 Yadhaiganas left.[71]

On 29 April 1896 Donald Mackenzie, the owner of Lakefield Station, some 80 kilometres north-west of Laura, was murdered by members of the Lamalama group and news was rapidly conveyed to Laura and telegraphed to Cooktown. The local school teacher at Laura wrote to a friend, that:

> A special train brought up a small army of black police who left here on April 31st & haven't come back since, though we've had news of them. Mackenzie's body was found in a waterhole, & niggers [*sic*] were tracked to a camp on the Normanby river, where a good many found a final resting place. Some took to the river & escaped but as the police are still after them they will have a warm time before it is over.[72]

An indication of how myriad smaller-scale killings took place comes from a report by Bishop Gilbert White in 1902. Halfway between Weipa and the Moreton Telegraph Station on Cape York Peninsula, His Reverence and the Northern Protector of Aborigines, Dr Walter Roth were on an expedition to investigate 'charges that were made with regard to the alleged murder of certain aborigines a few weeks ago'.[73] The Bishop wrote:

> The natives described to us the attack with extraordinary vividness. They were all bathing in a certain water-hole when suddenly the assailants galloped up from the south-west and opened fire; two old men, so old that they had to be carried on the shoulders of their grand-children, had fallen at the first discharge, and two young men, Charlie and Jimmie, had been shot as they were trying to get away. The rest had managed to escape by swimming under water to the farther end of the lagoon ... The natives had immediately removed the bodies of Charlie and Jimmie, and on the following day the attacking party had returned and burned the bodies of the two old men which had not been removed.[74]

White and Roth went on to inspect the killing-ground beside the water-hole, where they:

> ... found the recent tracks of shod horses at a gallop leading from the south-west. As there had never been any white man in this part of the country the fact was a strong corroboration of the statements we had heard, but we had further.
>
> On the banks of the creek we found the remains of a big fire, evidently made by a white man, as the natives never make a fire of big logs lighted in the centre. On searching the ashes we came upon several knee-caps and other human bones and two skulls. Under one of the skulls was a little lump of lead of the exact weight of the bullets which had been supplied, as we knew, to the assailants, a large and unusual size. We could find no cartridge-cases—they had evidently been carefully picked up—but we had sufficient evidence to induce the Commissioner of Police to make the journey up from Brisbane ...

How many of these incidents occurred across Queensland will probably never be known. That they happened is not really open to question, but the frequency and extent can in all probability never be surmised, even from a thorough review of original and oral history sources.

In a similar vein, the Kokoberran Elder, Kenny Jimmy, recalled an event that occurred in the first decade of the twentieth century, on the west coast of Cape York Peninsula between the Staaten and Nausau Rivers, on Cattle Creek:

> From Croydon on to Normanton, come along the coast, coast area, as far as Cattle Creek ... The Aboriginal people were there ... was camping out there; and happened out that they came along and shot them old people in the water there, while they were hunting in the water, swimming hunting for fish, turtle. All my Aboriginal people got shot there at Cattle Creek. The river was all bloodshed and they picked them bodies up and stack them up on the sand ridge; 'til today you can still see the bone.[75]

The tragedy is that in every district and region in Queensland, indigenous oral history recounts similar tales. Violence was ubiquitous. And to justify their behaviour, Europeans portrayed 'the blacks' as cannibals and 'bad' because they dared to resist the invasion of their homelands and fight a guerilla war.

Chapter 8

Dark Deeds in the Northern Rainforests
—the Tully and Cairns Districts

> When the past no longer illuminates the future,
> the spirit walks in darkness.
>
> *Alexis de Tocqueville (1805–1859),*
> *French political thinker and historian.*

In 1945, when Ernie Grant (a Jirrbal/Girramay descendant) was ten, old Mrs Butler, who owned the property where his mum and dad worked, usually had a cup of tea and a biscuit waiting for the kids when they arrived home from school. On one such day, being in a thoughtful mood, she pointed towards the Tully River and said, 'Dark deeds happened over there Ernest'. Ernie commented: 'I wasn't to know until much later in my life what she was getting at but I plainly know now.'[1]

Until 1848 four tribes inhabited the valley of the Tully River: the Girramay in the southern part, the Djiru along the north, the Gulngay along the Tully River and the Jirrbal to the west. The four tribes have been linguistically represented as 'Dyirbal'.[2] For thousands of years they hunted for food, held *buyas* (corroborees) to settle disputes and shared cultural events. On 4 July 1848 a dramatic change took place. On what is now known as Meunga Creek, the Girramay confronted white invaders. Edmund Kennedy's exploring party had arrived. During the confrontation four Girramay were shot. A week later, on 11 July, Kennedy was near the Murray River when he wrote that 'the fifteen or so aborigines following them did not know what had happened to their mates eight miles in front of them'.[3] That is, they had been shot. The rifle had arrived.

It was to be another sixteen years before George Elphinstone Dalrymple and party arrived in 1864 to establish the coastal township of Cardwell. Speaking Biri through his interpreter, James Morrill, a language not understood by the local Girramay, Dalrymple arrogantly informed the Girramagan that he had come to take the land and that they must not interfere.[4] John Ewen Davidson, who took up land at Bellenden Plains on the Murray River in 1865, recorded in his diary on 7 January the following year, that:

> ... it was a strange and painful sight to see a human being running for his life and see the black police galloping after him and hear the crack of the carbines; the gins and children all hid in the grass ... One little girl took refuge under my horse's belly and would not move: of course, I took no part in these proceedings, that being the duty of the [Native Mounted] police: it is the only way of insuring the lives of white men to shew that they cannot be attacked with impunity, for though the road party drove them off, if a dog had not given the alarm *they would most probably* all have been murdered as they slept. At 1 p.m. [we] stopped in the middle of a stream; discovered another wild black's camp, and secured their dinner—fish prawns, and scrub hen's eggs, all cooked to a nicety ...[5]

The Dyirbal-speakers and Girramay were to experience many violent encounters, particularly after the wreck of the *Maria* on the Barrier Reef in February 1872. After the wreck there were 75 men on board the brig,[6] of which thirteen were on a large raft, twelve on a smaller raft and an unknown number on two of the ship's boats,[7] one of which carried the captain. Fourteen survivors of the wreck were killed by local Aboriginal people which resulted in more than 43 Aboriginals being killed. The camp or village site of the people of Tam O'Shanter Point was located in a very rich food resource area and more than likely had 50 residents.[8] Assuming this to be the case then we can roughly gauge the overall numbers of Djiru who were killed. Combined with the numbers admitted officially, plus 45 from Tam O'Shanter Point, then one can suggest that somewhere in the vicinity of 88 Aboriginal men, women and children were killed. Charles Heydon, who was on the *Governor Blackall* sent from Sydney for the *Maria* search:

> ... had opportunities of becoming acquainted with the state of public opinion in North Queensland with regard to the blacks. I heard white men talk openly of the share they had taken in slaughtering whole camps, not only of men, but of women and children.[9]

A retribution party came from Cardwell, composed of Sub-Inspector Robert Arthur Johnstone of the Native Police and his troopers, and a posse of local settlers, who virtually annihilated the Djiru opposite Dunk Island.[10] A week later Johnstone confirmed to Lieutenant Gowlland the killings that had already occurred: 'I have also to state that I have severely punished the guilty parties having found the property of the missing men in their possession.'[11] Johnstone and his troopers shot a total of 43 Djiru.[12] Historian Arthur Laurie noted with regards to this, that 'there was grave suspicion that many of the blacks they killed were innocent'.[13] Chris Wildsoet, who arrived in the area in 1883 and spoke the local language, was interviewed in 1965 about further retribution and told how:

> ... they cut the niggers [*sic*] off at Tam O'Shanter Point ... [*pointing to the narrow neck*] And drove them out to sea and they shot women and kids and all—only five survived. Five of the old fellows and I got talking ... I said 'how did you fellows get away.' 'Well, we got in the caves, the tide was going out and when the white men and all the policemen had gone, we got up too, and cleared out.'[14]

Captain John Moresby of HMS *Basilisk* aided in the search for survivors, but appears to have found his involvement with carrying the retribution parties distasteful when he recorded that: 'several unfortunate blacks were shot down by the native troopers, who showed an unrestrained ferocity that disgusted our [Royal Navy] officers.'[15]

Over the Paluma Range, on the upper reaches of the Running River, Hidden Valley Station was established and an old Ravenshoe resident, Blue Wyatt, recalled a fellow who used:

> ... to actually shoot the Aborigines. The ones that played up, he would shoot them. He would take them to what they call the Break-aways which are on the flood plains in the wet seasons. He'd take the bodies up there, pile wood on them and burn them. When he had burnt them, he would get a stick and smack all their bones up. He would take all their teeth and put them in a milk tin, [and hide it] so when the Wet came it would wash all the [other] evidence away.
>
> The man who did it told me those stories and I didn't believe him, but he showed me the milk tin. He told me a story of how he put a body on the fire and turned his back on it and when he turned around it was sitting up looking at him, it had shrunk with the heat, you know. He also said ... when the heat got on, the finger-nails would fly off and he would run around and pick them all up and throw them back in the fire, so there wouldn't be any evidence left. ... He finally died of cancer.[16]

From the Alice River, 25 kilometres west of Townsville, Richard Bird Hall wrote to the *Brisbane Courier* in August 1872 criticising the Premier, Arthur Palmer, for making contradictory statements and fudging the truth in the Legislative Assembly. Hall, in his 'Cruelty to Blacks' letter states: 'The case I refer to is that near the Valley of Lagoons. If Mr Palmer desired to do justice, why did he not enquire into this matter, that even the squatters in the neighbourhood condemn.'[17] Unfortunately, no details are given, but he could well be referring to the Blencoe Falls or Kirrama massacres, which are 70 to 80 kilometres from the Valley of Lagoons. It is apparent from his letter that local atrocities were brought to the attention of the colonial government, but in such a vague fashion that one can see how it was able to overlook them. Hall goes on to identify another atrocity committed by Acting Sub-Inspector Robert Johnstone at Wyandotte Station belonging to the Scott Brothers:

> Lambing was taking place, and the shepherd and one white man were out two days looking for the blacks; they found them, and brought them in. I remonstrated with them. The only answer I got was—this mob of seven are always allowed in, and they will help us lambing. In a week after Mr. Johnson [Johnstone] came, and hunted them from lambing.* [Here it appears the editor has sanitized the accusation. His asterisked footnote reads: '*Mr Hall uses very strong language in describing the manner in which the blacks were treated at the woolshed, but to publish would subject us to an action for libel.']¹⁸

However, Alfred Davidson (1812–81), a representative of the Aborigines Protection Society based in Brisbane, wrote to the Colonial Secretary pointing out that:

> Mr Scott of Valley of Lagoons permitted a mob of Blacks mostly aged, to camp in that neighbourhood upon condition they would do no harm which condition they faithfully kept. One morning before daylight they were attacked by Native Police without any warning. Several were shot and two Gins taken away. The bodies of the Slain Gins appear to have been buried but the naked bodies of 8 dead men one grey headed—were left exposed on the roadside till they stank.¹⁹

The Reverend Edward Fuller tried to establish a mission on Hinchinbrook Island off the coast from Cardwell and informed the Scottish Catholic Missionary, the Reverend Father Duncan McNab, that he 'found only women and children all the men having been shot by the Native Police a few weeks previous to his arrival' in March 1874.²⁰ Yet seven years before, in the interior of the island, Captain Major and party counted some 40 or 50 huts spread out over about half a square mile (1.3 square kilometres).[21] Ernie Grant recalls:

> When I was a child there were between three and eight people per *mija* [hut] which gives an indication of the population of this one small part of Hinchinbrook Island before the killing-times began. This one village then, contained at least 200 residents and suggests that there were many more people living here prior to 1874. What happened to them?[22]

The Norwegian ethnologist, Carl Lumholtz (1851–1922), spent twelve months living on the upper Herbert River (1882–83) and recorded what he often heard from squatters in the region, that: 'The only treatment proper for the blacks is to shoot them all.' Lumholtz noted that one squatter 'acted on this principle', whereby:

> He shot all the men he discovered on his run, because they were cattle killers; the women, because they gave birth to cattle killers; and the children, because they would in time become cattle killers.[23]

Reports reached Brisbane from the north, and inland to George-town (1870) from a correspondent 'who admits that he has himself shot natives [and] ... as he says, he is 'not particularly prejudiced in favour of the natives or very soft-hearted'. The *Brisbane Courier* noted that 'our people have not yet been educated to the recognition of the human rights of the original possessors of Australia'. Their correspondent's:

> ... indictment touches mainly the districts lying between Cairns and Georgetown, where, he says, the blacks are being deci-mated, and by Government servants in the shape of black troopers and their masters, whose 'dispersion' of the aboriginals in particular localities has simply come to mean their slaughter. He speaks of men being kept for the sole purpose of hunting and killing the

aborigines; he gives instances of their camps being surrounded, and men, women, and children massacred for killing cattle, when, through the white man's presence, they could no longer find game; and he tells in detail one story of the extermination of a camp simply because some blacks had been seen passing a mining station where nothing had been stolen for months. Roundly he charges the 'grass dukes' and their subordinates with 'murdering, abducting children for immoral purposes, and stock whipping defenceless girls, and he condemns' each Government that comes into power for winking at the slaughter of our black fellow subjects of the Queen as an easy way of getting rid of the native question? The *Northern Miner* asserts that this picture is not overdrawn, and that the atrocities mentioned have even been exceeded. It refers to squatters branding blacks, keeping harems of black gins, and finding their slaughtering record no bar to advancement to high office in the State. The black trooper system is, in the view of this paper, legalised murder, which reckons the life of a bullock of more account than that of a score of blackfellows.[24]

The colonial government still managed to ignore these reports, but the author Arthur J Vogan reminded his readers in *The Black Police*, two years later in 1890, by quoting the above article and citing many other instances of brutality.[25] Fred Wimble, the newly elected inaugural member for Cairns, responded within 24 hours refuting that any atrocities of the nature mentioned had occurred in the Cairns area, although he could not offer an opinion beyond Herberton. Wimble, who arrived in Cairns in 1883 and established the *Cairns Post*, could not possibly have been unaware of the Skull Pocket/Mulgrave River/Skeleton Creek battue of December 1884– January 1885; nor the other massacres that occurred in the district during the 1880s. Wimble, however, did concur that the Native Police should be abolished and then proposed a series of 'reserves for the natives and placing them under the supervision of responsible Government agents'.[26] A decade passed before the government began thinking in terms of establishing

reserves, although the basis for it was still flawed as they showed no understanding of Aboriginal links to their traditional lands.

The oral history of the Jirrbal/Girramay people, like so many other
Aboriginal people and their associations to their traditional lands, is a
reality for their descendants. The killing-times still impact on their psychological well-being. Here is Ernie Grant's story as informed from the oral
history recollections of his relatives and ancestors.[27]

In May 1954, aged nineteen, Ernie Grant arrived at the Bilyana Railway
Station at 2 a.m. on the old Sunshine Express. He had been at the National
Servicemen's camp at Wacol in Brisbane. Ernie walked the seven miles
(11 kilometres) to his home at Yaban, arriving there four hours later. Sitting
at a campfire in front of his home was an old Aboriginal man who was
startled to see him arrive in army uniform. After greeting his parents and
siblings, Ernie's mother introduced him to the old man: he was his grandfather, Willy Lee. A couple of months later, the old fellow recounted the
following story to Ernie:

> The Native Police and settlers surrounded my mum and dad's camp
> and shot my parents and two brothers. Then we were chained up
> and marched towards Kirrima station to Horse-swamp camp about
> a mile from the station, until daylight. The camp was made up of
> Girramay, Jirrbal and Warungu people on Horse-swamp Creek.
> You can't miss it, a big clear sandy place.
>
> They rounded the old people up and women and children, and
> lined them up, children in one line, women in another and the men
> behind them in line. They then raised the British flag and proceeded
> to shoot all of the men, [and] smash all the children's heads against
> tree trunks. They then raped all the women and shot them, but one
> trooper went on to have sex with one of the dead women. He was
> unable to withdraw from her body as her pelvis had collapsed and
> as a result he was shot and left at the site.[28]

This recollection was also told by Joe Lee, Willy's brother, who was at the site and who informed Norman Tindale at Palm Island in 1938. The story is also mentioned in Tindale's genealogies from Palm Island.[29]

In 1954, Ernie was employed as a timber-getter by George Henry at Michael Creek (Jirin Creek). One day, while walking across the creek to look for timber, Ernie noticed a square patch of ground, approximately 60 square feet (5.7 square metres). Knowing that there was no machinery which had been on that side of the creek he later asked his mother why the patch was there.[30] This is what his mother (and later six other Jirrbal/Girramay) told him:

> The settlers and Native Police after massacring most of the tribe at Kirrima station in 1888, later turned their attention to Aboriginal's [sic] still killing cattle. They caught the old people and women and children, chained them together and brought them over the range and down to Michael Creek [Jirin]. In the three days they were there, they shot, raped and terrorised the two groups of people, as there was a large Jirrbal campsite located there. George Beeron told how, as the Native Police and settlers started to run out of bullets, they forced the men to have sex with the women so that they could shoot two at the one time. Over to the right of the camp, they took the young girls (11–14 years old) and raped them through the three days and nights. There were six young boys who survived: Wally Simpson, Joe Chalum, Harry Tully, Willy & Joe Lee, and Esau.[31]

The area on Jirin Creek has been surveyed as a memorial to those slain. The known settlers involved were: William Dallachy, Fred Robinson and Dick Lee, but there were others. Film and sound recordings of this oral history were made in 1987.[32]

A local Jirrbal, Tommy Warren, recalled the Mumbay Flat poisonings between 1906 and 1914, where his family and relatives:

> ... were walking over the mountains from the Kennedy Valley to the Murray Pocket, passing by the Guyurru [Murray Waterfall], as

we came over the top of the hill, the old people said: 'Hey, what's that smell coming up the hill.' They felt that something was wrong. We were still three or four miles from the camp. The closer we got, the worse the smell got. When we arrived at the camp site there were some people lying dead in the camp, but all the others were missing. So we followed the track down the river, about half a mile, and came out on the Mumbay Flat. Here we saw the whole flat covered by our people's bodies, all rotting away.[33]

Ernie remembers his great uncle, Wild Jimmy, telling how Arthur Blackman came up on a horse with two packhorses and six bags of flour. The flour, which was laced with strychnine, was given to his people, including Wild Jimmy's parents.

In 1952, just before Wild Jimmy died, Warajala (Jack Marita) told Ernie's uncle that it was the poisoning of his parents and his people which made him kill white and black people. During the 1930s he spent time in prison for killing Alick Brown, an Aboriginal from the Gulf Country. Ernie was working with his Uncle Jack for a saw-miller called Lenny Curry. A similar incident had happened a short way down the river, where water in a washing copper was boiled and tea made, but also laced with strychnine by William Dallachy. Dallachy wiped out all but one person from the Girramay and also some Jirrbal. Later on he was to try again using milk laced with strychnine. Dallachy told the Aboriginals to run as they drank the milk. This was at Gujiba on the north branch of the Murray River.[34] Long-term resident of Dunk Island (1897–1923), E J Banfield, tells of dispersals of Aboriginals involved with the murder of some of the crew of the brig *Maria*, and also wrote of Aboriginals being given a bucket of milk laced with strychnine.[35]

Dorothy Jones, in her book the *Cardwell Shire Story*, describes two dispersals on the Tully River.[36] The first one she identifies happened at Wiri ('Weary') Pocket, where a group of horsemen in a sporting mood shot up a group of Girramay and Jirrbal people on a sandbank known as Juluju-lumba. Willie Masina and Dave Barlow, two of Ernie's uncles, took him there around 1996 and told him what happened:

Uncle Willy says he saw some of the bodies and that they were white because the skin had peeled off. A 16 year old pregnant girl escaped by swimming across the river. She was the mother of Maggie Kinjun. Another old man escaped into the scrub up-river. The other massacre where the Tully River ran red with blood is located just below the Dip on Davidson Road. There is a large sandbank there and again the two old men told me that the native police waited until all the Aboriginals were in the river crossing before they opened fire. One little baby boy at the time, was being carried on his mother's shoulders and a bullet grazed his jaw. They said that the old people who managed to escape with the boy ... plastered clay over his mouth to help heal the wound. He became known as Broken Mouth.[37]

Ernie's two uncles, Uncle Dave and Uncle Willie, also took him to Kara Outstation on the head of Blunder Creek and showed him where Uncle Willie had seen the clearing full of skulls and bones. An old Aboriginal man known as Paddy Robinson said he and two white men were responsible. This man was also responsible for leading Native Police on other raids on the Jirrbal and other tribes of the area.[38] Another shooting of Jirrbal people took place at the head of the Tully River where sixteen Aboriginals were shot, but later found to be innocent of any misdeed.[39] Ernie has located where this happened near the head of Koombooloomba Dam on what the Jirrbal call the Jilgaring track in a pocket known as Numbal.

In the 1980s, Ernie's brother Earl, his wife and her mother Nora, were driving from Mt Garnet to the coast via Kirrima and pulled up at Blencoe Falls. Nora told how she survived a plunge into the gorge as a young girl because she fell on top of the bodies of Aboriginals who had been whipped and driven over the cliff by a party of white-men. Ernie was quite young when he noticed that Nora had a bad limp but he did not know why. Buck Bail, an elderly resident of Fringford where Ernie grew up, also told him that two Aboriginal women, one of whom was pregnant, were pushed over the falls to their death. The man who pushed them over was responsible for the pregnancy. Buck said it was common knowledge in the district. Ernie's Uncle Spider Henry was a little boy at the time and saw it happen. Another one of the persons Buck Bail told the story to was Michael Dickman who is still alive today.[40]

In response to the spearing of cattle on Wallace and Harry Grant's Woodleigh Station (between where Mt Garnet and Ravenshoe were later established in 1896), the brothers called in the Native Police from their Cashmere depot (c.90 kilometres south of Mt Garnet). At Wooroora Station (some 10 kilometres north-west of Tully Falls) on Blunder Creek, a posse:

> ... led by a white police inspector and guided by the Grants ... [went] in to punish and break up the guilty tribe. A surprise attack on the main camp was followed by terrible slaughter, the troopers galloping through the camp hacking down and shooting without mercy, men, women and children of their own race. Failing to check the orgy they were partially responsible for, the Grants, aghast at the dreadful scene, halted at the now deserted aborigines' camp where two small survivors of the massacre were huddled down in the wreckage of their gunyahs. It was fortunate ... that the Grants had paused where they did as just then a native trooper, mad with the lust to kill, rushed into the camp, seized the naked piccaninny by a leg and swung him up to dash his brains out against a tree. Harry Grant quickly grappled with the native and seizing the piccaninny put him out of harm's way in a dilly-bag ... A moment later Wallace Grant had saved the other piccaninny (a female) from a similar fate.[41]

The baby boy was Ernie's father's uncle, Boujeri. He was taken to Woodleigh Station which had been taken up by the Grant brothers. Luckily, Boujeri's father, Quingai, mother, Karingala, and older brother, Mutyeroo, escaped the massacre and later heard 'through the bush telegraph' that Boujeri (who the Grants had called 'Beadle') was alive and being treated well at the Woodleigh homestead. Ernie's ancestors' hard-working and productive life 'with the white people' was later recorded in an obituary in the *Cairns Post* in 1943.[42] It is apparent from this obituary that Ernie's family gained their English surname from the Grant brothers. Dolefully, Ernie ruminates that: 'The frontier treatment of my forebears has always been a source of acute bewilderment about the contradictory nature of brutal white violence and extremely kind and caring behaviour.'

In response to James Venture Mulligan's explorations inland from the future Cooktown, the colonial Queensland government anticipated a new goldrush to the region. George Elphinstone Dalrymple was put in charge of the 1873 north-east coast expedition, which traversed the coastal district from Cardwell, north to 'Cook's' Endeavour River. He was to report to the government about coastal resources.

At one stage, Dalrymple's expedition camped on Wangal Djungay (Double Island), and were aware that 'opposite where . . . the smokes of blacks' camps [were] . . . a supply of water would be obtained';[43] hence the excursion by Sub-Inspectors Johnstone and Tompson and troopers, along with the botanist, Walter Hill, to the shores of the future Palm Beach. They obtained a plentiful supply 'from a narrow lagoon nearly two miles long, running parallel to and only divided from the sea by the high sandy beach on which a number of blacks' camps were situated'.[44] To the Yirrganydji, the landing of the shore party was an imminent threat to the safety of their families and an obvious breach of etiquette regarding trespass. It is therefore not surprising that 'Immediately after landing a considerable mob of blacks came out of their camps, and in a most daring manner attempted to prevent Mr Johnstone's advance'.[45] The Europeans' intentions would have been no less clear to the Bama (rainforest Aboriginals), than those of the Bama would have been to Johnstone and his party, except that in anyone's language, the whites were intruding on what was obviously somebody else's territory.

To justify their behaviour during the incursion, in the brief time he was there, Johnstone managed to imply that the Bama were cannibals, possibly because they challenged the party's presence.[46] By interpreting cooked flesh as being human flesh, Johnstone could then by implication justify his violent response in claiming they were the worst of the worst: cannibals. However, the Yirrganydji were in fact giving a typical ritual greeting prior to acceptance into a village or camp.[47] Cooked flesh does not necessarily suggest cannibalism, but a misidentification of either local game (such as the cassowary) or the mortuary practice of carrying the remains of loved ones around in dilly bags.[48] The European party was ignorant of Bama cultural mores and made assumptions which suited their purposes. Dalrymple also attempted to justify the expedition's use of firearms:

> According to his instructions Mr Johnstone did not allow a shot to be fired, but this only appeared to add to their insolence and daring, as they advanced to within thirty yards, shipped their spears in the woomeras and poised them to throw; then, and not till then, the sniders opened upon them, but still they appeared utterly reckless as to the results, and their leader, a big hulking ferocious savage of over six feet in height, with several of his more daring fellows, tried still to throw their spears, and to induce the rest to come on when severely wounded.[49]

Dalrymple, somewhat hypocritically, accuses the Bama of being 'blood-thirsty bullying scoundrels' and suggests that *had* his men been a party of 'poor shipwrecked crew', the Bama would have mutilated and killed them 'as *many hundreds* of poor fellows have been'.[50] Unfortunately, this is mere supposition and there is an absence of evidence to support such an assertion.[51]

Thus, with their version of events recorded, the intrepid north-east coast expedition sailed north to Guugu Yimithirr territory, and the Endeavour River. Arriving on Friday 24 October 1873, the expeditioners were startled the next day 'by the sudden appearance of the tall masts and yards of a large steamer over the mangrove belt towards the point'.[52] It was the Austral-asian Steam Navigation company's *Leichardt*,[53] which promptly discharged some 70 'hardy' miners, as well as Mr Howard St George, the new Gold Commissioner for the Palmer diggings. With 'men hurrying to and fro, tents rising in all directions, horses and cargo, combined with the rattling donkey engine, cranes, and chains',[54] the fledgling port of Cooktown came instantly into being. Within four months there were 60 vessels riding at anchor in the Endeavour River.[55] The Palmer River gold 'rush' and European invasion of Cape York Peninsula had begun.

Over the coastal range, to the north-west, the frontier was beginning to expand at a rapid rate, for James Mulligan recorded on his second prospecting venture (6 July 1874), that 'up to now a few [white] men only have been here [at the Palmer River diggings], but these last few days men are coming in crowds'.[56] He was prospecting for a third time on 2 September when Mulligan named the river on which they were camped, the Hodgkinson. In 1875 Mulligan published his notes as a guide for prospective gold diggers, which not only gave mileage between 'centres' but also information about directions from which they may wish to travel, all this for 2/6.[57] Mulligan later recorded that 'the Hodgkinson Goldfield was reported by myself on 21st March, 1876'.[58]

With the stimulus of mining activities, white pioneers of the cattle industry were spurred to take up runs in the newly explored areas. Wrotham Park was established between the Walsh and Mitchell Rivers in 1873, Mt Mulgrave in 1875, Mitchell Vale in 1876 and Emerald End in 1877.[59]

East of the Hodgkinson goldfields, the port of Cairns was established in October 1876 to service the new mining ventures, which also attracted other forms of metal extraction, such as tin. Within eight years, in December 1884, one of Cairns District's best-kept secrets had occurred. At a site not far north of Allumbah Pocket (which became Yungaburra in 1910), eighteen-year-old Jack Kane, who had arrived in Cairns in 1882, told 'without an ounce of emotion, as plain fact',[60] how:

> ... [i]n 1884 he took part in a police raid which lasted a week, culminating in a round up at Skull Pocket and others following at Mulgrave River and near the Four Mile [Woree]. At Skull Pocket police officers and native trackers surrounded a camp of Idindji [Yidinydji][61] blacks before dawn, each man armed with a rifle and revolver. At dawn one man fired into their camp and the natives rushed away in three other directions. They were easy running shots, close up. The native police rushed in with their scrub knives

and killed off the children. A few years later a man loaded up a whole case of skulls and took them away as specimens.[62] [Old Jack stated] 'I didn't mind the killing of the "bucks" but I didn't quite like them braining the kids.' From Skull Pocket the raiders journeyed to the Mulgrave & again at [the] Four Mile, and shot other natives, some of them with wounds received in the raid at Skull Pocket.[63]

Michael O'Leary, writing as 'Coyyan', many years later recalled a 'most imposing sight was when we struck Skeleton Creek, for nearly every stump or tree had a nigger's [sic] skull as a trophy of the days when "dispersing" was the law. When we made camp, I strolled round and counted sixteen of these gruesome relics'.[64]

It is difficult to judge who was in charge of the Native Police detachment that started its dirty work at Skull Pocket and finished at Skeleton Creek, via the Mulgrave Valley. Suspicion could fall on Sub-Inspector William Austin Nichols who was based at Nigger Creek (now called Wondecla, south of Herberton), some 40 kilometres from the start of the fracas. Certainly, he was held responsible for his troopers killing 'two gins and a picaninny and a fellow called King Billy',[65] around 8 p.m. on Saturday 18 October 1884. Sub-Inspector Nichols was 'suspended in consequence of circumstances in connection with the recent murders at Irvinebank'.[66] White settlers had some sympathy for the Sub-Inspector, as Mrs Kate Atherton wrote to her daughter, Lucy: 'I suppose you will have heard that poor Nichol[s] has been arrested . . . we hear Garroway [sic] and the troopers were to be arrested also there is to be a hearing at Herberton[.] Today Isley and Carr went up . . . I hope there will not be anything done to them.'[67] Kate Atherton's wish came true: Nichols was acquitted.[68] It was not until 22 October 1885 that the troopers were discharged in Townsville, because no acceptable interpreters could be found.[69] One Herberton correspondent wrote: 'the fate of Nichols will be the salvation of any amount of murderous niggers [sic].'[70]

Sub-Inspector Ronald Garraway took over from his 'disgraced' associate, Nichols, who had been dismissed.[71] Certainly the 'battue' episode appears to have emboldened the male settlers of the district, for in mid-April 1885 a further 'outrage was committed', when Jamieson of Buchan

Estate's housekeeper was threatened by the Yirrganydji, and the homestead surrounded.[72] In response, Police in a customs boat were dispatched
to investigate, while '[a] number of townsmen rode over . . . armed with
revolvers and breachloaders in case of a collision, but no such luck was in
store'. The events caused great indignation.[73]

On the upper reaches of the Mulgrave River, a group of 100 Malanbarra
Yidinydji, while participating in a significant cockatoo ceremony, were
attacked by the explorer Christie Palmerston and his Ngadjanydji carriers.
Palmerston wrote on 8 September 1886, that Cockatoo Bora Ground was:

> . . . large and original, situated on the west bank of the Mulgrave. In
> the centre of the ground were dug two long parallel rows of oval-
> shaped holes, filled with crouching figures, that portion just below
> the armpits and upwards being the only part exposed. Quivering
> tufts of white and yellow cockatoo feathers decorated their nodding
> heads; bunches of larger white fluttering feathers were fixed along
> their arms and hands, which they worked in wing-wave fashion; the
> face and other parts of the body were formed in stripes of finer white
> down. Amid these stood two poles, up which many more niggers
> [sic] were perched and befeathered in a similar style. Their legs and
> arms were akimbo, and their nodding heads accompanied a banter-
> ing vein of cockatoo's screaches, [sic] which ended occasionally with
> roars of wild mirth . . . I placed my boys three parts round the borah
> ground, which I attacked shortly after day-dawn . . . After reducing
> heaps of war implements to ashes, we moved towards home, taking
> two young prisoners with us.[74]

Paul Savage analyses Palmerston's diary entries and makes the observation that Palmerston was 'embroiled by his [Ngadjanydji] carriers in a
feud with another tribe [the Malanbarra Yidinydji]', and that after writing
2200 words on the lead-up description, he passed over 'what should have
been the climax of the chase, the dawn attack', in just eight words. Savage
contends that 'As if to balance the understated violence of this episode,
CP [Christie Palmerston] ends his account of this part of the expedition

with a long, consciously gruesome account of funeral rites he witnessed'.[75] It is difficult to assess what the Malanbarra casualties were, but there can be no doubt they were sizeable.

Depredations were sometimes followed by the murder of a white man, which regularly led to a violent European response culminating in a massacre. Constable McLauglin from Herberton was instructed by Senior Constable Whelan[76] to investigate the disappearance of John Clifford from the Russell River gold diggings. Clifford's 'most trusted native, Jemmy, and his six other Aboriginals were known to have been sent at times to Mouril-yan Harbour without supervision to collect rations'. Clifford was reported to have returned from 'Salt Water' (Mourilyan Harbour) to his claim, in April 1889. In late July or early August, his body was found in 'Coopooroo Creek, buried in a hole ... covered with stones'. William Langdon held a Magisterial Inquiry at Boar Pocket on 9 September 1889, where it was found that 'John Clifford had been killed by the Blacks [probably for his supply of rations] ... Constable McLauglin stated, "I have every reason to believe from information I got from the Diggers that more murders have been committed as several other men were missing."' [77]

It appears likely that as a result of this murder, a massacre occurred at the site which became Butchers Creek.[78] The late Ngadjanydji Elder, Molly Raymond, recalled her mother, Granny Emily, finding her 'husband shot and hung up on a tree, but still alive, [he] tried to push his stomach back, but couldn't'. Molly's mother and grandmother found refuge with the Malan-barra Yidinydji on the Mulgrave River:

> ... as all their people up the top [of the range] had been attacked at [the] corroboree ground, [and because the] Police [were] around the district all the time—around Herberton way—hunting [and] killing people ... One girl [was] dragged through a blazing camp fire [by the Native Police], she escaped and hid in a log, but they found her and killed her and then [the Native Police] were sitting down and cutting her up like a meat.[79]

Over the Lamb Range (Bunda Djarruy Gimbal),[80] to the north and south of the middle Barron River, the Djabugay-speakers were giving trouble at Andrew Leon's selection on the range (c.May 1886), and it was suggested that a 'little "black birding" appears to be necessary, and if the limbs of the law do not look sharp and have some fun themselves, the selectors will be out skirmishing when "long pig" will probably be plentiful'.[81] The obscure nature of this reference does not hide the settlers' frustration, particularly as at least four settlers' camps on their selections had been 'cleaned out' in the previous two months.[82]

There appears to have been coordinated attacks by Bama groups from the coast to the ranges and onto the Atherton Tableland, which suggests that they were fighting a guerrilla war. A local historian, Bill Johnston, perceived that retribution by the new settlers, 'was seldom a matter of boasting, [a] knowledge of which was handed down from father to son, or ... gleaned from the glossed over official reports'.[83] Johnston noted the use of strychnine and arsenic with the Madjanydji on Babinda Creek and the 'armed bands and "nigger [sic] hunts" which wiped out men, women and children at Bones Knob and at Evelyn'.[84] He also recalled that 'Tommy Gilmore's brother Joe told him that when they were children, they used to collect bones around the Knob. This was in the early 1930s. I was told in the late 1930s'.[85]

During the early 1880s, an Irish prospector-turned-packhorse carrier, Patrick Molloy, worked the Port Douglas to Herberton road.[86] He and his wife established a home at the top of the range near the convergence of the traditional lands of the Djabugay and Kuku Yalanji.[87] At one stage he lost eight of his draught horses to the Djabugay. Molloy and a party of Native Mounted Police and some white settlers tracked the Djabugay group to Bunda Bugal (Black Mountain), at the head of Rifle Creek, where their 'camp was quickly surrounded [and] the blacks [sic] who showed fight were dispersed and taught a lesson that cured their taste for horse flesh for a considerable time. In fact some of them lost it altogether'.[88]

An early white 'pioneer', Grannie Reynolds, recalled when her 'family settled in the Mowbray Valley there was no trouble whatever with the Chabbuki [Djabugay] tribe. Another tribe ... camped at White Cliffs, reportedly a very ferocious tribe was the Yirkandja [Yirrganydji] tribe, who roamed as far as Spring Creek area',[89] the valley running north to the Mowbray River, about 4 kilometres from White Cliffs. It would appear that the 'ferocity' of the Djabugay-speaking Yirrganydji may have had something to do with them spearing cattle and taking:

> ... what meat they wanted and leav[ing] the carcasses to rot. After all threats and pleas had failed, some of the farmers went to the camp and fired shots in the air. The tribe fled the area. The next morning, Mr Robbins went to the camp and found a little baby girl that had been left in the camp. He took her home and a Mossman family reared her.[90]

Aboriginal oral history also tells of a massacre in the Spring Creek valley, where police from the Police Reserve, located on the south side of the mouth of the Mowbray River,[91] herded people into the valley, up where the old lime crusher is, on the eastern side. They chased them up to where the lime quarry is and killed them.[92]

Along the coast from Cooktown south to the Johnstone River, rainforest Aboriginals were badly treated by bêche-de-mer fishermen and other white men. George Demetries wrote to the Queensland Colonial Secretary in 1898, stating that he was:

> ... in Island Point [Port Douglas] from the day it was opened [1877] till 1899. About 12 to 13 years ago [c.1885] Beach de mere [sic] men were in the Mowbray river shooting the blacks, so they came and reported it in Town, but nobody seemed to take any interest in the matter ... and they done the same thing the other side of Cairns [on the Mulgrave River?].[93]

Demetries also makes reference to indiscriminate shootings and the nonchalant attitude of whites to the violence being perpetrated against the indigenous inhabitants of the coastal district and states that: 'A Frenchman named De Currie [Du Couret?] came there [to Island Point and] took up a bit of land and used to shoot them the same as others but the blacks shifted him.'[94]

Inland from Cairns in the Kuranda district, George Hobson was killed on his property, just opposite Myola Railway Station, on 20 July 1890.[95] Nearly 40 years later, the *Northern Herald* recalled that John Atherton:

> . . . while returning by the early day pack tracks from Cairns, accompanied by his two daughters, a camp was made at the wayside shack kept by Groves near the Clohesy. In the morning a pony ridden by one of the girls was missing, and its tracks followed, disclosed the fact that a number of the blacks were in possession . . . and finally, after penetrating the jungle for some distance, the natives were surprised in the act of cutting up the beast for an anticipated feast [at Guwulu, old Speewah, near today's Snake Gully].[96]

An elderly Djabugay called Buttercup remembered being present as a famished five-year-old who was salivating at the prospect of eating the *minya* (meat),[97] but as the pony was being prepared for *bayngga* (earth oven—hot rocks), in its death throes, it kicked a stone that hit young Buttercup in the chest. Her mother, Minnie, took her to the river to wash and cool the injury. The newspaper report ominously concluded: 'Needless to say, the banquet did not come off.' While down the river, Buttercup and Minnie heard gunshots and upon returning to the camp they saw the bodies of their people where they had been shot down. The terrified mother and daughter fled for their lives down to Crystal Cascades and the sanctuary of a white selector's family, that of the American, Andrew Banning.[98]

Professor Rentoul visited Kuranda in 1890 and later made reference in the *Brisbane Courier*:

> . . . to the recent murders by blacks of Hobson in the Cairns district [and] considers the Hobson tragedy was followed by tragedies of perhaps even a more terrible character, and that it is not improbable that several lives were taken perhaps of innocent persons

in avenging poor Hobson's death . . . for the stories that reached Professor Rentoul are open secrets in Cairns.[99]

Rentoul later wrote that the Barron tribe had:

> . . . nothing to do with Hobson's death . . . A black named Bismark shot him . . . The policeman and black trackers went and 'returned, not having made an arrest.' This is told you with a smile. The rule as to 'dispersing the blacks' is that no report is rendered. The other account, whispered in private around Cairns, is that the 'blacks camp' of the Barron tribe, towards which Bismarck's steps were traced, was surrounded; and without warning, the cordon of rifles fired into the camp and left eight aboriginals dead.[100]

Similar incidents occurred amongst the Djabugay-speakers in the northern part of the Cairns rainforest region. One such unconfirmed incident[101] is that of the Black Water Lagoon massacre,[102] which is believed to have taken place west of Wright's Crossing, south west of Mona Mona Mission (about 20 kilometres north-west of Kuranda). Another that Djabugay Elders recall took place at Mama's Camp[103] on Flaggy Creek, and yet another at Balilee (also on Flaggy Creek), where cattlemen believed the Bama to be killing and eating their bullocks. Elder, Florence Williams, remembered that after this episode, 'the water ran red with blood'.[104]

Chapter 9

The Gulf Country and Western Queensland

To realise the effect of these abuses on the Aboriginal men it would be necessary
for some race stronger than ourselves to come here and treat our own women and
children in a similar manner. What would the fathers, husbands and brothers do
under the circumstances?

Archibald Meston, 'Report on Aborigines of Queensland',
QV&P, 1896, p.4.

The Gulf Country was explored by Europeans during the 1860s, but those
who took up runs abandoned them as the western pastoral frontier completely collapsed. Between 1866 and 1870, about 159 stations in the Burke district
(i.e. the Gulf), 97 in South Kennedy, 78 in North Kennedy and 36 stations in
the Cook district (on Cape York) were abandoned.[1] This was a total of 370
runs abandoned in the four-year period to 1870. This collapse came with the
persistent depression from 1866 onwards. A series of crises—fiscal, political,
social, economic and environmental—shook the nascent colonial order to its
core.[2] A quarter of a century later, it was acknowledged that:

> ... the country was deserted to all intents and purposes, and the
> nigger [*sic*] had some ten or twelve years spell to recover himself, to

revel in the remains of the Whiteman's goods left at old stations and townships, and to fatten on the cattle which our pioneers had not thought worthwhile to travel south.[3]

Nevertheless, there were three overland trips made into the Northern Territory via north-western Queensland during the period 1872–78.[4] The construction of the overland 'telegraph line from Adelaide to Port Darwin in 1872 was to give a great impetus to pastoral settlement in the Territory',[5] and it also heralded a new wave of cattle drives via the Queensland and Territory Gulf Country, with a subsequent rapid increase in violence and dislocation for those Aboriginals whose traditional lands were being traversed by the cattlemen.

Tony Roberts gives an extensively researched coverage of the South-Australian–administered Northern Territory in *Frontier Justice*: it is balanced but horrifying. Roberts concludes that 'more than 50 massacres are known to have occurred',[6] and estimates that:

> ... at least 600 men, women, children and babies, or about one-sixth of the population were killed in the Gulf Country to 1910. The death toll could easily be as high as seven or eight hundred. Yet, no one was charged with these murders. By contrast, there were 20 white deaths, and not a single white woman or child was harmed in any way. The South Australian government . . . knew from a variety of reports that the region was heavily populated . . . In just four years, the Aboriginal population of at least 4000, composed of 15 tribes or language groups, was dispossessed of every inch of land . . . a peculiar dimension to this tragedy . . . [is that] the pastoral industry, for which the government had been willing to sacrifice hundreds of lives and dispossess thousands of people, was a failure. Six of the 14 stations were abandoned within ten years . . . [7]

Amazingly, the Darwin newspaper the *Northern Standard* published a biographical account of the colonial period in the Gulf in June 1934, some 48 years after the author Charley Gaunt's involvement in what became known as the Malakoff Creek massacre.[8] In 1886, Edward Lenehan, a stockman who had participated in previous dispersals, was tracking some Ngarnji tribesmen in order to 'teach them a lesson', but it was he who learnt a deadly lesson. A white reprisal party of 22 members was then organised. On the upper reaches of the McArthur River they chased the escaping Ngarnji into the Abner Range, about 120 kilometres south, south-west of Borroloola.[9] On the edge of a precipice, they took:

> ... up positions at every vantage point, M[ounted]. C[onstable].
> Smith [actually Constable William Curtis] gave the order,[10] he being
> in charge of the party: 'I'll lead off when it's light enough to see, and
> my shot will be the signal to open out on them.' ... [Gaunt], with a
> police boy, was lying on the easterly side of the camp, others in twos
> were stationed around the camp at intervals. It was a big mob by
> the look of the small fires and space it covered. The Abos [*sic*] were
> all sleeping peacefully. At times we could hear a piccaninny cry and
> the lubra crooning to it. The police boy and ... [Gaunt] were ...
> about fifteen or twenty yards away from the nearest fire. An Abo
> and his lubra were lying alongside of it. Higher and higher rose
> the Morning Star; the dawn was beginning to break in the east and
> those blacks slept peacefully on. A great many of them were not to
> see sunrise.
>
> It was now almost light enough to see and every man around
> that camp was feverishly awaiting the signal. At last the Abo at the
> fire nearest the boy and I sat up and threw his arms up to stretch
> himself. Just at that moment Smith fired and the police boy with me
> fired at the sitting Abo. The black bounced off the ground and fell
> over into the fire, stone dead. Then pandemonium started. Blacks
> were rushing to all points only to be driven back with a deadly fire.
> One big Abo, over six feet, rushed toward the boy and I dropped
> him in his tracks with a well directed shot. Later on when we went
> through the camp to count the dead and despatch the wounded, I
> walked over to this big Abo and was astonished to find, instead of
> a buck, that it was a splendidly built young lubra about, I should

judge, sixteen or eighteen years of age. The bullet had struck her on the bridge of the nose and penetrated to the brain. She never knew what hit her.

The blacks tried to break through at all points and when they found they were trapped the bucks grouped together and got the spears and boomerangs to work. Several spears went very close to the police boy and I but with the exception of a flesh wound in the arm the boy collected, we got clear. Later we found that Jack Gallagher and McClelland also got two light flesh wounds.

The camp was situated on a level piece of ground right on the edge of a cliff at the head of a big steep gorge, the extreme head of the Malakoff Creek. The cliff at the western side of the camp had a sheer drop of about five hundred feet [152 metres]. When the shooting began some of the Abos suddenly wakened out of their sleep, dazed and half asleep, rushed to the edge of the cliff and jumped over. Sudden death awaited them when they hit the jagged rocks at the bottom.[11]

Gaunt concluded that after the melee was over, 'we counted fifty-two dead and mortally wounded. For mercy's sake we dispatched the wounded. Twelve more we found at the foot of the cliff fearfully mangled'. Gaunt's coverage is one of the few detailed descriptions of whites massacring blacks and gives a horrifyingly accurate insight into the meaning of the word 'dispersal' and its application across Queensland.

Perhaps not surprisingly, the Queensland Native Police were involved in several of the Northern Territory killing expeditions and made forays across the Territory border. An arrangement was made in June 1888 whereby South Australian police based at Camooweal and Queensland police near the border were sworn in as constables of the respective colonies.[12] The remoteness of the area enabled their activities to be hidden and alternative versions of events to be promulgated. For example, in 1890 Thomas Perry, the manager and part-owner of Creswell Downs in the Territory, some 240 kilometres west of the border between Queensland and the Northern Territory, treated his Aboriginal stockmen with brutal disregard for their humanity and as a result was murdered. That he was targeted specifically can be deduced by the fact that three other white men camped nearby were unharmed.[13] One of the main suspects, Karrara, was a survivor of a previous massacre on Coanjula Creek, part of traditional Waanyi territory on the upper Nicholson River. So too was his brother, Yaribidja, whose son, Djagooridi (Duncan Hogan), had grown up on Creswell Downs and recalled:

> Mr Berry [Perry], he been shot at Bowgan. He was pinching young wife belonging to Old Man.[14] Them men asked a Queensland boy to shoot Mr Berry. Peter, he sneaked up night time and pinched a gun and shot Mr Berry—killed him dead. After Mr Berry been shot, soldiers shot a big mob down there, no one got away.[15]

By 'soldiers', Djagooridi is referring to the Queensland Native Police who wore military-style uniforms and most likely came from Turn-Off Lagoon, which had been established as a Native Police base in 1888.[16]

> Soldiers then went to Bowgan [an outstation on Creswell Downs] and Aborigines knew they would come, they all cleared out to Nicholson to Iringa ['Long Waterhole' east of Bowgan, on Creswell Creek] in the rough country. Soldiers went in and shot all they could find. Some of them old Bucks were made to go with the white men who made them track down their own colour.
> Old Strutton [Charlie Scrutton] white man he killed blackfellows up McArthur River. Ted Conson, whiteman, killed blackfellows along Brunette country.
> Harry Lanson whiteman killed a lot of blackfellows along [the waterholes of] Bowgan, Iringa, Woodoowala, Minyarga and Oogoora Well and all around Rajiji [on the Nicholson]. Harry Lanson came along with a mob of soldiers and killed a big mob of blackfellows from Bowgan, down into Nicholson River after Mr Berry been killed.[17]

For the next 30 years white pastoral settlement was attended by massacres across the entire Gulf region.[18] In 1875 the Palmerston (Darwin from 1911) newspaper readily acknowledged:

> We are invading their country, and they have a perfect right to—
> and it is but natural that they should—do their best to obstruct our
> passage through it. They look upon us as enemies, and we must do
> the same when they molest us. What is the crime with us is a virtue
> with them. They know nothing of our laws or our customs, and
> would be just as wise as to the true reason therefor [sic], when suffer-
> ing the extreme penalty of the law for these outrages, as would a
> dog ... Shoot those you cannot get at, and hang those that you do
> catch on the nearest tree as an example to the rest; *and let not the*
> *authorities be too curious and ask too many questions of those who may*
> *be sent to perform the service.*[19]

Much of the violence meted out by Europeans in the Northern Territory was based on the precedent of white Queenslanders' behaviour. The *Northern Territory Times* commenting in 1875 about a retribution party to the Roper River felt sure they should:

> ... save themselves the trouble of bringing their prisoners such a
> distance to serve no sensible purpose. The only things that have
> hitherto proved of any value in bringing the niggers [sic] to their
> senses have been dogs and the revolvers; and we trust the party
> now gone out will not be afraid to use them. The Queenslanders
> have been taken to task several times for their mode of dealing with
> them; but our Eastern neighbours have dearly bought their experi-
> ence; and it would be unwise of us not to profit by it.[20]

And learn they did, with teachers like Frank Hann, who went into partnership with Edward Edkins,[21] to re-establish Lawn Hill Station in 1875. Along with Jonathon Harold ('Jack') Watson, stockman/manager, they committed acts of extreme violence against the local Waanyi, Nguburinji and other Aboriginal people.

In February 1883, 22-year-old Caroline 'Carrie' Creaghe and her husband Harry (who was absent for the last six weeks of her stay), spent three months at Francis Shadforth's Lilydale Station (later Riversleigh), about 64 kilometres south of Lawn Hill. From the Shadforth women Carrie learnt that 'Mr Watson has forty pairs of blacks' ears nailed round the walls collected during raiding parties after the loss of many cattle speared by the blacks'.[22] Watson was a man who had been educated at Melbourne Grammar and came from a prominent horse-racing family. In 1896 he moved on to Victoria River Downs in the Territory,[23] where he was involved in slaughtering unknown numbers of tribespeople. He again demonstrated an extreme streak of sadism, when he punished 'an Aboriginal man, possibly for stealing, by impaling both hands on a tall sapling that had been sharpened to a point at the top'.[24] Similarly, he kept the skull of an Aboriginal man, with whom he once worked, as a spittoon.[25] An old Gulf prospector, John Tim Swann, wrote in December 1891:

> I seen Hann chain up a gin to a tree one leg on each side of the tree then [a] pair of handcuffs on her ancles [sic] for being too long out looking for horses. I went and looked at her the ants were running all over her person and his favourite gin pleaded for her release ... after two hours she was liberated.[26]

Hann noted in his diary on 11 October 1895 that 'Dora would not do as I wished so I chained her up'. On another occasion Frank Hann spent five consecutive days (from 7 to 11 March 1896) searching for 'Mary and Violet [who] ran away last night'.[27] He failed to find them. Previously, in 1880, Hann recorded how, about 240 kilometres west of the Queensland border, he: 'caught Ophal, the gin here' on Cresswell Creek.[28]

In 1885, Frank Hann claimed he was informed by Sub-Inspector Lamond that the Native Police 'have shot ... round this run alone over 100 blacks in three years and yet they still kill cattle',[29] which the dispersing was supposed to stop. It didn't, suggesting that it was a continued attempt to get rid of the whites, which the Aboriginals possibly thought they had achieved during the previous period of station abandonment.

Armstrong argues that 'It was when the Kalkadoons [local traditional owners] saw that the Europeans claimed their permanent waterhole as their private property, drove off the native game and shot any members of the tribe who speared cattle, that they [the Kalkadoons] decided the settlers must be kept out'.[30] This undoubtedly accounts for the tactics that were adopted, including scaring and spearing cattle and horses. Not to mention vulnerable lone individuals who were traipsing the outback frontier, including dray and bullock teamsters.

Around Christmas 1878 a party of four led by Russian cattleman, Bernard Molvo, were killed by Kalkadoon tribesmen at Woonamo (today Wonomo) Waterhole on Suliemen Creek, 30 kilometres south, south-west of the future Dajarra. Archaeologist Ian Davidson, and traditional owners, Isabel Tarragó and Tom Sullivan, noted that: 'Among the many . . . important Dreamings in the region are the Rainbow Serpent Dreaming that goes through Woodul Rockhole and the Yellowbelly Dreaming that begins at Wonomo Waterhole. A Dreaming connection [which] was probably the reason . . . Molvo was killed . . .'[31] The manager of Stanbook (today's Stradbroke?) Station, Luke Russell, was 'warned by his black boy' about the killings, and as cattle were being speared, he hastily mustered his cattle and 'waited in ambush till the blacks approached; then a well-directed fusillade caused them to withdraw'. The Native Police detachment at Boulia, some 150 kilometres to the south were informed, and rode north led by Second-Class Sub-Inspector Ernest Eglington to join forces with a white vigilante group, and Luke Russell and Alexander Kennedy (of Buckingham Downs, adjoining Stradbroke to the south).

A long trip into the hills followed, the native police hot on the trail and Kennedy as keen as the rest. A yell of defiance was heard, the pursuers were discovered by the retreating party and hurled threats from their supposed safety in the rugged hilly country [of the Selwyn Range]. However, they did not reckon on the deadly carbines of the whites and the native troopers, who speedily shot the warlike bucks down.[32]

Interestingly, Hudson Fysh immediately follows the above description with one of the supposed cannibalism and horrors of native mortuary practices, which is very similar to Christie Palmerston's coverage of the massacre of Malanbarra Yidinydji at Cockatoo Bora ground in the Goldsborough Valley south-west of Cairns, seven years later. Both reports seem to be deliberately designed to divert one's attention by highlighting mortuary practices, ill-understood but 'gory-fied' for effect and implied justification of the excessive violence dealt out to indigenous victims. Eglington does the same thing. Regarding the actual numbers of Kalkadoons killed in the Selwyn Ranges, Robert Clarke wrote to the *Pastoral Review* (12 August 1901) stating that 300 had been shot.[33] It is difficult to gauge how accurate or exaggerated this figure may be, but it has to be acknowledged that a great many Kalkadoons perished.

Alexander Kennedy believed: 'that the only way to survive in this wild country was to show conclusively who was master; to keep the bucks and fighting men at a distance, and at the least hint of trouble to get in first.'[34] In 1881 he went into partnership with James White Powell and took up Calton Hills Station on Gunpowder Creek, 70 kilometres north of the future Mt Isa (1924), which was still in the lands of the Kalkadoons. The traditional owners continued spearing and unsettling the station's cattle, and Kennedy travelled to Brisbane to complain to Police Commissioner Seymour. The double standards which applied at government level can be seen by the Commissioner telling him:

'Kennedy, if you touch one of those blacks we shall have you arrested!' Kennedy left the building feeling disgusted with the way the State was protecting her outlying settlers; but he had not gone far down the street when Seymour overtook him and, taking his arm, said, 'Look here, I could not tell you what to do in there. We shall do what we can to increase the number of police patrols in the bad area; meanwhile, *if you have trouble, you know what to do.*'[35]

After this meeting, a Native Police detachment, under the command of the inexperienced Sub-Inspector Marcus de la Poer Beresford, established a camp some 5 kilometres north-west of the township of Cloncurry. In January 1883, Sub-Inspector Beresford and four Native Police troopers went in search of the killers of a man called Britcher. Travelling to the south-east on the headwaters of the Fullarton River (roughly halfway between Farley Station and the future township of McKinlay, and about 60 kilometres south, south-east from Cloncurry), they disarmed a party of Kalkadoons and corralled them in a gorge. It seems the Kalkadoons had a cache of weapons hidden there and during the night they broke out, attacking the Native Police and crushing Beresford's skull. A wounded trooper managed to stagger 30 kilometres to an outstation of the Farleigh run (today's Farley?) and raise the alarm. This incident heralded a renewed phase of guerilla warfare with a major increase in cattle-spearing and contempt for the invading white pastoralists.

Sub-Inspector Eglington attempted to carry out reprisals when he and his troopers travelled from Boulia to Cloncurry and the surrounding area, while hunting for Beresford's killer. The Kalkadoons eluded Eglington's efforts, which later in 1883 resulted in Sub-Inspector Frederick Urquhart being sent from Gregory Downs Native Police camp (270 kilometres to the north-west) to replace him. It seems to have been at the behest of the Premier/Colonial Secretary, Sir Thomas McIlwraith, whose wife was sister to A F Mosman who had taken up White Hills Station (north-west of Cloncurry between Calton Hills and Kamileroi Stations), that Eglington was replaced.[36] Urquhart moved the Native Police camp 40 kilometres to the north-west of Cloncurry so that the barracks were further away from the town, and there trained and drilled his troopers.[37]

The following year on Mistake Creek, in the vicinity of White Hills Station, James Powell was mustering cattle with the help of George Mark (the manager of Kamileroi). He was driving the cattle back to Calton Hills when Powell met his end. His Aboriginal stockman, Jacky, although wounded by a spear, managed to get news of the affray to Calton Hills. Alexander Kennedy responded quickly to his partner's sudden demise by riding the 130-odd kilometres from Cloncurry in two days, joining Urquhart and his detachment on their dispersal patrol.

> The blacks were finally located in a gorge and, though . . . at first by hurling spears in an attempt to stay the approach of the party, they broke and fled at the first sign of rifle fire. There were natives behind boulders, behind trees, and up trees, and every now and then they made attempts to sneak away to better cover . . . Kennedy was like hell let loose that day . . . The work was done; Powell had been avenged, and a severe lesson had been taught the natives, which they were not likely to forget.[38]

'What really happened at Battle Mountain in 1884?' is a question Jonathan Richards asks, as he re-assesses the legendary version which paints the event as a 'stand-up military-style battle'. Richards considers this version as oversimplified and identifies the lack of primary source verification. He notes that:

> The patrol consisted of two Europeans and six troopers—not 110 as [Robert] Armstrong reckons. [Sub-Inspector] Urquhart said they encountered '150 blacks' not 600 as Armstrong claims. There was not mention of an almost fatal attack on Urquhart, as Armstrong says. The entire concept of a 'flanking movement' to defeat the Kalkadoon appears to have been solely Armstrong's invention. Besides, it was standard practice for the troopers to attack from both sides. Importantly, there are no references for this crucial detail.[39]

Richards also observes that the legend has been promulgated to other authors, including the *Encyclopaedia of Aboriginal Australia* which adopts the military-style analogy, and states: 'the Kalkadoons made a concerted but desperate downhill charge, holding their spears like lances, only to be cut down by rifle fire.'[40] There is no evidence for the supposed military formation mentioned here. Richards concludes that:

... a clash, or in nineteenth-century terms, a 'collision', took place after the Kalkadoon attacked a Chinese shepherd on Granada station [some 70 kilometres north of Cloncurry]. Urquhart, with civilian volunteers [which was against regulations] and his troopers, encountered a number of Kalkadoon warriors on a hill and called on them to surrender. They were met with rocks and spears, so dismounted and advanced, firing their rifles as they climbed the rocky ground. Urquhart, who was hit by a lump of rock and temporarily knocked out, [had] sent two troopers round the hill to attack the Kalkadoon from the side—a standard 'flanking' tactic. This tipped the balance, causing many casualties and a general retreat. Urquhart's troopers then pursued the fleeing Kalkadoon people, killing an unknown number of men, women and children.[41]

Granada was taken up in 1867 by P E Walsh, nephew of W H Walsh (who owned Degilbo Station on the Burnett River) and who was later Minister for Mines in Sir Arthur Palmer's administration (3 May 1870–7 January 1874).[42] One can see some quite strong links between station-owners and their investors, and the political elite down in Brisbane. This no doubt helps to account for the maintenance of a conspiracy of silence. The same attitude of collusion appears to apply to South Australian politicians with regard to the Northern Territory.[43] In 1885 the *South Australian Register* concluded: 'The perpetrators are not only those who shot down the wretched blacks, but the officials who authorized and concealed this disgraceful deed.'[44]

The ubiquitous nature of these frontier killing-times can readily be observed from recollections of many of the older generations of indigenous Australians. One anthropological survey team interviewed an elderly woman whose mother came from around the Lawn Hill Gorge area who recalled that: 'Police been shoot 'em lot of dark people. My mum used to tell me, they run away into the mountain when they heard that horse bell comin'—shoot 'em down—just like a dog.'[45] Ruby Saltmere told historian Tony Roberts how her Waanyi grandmother (Rosie) only just escaped a dawn raid at Lawn Hill Station by the Native Police:

They were tired—they'd been on the run for weeks. [The Native
Police] caught up with them one morning when they were sound
asleep. And she reckoned all she could hear were shots, and people
screaming and moaning.

Rosie was young. She had just reached puberty and along with a friend she
took cover under a windbreak of bushes:

They wouldn't shoot the pregnant women—they bayoneted them,
and saved the bullets. The dogs and pregnant women and kids—
they just whacked into them with bayonets. So, she had to live
with that.

Rosie was cut on a shoulder when the police prodded the windbreak: 'God
knows how they missed her: They just cut [her] here', said Ruby, who went
on to describe how the girls fled and then hid under water: 'put rocks on
their tummies, and get a straw to breathe out of . . . so the police wouldn't
see them.' They remained like this 'for three nights, they reckoned. It
rained, too. Yes, they had it tough, aye'.[46]

It was during the 1880s that another negative factor arose on the Gulf
frontier: white criminals—'real blood-thirsty' bushrangers. Literally, as
a local station manager described them, 'desperate and lawless' and 'vile
thieves'; and Ruby Saltmere remembered:

They did some terrible things even with white families. You
know, they used to get to the station and if only the women folk
was home they used to rape them. And the same thing they did to
black women, too. So they had to be very careful of them. It was
mainly the bushrangers that were shooting the Aborigines out [at
that time] . . . Granny talked about that a lot. She talked about the
bushrangers, and where they [she and her husband] worked. She
talked about that a fair bit.[47]

Not surprisingly, these fugitives and criminals were infamous for instigating and being involved in murder, cattle-stealing, horse-stealing and
highway robbery. These nasty desperadoes haunted the upper Nicholson
and Calvert Rivers across to a shanty run by a fellow named Anderson, at
Turn-Off Lagoon. Between 1882 and 1885 the coast cattle-droving track
was at its most active and cattle-duffing was rife. Even Frank Hann of
Lawn Hill Station acknowledged to the Police Commissioner that there
were 'only a few blacks about . . . the harm they do is to kill a few head of
cattle which they have a right to do as all their country has been taken away
from them, whereas hundreds of cattle are taken away by whites and not a
word about them'.[48]

In December 1878, near the junction of the Gregory and O'Shanassy
Rivers, the Native Police Carl Creek camp was established, with eight to ten
troopers stationed under the command of Sub-Inspector James Lamond.
Five years later Lamond married Amy Brook Shadforth, whose father
ran Lilydale Station, the precursor to Riversleigh and not far from Carl
Creek.[49] John Dymock, from his oral history research in this region, notes
that: 'Massacres occurred along the Gregory; the localities of some of these
events are still remembered by some of the older Wanyi [sic] people [in 1982]
whose parents later migrated to the Gregory River from further west.'[50]

During the early 1880s, newspaper correspondents for the Burke district
were reporting the need for a police presence along the cattle route through
to the Northern Territory.[51] Another role that Sub-Inspectors of the Native
Police played was as Inspector of Brands as large numbers of cattle were
being brought to the Territory without being inspected. This resulted in local
cattle not being cut out from the moving mobs and losses for Queensland
pastoralists. In 1882 Westmoreland Station was established 70 kilometres
from the Gulf and 30 kilometres inside the Queensland border. In the
following year, 10 kilometres west of the border, Wollogorang Station was
established and an upsurge in conflict between the local inhabitants and the
station people ensued.[52] It was not until 1886 that a Native Police barracks
was established at Corinda, several kilometres from Turn-Off Lagoon.[53]
It closed the next year with declining traffic on the coastal track, then
re-opened at the insistence of the pastoralists, finally moving to Turn-Off

Lagoon in 1889.[54] John Dymock's oral history research with indigenous people of the region in 1978 persuaded him that the ill-defined group called Gnyunga (of the Gungalida?), in the area from the Coast Track to the Gulf, accounts for:

> ... the name Massacre Inlet situated in the middle of where the Gnyunga were said to have had their territory [and] would suggest the answer as to why so little is known about them ... The absence of surviving members of the group who originally inhabited what is now known as the Upper Westmoreland Valley, may I suggest, could be directly related to punitive expeditions sent out from Westmorland Station, Queensland and Wollogorang Station, N.T., during the late 1890s in particular, and into the opening years of ... [the twentieth century].[55]

In 1872, a small party landed on Sweers Island (within sight of Bentinck Island) and their actions resulted in a Magisterial Enquiry early the following year. This enquiry gives an insight into the clumsy colonial attitude of the period and the fear the Europeans' presence and behaviour created with the local indigenes.[56] About 1914, a man named John [?] McKenzie made an unauthorised attempt to settle on Bentinck Island. Dibirdibi (Roma Kelly), a Kaiadilt descendant from Bentinck, told linguist Nicholas Evans what her parents had told her, that 'During his short time on Bentinck Island, McKenzie systematically tried to eliminate the Kaiadilt, riding across the island on horseback, and shooting down everyone but the girls he intended to rape'.[57] From oral sources, Norman Tindale compiled a detailed genealogy from which he estimates that in about 1918 eleven people were killed, which Evans identifies as 10 per cent of the Kaiadilt islander population.[58]

David Trigger carried out extensive fieldwork, living and researching at Doomadgee, north from Lawn Hill, between 1978 and 1983. He observed that Aboriginal oral history accounts of the late nineteenth century in the Gulf:

... describe vicious killings of Aboriginal men, women and children
by both Whites and members of the Queensland Mounted Native
Police Force. Recounted atrocities by native police include smashing
children against trees and rocks 'so their brains came out' and, after
shootings, cutting up bodies, burning bodies, and hanging up parts
of corpses in trees where other Aborigines would later find them.[59]

Les Skinner, when he lived in the Gulf Country, was informed by William
Malone, the then manager of Inverleigh Station (about 70 kilometres south-
west of Normanton), that:

> ... when he came to that station near the end of last century [late
> 1890s], the remains of some twenty to thirty skeletons of Aborigi-
> nes still littered the plain near the homestead. He disagreed with ...
> [Skinner's] suggestion that these people may have been shot by the
> native police, saying that they had been shot by 'station people'.[60]

The indigenous and non-indigenous recollections of what really happened
when Europeans settled in the north stand in stark contrast to the fabrication that is the Pioneering Myth.

From the mid to late 1860s, the tide of European invasion continued
its earlier efforts from the east and south-east of central Queensland and
west of Blackall (1868). In April 1866, John Ellis took up Portland Downs,
followed nine months later in January 1867 by Charles Lumley Hill, who
established Isis Downs roughly 20 kilometres to the south.[61] Conflict arose
between the local Kuungkari and John Fanning, who was part-owner
and manager of Isis Downs. He was fatally speared later in the year, and
Lumley Hill signed Fanning's death certificate.[62] Some 30 years later under
the heading 'Taming the Niggers', an 'old pioneer' calling himself 'H7H'
(the cattle brand for Isis Downs) wrote to the *Townsville Herald* (2 February
1907) describing two attacks on a large group of Kuungkari, who it was
presumed were responsible for station-owner Fanning's death. 'H7H'
brags of his involvement in the first retaliatory expedition:

It was estimated that over 150 myalls ['wild' Aboriginals] 'bit the dust' that morning, and unfortunately many women and children shared the same fate. In that wild, yelling, rushing mob it was hard to avoid shooting the women and babies, and there were men in that mob of whites who would ruthlessly destroy anything possessing a black hide.

Later, he describes a second stealthy early morning raid by the European party:

They slept soundly those myalls after their long march, and could have had no thought of us being so close to them, for we were within revolver shot of them before our presence was discovered, and then it was too late, for muddled with sleep, sore-footed, weary, and panic-stricken they offered no resistance, and many of them were 'wiped out' before they could gain their feet. Talk of the 'Furies of Hell', that night's work amongst those myalls with the white man's rifle and tomahawk would make 'Hell's Furies' blush. How those gins and kiddies shrieked when we got amongst them. The blood of the white man was up and nothing with a black hide escaped death that night . . . for when we had finished our work and drawn off, and in daylight came to view the white man's work of vengeance bucks, gins and piccaninnies were lying dead in all directions, and not a thing in camp moved or breathed.[63]

Henry Reynolds makes a pertinent observation of this recollection and its context:

It was printed in the daily paper of a major provincial city in 1907, six years after Federation. The writer confessed mass murder without the slightest concern about prosecution or even social approbrium.[64]

As the twentieth century unfolded, the Pioneering Myth took hold. The truth of Aboriginal massacres which was readily acknowledged in the nineteenth century started to be repressed and officially denied.[65]

In the early 1870s, in western central Queensland, on the northern banks of the Western River near where it junctions with the Diamantina, Elderslie Station was established. It was here that Acting Sub-Inspector John Carroll and his Native Police troopers from Aramac (c.300 kilometres to the east, south-east), 'slaughtered all the [Guwa] males they came across'.[66] Ironically, not long afterwards, Carroll was allowed to resign at Aramac, when he was charged with the assault and murder of one of his troopers.[67]

About 70 kilometres east of Elderslie Robert Allen established his run at Pelican Waterhole, which became a village in 1875, a township in 1879 and changed its name to Winton in 1880.[68] Bladensburg Station was established in 1877 about 19 kilometres to the south.[69]

George Fraser, who had arrived from Britain 18 months earlier, was driving 700 cattle to stock a new run that he wanted to establish at Bladensburg. Near the 20 Mile, Fraser left two new chums to look after the tucker and wagons, while he and the rest of the party went out to tend to the cattle. During their absence, a mob of Guwa (Koa) came across the plain to the waterhole and 'parleyed' for some flour, tea and sugar. While one of the new chums went to get their horses, the other was murdered and the wagons rifled through, 'taking whatever they fancied and throwing the firearms into the waterhole, where they were found years afterwards at the time of the big drought, when the waterhole went all but dry'.[70]

Fraser and his men tracked the large mob of Guwa from camp to camp as they made their way towards the Forsyth Ranges on the head of Mistake Creek. A week after the incident, Sub-Inspector Robert Moran and his troopers arrived.[71] Along with Fraser's party they numbered fourteen, and surrounded the Guwa camp on three sides. Hazelton Brock recalls:

> Never shall I forget that scene . . . when the shots poured into the
> camp; every being was up, and a general rush made for the hills and
> timber; but the troopers drove them back. I had often read of men
> becoming panic-stricken on the field of battle, and I now knew what

it meant. For a second that mob stood irresolute, men, women, and children huddled together, rending the air with piercing screams and cries of anguish. Then they broke for the creek, where there was a precipice of 30 ft. [9 metres] to the water. However, that didn't matter; they tore down the couple of hundred yards' slope . . . and without a moments hesitation jumped into the creek below . . .

There were about 200 blacks in the water, endeavouring to shelter themselves under the banks, but it was no use; the merciless troopers found them out, and lead poured thick and heavy on them. You could see the flash of a rifle and watch a head disappear; a few seconds, and some bubbles would rise, then a dark crimson spot would spread across the water, marking another soul sent home. After a little while the blacks were thinned out to about half, nearly all the men being killed; and now happened one of the most blood-curdling sights I ever saw.

The troopers had been getting more and more excited, until at last they threw down their guns and drew their sheath-knives, which they all carried, jumped into the water, and engaged in a hand-to-hand struggle. But it didn't last long; the blacks had only a nulla-nulla or two, and the troopers fought with the ferocity of tigers.[72]

In 1881, the Norwegian naturalist Carl Lumholtz described his visit to this same area several years after the massacre. Admittedly, he tries to disguise the name of the station by calling it 'Bledensbourne', but the story matches rather too closely Brock's coverage. The cause of the conflict that Lumholtz identifies is significantly different and has a ring of truth about it. He wrote:

I was shown a large number of skulls of natives who had been shot by the black police in the following circumstances:- A couple of teams with provisions for the far west, conducted by two white men, had encamped near the blacks. The latter were lying in ambush, and meant to make an assault, *as two black women had been ravished by the white men*. Instead of defending themselves with their weapons, the white men were cowardly enough to take flight, leaving all their provisions, oxen, tent, and all their other things in the hands of the blacks. The fugitives reported to the police that they had been attacked, and so the 'criminals' a few weeks afterwards were pursued far into a narrow valley and shot. I visited the spot in company with the manager of Bledensbourne station, and saw seven or eight skulls . . . nearly the whole tribe was killed, as there was no opportunity of flight.[73]

This site became known as Skull Hole and over 100 years later is still remembered in local history, albeit with a negative twist towards the original traditional owners.[74] The visiting Norwegian also noted that: 'This is one of the many cruelties perpetrated by the native police against the natives . . . Their cruelties constitute the black page in the annals of Australian colonisation.'[75]

Brock goes on to tell how after the massacre, he 'collared one of the youngsters and brought him up; he's alive yet, and most of you know him; it's Boomerang Jack that knocks about Collingwood [Station, 50 kilometres west of Winton]'. Similarly, he describes how a young man who later became one of the biggest squatters in Queensland (owning between 20 and 30 selections at one stage, before his 'come down, and is now [1901] managing for one of the large companies'), 'heard' about the massacre and was 'anxious to get some bones and specimens . . . Well, I took him over to the place and we collected all the bones he wanted'.[76] Brock gives the impression that this squatter had nothing to do with the massacre, but if that was the case why is he so coy about identifying this important member of colonial society, for he only refers to him as 'M—'. Clues given by Brock indicate that it was John Arthur Macartney, who went into partnership with Edward Graves Mayne for the leases on Bladensburg encompassing 2450 square kilometres (1100 square miles).[77] Macartney also held at different times 25 stations and four smaller properties in Queensland and four large runs in the Northern Territory. He got into difficulties and lost most of his holdings and became a station manager.[78] The Georgina River was named after one of Macartney's daughters, Georgina Mildred Macartney, who married the Governor of Queensland, Sir Arthur Kennedy.[79]

Collecting Aboriginal skeletal bones and skulls was a European activity that was consistently carried on throughout the nineteenth century. Museums in Europe, America and Australia were keen to obtain specimens of Aboriginal Australians as examples of their supposed lowest form on the human hierarchy. One can gain an insight to their approach from a letter by Kendall Broadbent to the Queensland Museum curator, C W de Vis in 1888, where Broadbent says he will get 'all the skulls I can' and asks for 'one Snider rifle and 700 ball cartridges. Blacks are bad here. [and almost as an afterthought and more than likely a red herring] Require rifle for alligator shooting'.[80]

The yet to be Southern Protector of Aborigines, Archibald Meston, in March 1887, replied to a request from the curator of Sydney's Australian Museum [E P Ramsay]: 'Re skulls &c. skeletons of the festive myall!! To what strange use are our noble primeval inhabitants to be devoted! At your prices I could have procured about £2000 worth in the last six years. I shall be on the warpath again! Hope to succeed in slaughtering some stray skeletons for you. Shall also see to weapons dilly bags &c. &c.'[81]

In September 1861 the area covering Central West Queensland was officially proclaimed the Mitchell Pastoral District.[82] The traditional lands of more than fourteen clan groups were declared 'as an area of unoccupied Crown lands open for selection'.[83] William Landsborough, while exploring this region with Nat Buchanan in 1859, named the area 'Ar-ar-mac' (R R Mac) 'in honour of the late Sir R R Mackenzie'.[84] This was to pay tribute to the very same man who was Chairman of the 1861 Select Committee on the Native Police who brought down what amounted to a verdict:

> ... evidence taken by ... [the] ... committee shews beyond doubt that all attempts to Christianize or educate the Aborigines of Australia have hitherto proved abortive ... invariably they return to their savage habits. Credible witnesses show that they are addicted to cannibalism; that they have no idea of a future state; and are sunk in the lowest depths of barbarism.[85]

This was undoubtedly nineteenth-century spin and demonstrates that the colonial Queensland government was not above rigging an interpretation in support of their policy of using the Native Police.[86] Meanwhile, pastoralists continued establishing their runs, including Joseph Raven who set up Stainburn Downs Station, about 20 kilometres north-west of Aramac. In the mid to late 1860s, members of the Iningai made several raids,[87] first taking sheep from Rule and Lacey's Eight Mile Lagoon Sheep Station and killing several of them, then later stealing 150 ewes from Stainburn, killing half before they were retrieved. According to Raven, shortly afterwards they killed a man working for Rule and Lacey and a posse followed them up to where a lot of caves were located.[88] This was Gray Rock Station, where later a hotel was established on the Cobb & Co track between Aramac and Clermont:

> ... in a vast amphitheatre. It stands at the base of a low cliff and rocky ramparts of red sandstone—not grey—encircle it on three sides, the radius being some miles in extent ... The rocks abound with caves, which used to afford shelter to the aborigines when in trouble. [After the murder of the white man] ... a small band of whites, well armed and led by the manager, started in pursuit ... and then traced to a cave about three miles [5 kilometres] from the side of the hotel. The entrance [to the cave] was low, and the leader, who left his followers behind, crawled into the cave on his hands and feet, when he found himself face to face with thirteen savages ... With two loaded revolvers he shot down the whole band, who, paralysed with fear, offered no resistance.[89]

We are probably never going to know the full extent of the violence on the moving frontier. That it took place can be seen by the rapidity with which the traditional owners disappeared, which hints at many unrecorded killings.

Chapter 10

Queensland's Disreputable Reputation

But the protests of the minority have been disregarded by the people of the settled
districts: the majority of outsiders who take no part in the outrages have been
either apathetic or inclined to shield their companions, and the white brutes who
fancied the amusement, have murdered, ravished, and robbed the blacks without
let or hindrance. Not only have they been unchecked, but the Government of the
colony has been always at hand to save them from the consequences of their crime.

The Way We Civilise', Cooktown Courier, *14 April 1880.*

During the convict period at Moreton Bay (1824–39), European encroachment onto the traditional owners' land was relatively minimal, although
there were some massacres of Aboriginals. It was not until the advent of the
pastoral era in the 1840s and 1850s, when the newcomers took possession of
large tracts of land and stocked it with great numbers of sheep and cattle,
that the scale and number of massacres greatly increased. NSW established their Native Police force in 1848–49 to operate in the border regions
across the Macintyre River in what was to become southern Queensland.
The British Colonial Office required dual usage of land which allowed
the Aboriginal inhabitants to hunt and access waterholes, but pastoralists
ignored this on the Darling Downs and subsequently on the expanding

Queensland frontier (post-1859). NSW colonial politicians, like their future Queensland colleagues, owned runs and saw their value increase with the removal of Aboriginal resistance. The pattern of white violence had already been established before the invasion of pre-separation Queensland with the taking up of lands on the coastal and inland areas of what is now northern NSW.[1] Similarly, the pattern of maintaining secrecy about killings on the frontier had been set after the trials and hanging of seven white men for the 1838 Myall Creek massacre of 28 Wirrayaraay old men, women and children.

Following the massacres of eleven whites at Hornet Bank (1857) and nineteen whites at Cullin-la-Ringo (1861), the degree of violence aimed at the Aboriginal inhabitants in Central and Southern Queensland became overwhelming. Between the seven detachments of Native Mounted Police and the private white revenge posses, the killings were pervasive and devastating. The pattern for the colonial government in dealing with the traditional owners had been well and truly set.

In 1863, James Morrill re-joined white colonial society after seventeen years living with Aboriginal clan groups to the south of Townsville. Two years later long-time pastoralist Gideon Lang acknowledged:

'Morrill hoped for the authority of the Government to act as a mediator between the whites and blacks, as Mr Gellibrand intended Buckley to do'.[2] Morrell [sic] not only wished, but, I am told, actually beseeched the Queensland Government to allow him to devote himself to arranging between the white men and the blacks . . . [but] They did what they do now—nothing; the blacks are the business of the native police in Queensland.[3]

The violence perpetrated by the Native Police and some settlers, and the role of the Queensland government in implementing this approach, was clearly identified and condemned within five years of the creation of the colony in 1859. Despite this, opportunities for adopting a more conciliatory approach were not acted upon and the carnage continued. Historian Robert Ørsted-Jensen has uncovered documentary evidence that 'Queensland's first Governor and his Executive Council took a series of steps to sanction and institutionalise key elements in the previous and highly questionable frontier policy'.[4]

The fact that the policy of extermination was acceptable to those in the Executive Council who directed and controlled the violent actions of the Native Mounted Police, gives credence to the likelihood that some settlers thought that they too could rid themselves of the encumbrance of Aboriginal occupation of their traditional lands. It meant that more psychopathic individuals could commit atrocities with the knowledge that the colonial government would not do anything to stop them.[5] This compounds the difficulty in accurately identifying the degree of involvement by private settlers. However, references to settler involvement can be found in the primary sources. They hint at nefarious acts, but rarely go into incriminating detail. There are some exceptions, such as Korah Halcomb Wills' diary; nearly 30 years after his involvement in several dispersals, he wrote: 'there is very little dispersing going on now in the colonies [1890s],' but cautioned that: 'what there is must be done very much on the quiet or you may hap get into trouble, but in my time [1860s] they were dispersed by hundreds if not thousands.'[6]

Wills writes as if dispersing (or shooting to kill) Aboriginals was an accepted common occurrence (see Chapter 6).[7] One example is the incident that took place after the Cullin-la-Ringo massacre of Horatio Wills' party, when a vigilante posse of squatters and settlers carried out six weeks of retribution, killing hundreds of Aboriginals. Similarly, historian Tony Roberts observed that the Queenslanders who crossed the border into the Northern Territory, brought their violent approach to Aboriginal people with them. Roberts identifies them as coming from central Queensland, which explains the disappearance of Aboriginal inhabitants in that region. We know from archaeological evidence that there were thousands of indigenous people living there, but it is difficult to identify exactly what happened to them. I could find no reports or references to epidemics in this region, although we do have at least five identified massacres. All of this suggests that settlers may well have been acting independently and cloaking their activities in a veil of silence.

In 1865, the Scottish-born pastoralist, Gideon Lang, who had been a squatter in Victoria and the Riverina area of southern NSW, an explorer in what became southern Queensland, and who was the inaugural president of the Riverine Association representing squatters' interests, wrote:

> In Queensland there has always been more destruction of the blacks in occupying new country than in any other colony, but within the last few years it has been wholesale and indiscriminate, and carried on with a cold-blooded cruelty on the part of the whites quite unparalleled in the history of these colonies. Among the Queensland frontier squatters now [1865] there are many men as benevolent and as anxious to civilize and save the blacks as in former years, but there are always a number of men among them, employed as well as employers, who only require suitable circumstances to develop their real character as cowardly cold-blooded murderers... these bad whites do as they please, from all accounts, simply because it is the rule and custom to arrange the black question by killing them off.[8]

Lang had canvassed squatters in southern Queensland and noted that 'their report is unanimous that there is no exaggeration in what I have said'.[9] His comments also confirm the serious involvement in the violence of an element of private settlers.

The 1860s, 1870s and 1880s, at the height of white territorial advance to the Gulf Country in the north-west and the tropics in the far north (and Cape York Peninsula), as well as the Channel Country to the south-west, saw the peak of violence against Aboriginal resistance.[10] European fire-power (breech-loading rifles superseded muzzle loaders in the 1870s),[11] rapidity of movement (horses, steamships and later trains) and modern tele-graphic communications, along with overwhelming numbers combined with introduced diseases, effectively destroyed clan groups' ability to fight back or defend themselves.

The coverage given to dispersals throughout this book shows that it is extremely difficult to tabulate the numbers of people killed on the nineteenth-century Queensland frontier; but the fact that large numbers perished can no longer be denied. Queensland historian, Raymond Evans, has devised a theoretical calculation which is pretty radical compared to past estimates, and gives a well-justified concluding figure. Evans has looked at the number of Native Police camps in existence between 1859 and 1898,[12] which amounted to '84 camps operating for an aggregate of some 596 years—or roughly seven years per camp'.[13] Assuming only one patrol a month, this gives a total of 7152 patrols, and allowing for illness, natural disasters etcetera, one could then round the figure down to 6000 patrols, thus allowing for an average of ten patrol reports per year. He has also managed to find 22 monthly reports from eleven Native Police officers (operating between 1865 and 1884). They estimate 57 dispersals or collisions, which averages out at 2.6 collisions per patrol.

Evans deduces that: 'Even if we once more play it incredibly safe here and suggest the extremely conservative figure of only two killed on average per dispersal, we find ourselves confronting an aggregate estimate of 24,000 violent Aboriginal deaths at the hands of the Native Police between 1859 and 1897 alone.'[14] Private killings were probably equal to those of the Native Police, but more in-depth research on a regional level, including overseas repositories and private records, would probably confirm this, or possibly show even worse figures.

Understandably, Evans is erring on the side of extreme caution, for we know that many more Aboriginals were killed in 'dispersal patrols' than just an average of two. He also suggests that at least an equal number of Aboriginal deaths were attributable to white settlers.[15] Thus it is very likely that an overall death toll for Aboriginal Queenslanders may well be in the range of 48,000 to 50,000 men, women and children.

In this book we have travelled the frontier and considered many violent clashes, and it does not seem unreasonable to accept Evans' higher estimate of 50,000, or possibly a quarter of Queensland's original indigenous population.[16] This is a startling revelation when one considers that Henry Reynolds was savaged (by *Quadrant* and the Murdoch press) for suggesting 20,000 were killed Australia-wide between 1788 and the 1930s.[17] The major point is that the violence was real, ubiquitous and demands recognition. The scholarly research of Raymond Evans demands that we take notice. From the coverage in this book of the role of private settlers in the killing-times, it is possible to observe the general public's attitude towards 'teaching the blacks a lesson'—the behaviour was supported, and if not condoned, then at least tolerated. Newspaper coverage across the colony throughout the nineteenth and early twentieth centuries, as well as private correspondence and recollections, gives an insidious insight into this prevalent attitude. The language used hints at quite dastardly acts of violence which are not fictionalised or exaggerated, but a part of the unwritten conspiracy of silence. The frontier settlers knew enough to realise that their behaviour was not acceptable to Mother England or to future generations of Queenslanders and Australians. The death toll was undoubtedly much greater than has previously been projected, and hence their need to be oblique about the outcomes of European invasion.

During the 1880s, Queensland's annexation of Papua, the then southern half of New Guinea, was nullified by the British Imperial Government due to the colony's treatment of Aboriginal Queenslanders and South Sea Islander labour. It had been noted that upon annexing the Torres Strait Islands, which had a pattern of land use and tenure similar to Papua, the first act of the Queensland government was to advertise the islands for sale at five shillings an acre, regardless of the fact that they were 'the homes and property of many hundreds of natives'.[18] The Times of London stated:

> While there might be exaggeration in many of the stories of atrocity in Queensland it was impossible to converse with any average colonist, to read local newspapers, to listen to speeches in parliament without perceiving that the native was 'regarded as simply an encumbrance on the soil', as being destitute of rights and existing 'only on sufferance, for which he should be grateful'. To allow Queensland to gain control of New Guinea would 'incur grave moral guilt'.[19]

Aboriginal Queenslanders across the state can confirm the truth of The Times' opinion, as do archival sources and white oral history. In other parts of Australia the generally accepted number of killings to qualify an event as a 'massacre' seems to be a tally of five or six,[20] and I have mapped many,

18. 'Mia mias', or mijas, Murray River North Queensland, 1908. Ernie Grant commented: 'When I was a child there were between three and eight people per mija [hut].'

19. The late Jack Cashmere (left) and Dr Ernie Grant at Blencoe Falls where their forebears were driven over the falls in the 1880s and their bodies piled up on the rocks below. (Courtesy of Dr Ernie Grant)

20. White civilian vigilantes in action as portrayed in the *Illustrated Christian Weekly*, 24 December 1880.

21. Hudson Fysh identified these skulls and skeletal remains as 'A Native Burial Place' in his *Taming the North*, (1933, first ed., p.162 but was deleted from later editions). No Aboriginal mortuary practices in the region of Alexander Kennedy's stations buried their dead in this manner, so it appears to have been done by a white man. To local Cloncurry district Aboriginals it would have been sacrilege to pile skulls in this way.

22. Illustration depicting the Skull Hole massacre on Bladensburg Station, south of Winton, from Carl Sophus Lumholtz's *Among Cannibals*, 1889.

23. A sign to Skull Hole today. (Photograph courtesy of the Winton Shire Council).

CIVILIZATION IN QUEENSLAND.

24. *Queensland Figaro*, 'Civilization in Queensland', 31 January 1885. The small print states: 'While expressing horrified indignation that kidnapping should take place in the South Seas, Samuel Walker Griffith pretends to be dispite [sic] the fact that the murder and kidnapping of Queensland natives is occurring under his very nose'.

25. When 'Jack' (Jonathon Harold) Watson was manager at Lawn Hill station he was violent towards the local Waanyi, Nguburinji and other Aboriginal people. Carrie Creaghe recorded that 'Mr Watson has forty pairs of blacks' ears nailed around the walls collected during raiding parties after the loss of many cattle speared by blacks [sic].' (Courtesy of Jan Cruikshank)

26. Snider Carbine lead bullets. Queensland placed an order in 1871 with the British War Office for 1 000 breech-loading Snider Carbines, many of which went to the Native Police. (R. Evans 'The Owl and the Eagle', *Fighting Words*, 1999, p.39)

but not all of the massacres in colonial Queensland. Nevertheless, it is my belief that it does not represent the full nature of violence on the frontier. One can understand why white colonial Queenslanders were ashamed of what they had allowed to happen, but why the conspiracy of silence since then? More pertinently, why does a vocal minority of contemporary white Australians persist in denying the truth? Their approach helps to continue to cast twenty-first century Australia as a myopic nation permeated by the sins of ignorance and jingoistic arrogance.

This book has investigated extreme violence perpetrated on the expanding nineteenth-century frontier. Although much research has already been done, more still needs to be done. Nevertheless, through mapping *some* of the massacre sites across Queensland (refer to maps 1.1–1.4) one can gain a clearer insight into the magnitude of the killing-times, as well as its ubiquity. Moving from region to region there are massacres in each, and when mapped across a sizeable proportion of the continent, the result is truly astounding. As the frontier moved to each new locality and the Aboriginal inhabitants realised that the whites were there to stay, resistance increased and bloody dispersals followed. What is even more astounding about the mapped massacres is that they don't represent all massacres, only a number which research to date could corroborate. There are undoubtedly many others that have yet to be recorded and authenticated. Robert Ørsted-Jensen believes that: 'we would be extremely lucky to map even 20 per cent of all massacres of blacks. Indeed, I rather think that the available records and hints, cover *less than 10 per cent in reality.*'[21] Regardless, one cannot help but acknowledge that maps 1.1–1.4 unambiguously confirm the pervasiveness of violence on the Queensland frontier and that a conspiracy of silence, both on an official and parochial level, was adopted in order to hide the true state of affairs. This involved, as Ørsted-Jensen notes, a: 'huge amount of records being destroyed and the record we may be able to uncover, thus covers only the tip of the iceberg.'

As noted in the Introduction, while we do have quantitative evidence of many killings, we do not have definitive evidence of the whole picture. However, it does appear that Queensland was more outstandingly violent than the other Australian colonies.[22] There can be no doubt that:

... the life of an Aboriginal person counted for little amongst white settlers and their government representatives ... [and] It is equally quite easily demonstrated that indigenous people were frequently massacred indiscriminately and with impunity in colonial Queensland and that their remains were treated with disrespect, if not outright contempt.[23]

The pivotal factor, as this work and Ørsted-Jensen's comprehensive research show, is that the evidence is overwhelming: 'the government and the colony's legislative institutions generally accepted and covertly condoned for decades a policy of taking no prisoners during decades of Native Police operations at the frontier.'[24] In confirmation of this, Ørsted-Jensen cites documentary evidence that he has recently uncovered:

... that Queensland's first Governor and his Executive Council took a series of steps to sanction and institutionalise key elements in the previous and highly questionable frontier policy. Later, facing the risk that three troopers, who had been accused of rape and murder, might be acquitted before a judge and jury, the Governor and his executives then decided in a meeting in the Executive Council that it was better to remove those troopers and deal with them summarily in the remote bush. This very decision was made during an Executive meeting held on 14 January 1861 and the participants were Governor [1859–68] Sir George Ferguson Bowen, Premier [1859–66] Sir Robert Herbert, Treasurer Sir Robert Ramsey Mackenzie [Premier 1867–68] and Attorney-General [1859–65] Radcliffe [sic] Pring.[25]

The new documents reveal: 'that Sir George Bowen went so far out in illegality that he ought to have been removed from office and that is by the standards of his own time.'[26] Here then is the key as to why Queensland was more violent than other Australian colonies.

Queensland was a colony that began with 7½ pence in its Treasury (which was then stolen).[27] It desperately needed more revenue and an obvious source was the renting out of land to squatters. Gold rushes also boosted population and revenue. Although Queensland did very well in the early 1860s before the 1866 financial crash, the subsequent impoverished nature of the state's finances partially explains the official attitude towards tolerating or ignoring frontier violence. What is particularly important is the fact that Queensland's early politicians were themselves the recipients of land-clearance. Regarding this, historian Bill Thorpe has concluded that they were:

> ... arguably the most comprador [i.e. agents of foreign powers] yet the most chauvinistic Queensland capitalist-politicians to emerge in the colonial era ... The ... alliance either owned, controlled or directed many of the major non-domestic economic activities in this period: pastoralism, mining, timber milling, sugar production, banking, shipping, trade, finance, land-speculation, railway construction and the ... [press].[28]

The avariciousness of the pastoral ruling elite enabled them to ignore the humanity of Aboriginal people and belittle or ignore the concerns of ex-frontiersmen who spoke out and condemned the treatment of Queensland's First Australians. Consider the response of Colonial Secretary (1879–81) Arthur Palmer to Anglican Bishop Matthew Hale's letter asking for particulars about the actions of Sub-Inspector O'Connor and six Native Police in Cooktown.[29] Palmer's notes written in the margin give an insight into the man and his actions: 'The Colonial Secretary is not in the habit of taking any notice of absurd paragraphs in newspapers and lectures being catechized ['to question closely'] on them.'[30] Palmer clearly chooses the word 'catechized' in order to diminish and needle the Anglican Prelate for daring to voice his objections. The response from the Colonial Secretary to Bishop Hale was 'a brief letter in reply declining to answer any questions'.[31] He is basically saying he has no time for religious do-gooders.

Palmer, like McIlwraith, Herbert and Mackenzie, and so many other Queensland colonial politicians, was investing in pastoral runs on the expanding Queensland frontier. There can be no doubt that these men had a vested interest in enabling their investments to make a profitable return, as too did most of the now lauded frontier money-makers, such as Oscar de Satgé, John Costello, Robert Collins, Patrick Durack, George Dalrymple, John Macartney and many others. They achieved their wealth, or attempted to, at the expense of Aboriginal sovereignty. They could do this, as Jane Lydon so succinctly put it, because:

> They believed in the inferiority of Aborigines, and objected strongly to the official principle that Aborigines were subjects of Her Majesty, and as such had rights, as well as to the related, although unofficial argument that this implied a right to the land and therefore to compensation for its loss—both of which seemed ludicrous to those in the bush.[32]

On a parochial level many saw the acquisition of land as their opportunity to 'make good'. For instance, in 1875, John Matthews refers to the Manumbar region where '42 [settlers] are to Start Dairying [*sic*] immediately, and 40 want more cows, by Hook or Crook, as we are determined to make money'.[33] Many such settlers had emigrated as an indirect result of post-Napoleonic events in Europe, involving the collapse of the Spanish wool industry, the industrialisation of Britain's textile industry (in part requiring more merino wool), and the rise of democratic/socialist ideals, particularly between 1830 and 1848.[34] This led to a ' . . . large-scale emigration to the Australasian colonies of entrepreneurial, ambitious, capitalist middle class and an impoverished, dispossessed working class—each aspiring to an improved lifestyle . . .'[35]

In Queensland's first five years Governor Bowen was able to boast that the white population had increased by 195 per cent, the revenue by 139 per cent, trade by 178 per cent and shipping by 189 per cent.[36] By this time (1865) there were some 100 squatters who 'owned' 1.5 million acres (600,000 hectares) and within a decade, some 3 million acres (1.2 million hectares) had been declared freehold, of which half was owned by pastoralists. Yet by 1885 only 1.68 per cent of this land (mainly in East and West Maranoa and the Darling Downs) was actually cultivated. In the mother colony of NSW

during roughly the same period (1861–84), three million acres of Aboriginal land had been sold, but only 1.7 per cent was cultivated. Of the 170,000
freehold applicants during this period, by 1884 some 87 per cent had not
economically survived, leaving only 21,000 who had.[37] One cannot help but
wonder: how many Aboriginal people died so that colonists could take the
land only to abandon it? Similarly, the contradiction between the colonial
claims that Aboriginals did not use the land because they did not cultivate
it, was never reconciled with the fact that they did practise domiculture and
had an intimate spiritual link to the land.[38]

The rapaciousness of the colonial frontier is well reflected in an 1885
advertisement in the *Cairns Post*, which proclaimed:

> Englishmen, Irishmen & Scotchmen—what brings you to Queens
> land, leaving home in the dear old island 1000's [*sic*] of miles away?
> It is not for love of country, is it? No, plainly I can hear you answer.
> It is to make money, & at no distant date to return . . . home.[39]

Interestingly, while the newcomers did not perceive their own acts of usurpation as being unjust, they did consider other newcomers like the Chinese
as unfairly exploiting the 'new' lands' resources,[40] which they ironically
considered their own.

The mindset of 'getting rich and going home' pervaded the thinking of
many nineteenth-century settlers. As Maurice French notes, most of these:

> . . . squatters (whether the sons of England/Scotland or colonial offi
> cials) were men on the make or rather men who had to make their
> own way—with a little help from the family . . . [They] were 'birds
> of passage', intending to make their fortunes in the colonies in as
> short a time as possible in order to return 'Home' to restore family
> estates or fortunes or to a leisured retirement.[41]

The cultural chasm between the newcomers and the indigenous inhabitants, combined with the mindset of the 'bird of passage' approach, as well as an ingrained perception of racial superiority, would appear to be a sure-fire recipe for aggression and violence on the frontier.

An assertion in *The Times* of London (10 March 1904), by a Mr Hogan, stated 'that the squatters were mainly responsible for the extermination of the blacks in Australia'. In response, Harold Finch-Hatton, a former frontier squatter, wrote to *The Times* (16 March 1904) from his club in London: 'I unhesitatingly declare that the blacks of Queensland have been almost entirely exterminated by a system carefully planned and deliberately carried out by the Government of the country.'[42] However, Finch-Hatton, as one of the prominent squatters, would hardly implicate himself, his brother or their 'colleagues'.[43] Certainly Finch-Hatton's assertion that it was government officials rather than squatters who orchestrated the killings is contradicted by oral history recollections, both black and white, as well as many diary entries, reminiscences and newspaper reports. Historian Noelene Cole has observed, '*If* police attempted conciliation [with Aboriginals] they were likely to be met with vigorous local opposition'.[44] The *Cooktown Courier* (25 January 1879) criticised Sub-Inspector Stanhope O'Connor for attempting to negotiate with Aboriginals, a stance endorsed by the frontier community. Similarly, five years later, Inspector Hervey Fitzgerald wrote to the Commissioner of Police from Cooktown, defending Sub-Inspector Charles Marrett against allegations of inefficiency made by the local pastoralists: 'It is utterly hopeless for him [Marrett] to expect the good feelings of the majority of his neighbours—humanity is unrecognized—their creed[:] extermination of the natives.'[45] This was indeed rich, coming from an officer of the Native Police, who had sixteen years' experience with an organisation that had been operating on the ever-expanding frontier for nearly three decades. The policy of both Native Police and squatters' private, vigilante squads was one of wholesale slaughter.

In late 1872, one correspondent for the *Queensland Times* reported that the blacks on the Paroo River, south-west of Charleville, had been:

> ... spearing cattle, and that they have wounded, though not killed, some white men. Police and black troopers are after them to hunt, shoot, and otherwise destroy them. But the *real truth is this*, that

the Government, or, perhaps more correctly speaking, the [white] people themselves, are responsible and to blame for every murder of a white man which has taken place, by their utter, shameless, brutal neglect of those savages whose land they ruthlessly occupy without remuneration, and for the bad example of drunkenness and profligacy and every vice too frequently set before them.[46]

Unfortunately, between the investors and pastoralists and their greed, and the rapidity of change for the Original Australians, there was little hope left for their traditional way of life.

Ian Clark, in his survey of massacres in western Victoria, found that most killings were in the one to three range,[47] whereas in Queensland we have so many examples of double- or even triple-figure massacres. Historian Richard Broome observes that:

> ... the Victorian frontier was still arguably less violent than some, for at least four reasons. Gun technology on this frontier, which had closed in almost all areas by 1850, was single shot and muzzle-loading guns. The native police force, with some expeditionary exceptions, was benign compared to the force found on the northern frontiers [that is, Queensland]. Thirdly, the Port Phillip District was unique in having a serious (albeit inadequate) protective effort, which meant that settlers were more under the eye of colonial officials, with instructions from London to try and apply British justice to Aboriginal people. Fourthly, racial ideas hardened after the 1850s, due to dominant ideologies about difference, shifting from environmental to racial explanations, and also due to a loss of optimism due to the apparent fading away of Aboriginal people.[48]

It was from Victoria that many of the investors and Queensland squatters came and with the peak of violence reaching its zenith during the 1860s and 1870s in northern and western Queensland, things had changed, as Broome notes. Gun technology advanced in the decades following the colonisation of Queensland, and breech-loading Snider carbines were far more effective killing implements. Evans considers:

> It was this, more than any other single item, which was responsible for tearing Aboriginal resistance into shreds: A short, bulky rifle with a caliber of 0.577 [inch]—something akin to an American buffalo gun—it discharged its leaden ball with tremendous impact leaving a ragged opening in its victim 'four times the diameter of the modern 0.303 [inch] bullet'... The Snider, never particularly accurate, would, at close quarters, simply tear apart anyone or anything it hit.[49]

Historian Libby Connors believes that 'Rather than bringing the blessings of English justice to the indigenous inhabitants, the colonization of Queensland proceeded on the basis of systematic extermination by a quasi-legal paramilitary force'.[50] The Native Police was a state instrument. It was not simply something operating with official knowledge. Jonathan Richards' extensive archival research has led him to conclude that:

> Successive governors, colonial secretaries, and ministers of the Crown knew what was going on in the force... The evidence clearly shows that the Native Police in Queensland operated under the direct control of the colony's most senior administrators—the Executive Council.[51]

Similarly, Alan Hillier notes that:

> Leading politicians, who tended to be squatters anyway, knew what the force did on the frontier. They had been eye-witnesses to murders and retaliation near, or on, their own runs and they secretly condoned the actions of this force. Ultimately, the Native Police survived because it offered the cheapest methods of controlling a hostile Aboriginal population which... [was] attractive because

they cost a fraction of a white force and their evidence could not be
turned against officers in the Queensland courts . . . [52]

Aboriginal evidence in court was prohibited until 1884.[53] Reading official
correspondence, especially within the Native Mounted Police, between
Sub-Inspector and Inspector and the Commissioner and Colonial Secretary
and members of the public, is weighty but irrefutable evidence of state-
backed violence.[54]

Circumstances had altered from the time of Victoria's establishment,
when the British Colonial Office 'kept an eye' on activities.[55] First, in the
new colony of Queensland the Native Police were financed by the colony
itself, and the ruling elite therefore felt that only they had a right to say
how the force was run. Secondly, British investment in the colony was such
that the institutions concerned did not want to hinder the opportunities of
greater financial returns. Thus an official British attitude of laissez-faire
was adopted as to how Queenslanders expanded their land-grab. Also, as
historian Alison Palmer notes, there was ' . . . no strong British military
presence in Queensland, to either implement or quell the genocide'.[56]
Broome's fourth point about why Queensland was more violent than
Victoria relates to polygenism.[57] The Spencerian and Darwinian concepts
of the 'survival of the fittest' and the perception of Aboriginals as vermin
and chattel labour were well-accepted concepts from the mid-nineteenth
century and through into the twentieth. These beliefs were used to confirm
the 'doomed race theory' or 'vanishing tribes' approach which was still
being promulgated up to the Second World War. It is these ideas which
gave permission for what happened in Queensland.

Queensland was a colony where the State apparatus operated official
'death squads' and allowed the corresponding operation of private, vigilante death squads, without the effective interference of the so-called 'rule
of law'. The politicians were heavily investing in land acquisition and the
Executive Council were privy to and directed the operations of the Native
Police. Furthermore, many of the ex-death squad officers became government officials, particularly Magistrates or Clerks of Petty Sessions, who
then effectively interfered with the 'rule of law' through further inhibiting

whistle-blowers. In this regard, former Sub-Inspector William Richard Onslow Hill (1844–1923), acknowledged in his reminiscences about his relationship and that of other officers to Sir Robert Herbert, that:

> The then Colonial Secretary was our steadfast friend, and he initi-
> ated every one of the officers so dispensed with [that is, those who
> left the service] would have preference in the first openings in the
> Government Service. Well and faithfully he kept his word, *for
> most of us afterwards* were given billets either as a Police Magistrate
> or C.P.S. [58]

Norwegian ethnologist, Carl Lumholtz (1851–1922), lived on the upper Herbert River (1882–84), inland from Ingham, and interacted with local Warrgamay. He noted that there were 'persons who look upon the blacks as human beings with a right to live in the land which is in fact their own'. He cites an Australian gentleman who despaired of being able to ameliorate the treatment of the natives:

> But alas! it were vain to hope for any improvement in their condi-
> tion; for it is an immutable law of nature that the strong will prey
> on the weak. I always look upon the condition of the lower order
> of 'whites' as a fearful satire on Christianity. The English nation
> is continually casting stones at other nations for the treatment of
> conquered races, but nothing could be more barbarous than their
> own treatment of the aborigines of Australia. [59]

There are masses of letters to newspapers throughout the latter half of the nineteenth century condemning the violence and treatment of Aboriginal people on the frontier, almost all signed with a nom de plume. [60] Correspondence to the Colonial Secretary, Police Commissioner and others in government tended to have signatures, but this also enabled intimidation and coercion.

In March 1895, sixteen settlers from Cardwell signed a petition to the Colonial Secretary requesting police protection from thieving blacks and reporting the burning of Mr W G Ewans' buildings, material and stores. This, the petitioners proclaimed 'is the seventh property in this locality that has been destroyed by fire by aboriginals'.[61] There can be no doubt that this action was part of an Aboriginal strategy of guerilla warfare.[62] It was certainly driving the colonial settlers to distraction, for six months later another letter of complaint was sent, this time to the Police Commissioner from the Clerk of the Cardwell Divisional Board, who did not mince his words:

> I have the honor [sic] by direction to bring to your notice the insufficient Police protection in this district and the way in which the aboriginals are taking advantage of it, they have not the slightest fear of the Police at present stationed in the district, and the way in which they have been robbing the selectors and others in this district of late, is a disgrace to the whole colony.[63]

The Clerk, P J Hull, lists an array of frustrating misdemeanours (such as pilfering and cattle-spearing) and ends requesting another (white) constable and more 'black trackers' to operate in the Tully and Murray Rivers area. Nearly six months later, William Craig from Niagara Vale Station (on the upper Herbert River, near the start of the gorge) via Cardwell, wrote to the Colonial Secretary drawing his 'attention to the treatment of the remnants of . . . aboriginals left in this district are receiving at the hands of the Cardwell Native Police'.[64] Craig paints a picture that is certainly at odds with Hull's letter and the petitioners from a year before:

> Though they have not killed cattle for years . . . and are now employed by settlers, and can be as easily arrested and punished as any white man in the district if they commit any petty depredations, which is the only ones they are usually accused of. Yet they are so terrorised by the fate of some of their companions who have disappeared . . . that they will not go hunting now but gather round the houses of the friendliest settlers to starve although there are miles

and miles of scrub unoccupied by any white man, where they can get a fair living.[65]

Craig also accused the Native Police of fabricating charges in order to remove unwanted relatives of women and children to whom they wanted access. He concludes that 'Surely if Native Police are necessary their officer should be a protector of the innocent as well as a punisher of the guilty, and not terrorise or allow others to terrorise and wrong the well behaved'. In response Police Magistrate Pears was asked to report on Craig's accusations within six weeks of the complaint. Pears' report addressed each of Craig's accusations, on which Craig amazingly reneged.[66]

In the way Craig repudiates his original statements you get the distinct feeling that he is being intimidated and coerced. This is also conveyed in Inspector Hervey Fitzgerald's telegram to the Police Commissioner. Fitzgerald was a man who had been suspended and 'severely reprimanded' for whipping an Aboriginal woman in 1876 and transferred. He was also in command of detachments involved in reprisals at Lizard Island after the death of Mrs Watson.[67] The Inspector's history and Craig's about face hint at possible coercion by officials. Certainly Fitzgerald seems to have made a habit of wanting to intimidate anyone criticising the Native Police. In the telegram he wired about Craig's accusations: 'Charges "absolutely groundless" I recommend prosecution [for] Criminal libel.'[68] Fitzgerald wrote on another occasion to the Police Commissioner regarding newspaper accounts, which he described as the 'attacks of scoundrels' on the Native Police. He again recommended that they be 'met by an action of criminal libel'.[69] At his rank he should have known better. Any court proceedings, as the Police Commissioner would have known, could very easily have opened Pandora's box as far as the Native Police were concerned. The ramifications for the incumbent government who denied and ignored violence on the frontier, could have been politically disastrous. Nevertheless, the suggestion that they might take legal action (if mentioned on the local level) could easily be construed as a form of intimidation by Fitzgerald.

Craig's volte-face needs also to be seen by the fact that two years later he again wrote to the Commissioner of Police, this time proposing a reserve for Aboriginals, 22 kilometres north-west of Cardwell. He was concerned that the hinterland group were making their way to the coastal region and being corrupted by opium charcoal smoking, prostitution and disease, and that if supplied with tobacco they would be protected from this depravity. Some three months later, Constable W R Holmes wrote confirming Craig's comments about the suitability of the site and its ability to supply native foods. It is apparent that Craig has lost none of his humanitarian zeal, but has taken a different tack by not commenting critically on the Native Police, and sticking to the more positive aspects that might protect the local Aboriginal people.[70]

If one looks at the bureaucratic paperwork generated by any incident and the long drawn-out politicking in responding, it is probably not surprising that officially, few colonists went to the trouble of reporting questionable behaviour on the frontier. However, at least two incidents of a similar nature had occurred previously in this region, the first 24 years earlier and the second twenty years earlier. The first was in the Cardwell area, in 1872 where a young Aboriginal woman was shot by Acting Sub-Inspector Charles Norman Sharpe.[71] An official response of reprimand was made and Sharpe was dismissed from the Native Police, quite likely because of his involvement in the 'gin' killing. Four years later (1876), just over the Cardwell Range on the Lower Herbert River, Thomas Barclay Miller made 'strong representations . . . respecting the conduct of certain white settlers towards the blacks'.[72] Miller, of Avoca Plantation, reported the savage murder of a twelve- or thirteen-year-old Aboriginal boy called Monday, who had been 'employed' by Sub-Inspector R A Johnstone, but had then been given to a fellow called Puddock who was a professional jockey and brick-maker. Miller felt it necessary to tell the Attorney-General that:

> You will understand that there are few in this district who look upon the willful killing of an Aboriginal as murder. The parties who held the enquiry are noted for their dislike to the blacks. If things take their usual course as regards the blacks, it might happen that the *boys* who intimately know particulars of the above sad story would be missing some day soon.[73]

Two of the 'most important [white] witnesses' were Sub-Inspectors R A Johnstone and G R Townsend. It is therefore not surprising that Miller retracted his allegations and Sub-Inspector Johnstone sent a telegram to the Police Commissioner: 'The whole of Mr Miller's statements were proved to be wrong and the evidence of former inquiry borne out.'[74] Again, the archival record of correspondence suggests that Miller's volte-face was influenced by locally applied pressure—or intimidation.

In the late 1800s, Queensland's white population was still small and the settlements that arose on the frontier were also small. To speak out against atrocities meant a very real possibility of ostracism, both socially and financially, which put a serious brake on the readiness of the morally outraged to identify themselves publicly. That there were persistent campaigns against the role of the Native Police and frontier violence is a tribute to the humanitarian element of some dedicatedly benevolent colonials. Nearly 40 years later, the Reverend J S Needham, Chairman of the Anglican Australian Board of Missions, publicly acknowledged that:

> There were many well-authenticated accounts of ill-treatment of aborigines which amounted to cold-blooded murder . . . There was a conspiracy of silence . . . Information was received that a certain outrage had been committed; but when the informant was asked to permit his name to be used, he refused. That was a common thing. White informants feared the resultant victimization. In these circumstances it was impossible to lay these complaints before the Government.[75]

In September 1897 'Stone Age' wrote to the *Queenslander* and observed:

> Mr Meston and others ask why on these subjects do persons persist in writing under noms de plume. The reason is that so demoralized have the bulk of Australians become on this subject that a person who advocates any amelioration of the condition of the blacks is in about the same position as an abolitionist in the Southern States before the Civil War, and would have a very bad time of it; for, though his

neighbours are very intelligent on other subjects, on this they are often as brutal and unreasonable as a gentlemanly Southern planter. Murrells's [*sic*] history describes our 'blood and bullet' methods of civilization; it shows also the natural kindness of the black.[76]

Morrill, as Bruce Breslin has noted, 'desired harmonious relationships between the Aboriginals and the settlers and he offered his services for the benefit of both peoples'.[77] Several versions of his life were subsequently published after he returned to colonial society in Bowen in 1863. Similarly, the Frenchman, Narcisse Pelletier,[78] who also spent seventeen years (1858–75) living with the local Aboriginals around Cape Weymouth,[79] was not consulted. Colonial officials singularly failed to capitalise on Morrill's and Pelletier's intimate knowledge of the original inhabitants' way of life. It was a lost opportunity to change from violence to a more humane and understanding interaction.

There were some colonists who tried a different tack. Men like Dr Henry Challinor, Duncan McNab and Alfred Davidson, strove to change government policy and attitudes, but to little avail. Davidson campaigned for twenty years (1861–81) advocating justice for Aboriginals and opposing the South Pacific Island labour trade. Davidson 'scanned the colonial newspapers, wrote letters to them himself as well as to the government, lobbied politicians and governors. He was forever frustrated, fobbed off, rebuffed'.[80] He was clearly aware that those opposed to the humanitarian cause were the employers whom he recognised, had a 'clear hold on the newspapers: the claims of capital are felt'.[81] There was also Frank Bridgman at Homebush Station, 20 kilometres south-west from Mackay. Bridgmen initially rescued orphaned survivors of massacres and then went on to develop a labour reserve of cheap Aboriginal workers based upon the idea that 'labour being valuable, there will be less wish to have them shot down'.[82] His reserve was working successfully, but political patronage evaporated with the election of the conservative McIlwraith government (1879–83).[83] Following this, the operation declined and eventually the land was sold.

The Scottish Catholic missionary, Duncan McNab (1820–96) raised his voice against seeing Aboriginals as 'a problem' and at Mackay proposed that they be able to own land and be treated as responsible adults by white-man's law as well as acknowledging their individuality. Unfortunately, his uncompromising manner did not endear him to government or his superiors, and his passionate spiritual Catholicism created suspicion on the part of the Protestant majority. After a period of illness he raised money for work among tribal groups just north of Brisbane and became a Commissioner for Aborigines. He antagonised his fellow Commissioners by promoting the acquisition of homesteads instead of reserves for Aboriginal Queenslanders. McNab unsuccessfully lobbied Rome and the Colonial Office in London, and journeyed across the USA, eventually moving to Western Australia in 1883 where he continued his pastoral care and promoted vocational training for Aboriginal prisoners which was only partially implemented. He laboured for two years near Derby, but eventually retired to Melbourne. Again his outspokenness, like so many others who objected to the treatment of Aboriginal people, was sidelined and his proposals for Aboriginal welfare fell on deaf ears.[84]

From Toowoomba in 1862, Western Wood, a member of the Queensland Legislative Council remarked:

> ... there is only one question that staggers me, that is taking their country at all, but if it is to be there arises the question, which is the best way of dealing with them. To effect this I would remark that we ought to try to acquire a knowledge of their Laws and Work accordingly at least as near as possible, I say this because this is the simplest and I think we may be able to learn theirs quicker than teach ours to them.[85]

Wood may well have been right, but Aboriginal Religion/Law remained an enigma to white Queenslanders.

It may have been inevitable that there would be some violence on the frontier with Aboriginal resistance, but much of the colonists' response went to extremes. There was some Aboriginal forbearance of the white intrusion. For example, ten years after Cullin-la-Ringo, Charlotte

May Wright while living at Nulalbin Station (c.20 kilometres south of the future Baralaba) in central Queensland, often wondered:

> ... why the blacks did not kill us all; we were so few, and there were hundreds of blacks in the camps, real wild 'myalls' who had never worn a garment or understood a word of English. There was a big camp on the creek, about half a mile from the homestead, and I often sat on the verandah watching the blacks trooping past for hours when moving camp.[86]

Wood and Wright independently identified that the Aboriginal character was by nature to some extent accommodating. No doubt pragmatism played a part, but one can't help thinking that Aboriginal cultural life revolved around performing right ritual, and that the encroachment by squatters was an irritating distraction, until the impact of their activities disrupted and then destroyed their ability to perform ceremony and conduct their usual way of life. Perhaps it took some time to understand white motivation: the invaders were not temporary visitors, they were usurpers.

The final blow to any form of Aboriginal independence came with the introduction of the *Aboriginals Protection and the Restriction of the Sale of Opium Act* in 1897, and successive legislation (1928, 1934, 1939, 1965, 1971), which increasingly became the means for further invasive, authoritarian and de-humanising control of indigenous Queenslanders and their children for the next 89 years (1897–1986). The Act, which was a result of a report by Archibald Meston and a slightly later report by Commissioner of Police, Parry-Okedon, appeared to be a measure meant to look after indigenous Queenslanders, but was in fact to have a deleterious effect on the very people it was supposed to safeguard. Historian Geoff Genever observes:

> In fact the Act was draconian and cruel. The institutionalized kidnapping of children, the incarceration of people whose crime was being black or part black, and the enforced, and sometimes permanent separation of husband from wife, can only be viewed as

inhuman. It also became the model for Western Australia and the Northern Territory.[87]

Only one member of Parliament voted against Clause 9 which enabled forced removal to reserves, arguing that it treated Aboriginals as 'criminals'.[88]

In 1900, a general history entitled *Queensland*, referred to the expanding frontier, citing an author who referred to settlement from the 1840s, and wrote:

> ... the progress of settlement was marred by the deadly conflict between the pioneer settlers and the blacks. It is a very sad story, and shows that the whites were no less savage than the blacks. The squatters, no doubt, suffered many annoyances from the blacks, such as sheep stealing and the theft of property. But were these offences sufficient justification for the inhuman revenge with which they pursued them? Native troopers officered by Europeans were added to the police to cope with the disorder. They displayed a savage joy in slaughtering their countrymen ... Whole-sale poisoning was not an uncommon method of freeing a run of aborigines. A barrel of flour, in which arsenic had been mixed, was given by the shepherd and hut-keepers of an out-station as a present to a tribe of blacks in their vicinity. Soon all those who had partaken of it might be seen suffering the most frightful agonies until death relieved them. What wonder if the blacks took a terrible revenge for acts so inhuman?

The editor then commented:

> The incidents referred to by this writer [above] are still fresh in the memory of Queenslanders [in 1900], and, although they must not be taken as universal examples of treatment meted out to the natives by the white population, still the record of such occurrences as these help us in coming to a conclusion as to the frequent cause of the native hostility, and go to prove that, under all circumstances, the blacks were not quite as somber [*sic*] in their characteristics as has

sometimes been painted. Indeed, it is a fact that the blacks were often just what their white brothers made them.[89]

A decade later, James Collier, who had been a researcher for the English philosopher and sociologist, Herbert Spencer,[90] published *The Pastoral Age in Australasia*, where he openly acknowledged that 'In all parts of Australia the advance of the white settlers was in the nature of an invasion, and was resisted by the blacks as invasions are resisted'.[91] The point about these historical interpretations is their original openness about how colonial Australia was acquired. Pamela Lukin Watson succinctly points to:

> What is uncontestable ... that 'black armband' histories are not modern-day rewrites, motivated in part by anti-British sentiment. On the contrary, apart from Aboriginal evidence, it is largely British opinions from the previous century which form the basis of current claims about the brutal nature of settlement. Nor were these nineteenth-century informants from the outer fringes of British colonial society. They included explorers, pastoralists, police, scrub-cutters, future parliamentarians and journalists.[92]

Unfortunately, the clergy in the colony remained remarkably quiet on this topic until the last decade of the nineteenth century.[93] Watson concludes that the Pioneering Myth is an: 'idyllic picture ... shafted by the sub-text. Here, land speculation, greed, the involvement of big business and chicanery over pastoral leases are integral to the British push into the region', as it was for the rest of the colony.[94] In the intervening century a more sanitised version supplanted the original honesty and developed into the revisionist falsehood that became the Pioneering Myth.

There can be no doubt that colonial Queensland under the auspices of the first Governor and the Executive Council put in place the necessary components that comply with the term 'genocide'. Each regional coverage in this book combines with one another for the whole of Queensland to confirm that the nineteenth century was indeed a planned killing-time. It is this aspect that makes Queensland different from other Australian colonies and it seems more than likely that the aftermath of this approach has had its impact on twentieth- and twenty-first-century Queensland. Certainly with regard to the contemporary denial of massacres on the Australian frontier, one cannot help but agree with Ørsted-Jensen, that:

> The entire construct seems to have one purpose only—namely that of systematically turning the craft of researching and writing history into an airbrushing act of edifying patriotism. They want triumphalist eulogies and heroes fit for their flag-raising national anthems. They will rather yield the knife and kill history as a social science discipline, than have to face the consequences of some unpleasant facts and the general uncertainties of a troublesome past. . . . there is no way of denying the fact that Queensland's government rapidly moved to take full control and thus also full responsibility of all aspects of its Native Police system almost from the day of the inauguration of the colony's first government. Moreover—probably no other colonial government in Australian history was better equipped to control its frontier indigenous policy than the government of colonial Queensland.[95]

A part of this is a social psychology that enables a kind of pervasive viciousness, accompanied by a denialism that ducks any responsibility that says, no, none of that ever happened—it's all lies! Combined with the advent of nationhood and the introduction of the *Commonwealth Immigration Restriction Act* (1901), the ugly truth could be subsumed under the guise of the 'White Australia Policy'. This, in combination with the fabrication of the Pioneering Myth would appear to be an ideal vehicle for the rewriting of frontier history, where the killers become the heroes.

Australians justifiably criticise Japan for not acknowledging the bad deeds its troops perpetrated before and during the Second World War and for not tackling these aspects in their history textbooks. The Japanese are just as parsimonious as some Australians when it comes to acknowledging the crimes of the Rape of Nanking, where between 260,000 and 300,000 noncombatant Chinese were killed, and 80,000 women raped then murdered.[96]

Plus the innumerable examples of torture and the perverse medical experiments in Manchuria, the inhumane treatment of Australians and their allies on the Burma Railway, and the forced prostitution of women from conquered territories. Germany on the other hand has re-written its history and acknowledged the vile and criminal behaviour of the Nazis, including concentration camps, death squads, stealing children and a blind-faith bureaucracy that merely followed orders.[97] The Germans have managed to do what the Japanese have been unable to do, and similarly what some Australians have also been unable to do with regards to our nineteenth-century frontier and the subsequent autocratic control of Aboriginal people in the twentieth century.

Acknowledging the truth about how white Australia was acquired involves a re-adjustment in how we portray our history since the colonial period. We have seen on numerous occasions a rampant greed where profit comes before people and the environment. This was the key approach taken by European powers in their need for colonies, from the Spanish and Portuguese in South America, to the Dutch in what became Indonesia and the British in North America, Africa, Asia and India. It was this approach that the British took in their colonisation of Australia.

Conclusion

Australian history . . . does not read like history,
but like the most beautiful lies.

Mark Twain, Following the Equator, *1897*.[1]

This book attempts a thorough look at violence on the Queensland frontier.
It is apparent that there were many more violent encounters for which there
are no written or oral history recollections, or that went to the grave with
the perpetrators and their victims and witnesses.[2] However, acknowledging violence on the frontier and the treatment of Aboriginal Queenslanders
provides an opportunity to embrace Aboriginal Australia, and as Noel
Butlin affirms:

> If Australian history is about human existence in Australia, it begins
> now at least 60,000 years ago . . . We are dealing with one of the
> very longest settled countries on earth, so far as *Homo sapiens* is
> concerned—not the longest but a very long history indeed. We can no
> longer approach Australian history as an 'area of recent settlement'.[3]

This is a truly exciting and intriguing approach to incorporate into recording our national story. It's an approach that I took when I wrote *A History of Cairns—City of the South Pacific 1770–1995*,[4] an integrated inclusive history, warts and all. This is what, as John Harris has acknowledged, 'modern historians . . . have been trying to do . . . to write back into history the story of Aboriginal Australians hidden for so long from our eyes'.[5]

The way Australian history has been portrayed has a ring of falsehood about it; something is missing. It is an idealised, triumphalist story of the Pioneering Myth-makers. Social scientist, Sarah Maddison considers that:

> Our 'narcissistic insecurities' about our place in the world rest in large part on our concern that there is an 'emptiness' at the centre of Australian identity. It would seem inevitable that such an emptiness will persist for as long as we feel the need to deny aspects of our history . . . Such an identity will always have a certain hollowness to it.[6]

It is interesting to ponder James Douglas Henry's comment in early 1983 to Judith Wright, in response to reading her frontier histories of central Queensland: *The Cry for the Dead* (1981, based on her grandfather's diaries), and her earlier work, *Generations of Men* (1959, based on family documents and diaries). James' father was born in 1881 not far from Nulalbin (about 20 kilometres south of the future Baralaba), when Judith Wright's parents lived there. He recalled that the truth about frontier violence was hidden in their childhood:

> The odd thing is, you know, that we always knew the theme in our bones, as only children can. Those legendary unspoken horrors, those sins cherished by successive generations, were essential to us; they added value to our conspiracy of silence.[7]

Many suspected the truth confirmed by Wright's work, something which Aboriginal Australians have always known. However, the truth has prevented certain Australians denying what occurred. Deborah Bird Rose makes a significant point for the Victoria River Downs area of the Northern Territory which is applicable elsewhere. Those who came:

> ... shortly after the first two or three decades of violence find accounts of earlier years difficult to credit. European violence, at one moment understood to be essential, was at a later moment denied or simply lost to memory. Taken together, the two moments—death and denial—shield the victors from the knowledge of the origins of their relationships to people and land.[8]

In the same way that our nation's convict heritage is no longer considered a birthstain, it is undoubtedly time to accept a more honest appraisal of our history since that era, and acknowledge the violence perpetrated in taking the land. This is particularly important, as the American sociohistorian, James W Loewen notes, because:

> History cannot be avoided. Understandings of the past seep into popular movies and television programs and determine public policies. Understandings of our past race relations are especially powerful influences in our public and private lives. It matters what students learn ... [9]

In the Australian context one merely has to consider Baz Luhrmann's portrayal of our history in the film *Australia* (2008) or the television series *Wild Boys* (2011)—both romanticised farces based on the 'Pioneering Myth'.

We can glimpse what Aboriginal clan groups experienced throughout this period by examining the words of the then Anglican Bishop of Tasmania, the Right Reverend Phillip Newell, who said in response to the 1996 Port Arthur massacre of 35 non-Aboriginal people: 'The destruction of beautiful lives and the wastefulness of it all have immersed us in a sorrow we have never known before.'[10] Aboriginal Queenslanders had known it, and what's more had experienced it over and over again during the nineteenth century. If the 'effects of post-traumatic stress disorder and clinical depression' for those surviving Port Arthur, 'were being felt throughout the community, and the recovery process could not be measured in days or weeks or months', what then of Aboriginal Australians? Add to this the concentration and total control of the surviving remnants who were until recently treated as children, and it is possible to see why Aboriginal Australia has so many contemporary problems.

Violence took place everywhere on the frontier. If we are to give the dead original Australians their rightful place in Australian history we owe them the truth, as we do ourselves and those to come. This honesty confirms the validity in being 'fair dinkum' and strengthens our national character by acknowledging our forebears' fallibilities and flaws.[11] Australian history has not been 'one success after another', which was the way it was depicted when I went to school. This is a lie which strikes through to the core of who we are as a people; it's dishonest. We already have a significant historical record. Although schools today teach about conflict on the frontier, it is repetitive and compartmentalised, and operates within a framework of continued denial, merely re-affirming to the world the miserly elements of our convict heritage. Being honest or 'true blue' may be clichéd, but it has been portrayed as a cornerstone of Australian identity. Perhaps this is merely empty rhetoric that flies in the face of the real history.

No Australian today is responsible for what happened on our colonial frontier. But we are responsible for not acknowledging what happened. If we do not, our integrity as a nation is flawed and we are shamed as a people for perpetuating a lie.

How we respond as a nation will reflect on our own maturity. British colonisation of this island continent resulted in several thousand whites being killed, and an enormous indigenous death toll, in Queensland approaching the numbers of Australians killed during the First World War. When the nation really understands the humanity and suffering of Aboriginal Australians, their spirited and justifiable defence of their territory, and gives full recognition to frontier crimes, along with their mistreatment 'under the Act' since then, then we can speak of truly genuine reconciliation and, truly, a more honest national spirit. The incredible part of all of this is that Aboriginal Australians have survived and twenty-first-century Australia will be the richer for their taking their rightful place in our national identity.

Endnotes

Introduction

1   Despite Carrington's concern for Aboriginals and the reporting of massacres, he, like others, was not beyond killing Aboriginals. He tells how, while shepherding, he was warned by his dog and fired into the long grass near to where the dog had been resting. He 'fired right into the middle of it, and immediately afterwards a black form bounded into the air and fell ... He was not dead ... the bullet had passed through him just above the hips, so I shot him through the head'. G Carrington, *Colonial Adventures*, Bell and Daldy, London, 1871, p.163.

2   Robert Ørsted-Jensen examines this aspect in *Frontier History Revisited* at <luxmundipub@ hotmail.com> and his forthcoming publication *The Right to Live*.

3   See T Taylor, *Denialism: History Betrayed*, Melbourne University Press, Carlton, 2008.

4   See R Evans, 'Done and Dusted', 'Hidden Queensland' in *Griffith Review*, South Brisbane, Spring 2008, pp.185–98; also R Evans, 'The country has another past: Queensland and the History Wars', in F Peters-Little, A Curthoys and J Docker (eds), *Passionate Histories*, ANU E-Press & Aboriginal History Incorporated, Monograph 21, 2010, <epress.anu.edu.au/passionate_histories>.

5   Robert Hughes observed of the convict era that: 'After abolition, you could (silently) reproach your forebears for being convicts ... The cure for this ... was amnesia—a national pact of silence. Yet the stain would not go away ...,' R Hughes, *The Fatal Shore*, Harvill Press, London (1987), 1996, p.xii.

6   W R Johnston, *The Call of the Land—A History of Queensland to the Present Day*, Jacaranda Press, Milton, 1982, p.40.

7   A McGrath (ed), *Contested Ground*, Allen & Unwin, St Leonards, 1995, p.170; H Reynolds (ed), *Race Relations in North Queensland*, Dept. of History & Politics, James Cook University (JCU), Townsville, 1993 and R Evans, K Saunders & K Cronin, *Race Relations in Colonial Queensland, A History of Exclusion, Exploitation and Extermination*, University of Queensland Press (UQP), St Lucia, 1993; Although it must be remembered that other Australian colonies behaved in an equally questionable manner, see McGrath; also for a regional study of Gippsland, D Watson, *Caledonia Australis—Scottish Highlanders on the frontier of Australia*, Vintage, Milsons Point, 1997; see also M Cannon, *Who Killed the Koories?*, 1990 (for Victoria) and H Reynolds, *Fate of a Free People*, Penguin, Ringwood, 1995, and L Ryan, *Tasmanian Aborigines*, Allen & Unwin, Crows Nest, 2012.

8   T Gurry, *The European Occupation*, Heinemann Educational Australia, Richmond, 1984, pp.68–9; P Grimshaw, M Lake, A Mcgrath & M Qartly, *Creating A Nation*, Penguin Books, Ringwood, 1996, pp.79–80; See also R McGregor, *Imagined Destinies, Aboriginal Australians and the Doomed Race Theory, 1880–1939*, Melbourne University Press (MUP), Carlton South, 1997, pp.1–8.

9   *The Concise Macquarie Dictionary*, Doubleday, Lane Cove, 1982.

10   R Evans, 'The Owl and the Eagle' in *Fighting Words: Writing About Race*, UQP, St Lucia, 1999, p.42. 'Philanthropist' wrote a long diatribe in the *Moreton Bay Courier* (Tuesday, 29 May 1860, p.2) which in part stated: 'The sensual and animal part of their being is almost entirely in the ascendant; and they seem only to be "at home" whilst revelling in all that is beastly and obscene.' There are many other examples in nineteenth-century Queensland newspapers.

11   *The Concise Macquarie Dictionary*, 1982.

12   McGregor, *Imagined Destinies*, 1997, p.8.

13   C Darwin, 'The Origin of Species—By Means of Natural Selection' in R M Hutchins (ed) *Great Books of the Western World—Darwin*, Vol.49; *Encyclopaedia Britannica*, Chicago, 1952. Similar ideas had been in circulation in the western world for at least a century prior to 1859.

14   'It was', the English philosopher, Herbert Spencer 'and not Darwin, who coined the phrase "survival of the fittest," though Darwin came to employ the expression in later editions of *Origin of the Species*,' W Sweet, Spencer, Herbert, <http://www.iep.utm.edu/spencer/>, p.2. R Evans, 'The Owl and the Eagle' in *Fighting Words*, 1999, p.41.

15   McGregor, *Imagined Destinies*, p.18. Nearly 60 years later, the editor of the Cairns newspaper *Northern Affairs*, in June 1931, was still referring to the North Queensland Aboriginal as 'dying out', p.17.

16   W E Hearn, *The Theory of Legal Duties and Rights: An Introduction to Analytical Jurisprudence*, Government Printer, Melbourne, 1883, p.60.

17   'Alleged Outrages Committed on the Aborigines in Queensland by the Native Mounted Police', *Queensland Votes and Proceedings (QV&P)*, Vol.1, 1875, p.623. See also *Sydney Morning Herald*, 2 February 1874, p.3. Heydon went on to become NSW Attorney General, and later a judge of the Industrial Court (1909). See *Australian Dictionary of Biography, ADB Online*.

18   There were other earlier military versions of Mounted Police in NSW, but it was the northern NSW Border Mounted Police who were established in 1848 and operated along the Macintyre River and then the Dawson and Burnett Rivers for eleven years until the new colony of Queensland came into being in December 1859. The new colony incorporated the Native Police into the Queensland Native Police and they were to continue operating for the next 51 years; a total, if one includes their operation under the authority of NSW, of 62 years (1848–1910). There is also a possibility that the force operated on Cape York up until the First World War. Personal communication with Jonathan Richards, 27 January 2011. See also J Richards, *The Secret War, A True History of Queensland's Native Police*, UQP, St Lucia, 2008, pp.8–10.

19   Richards, *The Secret War*, 2008, p.216.

20   Personal communication with Robert Ørsted-Jensen, email 24 March 2011.

21   *QV&P* Vol.1, 1861, p.83, questions (33–35) and response.

22   *QV&P* Vol.1, 1861, p.17, Q35 and p.99, Q53–54.

23   Personal communication with Robert Ørsted-Jensen, email 24 March 2011. See *Frontier History Revisited* and forthcoming publication *The Right to Live*.

24   For a coverage of whistle-blowers, see H Reynolds, *This Whispering In Our Hearts*, Allen & Unwin, St Leonards, 1998.

25   Personal communication with Raymond Evans, email 27 February 2011.

26   Vogan to APS, ASS, 18 Dec. 1892, 6.97 cited in Reynolds, *This Whispering In Our Hearts*, 1998, p.137, n.54.

27   J B Hirst, 'The Pioneer Legend', in J Carroll (ed), *Intruders in the Bush: The Australian Quest for Identity*, Oxford University Press (OUP), Melbourne, 1982, p.14.

28 Hirst, *Intruders*, pp.14–15.

29 In a similar vein, Aboriginal people today tend to refer to themselves as 'Aboriginals', not Aborigines, which is why I have adopted this approach.

30 Over 36 years ago historians began researching and writing about the violence on the Australian frontier. For example: H Reynolds, *Aborigines and Settlers*, Cassell Australia 1972; C D Rowley, *The Destruction of Aboriginal People*, Penguin Books, Ringwood, 1974; R Evans, K Saunders & K Cronin, *Race Relations in Colonial Queensland*, UQP, (1975, 1989) 1993; H Reynolds, *The Other Side of the Frontier*, JCU 1981, (Penguin 1982, 1983, 1984, 1986, 1988); A T Yarwood & M J Knowling, *Race Relations in Australia—A History*, Methuen, North Ryde, 1982.

31 B Barker, 'Massacre, Frontier Conflict and Australian Archaeology', in *Australian Archaeology*, No.64, June 2007, pp.12–13.

32 1898 to 1986 in the guise of the State Government Department of Native Affairs and its successors. See: R Kidd, *The Way We Civilise*, UQP, St Lucia, 1997; R Kidd, *Hard Labour, Stolen Wages*, ANTaR, 2007, <antar@antar.org.au>; T Blake, *A Dumping Ground: A History of the Cherbourg Settlement*, UQP, St Lucia, 2001; W Thorpe, *Remembering the Forgotten, A History of the Deebing Creek Aboriginal Mission in 1887–1915*, Seaview Press, Henley Beach, 2004; T Bottoms, *Djabugay Country: An Aboriginal History of Tropical North Queensland*, Allen & Unwin, St Leonards, 1999 (dealing with Mona Mona Mission); C Halse, *A terribly Wild Man: the Life of the Rev Ernest Gribble*, Allen & Unwin, Crows Nest, 2002; P Freier, '"Living with Munpitch"—A History of the Mitchell River Mission', PhD, JCU, Townsville, November 1999, K E Evans, 'Marie Yamba, Bloomfield and Hope Vale: The Lutheran Missions to the North Queensland Aborigines, 1886–1905', *Queensland Heritage*, Vol.II, No.6, 1972; D Craig, 'The effect of State policy and Queensland laws on an Aboriginal Reserve: A look at Yarrabah', in *Australian Institute of Aboriginal Studies*, No.11, March 1979; J Watson, *Palm Island Through a Long Lens*, Aboriginal Studies Press, Canberra, 2010; and others.

33 R Evans & J Scott, 'Fallen Among Thieves, Aboriginal Labour and State Control in Inter-War Queensland', in R Evans, *Fighting Words: Writing About Race*, UQP, St Lucia, 1999; R Kidd, *The Way We Civilise*, UQP, St Lucia, 1997; R Kidd, *Trustees on Trial*, Aboriginal Studies Press, Canberra, 2006; Kidd, *Hard Labour, Stolen Wages*, 2007.

34 *Queenslander*, 4 October 1890, p.654.

35 W Thorpe, 'Archibald Meston and Aboriginal Legislation in Colonial Queensland', in *Historical Studies*, Vol.21, No.82, April 1984, p.62.

36 See letters and correspondence etc. at: <www.aconspiracyofsilence.com.au>.

37 See R Broome, 'The statistics of frontier conflict', in B Attwood & S G Foster (eds), *Frontier Conflict: The Australian Experience*, National Museum of Australia, Canberra, 2003.

38 c.1830s to c.1914. See also: A Laurie, 'The Black War in Queensland', *Journal of the Royal Historical Society of Queensland (JRHSQ)*, Vol.VI, No.1, September 1959.

39 M Gilbert, *In Search of Churchill*, HarperCollins, London, 1994, p.246.

40 For example: W Coote, *History of the Colony of Queensland*, W Thorne, Brisbane, 1882; A J Vogan, *The Back Police: A Story of Modern Australia*, Hutchinson & Co, London, 1890; *The Way We Civilise; Black and White; The Native Police*, G & J Black (Late W Thorne), Brisbane, 1880; E O Hobkirk, *Queensland historical manuscripts—Vol.2* 'Original Reminiscences of South West Queensland', NLA MS3460 (1922).

41 J Richards, *The Secret War*, 2008, p.6.

Chapter 1   Post-Convict Era and the Future South-East Queensland

1   Norfolk Island's first penal settlement was established on 15 February 1788 and closed in 1808. It re-opened in 1825 for convicts guilty of further crimes while serving a sentence in NSW, and was renowned for harsh treatment of the prisoners. Norfolk Island closed as a penal settlement in 1856.

2   NSW Colonial Secretary Letters 28/8744. Logan wrote (20 October 1828) from Moreton Bay, that: 'Immediately on my return from Sydney I dispatched a military party to Point Danger and they have already sent in two runaways who had left the settlement ten days previously. I have every reason to believe that this measure will have the effect of checking absconding to a considerable extent . . .'

3   M O'Keefe, *A Brief Account of the Moreton Bay Penal Settlement, 1824–1839*, John Oxley Library (JOL), State Library of Queensland, Brisbane, 1974, pp.7–8; K Imbruglia, 'Paradise Stolen, A History of Aboriginal and European Relations in the Gold Coast Region to 1990', BA(Hons), University of Queensland, 1992, pp.28–31.

4   *The Times*, London, 27 November 1818.

5   O'Keefe, 'The Runaway Convicts of Moreton Bay', *Journal of the Royal Historical Society of Queensland (JRHSQ)*, Vol.X, No.1, 1975–76, p.52, p.70.

6   R Evans, 'The Mogwi Take Mi-An-Jin, Race Relations and the Moreton Bay Penal Settlement, 1824–1842' in *Fighting Words: Writing about Race*, University of Queensland Press (UQP), St Lucia, 1999, p.64, n.84; J Clunie, 27 February 1833, NSW Colonial Secretary Letterbook (CSL) micro.7 & 8.

7   Evans, 'The Mogwi Take Mi-An-Jin', *Fighting Words*, 1999, p.65, n.86: G Watkins, 'Notes on the Aborigines of Stradbroke and Moreton Islands', *Proceedings of the Royal Society of Queensland*, 8, 1892, p.43; cf. J J Knight, *In the Early Days*, Sapsford, Brisbane, 1898, p.36.

8   Evans, 'The Mogwi Take Mi-An-Jin', *Fighting Words*, 1999, pp.65–66.

9   Evans, 1999, p.66.

10   See Chapter 9, 'The Gulf Country and Western Queensland'.

11   R Fitzgerald, *A History of Queensland: From the Dreaming to 1915*, UQP, 1986, p.86.

12   Dr R B Walker in his history *Old New England* (Sydney University Press, 1966) wrote of the aftermath of Myall Creek, where 'To protect themselves and their property the squatters had recourse to violence which in view of the fate of Myall Creek murders was not publicized. There are just a few hints of this surviving . . . It is rumoured that two stations took the law into their own hands with expeditions that thoroughly scared the blacks . . .', G Blomfield, *Baal Belbora— The End of the Dancing*, The Alternative Publishing Co-operative Ltd, Chippendale, 1988, p.84.

13   Don Dignan, *The Story of Kolan*, Smith & Paterson, Brisbane, 1964, p.4.

14   F Uhr, 'September 12, 1843: The Battle of One Tree Hill—A turning point in the conquest of Moreton Bay', *JRHSQ*, Vol.18, No.6, May 2003, pp.250–51.

15   R Evans, *A History of Queensland*, Cambridge University Press (CUP), Melbourne, 2007, p.53.

16   Evans, *A History of Queensland*, 2007, p.53.

17   Evans cites Rogers' statements as coming from: 'A Hodgson, Report on Aboriginal Outrage, 27 October 1841, NSW Col. Sec., 41/9744, CSL micro 12, while Brown's is hidden away in the back of the Moreton Bay Book of Trials, 13 January 1842, Oxley Memorial Library; Gipps' responses in memo, 6 November 1841, 41/9745, and 10 November 1841, 41/9744.' October 1841 Attack, p.276 in Evans, *A History of Queensland*, 2007, p.53.

18 Letter from Christopher Rolleston, Commissioner for Crown Lands Darling Downs to Wickham PM (Police Magistrate), Moreton Bay, 28 October 1844, JOL: A2.14, frame 619. Letter number 44/8352.

19 *NSW Legislative Assembly Votes & Proceedings (NSWV&P)*, 1846, p.17.

20 Jan Walker, *Jondaryan Station: The Relationship Between Pastoral Capital and Pastoral Labour 1840–1890*, UQP, St. Lucia, 1988, p.35.

21 A version of the Native Police began in Victoria in 1842, and in 1848 in greater NSW, primarily in the northern districts, including the Moreton Bay region from 1853.

22 Queensland State Archives (QSA) COL/A188, 73/3005; B Breslin, *Exterminate With Pride*, James Cook University, Townsville, 1992, p.54.

23 *The Way We Civilise—A series of Articles Reprinted from the Queenslander*, G & J Black, Brisbane, 1880, p.3.

24 E B Kennedy, *The Black Police of Queensland: Reminiscences of Official Work and Personal Adventures in the Early Days of the Colony*, Murray, London, 1902, pp.34–36. For a contemporary comprehensive coverage, see J Richards, *The Secret War*, UQP, St Lucia, 2008.

25 R Evans and J Walker, ' "These Strangers, Where Are They Going?" Aboriginal–European Relations in the Fraser Island and Wide Bay Region 1770–1905', P K Lauer (ed), *Occasional Papers in Anthropology*, No.8, March 1977, p.52.

26 *Sydney Morning Herald*, 23 August 1842, p.3.

27 R Fisher, Chapter 2, 'From depredation to degradation: The Aboriginal experience at Moreton Bay 1842–60', in R Fisher (ed), *Brisbane: The Aboriginal presence 1824–1860*, Brisbane History Group, Paper No.11, 1992, p.32.

28 S Sheaffe, 'Justice in Moreton Bay through the eyes of criminal trials', in *Queensland History Journal*, Vol.20, No.11, August 2009, pp.649–50.

29 Personal communication with Robert Ørsted-Jensen, email 25 March 2011.

30 See Chapter 5, 'Poisonings and Sexual Exploitation'.

31 Paddy Jerome, '*Boobarran Ngummin*: The Bunya Mountains', in A Haebich (ed), 'On the Bunya Trail', *Queensland Review*, Vol.9, No.2, UQP, St Lucia, November 2002, pp.1–2.

32 Macarthur Papers, Mitchell Library, State Library of NSW, MS A2933, V.37B; 29.

33 The Baanyiy (bunya-bunya) 'fruit during three or four months of the year affords an ample feast for the tribes within a circuit of a hundred miles [161 kilometres]', Christopher Rolleston, Commissioner for Crown Lands, Darling Downs to NSW Colonial Secretary, 12 January 1849, JOL, A2.18, frames 383–87.

34 *New South Wales Government Gazette*, 1842, p.587.

35 C Rolleston to Chief Commissioner of Crown Lands (NSW), 17 April 1851, JOL, A2.22, frames 407–22.

36 R Evans, 'Against the Grain: Colonialism and the Demise of the Bunya Gatherings, 1839–1939', in *Queensland Review*, Vol.9, No.2, 2002, p.51.

37 Evans, 'Against the Grain', *Queensland Review*, Vol.9, No.2, 2002, p.51.

38 Evans, 'Against the Grain', *Queensland Review*, Vol.9, No.2, 2002, p.52.

39 Evans, 'Against the Grain', *Queensland Review*, Vol.9, No.2, 2002, pp.56–57.

40 Government Resident J C Wickham to Colonial Secretary (28 December 1858), NSW Col. Sec. correspondence, A2/41, endnote 9, cited in Richards, *The Secret War*, UQP, St Lucia, 2008, p.13.

41 W Rosser, *Up Rode the Troopers: The Black Police in Queensland*, UQP, St Lucia, 1990, p.59.

42 'Report from the Select Committee on the Native Police Force and the Condition of the Aborigines Generally', 1861, pp.12 & 66; D O'Donnell, 'The Ugarapul Tribe of the Fassifern

Valley', *JRHSQ*, Vol.XIV, No.4, November 1990, pp.149–60; Rosser, *Up Rode the Troopers*, 1990, p.59ff.

43   Rosser, *Up Rode the Troopers*, 1990, p.68.

44   *Moreton Bay Courier*, 18 July 1846.

45   J A Walker, 'Aboriginal-European Relations in the Maryborough District 1842–1903', Hons. University of Queensland, 1975, p.26.

46   Dignan, *The Story of Kolan*, 1964, p.10.

47   C Lack, *One Hundred Years Young—Bundaberg, the city of charm, 1867–1967, News-Mail*, Bundaberg, 1967.

48   Dignan, *Story of Kolan*, 1964, pp.10–11.

49   Lack, *One Hundred Years Young—Bundaberg*, 1967.

50   Australian Dictionary of Biography—Online.

51   A Halloran, Wide Bay to Col.Sec.(Sydney) 28 Nov.1853; First Report on Aborigines, Wide Bay Dec. 1853; Reports . . . 31 Aug.1855, 3 Oct.1855; Queensland State Archives (QSA) CCL3/G1. For a comprehensive coverage of this region, see R Evans and J Walker, 'These Strangers, Where Are They Going?' P K Lauer (ed), *Occasional Papers in Anthropology*, No.8, March 1977.

52   *Moreton Bay Courier*, 18 September 1852, pp.2,3.

53   F Walker, Maryborough, to NSW Colonial Secretary, Sydney, 5 January 1852, JOL Microfilm Reel A2.23 frames 820–21.

54   Evans and Walker, 'These Strangers, Where Are They Going?', p.54.

55   *Moreton Bay Courier*, 18 September 1852.

56   *Moreton Bay Courier*, 18 September 1852.

57   *Sydney Morning Herald*, Friday 4 June 1852, p.2.

58   Evans, 'Against the Grain', *Queensland Review*, Vol.9, No.2, 2002, p.53, n.36: R Kirkhove, *A Concise Aboriginal History of the Sunshine Coast*, typescript, 1986, pp.73–74; F Wheeler (Sandgate) to A W Manning, 1 December 1863, QSA, COL/A47 63/2889.

59   Queensland Parliamentary Papers, 'Annual Report of the Chief Protector of Aborigines', 1913, 'Appendix—Grammar, Vocabulary, and Notes of the Wangerriburra Tribe. Orthography', p. 23 (of report), pp.1035–36.

60   Queensland Parliamentary Papers, as cited in note 59, p. 23 (of report), pp.1035–36.

61   W E Roth, 'Annual Report of the Northern Protector of Aboriginals for 1903', Queensland Parliamentary Papers, Brisbane, 1904, p.18.

Chapter 2   European Invasion of the Future Southern Queensland

1   For a comprehensive coverage of this area, see M Copland, J Richards and A Walker, *One Hour More Daylight: A Historical Overview of Aboriginal Dispossession in Southern and Southwest Queensland*, The Social Justice Commission, Catholic Diocese of Toowoomba, 2006. See also, for the Maranoa, P Collins, *Goodbye Bussamarai: The Mandandanji Land War, Southern Queensland 1842–1852*, University of Queensland Press (UQP), St Lucia, 2002.

2   *Father Leo Haye's book of press cuttings*, No.36, p.40, Fryer Library Collection, University of Queensland Library.

3   H Reynolds, *Why Weren't We Told?* Viking, Ringwood, 1999, pp.210–11.

4   Personal communication with Raymond Evans, email 28 March 2011.

5   *Maitland Mercury*, 28 January 1843; William Gardner, *Production and Resources of the Northern and Western Districts of New South Wales*, Vol.1, 1854, Mitchell Library, State Library of NSW, p.80.

6   M Copland, 'A System of Assassination', BA Hons, University of Queensland, 1990, pp.98–99.

7   Gardner, *Production and Resources of the Northern and Western Districts of New South Wales*, 1854, Vol.1, p.78.

8   Lanarch claimed he had lost 900 cattle to 'depredations'. D Lanarch to Colonial Secretary, 24 November 1848, NSW State Archives, 4/2929, 48/13167.

9   Watts, *Personal Reminiscences*, n.d., John Oxley Library (JOL), Q994.33WAT.

10 R Milliss (ed), *The Wallabadah Manuscript, Recollections of the Early Days by William Telfer Jr.*, n.d. University of NSW Press (UNSW Press), Kensington, 1980, p.40.

11 *Sydney Morning Herald*, 15 October 1847; also Milliss (ed), *The Wallabadah Manuscript*, n.d. 1980; and R J Webb, *The Rising Sun: A History of Moree and District*, Moree Centenary Celebrations Committee, 1962.

12 Primary source data in Copland, 'A System of Assassination', 1990 Appendix II.

13 Milliss (ed), *The Wallabadah Manuscript*, 1980, p.42.

14 A E Tonge, 'The Youngs of Umbercollie: The First White Family in South-West Queensland', n.d. Mitchell Library, MSS 3821 5–537C, p.25.

15 Maitland Circuit Court Depositions, March–April 1849.

16 John Watts, 'Personal Reminiscences', JOL, n.d. Q994.33WAT. See also Walker to Colonial Secretary, 26 May 1849, NSW State Archives, 4/2920, 49/5554.

17 *NSW Legislative Assembly Votes & Proceedings (NSWV&P)*, 1858, Vol.2. p.880.

18 *NSWV&P*, 1858, Vol.2, p.880.

19 Morris to Walker, 18 October 1849, NSW State Archives, 4/2920, 49/10488.

20 Walker to Colonial Secretary, 31 December 1849, *NSW Legislative Council Votes & Proceedings*, 1850.

21 Milliss (ed), *The Wallabadah Manuscript*, 1980, p.176, endnote 31, quotes Walker's letter to Deas Thomson on 31 December 1849.

22 Milliss (ed), *The Wallabadah Manuscript*, 1980, p.41.

23 Evidence is sketchy, although there are two accounts leading up to the conflict. The first account is 'Davison's Diary' in E Browne, 'A Short History of Goondiwindi', *Goondiwindi Argus*, 1922, pp.10–11. The second is the 'Darky Flat Massacre' described in T Hall, *A Short History of the Downs Blacks*, Vintage Books, Toowoomba, 1987, pp.149–52.

24 Notes written by Colonial Secretary on Walker's report of 9 July 1849, NSW State Archives, 4/2920, 49/7305.

25 Colonial Secretary to Walker, 25 October 1850, NSW State Archives, copies of letters addressed to Bench of Magistrates, Justices of the Peace and Superintendents of Police beyond the Settled Districts, 4/3861: reel 2818.

26 Walker to Colonial Secretary, 7 November 1850, JOL, A2.18.

27 *NSWV&P*, 1852, p.790.

28 Milliss (ed), *The Wallabadah Manuscript*, 1980, p.42. Half a mile (0.8 kilometres) east of Callandoon Station or three-quarters of a mile (1.2 kilometres) west of Goondiwindi, there is a bend in the Callandoon branch of the Barwon River labelled 'Deaths Corner'. See *The Roads of Queensland*, compiled and published by Yates & Jones, Brisbane, 1913, p.16.

29 See N B Tindale, 'Distribution of Australian Aboriginal Tribes: A Field Survey', in *Transcripts of the Royal Society of South Australia*, Vol.54 (1), 1974, p.189.

30 Steele Rudd (collector), *Recollections of Thomas Davis*, in the possession of J T Bell, c.1908–9, <http://espace.library.uq.edu.au/QU:216890>, p.5.

31 *Recollections of Thomas Davis*, p.6.

32 *Recollections of Thomas Davis*, p.7.

33 Davis calls the station Bingera, but research by Patrick Collins suggests that there was no such station on the Balonne: 'However, Thomas Simpson Hall, from Dartbrook Station near Muswellbrook, held multiple properties on both sides of the Balonne as Yamboucal (or Yambugle) Station adjacent to Surat, and as Weribone Station a little further south. His family also held Bingera Station on the Gwydir. The town of Bingara developed from this. As Thomas Davis would have known of the Hall family's Bingara, I guess he confused it with another station known as Burgurrah [Burgorah]. Collins makes the point that 'The inaccuracies no doubt resulted from memory lapses by Thomas Davis when retelling events that took place around 50 years before his son recorded them.' Similarly with the supposed Waggor (Warroo?) Station. Personal communication with P Collins, email 9 October 2010.

34 *Recollections of Thomas Davis*, pp.8–9.

35 *Recollections of Thomas Davis*, p.9.

36 *Recollections of Thomas Davis*, p.10.

37 *Recollections of Thomas Davis*, pp.10–11. David Graham was born in Ireland in 1840. An Irish constable before joining Queensland's Native Police, also as a constable in 1865, before being promoted to sergeant in 1869; senior sergeant 1874; 2nd-class Sub-Inspector 1892; retired 1904, died 1933 aged 93. Richards, *The Secret War*, UQP, St Lucia, 2008, p.237.

38 P J Collins, 'Richard, Frederick and Robert: Three Militant Walkers on the Maranoa Frontier' in *Queensland History Journal (QHJ)*, Vol.20, No.10, May 2009, p.502.

39 P Collins, *Goodbye Bussamari: The Mandandanji Land War, Southern Queensland 1842–1852*, UQP, St Lucia, 2002.

40 *Recollections of Thomas Davis*, p. 16.

41 G Reid, *A Nest of Hornets*, Oxford University Press (OUP), Melbourne, 1982, p.55 n.20 & 21, citing O'Connell to 1861 Select Committee, p.87, and J D Wood, 12 March 1862, to Chief Secretary, Queensland State Archives (QSA) Col. Sec. 62/1118. Reid notes that 'Wood apparently had visited Hornet Bank some time after October 1860 and had questioned working men in the district about the massacre; he had also spoken to Nicoll'.

42 Reid, *A Nest of Hornets*, 1982, pp.54–55.

43 QSA: COL/A3, 60/381. 'Baulie' was not Jiman, but worked at the station.

44 E C Davies, 'Some Reminiscences of Early Queensland', *Journal of the Royal Historical Society of Queensland (JRHSQ)*, 6, No.1, 1958, p.36; also at: <espace.library.uq.edu.au/eserv/UQ:211811/s00855804_1959_6_1_29.pdf>.

45 Letter from G Serocold to C Serocold, 31 December 1857, 'Serocold Papers', John Oxley Library, Queensland Historical Retrieval Project 5–7.

46 Letter from G D Lang, Mitchell Library, State Library of NSW, A63, cited and quoted in F Williams, *Written in Sand—A History of Fraser Island*, Jacaranda Press, Milton, 1982, p.59.

47 D Cryle, *The Press in Colonial Queensland*, UQP, St Lucia, 1989, p.22–23. 'Phillip Lamb of Rocky Springs on the Auburn [River, c.80 kilometres west of Mundubbera] wrote on 3 December [1857] to his brother in Sydney that the blacks in his district were harbouring the Dawson tribe who had been committing atrocities equaled only by those of the Sepoys in India.' G Reid, 'From Hornet Bank to Cullin-La-Ringo' in *JRHSQ*, Vol.XI, No.2, 1980–81, p.65, also at <espace.library.uq.edu.au/eserv/UQ:205360/'s00>, footnote 8, quoting from Wiseman, Bungaban Station, Upper Dawson, 8 December 1857, to CCCL, in NSA Col. Sec. Special Bundle, 4/719.2.

48 Alex W Nahrung, 'The Life of Konrad Nahrung', manuscript 1902, typed by his son Alex, from a handwritten script written by his father. In the possession of R Evans.

49 'The Late Massacre of Blacks at the Cabulture', *Brisbane Courier*, 4 October 1862.

50 *Brisbane Courier*, 4 October 1862; a month earlier (1 September 1862), the *Courier* published a brief piece entitled 'The Blacks at the Cabulture', where it was acknowledged that they held off with the story until they could verify the particulars. Having done that, they reported the shooting of eight or ten 'supposed depradators' by Lt Wheeler and his troopers, but then allowed that there might be extenuating circumstances, although concluded, that whether the Native Police 'were justified in an act of slaughter remains to be seen'.

51 *Recollections of Thomas Davis*, pp.16–17.

Chapter 3 European Invasion of the Future Central Queensland

1 For more detailed coverage, see J Wright, *The Cry for the Dead*, Oxford University Press (OUP), Melbourne, 1981; G Reid, *A Nest of Hornets, The Massacre of the Fraser Family at Hornet Bank Station, Central Queensland, 1857, and Related Events*, OUP, Melbourne, 1982; L McDonald, *Rockhampton: A History of City and District*, University of Queensland Press (UQP), St Lucia, 1981.

2 Extract cited in S Rosenberg, 'Black Sheep and Golden Fleece: A Study of Nineteenth Century English Attitudes Toward Australian Colonies', Ann Arbor, Michigan, University Microfilms, 1954, pp.127–28.

3 F Sinnett, *An Account of the 'Rush' to Port Curtis, Including Letters Addressed to the Argus as Special Correspondent from the Fitzroy River*, Ray and Richter, Geelong, 1859, p.69.

4 R Fitzgerald, *A History of Queensland—From the Dreaming to 1915*, UQP, St Lucia, 1986, pp.112–13.

5 Captain John Coley's evidence, 'Royal Commission into the Native Police Force', 14 May 1861, No.20.

6 *Moreton Bay Courier*, 1 December 1860, p.3.

7 *Moreton Bay Courier*, 24 January 1861, pp.2–3. The implication is that Gulliver and Alma were disposed of by their colleagues.

8 R Ørsted-Jensen, *Frontier History Revisited*, Lux Mundi Publishing, 2011, pp.165–66.

9 *Moreton Bay Courier*, 1 December 1860, p.3.

10 *The Argus* (Melbourne), 7 February 1861, p.6; *Moreton Bay Courier*, 30 May 1861, p.2; *Moreton Bay Courier*, 2 April 1861, p.3.

11 Ørsted-Jensen, *Frontier History Revisited*, 2011, p.170.

12 Alex W Nahrung, 'The Life of Konrad Nahrung', manuscript 1902 (typed by his son Alex, from a handwritten script written by Konrad), in possession of R Evans.

13 There '... was enormous consternation in 1860 when male electors discovered that, due to an administrative blunder, they had been enfranchised under the New South Wales *Constitution Act* of 1855 rather than being granted the extended franchise of 1858. As a result, around one-third of those who had previously voted were debarred due to the property qualifications, leaving only some 19 per cent of the adult population exercising the suffrage ... Electoral reform did not proceed until 1873'. R Evans, *A History of Queensland*, Cambridge University Press (CUP), Melbourne, 2007, p.80.

14 Wright, *The Cry for the Dead*, 1981, pp.100–1.

15 F Walker to Col. Sec., letter dated 3 April 1861, Nullalbin [*sic*] Post Office, 'Complaint of Aggression by the Native Police on Planet Creek', *Queensland Votes & Proceedings (QV&P)*, 1862 (for 1861).

16   F Walker to Attorney-General, letter dated 10 July 1861, Nullalbin [*sic*] PO, Queensland State Archives (QSA), COL/A17 61/1469, p.3.

17   C B Dutton to Commandant Morisset, Bohinia [*sic*] Downs, 23 March 1861, QSA, COL 61/2545 with covering letter by J O'C Bligh cited in Wright, *The Cry for the Dead*, 1981, p.104.

18   Editorial, *Port Denison Times*, 23 September 1865.

19   Wright, *The Cry for the Dead*, 1981, pp.104–5.

20   'The Select Committee on The Native Police Force and the Conditions of the Aborigines in General' (Chairman: R R Mackenzie), *Queensland Parliamentary Papers (QPP)*, 8 May 1861.

21   *Moreton Bay Courier*, Tuesday 7 May 1861, p.2.

22   *Courier* (Brisbane), Thursday 30 May 1861, p.2.

23   *Courier* (Brisbane), Thursday 30 May 1861, p.2.

24   J Richards, *The Secret War*, UQP, 2008, p.249.

25   *Moreton Bay Courier*, 2 & 25 April 1861.

26   *Courier* (Brisbane), Thursday 25 July 1861, p.2.

27   Derived from a Spanish term, meaning 'sought and found', named by Peter McDonald who originally selected the run and transferred it to Horatio Wills. D J Mulvaney, *Encounters in Place*, UQP, St Lucia, 1989, p.98.

28   *Courier* (Brisbane), Thursday 25 July 1861, p.2. My emphasis.

29   F Walker to Attorney-General, letter dated 10 July 1861, Nullalbin [*sic*] PO, QSA, COL/A17 61/1469, p.2.

30   For a more detailed coverage, see G de Moor, *Tom Wills: his spectacular rise and tragic fall*, Allen & Unwin, Crows Nest, 2008; G Reid, *A Nest of Hornets*, OUP, Melbourne, 1982; L Perrin, *Cullin-la-Ringo: The Triumph and Tragedy of Tommy Wills*, self published, Stafford, Queensland,1998.

31   A M G Patrick was appointed to the Native Police in 1860 as a 2nd Lieutenant. He was shot in the leg while on duty and resigned with ill-health in 1862. He died in Brisbane in 1870. Richards, *The Secret War*, UQP, 2008, p.255.

32   Cedric Wills, *Morning Bulletin*, Rockhampton, 9 December 1912.

33   Native Police Commandant Bligh, Rockhampton, to Colonial Secretary, 2 December 1861, QSA, COL/A 23 61/2777.

34   Harry Arlington Creaghe, *Letters From Ireland*, 9 April 1867, p.29 in J Stewart, 'Emily Caroline Creaghe (1860–1944), Explorer', *Queensland History Journal*, November 2008, Vol.20, No.8, p.395.

35   *Morning Bulletin*, Rockhampton, Friday 4 August 1899, from the Central Queensland Collection of the Rockhampton Regional Council Libraries.

36   *Morning Bulletin*, Rockhampton, Friday 4 August 1899.

37   *Rockhampton Bulletin*, 18 July 1865; McDonald, *Rockhampton: A History of City and District*, 1981, p.196.

38   For example, on the 'Bump Track' near Port Douglas in 1880, The Reverend Tenison-Woods described a white couple who had built a small bark hut near the main track (going to the Hodgkinson goldfield). The Reverend and the woman and children in the hut for the night 'could see fire-sticks of a large party of natives crossing down towards the creek. They evidently had been watching the hut and perhaps the dogs scared them, for they came no nearer . . .' ('Notes Made in Northern Australia', *Sydney Mail*, 17 July 1880–25 December 1880). The colonists' fear enabled them to misinterpret the Aboriginal warriors' intentions. The Aboriginals were going about their business and if they had intended attacking, they would not have been using torches to light their way.

39   McDonald, *Rockhampton: A History of City and District*, 1981, p.196.

40 W H Corfield, *Reminiscences of Queensland 1862–1899*, A H Frater, Brisbane, 1921, p.13.

41 *Port Denison Times*, 3 April 1869.

42 *Port Denison Times*, 17 April 1869.

43 *Port Denison Times*, 1 May 1869. See also R L Evans, 'Queensland's First Aboriginal Reserve', Part 1—'The Promise of Reform', *Queensland Heritage*, Vol.2, No.4, May 1971, p.27.

44 *Port Denison Times*, 1 May 1869.

45 *Queenslander*, 18 March 1876, p.12.

46 *Port Denison Times*, 1 May 1869.

Chapter 4 South-West Queensland—The Channel Country

1 From their coverage of the Hospital Creek massacre, 21 kilometres from Brewarrina, and 100 kilometres from the future Queensland border, established after 1859.

2 M Pearson, <www.aicomos.com/wpcontact/uploads/Paroo-tracks-water-and-stock-routes-in-arid-Australia>, p.2. Maps of the region spell the waterway 'Cooper Creek'; locally at Windorah on either side of the waterway, it is signposted as 'Cooper's Creek'. Similarly, Alice Duncan-Kemp who wrote prolifically about the Channel Country, particularly around her family's property of Mooraberrie (c.60 kilometres north of Betoota) identified it this way. Therefore, as it seems that the locals spell it this way, this is the spelling that has been adopted.

3 'Canbar East, Canbar West, Lubrina and Nockatunga, were tiny outposts . . . where pioneer settlers S D Gordon, Alex Munroe and Pat Drynan were battling . . .', M Durack, *Kings in Grass Castles*, Vintage Classics (originally published in 1959), North Sydney, 2008, p.88.

4 Durack, *Grass Castles*, 2008, p.111. An interesting point from this event, as Raymond Evans noted, was 'that Harry Redford has been immortalised (there is presently a huge annual cattle muster in his honour and he was used as the model for Captain Starlight in *Robbery Under Arms*) and was never punished (as he was exonerated by a jury) for stealing 1000 head; and yet Aborigines would be slaughtered in Queensland for killing a single steer?' Personal communication with R Evans, email 30 March 2011.

5 B Hardy, *Lament for the Barkindji, the vanished tribes of the Darling River Region*, Rigby, Adelaide, 1976, p.119.

6 B Hardy, *Lament for the Barkindji*, 1976, p.119.

7 Cunnamulla Station was established in August 1859 by Samuel Smith and his son, Thomas Arkell Smith, from Dubbo (central western NSW), and the runs were accepted by the Queensland government in May 1863. D Webster, 'First Settlers and the Occupation of the Warrego', in *Warrego and South West Queensland Historical Society Collection of Papers, Cunnamulla and District*, Vol.1, 1969, p.2 (of paper).

8 Surveyor G C Watson, 'Building the Commonwealth, A Record of Forty Years in the Civil Service of Queensland', in *Warrego and South West Queensland Historical Society Collection of Papers, Cunnamulla and District*, Vol.1, 1969, p.3 (of paper).

9 Surveyor Watson, 'Forty Years', 1969, p.5 (of paper).

10 Durack, *Grass Castles*, 2008, pp.94, 98.

11 Durack, *Grass Castles*, 2008, p.110.

12 Durack, *Grass Castles*, 2008, p.156.

13 J St Pierie, '18. Some Information on the History of South West Qld,' in *Warrego and South West Queensland Historical Society Collection of Papers, Cunnamulla and District*, Vol.1, 1969, p.2 (of paper).

14   H McKellar, *Matya-Mundu, A History of the Aboriginal People of South West Queensland*, Cunnamulla Australian Native Welfare Association, 1984, p.57.

15   E O Hobkirk, *Queensland historical manuscripts—Vol.2 'Original Reminiscences of South West Queensland'*, NLA MS3460, (1922), pp.3–4. Cheshunt Station is located 20 kilometres south-west of Taro, or c.100 kilometres west of Dalby.

16   Hobkirk, NLA MS3460. Hobkirk noted: 'We found it hard to prevent the few that were employed on the station from . . . [running away into the ranges] . . . as they were so scared at what had taken place that we had to lock them up in the Hut—that was used as a store[,] for a short time.' p.4.

17   G Gooch (bookkeeper at Norley in 1911) cited by St Pierie, 'History of South West Queensland,' in *Warrego and South West Queensland Historical Society Collection of Papers, Cunnamulla and District*, Vol.1, 1969, p.3 (of paper).

18   R Evans, 'The Country Has Another Past', Chapter 1, in A Curthoys (ed), *Passionate Histories, Myth, Memory and Indigenous Australia*, <epress.anu.edu.au/aborig_history/passionate/pdf>, 2010, p.21 n.44: *The Stockwhip*, 22 April 1876; *Maryborough Chronicle*, 9 May 1876; see also R Evans, 'Queensland, 1859: reflections on the act of becoming', *Queensland Review*, February 2009.

19   McKellar, *Matya-Mundu*, 1984, p. 57. Thouringowa/Thuringowa Waterhole is located about 45 kilometres upstream for Bulloo Downs, on the Bulloo River.

20   *Moreton Bay Courier*, 17 September 1862, p.4, (Government advertisements for the Maranoa District). R Ørsted-Jensen observed that 'it was actually one of the stations initially taken up by Henry de Satgé [who paid £12/10/—for 20 square miles (52 square kilometres)], but he parted from it almost immediately, probably as he was in partnership or the financier behind the owner, who Chambers will not mention'. Personal communication with Robert Ørsted-Jensen, email 18 April 2011.

21   Ørsted-Jensen notes that 'a contemporary satirical contribution—about a series of failed Native Police dispersals from the *Brisbane Courier* (21 January 1865, p.5) entitled: 'The Tremendous Adventure of "Bombastes Furioso", No.14 By Will Weasal, was clearly written by someone who knew about Native Police work in great detail. He may have wished to smear the name and reputation of a particular officer, claiming that he was a useless liar or something. But here again we have some—this time contemporary—evidence of 'police' work in that particular area. If you read this you will notice that an area about Drummond and Chesterton range some 50 kilometres south of Carnarvon National Park was indeed known as Pigeon Creek, so that is where Blagden got it from. It was just his way of covering the name up a bit, just as he does not mention the real name and surname of anyone.' Personal communication with Robert Ørsted-Jensen, email 18 April 2011.

22   Personal communication with Robert Ørsted-Jensen, email 3 April 2011.

23   J Wright, Foreword to B Chambers, *Black and White*, Methuen, Richmond, 1988, p.9.

24   Wright, Foreword to Chambers, *Black and White*, 1988, p.7.

25   Chambers, *Black and White*, 1988, pp.18–28.

26   J Richards, '"A Question of Necessity": The Native Police in Queensland', PhD, Griffith University, Brisbane, 2005, Appendix A, pp.349 and 351.

27   'Friends and branches of the family, mostly from the Goulburn area, were now constantly arriving in big parties to take up the selections picked out for them, and often the Thylungra and Kyabra homesteads were filled to overflowing,' Durack, *Grass Castles*, 2008, p.130, see Chapter 14.

28   35,000 square miles (90,650 square kilometres), 17,000 square miles (44,000 square kilometres), 11 million acres (4.4 million hectares). Durack, *Grass Castles*, 2008, pp.128–29.

29 K Willey, *The Drovers*, Macmillan, South Melbourne, 1982, p.45; Durack, *Grass Castles*, 2008 (1959), pp.138–39.

30 A M Duncan-Kemp, *Our Sandhill Country*, Angus and Robertson, Sydney, 1933, pp.24–25.

31 P L Watson, *Frontier Lands and Pioneer Legends*, Allen & Unwin, St Leonards, 1998, p.60.

32 <http://www.derm.qld.gov.au/property/placenames/search.php?search=welford>.

33 Durack, *Grass Castles*, 2008, p.140; K Willey, *The Drovers*, 1982, p.45.

34 Durack, *Grass Castles*, 2008, p.140.

35 Richards, 'Question of Necessity', PhD, Griffith University, Brisbane, 2005, Appendix A, p.349.

36 H Tolcher, *Conrick of Nappa Merrie*, Linden Park, Adelaide, 1997, p.17.

37 T House of Currawilla Station, letter 28 April 1959, published in *Local Government* (magazine), October 1960. Personal communication with P Gorecki, article cited in email 1 April 2011.

38 Durack, *Grass Castles*, 2008, p.139.

39 B J Reyment, *My Towri*, Tabra Press, Morningside, 1970, p.7.

40 M Henry, *From City to the Sandhills of Birdsville*, Copyright Publishing, Brisbane, 1994, p.71.

41 D Huggonson, 'Cecil "Ngaka" Ebsworth', *Journal of the Royal Historical Society of Queensland (JRHSQ)*, Vol.XIV, No. 3, August 1990, p.113.

42 K Willey, *The Drovers*, 1982, p.45 & 47.

43 M Copland, J Richards and A Walker, *One Hour More Daylight*, Social Justice Commission, Catholic Diocese of Toowoomba, Toowoomba, 2006, p.78.

44 Tolcher, *Conrick of Nappa Merrie*, 1997, p.22.

45 J Richards, *The Secret War: A True History of Queensland's Native Police*, 2008, University of Queensland Press (UQP), pp.236–38.

46 H M Tolcher, *Seed of the Coolibah, A History of the Yandruwandha and Yawarrawarrka*, Linden Park, Adelaide, 2003, p.3; Tolcher, *Conrick of Nappa Merrie*, 1997, pp.17–23.

47 Tolcher, *Conrick of Nappa Merrie*, 1997, pp.20–24; Richards, *The Secret War*, 2008, p.261.

48 Willey, *The Drovers*, 1982, p.47.

49 E H McFarlane, *Land of Contrasts: Recollections*, W R Smith & Paterson, Fortitude Valley, 1976, p.16.

50 W Olliffe, *Adelaide Chronicle*, 23 May 1935, p.13. Surveyor G C Watson stayed with Dunne at the Thargomindah Native Police Barracks until the end of December 1875, 'Building the Commonwealth, A Record of Forty Years in the Civil Service of Queensland', in *Warrego and South West Queensland Historical Society Collection of Papers, Cunnamulla and District*, Vol.1, 1969, pp.18–19 (of paper).

51 Tolcher, *Seed of the Coolibah*, 2003, p.132. n.11 Queensland State Archives (QSA), Col. Sec. letter 76/812.

52 Richards, *The Secret War*, 2008, p.232. See also QSA, A/38756 file on W F Cheeke who identifies Dunne's condition, p.6.

53 McKellar, *Matya-Mundu*, 1984, p.57; Willey, *The Drovers*, 1950, pp.46–47; Tolcher, *Conrick of Nappa Merrie*, 1997, pp.63–64; Tolcher, *Seed of the Coolibah*, 2003, p.132: 'Accounts of what happened during their presence there have been passed down through the Conrick family, who were then Doyle's and Nutting's neighbours, with a consistency of detail which implies accuracy . . . According to the Conricks, the cattle-spearers were not local, but people from the "dry country" away from the river.'

54 Richards, *The Secret War*, 2008, pp.227–28. Cheeke went through a series of government appointments and was admitted to Dunwich in 1917 as he was destitute, 37 years after he finished with the Native Police.

55   McKellar, *Matya-Mundu*, 1984, p.19.

56   C G Austen, 'History of South-West Corner of Queensland', *JRHSQ*, Vol.II, No.1, September 1959, p.218.

57   Tolcher, *Conrick of Nappa Merrie*, 1997, p.46; Willey, *The Drovers*, 1950, pp.53–54.

58   *Queenslander*, 24 May 1879, p.668, 'Native Police Duty in the West'.

59   *Queenslander*, 24 May 1879.

60   Cited by C Nolan, *Sand Hills and Channel Country*, Diamantina Shire Council, Bedourie, 2003, pp.61–62.

61   Cited in Nolan, *Sand Hills and Channel Country*, 2003, pp.61–62.

62   G Farwell, *Land of Mirage, The Story of Men, Cattle and Camels on the Birdsville Track*, Cassell & Co, Melbourne, 1950, p.131.

63   Farwell, *Land of Mirage*, 1950, p.132.

64   McFarlane, *Land of Contrasts: Recollections*, W R Smith & Paterson, Fortitude Valley, 1976, p.16.

65   N Watton, 'Where Rivers Feed a Creek', in *Australian Shooters Journal*, July 1989, pp.34–35.

66   Farwell, *Land of Mirage*, 1950, p.160.

67   Richards, *The Secret War*, 2008, p.244. The Eyres Creek Native Police barracks operated from 1881 to 1889. Richards, "A Question of Necessity", PhD, Griffith University, Brisbane, 2005, p.350.

68   P L Watson, *Frontier Land and Pioneer Legends*, 1998, p. 61.

69   Durack, *Grass Castles*, (1959) 2008, p.138.

70   Durack, *Grass Castles*, (1959) 2008, pp.139–40.

71   H C Perry, *Pioneering, the Life of the Hon. R M Collins MLC*, Watson, Ferguson & Co., Brisbane, 1923, p.180.

72   S O'Neill & W Collins, 'Robert Martin Collins', *Australian Dictionary of Biography ADB Online*.

73   A J Vogan, *The Black Police, A Story of Modern Australia*, Hutchinson & Co, London, 1890.

74   L Hercus, 'Tales of Ngadu-Dagali' in *Aboriginal History*, 1977, Vol.1, p.55.

75   L Hercus in L Hercus & P Sutton (eds), *This Is What Happened: Historical Narratives by Aborigines*, Australian Institute of Aboriginal Studies, Canberra, 1986, pp.183–84.

76   M M Irinjili & L Hercus in L Hercus & P Sutton (eds), *This Is What Happened*, 1986, pp.187–90.

77   Farwell, *Land of Mirage*, 1950.

78   Tolcher, *Seed of the Coolibah*, 2003, p.130.

79   Hercus, 'Tales of Ngadu-Dagali' in *Aboriginal History*, Vol.1, p.55.

80   B Murray to L Hercus, 'Tales of Ngadu-Dagali', pp.60–62.

81   Personal communication with P Gorecki, email 1 April 2011.

Chapter 5 Poisonings and Sexual Exploitation

1   *Brisbane Courier*, 10 August 1872, p.5.

2   Queensland Museum Inwards Correspondence Archive 15/1043.

3   D Horne, *The Australian People*, Angus & Robertson, Sydney, 1972, pp.53–55.

4   For example, Jack Kane participated in the Skull Pocket–Mulgrave River–Skeleton Creek battue, from the southern Atherton Tablelands to the outskirts of Cairns in 1884 as an eighteen-year-old, and was interviewed by Dr Norman Tindale on the Birdsell/Tindale Expedition of 1938. T Bottoms, *A History of Cairns—City of the South Pacific 1770–1995*, PhD, Central Queensland University, Rockhampton, 2002, pp.148–54.

5   Clipping from the *Daily News and Mail*, 29 July 1933, Father Leo Haye's book of press cuttings, No.36, p.40, Fryer Library Collection, University of Queensland Library.

6   JVD Coutts, 'The Coutts Family', 1950, JOL P929.2 cou c1, p.1; Captain Thomas Coutts' family arrived at the Clarence River on *ss Phoenix* on 19th February 1848; *Maitland Mercury & Hunter River General Advertiser*, 26 February 1848, p.5; *Sydney Morning Herald*, 7 June 1848, p.4; J Hoff, *Bundjalung Jugan, Bundjalung Country*, Richmond River Historical Society, Lismore, June 2006, p.118.

7   J Lydon, '"no moral doubt . . . "': Aboriginal evidence and the Kangaroo Creek poisoning, 1847–1849', *Aboriginal History*, Vol.20, 1996, p.156, citing Fry 18 Jan 1848, Col. Sec. Corres. Rec. 48/1331; Att. Gen. to Col. Sec., 10 May 1848, 48/7126. See also 'Part II: Transcripts of nineteenth-century documents relating to Kangaroo Creek poisoning', *Aboriginal History*, Vol.20, 1996, pp.166–75.

8   Letter from C Tindal, 28 January 1848, cited by J Hoff, *Bundjalung Country*, 2006, p.119 and J Lydon, 'no moral doubt . . .', *Aboriginal History*, Vol.20, 1996, p.158.

9   Cited by Lydon, 'no moral doubt . . .', *Aboriginal History*, Vol.20, 1996, p.158.

10   Hoff, *Bundjalung Country*, 2006, p.119.

11   *Sydney Morning Herald*, 5 June 1856 and *Moreton Bay Courier*, 7 June 1856.

12   J V D Coutts, 'The Coutts Family', 1950, p.6, State Library of Queensland.

13   *Brisbane Courier*, 4 January 1870, p.3.

14   W Coote, *History of the Colony of Queensland: From 1770 to the close of the year 1881*, William Thorne, Brisbane, Vol.1, 1882, pp.45–46.

15   At the time of Hornet Bank (1857) R R Mackenzie was in partnership with Serocold in the station Cockatoo. Denholm has observed, that: 'His attitude to the blacks need not have followed logically from this fact, but in the event it did. His questioning of one witness constituted a restatement of the propositions of the 1840s, that the execution of the Myall Creek murderers in 1838 was "judicial murder", that the "Exeter Hall" influence in colonial affairs had been pernicious, and that the blacks understood only superior strength. ('Select Committee . . . Native Police', *Queensland Votes & Proceedings (QV&P)*, 1861, p.454.) D Denholm, 'Some Aspects of Squatting in NSW and Queensland, 1847–1864', PhD, Australian National University, Canberra, 1972, p.361. R R Mackenzie was Colonial Secretary 15 August 1867–25 November 1868 (after 1901 this position became 'Premier'). *Queensland Past and Present: 100 Years of Statistics, 1896–1996*, Government Statistician's Office, Brisbane, 1998, Table 4.7, p.112.

16   F Eldershaw in his *Australia As It Really Is*, 1851, estimated that there were about 200 Aboriginals in a group that had been cornered and he could not stop his men from shooting: 'Sick of the horrid carnage below, I fain would have retired from the dreadful spot, but all my efforts, entreaties, threats were utterly useless. Shot after shot, with curses wild and deep, the excited fellows launched at their hated foe—their butchered comrades blood was that night fearfully avenged.' G Blomfield, *Baal Belbora—The End of the Dancing*, Alternative Publishing Co-operative, Chippendale, 1988, p.121.

17   D Rye, *Newcastle Morning Herald*, 25 July 1964. Blomfield, *Baal Belbora*, 1988, pp.122, 124.

18   Report from the Select Committee on the Native Police Force, Legislative Assembly, *NSW Legislative Assembly Votes and Proceedings (NSWV&P)*, 1856–57, minutes of evidence, p.41.

19   *QV&P*, Select Committee on the Native Police Force, 1861, p.481.

20   Kilcoy Creek was established in late June–early July 1841. J MacKenzie-Smith, 'Kilcoy, the first six months—Sir Evan Mackenzie's Albatross', *Journal of the Royal Historical Society of Queensland (JRHSQ)*, Vol. XIII, No.12, November 1989, pp.437–39.

21 Dr Simpson, Commissioner for Crown Lands, wrote on 6 May 1843, to the NSW Colonial Secretary: '. . . the Giggarbarah Tribe the one said to have suffered [poisoning] I was not able to meet with . . .', P K Lauer (ed), *Cultural and Historical Records of Queensland*, No.1, October 1979, p.11.

22 Statement of Davis and Bracewell as to the supposed 'Administration of Poison to Some Blacks by White Men', June 1842, John Oxley Library (JOL) Microfilm frames 755–56, also in L P Winterbotham, 'Some Original Views Around Kilcoy', *Queensland Ethnohistory Transcripts*, Vol.1, No.1, G and B Langevad (eds), UQ Anthropology Museum, p.5; C. Petrie, *Tom Petrie's Reminiscences of Early Queensland* (1904), Lloyd Neil, Hawthorn, 1975. In December 1842, J D Lang reported that '50–60 natives' were poisoned at one station alone, and that, in retaliation, 'The neighbouring tribes . . . are going to attack and kill the whites whenever they meet with any under any circumstances'. J D Lang and R Ross, Moreton Bay to Col. Sec. Sydney, 16 December 1842, Moreton Bay, p.497. Fryer Collection, UQ ; R Evans and J Walker, '"These Strangers, Where Are They Going?" Aboriginal–European Relations in the Fraser Island and Wide Bay Region 1770–1905,' *Occasional Paper in Anthropology*, No.8, March 1977, Anthropology Museum, UQ, p.47.

23 *QV&P*, 1861, p.477.

24 J Mackenzie-Smith, 'The Kilcoy Poisonings Revisited', *Queensland History Journal (QHJ)* of RHSQ, Vol. 20, No.11, August 2009, p.603.

25 W Coote, *History of the Colony of Queensland*, William Thorne, Brisbane, 1882, Vol.1, p.48.

26 E Thorne, *The Queen of the Colonies; or, Queensland as I knew it, by an eight years' resident*, Sampson Low, Marston, Searle, & Rivington, London, 1876, p.341.

27 E Long, 'Early White Settlement on the Pine River', *JRHSQ*, Vol.16, No.5, February 1997, p.202.

28 D Cryle, *The Press in Colonial Queensland*, University of Queensland Press (UQP) St Lucia, 1989, p.8; R Fisher, 'From Depredation to degradation: The Aboriginal experience at Moreton Bay 1842–1860', in R Fisher (ed), *Brisbane the Aboriginal Presence 1824–1860*, Brisbane History Group, 1992, p.33.

29 *Moreton Bay Courier*, 21 November 1846, 24 April 1847.

30 C C Petrie, *Tom Petrie's Reminiscences of Early Queensland*, Watson Ferguson & Co, Brisbane, 1904, pp.147–48, cited in E Long, 'Early White Settlement on the Pine River', *JRHSQ*, Vol.16, No.5, February 1997, p.202, n.84.

31 Petrie, *Reminiscences*, p.148; also cited in Long, 'Early White Settlement', 1997, p.202.

32 *Sydney Morning Herald*, 13 April 1847; *Moreton Bay Courier*, 24 April 1847.

33 Long, 'Early White Settlement', 1997, p.202.

34 E Foreman, *The History and Adventures of a Queensland Pioneer*, Exchange Printing Co, Brisbane, 1928, pp.19–20.

35 William Stamer, *Recollections of a Life of Adventure*, Vol.2, Hurst & Blackett Publishers, London, 1866, p.98.

36 J Lennon's 'Workbook for History of Maryborough 1842–1924,' manuscript Maryborough Historical Society.

37 F Wheeler to Commissioner of Police, 1 August 1872, Queensland State Archives QSA, Col/A170 72/1484.

38 J Richards, *The Secret War: A True History of Queensland's Native Police*, UQP, 2008, p.266.

39 Personal communication with Ray Rex, email 1 March 2011. Ray was former Manager and Co-ordinator for the Cairns TAFE Ranger Program and in 1991–92 conducted a week-long fieldtrip with Aboriginal rangers and Elders at Battle Camp.

40 H Finch-Hatton, *Advance Australia*, W H Allen & Co, London, 1886, pp.133–34. Carl Lumholtz
    (*Among Cannibals*, 1889, rpt.1980) also mentions Long Lagoon (p.373).

41 Australian Dictionary of Biography, *ADB*, *Online Edition*.

42 Personal communication with Jim Foley, Mackay Historical Society, email 28 February 2010.

43 *Early Settlers of Mackay*, Mackay Historical Society, <www.mackayhistory.org>.

44 <http://finch.customer.netspace.net.au/fhhistory.html>.

45 S Babidge, *Written True, Not Gammon! A history of Aboriginal Charters Towers*, Black Ink Press,
    Thuringowa, 2007, p.5. Sally Babidge interviewed an array of Aboriginal informants who
    'referred to massacre sites they knew of in the Charters Towers Region'. Personal communication,
    email 18 January 2010. See also S Babidge, 'Family Affairs: an historical anthropology of state
    practice and Aboriginal age in a rural town, North Queensland,' PhD, James Cook University,
    Townsville, 2004.

46 N Loos, *Invasion and Resistance*, Australian National University Press (ANUP), Canberra, 1982,
    p.57.

47 *Hodgkinson Mining News*, 31 August 1878.

48 *Cairns Post*, 8 June 1887.

49 *Port Denison Times*, 21 February 1874; J Black, *North Queensland Pioneers*, CWA, Townsville,
    1931, p.57; Mrs Halpapp's recollections; 'One of the methods used to stop thieving was to put
    strychnine in the flour', F M Bell, 'Camboon Reminiscences', *Historical Society of Queensland
    Journal*, Vol IV, No.1, December 1948, p.58.

50 T Bottoms, 'History of Kowanyama', Kowanyama Land & Natural Resource Management
    Office, Kowanyama Aboriginal Council, Kowanyama Elders, Kowanyama, 1990, p.4.

51 PL Watson, *Frontier Lands and Pioneer Legends*, Allen & Unwin, St Leonards, 1998, p.89, citing
    the Vogan quote from 'The case for the Aborigines', unpublished manuscript, Hayes Collection,
    University of Queensland Library, 2/2579, undated.

52 B Hardy, *Lament for the Barkindji*, Rigby, Adelaide 1976, p.97.

53 'Select Committee on the Aborigines Bill', minutes of evidence, South Australian Parliamentary
    Papers, 1899, Vol.2, No.77, pp.113–14.

54 H Fisher, Letter to Archibald Meston, [Southern] Protector of Aborigines, QSA, COL/139-
    COL/144, 1900.

55 Watson, *Frontier Lands and Pioneer Legends* 1998, p.89, citing H Fisher, Letter to Archibald
    Meston, [Southern] Protector of Aborigines, QSA, COL/139-COL/144, 1900.

56 R Evans, '"Don't You Remember Black Alice, Sam Holt?" Aboriginal Women in Queensland
    History', *Hecate*, Vol.VIII, No.2, 1982, p.12.

57 A McGrath, 'Aboriginal Women Workers in the NT, 1911–1939', *Hecate*, Vol. IV, No.2, July
    1978. D Rose, *Hidden Histories. Black Stories from Victoria River Downs, Humbert River, and
    Wave Hill stations, North Australia*, Aboriginal Studies Press, Canberra, 1991. See also T Roberts,
    Frontier Justice, UQP, St Lucia, 2005.

58 *Recollections of Thomas Davis*, manuscript, collected by Steele Rudd, in the possession of J T Bell,
    c.1908–9, p.8 <http://espace.library.uq.edu.au/QU:216890>.

59 Wondai Gumbal was located on Tchanning Creek, about 20 kilometres south of the township of
    Jackson, south-east of Roma.

60 *Recollections of Thomas Davis*, p.9.

61 T Egan and R Ingpen, *The Drover's Boy*, Lothian Books, Port Melbourne, 1997.

62 John T Swann letter to C Lilley, Justice Department, 21 December 1891. QSA, COL/713
    92/12790.

63   Inspector A Douglas to Police Commissioner, 4 October 1892, QSA, COL/A713, 92/12790.

64   J Hamilton to Colonial Secretary, 1 November 1880, QSA, COL/A306, 81/296. Hamilton notes
      that the event took place some eighteen months earlier, probably in early 1878.

65   W E Roth, 14 August 1901, QSA, A/45400.

66   Inspector P D Galbraith 30 January 1904, QSA, A/44680/04/226.

67   'Alleged Outrages Committed on the Aborigines in Queensland by the Native Mounted Police',
      QV&P, 1875, p.623.

68   W E Parry-Okedon, *Report on North Queensland Aborigines and the Native Police with Appendices*,
      Government Printer, Brisbane, 1897, p.10.

69   'Shall we admit the blacks?', *Port Denison Times*, 1 May 1869.

Chapter 6   Early Gulf and Central Queensland

1   H McKellar, *Matya-Mundu, A History of the Aboriginal People of South West Queensland*,
     Cunnamulla Australian Native Welfare Association, 1984, p.19.

2   F Walker, 'Exploration Expedition, Copy of Mr Walker's Journal from Rockhampton to the
     Albert River, Gulf of Carpentaria', *Argus* (Melbourne), 15 April 1862, p.7. Stawell River named
     for the president of the Victorian Exploration Committee that sponsored Walker's Expedition. It
     is likely that it was the Mitjamba, as Tindale identifies their approximate traditional area which
     includes the Stawell River where this event occurred. N Tindale, *Aboriginal Tribes of Australia*,
     Canberra, 1974.

3   *Argus* (Melbourne) 16 April 1862, p.7.

4   Starting in mid-1863, McIntyre was delayed at the beginning of 1864 by the Upper Darling River
     being in flood. Queensland's quarantine restrictions meant that he could not move his stock
     north. He used the opportunity to explore the Paroo, Bulloo and Barcoo Rivers and then made
     his way to the Gulf. Along the way two trees with 'L' carved into them were observed, along with
     capturing two very old horses, which suggested to him that these might be an indication of the
     lost Ludwig Leichhardt. McIntyre returned to Melbourne and was then sponsored by the Ladies
     Leichhardt Search Expedition. *Brisbane Courier*, 17 January 1865, 'Late Exploration on the Shores
     of Carpentaria (From the *Riverina Herald*, Dec. 31)', p.7.

5   *Brisbane Courier*, 17 January 1865, 'From the Darling to Carpentaria (from the *Pastoral Times*)',
     p.10.

6   *Brisbane Courier*, 17 January 1865, p.10.

7   My emphasis. *Brisbane Courier*, 17 January 1865, p.10.

8   Roberts cites: *Brisbane Courier,* 20 March 1875, 20 November 1876; *Northern Standard*, 5 June 1934;
     T Traine, *Across the Barkly Tableland to the Kimberleys: Memories and Experiences of a Pioneer*,
     Unpublished manuscript, Northern Territory State Library, c.1920, p.13; A Chambers, *Battlers
     of the Barkly: The Family Saga of Eva Downs 1936–1960*, Central Queensland University Press,
     Rockhampton, 1998, p.55.

9   T Roberts, *Frontier Justice: A History of the Gulf Country to 1900*, University of Queensland Press
     (UQP), St Lucia, 2005, p.99.

10   Henry to his mother, 30 December 1863, *Henry Manuscript*, cited in A Allingham, *'Taming
     the Wilderness': the First Decade of Pastoral Settlement in the Kennedy District*, Studies in North
     Queensland History, No.1, History Department, James Cook University (JCU), Townsville, 1988,
     p.69, n.10.

11   G C Bolton, *A Thousand Miles Away*, Australian National University Press (ANUP), Canberra, 1975, p.16.

12   R Fitzgerald, *A History of Queensland: From The Dreaming To 1915*, UQP, St Lucia, 1986, p.134.

13   B Breslin, *Exterminate With Pride, Aboriginal–European Relations in the Townsville–Bowen Region to 1869*, Department of History & Politics, JCU, Townsville, 1992, p.55. See Dalrymple's evidence given on 12 July 1860, in 'Evidence Taken Before the Select Committee Appointed to Enquire Into the Efficiency and Management of the Police Force', 1860.

14   N Loos, *Invasion and Resistance—Aboriginal–European Relations on the North Queensland Frontier 1861–1897*, ANUP, Canberra, 1982, p.29.

15   T Bottoms, '"Djarrugan the Last of the Nesting": A Revisionist Interpretation of Aboriginal–European Relations in the Cairns Rainforest Region up to 1876,' MA(Qual), JCU, Cairns, 1990, pp.23–29. See also Queensland State Archives (QSA) A/45400, report of the Northern Protector of Aborigines for Queensland, Dr W E Roth, 14 August 1901, p.3: 'These Aboriginal trade routes have of course been adopted from times immemorial on account of the suitability of certain waterholes, grass, native foods, etc., and so in great measure have come to be utilized as stock routes indicated in the map by dotted lines.' Both the Coast and Hedley's tracks are shown on Roth's map.

16   G C Bolton, *A Thousand Miles Away*, ANUP, Canberra, (1963) 1975, p.37.

17   Breslin, *Exterminate With Pride*, 1992; p.60, see also pp.61–68.

18   J Kerr, *Black Snow and Liquid Gold, A History of the Burdekin Shire*, Council of the Shire of Burdekin, Ayr, 1994, p.35.

19   'Regulation 11: The officers are not to allow any person unconnected with the Native Police Force to interfere with or *accompany them*, or give orders to any of the troopers under their command.' Appendix 5: Native Police Regulations as published in *Queensland Government Gazette* (10 March 1866), J Richards, '"A Question of Necessity": The Native Police in Queensland', PhD, Griffith University, Brisbane, 2005, p.374. My emphasis. See: <www.aconspiracyof silence.com.au>.

20   Dalrymple to Colonial Secretary, 28 June 1862, QSA, COL/A30 62/1534.

21   *Courier* (Brisbane), Tuesday 10 November 1863, p.2.

22   *Australian Dictionary of Biography (ADB) Online*, Sir Robert George Wyndham Herbert (1831–1905) & Walter Jervoise Scott (1835–1890) and Arthur Scott (1833–1895). Herbert persuaded Scott to become a partner.

23   1 January 1864. Bolton, *A Thousand Miles Away*, (1963) 1975, p.27.

24   G C Bolton, William Hann (1837–1889), *ADB Online*.

25   *The Australasian Pastoralists' Review*, 15 June 1899, p.218.

26   *The Australasian Pastoralists' Review*, 15 June 1899, p.218.

27   S Babidge, *Written True, Not Gammon! A History of Aboriginal Charters Towers*, Black Ink Press, Thuringowa, 2007, p.5. Sally Babidge interviewed Harry Santo and Kevin Burdekin (August 2001), Kevin Burdekin (30 July 2004), Bob Masso (20 & 23 April 2004, 14 December 2005) and Willie Santo (17 August 2002) as part of her doctoral research, where 'the people listed referred to massacre sites they knew of in the Charters Towers Region'. Personal communication, email 18 January 2010. 'William Jones . . . who grew up on stations throughout the Charters Towers area was told by his grandparents stories of massacres that occurred on stations in the vicinity, and in particular that there were "many killings around the Lolworth area".' S Babidge, 'Family Affairs: an historical anthropology of state practice and Aboriginal agency in a rural town, North Queensland', PhD, JCU, Townsville, 2004, p.42.

28   Language name, J Dymock, 'Historical material relevant to Nicholson River Claim area', Northern Land Council, Darwin, 1982, p.75.

29   The brothers lost three-quarters of their horses and a quarter of their cattle. J Wenger, *The Etheridge, Studies in North Queensland History No.13*, JCU, Department of History, Townsville, 1990, p.12.

30   F J Byerley (ed), *Narrative of the Overland Expedition of Messrs Jardine, from Rockhampton to Cape York, North Queensland*, J W Buxton, Brisbane, 1867, facsimile: Bundaberg, Corkwood Press, 1995, p.34.

31   On west coast Cape York Peninsula. *Private Journal of the Surveyor Attached to the Messrs Frank and Alexander Jardine's Overland Expedition to Cape York*, 1867, Corkwood Press, North Adelaide, 1997, p.26.

32   L Hiddins (Intro), *The Journals of the Jardine Brothers and Surveyor Richardson on the Overland Expedition from Rockhampton to Somerset, Cape York*, 1867, Corkwood Press, North Adelaide, facsimile edition 1998, p.50.

33   *Private Journal of the Surveyor*, p.40.

34   D Day, *Claiming a Continent: A New History of Australia*, HarperCollins, Sydney, 1997, p.169.

35   Personal communication with Mrs Alma Wason, Okunjen Elder, Kowanyama, 5 May 1998.

36   A Laurie, 'The Black War in Queensland', *Journal of the Royal Historical Society of Queensland (JRHSQ)*, Vol.1, No. 1, September 1959, p.166.

37   R Cannon, *Savage Scenes from Australia: Being a Short History of the Settlement at Somerset, Cape York*, Helfmann, Valparaiso, 1885, p.30.

38   J Dymock, *Nicholson river (Waanyi-Garawa) land claim: historical material relevant to Nicholson River land claim area*, Northern Land Council, Darwin, 1982, p.14.

39   G Sutherland, *Pioneering Days, thrilling incidents across the wilds of Queensland, with sheep, to the Northern Territory, in the early Sixties*, W H Wendt & Co, Brisbane, 1913, p.12.

40   Dymock, 1982, p.17.

41   Sutherland, *Pioneering Days*, 1913, p.10.

42   E Palmer, *Early Days in North Queensland*, Angus & Robertson, Sydney, 1903, p.102.

43   Dymock, 1982, pp.15–25.

44   Uhr's friend, Arthur Ashwin, went on to state that ' . . . for years after there were about two hundred gins and no bucks'. Roberts considers that Ashwin exaggerated the numbers killed, but that they 'may well have acted excessively on this occasion, far from the nearest white witnesses, both to punish the presumed killers and to make the [stock] route safe for other travellers'. T Roberts, *Frontier Justice: A History of the Gulf Country to 1900*, UQP, St Lucia, 2005, p.12 n.27: A C Ashwin, *Gold to Grass: The Reminiscences of Arthur C Ashwin 1850–1930, Prospector and Pastoralist*, Hesparian Press, Victoria Park, 2002.

45   *Brisbane Courier*, 9 June 1868.

46   30+14+9+8=61.

47   J Richards, *The Secret War: A True History of Queensland's Native Police*, UQP, St Lucia, 2008, p.264.

48   Roberts, *Frontier Justice*, 2005, p.13.

49   W H Corfield, *Reminiscences of Queensland 1862–1899*, A H Frater, Brisbane, 1921, p.25.

50   H Fysh, *Taming the North*, Angus & Robertson, Sydney, 1933 (revised 1950), p.174.

51   W Turnbull, letter dated 10 March 1896 and published in *Science of Man*, 1 June 1911, p.40.

52   Bowen to Carnarvon, Despatch 61, 12 November 1866 (sub-enclosed in Enclosure 3), QSA, GOV/24.

53 Korah Halcomb Wills Diary Extracts, John Oxley Library, Henry Brandon Collection, Box 8946, OM 75–75.

54 C Fetherstonhaugh, *After Many Days: Being the Reminiscences of Cuthbert Fetherstonhaugh*, E W Cole, Melbourne, 1917.

55 Fetherstonhaugh, 1917, pp.270–74; K Willey, *The Drovers*, Macmillan, South Melbourne, 1982, p.44. Although Uhr's Christian name is not mentioned, we know the event happened in 1864. Reginald joined the Native Police the previous year and became a Sub-Inspector in 1864. His brother (Wentworth) D'Arcy Uhr was appointed to the same rank in 1865. Richards, *Secret War*, 2008, p.264.

56 Personal communication with Col McLennan, 18 March 2009.

57 J Wright, *The Cry for the Dead*, Oxford University Press (OUP) Melbourne, 1981, p.146.

58 Close to today's township of Moranbah. See Wright, *Cry for the Dead*, 1981, p.152. Fort Cooper was a Native Police Barracks from 1868 to 1879. See J Richards, '"A Question of Necessity": The Native Police in Queensland', PhD, Griffith University, Brisbane, 2005, p.349.

59 Wright, *Cry for the Dead*, 1981, inside dust jacket.

60 L McDonald, *Rockhampton—A History of City and District*, UQP, St Lucia, 1981, p.185.

61 'De Satge's elder sister, Ernestine, married Gordon Sandeman in 1862. In 1863 de Satge sold most of his leases but retained Wolfang Downs in partnership with James Milson, with whom he bought Coreena Station, near Aramac, in 1872. They sold Wolfang in 1875 for £100,000 . . . De Satge sold Coreena in 1881 for £70,000. With Milson and other partners, he purchased Carandotta (three-million acres [1.2 million hectares] on the Georgina River) and Augustus Downs on the Leichhardt River . . . While at Carandotta, de Satge formed a liaison with an Aboriginal woman and fathered two sons and a daughter. One of the sons, Thomas, followed his father's earlier calling as a drover but, being Aboriginal, neither he, nor subsequently his daughter, Ruby, were entitled, under the Queensland Aborigines Act, to own any of their father's vast holdings. Ruby de Satge was a drover.' <http://www.parliament.qld.gov.au/apps/formermembers/members/memberBio1.aspx?m_id=263 (accessed 23/10/12)>.

62 Oscar de Satgé, *Pages from the Journal of a Queensland Squatter*, Hurst & Blackett, London, 1901, p.147.

63 *ADB Online*. See also *Qld Parliamentary Debates*. 27 June 1866, Debate on Diseases in Cattle and Sheep Bill. Anne Allingham identified: 'The member for Burnett Mr Haly stated that the quality of native pasture diminished rapidly after initial stocking and cited instances . . . Oscar de Satgé agreed . . .' (p.102). Haly also 'pointed to overstocking as a form of pasture abuse, and denounced the current land legislation as "those miserable land laws", with a limit of fourteen year tenure which encouraged graziers to stock heavily and exploit the land for quick returns'. A Allingham, *'Taming the Wilderness': the First Decade of Pastoral Settlement in the Kennedy District*, Studies in North Queensland History, No.1, History Department, JCU, Townsville, 1988, p.103.

64 P L Watson, *Frontier Lands and Pioneer Legends—How pastoralists gained Karuwali land*, Allen & Unwin, St Leonards, 1998, p.24.

65 G A Mayers, *Behold Nebo, a history of the Nebo Shire*, R & R Publication, Nebo, 1996, pp.19–21; personal communication with Col McLennan, Jangga descendant, 18 March 2009.

66 G Carrington, *Colonial Adventures and Experiences by a University Man*, Bell & Daldy, London, 1871, p.153.

67 Carrington, *Colonial Adventures*, 1871, pp.152–53.

68 D Cryle, *The Press in Colonial Queensland*, UQP, St Lucia, 1989, p.61.

69 Cryle, *Press in Colonial Queensland*, p.61; *Maryborough Chronicle*, 12 December 1860, p.4.

70   QSA, 1867 A/36335; *QV&P*, 1867, p.985.

71   Inspector Murray to Police Commissioner (13 July 1867) QSA, Midlands Inspector's Letterbook, A/36335 67/113.

72   Richards, *Secret War*, 2008, p.104.

73   E Hatte, email to author 9 February 2011.

Chapter 7   Far North Queensland and Cape York Peninsula

1   John Fraser, *The Aborigines of Australia*, Institution Ethnographique, 1882, p. 3.

2   *Queenslander*, 23 October 1880.

3   *Townsville Daily Bulletin*, 13 April 1966, 'About this time [1871] . . . Robert Johnstone was appointed Inspector of the Native Mounted Police. He was stationed at Waterview, and [he and his] troopers were continually after hostile natives . . .' Waterview was a Native Police Barracks from 1872 to 1877. J Richards, '"A Question of Necessity": The Native Police in Queensland', PhD, Griffith University, Brisbane, 2005, p.349. See also, J Richards, *The Secret War: A True History of Queensland's Native Police*, University of Queensland Press (UQP), St Lucia, 2005, Appendix 2, p.241.

4   T Bottoms, 'Djarrugan—the Last of the Nesting', MA(Qual), James Cook University (JCU), Cairns, 1990, pp.174–81.

5   Queensland State Archives (QSA), COL/A184 73/1354.

6   Richards, *The Secret War*, 2008, p.241.

7   P Sutton, 'Gugu Badhun and Its Neighbours', MA, Macquarie University, 1973.

8   J Black, *North Queensland Pioneers*, CWA, Charters Towers, 1931, p.42a.

9   Black, *NQ Pioneers*, 1931, p.42. Jan Wegner identifies that: 'Ezra could not have been at Hornet Bank in 1857, when the massacre occurred; he may have been near Cullen-la-Ringo when the Wills family was killed by Aborigines in 1861. The tradition, however, is important in showing the Firths' attitudes to Aborigines even before reaching the Etheridge.' J Wegner, *The Etheridge, Studies in North Queensland History No.13*, JCU, History Department, Townsville, 1990, p.7 n.23.

10   H Fysh, *Taming the North*, Angus & Robertson, Sydney, 1933 (revised edition 1950), p.186.

11   *Croydon Mining News*, 27 August 1904, cited in P Freier, '"Living with *Munpitch*"—A History of the Mitchell River Mission', PhD, JCU, Townsville, November 1999, p.74.

12   G C Bolton, *A Thousand Miles Away*, Australian National University Press (ANUP), Canberra, (1963) 1975, p.44.

13   Bolton, *A Thousand Miles Away*, 1975, pp.45–46.

14   J V Mulligan, *To the Palmer River and Normanby Gold Fields, North Queensland*, George Slater & Co., Brisbane, 1875, p.5.

15   Mulligan's 5th Prospecting Expedition of June 1875 ['Mulligan's Palmer Expedition', *Queensland Votes and Proceedings (QV&P)*, 1876, Vol.3, (p.6 of report), p.400]. See R M W Dixon, & G Koch, *Dyirbal Song Poetry*, UQP, St Lucia, 1996, p.11; & T G Birtles, 'Trees to Burn: Settlement in the Atherton-Evelyn Rainforest', *North Australia Research Bulletin*, No.8, September 1982, figure 4, p.12.

16   Mulligan, *To the Palmer River and Normanby Gold Fields*, 1875, p.10.

17   Carrington is just outside the township of Atherton, to the south-west. Mulligan's 5th Prospecting Expedition of June 1875 ['Mulligan's Palmer Expedition', *QV&P*, 1876, Vol.3, (p.6 of report), p.400].

18   'It was also known as Gangaarr, which refers to a hexagonal shaped, quartz rock found in the
     area . . . Archibald Meston . . . refers to the place as Janellganell. But this refers to a rocky outcrop
     behind the beach.' H J Pohlner, *Gangurru*, Hope Vale Mission Board, Milton, 1986, p.20.

19   W J Webb in R L Jack, *Northmost Australia*, Vol II, George Robertson & Co, Brisbane, 1922, p.421.

20   *Brisbane Telegraph*, 22 January 1874.

21   N Kirkman, 'The Palmer Goldfield, 1873–1883', Honours Thesis, JCU, Townsville, 1984, p.268.

22   Statement of Members of the Expedition from the Endeavour River to the Palmer River before
     Police Magistrate Thomas Hamilton, 26 March 1874, QSA, COL/A194 74/701. If one considers
     the precedents of violence on the frontier since the late 1830s, one can only wonder why this event
     should be any different. See Kirkman, 'The Palmer Goldfield,' 1984, pp.268–72, as she offers an
     insight into the hollowness of the miners' declaration.

23   Webb in R L Jack, *Northmost Australia*, 1922, Vol II, pp.421–22.

24   Personal communication with Ray Rex, email 1 March 2011. Ray was former Manager and
     Co-ordinator for the Cairns TAFE Ranger Program and in 1991–92 conducted a week-long
     fieldtrip with Aboriginal rangers and Elders at Battle Camp. His informant was Jack Harrigan
     whose mother survived the killings.

25   *Queenslander*, 19 June 1880; reproduced in 'The Way We Civilise; Black and White; The Native
     Police', *Queenslander*, Brisbane, 1880, V, p.20.

26   Kirkman, 'The Palmer Goldfield,' 1984, p.274. See *Cooktown Herald*, 8 December 1875.

27   Kirkman, 'The Palmer Goldfield', 1984, p.278.

28   Richards, *The Secret War*, 2008, Appendix 2, p.229; see also QSA, JUS/N41, inquest 274/1874.

29   Richards, *The Secret War*, 2008, Appendix A: A nominal roll of the European members of the
     Native Police, pp.229–30, 231, 263. W H Corfield, 'Reminiscences of North Queensland,
     1862–1878', *Journal of the Royal Historical Society of Queensland (JRHSQ)*, Vol 2, 1935, p.91.

30   Kirkman, 'The Palmer Goldfield', 1984, p.278.

31   Corfield, 'Reminiscences of North Queensland, 1862–1878,' 1935, p.93. Corfield (1843–1927) gave
     this paper as a talk on 18 August 1920, when he was 77 years old.

32   W H Corfield, 'Reminiscences of North Queensland, 1862–1878', JRHSQ, Vol 2, 1935, pp.94–95.

33   'Close relatives might also carry remains of their loved ones around in their shoulder bags on their
     seasonal movements.' T Bottoms, 'Djarrugan—the Last of the Nesting', MA (Qual), JCU, Cairns,
     1990, p.84. See E Mjöberg, *Amongst Stone Age People in the Queensland Wilderness*, 1918, translated
     by S M Fryer for the John Oxley Library, Brisbane, 1986, pp.208, 210.

34   Corfield, 'Reminiscences', 1935, pp.94–95.

35   G Pike, *Chasing the Rainbow: The Golden Gullies of the Palmer*, Pinevale Publications, Mareeba,
     1993, p.29.

36   *Brisbane Courier*, 1 March 1879, 'Northern News'.

37   QSA, COL A/297 80/4039.

38   QSA, COL A/272 79/858 (Hale's letter dated 4 March 1879). In response from the Colonial
     Secretary, Bishop Hale 'received a brief letter in reply declining to answer any questions'. *Brisbane
     Courier*, 9 June 1880.

39   Both probable (20) and possible (22), with a potential total of 42. For specific details, see Kirkman,
     'The Palmer Goldfield, 1873–1883', 1984, pp.314–15.

40   Kirkman, 1984, p.322.

41   Interview with Mick McNamarra (2b) by Bruce & Jenepher Lingelbach, Mt Molloy, FNQ,
     12 August 1989 in R Edwards, *Fred's Crab*, Ramskull Press, Kuranda, 1989, p.24.

42   'Kaanju homelands (*ngaachi*) stretch from the township of Coen in the centre of Cape York
     Peninsula to around the former Moreton Telegraph Station to the north, covering the headwaters
     of the eastern- and western-flowing river systems that run off the Great Dividing Range.'
     B J Smith, 'Kaanju homelands', <epress.anu.edu.au/caepr_series/no_29/html>.

43   Jack, *Northmost Australia*, 1922, Vol.II, Chapter 88, p.675 & 677.

44   N Loos, *Invasion and Resistance*, ANUP, Canberra, 1982, p.61; See also QSA, A/49714, 89/9436.

45   *Cooktown Courier*, 14 May and 18 June 1889.

46   *Thargomindah Herald*, 30 May 1889 cited in A J Vogan, *The Black Police*, Hutchinson & Co,
     London, 1890, p.137.

47   Merluna Station is c.60 kilometres south, south-east of York Downs, or c.100–110 kilometres
     from Weipa via the Peninsula Developmental Road. QSA, A/49714 89/9436.

48   N Cole, 'Battle Camp to Boralga: a local study of colonial war on Cape York Peninsula,
     1873–1894', in *Aboriginal History*, Vol 28, 2004, p.179. See also Jack, *Northmost Australia*, 1922,
     Vol II, 1922, p.676.

49   Jack, *Northmost Australia*, 1922, Vol II, 1921, p.647.

50   Called Lynd Junction from 1885 until 1896, then Highbury. Lyndon Poingdestre was stationed
     there from 1889 to 1897. Personal Communication Jonathan Richards; see also Richards, *The
     Secret War*, 2008, pp.255–56. Police Inspector Lamond recommended Poingdestre's removal from
     Highbury as he was living with three Aboriginal women (one for 14 years, another for 10 years)
     with whom he had had children, and he was in his 'feeble' health. QSA, A/40323 97/00340.

51   Personal Communication with Viv Sinnamon, Kowanyama Land & Natural Resource
     Management Office, 8 February 2010. The baby girl who was taken from her dead mother's
     breast, died at Chilligoe in the late twentieth century. The grandchildren of other victims are still
     alive in Kowanyama today.

52   P Freier, '"Living with *Munpitch*"—A History of the Mitchell River Mission,' PhD, JCU,
     Townsville, November 1999, p.76. Source: Lofty Yam, tape-recorded interview, 12 November
     1987, Kowanyama, (n.244).

53   Lofty Yam, tape-recorded interview, 12 November 1987, Kowanyama, (n.233) in Freier, '"Living
     with *Munpitch*"', 1999, p.73. Philip Freier is now the Anglican Archbishop of Melbourne.

54   S Mullins, Torres Strait: A History of Colonial Occupation and Culture Contact 1864–1897,
     Central Qld Univ. Press (CQUP), Rockhampton, 1995, p. 22.

55   Mullins, 1995, p.30.

56   Mullins, 1995, p.34. n.30 Jardine to Lt. Genates, Rockhampton, 23 October 1861. Enclosed in
     Jardine to Colonial Secretary, 4 November 1861, QSA, COL/A23, in-letter 2812 of 1861.

57   'The Rev Jagg concluded in 1867, after some investigation, that the axe was not in fact stolen
     by the boy.' N Sharp, *Footprints: Along the Cape York Sandbeaches*, Aboriginal Studies Press,
     Canberra, 1992, p.36.

58   Sharp, 1992, p.36.

59   Sharp, 1992, p.37, n.11: Proceedings of the Executive Council of Queensland, 4 July 1865, p.306.

60   Sharp, 1992, pp.36–7. n.10: Proceedings of the Executive Council of Queensland, 4 July 1865,
     p.304.

61   Sharp, 1992, p.38. n.21: R Cannon, *Savage Scenes from Australia: Being a Short History of the
     Settlement at Somerset, Cape York*, Helfmann, Valparaiso, 1885, pp.27–28. Dr Cannon concludes
     this episode with a description of two of the bodies in the 'blood stained canoe' where:
     'A black hand clenched in the death agony hung over her side and into her got O'Regan and old
     Dan, and raised with difficulty the rigid body of Big nose whose glazed eyes stared at us, as if in

horror. His thigh was red and his bowels hung from another gash. One instant this ghastly sight presented itself. "I knew I gev' iy him in the stomach," said Dan. The next moment there was a plunge and we shuddered to see the distorted corpse go down, down slowly to the coral bottom where a grim shark sailed on like some pale ghost . . . Another poor wretch Tom Pannikan, lay in a pool of blood in the bottom of the canoe and him also they flung overboard to add to the same repast. This picture my friends may be drawn in strong colours but it is strictly true, indeed, too true.' pp.28–29.

62   Sharp, 1992, p.39.
63   Sharp, 1992, p.41.
64   C F Pascoe, *Two Hundred Years of the Society for the Propagation of the Gospel* (SPG), SPG, London, 1901, as cited in J Bayton, *Cross over Carpentaria, being the History of the Church of England in Northern Australia, from 1865–1965*, Smith and Paterson, Brisbane, 1965, p.17.
65   Sharp, 1992, pp.65–73.
66   Sharp, 1992, pp.66–67.
67   Sharp, 1992, p.71. Typescript notes of an interview with Bootles Jardine, taken by P Pinney and given to Nonie Sharp on 2 November 1981.
68   Sharp, 1992, p.72, n.38 Chester to Colonial Secretary, 14 April 1870. QSA, COL/A153 70/1655.
69   Sharp, 1992, p.73.
70   Sharp, 1992, p.78; Mullins, 1995, p.52. Both citing from C Beddome to Colonial Secretary, 11 November, Somerset Letter Book, 1874, QSA, CPS 13c/G1.
71   Sharp, 1992, p.79.
72   F Mackeith (ed), *Letters from Laura, Records of North Queensland History No 1*, History Department, JCU, Townsville, 1987, p.88; See also *Queenslander*, 9 May and 26 December 1896.
73   G White, *Thirty Years in Tropical Australia*, Society for Promoting Christian Knowledge, London, 1918, p.109.
74   White, *Thirty Years*, 1918, p.110.
75   K Jimmy recollection in T Bottoms and V Sinnamon, *An Introduction to Kowanyama*, radio documentary, Kowanyama Land & Natural Resource Management Office, 1991.

Chapter 8   Dark Deeds—The Tully and Cairns Districts

1   Personal communication with E Grant. Dr Ernie Grant is a Jirrbal/Girramay Senior Elder from the Tully region of far north Queensland, and has been researching the treatment of Aboriginal people for 45 years. His mother, Chloe Grant, was one of Professor Bob Dixon's language informants in the 1960s. Ernie was awarded a doctorate from James Cook University in 2009 in acknowledgement of his breadth of knowledge and his effective sharing of this as a teacher and lecturer.
2   R M W Dixon, *The Dyirbal Language of North Queensland*, Cambridge University Press, London, 1972.
3   Kennedy's retrieved notes from Escape River dated Tuesday, 11 July 1848, in Edgar Beale, *Kennedy's Workbook*, Wollongong University College, Wollongong, 1970, p.101.
4   James Morrill, who accompanied Dalrymple as interpreter, had spent seventeen years with Wulgurukaba, Bindal, Juru and Gia on the coastal woodland plains which stretched from about present-day Townsville in the north to Bowen in the south. This is over 200 kilometres from Cardwell. J Morrill, 'Journal of an Expedition to Rockingham Bay', *Port Denison Times*, 26 March

1864. See also B Breslin, *Exterminate with Pride*, James Cook University (JCU), Townsville, 1992; B Breslin, 'Prologue, James Morrill', Manuscript, 1999.

5   Emphasis added. 'Journal of John Ewan Davidson', 7 January 1866, North Queensland Collection, JCU, Townsville.

6   A Laurie, 'The Black War in Queensland', *Journal of the Royal Historical Society of Queensland (JRHSQ)*, Vol.VI, No.1, September 1959.

7   W T Forster, *The Wreck of the Maria*, J Reading and Company, Sydney, 1872, pp.13–14. Forster was on the large raft.

8   Personal communication with E Grant. See Gowlland's Diary, 1872 & Wildsoet Interview.

9   'Alleged Outrages Committed on the Aborigines in Queensland by the Native Mounted Police', *Queensland Votes and Proceedings (QV&P)*, 1875, p.622.

10   T Bottoms, 'Djarrugan—the Last of the Nesting', MA(Qual), JCU, Cairns, 1990, pp.174–79.

11   Sub-Inspector Johnstone to Captain Gowlland, Ship 'Governor Blackall,' 22 March 1872, Annexure No.3 , p.5 of J T Gowlland RN, 'New Guinea Expedition per Brig "Maria." (Correspondence Respecting Rescue and Arrival of Survivors of.)', *NSW Legislative Assembly Votes & Proceedings (NSWV&P)*, 1872.

12   On 21 March 1872, R A 'Johnstone and his trackers having given a very good account of the sixteen he came across' (p.21) and the next day 'Mr Johnstone's trackers [ie troopers] shot 27 of the Blacks in the Camp' (p.22). This totalled 43 Aboriginal people killed. Gowlland, 'New Guinea Expedition per Brig "Maria."', 1872.

13   A Laurie, 'The Black War in Queensland', *JRHSQ*, Vol.VI, No.1, September 1959, p.168.

14   F P Woolston & F S Colliver, 'The Wildsoet Interview—Some Recollections of the Aborigines of the Tully Area', *Queensland Heritage*, Vol.3, No.3, November 1975, p.11.

15   J Moresby, *New Guinea and Polynesia: Discoveries and Surveys in New Guinea and the D'Entrecasteaux Islands*, John Murray, London, 1876, p.42.

16   Interview with Blue Wyatt 18 August 1989 (7e), by C Haan, Ravenshoe, Qld, in R Edwards, *Fred's Crab*, Ramskull Press, Kuranda, 1989, p.133.

17   *Brisbane Courier*, 10 August, 1872.

18   *Brisbane Courier*, 10 August 1872.

19   Queensland State Archives (QSA), COL A/170 72/1289. Alfred Davidson owned a pottery and was a representative of the Aborigines Protection Society in Queensland. He was outraged by the treatment of Aboriginals and lobbied tirelessly against their continued abuse. H Reynolds, *This Whispering In Our Hearts*, Allen & Unwin, St Leonards, 1998, pp.102–5.

20   Queensland State Archives (QSA) COL A/316 81/2895; see also D Jones, *Cardwell Shire Story*, Jacaranda Press, Brisbane, 1961, pp.199–200.

21   *Cleveland Bay Express*, 2 November 1867.

22   Personal communication with E Grant.

23   C Lumholtz, *Among Cannibals*, John Murray, London, 1889, p.373.

24   *Brisbane Courier*, 15 September 1888.

25   A J Vogan, *The Black Police, A Story of Modern Australia*, Hutchinson & Co, London, 1890, pp.220–22. Vogan mis-identifies the date of the article as 16 September, when it was the 15th and it is difficult to identify the year, however, it had to be either 1889 or 1888; and perusal confirms the latter.

26   *Brisbane Courier*, 17 September 1888, p.3. Letter dated 16 September.

27 It has not been possible to independently corroborate Dr Grant's remembrances through primary
    source documentation. These recollections are nevertheless considered fact by the Jirrbal/
    Girramay people.

28 Personal communication to Ernie Grant by Willy Lee (Girramay Elder), May 1954. Personal
    communication by E Grant to T Bottoms, September 2011.

29 N Tindale & J Birdsell, 'Results of the Harvard–Adelaide Universities Anthropological
    Expedition 1938–39, Tasmoid Tribes in North Queensland', Records of the South Australian
    Museum, 7, 1941.

30 Personal communication by E Grant to T Bottoms, September 2011.

31 E Grant personal communication with Chloe Grant. See also R M W Dixon, Searching for
    Aboriginal Languages, Memoirs of a Field Worker, University of Queensland Press (UQP), St Lucia,
    c.1984. Grant knew Wally Simpson, Joe Chalum and Willy Lee (who was also his informant
    about the Kirrima massacre in 1888, where Willy's two brothers and mother and father were
    shot). The other informants who confirmed this: Jack Muriata, George Beeron, Bessy Jerry,
    Davey Lawrence, Tommy Warren and Chloe Grant, among others. Personal communication by
    E Grant to T Bottoms, September 2011.

32 Charles Silver, producer, director & cinematographer, Girrigan Cultural Oral History Recording,
    1987. The 23 hours of film recording of Elders' recollections is in the author's possession.

33 Grant, personal communication with Tommy Warren. Personal communication by E Grant to
    T Bottoms, September 2011.

34 Personal communication by E Grant to T Bottoms, 7 January 2011.

35 E J Banfield, Confessions of a Beachcomber, Angus and Roberston Ltd, 1933 Sydney, pp.279–80.

36 D Jones, Cardwell Shire Story, Jacaranda Press, Brisbane, 1961, p.279.

37 Personal communication with E Grant by his uncles Willie Masina (Innisfail) and Dave
    Barlow (Tully). Daradgee Environmental Centre, 1994. Personal communication by E Grant to
    T Bottoms, September 2011.

38 Personal communication by E Grant to T Bottoms, 8 January 2011.

39 D Jones, Hurricane Lamps and Blue Umbrellas: A History of the Shire of Johnstone to 1973,
    G K Bolton Printers, Cairns, 1973, p.188.

40 Personal communication by E Grant to T Bottoms, September 2011.

41 Cairns Post, 5 November 1943, 'Beadle', p.1.

42 The obituary noted: 'To those who know and appreciate the unfailing loyalty, patience and
    cheerfulness in adversity of the aboriginal [sic], his dogged courage, generosity and good humour,
    there will be nothing remarkable in the story of Beadle's [Boujeri's] rise from a wild myall
    state to that of a useful and highly respected member of a civilised community.' Cairns Post,
    5 November 1943.

43 'Queensland North East Coast Expedition', QV&P, 1874, p.18, para 246.

44 QV&P, 1874, p.18, para 246.

45 QV&P, 1874, p.18, para 247.

46 QV&P, 1874, p.44, 20 October 1873.

47 'There was a meeting of two tribes here this afternoon [at Trubanaman]. Each party bristled
    with spears and they advanced to meet each other short rushes giving vent to loud yells. One
    could think to look at them meeting thus, they were going to have a fight. When the two parties
    got together however the weird wailing began as friends from whom they had been long parted
    perhaps were recognised.' Aboriginal News, Vol.2, No.14, 15 January 1908.

48 Bottoms, 'Djarrugan—the Last of the Nesting', MA(Qual), JCU, Cairns, 1990, pp.195–96.

49   'Queensland North East Coast Expedition', *QV&P*, 1874, p.18, para 247.

50   My emphasis *QV&P*, 1874, p.18, para 248.

51   Between August 1861 and July 1873 there were 34 European deaths along the north Queensland coast, averaging 2.8 deaths per year over the twelve-year period. (Statistics derived from Appendix B, 'Settlers and their Employees Reported Killed as a Result of Aboriginal Resistance in North Queensland Between 1861 and 1897', N Loos, *Invasion and Resistance*, Canberra, 1982, pp.194–210.) It would seem the deaths of fourteen of the original survivors of the wreck *Maria*, and the then recent Green Island Killings, with a total of six non-Aboriginals, may have swayed Dalrymple to exaggerate the number to 'many hundreds'.

52   *QV&P*, 1874, p.20, para 280.

53   Named after Ludwig Leichhardt, the explorer, but 'through a painter's error the name was wrongly spelt', J W Collinson, *More About Cairns, 2.Echoes of the Past*, Smith & Paterson, Brisbane, 1945, p.18, n.1.

54   *QV&P*, 1874, p.21, para 283.

55   *QV&P*, 1874, p.34. 'Fortune seekers from Sydney to Cooktown paid £12 in return for which they had to sleep in a hammock slung in the stuffy and foul-smelling space between decks. Water was anything but good, while the tucker was mostly salt pork and biscuits. It generally took from three to four weeks to cover the distance, which wasn't surprising considering the barque used to drop anchor every night within the Barrier Reef.' *Northern Affairs*, 8 January 1932, p.9.

56   J V Mulligan, *To the Palmer River and Normanby Gold Fields*, George Slater & Co., Brisbane, 1875, p.12.

57   Mulligan, 1875, p.12. Included on the cover as a promotional point following his name was the statement 'Discoverer of the Palmer River Gold Field, and To Whose Party the Government Reward was Awarded'. The guide's sub-headings included: 'The Road to the Palmer via the Normanby Field,' 'Road to the Normanby Gold Field,' 'The Road to the Palmer From Townsville and Etheridge,' 'The Road From Cooktown to the Palmer Through Hell's Gates' and small discussion on 'Health—The Blacks, &c.'

58   *Queenslander*, 8 October 1904. This was a result of Mulligan's seventh prospecting expedition.

59   J W Collinson, *Early Days of Cairns*, Smith & Paterson, Brisbane, 1939, p.10; G Bolton, *A Thousand Miles Away*, ANUP, Canberra, 1963, pp.91–95; D Jones, *Trinity Phoenix*, Cairns and District Centenary Committee 1976, p.51.

60   Jack Kane to Dr N B Tindale, Tindale Expedition Diary, between 11 and 13 September 1938, Harvard–Adelaide Universities Anthropological Expedition, 1938, South Australian Museum, p. 417. Kane was 72 when he recalled these events in 1938. He arrived in Cairns as a sixteen-year-old in 1882.

61   *Dulgubarra* [*dulgu*—'scrub'/rainforest, *barra*—'people belonging to'] Yidinydji, roughly encompassing the area from old Top Gate (on the Gillies Highway) to Lake Barrine to Kulara and Skull Pocket. Personal Communication with respected Yidinydji Elder, Nganygabana (George Davis), 5 January 1999. See R M W Dixon, *Words of Our Country*, UQP, St Lucia, 1991, p.190; see also J Covacevich, A Irvine & G Davis, 'A Rainforest Pharmacopoeia' in J Pearn (ed), *Pioneer Medicine in Australia*, Amphion Press, Brisbane, 1988, pp.159–74.

62   The Acting Director of the Queensland Intelligence and Tourist Bureau in Brisbane, on 3 December 1917, requesting the Queensland Museum receive 'One (1) Case of Ethnological Specimens (Aboriginal skulls) forwarded from Cairns by Messrs Bolands Ltd. At the request of Mr A Meston.' [Queensland Museum, 00599, 5 December 1917 (HSC, D8979)]. Whether these were the bones of those massacred at Skull Pocket may be open to question, however, it does at

least confirm the collection of a large number of skulls and suggests the likelihood of a nefarious act(s) having taken place.

63   Tindale, Expedition Diary, 1938, pp. 413–17.

64   'Coyyan', *Cairns Post Jubilee Supplement*, 1 November 1926, p.19.

65   *Cairns Post*, 20 November 1884. 'The prosecution led conflicting evidence which could not be corroborated through the interpreters. There was strong evidence that Inspector Nicholls [*sic*] instructed the Native Troopers to shoot the Aborigines and burn them, and when their success was reported to Inspector Nicholls [*sic*], he apparently commended the Troopers. However, Judge Cooper discharged the prisoners and dismissed the case . . .' R S Kerr, 'Aborigines & Mining in North Queensland in the 1880s—The Police Commissioner's Dilemma', unpublished article, 1988, cites *Queenslander*, 13 & 24 December 1884, 17 January 1885, 7 February & 2 May 1885; *Herberton Advertiser*, 21, 24, & 28 January 1885; 4 March 1885; *Cairns Post*, 30 January 1885; and QSA, 1885/342, A/18293. Personal communication with Dr Ruth Kerr, 13 February 1999. See also QSA, A/40104, Nichols' Police File. In 1921, 35 years after his dismissal, Nichols tried to claim a pension for his nine years of service with the Native Police, but failed, as he had not resigned as he asserted.

66   *Cairns Post*, 20 November 1884. However, it appears that another incident prior to the Irvinebank killings, where Nichols let 'two prisoners whom he had arrested on warrant' escape, was the reason for his dismissal. QSA, A/40104, 85/1597.

67   Mrs Kate Atherton to Lucy Brown (née Atherton), 19 January 1885, John Oxley Library (JOL), OM67–26/2; An article in *Cairns Post*, 8 January 1885, gives support to Nichols, and then almost contradictorily states that 'although we do not for one moment countenance slaughtering inoffensive [A]boriginals, we maintain that it is a difficult question as to what means shall be resorted to when settlers are being murdered and homesteads plundered by cannibals such as the north Queensland [A]boriginals are'.

68   *Cairns Post*, 22 January 1885.

69   QSA, 1885/342.

70   *Cairns Post*, 15 January 1885. The Mulgrave settlers had been lobbying to have the Native Police Camp at Nigger Creek (now Wondecla) removed to the Mulgrave River where Gordonvale now stands. A week later [*Cairns Post*, 22 January 1885], the same reporter wrote that: 'If the police are removed the blacks will revert to their former murderous propensities . . . Of course the same evils exist in your district [Cairns] . . . [however] if aggressions are perpetrated in your district, a 'roll up' [meaning battue] will drive the niggers up this way, and the same condition of affairs will hunt them from here.' The Skull Pocket/Mulgrave River/Skeleton Creek battue appears to have taken place in late 1884, or early 1885. It is difficult to judge whether references to a 'roll up' were an oblique reference to deeds already done, but reversed (i.e. Cairns to Herberton), or that the action was simply contemplated. If further Bama aggression occurred, would it warrant another battue?

71   On a speculative note, could the dismissal have been a ruse to hide Nichols' role in the much more devastating Skull Pocket/Mulgrave River/Skeleton Creek battue? The linguist, Dixon, (R M W Dixon, *The Dyirbal Language of North Queensland*, Cambridge University Press (CUP), London, 1972, p.34) wrote 'thousands of European miners . . . [and] Chinese fossickers, . . . [were] responsible for the almost instant elimination of tribes such as Mbabaram'. Historian, Noel Loos, although acknowledging that Dixon does not give evidence to support this, felt that 'considering the petition of 1882 [signed by 257 people], it is not surprising'. N Loos, *Invasion and Resistance*, 1982, p.95. A local historian, the late W T Johnston, recalled the Evelyn massacre near Herberton.

However, due to the paucity of information relating to both the Evelyn massacre and that of the Mbabaram; and Nichols' apparent frequent association with Baan Bêro (see Atherton Papers, JOL, 67–26/2), and therefore likely familiarity with the district in-between, it suggests he may have been quite well placed to have led the Skull Pocket battue.

72   *Cairns Post*, 16 April 1885. Two or three Yirrganydji were wounded, although not before the cattle had been raided, a horse speared and 'all the ropes and sails in the store' had been destroyed.

73   *Cairns Post*, 16 April 1885. It was even suggested that the 'entire Northern population of blacks . . . should be massed together towards the north of [and opposite] Double Island, on an area admirably suited for a hunting ground . . . The native police . . . [to] see that their charge is kept strictly within a certain boundary. The present state of things is becoming intolerable'.

74   P Savage, *Christie Palmerston Explorer*, JCU, Townsville, 1989, pp.205–6.

75   Savage, *Palmerston*, pp.178–80.

76   Stationed at the Mulgrave Native Police Barracks. W T Johnston, 'John Clifford. Killed by Blacks on the Russell River Goldfield', Eacham Historical Society, Bulletin 124, September 1987.

77   Johnston, 'John Clifford Killed by the Blacks,' 1987.

78   E H Short, *The Nation Builders*, Self-published, Dimbulah, 1988, p.55. Interview with Molly Raymond, *Black Oral History Collection (BOHC)*, JCU, Townsville, 1989. M Raymond died 4 May 1992, aged 102 years. H & M E Tranter (eds), *Malanda: In the Shadow of Bartle Frere*, Eacham Historical Society (EHS), 1995, p.6. The name 'Butchers Creek' appears to stem from this event. See J May, *Eacham Shire Historical Data*, EHS, 1959, p.3A.

79   Molly Raymond, *BOHC* Black Oral History Collection, James Cook University, School of History and Politics, (accessed 1989).

80   'Bird Barrier Mountain', which was the general limit of coastal seabirds. A sign of an impending cyclone was the presence of seabirds west of Lamb Range on the Tableland. See Dixon, *A Grammar of Yidin*, CUP, 1977, p.10.

81   *Cairns Post*, 4 May 1886.

82   *Cairns Post*, 28 April 1886.

83   W T Johnston, 'Aboriginals', Historical Society of Cairns (HSC), Bulletin 106, February 1968, p.2.

84   Johnston, HSC, Bulletin 106. Mr Johnston stated that most of his references were based on local white folklore (personal communication, 28 September 1989). Another example in the district occurred when men were getting hickory logs for the railway, between the second selection (in the vicinity of modern Smithfield) and Jamieson's (at Buchan Point), they found the coastal Djabugay an 'intolerable nuisance'. They had to leave one man on guard in camp, 'otherwise every scrap of food is taken by the thieving rascals'. *Cairns Post*, 8 June 1887.

85   Personal communication with Bill Johnston, 28 September 1989.

86   Johnston, 'A Town with so much to Recall', *Sunday Mail Colour*, 14 November 1976; 'Tramp' [C A Jenkinson], 'The Path of the Pioneers', *Cummins & Campbell's Monthly Magazine*, May 1936, pp.13–15; J Black, *North Queensland Pioneers*, CWA, Charters Towers, 1931, p.75. However, it is possible that these events occurred earlier in 1877, with Christie Palmerston participating. '[John] Fraser said he was with Palmerston when he acquired Pompo on Rifle Creek near Mitchell Vale homestead. Blacks had been killing horses in the district and Palmerston had tracked a group of about 20 who were cutting up and roasting one of the animals. Pompo was the only black [*sic*] who did not attempt to run away and he readily conversed with Palmerston in the black's [*sic*] language [Kuku Yalanji] and then went with him to Palmerston's camp'. [P. Savage, *Christie Palmerston Explorer*, Records of North Queensland History No.2, JCU, Townsville, 1989, p.5.]

Although they may have been two separate incidents, the stories are remarkably similar and may have been one and the same.

87   Bottoms, 'Djarrugan', p.45A; T Bottoms, *Djabugay Country—An Aboriginal History of Tropical North Queensland*, Allen & Unwin, St Leonards, 1999, p.14.

88   'Tramp' [C A Jenkinson], *Cummins & Campbell's Monthly Magazine*, May 1936, pp.13–15.

89   'Tramp', *Cummins & Campbell's Monthly Magazine*, May 1936, p.45.

90   D M Connolly, *Chronicles of Mowbray and Port Douglas*, Self-published, Cairns or D M Connolly, June, 1984, p.45.

91   See the *Cook District, 2 Mile Map Sheet No.1, Port Douglas & Neighbourhood*, Brisbane, The Surveyor General's Office, September 1894.

92   'There was a massacre up there too . . . It wasn't the settlers who shot the Bama, it was the Police.' Personal communication with Djabugay Elder, Mrs Enid Boyle, Kuranda, 3 September 1997.

93   QSA, COL A791 4020/1895.

94   QSA, COL A791 4020/1895.

95   R C Mann, 'Some Early History of Kuranda', HSC, Bulletin 158, December 1972.

96   *Northern Herald*, 18 July 1928. Bottoms, *Djabugay Country*, 1999, pp.38–39.

97   Kelvin Hill, 'Outline of Origins of Buttercup Banning', unpublished manuscript in possession of the author. Ernie Grant confirmed that Buttercup had recounted the events of the massacre to Kelvin Hill who recorded her recollection, which is believed to be in the possession of Kelvin's widowed wife. Personal communication with Ernie Grant, 4 November 2003. The author had an opportunity to see Mr Hill's collection at Tully on 5 March 1993. *Djabugay Country*, pp.40–42.

98   Buttercup and *Binda Nyiwul* (Tambo Banning) brought their family up on Andrew Banning's selection. Andrew Banning was an American who with his wife ran a hotel in Abbott Street [W F Tierney, 'Cairns at the Turn of the Century', HSC, Bulletin 52, June 1963], before taking possession of his selection in the Freshwater Valley around 1886. The *Cairns Post*, 6 January 1892, reported that 98 acres (40 hectares) had been cleared and that he lived in an impressive house. Descendants of the Bama Bannings still live at Redlynch.

99   Quoted from the *Brisbane Courier* in the *Cairns Argus*, 22 August 1890; see also Bottoms, *Djabugay Country*, pp.40–42. An oblique reference to the time that the massacre occurred was made in the *Brisbane Courier*, 23 May 1892, where it was stated that 'Mr. Gribble informs us that the incident related occurred about twelve months prior to his [1891] visit to the Upper Barron, and was reported to him for the first time on that occasion'. The Rev. John Brown Gribble wrote in his notes on Saturday 22 August 1891, referring to the Djabugay-speakers near Myola, that: 'It seems that after the scrub murder [of Hobson] many were shot down by the Native police and they are all very timid.' 'Journal of J B Gribble 1891', Mitchell Library (Australian Board of Missions).

100 *Queenslander*, 19 September 1891. *North Queensland Herald*, 23 September 1891.

101 That is, no written source or documentation has been found. However, the oral history recollections of Djabugay Elders independently corroborated these tragic occurrences. Bottoms, *Djabugay Country*, 1999.

102 *Djabugay Country*, 1999, p.39; personal communication with Glen Williams, former Senior Djabugay Ranger.

103 *Djabugay Country*, 1999; personal communication with Senior Djabugay Elder, Selwyn Hunter, 19 September 1995.

104 *Djabugay Country*, 1999; personal communication with Senior Djabugay Elder, Florence Williams, 18 September 1998.

Chapter 9 Gulf Country and Western Queensland

1   D May, *From Bush to Station, Aboriginal Labour in the North Queensland Pastoral Industry 1861–1897*, History Department, James Cook University (JCU), Townsville, 1983, Table 1, p.7.

2   R Evans, *A History of Queensland*, Cambridge University Press, Melbourne, 2007, p.85.

3   A Turnbull, 10 March 1896, letter published in *Science of Man*, 1 June 1911, p.40.

4   1) Ex-Native Police Sub-Inspector Uhr in 1872 drove 163 cattle and 125 horses across to the construction camps of the NT Overland Telegraph; 2) In 1874 George Latour led a party via the Nicholson River; 3) Nat Buchanan in 1878 began overlanding large herds of cattle across to Glencoe Station in the Territory. J W F Dymock, *Nicholson River (Waanyi-Garawa) land claim: historical material relevant to Nicholson River land claim area*, Northern Land Council, Darwin, 1982, p.26.

5   G Buchanan, *Packhorse and Waterhole*, Angus & Robertson, Sydney, 1934, p.40.

6   T Roberts, *Frontier Justice, A History of the Gulf Country to 1900*, University of Queensland Press (UQP), St Lucia, 2005. Roberts, 'The Brutal Truth: What Happened in the Gulf Country', *The Monthly*, November 2009, No. 51, <http://www.themonthly.com.au>, Endnote 3, p.11.

7   Roberts, 'The Brutal Truth', November 2009, No. 51, pp.1–2.

8   *Northern Standard*, 1 June 1934.

9   Just north of the much larger Barkly Tableland, some 25 kilometres south-east of today's Cape Crawford.

10   Roberts argues very convincingly that Mounted Constable Smith was actually Constable William Curtis. In fact, his analysis of events is a tour de force of historical detective work. See Roberts, *Frontier Justice*, 2005, pp.174–81.

11   *Northern Standard*, 1 June 1934.

12   Roberts, *Frontier Justice*, 2005, pp.250–51. See n.53 *South Australian Police Gazette*, 6 June 1888, p.90. Although, as Roberts notes: 'The Queensland Solictor-General [*sic*] advised in November 1890 (QSA A/454000 29.11.1890) that such arrangements were unlawful, but cross-border patrols in pursuit of Aboriginal offenders continued, at least by the Queensland police, whether sanctioned informally or not . . .'

13   Roberts, *Frontier Justice*, 2005, pp.248–49.

14   'Old Man' is a term of respect for male Elders.

15   Dymock, *Nicholson River (Waanyi-Garawa) land claim*, 1982, p.52. Djagooridi's (Duncan Hogan's) account of these events was recorded by John Dymock in November 1978. Roberts observes that although transcribed as 'Gundoorana', the site of the massacre may in fact have been Goonadbra Waterhole on Puzzle Creek. Roberts, 2005, n.51, p.293.

16   J Richards, 'A Question of Necessity', PhD, Griffith University, 2005, Appendix 2, p.350; Roberts, 2005, p.250.

17   Dymock, *Nicholson River Waanyi-Garawa land claim*, 1982, p.52.

18   Roberts, 'The Brutal Truth', November 2009, p.3.

19   My emphasis. *Northern Territory Times*, 23 October 1875.

20   *Northern Territory Times*, 17 July 1875.

21   Shropshire-born Edkins (1840–1905) and his brother, ran a boiling-down works for the Scottish Australian Co. Ltd. at Burketown in 1866. He married Edwina Marion in Victoria in October 1867 and then managed Beamesbrook Station [c.50 kilometres south-west of Burketown]. Two of his eight children died here, and his brother-in-law, while visiting from India, was speared to death in 1871. The following year Edkins and family and 12,000 head of cattle abandoned the

run and moved some 800 kilometres to the south-east and the western lease of Bowen Downs. He went into partnership with several other pastoralists during the 1880s and 1890s, including Roxborough, Katandra and Dunrobin stations. *Australian Dictionary of Biography ADB Online.*

22   P Monteath (ed), *The Diary of Emily Caroline Creaghe, Explorer*, Corkwood Press, North Adelaide, 2004, Diary Entry 8 February 1883, p.26. Carrie Creaghe was the first white female to be involved in an exploration party across the Gulf region when she and her husband joined Ernest Favenc.

23   See D B Rose, 'Aboriginal life and death in Australian settler nationhood', *Aboriginal History* 25 (2001).

24   Roberts, 'The Brutal Truth', *The Monthly*, November 2009, Endnote 52, p.22.

25   Rose, 'Aboriginal life and death . . .', 2001, p.156.

26   J T Swann letter, 21 December 1891, Queensland State Archives (QSA) COL/713 92/12790.

27   Donaldson & Elliot (eds), *Do Not Yield to Despair*, 1998, pp.6, 12.

28   Diary entry 27 April 1895. M Donaldson & I Elliot (eds), *Do Not Yield to Despair: The Exploration Diaries of Frank Hann 1895–1908*, Hesperian Press, Carlisle, 1998, p.17.

29   Unconfirmed quotation in D Trigger & J Devitt, *A Brief History of Aboriginal Associations with the Lawn Hill Area*, Doomadgee Aboriginal Community Council, 1992, p.3 (letter from F Hann to A Howitt, 5 July 1885). Richards makes the salient point that: 'We will never know if Lamond was exaggerating or if Hann quoted him accurately, but clearly a large number of deaths occurred.' J Richards, 'Patrolling Another Northwest Frontier', *Law and History Conference*, Hamilton, New Zealand, July 2001, pp.6–7.

30   R E M Armstrong, *The Kalkadoons: A Study of an Aboriginal Tribe on the Queensland Frontier*, William Brooks & Co, Brisbane, 1981, p.126.

31   I Davidson, I Tarragó & T Sullivan, 'Market Forces', in V Donovan & C Wall (eds), *Making Connections, A journey along Central Australian Aboriginal trading routes*, Arts Queensland, Brisbane 2004, p.16.

32   H Fysh, *Taming the North*, Angus & Robertson, Sydney, 1933 (revised edition 1950), p.96.

33   Armstrong, *The Kalkadoons*, 1981, p.128.

34   Fysh, *Taming the North*, 1933, pp.113–14.

35   My emphasis. Fysh, p.125.

36   Armstrong interviewed Mosman's daughter in January 1974. Armstrong, *The Kalkadoons*, 1981, pp.132–36 (n.38, p.147). Combined with Police Commissioner Seymour's instructions to Urquhart 'to watch the Calton Hills district, owing to the protection asked for by Kennedy', this definitely suggests political influence being brought to bear. Fysh, *Taming the North*, 1933, p.143.

37   Later, the area where this site was became a railway siding called 'Urquhart'.

38   Fysh, *Taming the North*, pp.143–45.

39   J Richards, 'What really happened at Battle Mountain in 1884?', Unpublished paper, 2010, p.8. See also Armstrong, *The Kalkadoons*, 1981, pp.140–45.

40   I Howie-Willis, 'Kalkadoon', in *Encyclopaedia of Aboriginal Australia*, Vol. 1, Australian Institute of Aboriginal and Torres Strait Islander Studies, Canberra, 1994, p.529.

41   J Richards, 'What really happened at Battle Mountain in 1884?', Unpublished paper, 2010, p.11.

42   S E Pearson, 'The Prospector of Argylla—Being an Account of the Life of the Late E Henry', John Oxley Library (JOL), OM 77–16, p.20. *Queensland Past and Present: 100 Years of Statistics, 1896–1996*, Qld Government, Brisbane, 1998, p.112, Table 4.7.

43   Roberts, 'The Brutal Truth', November 2009, No.51, pp.8–9.

44   *South Australian Register*, 8 December 1885, cited in Roberts, 'The Brutal Truth', p.8.

45   Trigger & Devitt, *A Brief History of Aboriginal Associations with the Lawn Hill Area*, 1992, p.4.

46   Interview with Ruby Saltmere by Tony Roberts, 4 August 1997. Roberts notes: 'The Native Police officers were issued with swords and it is these that Rosie may have witnessed, rather than bayonets.' Roberts, *Frontier Justice*, 2005, pp.233–34.

47   Letter T McIntosh, 10 November 1887, QSA, A/45400, Ruby Saltmere to Tony Roberts, 4 August 1997, in Roberts, *Frontier Justice*, 2005, p.234.

48   F Hann to Commissioner of Police, Seymour, 8 October 1883, QSA, A/41523 83/2502 n.15, Roberts, *Frontier Justice*, 2005, p.235.

49   Amy Shadforth died in 1898 and Lamond later married Amie Edkins in 1902. Richards, *The Secret War*, 2008, p.243.

50   Dymock, *Nicholson River (Waanyi-Garawa) land claim*, 1982, p.41.

51   *Queenslander*, 22 April 1882; 20 December 1884.

52   Dymock, 1982, p.77.

53   26 kilometres west of the contemporary indigenous township of Doomadgee and several kilometres north of the Nicholson River.

54   See J Richards, 'Patrolling Another Northwest Frontier', July 2001, p.7; Roberts, *Frontier Justice*, 2005, p.237.

55   J W F Dymock, *Northern Land Council Kratos Report*, 1978, p.4, cited in Dymock, 1982, p.80.

56   QSA, COL/A182/849.

57   R Kelly & N Evans, 'The McKenzie Massacre on Bentinck Island', *Aboriginal History*, Vol.9, No.1, 1985, pp.44–45; N B Tindale, 'Some Population Changes Among the Kaiadilt People of Bentinck Island, Queensland', *Records of the S.A. Museum*, Vol.14, No.2, 27 July 1962, pp. 309–10.

58   N B Tindale, 'Geographical Knowledge of the Kaiadilt People of Bentinck Island, Queensland', *Records of the S.A. Museum*, Vol.14, No.2, 27 July 1962, pp.266–67.

59   D Trigger, *Whitefella Comin'—Aboriginal responses to colonialism in northern Australia*, Cambridge University Press (CUP), Melbourne, 1992, p.20. Ian Clark notes that in western Victoria in the late 1830s and early 1840s, Aboriginal skulls adorned entrances to European huts and walls. Assistant Protector, C W Sievwright, 'was at pains to stress that this abuse was not confined to hut keepers and shepherds: the practice was followed by "respectable" squatters as well. He was convinced the practice was intended to intimidate the Aborigines, and the strategic location of Aboriginal skulls was in effect declaring to local Aboriginal people that they approached these huts at their peril.' I Clark, *Scars in the Landscape*, Australian Institute of Aboriginal and Torres Strait Islander Studies (AIATSIS), Canberra, 1995, p.6.

60   L E Skinner, 'Pastoral Frontiers of Queensland Colony', in *Settlement of the Colony of Queensland*, Seminar, JOL, Library Board of Queensland, Brisbane, 1978, p.9 of article.

61   Apparently named after the upper reaches of the Thames River, back home in England. <Queenslandplaces.com.au/isisford-and-isisford-shire>.

62   Personal communication with Jocelyn Avery, local Isisford historian, email 27 June 2010.

63   Quoted in H Reynolds, *Why Weren't We Told?*, Viking, Ringwood, 1999, p.107.

64   Reynolds, *Why Weren't We Told?*, p.108.

65   See G W Rusden, *History of Australia*, 3 vols, G Robertson, Melbourne, 1883; and for a contrast see A Morgan, *Our First Half Century, A Review of Queensland Progress*, Queensland Government, Brisbane, 1909, especially Part IV, Chapter I where nary a word is written about how the land was acquired, or the traditional indigenous owners. They don't even rate as Queenslanders.

66   *Diary of R M Watson*, 1–2, Noel Butlin Archives Centre, Australian National University (ANU), N31/1(i) cited in J Richards, *The Secret War*, UQP, St Lucia, 2005, p.105 n.44.

67   Richards, 2005, p.227.

68   V S Barnes, L J Moore & A Oxenham, *The Modern Encyclopaedia of Australia and New Zealand*, Horwitz-Grahame, Sydney, 1964, p.1103.

69   Pearson, 'The Prospector of Argylla', JOL, OM 77–16, p.4.

70   *Queenslander*, 20 April 1901.

71   The coverage refers to one 'Sergeant M –'. Local Winton author V T Corbin (ed), *Winton Queensland (Originally Pelican Waterhole): one hundred years of settlement 1875–1975*, Winton Shire Council, Winton, 1975, p.58, refers to Sergeant M as being Morgan from Winton Police Station. However, it appears more likely that it was Sub-Inspector Robert Moran who was in charge of the Native Police barracks at Yo Yo Creek near Charleville. During the 1870s period three new townships came in to being: Tambo (1863), Blackall (1868) and Aramac (1872), and with the resignation of Acting Sub-Inspector Carroll at Aramac, it is not inconceivable that Native Police patrols were being staffed from other regions. In 1879, according to the *Brisbane Courier* (3 May 1879, reporting from 8 April), Sub-Inspector Moran was trapped by floods at Muttaburra, which suggests he was working the whole of the Mitchell district and Winton, despite being in the Gregory pastoral district, probably came under his ambit at one time. My thanks to Jonathan Richards for helping to identify Moran as the likely candidate.

72   *Queenslander*, 20 April 1901.

73   My emphasis. C Lumholtz, *Among Cannibals*, John Murray, London, 1889, pp.58–59.

74   Corbin, *Winton Queensland (Originally Pelican Waterhole)*, 1975, p.58.

75   Lumholtz, *Among Cannibals*, 1889, p.59.

76   *Queenslander*, 20 April 1901. The article is signed by P F H.

77   Macartney owned *Bladensburgh* from 1877 to 1896. J A Macartney, 'Reminiscences of the Early Days In Rockhampton and Elsewhere', *The Daily Record*, Rockhampton, 3 & 4 June 1909, p.28. W H Corfield, *Reminiscences of Queensland 1862–1899*, A H Frater, Brisbane, 1921, p.88. T Blake & P Marquis, *Bladensburg Conservation Management Plan & Interpretation Strategy*, A report for the Winton Shire Council, November 2003, p.6.

78   *ADB, Online*. J A Macartney was 'the son of the Dean of Melbourne, [and] was renowned as an enterprising pastoralist and a fearless rider who once rode from Broadsound to Rockhampton in one day and one night . . . Macartney . . . married Anne Wallace-Dunlop on 4 January 1861'. C Nolan, *Sandhills and Channel Country*, Diamantina Shire Council, Bedourie, 2003, p.38. See Appendix D: An example of one pastoralist's acquisitiveness.

79   See Appendix D, Nolan, *Sandhills and Channel Country*, 2003, p.XI; see also Nolan p.143 regarding Macartney's pastoral efforts in the Channel Country.

80   Letter from K Broadbent to C W de Vis, QM curator, 12 October 1888, *Queensland Museum Correspondence*, 88/2547. Six years earlier, on 29 July 1882, Broadbent had written to de Vis from Cardwell regarding his specimen collecting, and stated: 'Blacks are bad. I want a small revolver and 100 cartridges, not safe anywhere now out of Cardwell.' Broadbent might well have been of a nervous disposition, but there is no denying that he intended to use firearms; whether the Museum agreed to furnishing this form of protection I have not been able to confirm. However, the fact that in his later communication he requests a rifle for shooting alligators, having just identified that he can get more skulls and that the Blacks are bad, suggests that he may have been obtaining specimens in a much more aggressive fashion. Letter from K Broadbent to C W de Vis QM, *Queensland Museum Correspondence*, 82/164.

81   Meston to Ramsay, 15 March 1887, E P Ramsay Papers, Mitchell Library (State Library NSW), MS 1589/2. See P Turnbull, 'Theft in the name of Science', in *Griffith Review*, Edition 21:

Hidden Queensland: <www.griffithreview.com/edition–21/57-essay/613.html>; T Delamothe, 'Aboriginal skeletons in the closet', *British Medical Journal*, Vol.303, 21–28 December 1991: <www.ncbi.nlm.nih.gov/pmc/articles/PMC1676223/>; also: <http://www.creativespirits.info/aboriginalculture/people/aboriginal-remains.html>; The German naturalist Amalie Dietrich (1821–91) from 1863 to 1871 collected artefacts and fauna and flora in central Queensland for the Godeffroy Museum. In 1869 she wrote to her daughter: 'I am sending to Hamburg thirteen skeletons and several skulls.' C Bischoff (daughter), *The Hard Road: The Life Story of Amalie Dietrich*, Martin Hopkinson Ltd, London, 1931, p.290; also *ADB, Online*.

82   *Queensland Government Gazette*, Vol.2, No.74, 7 September 1864. G S Wharton, *Shire Aramac 1880–1980*, Aramac Shire Council, Townsville, 1980, p.3.

83   If one accepts Robert Christison's delineation of fourteen groups inhabiting the area, greater than the Mitchell District, which he drew of the Dalebura [*sic*] Tribe and sent to A Howitt, 31 October 1884, Howitt Papers, Box 1, Folder 2, National Museum of Victoria.

84   *Queenslander*, 20 September 1879, p.372.

85   'Report of the Select Committee on the Native Police', *Queensland Votes & Proceedings (QV&P)*, 1861.

86   See *Moreton Bay Courier*, 7 May 1862, p.2; also Chapter 3, Invasion of the future Central Queensland.

87   A Smith, *This El Dorado of Australia: A centennial history of Aramac Shire*, Studies in North Queensland History No.29, Dept. of History & Politics, JCU, Townsville, 1994, pp.15–17.

88   J W Raven, 'Reminiscences of a Western Australian pioneer', 1909, Mitchell Library, Microfilm MAV/FM4/3099, pp.14–15.

89   *Capricornian*, 13 July 1878, p.12.

Chapter 10   Queensland's Disreputable Reputation

1   See M D Prentis, 'Aborigines and Europeans in the Northern Rivers Region of NSW, 1823–1881', PhD, Macquarie University, Sydney, 1972; D Denholm, 'Some Aspects of Squatting in NSW and Queensland, 1847–1864', PhD, Australian National University (ANU), Canberra, 1972; G Blomfield, *Baal Belbora—The End of the Dancing, The Massacre of a peaceful people*, The Alternative Publishing Co-Operative Ltd, Chippendale, 1988.

2   'The Wild White Man and The Blacks of Victoria', by James Bonwick, 1863 (State Library of Victoria). This was Lang's original asterisked footnote. William Buckley (1780–1856) was taken as a convict to Port Phillip in April 1803 at the age of 23. He absconded and lived with the Watouring tribe for the next 32 years, surrendering in 1835. Buckley was employed as an interpreter, but due to his confused loyalties, left for Hobart in December 1837. He became an assistant storekeeper, married in 1840, sired two daughters and died at 76 years of age. M J Tipping, *William Buckley, Australian Dictionary of Biography, ADB Online*.

3   G S Lang, *Aborigines in Australia, in their Original Condition and in their Relations with the White Men*, Wilson & Mackinnon, Melbourne, 1865, p.82.

4   R Ørsted-Jensen, *Frontier History Revisited: Queensland and the 'History War'*, Luxmundipub@hotmail.com, 2011, p.165.

5   Interestingly, this still has relevance today, as Henry Reynolds has observed: 'The sanctioning of racism, the attacks on political correctness by the One Nation party and in a covert way by the Liberal and National parties, gave many bigots hope that the good old days had returned . . . when political leaders appeared to sanction or even promote racism, a minority would believe

thay had received approval to take action.' H Reynolds, *Why Weren't We Told*, Viking, Ringwood, 1999, p.254.

6   Korah Halcomb Wills Diary Extracts, John Oxley Library (JOL), Henry Brandon Collection, Box 8946, OM 75–75.

7   See also Ørsted-Jensen, *Frontier History Revisited*, Lux Mundi Publishing, 2011, and *The Right to Live*.

8   G S Lang, *Aborigines of Australia*, 1865, pp.45–46.

9   G S Lang, *Aborigines of Australia*, 1865, p.81.

10   See also R Evans, *A History of Queensland*, University of Queensland Press (UQP), St Lucia, 2007, p.94.

11   R Evans & B Thorpe, 'Indigenocide and the Massacre of Aboriginal History', *Overland*, 163, 2001, Winter, p.26.

12   Queensland established in 1859 and the *Aboriginals Protection and the Restriction of the Sale of Opium Act 1897* became operational in 1898.

13   J Richards, 'A Question of Necessity', PhD, Griffith University, Nathan Campus, 2005, pp.349–51.

14   R Evans, 'The country has another past: Queensland and the History Wars', in F Peters-Little, A Curthoys and J Docker (eds), *Passionate Histories*, ANU E-Press & Aboriginal History Incorporated, Monograph 21, 2010 <epress.anu.edu.au/passionate_histories>, pp.29–31.

15   Personal communication with Raymond Evans.

16   Evans does not include numbers killed from 1849–59. His estimates only cover the Native Police from 1859–97 and do not include any violence in the early part of the twentieth century. It therefore seems that the figure of 50,000 is very likely a conservative underestimate.

17   R Evans and B Thorpe, 'Indigenocide and the Massacre of Aboriginal History', *Overland*, 163, 2001, pp.21–39, <http://www.kooriweb.org/foley/resources/pdfs/101.pdf>; See also D Moses, 'Windschuttle, History Warriors and Real Historians', <www.onlineopinion.com.au/view.asp?article=3320&page=0>.

18   H Reynolds, *This whispering in our hearts*, Allen & Unwin, St Leonards, 1998, p.130.

19   *The Times*, London, 15 May 1883, in Reynolds, *This whispering in our hearts*, 1998, p.131.

20   See R Broome, 'The statistics of frontier conflict', in B Attwood & S G Foster (eds), *Frontier Conflict: The Australian Experience*, National Museum of Australia, Canberra, 2003.

21   Original emphasis. Personal communication with Robert Ørsted-Jensen, email 24 December 2011.

22   Evans, *A History of Queensland*, 2007, p.94.

23   Ørsted-Jensen, *Frontier History Revisited*, 2011, p.165.

24   Ørsted-Jensen, *Frontier History Revisited*, 2011, p.166. See also Ørsted-Jensen, *The Right to Live* (in eprint) 2011, Doctoral thesis, University of Queensland.

25   Ørsted-Jensen, *Frontier History Revisited*, 2011, pp.165–66. See n.286, see Queensland State Archives (QSA), EXE/E3/61/3. 'The final order to the commandant was dated "*14th of January 1861*" in the letter books QSA, COL/Q1 61/26. See further details in *The Right to Live*, chapter 3.' Ratcliffe Pring also served as Attorney-General in July–August 1866, 'under Mackenzie from 15 August 1867 to 25 November 1868; under Lilley from 12 November 1869 to 3 May 1870; under Palmer from 2 January 1874 for six days; and under McIlwraith from 16 May 1879 to 4 June 1880 . . .' see W Ross Johnston, 'Pring, Ratcliffe' (1825–85), *ADB Online*.

26   Personal communication with Ørsted-Jensen, email 5 October 2011.

27   R Evans, *A History of Queensland*, Cambridge University Press (CUP), Melbourne, 2007, p.78.

28   W Thorpe, *Colonial Queensland*, University of Queensland Press (UQP), St Lucia, 1996, p.159.

29   AH Palmer had originally been Colonial Secretary and Secretary for Public Works under R R Mackenzie's premiership (Aug 1867–Nov 1868). Palmer then went into opposition until the next election. He was Premier from 3 May 1870 to 6 January 1874, when he resigned because his own party voted against his proposed Education Bill, or possibly because he had breached etiquette by being drunk in parliament. When Thomas McIlwraith's ministry was elected in January 1879, Palmer became the Colonial Secretary and Secretary for Public Instruction (i.e. Education), but resigned on 24 December 1881 to become the president of the Upper House, the Legislative Council. He retained this position until his death in 1898 at the age of 78. *ADB Online*.

30   QSA, COL A272 79/858. Hale's letter dated 4 March 1879.

31   *Brisbane Courier*, 9 June 1880.

32   J Lydon, '"no moral doubt . . . ": Aboriginal evidence and the Kangaroo Creek poisoning, 1847–1849', *Aboriginal History*, Vol.20, 1996, p.153.

33   J Matthews, JOL, OM 74–17 8889, letter dated (Sunday) August 1875; Such phrases as 'dreams of big fortunes and lovely homes in the future were also a big incentive' (p.12) and, 'Then the settlers thought their days of hardships were over and fortunes ahead for all of them' (p.22) are dotted throughout. J Black, *North Queensland Pioneers*, CWA, Charters Towers, 1931.

34   See D Thomson, *Europe Since Napoleon*, Penguin Books, Ringwood, 1966, pp.127–288.

35   M French, 'Squatters and Separation: a synoptic overview', in *Queensland History Journal (QHJ)*, Feb 2010, Vol.20 No.13, p.804.

36   Oscar de Satgé, *Pages from the Journal of a Queensland Squatter*, Hurst & Blackett, London, 1901, p.227.

37   M French, 'Squatters and Separation', *QHJ*, Feb 2010, p.813.

38   Aboriginal informants have stressed that prior to European settlement food resources were managed or 'farmed' in the unconventional sense (i.e. 'domiculture'), with species being encouraged to re-generate after the food source had been harvested. This also tied in with 'fire-stick' farming. The landscape, as perceived by Aboriginal people, embodies their spiritual heritage, their religious beliefs pervade every aspect of their lives. The landscape itself is informed by the Storied Past. Features of the landscape have their place in the Creation Stories, and these Stories link each Aboriginal group to their homeland. It is this Storied Past which tells of the activities of the ancestors. Mirrored in these stories, the actions of the ancestors, their way of life is clearly outlined. Continuing in this 'way', the Aboriginal people have walked in confidence, secure in the knowledge that others have so walked in safety before them. See T Bottoms, *Bama Country*, Fishtail Solutions, Cairns, 2008, pp.9, 25.

39   *Cairns Post*, 15 October 1885.

40   See K Cronin, 'Part Three: "The Yellow Agony"', in R Evans, K Saunders, & K Cronin, *Race Relations in Colonial Queensland*, UQP, St Lucia, (1975) 1993, pp.235–318.

41   French, 'Squatters and Separation', 2010, pp.807–8.

42   <http://finch.customer.netspace.net.au/haroldfh.html>.

43   See Chapter 5 and the mass poisoning of Long Lagoon at Mt Spencer west of Mackay.

44   My emphasis. N Cole, 'Battle Camp to Boralga', *Aboriginal History*, Vol.28, 2004, p.173.

45   H Fitzgerald to Commissioner of Police 5 March 1885, QSA, COL/A422 85/1840; Cole, 'Battle Camp to Boralga', 2004, p.173.

46   *Queensland Times*, 19 November 1872, my emphasis.

47   I Clark, *Scars in the Landscape, A Register of Massacre Sites in Western Victoria, 1803–1859*, Aboriginal Studies Press for AIATSIS, Canberra, 1995.

48 Broome, 'Statistics of Frontier Conflict', 2003, p.7.

49 R Evans, 'Part One: "The Nigger Shall Disappear . . . "', in Evans, Saunders, & Cronin, *Race Relations in Colonial Queensland*, (1975) 1993, p.57.

50 L Connors, 'The theatre of justice: Race relations and capital punishment at Moreton Bay 1841–59', in R Fisher (ed), *Brisbane: The Aboriginal presence 1824–1860*, Brisbane History Group, Papers No.11, 1992, p.49.

51 J Richards, *The Secret War*, UQP, St Lucia, 2008, p.216.

52 A Hillier, 'An eye for an eye: Action of the Native Police in Central Queensland 1865–67', *Journal of the Royal Historical Society of Queensland (JRHSQ)*, Vol.16 No.2, May 1996, p.70.

53 Evans, *History of Queensland*, 2007, p.139.

54 See Reynolds, *This Whispering in Our Hearts*, 1998; also <www.aconspiracyofsilence.com.au>.

55 First British settlement for convicts was established in 1803; Melbourne in 1835 and the Port Phillip region became the colony of Victoria in 1851.

56 A Palmer, *Colonial Genocide*, Crawford House Publishing, Adelaide, 2000, p.19.

57 Broome, 'Statistics of Frontier Conflict', 2003, p.7.

58 My emphasis. Clerk of Petty Sessions from W R O Hill: *Forty-five years' experiences in north Queensland 1861 to 1905: with a few incidents in England, 1844 to 1861*, Pole & Co, Brisbane, 1907, p.25.

59 C Lumholtz, *Among Cannibals: An Account of Four Years' Travels in Australia and of camp life with the Aborigines of Queensland*, John Murray, London, 1889, pp.374–76.

60 For examples, see <www.aconspiracyofsilence.com.au>; See also *The Way We Civilise; Black and White; The Native Police: A Series of Articles and Letters Reprinted from the 'Queenslander'*, Printed by G. and J. Black (Late W. Thorne), Edward, Brisbane, 1880.

61 28 March 1895, QSA, COL/139 95/4225.

62 Petition from residents of Cardwell to Colonial Secretary, 11 March 1872, COL/A167 72/523; Article 'Travels in the North', *Brisbane Courier*, 16 April 1872:6; Letter from Walter Scott, Valley of Lagoons, to Acting Commissional of Police, 17 July 1872, COL/A170 72/1346 et.al.

63 P J Hull, Clerk of the Cardwell Divisional Board to the Commissioner of Police, 17 October 1895, QSA, POL A/45211 95/11462, p.1.

64 W Craig to Colonial Secretary, 4 April 1896, QSA, COL/139 96/5091.

65 W Craig to Colonial Secretary, 4 April 1896, QSA, COL/139 96/5091.

66 Craig fits the same profile as other Queenslanders who spoke out against the operations of the Native Police. Six years earlier, in 1888, a specimen collector for the Queensland Museum reported that he was 'going to Blackman's [station] at the Vale of Herbert because 'Mr Craig has hunted the natives off his place'. Whether Craig injured or killed any Aboriginal people is not clear, however, his change of attitude regarding the treatment of Aboriginals is consistent with other complainants. See Ørsted-Jensen, *Frontier History Revisited*, 2011, p.8, pp.126–45.

67 Richards, *The Secret War*, 2008, p.234.

68 H Fitzgerald to Police Commissioner, 14 May 1896, QSA, POL A/45211 96/5457.

69 Richards, *The Secret War*, 2008, p.234. Fitzgerald retired in 1905 and died in 1922.

70 QSA, COL/143 M1634 (Z1610), William Craig's proposal (26 January 1898) to the Commissioner of Police and letter (3 April 1898) from Constable Holmes to Inspector Fitzgerald, Townsville.

71 QSA, JUS/N 35 72/218 (QSA, Z/3388); See also Richards, *The Secret War*, 2008, p.259.

72 CS Cansdell at Bowen to Attorney-General (21 August 1876), QSA, JUS/A17 76/2163.

73 T Barclay Miller to CS Cansdell (12 June 1876), forwarded to Attorney-General, QSA, JUS/A17 76/2163.

74   R A Johnstone, Herbert River, to Commissioner of Police (17 August 1876), QSA, JUS/A17 76/2163.

75   *Sydney Morning Herald*, 18 July 1933, 'Atrocities by Whites', p.9.

76   'Stone Age', *Queenslander*, 29 May 1897.

77   B Breslin, 'The James Morrill Story', unpublished manuscript, 2000, p.2. This work is the most comprehensive and insightful coverage of James Morrill to date.

78   S Anderson, *Pelletier: The Forgotten Castaway of Cape York*, Melbourne Books, Melbourne, 2009.

79   On the central coast of eastern Cape York Peninsula.

80   Reynolds, *This Whispering In Our Hearts*, 1998, p.103.

81   Letters of A Davidson to F W Chesson, ASS, Rhodes House, Oxford, MSS. British Empire S. 18 C132, 1 October 1870, cited in Reynolds *This Whispering In Our Hearts*, 1998, p.103.

82   R Evans, *A History of Queensland*, CUP, Melbourne, 2007, p.97.

83   Also in 1888 and 1893. Denver Beanland argues that McIlwraith was a classical liberal, and gives a thoughtful comprehensive coverage of the man, but omits any mention of him making money from the expropriation of Aboriginal land. D Beanland, 'Sir Thomas McIlwraith: Queensland's visionary premier,' in *QHJ*, Vol. 21 No.1, May 2010, p.10. For a comprehensive coverage of the Mackay reserve, see R Evans, 'Queensland's First Aboriginal Reserve: Part I, The Promise of Reform', and 'Part II, The Failure of Reform', in *Queensland Heritage 2*, No.4 (May 1971), pp.26–37, and No.5 (November 1971), pp.3–14.

84   H J Gibbney, Duncan McNab (1820–1896), *ADB Online*.

85   QSA, COL/A28 62/1118. Wood was later dismissed for embezzlement as Police Magistrate at Bowen, but escaped to England before he could be tried. Personal communication with R Evans.

86   P A Wright (ed), *Memories of Far Off Days—The Memoirs of Charlotte May Wright 1855–1929*, self-published, PA Wright, Armidale, 1985, p.36.

87   T G Genever, 'Black and Blue—Aboriginal-Police Relations in Far North Queensland During the Currency of *The Aboriginals Protection and Restriction of the Sale of Opium Act 1897–1939*', Hons, James Cook University (JCU), Cairns, 1992, p.77.

88   N Loos, *Invasion and Resistance*, Australian National University Press (ANUP), Canberra, 1982, p.179, citing *QPD* of LA LXXVIII (1897), p.1629.

89   *Queensland 1900, a narrative of her past, together with biographies of her leading men*, Chapter X, 'The Aborigines of Queensland', Alcazar Press, Brisbane, 1900, pp.89–90.

90   Herbert Spencer (1820–1903) was a major figure in the intellectual life of the British Victorian era. He was one of the principal proponents of evolutionary theory in the mid-nineteenth century. See <http://www.iep.utm.edu/spencer/>.

91   J Collier, *The Pastoral Age in Australasia*, Whitcombe & Tombs Ltd, Melbourne, 1911, pp.124–25.

92   P L Watson, *Frontier Lands and Pioneer Legends, How Pastoralists Gained Karuwali Land*, Allen & Unwin, St Leonards, 1998, p.114.

93   Ørsted-Jensen, *Frontier History Revisited*, 2011, pp.107–11.

94   P L Watson, *Frontier Lands and Pioneer Legends*, Allen & Unwin, Crows Nest, 1998, p.113.

95   Ørsted-Jensen, *Frontier History Revisited*, 2011, p.164.

96   N Ferguson, *Empire: How Britain Made the Modern World*, Penguin, Camberwell, (2003) 2008, pp.338–39.

97   Today in Germany, perhaps one of the most emotionally moving memorials seen on a daily basis are the Stolpersteine, or Stumbling Stones, which are small metal plaques that are located in front of buildings where Nazi-era victims lived (see <http://www.stolpersteine.com/>). These metal plates powerfully engage people and offer a discrete yet constant reminder of the victims—not

as a homogenous mass, but as unique (and where possible) identifiable individuals with separate lives; lives lived and extinguished before their time. However, German colleagues have expressed reserve about the term 're-written' not being strong enough, which is reflected in the existence of the Zentrum fuer Antisemitismusforschung (Centre for Research on Antisemitism) at the Technical University of Berlin (see: <http://zfa.kgw.tu-berlin.de/english/publikationen_english. htm>).

Conclusion

1 Mark Twain, *Following the Equator*, 1897, Extracted in *Mark Twain in Australia and New Zealand*, Penguin, 1973, p.169.

2 N Loos, *Invasion and Resistance: Aboriginal European Relations on the North Queensland Frontier 1861–1897*, Australian National University Press (ANUP), Canberra, 1982, Chapter 5, pp.118–59. On a somewhat similar level was the impact of beche de mer fishermen and their need for labour (kidnapped or otherwise) from the coastal clans of Cape York Peninsula. Noel Loos examines this aspect in the chapter 'The Sea Frontier' in his work *Invasion and Resistance*.

3 N G Butlin, *Economics and the Dreamtime*, Cambridge University Press (CUP), Melbourne, 1993, p.viii; Since Butlin published this, the timeframe has altered to around 50,000 years. University of Copenhagen geo-geneticists have: 'By sequencing the genome, . . . demonstrate[d] that Aboriginal Australians descend directly from an early human expansion into Asia that took place some 70,000 years ago, at least 24,000 years before the population movements that gave rise to present-day Europeans and Asians. The results imply that modern-day Aboriginal Australians are in fact the direct descendents of the first people who arrived in Australia as early as 50,000 years ago.' <http://news.ku.dk/all_news/2011/2011.9/aboriginals-get-new-history/>.

4 Commissioned by the Cairns Regional Council in 1997 to research and write the history of Cairns, the work was completed in 2002. The Council refused to publish the work on the grounds that it was too expensive. This, despite their own independent reviewer, Adjunct Professor of History (University of Queensland), Dr Helen Gregory, concluding: 'It is likely to become a "classic" in Queensland history writing.'

5 J Harris, 'Hiding the bodies: the myth of the humane colonisation of Aboriginal Australia', *Aboriginal History*, Vol.27, 2003, p.99.

6 S Maddison, *Beyond White Guilt*, Allen & Unwin, Crows Nest, 2011, pp.148–49.

7 James Douglas Henry to Judith Wright, Jan/Mar 1983, NLA Box 30, Folders 228 & 229.

8 D B Rose, *Hidden Histories*, Australian Institute of Aboriginal and Torres Strait Islander Studies (AIATSIS), Canberra, 1991, p.34.

9 J W Loewen, 'Who controls the Past controls the future', *Crisis*, May/June 2000, p.8. See also J W Loewen, *Lies My Teacher Told Me, Everything Your American History Textbook Got Wrong*, A Touchstone Book, New York, 2007.

10 M Bingham, *Suddenly one Sunday, The Story of the Port Arthur Tragedy Based on Eyewitness Accounts*, HarperCollins, Pymble, revised edn 2000, p.136.

11 The term 'fair dinkum' may have originated on the Palmer River goldfields and the term 'din kum' was apparently a Cantonese expression for 'real gold'. J Hughes (ed), *Australian Words and their Origins*, Oxford University Press (OUP), Melbourne, p.166.

Index

The *Literary Heritage* *of* NORTHAMPTONSHIRE

An exploration by Ian Addis and Robert Mercer

DIAMETRIC PUBLICATIONS
2002

The Literary Heritage of Northamptonshire

ISBN 0 9533482 5 3

First published in 2002 by
Diametric Publications, 45 Grosvenor Road, Kettering, Northamptonshire

Printed & bound in the United Kingdom by Woolnough Bookbinding Ltd.,
Irthlingborough, Northamptonshire.

'Still I know every part,

From beginning to end,

Was conceived in the heart,

Or it ne'er had been penned.'

(Joseph Hawthorn *'Poems'* 1882)

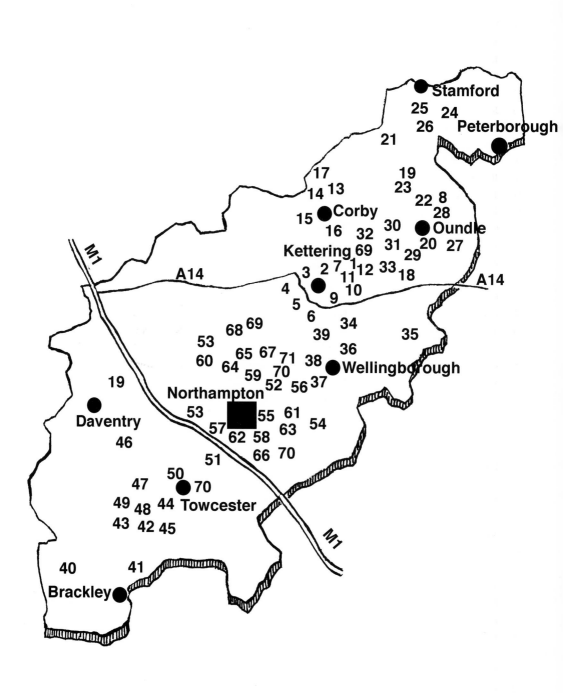

Dramatis Personae

1	David Townsend	Grafton Underwood
2	Joseph Hawthorn	Kettering
3	John Plummer	Kettering
4	Revd George Maunsell	Thorpe Malsor
5	John Leatherland	Kettering
6	John Alfred Gotch	Kettering
7	Chas H Montagu-Douglas-Scott	Geddington
8	Mary Queen of Scots	Fotheringhay
9	George Harrison	Kettering
10	JL Carr	Kettering
11	Tony Ireson	Kettering
12	John Bridges	Barton Seagrave
13	Colin Dexter	Corby
14	Jill McGowan	Corby
15	Andrew Cowan	Corby
16	Peter Hill	Corby
17	Charles Dickens	Rockingham
18	Revd Talbot Keene	Brigstock
19	Thomas Randolph	Newnham
		Blatherwycke
20	Peter Hausted	Oundle
21	William Law	Kings Cliffe
22	Julian Fane	Apethorpe
23	Mildmay Fane	Apethorpe
24	John Clare	Helpston
25	Charles Kingsley	Barnack
26	Henry Kingsley	Barnack
27	Bandula Chandraratna	Oundle
28	Miriam Rothschild	Ashton
29	Thomas Bell	Barnwell
30	Thomas Fuller	Aldwincle
31	John Dryden	Aldwincle
		Titchmarsh
32	Trevor Hold	Wadenhoe
33	Michael De-la-Noy	Slipton
34	Digby Mackworth-Dolben	Finedon
35	HE Bates	Rushden
36	John Askham	Wellingborough
37	Thomas Dexter	Wellingborough
38	Mary Lucy Pendered	Wellingborough
39	Thomas Vaux	Great Harrowden
40	William Bowles	Kings Sutton
41	Mary Leapor	Brackley
42	Edith Sitwell	Weedon Lois Weston
43	Sacherevell Sitwell	Weedon Lois Weston
44	Joseph Coles	Weedon Lois
45	Joseph Furniss	Weedon Lois
46	Benjamin West	Weedon Bec
47	Edward Bagshaw	Moreton Pinkney
48	Gilbert White	Moreton Pinkney
49	SJ Tyrrell	Eydon
50	Byron Rogers	Blakesley
51	Joan Wake	Courteenhall
52	RL Greenall	Northampton
53	James Harrington	Upton Holdenby
54	William Cowper	Northampton
55	Anne Bradstreet	Northampton
56	Leonard Welsted	Abington
57	Philip Doddridge	Northampton
58	John Ryland	Northampton
59	George De Wilde	Northampton
60	Christopher Hughes	Northampton
61	Joseph Rowlatt	Northampton
62	Susan Bostock	Northampton
63	Ray Gosling	Northampton
64	Jeremy Seabrook	Northampton
65	Pat Thomson	Northampton
66	Anne Fine	Northampton
67	George Whyte-Melville	Boughton
68	Thomas Isham	Lamport
69	Denys Watkins-Pitchford	Lamport Sudborough
70	William Carey	Paulerspury Hackleton Moulton
71	William Chown	Moulton

Acknowledgements

We are indebted to Trevor Hold, not only for *'A Northamptonshire Garland'*, the anthology of county poets and biographical notes which proved an invaluable source of information, but for his generous encouragement and support for our project.

Mary and Stephen Judd of Moulton, for their delightful company and informative notes on William Carey, Ron Greenall, Liz McBride at the Kettering Evening Telegraph, Andrea Pettingale and the staff of Kettering Public Library, staff at the Local Studies section at Northampton Central Library, Bridget Fairway, Bandula Chandraratna, Joan Carnell, Dorothy Webb, Mike Lymer, Martin Pendered and all who contributed, intentionally or otherwise, to the array of material we amassed in our 'exploration'.

Special thanks are due, as ever, to Mick Dean for his publishing skills and insistence that we work *"speedily but not in haste"*.

Introduction

For its size, a mere seventy miles long and twenty-five miles wide at its broadest point, Northamptonshire possesses a remarkably rich and varied literary heritage. From Brackley and the Wolds to the Soke of Peterborough, straggling as it does across the main watershed of midland England, its gentle uplands feed such fine rivers as the Avon, the Great Ouse, the Welland and, of course, the county's principal waterway, the River Nene. From earliest times, along the spring-line of these broad river valleys, settlements developed and eventually grew into handsome villages and towns. Resplendent, owing to some of the finest building stone in England, with splendid churches, mills, priories and manor-houses. Beyond, in the rolling country-side marked indelibly with Saxon ridge and furrow, fine estates and ancient castles dot the landscape. A picturesque setting, no less, where sheep truly 'could safely graze'.

Its landscape could never claim to be dramatic. It cannot compete with Hardy's Dorset, Du Maurier's Cornwall or Wordsworth's lake-land. Indeed, it is said that Northamptonshire's most famous poet saw neither a mountain nor the sea. However, emerging from this long heritage, we find much to delight from both Northamptonshire-born authors and those who came, liked the county, and stayed. Others have paused here for reasons many and various, drawing inspiration during their stay from its peaceful and secluded rivers, fields and woods.

It is obviously not possible to include every poet and writer in a work of this size. We have made a personal selection from those deemed to have contributed most to the county's literary heritage. Some from past centuries may now, due to changes in style and taste, be little read and are most probably out of print. However, having been introduced, the reader may feel them worthy of rediscovery and an enjoyable hunt through second-hand bookshops could ensue.

Two important influences have dominated the creative impulse. Firstly, a strong sense of place, a lyrical and historic delight in the rural romantic landscape, timeless and unspoilt. And secondly, there are the darker and more turbulent forces of Man in this landscape, the struggle for economic, social and religious reform.

We embrace all the emotions; the ecstasy of the dawn chorus and the beauty of sunlight on carved stone, the long hours of weary toil in field, kitchen and factory and the gentle humour of the dialect tradition.

The legacy endures. It resonates with the county's wide skies and rolling pasture. We offer it with delight for your enjoyment.

Ian Addis and Robert Mercer

Rambles Roundabout

'Rambles Roundabout' was the title given to a collection of essays and poems about Northamptonshire by George James de Wilde, an erstwhile editor of the Northampton Mercury, writer and patron of the arts, who made regular excursions around the county. Our explorations took similar form, although they were chiefly by motor-car rather than the steam locomotive favoured by our illustrious predecessor.

Roundabout Kettering

'Kettering is a market town,
And situate upon the crown
Of rather elevated ground,
With pleasant scenery around,
And you will find if you enquire
That it is in Northamptonshire.'

(David Townsend 1892)

We begin our literary tour of the county in Kettering, for no better reasons than it's where we both live and we have to start somewhere.

Kettering is predominantly a Victorian town. An ancient core of church and manor house surrounded by rows of red-bricked terraced houses, factory buildings, schools, chapels and churches, which proliferate around its centre.

The arrival of the railway in 1857, the development of the boot and shoe industry and, with the advent of the Singer sewing machine, the growth of the clothing trade, allied to printing and engineering, all contributed to the town's rapid expansion.

Industrial growth coincided with the final demise of silk-weaving and the onset of an agricultural depression, creating a large pool of cheap labour in and around the town. Workers needed housing, and the town's entrepreneurs – men like stay-maker John Turner Stockburn and boot and shoe manufacturers Tom Bird, William Meadows and John Bryan – put their money into real estate, purchasing vast areas of land close to their factories and selling it off advantageously as building plots.

The attractive combination of regular, secure employment and affordable, good quality accommodation contributed to a massive increase in population. Between 1861 and 1901, the number of inhabitants rose from 5,485 to 28, 683.

Many had forsaken the traditional country cottage, featured in a verse by Grafton Underwood poet, **David Townsend**, (born 6th October 1807),

> *'Our little cottage which was thatched,*
> *To large farm buildings was attached.*
> *And it contained, if you must know,*
> *A pantry and one room below.*
> *In family we numbered five*
> *And yet we always did contrive,*
> *To live and wash and bake and brew*
> *In that one room the whole year through.'*

in favour of the town's new working class estates. Townsend was a blacksmith who moved to Kettering after carrying on business at Geddington and Little Oakley. Obviously a man of some spirit and vision, and a staunch temperance advocate, it was whilst living in Geddington in 1842 that he began a Manuscript Magazine, entitled *'Sparks from Vulcan's Forge'*, which continued for only seven months. He published numerous booklets, including *'Jubilee Memories' (1887)*, *'Kettering; a Flourishing Town' (1889)* and the poem, quoted above, on *'the early Life of the Author'*. His death, on February 5th 1897, in his ninetieth year, prompted many warm tributes in the *Kettering Leader*. This, in verse, from **Mr Joseph Hawthorn**, recalls aspects of his personal appearance.

> *'No more he'll vend his simple rhymes,*
> *No more we'll hear him sing*
> *His songs of temperance, and the time*
> *When George the Third was King.*
>
> *And though in fancy we shall see*
> *His figure, tall and thin,*
> *With breeches buttoned at the knee –*
> *A bandage round his chin:*
>
> *His well-worn hat and coat of grey,*
> *A stocking on each wrist;*
> *Now that he's gone Death's trackless way,*
> *Old David will be missed'.*

Hawthorn published a collection of his own poetry in 1882. Entitled, *'Poems'*, the verses were printed by Goss Brothers of Gas Street, (now Meadow Road), cost ninepence and range over a variety of subjects. The preface, like so many of its kind, denigrates the quality of the work maintaining that the poems were, *'written under the disadvantages of a very limited education, and in the scanty intervals of leisure that come between a constant round of toil.'*

The theme is continued in the introductory poem, *'To the Reader'*, which begins

> *'Reader, I fear you'll question why*
> *That one so unendowed as I, -*
> *Possessing little save the will,*
> *Attempts to climb Parnassus' hill:*
> *A hill where poets labour long*
> *With poem, sonnet, ode, and song,*
> *To gain a footing; yet with all,*
> *Where one may stand, a dozen fall.'*

There are *'Letters written home'*, *'Songs of the Seasons'*, and *'Miscellaneous Poems'*, the last of which, fittingly entitled *'Conclusion'*, ends with the following simple lines,

> *'Still I know every part,*
> *From beginning to end,*
> *Was conceived in the heart,*
> *Or it ne'er had been penned.'*

By no means all the incomers were country folk like Townsend. **John Plummer** was born near Tower Hill, London, the son of a stay-maker, on June 3rd 1831. An impoverished upbringing restricted his formal education, and to add to his disabilities, a childhood attack of fever left him deaf and lame. He largely recovered from the latter, but deafness remained with him to the end of his life. Self-taught, mainly through devouring every scrap of print gleaned from street bookstalls, he enrolled in night classes at the Spitalfields School of Design. Despite showing remarkable artistic promise, he couldn't afford to continue his studies and in 1853 moved to Kettering with the rest of his family in search of work. John and his father found employment in Stockburn's stay factory in Tanner's Lane, the fore-runner of the larger premises opened in Northall Street in 1876.

The young man's eclectic knowledge and literary proficiency were recognised by local publisher, Charles Knight, whose *Town and Country* newspaper started in 1855 with Plummer a regular contributor. Influenced no doubt by Chartism, the national movement dedicated to fighting oppression in the workplace, and the socialist writings of local poet and essayist, John Ayre Leatherland, he was an outspoken political activist and champion of the emergent working classes.

In 1857-8, economic depression brought temporary closure of the stay-factory.

> *'With Foodless shelves, and Fireless grates,*
> *We scare no where to turn:*
> *There is no Work: we must forego*
> *The Bread we fain would earn.'*

A younger brother, Japtheth, discontented at the prospects in the stay trade, decided to become a shoemaker. When the Kettering branch of the Shoemakers' Union passed a bye-law to the effect that no one should be allowed to learn the art of shoemaking after attaining the age of seventeen, and Japtheth found himself unable to obtain employment, John took up his cause. A series of letters, in which he defended *'The Rights of Labour'*, attacked the Shoemakers' Union by every possible argument. A pamphlet, entitled the 'Freedom of Labour', attracted notice throughout the country, bringing him recognition from Lord Brougham, to whom a second edition was dedicated.

A collection of his writing, containing numerous verses, their subjects ranging from social issues, (as illustrated in the example above), descriptions of places in the locality, and an evocative autobiographical memoir of his early life was published in 1860, entitled *'Songs of Labour: Northamptonshire Rambles and*

Poems'. Its distinguished list of subscribers included George Ward Hunt, a future Chancellor of the Exchequer, and George de Wilde, editor of the *Northampton Mercury*, to which publication Plummer frequently contributed.

At about this time, he made the acquaintance of the Revd G E Maunsell, a clerical poet and rector of Thorpe Malsor. Plummer and his wife enjoyed, *'many a pleasant evening ramble to the Thorpe Malsor Rectory,'* later describing his association with the village as, *'some of the happiest hours in my chequered career.'*

Among articles submitted to the *Northampton Mercury* was an evocative piece entitled, *'The Forgotten Poet',* describing a memorable meeting with John Clare in the Northampton General Asylum in May 1861.

'Passing through several of the wards we were ushered into what we first deemed to be a gentleman's private sitting-room, but which was the ordinary sitting chamber of the better class of patients; and which appeared very cosy and comfortable with its mahogany chairs, table and couch, warm soft carpets, and cheerful fire……… and there sat John Clare'.

In his concluding paragraph, Plummer is philosophical about the great poet's fate.

'…it is perhaps better for him to be as he is, than to awaken to reason and find himself among a new generation who know, and yet know him not, so little is he in fashion with the present generation.'

That same year, he became English Social Affairs Correspondent of the *'Sydney Morning Herald'*.

In 1864 Plummer moved to London and pursued a highly successful career in journalism, working initially on the editorial staff at Messrs Cassell & Co., and later for as disparate publications as *The Mineral Trades Review*, and *The Non-Conformist,* for whom he was 'special commissioner'. In this role he was the first to direct public attention to the labours of William, (later General), Booth. He emigrated to Australia with his wife and family in 1879, combining duties as editor of the *'Sydney Morning Herald'* with those of drawing master at the city's State Training College. He rejected a possible political career in favour of writing and foremost among his considerable literary achievements was the *'Centennial Ode'*, written to celebrate Australia's first hundred years. His well-appointed home, set among camellias, magnolias and pelargoniums on the shores of Lane Cove River a steamer's ride from Sydney, was a far cry from his humble origins.

Interestingly, the house was named 'Thorpe Malsor', echoing sentiments recorded in one of his early verses.

> *'Oh! Dearest Thorpe, my thoughts are linked with thee!*
> *And ever in my dreams I view*
> *Thy winding walks, thy groves, and grassy lea –*
> *For ever old, yet ever new.'*

John Plummer died, aged 83, on March 9th 1914. He was survived by his widow, formerly Miss Stafford Jenkinson of Kettering, and two sons.

Revd George Edmond Maunsell, friend and supporter of the young John Plummer, was born on April 17th 1816. Educated at Christ Church Oxford, he embarked upon a career in the church, succeeding to the living of Thorpe Malsor in 1841 and remaining rector until his death on October 29th 1875. (Thorpe Malsor Hall had been the Maunsell family home since 1622, George Edmond eventually inheriting the estate in 1866).

'*Poems*', a collection of his work, was published in 1861, and includes verses on local subjects including '*Rushton Hall*' and the '*Execution of Mary, Queen of Scots.*'

Plummer's muse, **John Ayre Leatherland**, was born at Kettering on May 11th 1812. His father, a carpenter, died when John was about six, and his mother married again in 1822. His maternal grandfather was John Ayre, a Baptist minister at Walgrave and Braybrooke, and one of the thirteen founder members of the Baptist Missionary Society in 1792. Apprenticed first to a shoemaker and then to a ribbon weaver, he left the ribbon factory and learned to weave velvet. In 1838, after pursuing a lengthy course of self-instruction, he won first prize in a local essay-writing competition entitled, '*The Best Means of Improving the Condition of the Working Classes.*' After enthusiastically embracing Chartism,

> *'Base oppressors, leave your slumbers,*
> *Listen to a nation's cry;*
> *Hark! United, countless numbers,*
> *Swell the peal of agony -*
> *Lo! From Britain's sons and daughters,*
> *In the depths of misery -*
> *Like the sound of many waters -*
> *Comes the cry 'We will be free!'*

he later became disaffected with the cause. By 1848 he had begun manufacturing and marketing plain and fancy silk vests but turned to journalism as a means of livelihood after suffering serious injuries, incurred after falling from the Kettering and Northampton omnibus in July 1850. He worked on the staff of several local newspapers, including the *Northampton Herald*, and in 1862 published a collection of his *'Essays and Poems with a brief Autobiographical Memoir'*. He continued to contribute to local journals up to his death in December 1874.

Kettering's Charter Mayor in 1938 was **John Alfred Gotch**, great-grandson of Thomas Gotch, the pioneer of the town's shoe trade during the late eighteenth century. Born in 1852, a member of an illustrious and gifted family, which included his brother, the celebrated artist Thomas Cooper Gotch, J A became Kettering's first resident practising architect. Along with his partner, Charles Saunders, he designed many important buildings, both locally and nationally. Gotch buildings in the town include the Alfred East Art Gallery, the Borough Council Offices, (once the town's Grammar and High Schools) and the HSBC Bank, while the imposing yet elegant Post Office block in Gold Street was sacrificed during town centre development in the 1970s.

Honoured by the Royal Institute of British Architects as its first provincial president, Gotch was also a celebrated author and his books on architecture are standard works. Most notable are *'The Old Halls and Manor-houses of Northamptonshire'* (1936) and its companion volume, *'Squires' Homes and other Old Buildings of Northamptonshire'* (1939), which provide a wealth of information about the great families that helped shape the county's history. Gotch's long life was not without personal tragedy. His only son was killed in action in France during the First World War, and he was pre-deceased by his wife, who died in 1924, eighteen years before her husband. JA Gotch was buried in the tranquil setting of Weekley churchyard, just a short distance from the grave of another distinguished local writer who, coincidentally, had provided him with valuable details about the history and contents of nearby Boughton House.

Charles Henry Montagu-Douglas-Scott, the second son of Lord Walter Scott and grandson of the Fifth Duke of Buccleuch and Queensberry, was born in London on June 16th 1862. The preface to *'Tales of Northamptonshire'*, a collection of ballads published shortly after his death, provides a brief yet fascinating biography. It describes a true 'Renaissance Man' steeped in a love of the arts and the antiquities of Boughton House, the family's ancestral home where he spent most of his early life. After suffering from infantile paralysis at the age of three, he was crippled for life and unable to walk without crutches. Despite lacking a formal education he cultivated a natural love of art and literature, visiting all the important picture galleries of Europe. A keen student of modern languages, he was proficient enough in French, German and Italian to publish translations of several collections of poetry, including *'The Sonnets of Ceccio Angiolieri'*. Modestly, he regarded these efforts as inconsequential compared with the work of the great Gabriel Dante Rossetti whose, *'masterly renderings are naturally far beyond the powers of a mere bungler like myself.'*

Charles began composing poetry in his teenage years and by the turn of the nineteenth century had written sufficient verse to fill three volumes, entitled *'Northamptonshire Songs'*, and *'printed for private circulation at the Chiswick Press'* between 1904-6. The contents range over a variety of subjects and are by no means parochial. Consider this powerful stanza from *'HMS Saldanha'*, a poem describing the sinking of a frigate off the north-west coast of Ireland in 1811.

> *'Hear the wind, how it howls*
> *In the hollows of space,*
> *How it shrieks, how it growls*
> *And increases in pace;*
> *How it hunts through the dark*
> *With the hunger of shark –*
> *Lo! The flash of a light! – tis the chace!*
> *And now hark! –*
> *The storm smites the Saldanha!'*

Many of the poems with a local setting re-appeared in the afore-mentioned *'Tales of Northamptonshire'*, which the author edited and prepared for publication in the final months of his life. His introductory notes contain further evidence of characteristic self-deprecation.

'The following trifles were written many years ago, when I was very young and inexperienced. Most of the legends to which they refer were then current in the villages of north Northamptonshire. I understand this is no longer the case.'

The ballads have intriguing titles such as, *'The Curse of Rushton Hall'*, *'The Wild Huntsman of Whittlebury'* or *'The Bearded Lady of Bulwick'*. Apocryphal tales, like the drowning of a witch in Stanion, may well have inspired the stories in *'Northamptonshire Ghosts and Legends'* by Kettering writer, Marion Pipe, but others portray authentic historical events.

'Fotheringhay in Winter'

On Sunday the 5ᵗʰ February 1587, Master Robert Beale arrived at
Fotheringhay with the warrant for Queen Mary's execution. Three days
afterwards, she became immortal.

> *'The skies are grey o'er Fotheringhay*
> *The tottering church, the tumbled mound;*
> *The Nene meanders on its way*
> *Without a sound;*
> *The fields are flat on either bank;*
> *The ploughland rich, the meadow rank;*
> *The climate's gloomy, cold and dank.*
> *And this is all one notes today*
> *Around.*
>
> *And Scotland's queen beheld this Nene*
> *That oozes idly toward the main,*
> *And thought of many a fairer scene,*
> *Of Loire or Seine;*
> *Of dancing Tweed or dimpling Clyde,*
> *Of birchen bank and moorland side, -*
> *How sadly must she here have eyed*
> *This sulky, silent, sombre Nene,*
> *This drain.'*

As the above Montagu-Scott poem indicates, its subject has residential qualification for inclusion in this compilation of Northamptonshire writers, albeit a brief one. **Mary, Queen of Scots** spent the final months of her short life as a prisoner in the castle. The following lines, in which she contemplates the injustice of her fate, are taken from a sonnet written on the eve of her execution.

> *'And you, my friends who have loved me so true*
> *Remember lacking health and heart and peace,*
> *There is nothing worthwhile I can do;*
> *Ask only that my misery cease*
> *Being punished in a world like this*
> *I've earned my portion of eternal bliss.*

Charles Henry Montagu-Douglas-Scott died on March 4th 1936 at Geddington Priory, then part of the Boughton Estate and where he had lived a reclusive life in his later years, and was buried in Weekley churchyard close to many of his long line of ancestors.

If John Plummer travelled to the other side of the world in pursuit of his calling, **George Harrison**'s muse rarely led him beyond the boundaries of his own county. Born in 1876 in Kettering's Workhouse Lane, later re-named Dryland Street, Harrison was, like his father, a barber by trade. Business was conducted at a shop in Rockingham Road and it was not unusual for staff to work some fourteen hours a day, every day, except Sundays.

The young George had left the British School in the fittingly named, School Lane, at thirteen, but had already developed the love of art and literature which would sustain and inspire him throughout his life. Much of his own poetry and painting came from the writings of naturalists, such as Gilbert White, Richard Jefferies and WH Hudson, and their fine descriptive sketches of rural life. Fired with enthusiasm, and no little talent, he set off on his bicycle into the countryside every Sunday, with an easel strapped to his back and a notebook in his pocket.

Harrison's artistic ability quickly came to the notice of that most eminent of Kettering painters, Sir Alfred East, whose advice was gratefully received. John Trevitt Nettleship, another local artist and widely regarded as one of the greatest of Victorian animal painters, generously lent his support. To further his studies, friends, including Mr Frank Berrill, manager of the town's Midland Bank, financed a trip to Antwerp, then one of Europe's most prestigious art centres, under the supervision of Grammar School art master, William Bonner Gash. Another leading Kettering artist, Thomas Cooper Gotch, who had himself studied in the city, also contributed towards the young Harrison's expenses. In time, the hairdresser's paintings became highly collectible around the area and he held several successful exhibitions in the gallery that bears his mentor's name.

Harrison's poetry found expression in a series of collections illustrated with his own drawings. *'Poems' (1921),* was followed by five volumes of *'Poems and Sketches'*, published between 1927 and 1946. In 1948, a more substantial publication entitled *'A Wanderer in Northamptonshire'* delightfully brought together many articles, drawings and verses originally contributed to local newspapers between 1925 and 1945. (Curiously, many were subscribed to the *Kettering Leader*, a publication produced by the Northamptonshire Printing and Publishing Company whose premises stood close to the site in Dryland Street once occupied by the Harrison family home).

This book was republished in two volumes by John and Vera Worledge in the early nineteen-nineties and contains a lyrical account of his excursions around the county. One verse of a poem dedicated to his home-town extols the virtues of its most celebrated artist sons,

> *'East, Nettleship and Gotch are names that dwell*
> *With those who strive for art and loveliness,*
> *I joy to know that her first beauty fell*
> *Upon their hearts and woo'd with soft caress,*
> *To create for man a magic spell.'*

But nowhere is his affection for the town and its people more apparent than in the passage he wrote for Kettering's Charter brochure in 1938.

> *'The modern factory may be harsh with the discordant noises of this*
> *Machine Age, but on his way to it the factory worker, walking briskly down*

Almond Road or along Laburnum Crescent, glimpses the first flush on the face of Spring; and when he has washed off the grime of the day's toil, in an incredibly short space of time he can be 'over the hills and far away', where the birds have their concert hall, and the buttercups spread their cloth of gold.'

George Harrison died at his home, in the town's Bath Road, on the last day of December 1950.

The fine building of St Faith's Church Newton, standing in splendid isolation above the Ise valley, became the model for Oxgodby parish church, centre-piece for **JL Carr**'s master-piece, Booker short-listed and winner of the 1980 Guardian Fiction Prize, *'A Month in the Country'*. Indeed George Harrison has also penned a few lines illustrating its situation well.

> *'Thy lonely church confined by flowering fields*
> *Stands a wise symbol for a cherished creed,*
> *That lowly faith a comfort yields,*
> *To troubled hearts indeed.'*

Some forty years ago, and virtually redundant, its location rendered the building vulnerable to vandals. That it survived is due, in no small part, to Jim Carr's determined efforts to keep the building alive by holding poetry readings, concerts and other literary gatherings on the site.

Accessible only by road from the village of Newton Magna to the west or along a muddy track from Mill Farm to the east, today's visitors will find little evidence of its once proud heritage, apart from its fine spire. Many of the more interesting artefacts were removed to the Church of St Mary Magdalene at neighbouring Geddington when the building was converted into an educational field study centre during the nineteen-sixties. These include memorials to the Mulshos and Tanfields, distinguished ancestors of the Treshams of Newton Parva, for whom St Faiths was originally the family chapel. Nothing now remains of the great hall or the former village which once occupied the site between the church and Mill Farm save the dovecote, whose grandeur bears impressive testimony to the family's prominence during Tudor times.

In an affectionate obituary, *The Guardian's* Matthew Engel described James Lloyd Carr as *'a sort of one-man literary anti-establishment'* who brought forth a succession of books, maps and novels from his *'magnificently unglamorous address'* in Kettering's Milldale Road under the imprint of the Quince Tree Press.

The product of an idiosyncratic but uniquely gifted mind, the body of work provides a valuable insight into the life and times of Northamptonshire's Renaissance Man. Yet he was a true Yorkshireman, born in Thirsk in 1912, and educated at Carlton Minnion village school and Castleford Secondary School.

A schoolteacher by profession, in 1938 Jim spent a year working in a High School in, of all places, South Dakota.

'All snapped up... New York City, Beverley Hills, all them pretty little Christmas card spots in Vermont full of snow and churchgoers.....but it just happens there is one job left... not that you'd want it... dead in the middle... Palisades, South Dakota.'

The experience inspired his initial attempt at novel writing, although the original manuscript remained secreted in a shoe-box for many years before an updated, and no doubt much refined, version eventually appeared in 1985. Entitled *'The Battle of Pollocks Crossing'*, it was promptly nominated for a Booker Prize.

His writing first found expression as poetry, an evocative selection of which appears in *'JL Carr: some early poems and recent drawings'*, an addition to the lengthy list of Pocket Books published by Jim's son, Robert, who now manages the Quince Tree Press from his home in Bury St Edmunds.

'Rhyme and rhythm,
Rhythm and rhyme,
Rhyme makes music
Rhythm keeps time.

School for scholars,
Home for friends,
Life to live well
Till death all ends.'

(Hastings Road School 1940)

However, by the time he finally found a publisher for his first novel, *'A Day in Summer'*, Jim had been resident in Kettering for some thirteen years. He had moved to the town from Birmingham in 1950 as headteacher-designate at Highfields Primary School and before settling in Milldale Road, he lodged for a time at the then Chesham House Hotel in Lower Street. Fittingly, for one destined to become so immersed in the county's history, the building had once been home to the Gotch family, whose forebears had introduced the boot and shoe industry to the town at the end of the eighteenth century.

'A Day in Summer', was published in 1963 and tells the story of a bereaved father intent on avenging his son's death by a hit-and-run driver. It contains the genesis of several themes that would become recurrent throughout Jim's work, most notably the idiosyncratic and splendidly absurd nature of human-kind, reflected in wartime service, life in school, unfulfilled love, duplicity and deceit.

Three years later, having resigned from his position at Highfields to concentrate on writing, he remained solvent due to an income largely derived from sales of his intricate, and now very collectible, beautifully drawn county maps. A second novel, *'A Season in Sinji'*, based very closely upon his wartime experiences on an RAF station in West Africa, was published in 1967 by cricket aficionado Alan Ross, who described the book as, *'one of the lasting novels of the post-war years.'*

In the book, several of the leading characters are named after local places or personalities with whom Jim had an acquaintance. Hence Wakerly, Glapthorn and Turton, the last an erstwhile vicar of Geddington.

A small village on the outskirts of Northampton gave its name to the central character of his third, and arguably most amusing novel, *'The Harpole Report'*. The story made little impact when first published in 1972 and Jim stored a pile of remaindered copies, acquired from the publisher for a mere tenpence each, in a corner of his garage. Salvation came in the unlikely form of writer and comedian Frank Muir who, when appearing on 'Desert Island Discs', described the book as, *'The funniest and perhaps the truest story about running a school I have ever read.'*

Understandably, demand rocketed in the wake of the programme and Jim was able to resurrect his copies from the dusty recesses, disposing of them at a goodly profit. It proved the turning point in his writing career, bringing his work to a wider public and one more inclined to stump up a few bob for a book.

His next novel, *'How Steeple Sinderby Wanderers Won The FA Cup', (1975)*, is a modern fairy-tale in which a village football team, coached by the mysterious Dr Kossuth, schoolmaster and Hungarian political refugee, and comprising a rag-taggle bunch of has-beens and never-will-be's, defeats mighty Glasgow Rangers in the final. Strangely, the allegorical nature of the book resonates powerfully with recent concerns about the true spirit of the game and a stage version was successfully produced at London's Mermaid Theatre.

The afore-mentioned Booker short-listed novels, *'A Month in the Country'* and *'The Battle of Pollock's Crossing'* followed and then, in *'What Hetty Did' (1988)*, and *'Harpole & Foxberrow: General Publishers' (1992)*, Jim sought to resolve the fate of the rich crop of characters created in earlier stories.

Fame and a modest fortune came late to JL Carr, who never lost a certain bluff reticence. In later years he enjoyed sitting in his garden on summer afternoons, the weathered statuary peeping through abundant greenery so reminiscent of Oxgodby churchyard, and discussing two of his great obsessions -- education and cricket. He once told me that one of his greatest regrets in life was to have decided not to travel to Headingley Cricket Ground on the final day of the county match against Nottinghamshire in July 1932, fearing rain would prevent any play. To his everlasting sorrow, his over-caution caused him to miss watching the great Yorkshire bowler, Hedley Verity, take all ten wickets for just ten runs to conjure an unlikely victory.

Jim Carr died on February 26th 1994, leaving his books, his maps, his stone-carvings, several distinctive and remarkable large-format volumes of pictures and words depicting the glories of his adopted county entitled *'The Northamptonshire Record',* and a host of memories for those privileged enough to have known him. The Blakesley-based writer Byron Rogers, to whom Jim initially entrusted *'The Record',* compiled an illustrated memoir of his friend, *'The Life and Times of JL Carr',* in 1996 and is currently researching a fulsome biography which is eagerly awaited by devotees.

In the last paragraph of his final novel Jim lists some of the characters that populate his stories. They, *'slip and slide like shadows, are moody, unreliable, bothersome. They flounder about and need footnotes to keep them from sidling off. Whereas books have body; books (if you are listening) always will say what they said last time. Or stay silent when you shut them up.'*

An appropriate last word.

According to FW Bull's definitive *'History of Kettering', (1891)*, Tanner's Lane took its name from a certain Mr Wade, who had his tanning-yard in the vicinity. Today, the thoroughfare serves chiefly to provide a rear access to the Newlands shopping complex and multi-storey car-park. A short distance to the north, almost parallel to Tanner's Lane, runs Northall Street, now part of the town's inner ring-road system. Sandwiched between the two roads, its front door facing the entrance to the shopping mall, its back just feet from a line of aircraft hangar-like retail outlets, stands Beech Cottage, home from 1947 to Kettering-born writer and historian, **Tony Ireson**.

When he and his late wife Rene moved into the eighteenth century cottage it stood in its own grounds within *'a rough rectangle bounded by Gold Street, Newland Street, Northall Street and Lower Street'*. The area contained a rich variety of buildings including the Fuller Baptist chapel, a Victorian grammar school, shops, factories, a cinema, a brewery and two fine old houses, the Mission House and Beech House. In 1960, alarming plans for the comprehensive re-development of the area were made public. Over the next fifteen years, civic vandalism on a grand scale swept away all but the chapel, the Mission House which, in 1792 had witnessed the birth of the Baptist Missionary Society and, against all the odds, Beech Cottage.

Tony's remarkable account of the struggle between the developers and the town's embryonic Civic Society is recorded in *'Old Kettering and its Defenders', (1984).* This was published thirty years after his first foray into the book trade.

In 1953, when working as a journalist on a local newspaper, he had been approached by publishers, Robert Hale, to contribute a volume on *Northamptonshire* for their County Book series. The commission had originally been awarded to HE Bates, but pressure of work apparently prevented the Rushden-born writer from undertaking the task. For Tony it was very much a labour of love and one to be completed in his own inimitable style. He traversed the county developing his central theme – the story of simple human beings silhouetted against the colourful backcloth of history. Room is found, not only to describe matters of great moment, like the trial of Thomas a Becket at Northampton Castle in 1164, but to ruminate upon the distinctive taste of a boiled egg, cradled in the elm egg-cup produced by Kings Cliffe's last surviving wood-turner and acquired by Tony back in the nineteen-thirties.

Eventually published in 1954, all 2,500 copies sold out in just two weeks. Half a century later, the book remains essential reading for those with a thirst for local knowledge, but alas now only available to those prepared to browse in second-hand book-shops.

Although it is no longer entirely true that, *'many Northamptonshire town dwellers are almost countrymen who, a few minutes after slamming the front door, can be striding through woods or roaming along fragrant footpaths',* much of our county remains unspoilt and unappreciated. As Tony wrote, *'she reveals her charms only to those who have time for her.'*

In his illuminating introduction to the book, Tony describes himself as a *'small-town enthusiast'.* This is evident from, *'Old Kettering – A View From The Thirties',* which he published in 1988 at the age of seventy-five. *'Now is the time to gather memories',* he wrote. *'This book makes a start, and I hope it will be followed by some more aspects of Kettering life in the between-wars years.'*

Five volumes have been produced since, providing an informative and highly evocative glimpse into a distant age, through the author's own recollections and those of his contemporaries.

In the introduction to his county book, Tony Ireson expressed a desire to spend his twilight years residing in one of Northamptonshire's villages, writing, *'I do not know of one in which I could not live and be happy.'*

In 1974, following the demolition of the neighbouring Beech House, and despite the distressing annexation of his own garden and the prospect of encirclement, he decided to accept his friend Jim Carr's advice that, *'Human beings can get used to almost anything,'* and stay on at Beech Cottage. At the time of his death in Kettering General Hospital, at the age of eighty-eight on February 1st 2002, he was still living there.

In 1993, Tony Ireson wrote the foreword to *'Kettering Revisited'*, the first of three collections of photographs of the town compiled by his friend, Tony Smith. They had much in common. Both were born in Kettering, educated at the Grammar School and employed as local journalists. Fittingly, it was Smith who penned an affectionate obituary on his mentor's death. Entitled *'Passing of town's defender'*, it describes the venerable author as *'a true gentleman of the press who lived by old-fashioned values of decency, honesty and fair play'*. It also recalls fascinating, intimate details of an idiosyncratic lifestyle in which, among other things, modern technology was ignored in favour of a 1923 Remington typewriter!

The tribute ends with a truly marvellous 'Iresonism'. Looking out one day from his Beech Cottage window at the multi-storey carpark opposite, he said, *'If I so wish I can pretend it's Hampton Court. It's the same colour.'*

A plaque over the north door in St Botolph's church, Barton Seagrave commemorates the life of **John Bridges**, the Lincoln's Inn lawyer who compiled the first significant historical record of the county. His father had purchased the Barton Seagrave estate in 1665 and the family lived in a large house, which occupied the site of the present hall on Barton Road. John, one of twelve children, was born in 1666, and raised in the village.

Having elected for a career in the law, he was appointed Solicitor of the Customs in 1695, Cashier of Excise in 1715, became a governor of the Bridewell Prison and the Bethlehem Hospital, and a Fellow of the Royal Society of Antiquaries. In 1719 he began the work for which he is best remembered. Travelling around the county at considerable personal expense, he accumulated transcripts containing drawings, records and copious information relating to every parish in Northamptonshire. These were compiled under the headings of the twenty Saxon Hundreds dating from the reign of Edward the Second. Originally numbering thirty, the hundreds were administrative districts indicating limits of jurisdiction by the Lord of the Hundred, the Sheriff of the County's representative.

On Bridges' death in 1724, the thirty or forty manuscript volumes passed first to his brother, William, then, via a 'committee of county gentlemen', to the

Revd Peter Whalley, late Fellow of St John's College, Oxford. Whalley spent years in careful scrutiny and, in 1791, published two volumes, entitled *'The History and Antiquities of Northamptonshire, compiled from the manuscript Collections of the late learned antiquary, John Bridges Esq'*. Whalley's admiration for Bridges' scholarship is apparent in the book's introduction, where he describes him as *'A man of the highest degree qualified to direct such an undertaking'*.

Each chapter contains detailed descriptions of the main features of all the settlements within the designated area and each follows the same pattern. Most notable are population figures, references from the Domesday Book, (here called the 'General Survey'), changes in land-ownership and the genealogy of leading families, architectural features of the local church, records of incumbents and important monuments.

A magnificent copy of the work, enlarged to five volumes by the addition of numerous sketches was formed by Kettering printer Mr Thomas Dash, and bequeathed by his son to the British Museum in 1883.

Roundabout Corby

Writers have long extolled the virtues of Oxford. Matthew Arnold writes famously of its *'dreaming spires'* and Gerard Manley Hopkins of a,

'Towery city and branching between towers
Cuckoo-echoing, bell-swarméd, lark-charméd, rook-racked, river-rounded....'

Yet one author more recently associated with the university town spent part of his life in a world far removed from the gilded halls of academia.

Set in gently rolling farmland, Corby transformed itself with the discovery of iron-ore from a small sleepy village to a thriving industrial steel town eventually dominated by Stewarts and Lloyds.

Growth continued after World War Two and in 1950 it was designated as one of England's first post-war new towns.

Prior to 1955, and the opening of the town's grammar school, Corby's eleven-plus successes were required to travel to Kettering. The new building, a significant step forward for the town, was a brick, concrete and glass construction, typical of the period and entirely congruous with the new town uniformity of architect-designed housing estates and municipal buildings.

Colin Dexter, the Stamford-born son of a taxi-driver, was appointed to the school staff in 1959 as senior classics master, after beginning his career teaching Latin and Greek at schools in Leicester and Loughborough. He spent seven happy years in Corby, during which he played for the town's hockey side. However, educational concerns over the grammar school's change to comprehensive status and a worsening hearing impairment which was beginning to affect his teaching, led to a move to Oxford in 1966, where he took up a position with the University Examination Board. He continued setting and grading examination papers until his retirement in 1988 at the age of fifty-nine.

Colin's literary output had begun nearly a quarter a century earlier with the publication of *'Liberal Studies: An outline course'*, a textbook in two volumes, which he co-authored with Edgar Rayner, senior history master at Leicester's Wyggeston Grammar School. He made his first venture into fiction during a wet week in Wales. The detective story he was reading proved disappointing and he resolved to do better himself. It's uncertain whether this was the genesis of *'Last Bus to Woodstock'*, his first novel, which eventually appeared in 1975, after rejection by publishing giants, Collins. The book featured Dexter's most famous creations, the misanthropic and world-weary Inspector Morse and his long-suffering sergeant, Lewis. Devotees of the long-running television series will recognise in the following extract taken from the novel's opening pages, many characteristics of the protagonists played so definitively by actors John Thaw and Kevin Whateley.

> *'By a quarter to midnight Lewis had finished his task and he reported to Morse, who was sitting with The Times in the manager's office, drinking what looked very much like whisky.*
>
> *'Ah Lewis.' He thrust the paper across. 'Have a look at 14 down: Take in bachelor? It could do (3).' He saw what Morse had written into the completed diagram. BRA. What was he supposed to say? He had never worked with Morse before.*
>
> *'Good clue don't you think?'*
>
> *Lewis, who had occasionally managed the Daily Mirror coffee-time crossword was out of his depth, and felt much puzzled.*
>
> *'I'm afraid I'm not very hot on crosswords, sir.'*
>
> *'Bachelor – that's B.A. and 'take' is the letter 'r'; recipe in Latin. Did you never do any Latin?'*
>
> *'No, sir.'*

Morse's fondness for crossword puzzles, like his love of classical music, reflects that of his creator, a former national champion in the Ximenes clue-writing competition. No less than 29 out of the 30 characters in his initial book were named after first prize-winners in various crossword competitions, the odd one out being the villain. However, perhaps his most intriguing conundrum was the mystery surrounding his hero's unlikely Christian name, Endeavour, which was only revealed in *'Death is Now My Neighbour'*, published in September 1996 and originally intended to be Morse's swan-song.

Dexter followed up *'Woodstock's'* success with a series of acclaimed novels, several of which earned recognition by the Crime Writers Association, and in 1997 he was awarded the association's Diamond Dagger for his outstanding contribution to the genre.

In 1999, to the intense disappointment of his legion of fans, comprising both readers and viewers, Dexter signalled his own 'retirement' by 'killing-off' the cantankerous detective in his final novel, its title, *'The Remorseful Day'*, further evidence of the author's fondness for word-play.

Should detectives Lloyd and Hill succeed Morse and Lewis as the nation's favourite policemen it would be proof that truth is often stranger than fiction. The Bartonshire sleuths are the creation of county writer, **Jill McGowan**, who once attended Colin Dexter's Latin classes as a pupil at Corby Grammar School. Curiously, the coincidence was lost on Jill until she discovered they shared the same publisher.

Jill McGowan moved to Corby from Argyll in 1957 at the age of ten. On leaving school she, like many contemporaries, worked at British Steel until the plant's closure brought redundancy in the early nineteen eighties. She used her new-found 'free time' to write, completing her first novel, *'A Perfect Match'* in 1983. Although she denies basing her characters on real people, Jill admits that Stansfield, the setting for her stories, is the former steel town where she has lived for the past forty-five years.

In 2001, her detective duo were introduced to a television audience when Carlton TV broadcast a two hour adaptation of, *'A Shred of Evidence'*, originally published six years earlier. No stranger to the demands of television, Colin Dexter gave valuable advice when Jill approached him regarding editorial control over the story. *'Whatever they want you to do, say yes'*, was his pragmatic response. Should producers decide to turn the pilot into a series there is no shortage of material, Jill having written fifteen novels in all since her writing debut nineteen years ago.

There is no doubting the location of *'Pig'*, **Andrew Cowan**'s novel first published in 1994. The setting, described in this extract from the book's fourth chapter, will be instantly recognisable to readers familiar with Corby's eastern outskirts during the late nineteen-eighties.

> *'Far away in the distance I could see the Enterprise Zone, a cluster of tiny white factories and conifer trees. It looked like a planner's scale model and I couldn't imagine that people would work there.........At about the same time a hoarding appeared on the far side of the railway cutting, facing across Gran's garden. It stood at the head of the tip and said LeisureLand in large cheerful letters. Helicopters and rockets arched over the words. Beneath them was a line of children and adults about to enter a dome. Similar signs faced out onto every road that skirted the old site of the steelworks, and sometimes in the evening paper there were letters asking when the work was supposed to begin. One was headlined 'Fantasy Land?' I preferred to read the company's replies, which were more optimistic.'*

Those who remember 'WonderWorld', and the added 'Wonder When', will understand.

The son of a steelworker, Andrew Cowan was born in Corby in 1960. As a child he was a voracious reader who enjoyed writing and, after attending Beanfield School and Nene College, Northampton, he completed his formal education at the University of East Anglia, where he came under the influence of the renowned novelist and creative writing tutor Malcolm Bradbury. Like many aspiring authors, Andrew spent several years in menial jobs, including cleaning in a cake factory, to fund his writing and in 1989 moved to Glasgow to work as a school librarian. The eventual publication of *'Pig'*, after countless rejections, changed his whole life. The book, which won the Betty Trask Award (for British and Commonwealth writers under the age of 35), the Sunday Times Young Novelist of the Year award and the Ruth Hadden Memorial Prize, attracted great media attention. Andrew's sympathetic, but realistic, treatment of the book's central themes of first love and racial conflict won widespread critical acclaim, fellow author, the crime-writer Michael Dibdin, describing it as *'a first novel of extraordinary poise and accomplishment.'*

A second novel, *'Common Ground'*, was published in 1996, by which time Andrew had moved to Norwich and become a full-time writer. Ostensibly the topical story of a campaign against a motorway, the book also addresses issues of parental responsibility which resonate strongly with the author's recent experiences of fatherhood. Commenting on the subject in a newspaper interview, he said, *'It is best to write about what you know, and at the time I started the novel my daughter loomed large in my life.'*

Now an established and respected author, Andrew Cowan produced a third novel, *'Crustacean'*, in 2000. Doubtless there will be more for, as he confesses, *'I write because I have to: it's a mental illness, an obsessive-compulsion disorder. I'd much rather be a potter.'*

Another incomer, albeit one who arrived in the area somewhat later in life than Jill McGowan, soon became immersed in local history and quickly established a considerable reputation as researcher, writer and broadcaster. **Peter Hill** was born in Brighton, grew up in Surrey and travelled widely after graduating from the University of East Anglia. He became fascinated with Rockingham Forest and its environs during visits in the mid nineteen-seventies and, after settling in Great Oakley in 1989 and discovering the dearth of published material on the locality, determined to make good the deficit. His first venture was a series of books on his adopted village but in 1995, aided by contributions from over two hundred local people from all walks of life, he compiled *'Rockingham Forest – Then and Now'*. An extended version, which can be regarded as the definitive record, was published in 1998 as *'Rockingham Forest Revisited'*. The book also includes a comprehensive bibliography of county books relevant to the area, including key reference material, individual village and town histories and personal memoirs. Three photographic histories of the Forest followed.

In September 1997, an exhibition entitled *'Wood, Trees and the Green Man'* was staged at Oundle School. When Peter Hill was approached to deliver a complementary lecture on the mysterious pagan symbol, found chiefly in a profusion of medieval churches and public buildings in the north of the county, he could scarcely have imagined the effect it would have on his life. After researching the subject in detail he recorded his findings in *'In Search of the Green Man in Northamptonshire' (1996)*. Interest in the topic is now international and has led to world-wide lecture tours and an up-dated and enlarged edition of the original book is due for publication in 2003.

Peter Hill's contribution was officially recognised in September 1999 when he received a 'services to local history' award from the British Association of Local History at the Guildhall, Northampton.

Renowned author, **Charles Dickens**, was a regular visitor to Rockingham Castle during the nineteenth century as a guest of its owners, Mr and Mrs Richard Watson. Dickens was inspired to write *'Bleak House'* while resident there, basing Chesney Wold on Rockingham. According to Tony Ireson's *'Northamptonshire'*, Dickens *'strode up its steep street thinking out the plot for 'David Copperfield'* and created much of the story in a room overlooking Yew Walk. The novel is, indeed, dedicated to the Watsons.

Dickens had first become familiar with the area in 1835, when as a fledgling reporter on the *Morning Chronicle* he came to Kettering to cover the general election, staying at the town's 'White Hart Inn', (later re-named 'The Royal Hotel' in honour of Queen Victoria's visit in November 1845). A similar association led the famous writer to locate the comic duel between the rival editors of the *Eatonswill Gazette* and the *Eatonswill Independent* in the *'Pickwick Papers'* at Towcester's 'Saracen's Head' hotel.

> *'The author begs leave to inform the courteous Reader, that the publication of the following trifling pieces, was intirely owing to the encouragement of a most worthy friend, who by chance having seen some of them, thought they might not be unworthy of the public eye.*
> *That so far from any such idea ever having struck himself, he actually had scarce a single copy by him, but was obliged to have recourse to those friends to whom they had occasionally been written, and (more than the author could deserve, or even have thought of) had most of them still respectfully in their possession – And to whose kind assistance also, he is happy as well as bound to acknowledge some of the chief embellishments in the following volume.'*

So reads the introduction to *'Miscellaneous Pieces: Original and Collected' by a Clergyman of Northamptonshire'*, and published anonymously in 1787. The mysterious cleric was **Talbot Keene**, the vicar of Brigstock with Stanion from his appointment in April 1773 to his death, at the age of eighty-nine, in February 1824. An Irishman, educated at Westminster School and a Fellow of Trinity College, Cambridge, Keene's anthology contains some wonderfully pithy verses, such as this example entitled, *'To a Lady: With a Phial of Ink.'*

> *'Fair lady, do not me despise,*
> *Tho' black, I'm honest, true and kind;*
> *Thro' damask cheeks, or sparkling eyes,*
> *What mortal yet e'er read the mind?*
>
> *Yet fair ones then be sure to write,*
> *In down-right honest black and white.'*

Typical of Keene's adroit sense of humour, is the amusing disclaimer printed in the frontispiece.

'The reader, it is hoped, will pass over with an indulgent eye, any inaccuracies he may meet with, as the author was 80 miles from the press when the book was printed.'

Any reader who has ventured into print will appreciate the sense of apprehension and mild neurosis embodied in these lines.

Talbot Keene was buried in the south chancel of St. Andrew's church, Brigstock below a memorial tablet which vertically challenged visitors have little hope of reading. The inscription, on the blackened plaque located high on the wall, includes an epitaph, which Trevor Hold, in his definitive work, *'A Northamptonshire Garland'*, speculates may have been written by the vicar himself.

'Lie lightly here, O! cold and cheerless dust.
For he was virtuous: he was kind and just.
Death drops the curtain! hides the fleeting scene:
And only Mem'ry tells that he has been.
Yet all our sorrows cry. 'Ah! here lies Keene.'

Brigstock Rectory

Roundabout King's Cliffe

Follow the quiet road that meanders from Bulwick to Apethorpe and there is little to suggest that the area was once part of the great Rockingham Forest which extended from Stamford in the north, to the rivers Welland and Nene in the west and east respectively, and down to Northampton in the south. Large open fields pre-dominate with many of the hedges and fences that accompanied enclosure in the early nineteenth century recently swept away by the demands of modern farming methods.

But for the interested visitor, echoes of the past are seldom far away. Red kites wheel in the sky above the Norman tower of Blatherwycke's Holy Trinity Church, redundant since 1978, and now the responsibility of the Churches Conservation Trust. There are two ways to access the churchyard. A signpost on the right as you enter the village from Bulwick points out a public footpath through fields to the east of the church building. Alternatively, drop down through the village and pass through the old stone gate-way on the right which led to Blatherwycke Hall, following the narrow gently-rising path to the oak churchyard gates decorated with monogrammed letters. Obtaining a huge iron key from Glebe Farm on the King's Cliffe road will enable you to gain entry to the church itself.

Holy Trinity is a shrine to the great families who lived at Blatherwycke, from the Engaines during the early 14th century to the Stafford-O'Briens, resident in the village until the nineteen-fifties. Descendants of Humphrey Stafford, who inherited the manor in the time of Edward III, consolidated the family's position in the village, and are commemorated in a number of fine brass and stone memorials in the North Chapel. When Irishman, Henry O'Brien, married a Stafford co-heiress early in the eighteenth century, he built a Palladian style mansion to replace the Staffords' large, but unfinished Elizabethan house. In 1840 the population of Blatherwycke is recorded in Lewis's Topographical Dictionary as 227 – most dependant upon the Stafford-O'Briens for their livelihood. By 1901, the number of residents had fallen to 101.

The Irish Land Acts, following the country's partition in the nineteen-twenties, forced the sale of the O'Briens' 25,000 acres in County Clare, and signalled the beginning of the family's demise. This culminated in the razing of Blatherwycke Hall in 1948. The building had been commandeered by the army during the Second World War and abandoned in a state of dereliction, leaving the surviving impecunious Stafford O'Brien sisters with little alternative but to sell for demolition.

Among the many fine monuments in the church is a wall memorial commemorating **Thomas Randolph**, a seventeenth century poet and dramatist. Born at Newnham near Daventry in 1605, Randolph was educated at Westminster School and at Trinity College, Cambridge. A skilled versifier in English and Latin, he wrote two plays, *'The Conceited Pedlar'* and *'Aristippus or the Joviall Philosopher'*, that were performed in Cambridge in 1631. In 1632, King Charles I visited the city and attended a performance of Randolph's comic play, *'The Jealous Lovers'*. Reputation much enhanced, the young playwright moved to London later that year and, on becoming a disciple of Ben Jonson, produced his most accomplished work, *'The Muses Looking Glass'*.

However, a life of debauchery and excess in the capital seriously impaired his health, and in 1634 he retired to the comparative quiet of Blatherwycke in the Northamptonshire countryside. There he became tutor to Master Anthony Stafford, fifth son of John Stafford, whose magnificent stone memorial occupies a prominent position in Holy Trinity's North Chapel. Randolph's belated recognition of the shallowness of London life is apparent in the opening verse of a cautionary poem, dedicated to his young pupil.

> 'Come, spur away!
> I have no patience for a longer stay;
> But must go down,
> And leave the chargeable noise of this great town.
> I will the country see;
> Where old simplicity,
> Though hid in grey,
> Doth look more gay
> Than foppery in plush or scarlet clad.
> Farewell, you city-wits that are
> Almost at civil war!
> Tis time that I grow wise, when all the world grows mad.'

Thomas Randolph died of smallpox in 1635 at the age of twenty-nine. Some of his work appeared posthumously three years later and a more comprehensive anthology, compiled by William Hazlitt, was published in 1875.

The inscription on Randolph's marble memorial, donated by Sir Christopher Hatton of Kirby Hall and made by eminent sculptor Nicholas Stone in 1640 for £10, is attributed to a friend and contemporary, **Peter Hausted**. The words contain many conceits, or verbal puzzles, typical of metaphysical poetry of the period.

> 'Here sleepe thirteene together in one Tombe
> And all these greate, yet quarrell not for rome.
> The Muses and ye Graces teares did meete
> And grav'd these letters on ye churlish sheete
> Who having wept, their fountaines drye,
> Through the Conduit of the Eye
> For their friend who here does lye,
> Crept into his grave and dyed,
> And soe the Riddle is untyed……….'

This implies that the great writer was not alone in his final resting-place but shared eternity with numerous distressed muses and graces, all mourning the loss of their late friend.

Peter Hausted was born in Oundle at the turn of the 16th century and educated at Queen's College, Cambridge. His satirical play, *'The Rival Friends'*, had been performed along with Randolph's, *'The Jealous Lovers'*, at the same Cambridge concert attended by King Charles I. Although the established church was often the target for his acerbic wit, Hausted held two clerical appointments in the county, as Vicar of Gretton (1639-40) and Rector of Old (1642-43). During the Civil War he became chaplain to Spencer, Earl of Northampton, and died during the siege of Banbury Castle in 1645.

The road from Blatherwycke arrives at King's Cliffe, where it divides into two. The right-hand fork leads to the Parish Church of All Saints and St James, which lies at the heart of the village.

Once the largest settlement in Rockingham Forest after Brigstock, King's Cliffe was created a Royal Manor by William I, became popular with medieval kings who stayed in the royal hunting lodge once located behind the church, and was the centre of control for the 'Bailiwick' or administrative district of the forest. Much of the original village, then situated to the south of the church, was destroyed by fire in 1462 and rebuilt on its present site.

Entering the churchyard by the gate near the north transept, it is impossible not to notice a large, unusual tombstone in the shape of a writing desk. It marks the burial place of **William Law**, born the son of a King's Cliffe grocer in 1685, who died in the manor house opposite in Hall Yard seventy-five years later.

A Fellow of Emmanuel College, Cambridge, Law took Holy Orders, but was unwilling to compromise his support for the Jacobite cause and refused to take the Oath of Allegiance to George I. He moved to London, becoming tutor to Edward Gibbon, father of the historian, and began to write about the importance of living out one's faith through one's actions.

Describing Law's work, the younger Gibbon damns with faint praise.

'Had not his vigorous mind been clouded by enthusiasm he might be ranked among the most agreeable and ingenious writers of his time.'

Nevertheless, the most important of his books, *'A Serious Call to a Devout and Holy Life'*, is said to have influenced many religious thinkers including Cardinal Newman and the evangelist, John Wesley.

On his return to Northamptonshire, first at Thrapston and later in his home village, Law and his acolytes, wealthy benefactors Mrs Elizabeth Hutcheson and Mrs Hestor Gibbon, put into practice the unselfish principles of the *'Serious Call'*. Their generosity made King's Cliffe, and the manor house in particular, a focal point for beggars, who invaded the village in great numbers, much to the annoyance of the local populace. However, Law persevered, the hostility eventually died down, and his reputation for charitable works reigned supreme. Schools and almshouses were established, and a library of ecclesiastical literature founded in a house on the Apethorpe road, whose front doorway still bears the inscription,

'Books of Piety are here lent to any
Perfons of this or y Neighbouring Towns'.

'The moss-grey mansion of my
father stands
Parked in an English
pasturage as fair
As any that the grass-green
isle can show'.

Three lines of poetry celebrating the quiet, yet exquisite, beauty of this county were written by **Julian Fane** of Apethorpe Hall in 1860. He would most surely be saddened by the current condition of the great and beautiful house granted, in 1550, to his ancestor, Sir Walter Mildmay, founder of Emmanuel College, Cambridge, and Commissioner for receiving the surrender of property during the Dissolution of the Monasteries in the reign of Henry VIII.

Visitors may observe, from a discreet distance, the bay-windows, porches, archways, ornamental pinnacles and curved gables which reflect the many architectural styles added during its first three hundred years, and wonder how much longer its neglect will be tolerated.

Sir Walter served four monarchs, Henry, Edward, Mary and Elizabeth, whose Chancellor of the Exchequer he was and, according to contemporary historian William Camden, *'for his virtue, wisdom, piety, and favour to learning and learned men hath deserved to be register'd among the best men of his age'*. To others, he was an uncompromising 'establishment' man who amassed a personal fortune through his service to the State.

He died in 1589 and was succeeded by his son, Anthony, who became Queen Elizabeth's ambassador to France. Sir Anthony (died 1617) and his wife, Lady Grace (died 1620) are buried in the Mildmay Chapel in St Leonard's Church, the tomb being one of the finest and most imposing in the county. Their effigies lie on a black and white marble tomb chest under a great domed canopy, surrounded by figures of Piety, Charity, Wisdom and Justice.

Sir Anthony's only daughter and heiress Mary married Sir Francis Fane, who became the first Earl of Westmorland in 1624. Their son, **Mildmay Fane**, (born 1602), was educated at his great-grandfather's college at Cambridge, became a devout Royalist and was lodged in the Tower shortly after the outbreak of the Civil War. On his release the following year, he returned to Apethorpe to develop the estate and further his love of poetry, which had received encouragement from no less a figure than Robert Herrick. In 1648, he printed for private circulation a volume of verse, *Otia Sacra*, which includes *'My Happy Life'*, a hymn to rural tranquillity and the myriad birds familiar on his estate. As Trevor Hold notes in *'A Northamptonshire Garland'*, the observations anticipate the writing of poet and naturalist, John Clare, almost two hundred years later.

> *'The Auger Hern, and soaring Kite,*
> *Kalendar weather in their flight;*
> *As doe the Cleanlier Ducks, when they*
> *Dive voluntary, wash, prune, play;'*

Left among his papers after his death in 1666 was a volume of *'Fugitive Poetry'* consisting of epigrams, acrostics and anagrams in English and Latin.

Julian Fane, born in Florence in 1827, was the younger son of John Fane, 11th Earl of Westmorland. Fane lived abroad for much of his life, following his father into the diplomatic service. While based in Vienna from 1858-65 as Secretary of the British Legation and Embassy, he met Robert Lytton, (the poet Owen Meredith, later Lord Lytton). On Fane's death in 1870, Lytton published a memoir containing a large selection of his poetry, including the *'Apethorpe'* poem, which was considered by John Betjeman many years later to be one of the finest ever written about Northamptonshire.

The Apethorpe estate was acquired by Leonard Brassey, nephew of Sir Thomas Brassey the Victorian railway magnate, in 1904. Today, his descendants live in the manor house, originally built by the sixth Earl of Westmorland for his agent in 1736, which stands alongside the church.

Meanwhile, the great hall, purchased by an absentee landlord, Libyan Wanis Burweila, in 1982, falls increasingly into disrepair. Hopefully, now that a new buyer has been found, the building will soon be restored to its former glory.

Roundabout Helpston

Changes in county boundaries have moved Helpston from Northamptonshire into Cambridgeshire, but our neighbours cannot be allowed to claim the village's most famous son as their own. As the title of his first collection of poems, published in 1820, clearly indicates, the *'Poems Descriptive of Rural Life and Scenery: Pastoral sketches in songs, ballads and sonnets'* are by '**John Clare**, A Northamptonshire Peasant.'

Edward Storey's *'A Right to Song'* provides a comprehensive biography of a remarkable life but you will find it neatly encapsulated in Cornishman Charles Causley's evocative poem, *'At the Grave of John Clare'*, extracts from which are quoted below.

The thatched cottage in Causley's *'dove-grey village'*, where John was born in July 1793, is now part of a larger house. Neither his father, Parker, a farm labourer, nor his mother Anne, were literate and the boy left school at the age of twelve destined, it seemed, for a similar life of drudgery and hardship. Encouraged by a local schoolmaster, he had already developed an unusual love of books, but opportunities to pursue his interest in literature were minimal. From early childhood he would have helped with seasonal farming tasks such as stone-picking, crow scaring, sheep tending, weeding, threshing, winnowing. Now he had to earn money to help support his ailing parents and younger sister, Sophie. By this time, Parker Clare, a former champion wrestler, was crippled with arthritis. John began his working life haymaking and learning to plough the fields around his home, or by running errands such as fetching flour from the nearby village of Maxey. In winter, often returning after dark, when marsh gas in the surrounding fields created hobgoblins in the boy's fertile imagination, he would make his tremulous journey home, as Causley says, *'expecting at every turn a Caliban'*.

Clare, of course, was no ordinary ploughboy. As he wandered the heathland, the woods and the river banks around his Helpston home he developed a naturalist's eye for detail and an ornithologist's ear for birdsong. When prompted to write seriously in his early teens, following chance exposure to James Thomson's collected poems, entitled *'The Seasons'*, he displayed a remarkable ability to express his ideas in succinct yet lyrical form, *'..the poetry, bursting like a diamond bomb'*. The revelatory experience shaped the rest of his life.

He wrote prolifically and by 1819, aged twenty-six, was producing six or seven poems a day. After an alarming discovery that dozens, written on scraps of paper and secreted in an alcove by the fireside, were being used as fire-lighters by his mother, he decided his best poems deserved a more permanent home. Consequently, he visited Market Deeping bookseller, John Henson, to get blank paper bound into a book.

It was at about this time, while working fourteen hours a day as a labourer in a lime-kiln at Bridge Casterton in Rutland, that he met Martha (Patty) Turner, his future wife, of whom he wrote,

'What are riches? not worth naming
Though with some they may prevail
Theirs be choice of wealth prevailing
Mine be Patty of the Vale.'

Perhaps inspired by this romantic association he shortly afterwards renewed his contact with Henson in a bid to get into print. Eventually the bookseller agreed to produce for £1, three hundred prospectuses inviting subscribers for a small collection of *'Original trifles by John Clare'*. Clare, himself, made no pretensions for their worth in his self-deprecating introduction.

'...the public are requested to observe that the trifles hereby offered for their candid perusal can lay no claim to eloquence of poetical composition...'

One hundred subscribers were required to make publication viable but, despite Clare's vigorous distribution of the leaflets, only seven were forthcoming.

It was understandably a bitter outcome and, indeed, a low point, Clare having quarrelled with Patty and also lost his job. He returned to Helpston, where he was forced to seek Parish Relief. He saw only one solution. To take the King's shilling and join the Royal Artillery, who were recruiting at Stamford. It wouldn't be his first experience of military life. Seven years earlier he had endured untold embarrassment when found to be profoundly unsoldierly while briefly enlisting in the militia during a Napoleonic 'invasion' scare. This time he was to be spared the ill-fitting uniform and harsh discipline. His half-hearted application was rejected and he returned to Helpston, where a surprise awaited. His prospectus had found an interested reader. Edward Drury of Stamford acquired the poems from Henson and after obtaining verification of their promise from Sir John English Dolben of Finedon, passed them to a relative, a London publisher named John Taylor.

It was Taylor who created the familiar image of a peasant poet. His introduction to *'Poems Descriptive of Rural Life and Scenery'*, published on January 16th 1820, maintains, *'The poems are the genuine productions of a young peasant, a day labourer in husbandry.'*

The collection was a great success and Clare was invited to London, where he was initially feted among the leading literary figures of the day. Charles Causley refers to, *'London, Charles Lamb and Hazlitt'*.

But sadly these heady days were not to last. Clare's second volume of poems, originally titled *'Ways in a Village'*, appeared as *'The Village Minstrel'* a year later in 1821. It sold poorly. Frustrations and disappointments, some related to his deteriorating health, delayed the publication of the ambitious *'Shepherd's Calendar'* until 1827, but this also made little impact. Already prone to bouts of intense melancholia, the most plausible diagnosis being a manic-depressive condition in which he became periodically psychotic, Clare suffered his first attack of delusions in 1830.

There are many explanations for the cause. Ten years earlier, he had married Patty Turner, and little more than a month after the wedding the first of their eight children was born. Although his wife proved a great source of support, displaying the virtues of industry, frugality, good temper and love for her husband, she could not share his life as a poet. Such esoteric needs and longings were the preserve of his first great love, school friend Mary Joyce, albeit only in a fantasy world of his own making. Mary was a local farmer's daughter deemed generally to be too high in the social scale for his aspirations. Her presence haunted his thoughts for the remainder of his life and inspired hundreds of love poems.

Their first meeting is recalled in *'First Love'*, written some forty years later

> *'My face turned pale a deadly pale*
> *My legs refused to walk away*
> *And when she looked what I could ail*
> *My life and all seemed turned to clay.'*

Never-ending financial troubles added to his problems. Little of the money made during his fleeting period of fame reached his pocket. Friends and patrons continued to be supportive and were instrumental in moving the Clare family to a larger cottage at Northborough some three miles from Helpston. Paradoxically, their good intentions contributed to the poet's sense of dislocation, as these lines from *'The Old Man's Song'* suggest. Straddling two worlds he was estranged from both his intellectual London acquaintances and his envious and limited village contemporaries.

> *'Life smiled upon me once as the sun upon the rose*
> *My heart so free & open guessed every face a friend*
> *Though the sweetest flower must fade & the sweetest season close*
> *Yet I never gave it thought that my happiness would end*
> *Till the warmest seeming friends grew the coldest at the close....'*

In the introduction to his anthology of Clare's work, published by the Penguin Poetry Library (1990), Geoffrey Summerfield offers a perceptive analysis of the poet's state of mind.

'All aspects of his experience, all his social and literary relationships, served to enforce his sense of having left familiar ground yet not of having securely arrived somewhere else........Even his sacral landscape had proved impermanent despoiled often beyond recognition by the 'improvements' of enclosure.'

The mature Clare targeted these distressing changes he observed in the surrounding countryside in poems like '*The Mores*'

> *'Now this sweet vision of my boyish hours*
> *Free as spring clouds and wild as summer flowers*
> *Is faded all – a hope that blossomed free,*
> *And hath been once, no more shall ever be*
>
> *Inclosure came and trampled on the grave*
> *Of labour's rights and left the poor a slave.'*

The publication of '*The Rural Muse*' in 1835 did little to improve his state of mind. Clare had sold the copyright for £40. Back in 1832, disenchanted by the lack of interest in his work, and tired of editorial intervention, he had intended to publish this and a vast collection of poems under the title, '*A Midsummer Cushion*'. Insufficient subscribers could be found, and it was not until 1979 that the book finally appeared under the editorship of Anne Tibble who, with her husband Professor J W Tibble, wrote '*John Clare: A Life*' *(1932)*, which is still widely regarded as the authoritative biography. In 1837 Clare was admitted to a private asylum in Epping, where he received treatment from an enlightened Doctor Allen. Over the next four years his physical health improved, but his mental condition remained disturbed. He finally absconded from the hospital in July 1841 and walked all the way back to Northborough without a penny in his pocket. He arrived several days later, starving and near to exhaustion, to write in his journal:

'Returned home out of Essex, and found no Mary.'

Convinced that he was married to two women, his first wife, Mary, and Patty his second, he refused to believe that the object of these misplaced affections had died, a spinster, in 1838.

Clare's situation continued to worsen, deeply disturbed by his many problems and disappointments and exacerbated by bouts of heavy drinking and the ever-mounting pressures of his large family. By December 1841 his wife could no longer cope and John was committed to Northampton General Lunatic Asylum, (now St Andrews Hospital in Billing Road), where he spent the rest of his life.

Never violent or 'mad' in the accepted sense of the word, he was treated with kindness and consideration, but the abandonment by his family contributed to his growing melancholy. John Plummer, the Kettering journalist who visited Clare in 1861, referred to him as *'A forgotten poet'*.

Clare's earliest biographer, Frederick Martin, writing in 1865, the year after his death, reports that *'Patty never once showed herself in the twenty three years, nor any of her children, except the youngest son who came to see his father once.'*

No words capture his sense of desertion and isolation better than the opening lines of the celebrated poem *'I Am'*, one of the thousand or more he wrote over those final twenty three years.

'I am – yet what I am none cares or knows
My friends forsake me like a memory lost:'

John Clare died on May 20th 1864, aged seventy-one. His body was, in Causley's words, *'trundled home to Helpston'* and buried in the local churchyard beneath a *'stone of grey cheese'* inscribed with the epitaph 'A poet is born not made.'

A monument, its panels inscribed with quotations from his poems, stands on the nearby village green.

On June 13th 1989 a memorial to Clare was unveiled in Poets' Corner, Westminster Abbey. Though still excluded from the premier line-up of the romantics, a formidable gathering of modern poets, including Robert Graves, Dylan Thomas and Ted Hughes, have recorded their personal debt to the Northamptonshire 'peasant'. As Seamus Heaney has written,

'It was the unique achievement of John Clare to make vocal the regional and particular, to achieve a buoyant and authentic lyrical utterance at the meeting point between social realism and conventional romanticism.'

A fitting tribute to a genius.

The poem *'A Wayside Encounter Near Helpston (1828)'*, published in Trevor Hold's collection of his own work, *'Chasing the Moon' (2001)*, describes an imaginary casual meeting on the high road between John Clare and a near neighbour, **Charles Kingsley** of Barnack. Kingsley, who would have been just nine years old at the time, lived in the village from 1824-30 during his father's incumbency as rector.

> *'Did it take place?*
> *parson's son and poetic ploughman,*
> *one on a keeper's horse*
> *bringing back the game bag,*
> *the other watching*
> *the sky and reeds?*
> *We'll never know,*
> *But if so,*
> *Probably neither*
> *Took the slightest interest*
> *Nor recognised the brother*
> *poet in the other.'*

The lasting effect of those formative years spent in Northamptonshire is evident in much of Charles Kingsley's writing, most notably in *'Hereward the Wake'* (1865), his last novel, which is set in the fen-land landscape so familiar during his childhood. One of his best known poems, *'Ode to the North-East Wind'*, pays ironic homage to the *'jovial wind of winter'*, which no doubt rattled around the Barnack Rectory, while *'Prose Idylls' (1873)* is a collection of writing based on his observations at home and abroad. This book includes an evocative essay entitled *'The Fens'*, in which Kingsley describes the transformation of the Great Fen from *'a waste and howling wilderness'* into a *'garden of the Lord'* where

'instead of mammoth and urus, stag and goat, that fen feeds cattle many
times more numerous than all the wild venison of the primaeval jungle; and
produces crops capable of nourishing a hundred times as many human
beings; and more – it produces men a hundred times as numerous as ever it
produced before; more healthy and long-lived – and if they will, more
virtuous and more happy – than ever was Girvian, (a man of the marshes
from Hereward the Wake's time), or holy hermit in his cell. So we, who knew
the deep fen, will breathe one sigh over the last scrap of wilderness, and say
no more; content to know that –

> *'The old order changeth, yielding place to new,*
> *And God fulfils himself in many ways,*
> *Lest one good custom should corrupt the world.'*

Although Kingsley was a lifelong believer in the need for radical social reform and regularly contributed to Christian Socialist publications, it is for novels such as *'Westward Ho!'* (1855), *'The Water Babies'* (1863), and his retelling of Greek myths in *'The Heroes'* (1856), that he is usually remembered.

He died on January 23rd 1875 at Eversley in Hampshire, where he had been rector for thirty one years.

> *'Barnack, you say? Do I remember Barnack?*
> *Not a thing.*
> *All I know is what I've been told.*
> *No, I've never been back, but that's where I was born –*
> *and where I almost said goodbye.*
> *I was lucky the gardener needed his barrow,*
> *or my career would have come to a premature end,*
> *aetatis six months.'*

These lines from Trevor Hold's amusing poem, also published in *'Chasing the Moon'*, refer to an incident involving another celebrated member of the Kingsley family during their brief tenure of Barnack Rectory. **Henry Kingsley** was born, the fifth and youngest son of the Revd Charles Kingsley, on January 2nd 1830. According to Hold's poem, sibling jealousy probably caused his sister Charlotte and her brother George to wheel their baby brother in a garden barrow into a pond and abandon him there, only the gardener's fortuitous need of the barrow preventing a tragedy.

After establishing a reputation as a sportsman, this flamboyant character once won a wager that he could *'run a mile, row a mile and trot a mile'* within fifteen minutes. Henry emigrated to Australia in 1853 to prospect for gold. His literary career began with *'Geoffrey Hamlyn'* (1859), largely based on the author's experiences as a trooper in the Sydney Mounted Police and now regarded as the first great Australian novel. It was eventually completed on his return to England and followed by *'Ravenshoe' (1862)*, *'Austin Elliott' (1863)* and another Australian-based novel, *'The Hillyers and the Burtons' (1865)*, books which charted the opening up of this exotic and unforgiving continent. When mounting debts forced him to accept the editor-ship of the *Edinburgh Daily Review* in 1869, he nevertheless abandoned the post's sedentary role to report the Franco-Prussian War from the Prussian side, and was present at the entry into Sedan when the French city capitulated.

Henry Kingsley was a prolific writer whose novels achieved popular success in their day. He was also a fine poet, his best-known work being *'The Boy in Grey'* (1871). He died, having packed a great deal into a short life, at Cuckfield in Sussex on May 24th 1876 aged forty-six.

Roundabout the Nene Valley

The River Nene, the principal waterway of the county, meanders under wide skies from Staverton in the west, to Oundle and, eventually, the North Sea. Its valley is gentle and wide, more than two miles in places, and since Roman times has been a settled and productive landscape of woods, broad river pastures, stone villages and small towns, complemented by fine ancient bridges and splendid water-mills.

Despite ever-increasing traffic through the county, some servicing utilitarian warehouses which now often dominate the valley sides, away from the main arteries it is still a largely unspoilt and magical place. Beyond, the village roads are quiet, the countryside beguilingly empty, still dreaming under warm sun or dramatic cloud-scapes of a more leisured time.

*'I myself had an especial predilection for 'Mirage' by **Bandula Chandraratna**, which was not only very moving, but also had that special quality I was looking for in a potential Booker prize winner. For me a first rate novel.'*

Gerald Kaufman, the Chairman of the Judges, paid this glowing tribute to the Sri-Lankan born writer's first novel at the Booker Prize Award ceremony in 1999. It didn't make the short-list, but was among the last ten of the one hundred and twenty nine books entered for the competition. If you're wondering why the odd number, there is a simple explanation that reveals so much about the unassuming, softly-spoken man who combines his writing with running a residential home for the elderly in a large Edwardian house in Oundle overlooking the Nene valley. *'Mirage'* was five years in the making, but on completion was rejected by countless agents and publishers. However, Bandula's belief in the book was so strong that when he learned that, while individual authors were not allowed to enter their work for literary competitions, publishers could, he decided to set up his own publishing company. It was named, optimistically, Serendip.

He type-set the manuscript, sent it to Sri-Lanka for printing, and had a thousand copies shipped back to England. When he received the books, and gave one to a friend to read, he was politely informed that the unaccountable name-change of a central character from chapter ten onwards, rendered the story incomprehensible. Undaunted, he made the necessary amendments, contacted the printers, and ordered another thousand copies. Publishers are allowed to enter just two books each for the prestigious Booker Prize. Bandula sent the only title his company owned. Hence the odd number of entries.

Kaufman's highly perceptive remarks encouraged many favourable reviews. Boyd Tonkin in *The Independent* wrote, *'we need novels as lucid, moving and compassionate as this one. I would urge you to read it.'* And people did, including top literary agent Giles Gordon, who soon acquired a mainstream publisher for Bandula and the offer of a two-book deal with the Orion Publishing Group.

'Mirage' is set in a closed middle eastern country, transparently Saudi Arabia, where Bandula and his wife Indra spent some time in the early nineteen eighties. Like his central character, Sayeed, they worked in a hospital alongside both local and foreign workers, but there the similarities end for the Arab porter of the novel lived in a shanty town on the city's edge whereas Bandula enjoyed a privileged lifestyle in the sleek new medical complex. His descriptions of life in the unnamed capital are beautifully observed. It's a world in which, as Francis King writes in the *Literary Review*, *'Ramshackle trucks, not camels, now transport the Bedouin around the desert: the unmade roads are crammed with gas-guzzling, constantly hooting cars: cigarettes increasingly take the place of the narghile, Coca-Cola that of mint tea; and children watch television programmes dubbed from the Japanese.'* But Arab law remains cruelly uncompromising when Sayeed's young wife is seduced by a ne'er-do-well.

His second novel, *'An Eye for an Eye' (2001)*, continues the tragic story of Sayeed's doomed marriage. This book also won critical acclaim in high quarters. Doris Lessing chose it among her three international books of the year, writing *'this is a little master-piece, beautiful, a testimony to decency and courage in the face of such oppression, such hardship.'*

Bandula's writing style is economical, even terse at times, but his words are weighed carefully to convey subtle shades of meaning. In the following extract from *'An Eye for an Eye'*, he describes the build-up of the crowd in the city square, awaiting the execution of Hussein the adulterer.

'It was after one. The sun was blazing down on the crowd in the square. Some patches of the tarred car park were melting. In the potholes and cracks some resilient parched grass bushes were growing, outstretched blades squashed by the tyres and embedded in the tar. The big clock at the top of the tower was showing the time, a long time ago, when it had stopped running. The crowd were careful not to expose their wristwatches to the direct sunlight for fear it would melt the electronics inside and stop them. All watches and clocks in the now shut, air-conditioned row of shops from the clock tower towards the sconce were running smoothly. The crowd was squinting towards the Palace of Justice for any movement. Some were wiping the sweat from their faces with their gutras and fanning themselves with whatever they had in their hands. They were quiet and the air was still.'

If Bandula's experiences in Saudi Arabia were the creative main-spring of his novels, other episodes from his life read like pages of fiction. In June 1967, when he was twenty-two, his father mortgaged property in Sri-Lanka to buy a ticket to send his son to England. Passage on the *SS Vietnam* from Colombo to Marseilles, across France to Calais by rail, and on to Victoria Station cost £75, which was a fortune to the father of eight. It was a journey the young man never forgot. The day after the ship passed through the Suez Canal it was closed due to the outbreak of the Six Day War. Delayed by just twenty-four hours and his whole life might have been different. He arrived in London alone and friendless, spent his first night in the Ceylon Students' Centre and travelled the next day to Eastbourne to begin his training as a student nurse at the town's general hospital. After a few months he met Indra, who had newly arrived from Sri-Lanka to work at the hospital, and a short time later they were married. By then he had switched from nursing to laboratory work at the Royal East Sussex Hospital at Hastings. The couple were so hard up on their marriage that they bought their wedding rings on hire purchase, lived in a one-roomed bedsit in Eastbourne which was often without water or electricity and, had it not been for the kindness of an English couple, Joyce and Joe Neate, who befriended them, would have become homeless.

Desperate to return to Sri Lanka to show off his wife and new daughter, he approached his bank manager for an overdraft. It was refused, but advice received was not forgotten.

'You're overdrawn every month as it is,' the manager said. *'Cut the suit according to the size of the cloth.'* Bandula resolved to adopt a more prudent approach, saved assiduously, and the following year took his family home to meet his parents, brothers and sisters.

In 1978 the Chandraratnas moved to the Middle-East. On their return in 1983, Indra found work at the new Milton Keynes hospital, the family moved to the town and, after a year of rejected job applications, Bandula became employed at Great Ormond Street. The shifts were long and he was often exhausted at the end of his working day, but it was then that he began to write the first chapters of *'Mirage'*. Five years later, when the couple had invested the proceeds from the sale of their Milton Keynes house and all their savings into the business at Oundle, he finally finished the last few chapters. He says that he had always intended to rewrite the book, but the published version is in fact the first draft. Remarkably, *'Mirage'* has now been published world-wide. Bandula has copies written in many languages including Hebrew , but the edition of which he is most proud is the Sri-Lankan version. *'It's written in Singhalese,'* he says. *'And my mother can read it.'*

Ashton, with its oddly rustic hostelry and neat village green, lies across the water-meadow to the east of Oundle and is best known today for the annual 'conker' competition which attracts entries from all over the world.

The pub's unusual name, 'The Chequered Skipper', is a reminder of the village's most celebrated resident, the eminent zoologist and entomologist **Dame Miriam Rothschild** DBE, CBE, FRS. Her father, (Nathaniel) Charles, son of the first Baron Rothschild of Tring, settled in Ashton in 1900 and entirely recreated the village in a style which the *'Shell Guide'* likens to E Nesbit's Arden in *'Harding's Luck'* – *'picturesque, thatched houses, but with a bathroom and good plumbing in every cottage'.*

Miriam was born on August 6th 1908 and, in the fashion of the day, educated at home. Her long and distinguished career as a naturalist owes much to the influence and example of both her father and her uncle, Lord Walter Rothschild, the subject of her immensely enjoyable biography, *'Dear Lord Rothschild: Birds, Butterflies and History.' (1983).*

Charles Rothschild combined his responsibilities as head of the family's famous banking firm with a range of civic duties, yet still found time to pursue his passion for entomology and as a pioneering conservationist. Miriam provides a brief, but illuminating, account of her father's life and work in the opening chapter of *'Rothschild's Reserves; Time and Fragile Nature' (1997).* She recalls how Charles, who had published his first paper on the moths and butterflies of Harrow while still at school,

> *'greatly feared the depredations of ruthless, commercial collectors. His own collecting had a strictly scientific objective. As a child, I was encouraged to catch butterflies but was not allowed to catch female specimens which had to be released. 'Even if I catch a Purple Emperor?' Yes, even a Purple Emperor.'*

The book investigates the disturbing fate of the 182 potential nature reserves presented to the Government by her father in 1915 and eventually established forty years later with the founding of the Nature Conservancy. It makes a compelling case for the need to protect the natural world by the application of science combined with adequate financial support from the government if we are not to experience, *'a silent Spring in England'.*

An honorary fellow of St Hugh's, Oxford, Miriam Rothschild has published about 250 scientific papers which include a quarter of a million words on fleas. Her researches also touch on butterflies, plants, birds, snails, worms and wild flowers, and publications include *'Fleas, Flukes and Cuckoos' (1952), 'The*

Butterfly Gardener' (1983) and *'Butterfly cooing like a Dove' (1991).* Despite the technical detail of much of her work, her writing is often beautifully crafted, like this opening extract from her uncle's biography.

> *'It is not easy to be born. The average man is squeezed out into the world with blood to lubricate his passage and wild shrieks of anguish to speed him on his way. If, as an added complication, he arrives on the scene with a theoretical silver spoon in his mouth, the life awaiting him beyond the draw-sheet is fraught with extra hazards. Walter Rothschild, however, was born in serene silence.'*

An inscription on a gravestone in the churchyard of Barnwell St Andrew preserves the memory of **Thomas Bell**, schoolmaster, historian and poet, who spent the greater part of his seventy-nine years in the village.

The inside cover of his final book, *'Winter Evenings at Home'*, *(1856)*, reminds readers of his two previous publications. Described as *'Mr Bell's Poetical and Historical Works'*, the first, *'The Ruins of Liveden, (1847)*, provides significant details of the history of the Tresham family, its buildings and involvement in the Gunpowder Plot. The second, *'The Rural Album'*, *(1853)*, consists of *'original poems, and historical notices of Barnwell and Fotheringhay castles, and other localities in the county of Northampton.'* These publications were, *'to be had only of the author, at Barnwell, near Oundle, who will forward Copies, free of carriage, to Purchasers.'*

Judging from his preface to *'Winter Evenings at Home'*, Bell was extremely gratified by the response to these earlier *'labours'*, and maintains that *'his greatest pride is to retain the patronage that has been so liberally extended in the past'*. The work is divided into sections, or evenings, each *'complete and distinct in itself'* and ranges over a variety of subjects, including such diverse topics as *'The Milton Hunt', Village Weddings and Funerals', 'The Voyages of Captain Cook'*, and *'Hindoo Idolatory'*. Most is written in blank verse, which he describes as *'the poetry of the heart'*, although he reverts to rhyme, or *'the poetry of the ear'*, in the final lines expressing sentiments concerning life's vulnerabilities over the previous year that we can all share.

> *'But to my God I bow in silent pray'r,*
> *With lowly heart to reverence His name,*
> *Whose mercy thus has brought my shatter'd frame*
> *Through all the changes of another year.*
> *To see the Spring, with blossoms gay, once more;*
> *And Summer shed its balmy fragrance round;*
> *And Autumn richly yield its golden store;*
> *And Winter's garb conceal the frozen ground;*
> *And Christmas, smiling through its veil of snow,*
> *Shine with a brighter ray to cheer the world below.'*

The Roman Gartree road from Huntingdon to Leicester crossed the River Nene at Aldwincle, linking Ermine Street with the Fosse Way. The village has two churches, St Peter's and All Saints, suggesting it must also have been an important place in medieval times, but its significance for devotees of English literature is due to a remarkable coincidence. Two of the seventeenth century's finest writers were born in the village, less than half a mile and a mere twenty three years apart.

The building where **Thomas Fuller**, the son of the rector of St Peter's, was born in 1608, has long since disappeared, but a memorial window in the west wall of the church describes him as, *'a scribe instructed into the kingdom of heaven'*.

Fuller was educated at Cambridge University, becoming its youngest ever MA, and embarked upon a career in the church. A committed Royalist and Anglican, he was appointed preacher to the Chapel Royal in 1641. During the Civil War, he served as chaplain to Sir Ralph Hopton, the commander of King Charles' forces. He made no secret of his sympathies, directing a bitter satire, *'Andronicus or the Unfortunate Politician'*, at Oliver Cromwell in 1646. After the King's defeat at Exeter, Fuller, rather surprisingly considering the fate of many, was allowed to continue preaching, eventually regaining his old preferments with the Restoration in 1660. A witty and sometimes irreverent orator, he was popular with London congregations, and the humour which often enlivened his sermons is apparent in his writings.

A good example of his amusing and epigrammatic brevity is this epitaph for Thomas Bannister and his wife, who died the day after her husband.

'He first deceased: she for few hours try'd
To live without him, lik'd it not, and dy'd.'

A prolific poet, historian and theologian, his works include an account of the Crusades entitled *'The Historie of the Holy Warre', (1639-40)*, *'The Holy State and The Profane State', (1642)* and *'The Church History of Britain: from the Birth of Christ till 1648', (1655)*.

His most highly regarded book, *'The History of the Worthies of England'*, was never completed and was not published until 1662, the year after his death. Much more than the biographical encyclopaedia suggested by the title, the book contains descriptive accounts of Fuller's journeys around England, including affectionate references to his native county.

'Northamptonshire is an apple without a core to be cut out or a rind to be pared away.'

The house where **John Dryden**, Poet Laureate and initiator of modern English prose, was born in 1631, stands opposite the handsome but redundant church of All Saints, where his maternal grandfather, the Reverend Doctor Pickering, was rector.

John's parents, Erasmus, a baronet and member of the Dryden family from Canon's Ashby, and Mary, had fourteen children of whom he was the eldest.

Educated first at Westminster School, where he gave early notice of his writing talent with an elegy, *'Upon the Death of Lord Hastings', (1649)*, he went to Trinity College, Cambridge in 1650, taking his BA in 1654. Little is known of Dryden's activities from then until 1659 when he published a poem on Oliver Cromwell. This was the first of many works celebrating the 'great and the good' of the day; a pursuit which earned him both a reasonable income and the subsequent contempt of Samuel Johnson. Johnson, who had high regard for his writing, *'he had all the forms of excellence……combined in his mind, with endless variation,'* was angered by what he saw as a prostitution of Dryden's talent through flagrant and self-seeking opportunism. This had not been the view of the Court, however. Poems such as *'Annus Mirabilis, The Year of Wonders, 1666,'* and various ventures into the theatre enhanced his reputation, and when Sir William Davenant died in April 1668, Dryden succeeded him as Poet Laureate. His productivity was both prolific and diverse. Over the next thirty years he wrote plays, critical essays, lyrical, didactic and satirical poetry, translations of classical text and operatic librettos. Although his refusal to take the oath of allegiance to William and Mary following the Revolution of 1688 led to deprivation of the laureateship, he remained the major literary figure of his age until his death on May 1st 1700.

A few choice examples must suffice to demonstrate the quality and range of Dryden's work.

His ode, entitled *'To The Pious Memory Of The Accomplisht Young Lady, Mrs Anne Killigrew', (*an artist and poet tragically drowned in the Thames in 1686*)*, was regarded by Johnson, as the finest in the language.

> *'Art she had none, yet wanted none,*
> *For Nature did that want supply:*
> *So rich in treasures of her own,*
> *She might our boasted stores defy:'*

The elegance and clarity of his prose is evident in this description of Shakespeare from *'Essay of Dramatic Poesy'*.

> *'He was the man who of all modern, and perhaps ancient poets, had the largest and most comprehensive soul. ...He was naturally learn'd; he needed not the spectacles of books to read Nature; he looked inwards, and found her there...He is many times flat, insipid; his comic wit degenerating into clenches, his serious swelling into bombast. But he is always great, when some occasion is presented to him.'*

Like the subject of that essay, Dryden was also a master of the rhyming couplet, as in this example from *'Palamon and Arcite'*.

> *'Like pilgrims to th' appointed place we tend;*
> *The world's an inn, and death the journey's end.'*

John Dryden's own journey ended at Poets' Corner in Westminster Abbey, where he was buried in the same grave as Geoffrey Chaucer.

One of the many mourners at the funeral was his cousin, Elizabeth Creed from Titchmarsh.

In the north chapel of the splendid Church of St Mary the Virgin, in the village where Dryden spent much of his childhood, a wooden wall-monument painted by Mrs Creed commemorates the life of the writer and his parents, both of whom are buried in the church.

The words make specific reference to the importance of John's Northamptonshire upbringing in his future career,

> *'.. his bright parts and learning are best seen in his own excellent writings*
> *on various subjects and we boast that he was bred and had his first learning*
> *here'.*

They also express family pride at his subsequent achievements, reflected in his final resting place.

> *'His body was honourably interred in Westminster Abbey among the*
> *greatest wits of divers ages.'*

No further epitaph is required.

The fifteenth century Perpendicular tower of Titchmarsh church is clearly visible from the hillock above the Nene at Wadenhoe, where stands its Norman counterpart.

Wadenhoe is home to author, poet and composer, **Trevor Hold**. Born in Northampton in 1939, and educated at the town's Grammar school and the University of Nottingham, Trevor held appointments as Lecturer in Music at the Universities of Aberystwyth and Liverpool before joining the staff of the Department of Adult Education at the University of Leicester in 1970. This appointment enabled him to move back to his native county, whose under-rated glories are recorded with affection in, *'In Praise of Northamptonshire'*.

> *'But it is to that unassuming shire*
> *Where I was born that my own spirit flies,*
> *Homing to her parks and ancient trees,*
> *The sandstone manor and the weathered spire,*
> *The steady river ambling to the seas.*
> *Wherever I may live, my exiled eyes*
> *Will seek that landscape and those gentle skies.'*

The poem prefaces his anthology entitled, *'A Northamptonshire Garland'* *(1989)*, an authoritative work containing biographical details, bibliographies and examples from the works of over sixty poets who were either born or resided for a considerable time in the county.

Collections of his own poetry, *'Time and the Bell'* *(1971)*, *'Caught in Amber'* *(1981)*, *'Mermaids and Nightingales'* *(1991)* and *'Chasing the Moon'* *(2001)*, provide further evidence of Trevor's appreciation of the Northamptonshire countryside, its rich heritage and their profound influence upon his own destiny.

An enduring love of music is revealed in his critical studies of twentieth-century English song-writing, some of which are included in *'Parry to Finzi: 20 English Song Composers'* *(2002)*. Among the many examples of setting his own poems to music is *'A Villanelle for Kirby Hall'* *(2002)*, dedicated to the memory of JL Carr, whom he first met at a poetry reading at Kirby in 1974.

For twenty years the village of Slipton was the weekend retreat for author and journalist, **Michael De-la-Noy**, whose fulsome obituary appeared in *The Guardian* following his death in August 2002. Sub-titled, *'The mercurial writer at the centre of an Anglican dispute about sexual tolerance'*, it detailed the life of a prolific author who *'never achieved critical acclaim because he was far more interested in gossip than scholarship.'*

Born Michael Walker in Hessle, Yorkshire in 1934, he later adopted the name De-la-Noy from uncertain sources as a nom de plume. Educated at Bedford School, he began his literary career as a journalist on the *Bedfordshire Times* and later the *Brighton and Hove Herald* before joining the radical magazine *Prism* as assistant editor in 1961. Six years later he became Press secretary to Michael Ramsey, the Archbishop of Canterbury. Ramsey tolerated his representative's unconventional sexual proclivities for three years before an ill-advised magazine article about a bisexual, transvestite colonel from Earl's Court caused the liberal archbishop such embarrassment that he had little option but to bow to pressure and 'release the secretary from his duties'. De-la-Noy described his sacking in *'A Day In The Life Of God' (1971)*, bitterly referring to what he saw as the work of a bigoted and intransigent ecclesiastical establishment.

'It was revealing of even the archbishop's apparent impotence to match actions with words in the face of opposition from an establishment collectively more powerful than he had ever realised.'

Between 1971 and 2001 De-la-Noy wrote more than twenty books, including an intimate life of Archbishop Ramsey entitled, *'Michael Ramsey: A Portrait' (1990)*, which brought a degree of notoriety, and biographies of Elgar and Edward Sackville-West. His one major commercial success was, *'The Queen Behind the Throne' (1994)*, in which he explored the matriarchal role of Queen Elizabeth the Queen Mother. A final book, *'Queen Victoria at Home'*, is expected to be published posthumously in 2003.

Roundabout Wellingborough

Drive through Finedon on the A6 towards Irthlingborough and immediately after negotiating the roundabout at the foot of the hill you will pass on your right a mound surmounted by a stone obelisk.

John Bailey's meticulously researched history of the town, *'Finedon otherwise Thingdon',* (1975), informs its reader that the monument was erected in 1789 by Sir John English Dolben as *'a Direction Pillar and to record the many blessings'* of that year. These are believed to include, King George III's recovery from a second attack of insanity, which was celebrated at Finedon by a *'ringing of bells and other demonstrations of joy',* the birth of John Dolben's daughter, Louisa, and the second marriage of his father, Sir William Dolben.

The Dolben family had originally settled at Finedon Hall in 1682 following the marriage of Gilbert Dolben to Anne Mulso, who inherited the estate from her late father. Sir John English, great-grandson of Sir Gilbert, lived there from 1750 to 1837. During his long life he was an active patron of the arts, particularly literature, and was described in his obituary as *'a walking library'.* It was to Sir John that the Stamford bookseller, Edward Drury, first sent copies of John Clare's poetry in a bid to determine their worth. To his everlasting credit, Dolben recognised their quality and agreed to subscribe to their eventual publication.

On his death, the estate passed to his grand-daughters, Ann Julia and Frances, the younger of whom had married William Harcourt Isham Mackworth, two years previously. The Mackworth-Dolbens, as they became known, had one daughter, Ellen, and three sons, William, Herbert and Digby.

Digby Augustus Stewart Mackworth-Dolben, to give him his full name, was born in Guernsey in 1848. Educated at Eton, he wrote a considerable number of poems, many of which reflect his strong affinity to the Roman Catholic faith and bear a similarity to the work of Gerard Manley Hopkins, both in style and content,

> *'Poetry, the hand that wrings*
> *(Bruised albeit at the strings)*
> *Music from the soul of things.'*

During 1867, aged nineteen, Digby spent several months at the home of the Rector of Luffenham, the Revd. Prichard, receiving private tuition in the hope of gaining a place at Christ College, Oxford. While carrying the rector's son, Walter, who could not swim, across the River Welland on his back, he suddenly sank below the water. Walter was rescued, but Digby's body was not found for several hours. Apparently, he had fainted and consequently drowned.

Hopkins, on learning of his death, wrote to Robert Bridges, the future Poet-Laureate and Digby's contemporary at Eton, expressing his regret at the *'loss of so much beauty (in body and mind and life) and the promise of still more'*.

The tragedy merely compounded the suffering felt by his parents, who had already lost their eldest son, William, drowned off the coast of Africa in 1863, while serving in the Royal Navy. Herbert, the last of the male heirs succumbed to tuberculosis in 1870 and, as their daughter, Ellen, died unmarried in February 1912, the Mackworth-Dolben line came to a sad end. Four months later, the Hall estate was sold by auction.

Reminders of the family still proliferate around the town, including the aforementioned obelisk, the vault under the east window of St Mary's Church which houses several of the Dolben dead, and copious mock-Gothic constructions designed by the tragic Mr Mackworth-Dolben, who was a gentleman architect. The re-designed Bell Inn, the Star Hall house, the Ice Tower and other buildings survive, but the Volta Tower, erected in memory of his eldest son in 1863, collapsed in a storm eighty-eight years later, killing one of its occupants.

Digby Mackworth-Dolben lies in the churchyard extension opposite the church on Church Hill.

Robert Bridges, with assistance from Miss Ellen, compiled a collection of his poetry, which was published by Oxford University Press in 1911.

It contains this prayer.

> 'From falsehood and error,
> From darkness and terror,
> From all that is evil,
> From the power of the devil,
> From the fire and the doom,
> From the judgement to come –
> Sweet JESU, deliver
> Thy servant for ever.'

Leaving Finedon, the journey south down the A6 leads along the Irthlingborough by-pass, across the bridge over the Nene and up the hill into Higham Ferrers. The ancient market-town was the birth-place of Henry Chichele, *'Henry V's great archbishop at the time of Agincourt, who has a part in Shakespeare's play and whose tomb may now be seen in Canterbury Cathedral.'*

That description of Higham's most famous son is taken from *'The Vanished World'*, the first volume of the autobiography of Northamptonshire's celebrated novelist and master of the short story, **Herbert Ernest Bates**. H.E. as he preferred to be known, was born on May 16th 1905, just a mile or so up the A6 from his illustrious predecessor Chichele. A plaque on the wall marks the terraced house in Grove Road, Rushden, where the Bates family lived.

His father, like so many in the county at the time, worked in the boot and shoe trade. Bates recalls Rushden's mean streets where, *'some shoemaking dictator had insisted that for every hundred yards of dwelling house there should be thirty or forty of factory sandwiched between them.'*

The impressionable youngster was also greatly influenced by trips into the countryside in the company of his grandfather, who taught him the minutiae of the natural world. The most frequent, and best remembered, forays were to the village of Chelveston-cum-Caldicott, *'where a little tributary of the Nene twice made a water splash across the road, white in summer with water ranunculus, green with brook-lime and cress and alive with gudgeon and stickle-backs.'* Like his exact contemporary, Denys Watkins-Pitchford, the flavour of Bates' childhood can be captured in his stories. *'The Watercress Girl'* is a hugely romantic evocation of an idyllic world full of sun, streams, wheat, flowers and strange colourful relatives. But unlike the young 'BB', who knew only the countryside around Lamport, 'HE' was familiar with the harsh reality of life in an industrial town. A short story called *'The Barber'* recreates the plight of two small boys waiting in a corner shop for a haircut, amongst intimidating, rough and vulgar shoeworkers.

After attending his local school in Newton Road, Bates progressed to the Grammar School at Kettering. There he was rescued from what he described as *'a miserable existence',* by his inspirational English teacher, Edmund Kirby, who quickly recognised HE as a responsive, keen and sensitive pupil. The feeling was mutual. Of his first lesson with the battle-scarred, former infantry officer, Bates writes, *'If it is possible to change human vision or at best waken it, by the stimulus or even shock of a single experience, then this is the perfect example of it……..fanciful as it might sound, I date my literary career from that moment.'*

Bates' first appearance in print was in December 1920, when a poem entitled *'Armistice Day, November 11th 1920'*, was published in the school magazine, *'that universal graveyard of budding poets.'* He continued to write poetry, later condemning it as *'infinitely and execrably bad,'* adding, *'mercifully all of it is now lost.'* Thankfully, Bates recanted and these early poems, together with a number of later compositions were rediscovered, collated and edited by Bates' biographer, Peter Eads, a retired Detective Chief Superintendent with the county police force and great admirer of the Rushden writer's work. They were eventually published as a limited edition in 1990 under the title, *'Give them their life'*, the opening line of a poem which first appeared in *'Air Force Poetry'*, an anthology edited by John Pudney and Henry Treece in 1944.

> *'Give them their life:*
> *They do not know how short it grows;*
> *So let them go*
> *Young-winged, steel-fledged, gun-furious,*
> *For if they live they'll live,*
> *As well you know,*
> *Upon the bitter kernels of their sweet ideals'*

Beautifully illustrated by Lynne Evans, the book also contains two prose passages on John Clare. The first, under the rather grandiose title, *'Northamptonshire Men of Letters. No.1 John Clare: The Peasant Poet,'* originally appeared in the Kettering Grammar School Magazine in December 1921. The second, a review of *'The Poems of John Clare'* edited by JW Tibble, was published in *The London Mercury* in May 1935.

There was no *'Men of Letters No. 2'*. Bates left school in December 1921, forsaking the opportunity of a university place, to become a *'very junior'* assistant reporter at the *Northampton Chronicle* offices in Wellingborough. He was temperamentally unsuited for the hum-drum life of a provincial journalist and resigned after a few months, but unexpected benefits had accrued. Several characters and incidents from that period appear, thinly disguised, in later stories. In *'The World in Ripeness'*, the third volume of his autobiography published in 1972, he recalls two episodes which proved the catalyst for the plot of *'Love For Lydia'*, the hauntingly atmospheric novel written thirty years after the event.

'It had been many years since I had seen the figure of a strikingly beautiful young girl in a black cloak lined with scarlet arrive at the station at Rushden in a smart pony-drawn gig in order to catch a train and almost as many since, on a freezing winter night, I had gone to an assignment as a young reporter to Rushden Hall, totally unaware at the time that I was sitting in the same room in which the poet Robert Herrick must have sat, three hundred years before, on his visits to the ever-hospitable Sir Lewis Pemberton.'

In his new post, undemanding employment and agreeable working conditions as a clerk in a boot and shoe warehouse situated close to the Essex Street villa that had been the family home since 1914, H.E. indulged his passion. He contributed poems to a weekly literary magazine, *'The Kettering Reminder'*, wrote plays, and completed a novel, *'The Two Sisters'*, which he forwarded to a number of publishing houses. December 1925 might well have proved a miserable time for the aspiring writer. Out of work once more, and hugely disappointed at publishers' general lack of interest in his novel, he received the best possible Christmas present. Jonathan Cape expressed a wish to publish the book, which appeared in June the following year.

After his marriage to Marjorie (Madge) Cox in July 1931, Bates left Northamptonshire for Kent, where he set up home in a converted granary in the village of Little Chart. There he continued to write prolifically, indeed twenty books were produced between 1925 and 1940, but despite his widespread reputation as a short story writer he was still not a profitable author. Commissioned to describe the vital role of the RAF under the pseudonym, 'Flying Officer X', his stories captured the spirit and character of the times, boosting morale and selling in hundreds of thousands. Despite these huge sales, his financial rewards remained meagre and there was a rift with his long-established publisher, who Bates felt had not acted in his best interests. He accepted an advance from Michael Joseph for a new novel, *'Fair Stood the Wind for France'*, which was published to great acclaim in November 1944. (Fittingly, a dramatised version, adapted by Gregory Evans and Michael Napier Brown had its world-wide premiere at Northampton's Royal Theatre in 1986).

An assignment in the Far East provided the inspirational source for several post-war novels, including *'The Purple Plain'* and *'The Jacaranda Tree'*, but in 1952 Bates returned to his Nene valley roots with the afore-mentioned *'Love for Lydia'*, regarded by many critics as his most satisfying and aesthetically complete novel.

Readers were introduced to his most popular creation, the Larkin family, in *'The Darling Buds of May'*, which he described as, *'English as pubs, steak and kidney pie and the Canterbury Tales of Chaucer.'* Dramatised versions of the stories have since delighted a huge television audience. However, an attempt in 2001 to bring *'Uncle Silas'*, portrayed by Albert Finney, to the small screen met with only limited success. For those who had enjoyed the privilege of watching local actor David Neal's interpretation of the rapscallion countryman, Finney's version was sadly flawed.

Awarded the CBE in June 1973, H.E. died in January of the following year. An obituary in *The Times* maintained that Bates, *'stood in the direct line of succession of fiction writers of the English countryside that includes George Eliot, Thomas Hardy and DH Lawrence.'*

Splendid company indeed.

A dual-carriageway now links Rushden with Wellingborough - *'the town of a hundred wells'* - following the route through the Nene valley countryside so familiar to the young Bates. Like many Northamptonshire towns, Wellingborough's first major expansion occurred during the nineteenth century, when it grew six-fold from a 'village' of 3,000 to an industrial town of 18,000, and from 1850 to 1950 it enjoyed prominence as the third largest maker of boots and shoes in the county. The most recent history, compiled by Joyce and Maurice Palmer in 1972, contains a comprehensive account of its development during the Victorian period including a lengthy section on the growth of the boot and shoe trade.

One important factor during the middle of the century was the increased mechanisation, which converted a 'cottage-industry', where much of the labour was carried out by 'out-workers', into an intensive, factory-based occupation. Among those affected by this cataclysmic change was **John Askham**.

Born in Wellingborough on July 25th 1825, John was the youngest of a family of seven, of whom only two survived to adulthood. Memories of his early childhood are contained in a reverential article, entitled *'John Askham the Forgotten Poet'*, by Joyce Palmer, and recall the day his sparse education began at a Dame School, an experience not dissimilar to that later described by Gloucestershire's Laurie Lee in *'Cider with Rosie'*.

'I am set down almost at the threshold of life a struggling, wondering, chill-toed child, experienced in sugared bread and butter, treacle tarts, toys and toffee, at the door of 'an old dame's school'.

After a brief period at Freeman's School, sadly the extent of his formal education, at the age of nine he was apprenticed to his shoemaker father.

Comparisons also with John Clare are inevitable but unfair. Both were the sons of poor, working class parents. Both spent youthful hours of recreation wandering the fields and woods around their homes, Askham as respite from the rigours of his apprenticeship. Both were largely untutored. Yet while Clare's writing is blessed with originality, born of acutely perceptive observation, succinct and economical, Askham's fondness for rhyming couplets and occasionally ponderous imagery can pall with the modern reader. He was, however, merely in tune with the Victorian era and the ideas and sentiments behind his poetry are often inspirational and insightful. Some, like his first major poem, *'The Dignity of Labour',* reflect his concern with social issues.

'Working men, ye are not slaves;
Those who tell you so are knaves,
Seeking but their selfish ends
Under guise of labour's friends.'

Although he strongly believed in the rights of working people he was no Chartist rioter or machine-breaker. He responded positively to the advent of the Singer sewing machines, which could do the work of dozens of hand-sewers in the clothing and boot and shoe trade,

'...to me there is harmony in their song
As they clatter and spin along:
You may deem them harsh, but their notes to me
Are sweet as the softest minstrelsy;

For why? Because in their every turn
Is a little of the bread we earn;
And the loaf would be small, and the
hearthstone chill,
If the lays of the 'Singers' were hushed and still.'
(*'The Singers'* from Descriptive Poems, 1866)

His admiration for John Clare is evident from a sonnet, dedicated to the poet and written in 1863 when Clare was a long-term patient in the County Asylum. The pathos of its final couplet is reminiscent of Shakespeare.

'Alas! We mourn thy fate, poor hapless Clare,
That such a night should follow morn so fair.'

Askham's work was first printed in the *Wellingborough Independent* and impressed the newspaper's editor, the liberal aesthete, George James de Wilde. De Wilde, who was also the editor of the *Northampton Mercury*, became a friend and patron, installing him as correspondent to several papers, thus supplementing a frugal income from shoemaking. Askham published five volumes of poetry between 1863 and 1893, including *'Sonnets on the Months' (1863),* which included the tribute to Clare, *'Poems and Sonnets (1866),* dedicated to De Wilde, and the acclaimed *'Sketches in Poems and Verse (1893).* In addition to his journalistic work, John Askham was co-founder of Wellingborough's Literary Institute and a member of the School Board, formed in 1871 in consequence of the Forster Education Act. From 1875-87 he was, surprisingly, the town's Sanitary Inspector!

Askham's personal life was not without tragedy. The death of his first wife in 1860 was a major blow compounded some years later when his beloved daughter, *'his little maiden',* died at the age of eight. In 1874 he suffered both the loss of an infant son and his own mother at the advanced age of eighty-three.

He lived for many years at number 1 Church Way, died in 1894, and is buried in Wellingborough's London Road cemetery.

An inscription on his gravestone reads,

'John Askham. Whom God hath blessed with the gift of poesy'.

The road from Wellingborough to Great Harrowden is still called Red Hill. The name is a reference to the waters of the town's most celebrated well, the Red Well, which was situated a mile to the north-west of the town centre in meadows close to the Hatton Brook near Kilborn Road. Its chalybeate, or sparkling spa water, was considered so efficacious that King Charles I and his Queen, Henrietta Maria, visited in 1628 and 1637.

In 1813, a watermill, later known as Kilborn Mill, was built not far from the site. At its opening, a poem by local writer, **Thomas Dexter**, was read to the large gathering. It contained these verses.

'That well, which in days that are gone
Was held in such note and esteem
That Royalty stoop'd from her throne
To drink its salubrious stream.

But, alas, as the years rolled along
Forsaken was yon little spot!
No more the resort of the throng –
Neglected, despised and forgot.'

Some forty years later, George James de Wilde located the well in the course of one of his celebrated *'Rambles Roundabout'*.

'It is in an arable field, lying between the Kettering and the Hardwick roads
- a spot thoroughly secluded and very picturesque. The spring is strong, and
the water bubbles up abundantly, leaving a red deposit on the stones and
earth over which it flows……There is not a vestige of a building about it.'

Tradition maintains that during his visits the court of King Charles lived in tented pavilions erected in fields overlooking the spring. On this site, some two hundred and fifty years later, Thomas Pendered built his house named, fittingly, 'Redwell'. It was the Pendered family home until 1987, when Dudley, an uncle of the prominent Wellingborough estate agent, died and the property was sold.

Redwell was also the pseudonym adopted by Thomas's daughter, the author and poet, **Mary Lucy Pendered**, for the many articles she provided for the local press, including a lyrical example published in the *Kettering Reminder* in the early nineteen twenties describing her father's garden.

'There are no curved or winding paths in this garden. My father loved long straight lines and despised the so-called 'landscape' garden. He liked the open space and wide views; and so we have them, seeing across the fields to Orlingbury to the west and across to Finedon on the north-east where, on clear days, its church's beautiful spire, soft in the blue distance, is set in the arch of a blush rambler.'

Born in 1859, Mary Pendered died at Great Addington aged eighty-three. She wrote several historical novels set in the locality. *'Herriot of Wellingborrow'* was published in 1936 and tells the story of a family riven by divided loyalties during the English Civil War. *'An Englishman'* is also based in Wellingborough, but her finest work is considered to be *'Fair Quaker'*, the tale of Hannah Lightfoot, an alleged wife of George III, who vanished mysteriously soon after the marriage.

Eighteenth century Harrowden Hall, situated in the hamlet of Great Harrowden two miles north of Wellingborough on the Kettering road, has housed the local golf club since 1975. It was once home to the celebrated Vaux family, staunch Roman Catholics, whose ancestors had possessed the estate, and built the original house, from early in the fifteenth century.

Sir Nicholas Vaux's personal history included attending the marriage of Prince Arthur, son of Henry VII, to Katherine of Arragon in 1501, and being one of the two Northamptonshire knights on the Field of the Cloth of Gold. In 1523 he was created the first Lord Vaux of Harrowden for services to the Court by Henry VIII. However, he died within weeks of receiving the title and his son, Thomas became the second Baron at the age of fourteen, inheriting a troubled and turbulent legacy.

The story of Thomas Vaux is told in Geoffrey Anstruther's highly readable biography, *'Vaux of Harrowden: A Recusant Family' (1953)*. He describes his subject as,

> *'one of the old Catholic nobility, deeply disturbed by the prevailing religious chaos, and singing in the midst of the ruins.'*

According to Anstruther, having maintained something of a high-profile at court during Henry's reign, Vaux opted to *'keep his head on his shoulders and his hands clean'* after the king's death. He lived quietly at Harrowden, *'writing his plaintive songs and singing them to his friends'*, until succumbing to the plague in October 1556. Interestingly, the family's Catholic tradition was strengthened by his son, William, who married Mary Tresham, sister of Sir Thomas, the now celebrated builder of Triangular Lodge, Lyveden New Bield and Rothwell Market House.

None of Thomas Vaux's poems were published during his lifetime, but two appeared in *'Songes and Sonnettes' (1557)* and, nineteen years later, another fifteen in *'The Paradise of Dainty Devices'*. The former includes *'The Aged Lover Renounceth Love'*, whose opening stanza,

> *'I loathe that I did love,*
> *In youth that I thought sweet;*
> *As time requires, for my behove,*
> *Methinks they are not meet.'*

is one of several from the poem cleverly parodied by Shakespeare, no less, in the grave-yard scene from *'Hamlet'*. The gravedigger's version reads,

> *'In youth, when I did love, did love*
> *Methought it was very sweet,*
> *To contract, O, the time, for, ah, my behove,*
> *O, methought there was nothing meet.'*

Desdemona's, *'Sing all a green willow'* in *'Othello'*, is also 'borrowed' from a Lord Vaux poem.

There can be no greater tribute.

For over two hundred years from the middle of the 17th century, the Vaux title remained in abeyance and it was not until 1895 that Hubert, the seventh Lord Vaux was able to buy back the ancestral estates. He died in 1935.

Golfers suffering a frustrating round on the pleasant course that now occupies the grounds of Harrowden Hall might reflect upon these words from a Thomas Vaux poem.

'When all is done and said,
In the end thus shall you find,
He most of all doth bathe in bliss
That hath a quiet mind.'

Roundabout Brackley

It is now necessary to embark on the lengthy drive to Northamptonshire's south-western extremes to investigate the rich crop of writers associated with that part of the county.

The village of King's Sutton, located on the Oxfordshire border, is noted particularly for the beauty of its church-spire, described by Bridges as *'remarkably elegant and neat.'* It was the birthplace, on September 24th 1762, of the divine, poet and antiquary, **William Lisle Bowles**, whose father was the vicar. Like the Kingsleys, Bowles spent only a few years in Northamptonshire, joining Winchester School at the age of twelve and later Trinity College, Oxford. He entered holy orders, first as curate at Donhead St Andrew in Wiltshire and, from 1804, vicar of Bremhill, where he resided for the best part of his long life. In 1818 he was appointed chaplain to the Prince Regent, and ten years later became canon residentiary at Salisbury Cathedral.

Bowles had given early notice of his literary potential when his poem, *'Calpe Obsessa,* or the *'Siege of Gibraltar'*, won his college chancellor's prize for Latin verse. However, his reputation was founded on a small volume, originally published anonymously in 1789, entitled, *'Fourteen Sonnets written chiefly on Picturesque Spots during a Journey,'* and inspired by a tour through the north of England, Scotland and parts of the continent. The book was a spectacular success and won effusive praise from critics, including the seventeen year old Samuel Taylor Coleridge, who later recorded his admiration for Bowles in a fine sonnet, beginning

> *'My heart has thank'd thee, BOWLES! For those soft strains*
> *Whose sadness soothes me, like the murmuring*
> *Of wild bees in the sunny showers of spring!*
> *For hence not callous to the mourner's pains*
> *Through Youth's gay prime and thornless paths I went:'*
>
> (second version, pub 1796)

A prolific writer, Bowles produced fourteen volumes of poetry between 1789 and 1837. Their range is various and wide, including *'The Battle of the Nile',* *'The Spirit of Discovery'* and *'The Grave of the last Saxon'*. His biography of Alexander Pope, published in 1806, provoked extreme controversy. Byron was particularly critical of Bowles' censorious approach which, *'omitted no detail that could harm Pope's memory, but left out or mentioned coldly such facts as did him honour,'* and Bowles was subjected to stinging assaults in verse and prose from all quarters of the literary establishment.

A respected antiquary, Bowles' most important work in this field is considered to be *'Hermes Britannicus'*, published in 1828.

Several volumes of his work can be found among the collection of poetry in the Northamptonshire Studies section of the Central Library in Northampton. The copies are extremely fragile and can only be perused under the supervision of library staff; however, the effort will prove well worthwhile. In this untitled sonnet, reflections on the journey through life mirror beautifully observed ruminations on his travels through the countryside.

> *'Languid, and sad, and slow from day to day,*
> *I journey on, yet pensive turn to view*
> *(Where the rich landscape gleams with softer hue)*
> *The streams, and vales, and hills, that steal away.*
> *So fares it with the children of the earth:*
> *For when life's goodly prospect opens round,*
> *Their spirits beat to tread that fairy ground,*
> *Where every vale sounds to the pipe of mirth.*
> *But them vain hope, and easy youth beguiles,*
> *And soon a longing look, like me, they cast*
> *Back on the pleasing prospect of the past;*
> *Yet fancy points where still far onward smiles*
> *Some sunny spot, and her fair colouring blends,*
> *Till cheerless on their path the night descends.'*

A more personal note is introduced in *'Scenes and Shadows of Days Departed' (1837),* which includes references to his early life, but sadly makes no mention of his King's Sutton childhood.

Bowles died in 1850, aged eighty-eight, and five years later a collected edition of his poetry was published in two volumes by the Rev George Gilfillan.

Its situation straddling the main Oxford to Northampton road has given Brackley a degree of prosperity and importance since the Middle Ages. Consequently, it still contains some fine buildings in both stone and brick including Magdalen College School and the Duke of Bridgewater's Town Hall. The town has certainly benefited from a by-pass and now, with its tree-lined main street and old houses, preserves its quiet country atmosphere.

An unmarked grave in the churchyard of St Peter's contains the remains of the celebrated poet, **Mary Leapor**.

Mary was baptised on 26 February 1722 at Marston Hall in the nearby village of Marston St Lawrence where her father was gardener to Sir John Blencowe, a judge in the court of Common Pleas.

After the judge's death in 1726, the family moved to Brackley, her father setting up as a nurseryman, occupying the old castle site on the banks of the Ouse.

As a young girl, Mary was employed by Blencowe's daughter, Susanna (nee Jennens), as a cook-maid at the hall in her mother's home village of Weston by Weedon before taking up a similar position at Edgcote House near Banbury. Her poetry, which she began to write from the age of ten or eleven, contains sensitive, if rather cynical, observations of her life in service. Unusually for the time, many have a feminist perspective and bemoan the limitations placed upon her sex.

> *'Woman, a pleasing but short-lived flower,*
> *Too soft for business and too weak for power:*
> *A wife in bondage, or neglected maid:*
> *Despised, if ugly; if she's fair, betrayed.'*

There is confusion about circumstances surrounding her dismissal from her post as kitchen maid. Some authorities link the incident with Weston while others attribute it to Edgcote. We must assume that a fondness for the household cook, who appears as 'Sophronia' in *The Disappointment'*, was not the principal reason. As the following self-deprecating lines suggest, her dismissal was due to negligence of duties owing to her preoccupation with writing.

> *'Then comes Sophronia, like a barbr'ous Turk;*
> *You thoughtless Baggage, when d'ye mind your Work?*
> *Still o'er a Table leans your bending neck:*
> *Your head will grow preposterous, like a Peck.*
> *Go, ply your Needle; You might earn your Bread;*
> *Or who must feed you when your Father's dead?'*

Edgcote House, then the home of Sir Richard Chauncey, was originally constructed at the end of the sixteenth century. It was extensively re-modelled shortly after Mary's death in 1746 and is believed to have been the inspiration for her masterpiece, *'Crumble Hall'*.

> *'Of this rude Palace might a poet sing*
> *From cold December to returning Spring;'*

Mary's familiarity with her main place of work which, according to Bridges, contained, *'two chimneys of stone, vastly large'*, is encapsulated in the almost Shakespearean lines,

> *'The sav'ry Kitchen much Attention calls:*
> *Westphalia Hams adorn the sable Walls:*
> *The Fires blaze; the greasy Pavements fry;*
> *And streaming Odours from the Kettles fly.'*

In *'Eyebright in the kitchen'*, an appreciation of Mary's life and work written in 1996 on the 250th anniversary of her death, Trevor Hold selects examples from *'Crumble Hall'* demonstrating poetic skills reminiscent of the great John Clare.

> *'Grey Dobbin's gears (the harness), and drenching-horns enow;*
> *Wheel-spokes – the iron of a tatter'd plough'.*

In 1745, Mary returned to Brackley to keep house for her widowed father. It was during this year that she was befriended by Bridget Freemantle, the daughter of a former rector of Hinton-in-the-Hedges. Bridget, or Artemesia as she was referred to in Mary's poems, did much to promote her friend's career by bringing her to the attention of wealthy and influential friends.

Despite a brief life, lived with a complete lack of any formal education and ending at the age of twenty-four with a bout of measles, Mary produced a wealth of verse good enough to earn the admiration of William Cowper and Robert Southey and recognition in the Dictionary of National Biography. Her first poem to appear in print, *'The Rural Maid's Reflexions'* by A Gardener's Daughter, was published in the London magazine in 1747, the year following her death. After a successful appeal for subscribers, backed by David Garrick, two volumes of her poetry, and a biographical memoir by Artemesia, were edited by Isaac Hawkins Browne and published as *'Poems upon Several Occasions'* in 1748 and 1751.

Later admirers of her work include Edmund Blunden and, more recently, David Powell, who places her among the 'Five Best' poets born in the county alongside Randolph, Dryden, Clare and Bowles. Describing her particular qualities, Powell writes,

> *'Her poems are mainly concerned with the human comedy, the wisdom and folly of men and women, and she is specially delighted when poking gentle fun at herself.'*

Modern readers marvelling at the abundance of references to classical literature, her wry, perceptive view of human nature, and her anticipation of feminism, will share Blunden's appraisal that she was, indeed, *'an eighteenth century prodigy'*.

'An epistle to Mary Leapor', a poem in Trevor Hold's anthology of his own poetry entitled *'Chasing the Moon' (2001)*, contains interesting conjecture upon the poetess's physical appearance.

> *'I've often wondered what you looked like,*
> *but sadly no pictures exist –*
> *who would bother to paint a kitchen-maid? –*
> *and hardly a description except*
> *those mocking ones you wrote yourself –*
> *furze-faggot brows, decaying teeth*
> *and hunch-back shoulders –*
> *or that ungallant memoir by your employer:*
> *'extremely swarthy....quite emaciated...*
> *a long-crane neck and a short body,*
> *much resembling in shape a bass-viol'.*
> *These are no more than cruel squibs;*
> *I wish we had a true likeness, even a sketch*
> *So that I could get to know you better.*
> *But no matter: it's the poems that count in the end.'*

A short drive north-east from Brackley along winding lanes through rolling countryside will lead to the village of Weedon Lois and the church of St Mary and St Peter. In the churchyard extension across the road from the twelfth century building, lie members of the distinguished Sitwell family, descendants of the Jennens, who lived at the afore-mentioned hall in nearby Weston by Weedon.

Edith, Osbert and **Sacherevell**, the three children of Sir George and Lady Ida **Sitwell** all achieved literary prominence. Raised in the family home, Renishaw Hall in Derbyshire, and living and working mostly in London, Dame Edith can hardly be called a true Northamptonshire writer but, like her younger brother who lived at Weston Hall, she is buried in this quiet corner of the county and therefore merits inclusion.

Edith Sitwell's grave is marked with an impressive stone pillar inset with a Henry Moore bronze chosen by her younger brother from his studio. It depicts the hands of Youth and Age, a child's hand encircling a woman's thumb. The following lines from her poem *'The Wind of Early Spring'* are inscribed below it.

> *'The past and present are as one*
> *Accordant and discordant*
> *Youth and age*
> *And death and birth*
> *For out of one came all*
> *From all comes one.'*

Edith Sitwell was born in Scarborough on 7th September 1887. When she died at the age of seventy-seven she was widely recognised as one of the most celebrated writers of her age. Her early poetry earned the praise of WB Yeats, she was the first to publish the work of Wilfred Owen and her circle of friends included Aldous Huxley, TS Eliot, Virginia Woolf and Roger Fry. A controversial collaboration with the composer William Walton, entitled *'Façade' (1922)*, added notoriety to her increasing fame. During the 'thirties she broadened her scope by writing biography and a single novel, *'I Live Under a Black Sun' (1937)*, based on the life of Jonathan Swift. With maturity, her work acquired a deepening religious and social dimension. She conveyed the horrors of war, most notably in *'The Shadow of Cain' (1947)*, provoked by an eye-witness account of the first nuclear bomb on Hiroshima. She became a Dame of the British Empire in 1954 and continued her remarkable output until her death ten years later. A witty, self-deprecating autobiography, *'Taken Care Of'*, was published posthumously in 1965.

Her brother, Sacheverell, was born in 1897, educated at Eton and served with the Grenadier Guards during the First World War. His first claim to literary distinction was as a poet and followed the publication of *'The People's Palace'* in 1918. He contributed to *'Poor Young People' (1925)* with Edith and his brother Osbert, whose work is also included in later anthologies, *'Collected Poems' (1936)* and *'Selected Poems' (1948)*.

Sacherevell earned a considerable reputation as a critic of art and architecture, and wide-ranging and entertaining essays on art, music and travel form the contents of a number of prose volumes including, *'The Dance of the Quick and the Dead' (1936), 'Sacred and Profane Love' (1940), 'Primitive Scenes and Festivals' (1942), 'Splendours and Miseries' (1943*) and *'Cupid and the Jacaranda' (1952)*.

On the death of his elder brother in 1969, Sacherevell became the sixth baronet. *'An Indian Summer, poems'* was published in 1982, six years before he too died.

If Weedon Lois now boasts the final resting place of the distinguished Sitwells, two writers of far humbler origin were born, raised and lived their lives in the village a century or so before. Shoemakers **John Coles** (born 1775) and **Joseph Furniss** (born 1783) collaborated in the publication of *'Poems Moral and Religious'* in 1811. The preface, attributed to both authors, is typically apologetic, apprising the reader that,

> *'we are plain and unlettered men, having never received the advantages of an education, therefore, what little knowledge we possess has been self-acquired; and even in this respect our opportunities for improvement have been but small, for from our childhood to the present time we have been under the necessity of labouring hard for our daily support.'*

John Coles expands on this in the opening verses of his *'Address to the Reader'*

> *'Ye sons of learning and of taste*
> *To whom this work may fall,*
> *Pardon my leaving this my Last*
> *My Hammer, Knife and Awl.*
>
> *Unknown I am to public schools,*
> *Where science takes its seat;*
> *Nor understand their forms and rules,*
> *Which lead to learning sweet.'*

As the preface informs, the poems were written *'at different times, and on different occasions; sometimes to pass away a leisure hour, and sometimes to divert the mind from other gloomy and disagreeable objects.'* The writers were keen to satisfy all tastes and *'endeavoured to diversify the pieces in such a manner that there will be some found upon almost every subject.'*

The poems do, indeed, cover a wide range of topics from Coles' fashionably romantic yet well-observed lines *'On Winter'*.

> *'The northern winds now fiercely blow,*
> *And fields and meads are clad with snow;*
> *Each naked tree and barren plain,*
> *Proclaim tyrannic Winter's reign;*
> *The birds no longer thro' the grove,*
> *Sing to charm me as I rove;*
> *No verdant beauties now I find,*
> *To entertain and please my mind;*
> *'Tis now the flocks for shelter seek,*
> *To screen them from the dreadful wreak*
> *Of the cold winds that fiercely blow,*
> *Of beating rains and driving snow.'*

to the intense, religious fundamentalism of Furniss's *'Elegy on the death of an infant of Mr W West's of Weedon Beck: which happened on the 5th Day of July 1808'.*

> *'Then cease, fond parents, grieve not for your child,*
> *Let reason guide you thro' this scene of woe;*
> *The God of peace has call'd your infant mild*
> *To realms where endless pleasures ever flow.'*

It is likely that the bereaved Mr W West was related to Benjamin West, schoolmaster and poet from Weedon Bec, whose daughter subsequently married Joseph Furniss. The Furniss's son, Joseph junior, also produced a volume of verse, *'Miscellaneous Poems'*, which was published in 1841.

Weedon Bec is located some eight miles from Weedon Lois. **Benjamin West**, *'the Weedonian Bard'*, was born in the village in 1740 and died there 51 years later. Respected by county poets of the time, West's *'Poems, Translations and Intimations' (1780)* attracted a large number of subscribers and was widely read.

The church of St Mary's at Moreton Pinkney contains the remains of **Edward Bagshaw**, a Derbyshire man who achieved prominence during the seventeenth century as a religious and political author. Like the illustrious John Dryden, he flirted with both sides of the political divide, entering Cromwell's 'Long Parliament' as the member for Southwark in 1640. When the king was forced to leave London in 1644, Bagshaw left the Parliamentarian faction and sat in the king's 'anti-parliament' at Oxford. Captured and imprisoned by parliamentary forces later that year, he spent his confinement writing the ecclesiastical and political books which confirmed his reputation. The best known chronicles the life of Robert Bolton, one of the greatest religious thinkers of the day and Bagshaw's tutor at Oxford. After his release in 1646, Bagshaw retired from public life and spent the remaining sixteen years of his life on his Moreton Pinkney estate.

A century later, a more celebrated literary figure had tenuous associations with the village church. On retiring as Dean of Oriel in 1758, the **Rev Gilbert White** was granted the non-resident living of St Mary's by the Oxford College. However, he eventually returned to his native village of Selbourne in Hampshire, where he recorded the observations of wild life and the changing seasons, published in 1789 as the classic, '*The Natural History of Selbourne*'.

In general, we have restricted any reference to the many informative village histories produced in recent years to those containing specific details about literary figures from the area. A notable exception is *'A Countryman's Tale' (1973)*, **Syd Tyrrell**'s evocative and beautifully written account set in the south Northamptonshire village of Eydon, situated *'on the southern slope of a 580-foot hill on one of the last uplands of the Cotswolds just before they merge into the valley of the Nene and the Fen country'*. Although the author maintains in the prologue that *'much of the book is scrappy, and I make statements I cannot verify'*, he certainly achieves his stated intention to *'put flesh on the dry bones of recorded history.'*

While relating factual events Syd Tyrrell enlivens the narrative with personal asides and carefully chosen quotations from contemporary sources. Typical is the fascinating chapter describing the Annesley family, which settled in the village in 1788.

> The Rev Francis Annesley *'was a shrewd customer if ever there was one: with all his money he went into the Church and became rector of Chedzoy (Somerset). Then he played the game so many clergymen played in those days. He had the belly-ache and sent for the doctor. He knew very well what he was expected to say, so he said it: 'You will never be well here, the place don't suit you.' Here it is in black and white; 'Rector of Chedzoy Somerset. The place did not agree with Mr Annesley.'*

The upshot was that Annesley became an absentee rector with a living of £100 per annum, moved to Eydon, purchased and immediately demolished the old manor house, and built a new four-storeyed mansion some two hundred yards from the original site. The clergyman's impact upon Eydon was not without controversy, as Tyrrell relates. *'While Annesley was building his mansion and living on the fat of the land, the poor folk in the village were sinking lower and lower into abject poverty.'*

Whether due to an argument with his gamekeeper over unpaid wages or a dispute over land Annesley had purchased in neighbouring Moreton Pinkney, the unpopular rector received death-threats from an anonymous *'combination of persons'*. However, no blood was shed. Annesley survived the *'cheeky servants'* and *'cunning poachers'* and lived, like his wife Mary, until 1811 when he was succeeded by his nephew, who placed a marble tablet in the nearby church in memory of his uncle, 'with pious and unfeigned gratitude.' *'I should jolly well think he did'*, writes Tyrrell, *'bearing in mind he had inherited the new mansion and estate, free of encumbrance.'*

Other chapters recall incidents in the lives of villagers, often supported by oral accounts. In addition, there is a lengthy section on Syd's own family history covering almost a hundred years from one Joseph Tyrrell, (his father), to another, (his son). Graphic and well-observed, the autobiographical details begin with his own birth;

> *'When I arrived in 1889, it's said that Grandmother Tyrrell remarked, 'Poor thing, he ain't come for long.'*

and continue through childhood, work, memories of the First World War and the 'twenties, to the death of his father and birth of his son in 1930. One particularly colourful account describes the annual ritual of killing the family pig for Christmas. He acknowledges the butcher's skill; *'John Howard was an artist at his job. Of course he could not do it without a squeal, but it was not prolonged and there was no shouting'*. However, it's obvious that the practice caused Syd considerable soul-searching. *'I hated it and also Father's apparent indifference to the suffering caused....he went down considerably in my opinion.'* But as he then admits, within days he would be *'enjoying the good things that Mother put on our table. For about three weeks we lived on what Father called 'the fat of the land'. He would smack his lips over the pork pie and say, 'This is the best pig we ever had.' 'Sure enough', one of us would reply, 'Why you said that last year.' 'Ah well,' he'd say, 'it's true all the same.'*

The book took fifteen years to write and a further five to find a publisher. When **Byron Rogers** unearthed a copy in a second-hand bookshop in 1990 it had already been out of print for seventeen years and its author dead for twenty-four. Byron championed its cause in the *Guardian*, stating *'how absurd it was that 'Cider with Rosie' was on the reading lists of most schools in England, while 'A Countryman's Tale' had not gone into a second edition.'*

The prologue ends with the following lines,

> *'Now I lay down my pen, with the fervent prayer that one of the bright sparks now at school will, in a few years, carry on this story of a village in the heart of old England.'*

In fact, the cunning countryman did write a second book in which he brought his story up to date. Its belated discovery delighted the man who had done so much to promote the original. Byron Rogers contributed an intriguing introduction to *'Syd Tyrrell's Eydon'*, the sequel edited and published by Syd's family and the Eydon Historical Research Group in 2001. Its contents are more controversial than the first for, as Rogers notes, *'while it is one thing to sit in judgement on the dead in a small village, it is quite another to fill a court-room with contemporaries.'*

Roundabout Northampton

In the introduction to his book, *'The Wakes of Northampton', (1992),* author Professor Peter Gordon refers to a letter from Sir Hereward Wake to his sister Joan, in which he writes, *'We are worth a proper Family History if only because we have carried on for nearly eight centuries in unbroken, undisputed, legitimate male descent from a Norman baron.'* Despite being ideally qualified to undertake the task, she declined the request stating, *'There is no such boring thing in the world as ancestor worship to other people, and I was determined not to become that particular kind of bore.'*

As Gordon's engaging account demonstrates, the family was certainly worthy of a detailed history, but the remarkable Miss Wake was more concerned with the bigger picture and devoted much of her life to preserving the heritage of her beloved county.

Born at Courteenhall, home to five generations of Wakes, on February 29th 1884, **Joan Wake** was the first of that name in her family since her famous forebear, Joan of Kent, some five hundred and fifty years before. 'The Fair Maid' would have been Queen of England had her second husband, the renowned Black Prince, lived a year longer. As it was, their surviving son was crowned King Richard II in July 1377 at the age of ten. Little wonder, with such a celebrated antecedent, that the more recent Joan should develop a passion for history.

Unlike two of her brothers, Hereward and Godwin, who were sent to Eton, Joan and her sisters were educated by governesses and tutors at Courteenhall. Aware of deficiencies in her formal education, particularly in literature and art, she began to read widely and by her late twenties had earned something of a reputation as a literary critic. One who was grateful for such honest appraisal was her cousin, Edith Sitwell, who later dedicated a number of poems to Joan as a mark of gratitude.

Joan was twenty-nine when she enrolled on a two year course in palaeography and diplomatic and medieval economic history at the London School of Economics and Political Science. On completing the course, she immediately put her newly gained knowledge to good effect when a neighbour, Sir Thomas Fermor-Hesketh asked her over to Easton Neston to look at some boxes of old deeds in his possession. Among them she found, *'a scrap of parchment under nine inches by four in measurement',* which dated from the twelfth century and the reign of King Stephen and related to a grant to the Abbey of St James in Northampton.

This tangible link with the distant past had immense significance for Joan, who expressed her feelings in a graphic quote,

> *'Could this wonderful and exciting business we were up to, this intimate contact with real people in the remote past, have anything to do with the dull and prosy stuff called history which I used to learn out of books in the schoolroom? Yet so it was.'*

Joan recognised the need to preserve these records before, *'the dustcart rumbled by, laden with valuable family manuscripts, and people lighted their pipes with twelfth century charters.'* Her efforts led to the establishment of the Northamptonshire Record Society on December 20th 1920. Its aims were to accumulate manuscripts, as well as copies and photographs of them; to arrange lectures; to train students; to make lists of local records; and to recommend the publication of manuscripts. The work became ever more urgent between the wars with the disintegration of many of the larger estates and often the demolition of the actual buildings. Joan's privileged position as a member of one of the county's oldest families enabled her to access the estate and family records of Northamptonshire's great houses. Her Diary for 1932 contains this record of her visit to Burghley.

> *'I went on my motor bike…dinner at eight in a small dining room…we ate off silver plates – four courses and a dessert.....Next day, Lord Exeter (President of the Record Society) said to me, 'I have complete confidence in you'. I bowed low, and was very pleased as this is not the first unsolicited testimonial I have had. The Duke of Buccleuch has said the same thing ……Result, I can borrow what I want from these places… So (the next day) I made a list, stuffed an armful of documents into my suitcase, said goodbye, and left on my motor bike with the precious burden.'*

Her travels took her to the splendour of Althorp, Rockingham Castle, Drayton and Canon's Ashby, but she didn't neglect more humble locations. In the early thirties, she recorded and investigated the village of Corby, when the impending arrival of the steelworks and attendant large-scale housing development threatened to engulf the original settlement. She had already acknowledged the importance of local people recording local history, having produced a booklet in 1925 entitled, *'How to Compile a History and Present-Day Record of Village Life'.* Sold for a shilling, and intended primarily for Women's Institutes throughout the county, it became a standard reference work for would-be village chroniclers.

Largely due to Joan's efforts, with valuable support from JA Gotch and the Marquess of Exeter, in March 1930 the Record Rooms of the Society, comprising a fireproof strongroom, a students' room and a general store-room, were opened at

County Hall. Staffed by Joan, as honorary custodian, and two assistants, they were available to students for six days a week. The growing amount of archive material eventually put pressure on storage. From 1939 and the outbreak of World War Two, thirteen tons of records were re-located for safe-keeping under Joan's supervision at her own house in Cosgrove and at Brixworth Hall. At the end of hostilities, a new home was found at Lamport Hall, by kind permission of Sir Gyles Isham, an active member of the Society. There, records were kept in every conceivable kind of container from old trunks to hat boxes and by 1950 filled ten rooms.

The financial demands associated with maintaining an administrative staff and publishing Record Society volumes were greatly eased by Joan's initiative in selling local firms advertising space in the Society's new magazine, *'Northamptonshire Past and Present',* which she edited for eleven years from its first issue in 1948, not surprisingly contributing many articles herself.

Her busy, peripatetic lifestyle mitigated against much sustained writing but in 1953, after a gestation period of some twenty years, she published *'The Brudenells of Deene'*. It won great acclaim. One notable reviewer, Anthony Powell in *Punch*, wrote,

> *'Miss Joan Wake has used her material with remarkable skill; and the Brudenells themselves, partly from their habit of preserving records, partly from the individuality – not to say eccentricity – of various members of their race, provide all the elements of an enthralling narrative.'*

Perhaps Joan's greatest achievement was in leading the successful campaign to save Delapre Abbey from demolition in the mid nineteen-fifties. Many years earlier, she had ear-marked the former Cluniac nunnery at Hardingstone, which was purchased by the Town Council in 1946, as a permanent home for the Record Society and its records. After a remarkable fund-raising project which enabled essential repairs to the building to be carried out, the Society was granted a ninety-nine year lease of the Abbey at a minimal rent of £100 per annum. The official opening, on 9th May 1959, or Delapre Day as Joan called it, was a triumph. The Abbey housed the forty tons of archives relating to Northamptonshire, (and since moved to Wootton Hall), together with the Record Society itself, and a leading article in *The Times* made reference to her achievement.

'Northamptonshire has developed a sense of the vitality of history, a pride in its own traditions, and a determination to preserve them for posterity; and that is the fruit of the shire's most distinguished antiquary, MISS JOAN WAKE.'

Numerous honours were bestowed upon her. Elected to the Society of Antiquaries in 1945, she received an honorary MA from Oxford University in 1953, a degree of Doctor of Laws from Leicester University in 1959 and a CBE the following year. Shortly after receiving her Oxford degree, she moved to a house in the city close to the River Cherwell, whose source she would remind visitors was at Charwelton in her beloved Northamptonshire.

In the summer of 1971, and rather frail, she attended the fiftieth anniversary celebrations of the Society she had done so much to promote. She died on 15th January 1974, five weeks before her ninetieth birthday, and was buried in the churchyard at Courteenhall alongside other members of the distinguished Wake family. Yet the true memorial is the thriving interest in the county's rich historical heritage, which owes so much to her tireless commitment and devotion.

It is fitting that **RL Greenall**, one of Joan's successors as editor of *Northamptonshire Past and Present,* has helped to perpetuate her work. A familiar and much respected figure to devotees of local history, Ron worked as a lecturer in the Department of Adult Education at Leicester University from 1965-96 rising through the ranks to become Deputy Director and, following his retirement, an Associate Senior Lecturer. From 1967-78 he combined his duties with the position of Warden at the University Centre in Northampton's Barrack Road.

His writings have added to the accessibility of a store of material about the county, most notably *'A History of Northamptonshire and the Soke of Peterborough'*, which was revised and up-dated in 1999, twenty years after its original publication. A highly informative, carefully illustrated, account which *'sets local events against the backcloth of broader national history and in relation to economic and social developments'*, the book has become an essential part of the local historian's library.

True to the spirit of Joan Wake, he has also produced histories of individual towns and villages in the county. He edited *'The Population of a Northamptonshire Village in 1851: A Census Study of Long Buckby' (1971)* and *'Naseby: A Parish History' (1974)*, compiled *'Daventry Past' (1999)*, and a similarly titled volume on Kettering is expected to be published in 2003. He has also written extensively about religious nonconformity in the area, editing *'Philip Doddridge, Nonconformity and Northampton' (1981)*, and *'The Kettering Connection: Northamptonshire Baptists and Overseas Missions' (1993)*. The latter originated as a series of weekly lectures delivered in Kettering's Fuller Baptist Church as part of the celebrations to mark the bi-centenary of the founding of the Baptist Missionary Society in the town in 1792.

Like Joan, Ron Greenall has made important personal contributions to *Northamptonshire Past and Present*, submitting articles on *'The Rise of Industrial Kettering'*, *'The History of Boot and Shoemaking in Long Buckby'*, *'Three Nineteenth Century Agriculturalists'* and *'The Parson as a Man of Affairs; The Revd. Francis Litchfield of Farthinghoe'*.

Although a Lancastrian with roots in Salford, who has spent most of his life resident in Leicester, RL Greenall's professional dedication and fascination for this county make him an honorary Northamptonshire Man.

The manor of Holdenby came into the possession of the Hatton family during the sixteenth century. Only two gateways of the outer courtyard of the great palace, built in 1583 by Sir Christopher, Queen Elizabeth's Chancellor survived its demolition after the Civil War, and the present hall which dates from the nineteenth century is built on a small remnant of its predecessor.

In 1647, Charles I was brought to Holdenby, in the safe-keeping of Parliament, after he had been surrendered to them by the Scots. During his four month honourable confinement, the King renewed his acquaintance with one **James Harrington**.

Harrington was born at Upton, near Northampton, in 1611 and, as a tablet in the village church informs, he died in 1677 and is buried in St Margaret's, Westminster. His life was a series of contradictions. On leaving Oxford University, he embarked upon an unusual grand tour of the continent. During this time, he consorted with various royal exiles, studied in Holland, refused to kiss the Pope's toe in Rome and became so in awe of the republic of Venice that he maintained *'it could perish only with mankind'*. A Republican at heart, he accompanied Charles I to Scotland as one of his privy-councillors developing a lasting affection for the monarch. During the Civil War, despite being a declared Parliamentarian but taking no part in the conflict, he eventually became re-united with Charles at Holdenby where he was appointed groom of the royal bedchamber. The two are supposed to have talked freely together, Harrington expressing his views on the benefits of Republicanism. Nevertheless, he was dismissed from his post for appearing to be too favourably impressed with the King.

After Charles' execution, which had a profound effect upon his former confidant, Harrington retired from public life and began work on *'The Commonwealth of Oceana'*, the book for which he is best remembered. Considered to be a reply to Thomas Hobbes' *'Leviathan'*, *'Oceana'* was published in 1656 and offered a positive and constructive view of an ideal Commonwealth. According to a passage in Arthur Mee's *'Northamptonshire'*, the manuscript of the book was seized at the printers on Cromwell's orders. Apparently the Lord Protector took offence at passages relating to the dangers of the excessive growth of power of one man or one class, but relented when the author pleaded with Lady Claypole, Cromwell's daughter, who eventually secured the release of the manuscript. A remarkable number of Harrington's ideas such as - limitations on inherited property and on income; the principle of rotation in office at regular intervals; the selection of representatives by the people themselves – are fundamental to modern democracy, and the book had a powerful influence on the thinking of the early settlers in North America.

A friend of literary notables such as John Aubrey, Andrew Marvell and Samuel Pepys, he was arrested on a groundless charge of treason during the Restoration and imprisoned for some years in the Tower. As a result Harrington's health became severely impaired and he died in 1677 at the age of sixty-six.

The map of medieval Northampton reproduced in Ron Greenall's definitive, *'A History of Northamptonshire and the Soke of Peterborough,'* (1979), provides compelling evidence of the town's prominence during the Middle Ages.

The town centre was surrounded by huge stone walls with five gates providing access. All have long-since disappeared. The construction was the work of the first Simon de Senlis, Earl of Northampton, and husband of Maud, the daughter of William the First's niece. The Conqueror had been quick to recognise the importance of Northampton's strategic position in the middle of his kingdom and charged de Senlis with responsibility for creating a fortress town. In addition to the walls, he built an imposing castle on the site of the present railway station, which later became a seat of national government and the setting for the famous trial of Henry II's archbishop, Thomas a Becket in 1164. In 1095, with much of his building work complete, de Senlis set out on the First Crusade to the Holy Land. The busy road network that carries traffic along Sheep Street passes within yards of the Holy Sepulchre, the round church modelled upon its revered counterpart in Jerusalem, and built soon after 1100 by de Senlis on his safe return. He would not be so fortunate on his second pilgrimage, dying of disease in France. By the Middle Ages, the town bore little resemblance to the cluster of mean buildings in the vicinity of modern Marefair that had formed the original Saxon settlement of Hamtune. Although a great fire in 1675 ravaged much of the town, many of these medieval features survive. Most notable are three great churches, the afore-mentioned Holy Sepulchre, St Peter's in Marefair, described in the *'Shell Guide'* to the county, (1968), as *'Northamptonshire's most impressive and complete Norman parish church,'* and St Giles in the street that bears its name. Most of the original All Saints Church in the Drapery was largely destroyed in the conflagration and rebuilt with a generous gift of timber from King Charles II.

During his enforced sojourn at the town's asylum during the nineteenth century, the celebrated poet, John Clare, spent hours sitting under its portico. A further literary connection links another local luminary, **William Cowper**, to the building. The Olney poet supplied little moral sermons in verse for the parish clerk to accompany his Bill of Mortality, an important source for calculating insurance claims in the eighteenth century. As he wrote,

> *'A fig for poets who write epitaphs on individuals,*
> *I have one that serves 200 people.'*

When the clerk supplied Northampton's Mayor with his list of recorded deaths in the Parish of All Saints during 1787, it was embellished by Cowper's reflections on mortality, beginning

'While thirteen moons saw smoothly run
The Nen's barge-laden wave
All these, life's rambling journey done
Have found their home, the grave.'

By the late fourteenth century, Northampton had lost the pre-eminence enjoyed when court and parliament were regular visitors. Students loyal to the cause of the defeated rebel, Simon de Montford, had ended the possibility of establishing a university in the town to rival Oxford and Cambridge. The last parliament met at the castle in 1380, its most significant legacy being the decision to impose a burdensome Poll Tax to finance the endless wars in France leading directly to the Peasants' Revolt in June the following year. Northampton was already a centre of religious dissent, and several Lollards, supporters of the celebrated Dissenter, John Wycliffe, had gained access to important civic and ecclesiastical positions in the town. During the reign of Mary Tudor, extreme measures were taken against 'heretics' who denied the doctrine of transubstantiation. One such victim was John Kurde, a Syresham shoemaker who, in 1557, was burnt to death in a stone-pit close to Northampton's North Gate.

After Elizabeth's comparatively tolerant view of religious non-conformity, her successor, King James I was less accommodating and many Puritans sought refuge in the New World.

Two non-conformist families, the Dudleys of Yardley Hastings, and the Bradstreets from Lincolnshire, were among a number of leading Puritans who emigrated to Massachusetts Bay, New England in March 1630. **Anne Bradstreet** was the daughter of Thomas Dudley, once page to Lord Compton and then steward to the Earl of Lincoln. Her husband, Simon, the son of a Lincolnshire non-conformist minister, had been eight years in the Earl's service under her father. Born in or near Northampton in 1612, Anne had been a sickly child, stricken with smallpox and also lame, and continued to suffer from ill-health in her new home-land. Nevertheless, she gave birth to eight children,

'I had eight birds hatcht in one nest
Four cocks there were and hens the rest'.

before eventually succumbing to consumption in 1672 at the age of sixty.

Her fame as a poet originated in a collection of her works, which was first distributed in manuscript form and eventually published in London in 1650 under the title, *'The Tenth Muse Lately Sprung up in America.... By a Gentlewoman in Those Parts.* The volume included an *'Elogie on Sir Philip Sidney' (1638),* and *'The Four Elements' (1642*), which was dedicated to her father.

Many of her later poems express her emotional response to significant domestic events such as the deaths of three grandchildren. Of one, Elizabeth, *'who deceased August, 1665, being a year and a half old,'* she wrote

> *'Farewell, sweet babe, the pleasure of mine eye*
> *Farewell, fair flower, that for a space was lent,*
> *Then ta'en away into eternity.'*

Arguably the most interesting from a modern perspective, are the acute observations of her New England environment, written from a woman's viewpoint in what was then very much a man's world. When contemporary critics questioned her right to *'wield a poet's pen'*, she responded thus,

> *'I am obnoxious to each carping tongue*
> *Who says my hand a needle better fits,*
> *A poet's pen all scorn I should thus wrong,*
> *For such despite they cast on female wits;*
> *If what I do prove well, it won't advance;*
> *They'll say it's stol'n, or else it was by chance.'*

Her devotion to her husband, who like her father became State Governor, is demonstrated in the final couplet of the poem, *'To My Dear And Loving Husband'*.

> *'Then while we live, in love let's persever,*
> *That when we live no more, we may live ever.'*

A second edition of her poems was printed by John Foster at Boston, Massachusetts, six years after her death and, one hundred and ninety five years later in 1867, John Harvard Ellis published an enlarged version, entitled *'Several Poems Compiled with a Great Variety of Wit and Learning'*. Described as a *'monument for her memory beyond the stateliest marbles'*, the writings confirmed Anne's reputation as America's first major English poet.

> *'But Welsted most the poet's healing balm*
> *Strives to extract from his soft, giving palm;*
> *Unlucky Welsted! Thy unfeeling master,*
> *The more thou ticklest, gripes his fist the faster.'*

This scornful passage from Alexander Pope's *'The Dunciad'* refers to **Leonard Welsted**, poet and satirist, who was born at Abington, Northampton in 1688. Incidentally, a gravestone in the south chapel of the church where his father was the rector commemorates the life of Sir John Barnard and his wife, Elizabeth, grand-daughter and last descendant of William Shakespeare, who died in 1669.

Welsted, who wrote his first poem, *'Apple-Pye'* while a sixteen year old pupil at Westminster School, joined the Civil Service on leaving Trinity College Cambridge, became a commissioner engaged in the management of the state lottery in 1731, had an apartment in the Tower of London and married the daughter of the composer, Henry Purcell. A prolific writer, he was described by one critic as *'an indefatigable poetaster'*, while other opinion suggests that he wrote with, *'varying degrees of goodness and badness'*. *'The Triumverate'* (1717), a letter in verse from Palaemon to Celia, was a thinly disguised satire on Pope, Gay and Swift, but it was his libellous attack on Pope in *'One Epistle' (1730)*, that provoked the retaliation quoted above. Welsted died in his grace-and-favour residence at the Tower in August 1747.

> *'Live, while you live, the epicure would say,*
> *And seize the pleasures of the present day.*
> *Live, while you live, the sacred preacher cries,*
> *And give to GOD each moment as it flies.*
> *Lord, in my views let both united be:*
> *I live in pleasure, when I live to thee.'*

The motto of the Doddridge family, *'Dum vivimus, vivamus'* quoted above, gave title to this verse, regarded by Dr Johnson as, *'one of the finest epigrams in the English language.'* Its author, **Philip Doddridge**, arrived in Northampton on Christmas Eve 1729, to take up the pastorate at the Church of Christ on the town's Castle Hill.

Malcolm Deacon's highly readable biography, *'Philip Doddridge of Northampton', (1980),* provides detailed insight into the life of a remarkable man, whose tolerance, philanthropy and generous disposition have earned him a place amongst Northamptonshire's finest.

Born in London on June 26th 1702, he and his sister Elizabeth were the only surviving children of twenty born to Daniel Doddridge, a successful merchant, and his wife, Monica, the daughter of John Bauman, a German Protestant who had fled his native country in 1626 to escape religious persecution. A respected academic, Bauman eventually settled in England in 1646, seventeen years before Philip's paternal grandfather, John Doddridge, resigned his living as Rector of Shepperton following a crisis of conscience over the Act of Uniformity. Aimed at rooting out Puritanism in the established church, the act required every incumbent to declare their *'unfeigned Assent and Consent to all and everything contained and prescribed within'* The Book of Common Prayer. Some two thousand clergymen left their livings rather than be bound by such regulations and, like many others, John Doddridge became pastor of a small Dissenting congregation which worshipped clandestinely in a private house.

Philip, therefore, was well-versed in the stories of his Nonconformist forebears.   He inherited a Lutheran Bible, spirited out of Germany by his grandfather Bauman, and was influenced further by the Revd Daniel Mayo, his teacher at the Grammar School in Kingston-upon-Thames, a writer of religious treatises and eloquent minister of the Nonconformist congregation, which assembled at, of all places, the town's gravel pit. Orphaned at the age of thirteen, and placed under the nominal guardianship of a Mr Downes, the young Doddridge was removed to a school in St Albans. There, under the tutelage of Dr Nathaniel Wood and local Presbyterian minister, Samuel Clark, he acquired and developed the disciplined working habits, which characterised his later life in the ministry.

However, three years later, his studies were rudely interrupted by his guardian's bankruptcy. The financial crash ruined the several wardships for which Downes was responsible, and virtually destroyed the Doddridge inheritance, causing Philip to leave St Alban's and seek the comfort and shelter of his sister's home on Hampstead Heath. Elizabeth, and her husband the Revd John Nettleton, a Dissenting clergyman, actively supported his expressed ambition to become a minister of religion. After several disappointments, he was re-acquainted with Samuel Clark who, in October 1719, secured and financed a place for Philip at a Dissenting Academy, newly established at Kibworth in Leicestershire under the leadership of the inspirational Revd John Jennings.

After four years of intensive study, in which Doddridge strove to meet the self-imposed high standards for his conduct as a student, he was accepted into the Christian ministry. He was soon called upon to preach in the area, quickly winning a large following on his travels. Within months he had accepted the unanimous call of the Kibworth congregation to succeed to the pastorate following Jennings' premature death through small-pox. His tutor's tolerant and enlightened approach to ecumenical issues flew in the face of contemporary religious thinking and had helped shape Doddridge's own outlook, causing him to eschew doctrinal bigotry.

In the summer of 1729, after encouragement from the celebrated Isaac Watts and local Dissenting preacher, David Some, Doddridge set up an academy at Market Harborough, but within months had left his new position for the pastorate at Castle Hill.

The parting was not without acrimony, his many friends in Harborough expressing their sense of desertion, and Philip was greatly distressed. However, early in the new year he had settled in the house in Marefair that would be his home for the next ten years. During his summer vacation, he met and fell for Mercy Maris, an orphan like himself, and after a brief courtship the couple were married on December 22nd 1730. Their love was deep and enduring, although neither enjoyed good health or a robust constitution. His demanding life-style, travelling hundreds of miles by coach or on horseback, caused his wife and friends great anxiety. One, John Barker, wrote, *'You need not fear living too long, doctor; and therefore, pray do not live quite so fast.'*

When their first child, Elisabeth, died of consumption at the age of four in October 1736, Doddridge preached her funeral sermon, composed with *'more tears than ink'*. Entitled, *'Submission to Divine Providence in the Death of Children',* it was published the following year in an attempt to bring comfort to others similarly distressed. Despite numerous miscarriages, premature births and early deaths, four children survived beyond infancy.

So popular was Doddridge's Dissenting Academy that the building in Marefair became too small to accommodate the growing number of students keen to enter the non-conformist ministry. In 1740, the enterprise moved to a large town house (now marked with a memorial plaque) in Sheep Street, the property of his patron, the Earl of Halifax. For the next eleven years, Doddridge tirelessly combined his teaching responsibilities with his duties at the Castle Hill church.

There, he reiterated the main points of his sermons by utilising congregational hymn singing, a convention widely adopted by Dissenters following the publication of Isaac Watts's *'Hymns and Spiritual Songs'* in 1707. Doddridge wrote over 400 hymns which were published posthumously in 1755. As the title, *'Hymns founded on Various Texts in the Holy Scriptures,'* suggests, each is prefixed with a scriptural text from which the hymn is derived. The best known, *'Hark the Glad Sound'*, is taken from Luke IV vv 18-19.

> *'Hark the glad sound! The Saviour comes!*
> *The Saviour promis'd long!*
> *Let ev'ry heart prepare a throne,*
> *And ev'ry voice a song.'*

His writing was not restricted to verse. In 1745, *'The Rise and Progress of Religion in the Soul',* was published, in which Doddridge confronts the many earthly trials and tribulations faced by Christians in their journey along John Bunyan's path to the 'Celestial City'.

Eight years before his death, Doddridge preached at the funeral of Mrs James Stonhouse, the wife of Dr Stonhouse, who had recently settled in Northampton. Despite the physician's initial antipathy to the Christian faith, the two men became friends and co-operated in a major venture to establish an infirmary in the town. Doddridge, already an outspoken advocate in favour of inoculation against smallpox, succeeded in involving influential public figures, such as the Duke of Montagu and the Earl of Northampton. He subsequently published a plan, *'for the more immediate Execution of the Proposals for Establishing a County Hospital at Northampton,'* and preached an impassioned sermon, *'In favour of a design to erect a COUNTY INFIRMARY there for the Relief of the Poor, Sick and Lame.'*

Within a year of remarkable fund-raising, the infirmary, a fore-runner of the present General Hospital, was opened in George Row. Doddridge continued to work actively for the hospital, generating charitable contributions, donating part of his annual stipend, making regular visits and serving on its numerous management committees.

In late September 1751, with his health severely impaired by a weak constitution and over-work, Philip and Mercy took advantage of the generosity of friends, including the Castle Hill congregation, to travel to Lisbon, then a fashionable health resort. Respite was short-lived. Within a month, Doddridge was dead and buried in the British Cemetery in the city.

The Northampton Mercury reported the death in its edition published on November 23rd 1751. It includes this tribute,

> *'...He was a Man of fine Genius, rich in the Stores of Learning, and of unexampled Activity and Diligence – His Piety was without Disguise, His Love without Jealousy, His Benevolence without Bounds...'*

It is surely no coincidence that Doddridge's biographer, Malcolm Deacon, born and raised in Kettering and formerly a Northampton headteacher is, in 2002, the minister at Castle Hill.

The non-conformist tradition was upheld in Northampton during the second half of the eighteenth century by fervent Baptists such as **John Ryland**, who succeeded his father, John senior, as pastor at College Street Church in 1786. He remained in Northampton until 1794, when he moved to Broadmead, Bristol, subsequently becoming Principal of Bristol Baptist College, where he remained until his death in 1825 at the age of seventy-two. John Ryland is best remembered for carrying out the baptism of *'a poor journeyman shoemaker'* named William Carey in the waters of the River Nene in October 1783 and as a founding father of the Baptist Missionary Society which sent the young missionary to India in 1793.

Educated at home by his father, who had moved to his College Street living in 1759, John was a precocious scholar, who had read and translated the whole of the New Testament from Greek by the age of nine. He wrote on philosophical religious themes from a very early age, and the Northamptonshire Studies collection contains a volume of hand-written poems composed when he was about thirteen. The following extract is taken *from 'A Supposed Conference between a Temporal King and a Spiritual Christian'*.

King

Can anyone more happy be
Than I array'd in majesty
Has anyone more cause to sing
Than I an arbitrary king?

Christian

Yes I am happier far than you
And Riches greater nobler too
With costlier by far array'd
Robes from more distant countries had.

An anthology of John Ryland's work, entitled *'Hymns and Verses on Sacred Subjects'*, was eventually published in 1862, thirty-seven years after his death.

'No human being, to the best of my belief, was ever the worse for having known **George James De Wilde***: there were few who were not better for the knowledge: and than this I know of no higher and I can add no truer epitaph.'*

'In Memoriam' was Edward Dicey's remarkably warm tribute to the late editor of the Northampton Mercury, and acknowledges a life dedicated to public service and the promotion of the arts. It also provides a biographical preface to a

compilation of writings, entitled *'Rambles Roundabout and Poems'*, published shortly after De Wilde's death in September 1871.

The De Wilde family had originally arrived in England from Holland during the early 18th century, eventually settling in London's St Giles-in-the-Fields. George's father, Samuel, was an accomplished artist who regularly exhibited at the Royal Academy during the latter years of the century, and also established a reputation as the leading theatrical portrait painter of the time. His work, featuring many of the great actors and actresses of the day, consistently appeared in the leading publications, and from his studio in Tavistock Row he circulated among the city's great theatres.

It was into this colourful background that George James de Wilde was born on January 19th 1804, the elder of two children. Unsurprisingly, he was *'originally destined to become an artist'*, and a boyhood sketchbook demonstrates his early promise as a draughtsman. His formal, classical education was limited, however George did develop a love of letters, becoming through theatre connections intimately acquainted with Leigh Hunt and other notable literary personages of the day.

At the age of twenty-one he took a temporary secretarial post at the Colonial Office, where his outstanding abilities and diligence attracted the attention of Sir James Stephen, Assistant Secretary for the Colonies. Stephen's sister had married Thomas Edward Dicey, a member of the newspaper publishing family which had owned the *Northampton Mercury* since 1720. When the editorship of the paper became vacant in the town, Stephen recommended De Wilde, then only twenty-four. He was appointed and retained the post until the day of his death over forty years later.

Once installed, he became a 'workaholic', seldom leaving the *Mercury* offices except on editorial business. There he earned the respect and admiration of all for, as Edward Dicey recalls, *'he never wrote or said an unkind word, never lost a friend or made an enemy, never asked a favour or refused a service.'*

His literary output was largely restricted to editorial duties, but he found time to contribute items to a number of publications including *'The Gentleman's Magazine'* and *'Notes and Queries'* under a variety of imaginative nom-de-plumes. These included Sylvan Southgate, Camden Somers and, particularly amusing considering his artistic antecedents, one Vandyke Brown.

As mentioned above, *'Rambles Roundabout'* was not written for publication as a complete work, but was originally published at various intervals and over a period of years in the *Mercury*. Some articles describe nearby locations, like Abington, Kingsthorpe, Weston Favell and market day in the Drapery in the very heart of Northampton.

> '...up-piled peas, mounds of gooseberries, all fruits of the season, and, above all, crowning all, intersecting all, adorning all, - flowers. Flowers everywhere, of every hue and odour; flowers in all forms; flowers in pots; flowers in bouquets.'

Others were visited during summer holiday excursions to outposts such as Blisworth, Gayton, Rothersthorpe and Cotterstock, apparently a random choice but all accessible in those days by rail.

It's interesting to read de Wilde's words and compare his descriptions with the modern day scene. Arriving at the station of Barnwell All Saints, then a stop on the Northampton to Peterborough line, he paints an idyllic picture of the station-master's lot in this rural backwater, *'this by-way station which only the slowest trains discover.'*

> 'The station-master must have, one thinks, a pleasant time of it, working tranquilly at his little garden plot. Through the loop-holes of his retreat he sees the stir, without feeling the crowd. Better be a cyclop in Vulcan's own caverns than a station-master at a first class station, where intersecting lines cross each other in bewildering confusion; where all is clamour and noise, the thundering of wheels and the shrieking of whistles, and the ringing of railway bells and the bawling of newspaper boys, and the dread of careless switchmen and reckless platelayers, and the horrible anticipation of trains running into each other; but here there is quiet and, one imagines, leisure, and time for thought and tranquil enjoyment. One wouldn't object to being a station-master here with one's books and pencils.'

De Wilde would have difficulty recognising the place today. One hundred and forty years later the Old Station House still stands on a corner plot where the Barnwell Road leaves the busy A605, but only an abandoned goods van in a nearby field suggests the erstwhile proximity of a railway line. The track lies buried beneath the ribbon of tarmac that carries speeding motor traffic between Thrapston and Oundle, while the station building was dismantled board by board and lovingly restored at the Nene Valley Railway terminus at Wansford.

'Rambles Roundabout' also contains twenty five poems among the prose pieces. This extract, from 'Sudden Winter', gives a flavour of their subject matter -- pastoral, classical, romantic.

> 'Yesterday, glowing Autumn; and today,
> Winter. In one fierce night the yellow plains
> Are whitened, and the rivulet's pleasant way
> Is stayed; the woods, beneath a double weight,
> Are bending to the ground.
>
> Heap high the grate,
> And gather round the hearth dear friends, and loves
> Domestic; wheel the glad piano round,
> So that the hand that o'er the ivory roves
> May feel the generous warmth, and livelier bound.'

The tragic death of his wife, Mary, in 1841, shortly after the birth of a fifth child who also succumbed only months later, caused the distraught de Wilde to immerse himself even more fully in his work. He widened his interests in civic affairs, supporting Northampton's Mechanics' Institute by promoting a fund-raising exhibition including items from his own personal collection of paintings, curiosities, artefacts and autographs of such famed figures as Wordsworth, Byron and his old acquaintance, Leigh Hunt.

During the late eighteen-fifties, he became a patron of John Askham, supplementing the poet's meagre income by appointing him Wellingborough correspondent of *The Mercury* in 1860. Six years later, Askham showed his appreciation by dedicating 'Poems and Sonnets', a collection of his verse, to his influential friend. De Wilde compared favourably Askham's work with that of John Clare, whom he knew and who was benignly nearing the end of his life in Northampton Lunatic Asylum. 'Rambles Roundabout' contains a sensitive tribute to the great poet, including a splendid example of the rustic's acute discomfort in high society.

'When he became for a time a wonder in the fashionable world he was bewildered, and when dinner was over he would rise, thrust his hands in his pockets and saying, 'Well I'll goo,' would goo accordingly.'

De Wilde's devotion to his adoptive Northampton was characterised by his work as governor of the town's Infirmary and co-founder of its museum. His death at home above *The Mercury* offices in the Parade on September 16th 1871, prompted many eulogies, including this by his friend and fellow poet, Northampton solicitor, **Christopher Hughes**. *('Poems Early and Late' 1871)*

'Est Qui' – Horace
*I know the Man – who as he lives
Still better proof of manhood gives:
A man the longer I have known
Still dearer to myself hath grown:
Year after year with him gone by
Seem age and labour to defy.
A man so good, so just, so true,
And then, he's so hard-headed too –
But that's the secret (but in part)
Add to it all a warm, kind heart;
In brain a Nestor, heart a child,
Need I declare his name? – DE WILDE?*

Yet another poet to reflect upon the sad demise of John Clare was **Joseph Rowlatt**, librarian at the Northampton Mechanics Institute situated in the town's Corn Exchange building. Rowlatt held the post, which involved responsibility for some 1300 volumes, from 1873 until his death two years later. His collection of verse, entitled *'First Fruits'*, published in 1874, includes *'Abington Abbey – a reverie'*. The poem mused on the fate of those patients committed to the mental hospital, which was housed within the abbey from 1845 to 1892. Doubtless an earlier line, *'Lost to friends and to the world'* prompted this reference to Clare,

'......................*a king of men,
A bright, bright star, though set among the slough.
In an obscure and lowly village born,
Of humble birth, with yet an heritage
A king might rank amongst his noblest gifts.
He rose from out his lowly village home,
He shone a star among his fellow men,
Upon his forehead Poesy had set
Her broad distinctive seal; and in his eye,
That large blue eye, so full of love and truth,
The light of genius glowed......'*

In the introduction to his book, Rowlatt acknowledges the dubious merit of much of the poetry that flooded bookshops at the time. *'Numberless are the volumes of verse that afflict the public'*, nevertheless, *'I send my little volume forth, like a wise father, conscious of the faults of his children, but making allowance for their imperfections.'*

In the tribute to Clare, as with many other examples in the collection, the modern reader may feel his unquestionable sincerity and worthiness are somewhat marred by over-sentimentality. This is amply reflected in the opening lines of *'I am a boy again,'* a poem addressed possibly to a mother or lover.

> *'Do not mine eyes the thoughts reveal*
> *That deep within me lie,*
> *Or the sweet torment that I feel*
> *Whene'er I meet thine eye.*
> *Thy smile tears down the veil of years*
> *Wipes out time's darkling stain,*
> *When thy dear voice falls on mine ears*
> *I am a boy again.'*

But like John Askham, his Wellingborough contemporary, Rowlatt is merely following the conventions of the age, which are further reflected in such familiar subjects as the vagaries of the weather, the seasons, untimely and tragic deaths and unrequited love.

Susan Bostock's origins were far removed from those of Joseph Rowlatt and other local working class poets. Her father, Frederick Bostock, had founded one of Northampton's first boot-and-shoe manufacturing firms in 1835 and she grew up in comparative comfort. Born in the town in 1862, Susan contributed poems to the *Northampton and County Independent* and the *Northampton County Magazine* and published three volumes of verse, all rich in variety of form and content. The first, *'Spring Notes and other poems'* appeared in 1912 and includes *'A Yorkshire Mill Girl'*, a hymn to an indomitable spirit, unbroken by the harshness of her daily grind.

> *'It is an earnest face. Her shawl, close drawn*
> *O'er head and shoulders, frames it like a hood*
> *And shapes her upright figure. Stalwart, tall,*
> *She walks with swinging stride. No timid fawn*
> *My Mill girl.'*

The lyrical *'Snow'*, another poem from the same collection, provides a marked contrast.

> *'Hark! Not a footfall*
> *Sounds upon its whiteness*
> *Shroud-like over all*
> *With an airy lightness*
> *Steals the silent snow.*
> *Like a muted string*
> *Held almost to dumbness*
> *Like a hunted thing*
> *Stupefied to numbness*
> *By a cruel blow.'*

The following year saw the publication of *'The Call of the Uplands'* and a final volume, *'The World of Heart's Delight'*, appeared in 1930. Susan Bostock died at her home in Kingsthorpe in August 1948.

'I spent all my childhood in one place, Northampton, a market and factory town surrounded by countryside.'

A Radio 4 controller once described writer and broadcaster, **Ray Gosling**, as *'one of those singular and particular voices that we need to cherish.'*

Gosling, who rose to prominence during the nineteen seventies and eighties through his affectionate portraits of working class culture, was born in Northampton in 1939. His childhood is evocatively recalled in two collections of memoirs, *'Sum Total'*, published in 1962 and its more colourful follow-up, *'Personal Copy: A Memoir of the Sixties' (1980)*.

Readers of a certain age, regardless of origin, will readily identify with many of Gosling's early reminiscences; indeed, they are similar to those recalled by this writer in *'A Kettering Kaleidoscope' (1999)*. The privations of the outdoor lavatory and unheated bedrooms, home cooking, the rigours of washday, medium-wave radio and summer holidays in cheap boarding houses at east coast resorts.

The narrative ranges, almost randomly, over many issues. There are rather jaundiced views on the *'endemic'* snobbery encountered during his days as a 'scholarship' boy at Northampton Grammar School during the 'fifties, and light-hearted recollections of visits as a teenager to impresario Paul Raymond's revue, 'Strip Strip Hooray', at the town's New Theatre. One particularly amusing anecdote describes the time an errant rat crossed the stage in front of the deliciously named nude, Peaches Page, who, abandoning her statuesque pose, rushed for the safety of the wings. As a model's slightest twitch was sufficient to incur the wrath of the law in those days, the show was immediately closed and the theatre shut for a week!

He describes a period of adolescent rebellion, during which he purports to reject both the staid, fore-lock tugging deference of his working class background and the privileged conformity of grammar school. Here he presages his future career, revealing how the books in the back cupboard of the English room at school opened up new horizons – Auden, Isherwood, Waugh, Forster, Woolf, Spender and particularly Graham Greene who, *'seemed to have succeeded in the art of getting across to the common reader without having to talk down.'* They were part of an alternative curriculum, like the juke-box *'caffs'* and pubs he frequented and the influential *Picture Post* magazine, which fed his growing belief in the importance of an individualised approach to mass communication,

> *'getting across to the broadest public without having to be a servant to an intellectual discipline or a commercial tone. The whole idea of being popular while not sacrificing any of one's ideas, methods, or facts fascinated me.'*

He worked sufficiently hard at school to gain a place at Leicester University, which *'was the final end of Northampton as being a home.'* There was never any real likelihood that he would return.

> *'The roots had by then been torn up. I'm glad they got torn up. I don't want to put them down in this town again. But I'm glad for being born here. I'm glad I went away. Glad I went the way I did. I want to travel on….'*

If *'Sum Total'* is pure 'stream of consciousness', *'Personal Copy'* is more structured. It adds flesh to the early years before describing Gosling's brief University career, his involvement with a revolutionary Leicester Youth Club which won national acclaim, the New Left, London and the influence of novelist Colin MacInnes, his work for a tenants' and residents' association in his adoptive city of Nottingham, and his initial success as a writer and broadcaster.

At his peak, Gosling was earning £50,000 a year, but sometime in the nineteen-nineties the work dried up. His idiosyncratic portraits of working-class life became unfashionable. He stopped his pension plan, cashed in his savings and carried on submitting proposals, but no one wanted *'some old geezer offering a half hour documentary on people's sheds and who wants the money up front'*. He retired to the semi-detached Victorian house in Nottingham where he has lived for over thirty years, and now survives on social security payments.

A television film, broadcast in April 2002, focused on his bankruptcy originating, it appeared, from accumulating debts accrued from the non-payment of a VAT bill for £5,000. The programme traced these mounting debts and the government trustees' attempts to seize assets and repay creditors. Fortunately for Gosling, he had paid off the mortgage on his house during the good years, saving him from a bank repossession order, and he's safeguarded against eviction by the presence of his lodger, or 'unprotected tenant'. However, he's convinced that *'once I'm out of the public eye, they'll get me out'*. Ironically, the money he received from the BBC for the documentary – his first paid work in years – has been claimed by Nottingham council bailiffs as unpaid council tax.

Despite his difficulties, the programme contained flashes of the old Gosling wit.

> *'What about this for an epitaph to my career,'* he said. *'Latepayers will be penalised.'*

Coincidentally, **Jeremy Seabrook**, the author, *Guardian* correspondent and celebrated commentator on working class culture, was also born in Northampton in 1939 and educated at the town's grammar school. His autobiography, *'Mother and Son; A Memoir' (1979)*, which describes a Northampton childhood, has obvious similarities with Gosling's account of growing up. But for Seabrook it was a cathartic undertaking. As he writes, *'For twenty years, I carried my childhood as something frozen inside me.'* The story of his upbringing, the son of a working-class, single parent on the newly constructed White Hills estate off the Market Harborough Road, makes for riveting reading. However, within the fluent and humorous narrative, is a clever unravelling of the relationship between the son and his mother, who shapes, out of her own loneliness and need, the boy's alarming dependence upon her.

On leaving Northampton Grammar School, Seabrook attended Gonville and Caius College, Cambridge, before returning to his home town to teach in a local secondary modern school. He obtained a Diploma in Social Administration from the London School of Economics in 1967 and for two years was employed as a social worker with the Inner London Education Authority. In 1969, a play, *'Life Price'*, co-written with Michael O'Neill, was performed at the Royal Court Theatre. This was followed by a string of publications including *'The Unprivileged'*, *'City Close-Up'*, and *'What Went Wrong?'* (an analysis of the demise of the Labour Movement). *'Working Class Childhood: an oral history' (1982)*, is a collection of the personal memories of members of different age-groups from around Britain. Most interesting from a local perspective are the reminiscences of a certain Mr Baines, who was born in Northampton in 1887. Recollections of this gentleman's great-grandmother's life in service at Ecton Hall, his grandfather's conversion from cottage-based cordwainer to factory-based boot and shoe employee and descriptions of his own working life as a railway clerk in the Goods Department at Northampton's Castle Station are fascinating social history.

More recent publications include *'The Leisure Society'* and *'Landscapes of Poverty'*.

Seabrook has been described as *'the most powerful and passionate writer on the condition of modern society.'* The books generally reflect his fundamental beliefs that, *'growing appetites ensure the dynamic of the capitalist economy will be sustained'*, and that modern culture is, *'a kind of by-product of the process of selling-things'*.

Several eminent county writers have written for younger readers. Charles Kingsley's *'Water Babies'* is a children's classic, readers of a certain age will no doubt be familiar with John Clare's *'Little Trotty Wagtail'*, Denys Watkins-Pitchford (BB) created his *'Little Grey Men'*, H E Bates produced a novel, entitled *'The White Admiral'*, while JL Carr's stories, *'The green children of the woods'* and *'The red windcheater'* are worthy of reprinting. But by far the most prolific is **Pat Thomson** who, since her arrival in Northamptonshire in the nineteen eighties, has gained a reputation among the finest exponents of this burgeoning art.

A Librarian with special responsibility for the work of the School of Education at University College Northampton, Pat's literary life has a number of strands, but as author, anthologist, reviewer, lecturer and teacher, her primary aim is to promote children's love of literature.

'In the end, it all comes back to books. I want children to read. And I want to share what I have with them.'

Her own writing for publication began as a positive response to jibes that she was inclined to, *'lay the law down about what children's books should be.'*

The implied challenge to do better herself resulted in *'The Treasure Sock'*, *(1986)*, a story which was turned into the *'Share A Story'* series and later published in Spanish, French and on an English language teaching CD in Japan. Pat writes mainly for Primary aged children and has particular sympathy with early readers. Many stories are full of jokes, but she is never patronising or reluctant to use sophisticated themes with younger readers. One such story is *'A Ghost-light in the Attic,'(1995)*, a Civil War story set in Sulgrave Manor, Northamptonshire's celebrated ancestral home of the Washington family.

Recent publications include the adventures of Superpooch, that *'canny, canine, righter-of-wrongs', 'The Silkworm Mystery',* (a biography of Louis Pasteur, *1998), 'Ghoul School' (2000)* and her only book thus far for teenage children, *'Strange Exchange' (2002).*

Books cross all kinds of boundaries and Pat is currently working on picture books with two publishers in New York, though both have a very traditional, English feel and encourage the young listeners to join in.

Like many children's writers, she actively generates an interest in literature by visiting primary schools and working with the pupils.

'I like the way their minds work at that age', she says, *'and although my thoughts do turn increasingly to longer books and larger themes, I shall probably always value that chance to play with creativity and language that is permissible in books for younger children.'*

Unlike Pat Thomson, the novelist **Anne Fine**'s connection with Northampton occurred much earlier in her life. The popular writer, who succeeded illustrator Quentin Blake as children's laureate in May 2001, was a pupil at the town's High School for Girls in the Derngate. The Laker family had moved to Hardingstone from Fareham in the late nineteen-fifties when Anne was in her early teens. The eldest of five sisters, including triplets, Anne's precocious talent as a writer was carefully nurtured by the school staff and she remains appreciative of the support she received particularly from headmistress, Miss Marsden, and Miss Sinton, her English teacher.

On leaving the High School, Anne studied history and politics at Warwick University before undertaking a variety of jobs including teaching, secretarial work and as an information officer with Oxfam. Rather like JK Rowling, the creator of Harry Potter, Anne began writing seriously when her eldest daughter was a baby, as an antidote to the misery of being trapped in a cold Edinburgh flat during a snowstorm. The book, *'The Summer House Loon'* was published in 1978, and was the first of over forty, including *'Goggle-Eyes',* winner of both the Guardian Children's Fiction Award and the Carnegie Medal, and *'Flour Babies',* which also won the Carnegie Medal as well as the Whitbread Children's Novel Award. The books often draw on personal experience. *'Madame Doubtfire',* which deals with the issues of parental separation and divorce, was made into a full-length feature film starring Hollywood actor, Robin Williams, while *'Telling Liddy'* is a fictionalised account of a family comprising four sisters.

Of her motivation she says, *'I write books for me. Me at five, me at eleven, me at fourteen...'*

Her advice to would-be writers echoes the experience of many exponents featured in these pages.

'The practice for writing is to 'read, read, read. If you don't have a library card you cannot be serious.'

Anne now lives in County Durham, but returns to Northamptonshire regularly to visit her widowed mother.

The Whyte-Melville Inn in the centre of the village of Boughton takes its name from **Captain John Whyte-Melville**, a Scottish-born former Coldstream Guardsman who saw active service in the Crimean War and became one of the most popular novelists of the late nineteenth century. In 1847, at the age of twenty-six, Whyte-Melville married Charlotte Hanbury of Kelmarsh Hall and eventually settled in Boughton, *'devoting his days to hunting and his evenings to literary work.'* A prolific writer, who donated the proceeds from his work to charity, including a working men's club in St Giles' Street Northampton, he produced twenty-four novels, four volumes of verse, a translation of Horace, a book of riding recollections and a lecture.

His historical novels include *'Holmby House'*, set at Holdenby during the English Civil War. And, as befits a writer dubbed *'The Poet-Laureate of the Hunting Field'*, in *'Kate Coventry'* and *'Market Harborough'* he creates a vivid and amusing picture of Victorian sporting and social life set in familiar Fernie and Pytchley Hunt country. However, not all his poems are roistering romps in hunting pink. The final verse of *'Goodbye!'* from the *'Whitehall Annual'* is a passionate evocation of parting lovers.

> *'What are we waiting for? Oh! my heart!*
> *Kiss me straight on the brows! And part!*
> *Again! Again! – my heart! my heart!*
> *What are we waiting for, you and I?*
> *A pleading look – a stifled cry.*
> *Goodbye, for ever? – Goodbye, Goodbye!'*

After a brief residence at Wootton Hall, Whyte-Melville moved to London and finally to Tetbury in Gloucestershire where, after suffering a fatal fall while hunting in 1878, he lies buried.

The landscape around Lamport has changed little since the middle of the seventeenth century when enclosure of the fields was already well under way. Two hundred years later, a railway line linking Northampton with Market Harborough was constructed some miles to the north of the village while widespread ironstone excavations in the neighbourhood in the last century fortunately stopped short of Lamport and are now virtually unnoticeable. The road, (now called the A508) winding northwards is, as then, the main artery of communication.

A narrow village street separates the birthplaces of two Lamport men who, in very different ways, made important contributions to Northamptonshire's literary heritage.

Thomas Isham was born at Lamport Hall in 1656, the eldest child of Sir Justinian Isham and his second wife, Vere Leigh, while almost two hundred and fifty years later, the author and naturalist, Denys Watkins-Pitchford was born at the rectory opposite.

From November 1st 1671 to September 30th 1673, the fifteen year old Thomas kept a diary, written in Latin, whose entries provide a fascinating insight into late seventeenth century life. The manuscript was translated two-hundred years later by the Revd Robert Isham, Rector of Lamport, a cousin of Thomas's descendant, Sir Charles, and first edited and printed in 1875 by the antiquarian, Walter Rye. Although it attracted considerable interest among scholars, only 100 copies were printed and it wasn't until 1971 that a second version, entitled *'The Diary of Thomas Isham of Lamport: 1671-73'*, was published by Gregg International of Farnborough. Translated from the original by Norman Marlow, Senior Lecturer in Latin at Manchester University and with an introduction and detailed appendixes by Sir Gyles Isham, this edition corrects many of the inaccuracies in Rye's earlier *'Journal'* and can be regarded as the definitive version.

In his highly informative introduction, Sir Gyles describes the original diary as a small, neatly written volume, (4 by 6 inches) bound in contemporary leather with a gold border. He traces its genesis to a letter from the boy's father, Sir Justinian, dated 21st November 1667, which suggests that he *'goe on with a line or two most dayes, setting down ordinary matters as they happen about the house, garden, towne, country or field, nothing can come amiss for you to turne into Latin: even your talke in the nursery....'* If there was an earlier diary, it was never found. The surviving edition certainly contains much of those *'ordinary matters'* but widens its scope to include opinions of county affairs and news in the greater world. Sir Gyles speculates that Sir Justinian's offer of £6 a year and Thomas's maturer age are responsible for the change.

Whatever his motivation, the entries paint a vivid picture of the times. Descriptions of members of the household at Lamport abound. There are beautifully penned sketches of local gentry, clergy, lawyers and doctors. No event is too trivial to be disregarded by young Thomas's fresh and perceptive eye.

December 5th 1671: *'A girl called, quite well dressed, and said that she was skilled at all kinds of women's clothes and offered her services to Mother.*

Many entries are intriguing;

January 29th 1672: *'Mr Clerk* (Revd Gilbert Clerk of Bleakhall, Loddington) *came to dinner and said that a new telescope,* (probably the reflecting telescope presented to the Royal Society by Sir Isaac Newton in December 1671)*, far more perfect than previous ones, had been invented.'*

Others disturbing;

January 27th 1672: *'John Chapman,* (bailiff at Lamport Hall)*, told us that a woman convicted of clipping coin of the realm has been condemned and burned alive in the cattle market at Smithfield, London.'*

Much is made of country sports;

September 5th 1672: *'We went to Rowell* (Rothwell) *races, which are held in a suitable spot enclosed by hills from which there is a view down on to a level stretch two miles long and four hundred yards wide.'*

(Rothwell's racecourse was called 'The Slade' owing to its proximity to the Slade brook which runs through the valley to the south of the town. Thomas vividly describes a race for a prize of two silver candlesticks, won by Colonel William Lisle for Lord Exeter, as the *'whole amphitheatre resounded with applause and the shouts of men.'*)

November 11th 1672: *'Maidwell was beaten in the cock fight.'*

February 20th 1673: *'While father was riding along the main road towards Brixworth he met Sir William Haslewood* (of Maidwell Hall), *who was chasing a hare with Mr Saunders* (squire of Brixworth) *and Mr Tyrrell.'*

(According to Sir Gyles Isham, the Market Harborough to Northampton road came nearer to the Hall and at the corner, in what is now the park, stood the inn and a group of cottages. These were removed in landscaping carried out by the eighth baronet during the reign of George IV. The Swan Inn, named after the Isham crest, was relocated on its present site to the west of the road in 1830, but nowhere in the diary does Thomas use its name; it is simply *'Fisher's house'* after the name of the innkeeper).

4th November 1672: *'Bamford of* (Hanging) *Houghton had a bull, and they set dogs on it.........After it was all over the men who had assembled to watch had wrestling bouts till five o'clock.'*

17th October 1672: *'I went hawking with Lewis* (a servant) *at Sir William Haslewood's invitation.'*

But more serious matters are not neglected. A major source of concern was the Third Dutch War, which broke out some five months after Thomas had begun his diary. Apparently the war was not popular with the Ishams. In an entry dated 5th June 1672, he notes sententiously that, when a dark cloud arose and prevented the Duke of York pursuing the Dutch at the Battle of Solebay, *'I believe (nor shall I be ashamed to confess it) that God Himself was angry at the War.'*

These comments follow an earlier reference to an exchange of gunfire between English and enemy ships during the battle,

May 28th 1672: *'Heavy firing was distinctly heard at our house.'* (This surprising observation is corroborated in a letter written by Lady Isham to her husband a few days later.)

News of the war, and other foreign matters, were eagerly read at Lamport and recorded by Thomas in his diary. His primary source was *The Gazette*, the only official newspaper from 1666 to 1688, which devoted three-quarters of its space to foreign news. Sir Gyles Isham disagrees with historians who regard *The Gazette's* contents as *'the object of contempt and parody'*, stating that, *'whatever objections there may be to the official supplying of news, only the state was equipped to collect reliable news. Thomas's diary is evidence of how well-informed about international affairs a family living in the heart of England could be.'*

On the home front, there are regular references to domestic issues.

May 22nd 1672: '*A sweep came here who could climb chimneys without instruments and clean them instantly.*'

August 29th 1673: '*Carter brought a machine on a cart; it throws up a powerful jet of water and is very useful for putting out a fire. Father gave nine pounds for it.*'

One lengthy entry retells an apparently true story, attributed to Matthew Coles of Clipston, which is somewhat reminiscent of the great Chaucer.

March 2nd 1672: '*...it concerned a tinker who was in the habit of frequenting the house of an innkeeper with whom he was very friendly. One day he caught sight of the innkeeper counting a fairly large sum of money which he was going to pay to his master the next day or the day following. The tinker planned to steal the money from the innkeeper....*'

As Thomas relates, the robbery is foiled by the innkeeper's wife, but its aftermath has near tragic consequences for the couple's young son which are only averted by the mother's bravery.

The Diary ends on September 30th 1673 with an appropriate and unexpectedly poetic entry.

'*The harvest was gathered in and the boys raised their customary shouts.*'

Thomas Isham was now a young gentleman with his sword and his servant. He had also come to the end of the book in which he had been keeping his diary for almost two years.

Thomas succeeded to the title and estates on the death of his father in 1675. He was seventeen years old. The following year he travelled to the continent visiting France, Switzerland and Italy, where he acquired a small collection of contemporary paintings, cabinets, marble tables, prints, books and a considerable wardrobe of fine clothes. But, according to the custom of the time, it was essential that he married well for his own sake and that of his estate. On his return to England, he turned seriously to the matter of finding a wife of substantial means. After a number of aborted alliances, including Henrietta, Baroness Wentworth of Toddington, later a mistress of the ill-fated Duke of Monmouth, Thomas became engaged to Mary Van den Bemde. Mary was the daughter of a wealthy London merchant of Dutch origin and the wedding date was fixed for July 1681. Preparations went ahead at great speed, Thomas demonstrating his taste for finery by having a wedding suit made for himself of white brocade, woven in silk and gold. This, with other Isham clothes, was acquired by the Victoria and Albert Museum in 1899. But, sadly, the wedding never took place. On July 26th Thomas died in London of smallpox aged twenty-five. He was buried at Lamport on August 9th, his brother Justinian succeeding to the title.

In 1700, Sir Justinian Isham, 4th Bart, erected a splendid monument in the parish church to the memory of his father, children, sisters and brothers. The inscription pays special tribute to Thomas. Yet the most lasting legacy is the youthful author's diary, a Latin exercise that provides a unique glimpse into life in rural Northamptonshire in the seventeenth century.

'I have no business writing an autobiography; only the great and famous should do so, and those politicians who have worn out their shoe leather treading the 'corridors of power' and wish to make a bit on the side....'

These opening lines of the foreword to *'A Child Alone: The memoirs of 'BB',* do scant justice to **Denys Watkins-Pitchford**'s accomplishments as an author and illustrator. He was born at Lamport Rectory on July 25th 1905, the same year as another illustrious Northamptonshire writer and novelist, HE Bates and, like the great John Clare, 'BB' spent most of his life in his native county. Some years earlier, his parents had moved from Gloucester, where his clergyman father had been a minor canon of the Cathedral, to the elegant Queen Anne edifice situated opposite Lamport Hall, then home to the Isham family.

Like both Clare and Bates, the young Watkins-Pitchford spent much of his formative years wandering the countryside around his home. A bout of the then deadly appendicitis confined the already sickly boy to the rectory when his brothers, Engel and twin Roger, went away to prep school in Scotland, and he was destined never to receive any formal schooling. His father undertook responsibility for his education and, during long winter evenings, would read to him from the works of Richard Jefferies and WH Hudson, the same writers incidentally who had inspired the youthful George Harrison.

But not surprisingly summer morning lessons were full of distractions,

'like the sight of the big lime trees on the drive – motionless and misty green in the early heat of a peerless June morning, with flies shuttling back and forth, and occasionally a swallow sweeping by or a distant cuckoo calling.'

He loved the great outdoors, preferably in the company of his brothers during the school holidays, but more often alone birds'-nesting in the park of the Hall or venturing further afield to follow the Nene brook from Lamport Station to its source at Draughton. This magical stream made a lasting impression,

' The intimate bends where old oaks leaned, fairy shingle spits, gurgling runs where some fallen branch had diverted the main current, how the brook coiled and doubled on itself, its banks lined with bird-sown hawthorns. Silver dace dwelt in this stream and numerous sticklebacks… ',

and was the inspiration for the setting of *'The Little Grey Men',* that delightfully imaginative series of stories that earned their author a Carnegie Medal in 1942.

Other childhood influences also ran deep. As a very small boy still tucked up in bed in the rectory nursery, Denys listened to the early morning rattle and clatter of hunters in the stable courtyard across the road as they were led out for exercise by a red-jerseyed groom. It was the heyday of hunting and the Pytchley pack, one of the most famous in the Shires, was kennelled just a short distance away. The hounds feature in *'Wild Lone',* a novel originally published in 1939, which tells the story of Rufus, a one-eared motherless fox cub who frequents the trackways, woods, fields and hedgerows around Lamport. A particularly vivid passage from the book, based upon a real-life event at distant Fawsley Park, describes the tragic fate of some pack-members, drowned after falling through ice. Incidentally, many years later, after Fawsley Hall fell into decay, a memorial stone commemorating the incident was re-discovered among tangled shrubbery by a 'BB' enthusiast. It was cleaned and restored before being re-sited near the huntsman's house at the Pytchley Kennels in Brixworth.

Another fine book, *'Brendon Chase',* based on both Salcey Forest and Geddington Chase, places he knew intimately and where in younger days he had hunted the rare Purple Emperor butterfly, was, to the author's obvious pride, described in *Punch* as the finest thing since Richard Jefferies *'Bevis'.*

At the age of fifteen he had enrolled at the Northampton College of Art, then in Abington Street, and while there won a travelling scholarship to Paris before proceeding to the Royal College of Art in London where he honed the artistic skills which enliven his books. After graduation in 1928, he took up a post in the art department at Rugby School, where he was to teach for many years. He pursued his love of the countryside travelling extensively during the holidays and widening his vast knowledge as a naturalist. But he was never happier than when at home in Lamport.

One weekend in 1938 he began the story of the one-eared fox called Rufus, his first attempt at fiction. This typed manuscript, together with reprints of articles from the *Shooting Times* and retitled, *'The Sportsman's Bedside Book'*, were forwarded to publishers Eyre and Spottiswoode. Both were accepted for publication with illustrations by the author. It was the beginning of a prolific writing career. His vivid descriptions of wild-life earned wide critical acclaim and, as the Observer recorded, *'he is, as all good naturalists should be, a bit of a poet.'*

After leaving the security of his job at Rugby School, 'BB' moved to Woodford near Kettering, renting a house on a large country estate. His experiences there are described graphically in *'An Idle Interlude'*, a most revealing chapter of a book entitled *'Ramblings of a Sportsman-Naturalist'*, published in 1979. The owner of the estate, the widow of a former champion fly caster of Britain, allowed 'BB' the run of the place with permission to shoot and fish whenever he chose. It was an apparently idyllic existence, but one that he clearly looked back on with mixed emotions, perhaps generated by a creative block.

'Free from the sometimes irksome and mentally tiring job of teaching at Rugby, I seemed to want to unwind. I did not even paint or write – I was completely idle.'

However, in the ensuing years, he overcame this ennui by putting his considerable energies to work in restoring the estate's long-neglected *'tree-girt lake of about three acres.'* After repairing the boat-house and clearing a passage through the dense reeds into the main lake, he re-stocked the pool with carp and tench, ordered from a London firm and collected from Kettering railway station in a big can. A combination of pressures eventually conspired to bring this lengthy sojourn to an end. Deprived of his writing income, the years at Woodford brought financial hardship, agricultural sprays were destroying his beloved wild birds and, with the demise of its owner, the estate was to be sold.

'Had I the means to buy it,' he wrote, *'I would have done so, and employed a keeper to police it.'*

On a deeply personal level, the trauma of his son Robin's early death coupled with lack of money, there was, he felt, a need to be gone. He and his family moved out, leaving the estate to the vandals, poachers, developers and nature itself, and arrived at the picturesque Round House at Sudborough. This distinctive building located on the eastern edge of the village is now close to the busy road that links the A14 west of Thrapston with the A43 at Stanion. The house dates from the early seventeenth century and is a reminder of the more leisurely days of the turnpike and toll road.

'BB' cut a familiar figure in and around the area in his country-man's deerstalker and plus-fours. Sadly, his personal life continued to be stalked by tragedy. In his memoirs he even recalls a curse placed upon the family by a beggar, whose appeal for alms had been rejected by his father during a pilgrimage to the Holy Land. Coincidentally, Engel, Denys' elder brother had died in adolescence of Bright's Disease and his own son, Robin, as mentioned above, from a rare and incurable illness at the age of eight. In 1974, Cicily, his beloved wife of thirty-five years, succumbed suddenly to an unexplained illness, which Denys attributed to her inhaling pesticides sprayed on the field adjoining their garden.

Despite all, he wrote well over fifty books, illustrated some thirty others and painted skilfully in oil and water-colour. His final production, *'Indian Summer'*, was published in 1984. Five years later, his contribution to literature was formally recognised when he was appointed an MBE.

Denys Watkins-Pitchford MBE died on September 8th 1990, aged eighty five. A fitting epitaph might well be the lines, borrowed from a tombstone in a north-country churchyard, which are quoted in the front of all his books.

> *'The wonder of the world*
> *The beauty and the power,*
> *The shapes of things,*
> *Their colours, lights, and shades,*
> *These I saw.*
> *Look ye also while life lasts.'*

'An obscure village in the dullest period in the dullest of all centuries'.

This description of Paulerspury in the eighteenth century is taken from George Smith's *'The Life of* **William Carey**: *Shoemaker and Missionary' (1885).* The accuracy of the quotation is suspect on several counts. No-one could describe an age which heralded American Independence or the French Revolution as dull. And the birth of the great Christian missionary, scholar and translator in the village on August 17th 1761 ensured Paulerspury's place in history and, because of his sublime legacy of words and deeds, Carey's deserved inclusion in this book.

Sadly, little survives to commemorate Carey's association with the area where he spent his early years. The cottage where he was born in the tiny settlement of Pury End, some half-mile from the main village, was demolished in 1965. However, stone salvaged from the building was used to construct a small cairn, complete with memorial plaque, marking its location in Careys Road.

A wall tablet inside the porch of the parish church of St James the Great commemorates the life of the Missionary and Orientalist. But strangely, *'The Northamptonshire Village Book',* that comprehensive county guide lovingly compiled by Women's Institute members in 1989, makes no mention of William Carey under the entry for Paulerspury. The omission is remedied in the entry for Hackleton and Piddington where the mean cottages and shoemaker's shops in which he scraped a living during the seventeen-eighties have been supplanted by neat new housing.

Fortunately there are more fitting memorials at Moulton, the large village on the outskirts of Northampton where Carey worked as shoemaker, teacher and minister from 1785 to 1789. The cottage where he, his wife Dorothy and their three children lived has been preserved as a museum, and the neighbouring chapel contains a modern mural depicting a pictorial journey through his life and works. Below the oft-quoted line from a Carey sermon, *'Expect great things from God. Attempt great things for God,'* the important phases of this remarkable story are revealed in six illustrated panels.

The son of a poor journeyman weaver who became the village schoolmaster and parish clerk, the young William had privileged access to the school's collection of books. He wrote later that, *'I chose to read books of science, history, voyages etc. more than any other.'* His passion for journeys of exploration earned him the nickname 'Columbus' among his peers. Another major influence on his early life was his uncle, Peter Carey, who had returned to live and work in the village as a gardener after serving as a soldier in Canada. It was he who nurtured his nephew's love of plants and flowers, and stimulated his appetite for stories of travel to far-off places.

His ambition to emulate his uncle and become a gardener was thwarted by a skin disease generated by exposure to sunlight and at the age of fourteen he was apprenticed to a Clarke Nichols, a Piddington cordwainer, or craftsman shoemaker. Although raised an Anglican, at work Carey came under the influence of one John Warr, a senior apprentice and religious Dissenter, who introduced him to non-conformity. On 10th February 1779 at a service at the Meeting House at Hackleton, Carey made the decision to cease attending a *'lifeless, carnal ministry'* in preference for one *'more evangelical'*. Later that year Clarke Nichols died and Carey's apprenticeship was transferred to Thomas Old of Hackleton. On 10th June 1781 Carey married his new master's sister-in-law, Dorothy Plackett, a girl from a Puritan background and daughter of the leader of the Hackleton Meeting. Some biographers have been highly critical of Dorothy Carey. George Smith writes, *'Never had minister, missionary or scholar a less sympathetic mate ... ... not only did she remain to the last a peasant woman with a reproachful tongue....the marriage did not prove suitable.'*

Despite this disparaging view, Dorothy proved a loyal wife and devoted mother who over the years suffered alarming privations in support of her husband's calling.

1783 was a momentous year for William. Following the death of his baby daughter from a fever which also threatened his own life, the family were re-housed in a cottage at neighbouring Piddington, due largely to the generosity of his parents who were appalled at the impoverished circumstances in which their son and his wife lived. By this time, Carey was preaching regularly at Earls Barton, a round trip of sixteen miles, and in October of that year the *'poor journeyman shoemaker'* was baptised by the Rev John Ryland in the River Nene below the ruined walls of Northampton Castle.

On 25th March 1785, Carey moved to Moulton. The Baptist church had been without a minister for ten years, services had become infrequent and the building had fallen into disrepair.

As the former schoolmaster had recently left the village, William supplemented his meagre stipend by teaching.

The scholarly Carey, who had already taught himself sufficient French and Dutch to be able to read books in those languages, gave high priority in his curriculum to geography. Borrowed volumes of Captain Cook's Voyages had stimulated his love of travel and, according to a popular story, he traced the explorer's routes for his pupils on a globe crudely fashioned from coloured pieces of scrap leather. A wall map, consisting of sheets of paper pasted together, recorded details of every nation in the known world. Part of the entry for the Indian sub-continent, where he was destined to spend so many fruitful years, displays how little he knew of its peoples.

'8,000,000 Indians are Pagans, vigilant, cruel, warlike.'

His school didn't last long. The former schoolmaster, the popular William Chown, returned to the village and set up a rival establishment. Carey's pupils defected and he reverted to shoemaking to make good his income. It proved fortuitous. He began working for Kettering-based manufacturer Thomas Gotch, regularly walking the dozen miles to his headquarters at Chesham House in Lower Street to collect leather and deliver his finished shoes. Gotch was a Baptist and friend of Andrew Fuller, the Kettering minister who had officiated at Carey's ordination in May 1787. When he learned of the young man's talent for languages, the manufacturer was sufficiently impressed to inform Carey that,

'I do not intend you should spoil any more of my leather, but you may proceed as fast as you can with your Latin, Greek and Hebrew, and I will allow you from my own private purse 10 shillings a week.'

Carey Baptist Chapel, Moulton

Carey's Cottage, Moulton

Carey spent only four years at Moulton before accepting a position at Harvey Lane Church in Leicester. At the Northampton Association Easter Meeting of ministers, held at Clipston on 27th April 1791, John Sutcliffe of Olney and Fuller of Kettering preached on the importance of missionary work. Moved by their words, Carey published a paper written five years earlier, under the cumbersome title, *'An Enquiry into the Obligation of Christians to use means for the Conversion of the Heathens in which the Religious State of the Different Nations of the World, the Success of Former Undertakings and the Practicability of Further Undertakings, are Considered.'*

The literary quality of the work may be questionable, but its impact was immense. The publication led directly to the formation of the Baptist Missionary Society, originally named, 'The Particular Baptist Society for the Propagation of the Gospel among the Heathen', in the small back parlour of Mrs Beeby Wallis's house in Lower Street Kettering on 2nd October 1792.

There is no doubting Carey's willingness to become the first from the newly formed society to spread the 'Word'. When Andrew Fuller exclaimed, *'there is a gold-mine in India but it seems as deep as the centre of the earth,'* Carey replied*: 'I will venture down but remember that you must hold the ropes.'*

And in June the following year, Carey, his wife and sister-in-law, four children including a tiny baby, together with Dr John Thomas, a Baptist and former naval surgeon, set sail for the sub-continent. Thomas had previously gone out to Bengal in the service of the East India Company as a ship's doctor, but had stayed on ministering to the sick, preaching the gospel and endeavouring to translate the Bible into Bengali. Now he was returning, intent upon establishing a mission.

Carey eventually reached India in November 1793, after a hazardous five-month journey during which he passed the long days at sea studying Bengali with Thomas. There were certainly no brass bands to greet them. The event was recorded in the *Calcutta Gazette*, which noted the arrival in the River of the *Kron Princessa Maria*, the Danish ship on which they'd travelled, and a cargo of 'Sundries', which presumably included Carey and his entourage. So Carey began his association with the country which would become his home. He was then thirty-two years old and never returned to England again.

Space, and the remit of this book, preclude but the briefest summary of Carey's remarkable life in India, but a highly readable version can be found in Mary Drewery's biography, *'William Carey' (1978)*. Not only did he fulfil his primary aim and establish a strong Christian church, but he contributed greatly to social improvement. He improved educational opportunity, initiated agricultural projects, alleviated the suffering of lepers and helped to make sati, (the barbaric ritual burning of widows on their husbands' funeral pyres), illegal and criminal.

In January 1800, Carey was appointed to the staff of Fort William College, founded by the enlightened Governor-General, Lord Wellesley, brother of the Duke of Wellington, for new recruits to the East India Company, as a teacher of Bengali and Sanskrit. Carey divided his time between Serampore and Calcutta, leaving the mission at dusk on Mondays and returning late on Friday evenings. In later years, with the aid of Indian scholars known as pundits, he greatly extended his role. Among his many works were vernacular text-books and grammars for his students, (in Bengali, Sanskrit, Marathi, Panjabi, Telagu, Kanarese and Bhutia), *'Colloquies' and 'Garland of Indian Stories'*, described by Professor HH Wilson of Oxford University as *'a lively picture of the manners and the notions of the people of Bengal'*, and a series of Indian classics including the epic *'Ramayana',* with text, English translation and notes, to make *'the western World partakers of India's literary riches.'*

The Mission also benefited from Carey's appointment, particularly its press, which published the afore-mentioned texts together with translations of the Bible in forty languages including Chinese.

In 1818, Carey and the mission staff, most notably Joshua Marshman and William Ward, established a new college at Serampore close to the Baptist Mission. It offered higher education to Indians regardless of caste or creed and, in addition to western subjects, gave instruction in Sanskrit and Arabic, so opening the door to knowledge of India's ancient literature and philosophy and to the literature of Islam. Of course, this generous provision had an ulterior evangelical motive. Carey believed that Indians would only grasp for themselves *'the message of truth'* if they were sufficiently well-educated.

Today, it is difficult to reconcile Carey's achievements with the personal cost to his family. Within a year of arrival in India, Dorothy and their eldest son Felix were stricken with dysentery, William became gravely ill with 'fever' and their third son, five-year old Peter, contracted the disease and died. To add to their grief, strict rules among the Indians concerning contact with the dead - and especially the unorthodox dead - meant that it was some time before a coffin could be made, a grave dug, or bearers found to carry the infant to his final resting place. The locals feared being outcast. The woe of bereavement told heavily upon his wife, who never recovered from the tragedy and from that point became, in Carey's words, *'my domestic affliction.'* Dorothy lived on, deranged and unstable, until 1807 when she finally succumbed to the illness that had taken her son. The following year, Carey re-married. His new bride was Lady Charlotte Emilia Rumohr, a wealthy invalid Danish Countess, who had settled in Calcutta some eight years earlier, and the couple enjoyed *' thirteen years, three weeks'* of happiness before her death in 1821 at the age of sixty.

Although he found some solace with a third wife, a widow named Grace Hughes whom he married in 1823, Carey's final years were marked by sadness. By now his health was seriously impaired, floods had overwhelmed much of lower Bengal destroying his home, washing away his beautiful garden and seriously damaging the school buildings. Krishna Pal, the Mission's first native convert had died of cholera in 1822 and later that same year his son Felix contracted a fatal liver complaint. In 1825 came news of the death of John Ryland, the last of the 'ropeholders', while a bitter dispute with Baptists in England over slanderous accusations about the 'personal aggrandisement' of some of the Serampore missionaries, added further to his unhappiness.

William Carey died on June 9th 1834, aged 72, and was buried at Serampore. A simple tablet marks the grave.

> *'A wretched, poor, and helpless worm,*
> *On thy kind arms I fall,'*

William Chown, whose return to Moulton in the late seventeen-eighties ended Carey's brief career as village schoolmaster, was himself a writer. An edition of his poetry, entitled *'Original Miscellaneous Poems on Moral, Religious and Entertaining Subjects'* was published in 1818, a few years before his death. In the opening address the pedant Chown *'humbly hopes that accomplished Critics will spare their rod, and esteem him sincere if not learned...'* Such was his reputation that over two hundred and fifty subscribers contributed to the costs of publication. It's interesting to compare this generous response with that received by the young John Clare, whose origins were somewhat more rustic. The book contains ninety-eight poems on a range of subjects, including

'The Tutor's Address to his Pupils, on breaking up at the Vacation'.

> *Ye gentle youths, accept my grateful lay,*
> *Which I presume to offer you this day;*
> *Fraught with a sympathetic love to you,*
> *Your kind attention let me crave as due.*
>
> *Your minds to form has been my constant aim,*
> *To prompt your souls to emulate in fame,*
> *And every virtue that adorns the soul,*
> *That all your wayward passions might controul.*
>
> *Your duty to your God, and parents too,*
> *Hath been the only aim I kept in view,*
> *Fair virtue's cause I always recommend,*
> *And pure religion as your closest friend.*
>
> *Ye docile youths, oh let it be your care,*
> *T'embrace her precepts, with attentive ear;*
> *They'll teach you with propriety to please;*
> *Her end is happiness! – her paths are peace.*
>
> *When keen affliction wounds your tender hearts,*
> *'Tis she alone that can repel the darts!*
> *Becalm your souls at your departing breath,*
> *And soothe the keenest agonies of death.'*

It makes rather a change from the usual end of term warnings about road safety and not playing on construction sites!

A dozen miles down the A43 from Moulton and we're back in Kettering, only too aware that time and space have constrained our efforts to do justice to all.

To quote TS Eliot, who would have crept into the book had Little Gidding been a few miles to the west,

> *'We shall not cease from exploration*
> *And the end of all our exploring*
> *Will be to arrive where we started.'*

Index

Bibliography

The text of the book contains references to many of the key works associated with the writers detailed in the preceding pages. The following list restricts itself to identifying such source material that proved invaluable in providing essential background information.

I Addis & R Mercer	*'Moments of the Rose'*
Geoffrey Anstruther	*'Vaux of Harrowden: A Recusant Family'*
John Bailey	*'Finedon otherwise Thingdon'*
HE Bates	*'The Vanished World'*
	'The World in Ripeness'
	'Give them their life'
John Bridges	*'The History and Antiquities of Northamptonshire'*
FW Bull	*'History of Kettering'*
Richard Cowley	*'Who's buried where in Northamptonshire'*
Malcolm Deacon	*'Philip Doddridge of Northampton'*
Mary Drewery	*'William Carey'*
George de Wilde	*'Rambles Roundabout and Poems'*
Peter Eads	*'H E Bates – A Bibliographical Study'*
Peter Gordon	*'The Wakes of Courteenhall'*
JA Gotch	*'The Old Halls and Manor House of Northamptonshire'*
	'Squires' Homes and other Old Buildings of Northamptonshire'
RL Greenall	*'The Rise of Industrial Kettering'*
	'A History of Northamptonshire and the Soke of Peterborough'
Peter Hill	*'Rockingham Forest Revisited'*
Trevor Hold	*'A Northamptonshire Garland'*
	'Chasing the Moon'
Tony Ireson	*'Northamptonshire'*
	'Old Kettering and its Defenders'
Thomas Isham	*'The Diary of Thomas Isham of Lamport'*
Ian Mayes	*'The De Wildes'*
Arthur Mee	*'Northamptonshire'*
Joyce & Maurice Palmer	*'A History of Wellingborough'*
Byron Rogers	*'The Life and Times of JL Carr'*
Chas Montagu-Douglas-Scott	*'Tales of Northamptonshire'*
George Smith	*'The Life of William Carey: Shoemaker and Missionary'*
Michael Stapleton	*'The Cambridge Guide to English Literature'*
Edward Storey	*'A Right to Song'*
Denys Watkins-Pitchford	*'A Child Alone: The Memoirs of BB'*
A&JW Tibble	*'John Clare: A Life'*
John & Vera Worledge	*'A Wanderer in Northamptonshire'*
A Shell Guide	*'Northamptonshire'*
Northamptonshire Federation of Women's Institutes	*'The Northamptonshire Village Book'*

Ian Addis was born in Kettering and has lived in the town for all but a few years. A former primary school headmaster, he now works at University College Northampton teaching would-be teachers, is a tutor for the Workers' Educational Association and indulges his peculiar views on matters varied in a local newspaper column co-written with his publisher.

Previous publications reflect his main pre-occupations and include a history of county football, a collection of Northamptonshire tales and reminiscences of a Kettering childhood.

His father's fire-side stories about 'Bert' Bates, a flying winger, who cycled from his Rushden home to play football against Finedon St Mary's choirboys' team, provided an early introduction to one of the county's most celebrated writers and helped spark a lasting enthusiasm for literature. This book, the result of another fruitful collaboration with Kettering artist, former headteacher colleague and friend, Robert Mercer, has provided a welcome opportunity to express that interest.

Robert Mercer also lives in Kettering. He too has spent much of his career in education. Luckily his obligation ended a decade ago just as much of the delight and valuable independence of mind were finally being squeezed out of the system! Despite the demands of earning a living, he has always ensured that art materials were close at hand. He has remained committed to art in education at all levels and among much else has taught for the Adult Education Service for nearly thirty years without a break.

Over the years he has exhibited widely with both solo shows and in a variety of mixed exhibitions.

At intervals, as an interesting diversion from absorption in his own painting, his collaborations with Ian have continued to stimulate and intrigue, often carrying him to unusual 'spiritual' places and rewarding explorations of little known corners of the county.

Other publications by Ian Addis and Robert Mercer:

'Moments of the Rose'   Jema Publications, 1994

'Kettering Then and Now'   Jema Publications, 1997

'A Kettering Kaleidoscope'   Diametric Publications, 1999
(with Barrie Chambers)

'Corby Remembers'   Diametric Publications, 2000

Concise Atlas
OF THE
WORLD

and

Contents

Published by AND Cartographic Publishers Ltd.
Alberto House, Hogwood Lane
Finchampstead, Berks, RG40 4RF
United Kingdom

email: info@andmap.co.uk
www: http://www.and.com

First edition 1999
Copyright © 1999 AND Cartographic Publishers Ltd.

Based on the AND World Reference Database.

ISBN 00 9533246 5 6
HRR
9 8 7 6 5 4 3 2 1

Originated by AND Cartographic Publishers Ltd.
Printed in Italy by Editoriale Lloyd srl.

*Wherever possible the latest comparable data has been used in
the compilation of the World flags and statistics section.*

*The map section uses local spellings. The World flags and statis-
tics section uses the conventional English translation where it is
different from the local form of the name.*

Legend and key map

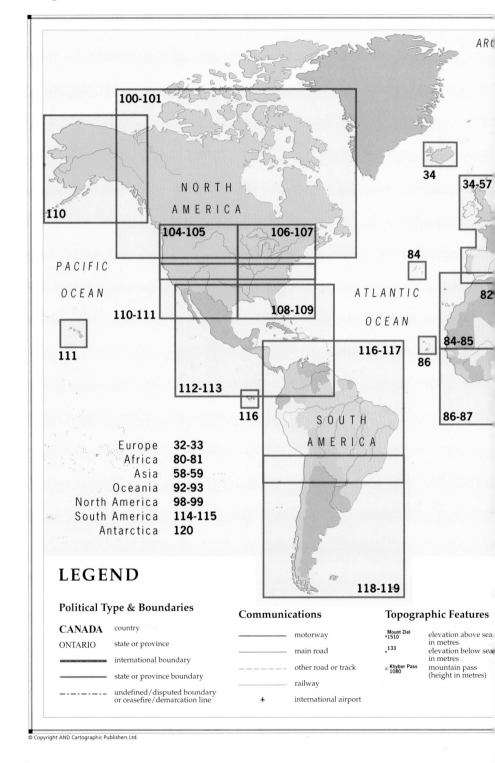

ARC

100-101

34

34-57

NORTH
AMERICA

104-105   106-107

110

84

PACIFIC

OCEAN

ATLANTIC

82

110-111   108-109

OCEAN

111

116-117

84-85

86

112-113

116

SOUTH
AMERICA

86-87

Europe	32-33
Africa	80-81
Asia	58-59
Oceania	92-93
North America	98-99
South America	114-115
Antarctica	120

118-119

LEGEND

Political Type & Boundaries

CANADA   country

ONTARIO   state or province

━━━━━━   international boundary

━━━━━━   state or province boundary

━·━·━·━   undefined/disputed boundary
or ceasefire/demarcation line

Communications

────────   motorway

────────   main road

── ── ──   other road or track

────────   railway

✦   international airport

Topographic Features

Mount Ziel
▲1510   elevation above sea
in metres

,133   elevation below sea
in metres

╳ **Khyber Pass**
1080   mountain pass
(height in metres)

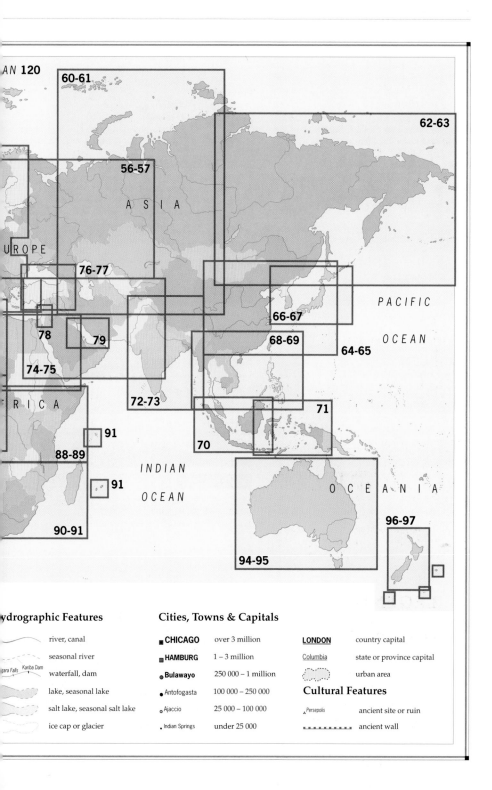

AN 120

60-61

62-63

56-57

A S I A

U R O P E

76-77

P A C I F I C

78

79

66-67

O C E A N

68-69

74-75

64-65

72-73

71

F R I C A

70

91

88-89

96-97

91

I N D I A N

O C E A N

O C E A N I A

90-91

94-95

ydrographic Features

river, canal	
seasonal river	
ara Falls Kariba Dam waterfall, dam	
lake, seasonal lake	
salt lake, seasonal salt lake	
ice cap or glacier	

Cities, Towns & Capitals

■ CHICAGO	over 3 million
▣ HAMBURG	1 – 3 million
● Bulawayo	250 000 – 1 million
● Antofogasta	100 000 – 250 000
○ Ajaccio	25 000 – 100 000
· Indian Springs	under 25 000

LONDON	country capital
Columbia	state or province capital
⬭	urban area

Cultural Features

▲ Persepolis	ancient site or ruin
··········	ancient wall

5

World flags and statistics

EUROPE

Iceland

Area: 103,000 km²
Population: 269,000
Capital: Reykjavik (*pop:* 153,210)
Religions: Evangelical, Lutheran, others
Languages: Icelandic, Danish
Political system: Republic
Economy: Fishing
GNP per capita: US$27,580
Currency: Icelandic króna

Finland

Area: 338,145 km²
Population: 5,108,000
Capital: Helsinki (*pop:* 1,016,291)
Religions: Evangelical, Lutheran, Greek
Orthodox
Languages: Finnish, Swedish
Political system: Republic
Economy: Engineering
GNP per capita: US$24,080
Currency: Euro/Markka

Norway

Area: 323,877 km²
Population: 4,360,000
Capital: Oslo (*pop:* 758,949)
Religions: Evangelical, Lutheran, others
Main language: Norwegian
Political system: Constitutional monarchy
Economy: Oil, gas
GNP per capita: US$36,090
Currency: Krone

Estonia

Area: 45,100 km²
Population: 1,530,000
Capital: Tallinn (*pop:* 447,672)
Religions: Evangelical, Lutheran
Languages: Estonian, Russian
Political system: Republic
Economy: Machinery, shipping
GNP per capita: US$3,330
Currency: Kroon

Denmark

Area: 43,094 km²
Population: 5,228,000
Capital: Copenhagen (*pop:* 1,353,333)
Religions: Evangelical, Lutheran, others
Main language: Danish
Political system: Constitutional monarchy
Economy: Industry, agriculture
GNP per capita: US$32,500
Currency: Kroner

Latvia

Area: 64,600 km²
Population: 2,515,000
Capital: Riga (*pop:* 847,976)
Religions: Evangelical, Lutheran, others
Languages: Latvian, Russian
Political system: Republic
Economy: Transport, defence equipment
GNP per capita: US$2,430
Currency: Lats

Sweden

Area: 449,964 km²
Population: 8,831,000
Capital: Stockholm (*pop:* 1,532,803)
Religions: Evangelical, Lutheran, Roman Catholic
Main language: Swedish
Political system: Constitutional monarchy
Economy: Car industry, electronics
GNP per capita: US$26,220
Currency: Swedish krona

Lithuania

Area: 65,200 km²
Population: 3,715,000
Capital: Vilnius (*pop:* 581,500)
Religions: Roman Catholic, others
Languages: Lithuanian, Russian
Political system: Republic
Economy: Textiles, engineering
GNP per capita: US$2,230
Currency: Litas

See page 121 for an index to flags

Poland

Area: 323,250 km²
Population: 38,588,000
Capital: Warsaw (*pop:* 1,643,203)
Religions: Roman Catholic, others
Main language: Polish
Political system: Republic
Economy: Heavy industry
GNP per capita: US$3,590
Currency: Zloty

Republic of Ireland

Area: 70,254 km²
Population: 3,582,000
Capital: Dublin (*pop:* 952,700)
Religions: Roman Catholic, Protestant
Languages: English, Irish
Political system: Republic
Economy: Agriculture
GNP per capita: US$18,280
Currency: Euro/Punt

Germany

Area: 356,733 km²
Population: 81,642,000
Capital: Berlin (*pop:* 3,472,009)
Religions: Protestant,
Roman Catholic
Main language: German
Political system: Republic
Economy: Cars, engineering
GNP per capita: US$28,260
Currency: Euro/Deutsche mark

United Kingdom

Area: 244,101 km²
Population: 58,258,000
Capital: London (*pop:* 6,962,319)
Religions: Protestant, Roman
Catholic, others
Main language: English
Political system: Constitutional monarchy
Economy: Financial services, defence
GNP per capita: US$20,710
Currency: Pound

Netherlands

Area: 40,844 km²
Population: 15,451,000
Capital: Amsterdam (*pop:* 1,100,764)
Religions: Roman Catholic,
Protestant, others
Main language: Dutch
Political system: Constitutional monarchy
Economy: Machinery, chemicals
GNP per capita: US$25,820
Currency: Euro/Guilder

France

Area: 551,500 km²
Population: 58,143,000
Capital: Paris (*pop:* 9,319,367)
Religions: Roman Catholic, Protestant
Main languages: French
Political system: Republic
Economy: Steel, chemicals
GNP per capita: US$26,050
Currency: Euro/Franc

Belgium

Area: 30,519 km²
Population: 10,113,000
Capital: Brussels (*pop:* 960,324)
Religions: Roman Catholic, others
Languages: Flemish, French
Political system: Constitutional monarchy
Economy: Steel, glassware
GNP per capita: US$26,490
Currency: Euro/Belgian franc

Luxembourg

Area: 2,586 km²
Population: 406,000
Capital: Luxembourg (*pop:* 76,446)
Religions: Roman Catholic, others
Languages: Letzebuergesch, French, German
Political system: Constitutional monarchy
Economy: Steel-making
GNP per capita: US$45,440
Currency: Euro/Luxembourg franc

Monaco

Area: 1 km²
Population: 32,000
Capital: Monaco (*pop:* 27,063)
Religions: Roman Catholic, others
Languages: French, Italian
Political system: Constitutional monarchy
Economy: Tourism, gambling
GNP per capita: US$16,000
Currency: French franc

Italy

Area: 301,268 km²
Population: 57,187,000
Capital: Rome (*pop:* 2,693,383)
Religions: Roman Catholic, other
Main language: Italian
Political system: Republic
Economy: Industry design, textiles
GNP per capita: US$20,120
Currency: Euro/Lira

Andorra

Area: 453 km²
Population: 68,000
Capital: Andorra la Vella (*pop:* 16,151)
Religions: Roman Catholic, others
Languages: Catalan, French, Spanish
Political system: Constitutional principality
Economy: Tourism, banking, commerce
GNP per capita: US$14,000
Currency: French franc/Spanish peseta

Vatican City

Area: 0.44 km²
Population: 1,000
Capital: Vatican City (*pop:* 766)
Religion: Roman Catholic
Main language: Italian
Political system: Absolute rule
Economy: Investment
GNP per capita: not available
Currency: Italian lira

Portugal

Area: 91,982 km²
Population: 10,797,000
Capital: Lisbon (*pop:* 2,561,225)
Religions: Roman Catholic, Protestant
Main language: Portuguese
Political system: Republic
Economy: Agriculture, wine
GNP per capita: US$10,450
Currency: Euro/Escudo

Malta

Area: 316 km²
Population: 371,000
Capital: Valletta (*pop:* 9,144)
Religions: Roman Catholic, Anglican
Languages: Maltesse, English
Political system: Republic
Economy: Tourism
GNP per capita: US$11,000
Currency: Maltese lira

Spain

Area: 505,992 km²
Population: 39,210,000
Capital: Madrid (*pop:* 3,084,673)
Religions: Roman Catholic, others
Languages: Spanish, Basque
Political system: Constitutional monarchy
Economy: Agriculture, industry
GNP per capita: US$14,510
Currency: Euro/Peseta

San Marino

Area: 61 km²
Population: 25,000
Capital: San Marino (*pop:* 4,251)
Religions: Roman Catholic, Protestant
Main language: Italian
Political system: Republic
Economy: Tourism, light industry
GNP per capita: US$20,000
Currency: Italian lira

See page 121 for an index to flags

Switzerland

Area: 41,284 km²
Population: 7,040,000
Capital: Berne (*pop:* 321,932)
Religions: Roman Catholic, Protestant
Languages: German, French, Italian
Political system: Republic
Economy: Banking, tourism
GNP per capita: US$44,430
Currency: Swiss franc

Liechtenstein

Area: 160 km²
Population: 31,000
Capital: Vaduz (*pop:* 5,072)
Religions: Roman Catholic, Protestant
Main language: German
Political system: Constitutional monarchy
Economy: Banking, dental products
GNP per capita: US$33,500
Currency: Swiss franc

Austria

Area: 83,859 km²
Population: 8,053,000
Capital: Vienna (*pop:* 1,806,737)
Religions: Roman Catholic, Protestant
Main language: German
Political system: Republic
Economy: Manufacturing industry
GNP per capita: US$27,980
Currency: Euro/Schilling

Hungary

Area: 93,032 km²
Population: 10,225,000
Capital: Budapest (*pop:* 2,002,121)
Religions: Roman Catholic, Protestant
Languages: Magyar, German
Political system: Republic
Economy: Industry, agriculture
GNP per capita: US$4,430
Currency: Forint

Czech Republic

Area: 78,864 km²
Population: 10,331,000
Capital: Prague (*pop:* 1,216,568)
Religions: Roman Catholic, Protestant
Languages: Czech, Slovak
Political system: Republic
Economy: Heavy industry
GNP per capita: US$5,200
Currency: Koruna

Slovakia

Area: 49,012 km²
Population: 5,364,000
Capital: Bratislava (*pop:* 451,272)
Religions: Roman Catholic, Protestant
Languages: Slovak, Hungarian, Czech
Political system: Republic
Economy: Heavy industry
GNP per capita: US$3,700
Currency: Koruna

Slovenia

Area: 20,256 km²
Population: 1,984,000
Capital: Ljubljana (*pop:* 330,000)
Religions: Roman Catholic, Muslim
Languages: Slovene, Hungarian, Italian
Political system: Republic
Economy: Manufacturing, tourism
GNP per capita: US$9,680
Currency: Tolar

Croatia

Area: 88,117 km²
Population: 4,495,000
Capital: Zagreb (*pop:* 867,717)
Religions: Roman Catholic, Protestant
Languages: Croato-Serb, Serbo-Croat
Political system: Republic
Economy: Manufacturing
GNP per capita: US$4,610
Currency: Kuna

Bosnia-Herzegovina

Area: 51,129 km²
Population: 4,484,000
Capital: Sarajevo (*pop:* 415,631)
Religion: Muslim
Languages: Serbo-Croat, Croato-Serb
Political system: Republic
Economy: Manufacturing industry
GNP per capita: US$2,600
Currency: Convertible marka

Bulgaria

Area: 110,912 km²
Population: 8,402,000
Capital: Sofia (*pop:* 1,188,563)
Religions: Christian, Muslim, Jewish
Languages: Bulgarian, Turkish
Political system: Republic
Economy: Agriculture, wine
GNP per capita: US$1,140
Currency: Lev

Yugoslavia

Area: 102,173 km²
Population: 10,544,000
Capital: Belgrade (*pop:* 1,136,786)
Religions: Orthodox Catholic, Muslim
Languages: Serbo-Croat, Albanian, Hungarian
Political system: Republic
Economy: Largely barter
GNP per capita: US$1,400
Currency: New dinar

Greece

Area: 131,957 km²
Population: 10,458,000
Capital: Athens (*pop:* 3,027,922)
Religions: Greek Orthodox, Muslim
Main language: Greek
Political system: Republic
Economy: Tourism, shipping
GNP per capita: US$12,010
Currency: Drachma

Albania

Area: 28,748 km²
Population: 3,645,000
Capital: Tirana (*pop:* 244,153)
Religions: Muslim, Greek Orthodox
Languages: Albanian, Greek
Political system: Republic
Economy: Oil, gas
GNP per capita: US$750
Currency: Lek

Romania

Area: 238,391 km²
Population: 22,680,000
Capital: Bucharest (*pop:* 2,060,551)
Religions: Romanian Orthodox, Roman Catholic
Main language: Romanian
Political system: Republic
Economy: Heavy industry
GNP per capita: US$1,420
Currency: Leu

Macedonia

Area: 25,713 km²
Population: 2,163,000
Capital: Skopje (*pop:* 448,229)
Religions: Christian, Muslim
Languages: Macedonian, Serbo-Croat
Political system: Republic
Economy: Reliant on foreign aid
GNP per capita: US$1,090
Currency: Dinar

Moldova

Area: 33,700 km²
Population: 4,432,000
Capital: Kishinev (*pop:* 667,100)
Religions: Romanian Orthodox, Jewish
Languages: Moldovan, Russian
Political system: Republic
Economy: Wine, tobacco, cotton
GNP per capita: US$540
Currency: Leu

See page 121 for an index to flags

Belarus

Area: 207,600 km²
Population: 10,141,000
Capital: Minsk (*pop:* 1,687,400)
Religions: Russian Orthodox, Roman Catholic
Languages: Belarusian, Russian
Political system: Republic
Economy: Food processing
GNP per capita: US$2,150
Currency: Rouble

Armenia

Area: 29,800 km²
Population: 3,762,000
Capital: Yerevan (*pop:* 1,254,000)
Religions: Armenian Apostolic, others
Languages: Armenian, Russian
Political system: Republic
Economy: Mining, agriculture
GNP per capita: US$530
Currency: Dram

Ukraine

Area: 603,700 km²
Population: 51,639,000
Capital: Kiev (*pop:* 2,646,100)
Religions: Ukrainian Orthodox, others
Languages: Ukrainian, Russian
Political system: Republic
Economy: Heavy industry
GNP per capita: US$1,040
Currency: Hryvna

Turkey

Area: 774,815 km²
Population: 61,644,000
Capital: Ankara (*pop:* 3,103,000)
Religion: Muslim
Main language: Turkish
Political system: Republic
Economy: Textiles, manufacturing
GNP per capita: US$3,130
Currency: Turkish lira

Russia

Area: 17,075,400 km²
Population: 147,855,000
Capital: Moscow (*pop:* 8,663,142)
Religions: Russian Orthodox, Jewish, Muslim
Main language: Russian
Political system: Republic
Economy: Oil, gas
GNP per capita: US$2,740
Currency: Rouble

Georgia

Area: 69,700 km²
Population: 5,457,000
Capital: Tbilisi (*pop:* 1,268,000)
Religion: Georgian Orthodox
Languages: Georgian, Russian, Armenian
Political system: Republic
Economy: Food processing
GNP per capita: US$840
Currency: Lari

ASIA

Azerbaijan

Area: 86,600 km²
Population: 7,499,000
Capital: Baku (*pop:* 1,149,000)
Religions: Muslim, Armenian Apostolic
Languages: Azerbaijani, Russian
Political system: Republic
Economy: Oil, gas
GNP per capita: US$510
Currency: Manat

Lebanon

Area: 10,400 km²
Population: 3,009,000
Capital: Beirut (*pop:* 1,500,000)
Religions: Muslim, Christian
Languages: Arabic, French, English
Political system: Republic
Economy: Banking, services
GNP per capita: US$3,350
Currency: Lebanese pound

Syria

Area: 185,180 km²
Population: 14,315,000
Capital: Damascus (*pop:* 1,549,000)
Religions: Sunni Muslim, Christian
Languages: Arabic, Kurdish, Turkish
Political system: Republic
Economy: Oil
GNP per capita: US$1,150
Currency: Syrian pound

Saudi Arabia

Area: 2,149,690 km²
Population: 17,880,000
Capital: Riyadh (*pop:* 1,800,000)
Religions: Sunni Muslim
Languages: Arabic, English
Political system: Absolute monarchy
Economy: Oil, gas
GNP per capita: US$7,040
Currency: Saudi riyal

Cyprus

Area: 9,251 km²
Population: 742,000
Capital: Nicosia (*pop:* 188,800)
Religions: Greek Orthodox, Muslim
Languages: Greek, Turkish
Political system: Republic
Economy: Tourism, shipping
GNP per capita: US$11,500
Currency: Cyprus pound

Yemen

Area: 527,968 km²
Population: 14,501,000
Capital: San'a (*pop:* 926,595)
Religion: Sunni Muslim
Main language: Arabic
Political system: Republic
Economy: Oil, gas
GNP per capita: US$270
Currency: Riyal

Israel

Area: 21,056 km²
Population: 5,545,000
Capital: Jerusalem (*pop:* 662,700)
Religions: Jewish, Muslim
Languages: Hebrew, Arabic
Political system: Republic
Economy: Industry, agriculture
GNP per capita: US$15,900
Currency: Shekel

Oman

Area: 212,457 km²
Population: 2,163,000
Capital: Muscat (*pop:* 400,000)
Religions: Ibadi Muslim, Hindu
Languages: Arabic, Qarra, Mahra
Political system: Absolute monarchy
Economy: Oil, gas
GNP per capita: US$4,820
Currency: Rial

Jordan

Area: 97,740 km²
Population: 5,439,000
Capital: Amman (*pop:* 1,270,000)
Religions: Muslim, Christian
Languages: Arabic, English, French
Political system: Constitutional monarchy
Economy: Phosphates, chemicals
GNP per capita: US$1,570
Currency: Jordanian dinar

United Arab Emirates

Area: 83,600 km²
Population: 2,314,000
Capital: Abu Dhabi (*pop:* 450,000)
Religion: Sunni Muslim
Languages: Arabic, English
Political system: Federation of absolute monarchies
Economy: Oil, gas
GNP per capita: US$17,400
Currency: Dirham

See page 121 for an index to flags

Qatar

Area: 11,000 km²
Population: 551,000
Capital: Doha (*pop:* 217,294)
Religions: Sunni Muslim, Hindu
Languages: Arabic, English
Political system: Absolute monarchy
Economy: Oil, gas
GNP per capita: US$11,600
Currency: Qatar riyal

Bahrain

Area: 694 km²
Population: 586,000
Capital: Manama (*pop:* 140,401)
Religions: Shi'a Muslim, Christian
Languages: Arabic, English
Political system: Constitutional monarchy
Economy: Oil, gas
GNP per capita: US$7,840
Currency: Bahraini dinar

Kuwait

Area: 17,818 km²
Population: 1,691,000
Capital: Kuwait (*pop:* 400,000)
Religions: Muslim, Christian
Languages: Arabic, English
Political system: Constitutional monarchy
Economy: Oil, gas
GNP per capita: US$17,390
Currency: Kuwaiti dinar

Iraq

Area: 438,317 km²
Population: 20,449,000
Capital: Baghdad (*pop:* 3,841,268)
Religion: Shi'a Muslim
Languages: Arabic, Kurdish, Turkic, Aramaic
Political system: Republic
Economy: Oil, collapsed due to UN sanctions
GNP per capita: US$1,800
Currency: Dinar

Iran

Area: 1,633,188 km²
Population: 67,283,000
Capital: Tehran (*pop:* 6,750,043)
Religion: Shi'a Muslim
Languages: Persian, Turkish, Kurdish, Arabic
Political system: Republic
Economy: Oil
GNP per capita: US$1,780
Currency: Rial

Turkmenistan

Area: 488,100 km²
Population: 4,099,000
Capital: Ashkhabad (*pop:* 407,000)
Religion: Muslim
Languages: Turkmenian, Russian, Uzbek
Political system: Republic
Economy: Cotton, gas
GNP per capita: US$630
Currency: Manat

Uzbekistan

Area: 447,400 km²
Population: 22,843,000
Capital: Tashkent (*pop:* 2,094,000)
Religions: Muslim
Languages: Uzbek, Russian
Political system: Republic
Economy: Agriculture, oil, gas
GNP per capita: US$1,010
Currency: Sum

Kazakhstan

Area: 2,717,300 km²
Population: 16,590,000
Capital: Astana (*pop:* 292,000)
Religions: Muslim, Russian Orthodox
Languages: Kazakh, Russian
Political system: Republic
Economy: Gas, oil, coal, uranium
GNP per capita: US$1,340
Currency: Tenge

Mongolia

Area: 1,566,500 km²
Population: 2,410,000
Capital: Ulan Bator (*pop:* 515,100)
Religions: Buddhist, Muslim
Languages: Mongolian, Kazakh
Political system: Republic
Economy: Agriculture, oil, coal
GNP per capita: US$390
Currency: Tugrik

Pakistan

Area: 796,095 km²
Population: 129,808,000
Capital: Islamabad (*pop:* 350,000)
Religions: Sunni Muslim, Hindu
Languages: Punjabi, Urdu, Sindi, Pushto
Political system: Republic
Economy: Cotton, rice, oil
GNP per capita: US$490
Currency: Pakistan rupee

Kyrgyzstan

Area: 198,500 km²
Population: 4,668,000
Capital: Bishkek (*pop:* 627,800)
Religions: Muslim, Russian Orthodox
Languages: Kirghiz, Russian
Political system: Republic
Economy: Collective farming, coal
GNP per capita: US$440
Currency: Som

Nepal

Area: 147,181 km²
Population: 21,918,000
Capital: Kathmandu (*pop:* 419,073)
Religions: Hindu, Buddhist
Main language: Nepali
Political system: Constitutional monarchy
Economy: Agriculture
GNP per capita: US$210
Currency: Nepalese rupee

Tajikistan

Area: 143,100 km²
Population: 5,836,000
Capital: Dushanbe (*pop:* 602,000)
Religion: Sunni Muslim
Languages: Tajik, Uzbek, Russian
Political system: Republic
Economy: Carpet-making
GNP per capita: US$330
Currency: Tajik rouble

Bhutan

Area: 47,000 km²
Population: 1,638,000
Capital: Thimphu (*pop:* 15,000)
Religions: Buddhist, Hindu
Languages: Dzongkha, English
Political system: Absolute monarchy
Economy: subsistence farming
GNP per capita: US$400
Currency: Ngultrum

Afghanistan

Area: 652,090 km²
Population: 20,141,000
Capital: Kabul (*pop:* 1,424,400)
Religions: Sumi, Muslim
Languages: Dari, Pushtu
Political system: Republic
Economy: Agriculture
GNP per capita: US$300
Currency: Afghani

India

Area: 3,287,590 km²
Population: 935,744,000
Capital: New Delhi (*pop:* 301,297)
Religions: Hindu, Muslim, Christian
Languages: Hindi, English, others
Political system: Republic
Economy: High-tech industry, clothing
GNP per capita: US$390
Currency: Indian rupee

See page 121 for an index to flags

Maldives

Area: 298 km²
Population: 254,000
Capital: Male (*pop:* 62,973)
Religion: Sunni Muslim
Main language: Maldivian
Political system: Republic
Economy: Tourism, fishing
GNP per capita: US$1,150
Currency: Rufiyaa

Thailand

Area: 513,115 km²
Population: 60,206,000
Capital: Bangkok (*pop:* 5,876,000)
Religions: Buddhist, Muslim
Languages: Thai, Chinese, Khmer, Malay
Political system: Constitutional monarchy
Economy: Manufacturing, rice, rubber
GNP per capita: US$2,800
Currency: Baht

Sri Lanka

Area: 65,610 km²
Population: 18,354,000
Capital: Colombo (*pop:* 615,000)
Religions: Buddhist, Hindu, Christian
Languages: Sinhala, Tamil, English
Political system: Republic
Economy: Tea, tourism
GNP per capita: US$800
Currency: Sri Lankan rupee

Laos

Area: 236,800 km²
Population: 4,882,000
Capital: Vientiane (*pop:* 120,000)
Religions: Buddhist, Christian
Languages: Lao, French
Political system: Republic
Economy: Timber, mining
GNP per capita: US$400
Currency: Kip

Bangladesh

Area: 143,998 km²
Population: 120,433,000
Capital: Dhaka (*pop:* 3,397,187)
Religions: Muslim, Hindu
Languages: Bengali, English
Political system: Republic
Economy: Foreign aid, jute
GNP per capita: US$270
Currency: Taka

Cambodia

Area: 181,035 km²
Population: 9,836,000
Capital: Phnom Penh (*pop:* 832,000)
Religions: Buddhist, Muslim
Languages: Khmer, Chinese, Vietnamese
Political system: Constitutional monarchy
Economy: Rubber, timber
GNP per capita: US$300
Currency: Riel

Myanmar (Burma)

Area: 676,578 km²
Population: 46,527,000
Capital: Rangoon (*pop:* 2,513,023)
Religions: Buddhist, Muslim
Languages: Burmese, English, Shan, Karen
Political system: Republic
Economy: Teak, rice
GNP per capita: US$1,000
Currency: Kyat

Vietnam

Area: 331,689 km²
Population: 74,545,000
Capital: Hanoi (*pop:* 3,056,146)
Religions: Buddhist, Roman Catholic
Languages: Vietnamese, French, English
Political system: Republic
Economy: Steel, gas, oil
GNP per capita: US$320
Currency: Dông

Malaysia

Area: 329,758 km²
Population: 20,140,000
Capital: Kuala Lumpur (*pop:* 1,145,075)
Religions: Muslim, Buddhist
Languages: Malay, English, Chinese, Tamil
Political system: Constitutional monarchy
Economy: Electronics, cars
GNP per capita: US$4,680
Currency: Malaysian dollar

Philippines

Area: 300,000 km²
Population: 70,267,000
Capital: Manila (*pop:* 8,594,150)
Religions: Roman Catholic, Protestant
Languages: Filipino, English
Political system: Republic
Economy: Agriculture
GNP per capita: US$1,220
Currency: Philippine peso

Indonesia

Area: 1,904,569 km²
Population: 193,750,000
Capital: Jakarta (*pop:* 9,160,500)
Religions: Muslim, Christian, others
Languages: Bahasa Indonesian, Dutch, English
Political system: Republic
Economy: Timber, minerals
GNP per capita: US$1,110
Currency: Rupiah

Taiwan

Area: 35,742 km²
Population: 21,450,183
Capital: Taipei (*pop:* 2,607,010)
Religions: Buddhist, Confucian, Taoist
Languages: Mandarin Chinese, Taiwanese
Political system: Republic
Economy: Manufacturing, electronics
GNP per capita: US$12,000
Currency: New Taiwan dollar

Singapore

Area: 618 km²
Population: 2,987,000
Religions: Buddhist, Christian, Muslim
Languages: Malay, Mandarin, Tamil, English
Political system: Republic
Economy: Finance, banking
GNP per capita: US$32,940
Currency: Singapore dollar

China

Area: 9,596,961 km²
Population: 1,221,462,000
Capital: Beijing (*pop:* 7,362,426)
Religions: Confucian, Buddhist
Languages: Mandarin Chinese, Cantonese
Political system: Republic
Economy: Agriculture, industry
GNP per capita: US$860
Currency: Yuan

Brunei

Area: 5,765 km²
Population: 285,000
Capital: Bandar Seri Begawan (*pop:* 49,902)
Religions: Muslim, Buddhist, Christian
Languages: Malay, English
Political system: Absolute monarchy
Economy: Oil, gas
GNP per capita: US$14,500
Currency: Brunei dollar

North Korea

Area: 120,538 km²
Population: 23,917,000
Capital: Pyongyang (*pop:* 2,000,000)
Religions: Traditional beliefs, Buddhist
Main language: Korean
Political system: Republic, one-party state
Economy: Manufacturing, agriculture
GNP per capita: US$1,000
Currency: Won

See page 121 for an index to flags

South Korea

Area: 99,274 km²
Population: 44,851,000
Capital: Seoul (*pop:* 10,776,201)
Religions: Mahayana Buddhist, Protestant
Main language: Korean
Political system: Republic
Economy: Ship-building, cars
GNP per capita: US$10,550
Currency: Won

Tunisia

Area: 163,610 km²
Population: 8,896,000
Capital: Tunis (*pop:* 1,394,749)
Religions: Muslim, Christian
Languages: Arabic, French, English
Political system: Republic
Economy: Oil, gas
GNP per capita: US$2,090
Currency: Tunisian dinar

Japan

Area: 377,801 km²
Population: 125,197,000
Capital: Tokyo (*pop:* 11,927,457)
Religions: Shinto, Buddhism
Main language: Japanese
Political system: Constitutional monarchy
Economy: Electronics
GNP per capita: US$37,850
Currency: Yen

Libya

Area: 1,759,540 km²
Population: 5,407,000
Capital: Tripoli (*pop:* 1,000,000)
Religions: Muslim, others
Languages: Arabic, Tuareg
Political system: Republic
Economy: Oil
GNP per capita: US$7,000
Currency: Libyan dinar

AFRICA
Morocco

Area: 446,550 km²
Population: 27,111,000
Capital: Rabat (*pop:* 1,220,000)
Religion: Muslim
Languages: Arabic, Berber, French, Spanish
Political system: Constitutional monarchy
Economy: Phosphates, tourism
GNP per capita: US$1,250
Currency: Dirham

Egypt

Area: 1,001,449 km²
Population: 59,226,000
Capital: Cairo (*pop:* 13,000,000)
Religions: Muslim, others
Main language: Arabic
Political system: Republic
Economy: Oil, gas
GNP per capita: US$1,180
Currency: Egyptian pound

Algeria

Area: 2,381,741 km²
Population: 28,548,000
Capital: Algiers (*pop:* 3,250,000)
Religions: Muslim, Christian
Languages: Arabic, Berber, French
Political system: Republic
Economy: Oil, gas
GNP per capita: US$1,490
Currency: Algerian dinar

Sudan

Area: 2,505,813 km²
Population: 28,098,000
Capital: Khartoum (*pop:* 924,505)
Religions: Muslim, traditional beliefs
Languages: Arabic, English
Political system: Republic
Economy: Cash crops
GNP per capita: US$280
Currency: Sudanese dinar

Eritrea

Area: 117,600 km²
Population: 3,531,000
Capital: Asmara (*pop:* 358,100)
Religions: Coptic Christian, Muslim, others
Languages: English, Arabic
Political system: Republic
Economy: Subsistence farming, gold
GNP per capita: US$210
Currency: Nakfa

Uganda

Area: 241,038 km²
Population: 21,297,000
Capital: Kampala (*pop:* 750,000)
Religions: Roman Catholic, Protestant, others
Languages: English, Swahili
Political system: Republic
Economy: Coffee, mining
GNP per capita: US$330
Currency: Uganda shilling

Djibouti

Area: 23,200 km²
Population: 577,000
Capital: Djibouti (*pop:* 340,700)
Religions: Christian, others
Languages: Arabic, French, Somali
Political system: Republic
Economy: Sea trade
GNP per capita: US$1,000
Currency: Djibouti franc

Kenya

Area: 580,367 km²
Population: 30,522,000
Capital: Nairobi (*pop:* 1,400,000)
Religions: Roman Catholic, Protestant
Languages: Swahili, English
Political system: Republic
Economy: Tourism, tea
GNP per capita: US$330
Currency: Kenya shilling

Ethiopia

Area: 1,104,300 km²
Population: 56,677,000
Capital: Addis Ababa (*pop:* 2,316,400)
Religions: Muslim, Christian
Languages: Amharic, English, Arabic
Political system: Republic
Economy: Subsistence farming
GNP per capita: US$110
Currency: Ethiopian birr

Rwanda

Area: 26,338 km²
Population: 7,952,000
Capital: Kigali (*pop:* 156,000)
Religions: Roman Catholic, traditional beliefs
Languages: Kinyarwanda, French, English
Political system: Republic
Economy: Coffee, oil, gas
GNP per capita: US$210
Currency: Rwanda franc

Somalia

Area: 637,657 km²
Population: 9,250,000
Capital: Mogadishu (*pop:* 1,000,000)
Religions: Sunni Muslim, others
Languages: Somali, Arabic, English
Political system: Republic
Economy: Foreign aid
GNP per capita: US$500
Currency: Somali shilling

Burundi

Area: 27,834 km²
Population: 5,982,000
Capital: Bujumbura (*pop:* 235,440)
Religions: Roman Catholic, traditional beliefs
Languages: Kirundi, French, Kiswahili
Political system: Republic
Economy: Agriculture
GNP per capita: US$180
Currency: Burundi franc

See page 121 for an index to flags

Central African Republic

Area: 622,984 km²
Population: 3,315,000
Capital: Bangui (*pop:* 473,817)
Religions: Christian, traditional beliefs
Languages: French, Sango
Political system: Republic
Economy: Subsistence farming, gold
GNP per capita: US$320
Currency: Franc CFA

Mauritania

Area: 1,025,520 km²
Population: 2,284,000
Capital: Nouakchott (*pop:* 850,000)
Religion: Muslim
Languages: Arabic, French, Pulaar
Political system: Republic
Economy: Agriculture, mining
GNP per capita: US$450
Currency: Ouguiya

Democratic Republic of Congo

Area: 2,344,858 km²
Population: 43,901,000
Capital: Kinshasa (*pop:* 2,664,309)
Religions: Christian, traditional beliefs
Languages: Swahili, Lingala, French
Political system: Republic
Economy: Minerals
GNP per capita: US$110
Currency: Congolese franc

Mali

Area: 1,240,192 km²
Population: 10,795,000
Capital: Bamako (*pop:* 658,275)
Religions: Muslim, traditional beliefs
Languages: French, Bambara, Fulani
Political system: Republic
Economy: Farming, herding, fishing
GNP per capita: US$260
Currency: Franc CFA

Niger

Area: 1,267,000 km²
Population: 9,151,000
Capital: Niamey (*pop:* 392,169)
Religions: Muslim, traditional beliefs
Languages: French, Hausa, Djerma, Fulani
Political system: Republic
Economy: Uranium
GNP per capita: US$200
Currency: Franc CFA

Senegal

Area: 196,722 km²
Population: 8,312,000
Capital: Dakar (*pop:* 1,641,358)
Religions: Muslim, traditional beliefs
Languages: French, Wolof, Fulani, Serer
Political system: Republic
Economy: Farming, mining
GNP per capita: US$550
Currency: Franc CFA

Chad

Area: 1,284,000 km²
Population: 6,361,000
Capital: N'Djaména (*pop:* 179,000)
Religions: Muslim, Christian
Languages: French, Arabic, Sara
Political system: Republic
Economy: Subsistence farming
GNP per capita: US$240
Currency: Franc CFA

The Gambia

Area: 11,295 km²
Population: 1,118,000
Capital: Banjul (*pop:* 109,986)
Religions: Muslim, Christian
Languages: English, Mandinka, Fula, Wollof
Political system: Republic
Economy: Agriculture, fishing
GNP per capita: US$350
Currency: Dalasi

Cape Verde

Area: 4,033 km²
Population: 392,000
Capital: Praia (*pop:* 80,000)
Religions: Roman Catholic, Protestant
Languages: Portuguese, Creole
Political system: Republic
Economy: Subsistence farming
GNP per capita: US$1,090
Currency: Escudo

Liberia

Area: 111,369 km²
Population: 2,760,000
Capital: Monrovia (*pop:* 421,053)
Religions: Traditional beliefs, Muslim
Languages: English, many ethnic languages
Political system: Republic
Economy: Unstable
GNP per capita: US$850
Currency: Liberian dollar

Guinea-Bissau

Area: 36,126 km²
Population: 1,073,000
Capital: Bissau (*pop:* 109,214)
Religions: Traditional beliefs, Muslim
Languages: Portuguese, Creole
Political system: Republic
Economy: Subsistence farming
GNP per capita: US$240
Currency: Franc CFA

Ivory Coast

Area: 322,463 km²
Population: 14,230,000
Capital: Yamoussoukro (*pop:* 126,191)
Religions: Traditional beliefs, Muslim
Main language: French
Political system: Republic
Economy: Cash crops, timber
GNP per capita: US$690
Currency: Franc CFA

Guinea

Area: 245,857 km²
Population: 6,700,000
Capital: Conakry (*pop:* 763,000)
Religions: Muslim, Christian
Languages: French, Susu, Malinké
Political system: Republic
Economy: Cash crops
GNP per capita: US$570
Currency: Guinea franc

Burkina

Area: 274,000 km²
Population: 10,200,000
Capital: Ouagadougou (*pop:* 634,479)
Religions: Traditional beliefs, Muslim
Languages: French, Mossi, Fulani, Tuareg
Political system: Republic
Economy: Agriculture
GNP per capita: US$240
Currency: Franc CFA

Sierra Leone

Area: 71,740 km²
Population: 4,509,000
Capital: Freetown (*pop:* 469,776)
Religions: Traditional beliefs, Muslim
Languages: English, French, Krio
Political system: Republic
Economy: Subsistence farming
GNP per capita: US$200
Currency: Leone

Ghana

Area: 238,533 km²
Population: 17,453,000
Capital: Accra (*pop:* 738,498)
Religions: Traditional beliefs, Muslim
Languages: English, Twi, Fanti
Political system: Republic
Economy: Cocoa, timber, gold
GNP per capita: US$370
Currency: Cedi

See page 121 for an index to flags

Togo

Area: 56,785 km²
Population: 4,138,000
Capital: Lomé (*pop:* 366,476)
Religions: Traditional beliefs, Christian
Languages: French, Ewe
Political system: Republic
Economy: Agriculture, coffee
GNP per capita: US$330
Currency: Franc CFA

Benin

Area: 112,622 km²
Population: 5,561,000
Capital: Porto Novo (*pop:* 179,138)
Religions: Traditional beliefs, Muslim
Languages: French, Fon, Bariba, Yoruba
Political system: Republic
Economy: Subsistence farming
GNP per capita: US$380
Currency: Franc CFA

Nigeria

Area: 923,768 km²
Population: 111,721,000
Capital: Abuja (*pop:* 378,671)
Religions: Muslim, Christian
Languages: English, Hausa, Yoruba, Ibo
Political system: Republic
Economy: Oil
GNP per capita: US$260
Currency: Naira

Cameroon

Area: 475,422 km²
Population: 13,277,000
Capital: Yaoundé (*pop:* 653,670)
Religions: Traditional beliefs, Christian
Languages: French, English
Political system: Republic
Economy: Oil, timber, cocoa
GNP per capita: US$650
Currency: Franc CFA

Equatorial Guinea

Area: 28,051 km²
Population: 400,000
Capital: Malabo (*pop:* 30,418)
Religions: Roman Catholic, others
Languages: French, Spanish
Political system: Republic
Economy: Timber, cocoa, oil
GNP per capita: US$1,050
Currency: Franc CFA

São Tomé and Príncipe

Area: 964 km²
Population: 127,000
Capital: São Tomé (*pop:* 43,420)
Religions: Roman Catholic, others
Languages: Portuguese, Creole
Political system: Republic
Economy: Cocoa, coffee, palm oil
GNP per capita: US$270
Currency: Dobra

Gabon

Area: 267,668 km²
Population: 1,320,000
Capital: Libreville (*pop:* 251,000)
Religions: Roman Catholic, Protestant
Languages: French, Fang, Eshira
Political system: Republic
Economy: Oil, timber, cocoa
GNP per capita: US$4,230
Currency: Franc CFA

Congo

Area: 342,000 km²
Population: 2,590,000
Capital: Brazzaville (*pop:* 596,200)
Religions: Roman Catholic, traditional beliefs
Languages: French, Lingala, Kikongo
Political system: Republic
Economy: Oil, sugar, coffee
GNP per capita: US$660
Currency: Franc CFA

Angola

Area: 1,246,700 km²
Population: 11,072,000
Capital: Luanda (*pop:* 475,328)
Religions: Roman Catholic, Protestant
Main language: Portuguese
Political system: Republic
Economy: Oil, diamonds
GNP per capita: US$340
Currency: Readjusted kwanza

Zimbabwe

Area: 390,757 km²
Population: 11,526,000
Capital: Harare (*pop:* 1,189,103)
Religions: Christian, traditional beliefs
Languages: English, Shona, Ndebele
Political system: Republic
Economy: Self-sufficient
GNP per capita: US$750
Currency: Zimbabwe dollar

Zambia

Area: 756,618 km²
Population: 9,373,000
Capital: Lusaka (*pop:* 982,362)
Religions: Christian, traditional beliefs
Languages: English, Nyanja, Tonga, Beruba
Political system: Republic
Economy: Subsistence farming
GNP per capita: US$380
Currency: Kwacha

Mozambique

Area: 801,590 km²
Population: 17,423,000
Capital: Maputo (*pop:* 882,601)
Religions: Traditional beliefs, Christian
Main language: Portuguese
Political system: Republic
Economy: Foreign aid
GNP per capita: US$90
Currency: Metical

Tanzania

Area: 883,749 km²
Population: 30,337,000
Capital: Dodoma (*pop:* 88,474)
Religions: Traditional beliefs, Muslim
Languages: Swahili, English
Political system: Republic
Economy: Agriculture, cash crops
GNP per capita: US$210
Currency: Shilling

Namibia

Area: 824,292 km²
Population: 1,540,000
Capital: Windhoek (*pop:* 147,056)
Religions: Christian, others
Languages: English, Afrikaans, German
Political system: Republic
Economy: Uranium, diamonds
GNP per capita: US$2,220
Currency: Namibian dollar

Malawi

Area: 118,484 km²
Population: 9,788,000
Capital: Lilongwe (*pop:* 233,973)
Religions: Protestant, traditional beliefs
Languages: Chichewa, English
Political system: Republic
Economy: Tobacco, tea
GNP per capita: US$220
Currency: Kwacha

Botswana

Area: 581,730 km²
Population: 1,456,000
Capital: Gaborone (*pop:* 133,468)
Religions: Traditional beliefs, Anglican
Languages: Setswana, English
Political system: Republic
Economy: Diamonds, copper
GNP per capita: US$3,260
Currency: Pula

See page 121 for an index to flags

Lesotho

Area: 30,355 km²
Population: 2,050,000
Capital: Maseru (*pop:* 288,951)
Religions: Roman Catholic, Protestant
Languages: Sesotho, English
Political system: Constitutional monarchy
Economy: Subsistence farming
GNP per capita: US$670
Currency: Loti

Comoros

Area: 2,235 km²
Population: 653,000
Capital: Moroni (*pop:* 17,267)
Religions: Muslim, Roman Catholic
Languages: French, Arabic, Comoran
Political system: Republic
Economy: Subsistence farming
GNP per capita: US$400
Currency: Comorian franc

Swaziland

Area: 17,364 km²
Population: 908,000
Capital: Mbabane (*pop:* 38,290)
Religions: Protestant, others
Languages: Siswati, English
Political system: Absolute monarchy
Economy: Cash crops, asbestos
GNP per capita: US$1,440
Currency: Lilangeni

Madagascar

Area: 587,041 km²
Population: 14,763,000
Capital: Antananarivo (*pop:* 377,600)
Religions: Traditional beliefs, Christian
Languages: Malagasy, French
Political system: Republic
Economy: Coffee, vanilla
GNP per capita: US$250
Currency: Franc malgache

South Africa

Area: 1,221,037 km²
Population: 37,900,000
Capital: Pretoria (*pop:* 525,583)
Religions: Protestant, Roman Catholic, others
Languages: English, Afrikaans, Zulu, Xhosa
Political system: Republic
Economy: Manufacturing, agriculture
GNP per capita: US$3,400
Currency: Rand

Mauritius

Area: 2,040 km²
Population: 1,122,000
Capital: Port Louis (*pop:* 144,776)
Religions: Hindu, Roman Catholic, Muslim
Languages: Creole, English, French, Hindi
Political system: Republic
Economy: Sugar, tourism
GNP per capita: US$3,800
Currency: Mauritius rupee

AUSTRALIA AND OCEANIA

Australia

Area: 7,741,220 km²
Population: 18,054,000
Capital: Canberra (*pop:* 307,100)
Religions: Protestant, Roman Catholic
Main language: English
Political system: Constitutional monarchy
Economy: Mining, agriculture
GNP per capita: US$20,540
Currency: Australian dollar

Seychelles

Area: 455 km²
Population: 75,000
Capital: Victoria (*pop:* 24,324)
Religions: Roman Catholic, others
Languages: French, English, Creole
Political system: Republic
Economy: Tourism
GNP per capita: US$6,880
Currency: Rupee

Vanuatu

Area: 12,189 km²
Population: 165,000
Capital: Port Vila (*pop:* 26,100)
Religions: Protestant, Roman Catholic
Languages: Bislama, English, French
Political system: Republic
Economy: Copra, cocoa
GNP per capita: US$1,310
Currency: Vatu

Palau

Area: 459 km²
Population: 17,000
Capital: Koror (*pop:* 10,493)
Religions: Christian, traditional beliefs
Languages: Palauan, English
Political system: Republic
Economy: Coconuts, US aid
GNP per capita: US$2,260
Currency: US dollar

Fiji

Area: 18,274 km²
Population: 796,000
Capital: Suva (*pop:* 141,273)
Religions: Christian, Hindu, Muslim
Languages: Fijian, Hindi
Political system: Republic
Economy: Sugar, gold, timber
GNP per capita: US$2,470
Currency: Fiji dollar

Federated States of Micronesia

Area: 702 km²
Population: 105,000
Capital: Palikir
Religions: Roman Catholic, Protestant
Languages: English, Yapese, Ulithian, Woleaian
Political system: Republic
Economy: Fishing, US aid
GNP per capita: US$1,980
Currency: US dollar

Papua New Guinea

Area: 462,840 km²
Population: 4,074,000
Capital: Port Moresby (*pop:* 173,500)
Religions: Christian, others
Languages: English, Pidgin English
Political system: Constitutional monarchy
Economy: Gold, copper, oil
GNP per capita: US$940
Currency: Kina

Marshall Islands

Area: 181 km²
Population: 56,000
Capital: Dalap-Uliga-Darrit (*pop:* 20,000)
Religions: Protestant, Roman Catholic
Languages: Marshallese, English
Political system: Republic
Economy: Copra, tuna-fishing
GNP per capita: US$1,770
Currency: US dollar

Solomon Islands

Area: 28,896 km²
Population: 378,000
Capital: Honiara (*pop:* 40,000)
Religions: Christian, others
Main language: English
Political system: Constitutional monarchy
Economy: Palm oil, copra, cocoa
GNP per capita: US$900
Currency: Solomon Islands dollar

Nauru

Area: 21 km²
Population: 11,000
Capital: Nauru
Religions: Christian, others
Languages: Nauruan, English
Political system: Republic
Economy: Phosphate
GNP per capita: US$10,000
Currency: Australian dollar

See page 121 for an index to flags

Kiribati

Area: 726 km²
Population: 79,000
Capital: Tarawa (*pop:* 17,921)
Religions: Roman Catholic, Protestant
Languages: I-Kiribati, English
Political system: Republic
Economy: Coconuts, copra
GNP per capita: US$910
Currency: Australian dollar

Tuvalu

Area: 26 km²
Population: 10,000
Capital: Funafuti (*pop:* 2,856)
Religions: Protestant, others
Languages: Tuvaluan, English
Political system: Constitutional monarchy
Economy: Fishing, foreign aid
GNP per capita: US$600
Currency: Australian dollar

Samoa

Area: 2,831 km²
Population: 171,000
Capital: Apia (*pop:* 36,000)
Religions: Protestant, Roman Catholic
Languages: Samoan, English
Political system: Constitutional monarchy
Economy: Agriculture, banking
GNP per capita: US$1,150
Currency: Tala

Tonga

Area: 747 km²
Population: 98,000
Capital: Nuku'alofa (*pop:* 29,018)
Religions: Protestant, Roman Catholic
Languages: Tongan, English
Political system: Constitutional monarchy
Economy: Cash crops
GNP per capita: US$1,830
Currency: Pa'anga

New Zealand

Area: 270,534 km²
Population: 3,542,000
Capital: Wellington (*pop:* 326,900)
Religions: Protestant, Roman Catholic
Languages: English, Maori
Political system: Constitutional monarchy
Economy: Agriculture, wool
GNP per capita: US$16,480
Currency: New Zealand dollar

NORTH AND CENTRAL AMERICA

Canada

Area: 9,970,610 km²
Population: 29,606,000
Capital: Ottawa (*pop:* 1,010,288)
Religions: Roman Catholic, Protestant
Languages: English, French
Political system: Constitutional monarchy
Economy: Light industries
GNP per capita: US$19,290
Currency: Canadian dollar

United States

Area: 9,363,520 km²
Population: 263,034,000
Capital: Washington DC (*pop:* 7,051,495)
Religions: Protestant, Roman Catholic, Jewish
Languages: English, Spanish
Political system: Republic
Economy: Manufacturing, agriculture
GNP per capita: US$28,740
Currency: US dollar

Mexico

Area: 1,958,201 km²
Population: 90,487,000
Capital: Mexico City (*pop:* 15,047,685)
Religions: Roman Catholic, Protestant
Languages: Spanish, Indian languages
Political system: Republic
Economy: Oil, cash crops
GNP per capita: US$3,680
Currency: Peso

Guatemala

Area: 108,889 km²
Population: 10,621,000
Capital: Guatemala City (*pop:* 1,675,589)
Religion: Christian
Languages: Spanish, Indian languages
Political system: Republic
Economy: Agriculture, sugar
GNP per capita: US$1,500
Currency: Quetzal

Nicaragua

Area: 130,000 km²
Population: 4,539,000
Capital: Managua (*pop:* 608,020)
Religions: Roman Catholic, others
Languages: Spanish, English
Political system: Republic
Economy: coffee, sugar
GNP per capita: US$410
Currency: Córdoba

Belize

Area: 22,696 km²
Population: 217,000
Capital: Belmopan (*pop:* 44,087)
Religion: Christian
Languages: English, Spanish, Creole
Political system: Constitutional monarchy
Economy: Agriculture, tourism
GNP per capita: US$2,740
Currency: Belize dollar

Costa Rica

Area: 51,100 km²
Population: 3,333,000
Capital: San José (*pop:* 1,186,417)
Religion: Roman Catholic
Languages: Spanish, English, Creole
Political system: Republic
Economy: Agriculture, coffee
GNP per capita: US$2,640
Currency: Costa Rican colón

El Salvador

Area: 21,041 km²
Population: 5,768,000
Capital: San Salvador (*pop:* 422,570)
Religions: Roman Catholic, Protestant
Main languages: Spanish
Political system: Republic
Economy: Coffee, foreign aid
GNP per capita: US$1,810
Currency: El Salvador colón

Panama

Area: 75,517 km²
Population: 2,631,000
Capital: Panama City (*pop:* 445,902)
Religions: Roman Catholic, others
Languages: Spanish, Creole
Political system: Republic
Economy: Banking, insurance
GNP per capita: US$3,080
Currency: Balboa

Honduras

Area: 112,088 km²
Population: 5,953,000
Capital: Tegucigalpa (*pop:* 670,000)
Religions: Roman Catholic, others
Languages: Spanish, English
Political system: Republic
Economy: Bananas, coffee
GNP per capita: US$700
Currency: Lempira

Jamaica

Area: 10,990 km²
Population: 2,530,000
Capital: Kingston (*pop:* 103,962)
Religions: Christian, others
Languages: English, Creole
Political system: Constitutional monarchy
Economy: Bauxite, tourism
GNP per capita: US$1,560
Currency: Jamaican dollar

See page 121 for an index to flags

Cuba

Area: 110,861 km²
Population: 11,041,000
Capital: Havana (*pop:* 2,175,888)
Religion: Roman Catholic
Languages: Spanish, English
Political System: Republic
Economy: Sugar
GNP per capita: US$1,250
Currency: Cuban peso

Bahamas

Area: 13,878 km²
Population: 278,000
Capital: Nassau (*pop:* 172,196)
Religions: Protestant, Roman Catholic
Languages: English, Creole
Political system: Constitutional monarchy
Economy: Tourism, banking
GNP per capita: US$11,940
Currency: Bahamian dollar

Haiti

Area: 27,750 km²
Population: 7,180,000
Capital: Port-au-Prince (*pop:* 690,168)
Religions: Roman Catholic, Protestant
Languages: Creole, French
Political system: Republic
Economy: Dependent on foreign aid
GNP per capita: US$330
Currency: Gourde

Dominican Republic

Area: 48,734 km²
Population: 7,915,000
Capital: Santo Domingo (*pop:* 2,134,779)
Religions: Roman Catholic, Protestant
Main language: Spanish
Political system: Republic
Economy: Mining, sugar
GNP per capita: US$1,670
Currency: Dominican Republic peso

St Kitts and Nevis

Area: 261 km²
Population: 41,000
Capital: Basseterre (*pop:* 14,161)
Religion: Protestant
Languages: English, Creole
Political system: Constitutional monarchy
Economy: Sugar, tourism
GNP per capita: US$6,160
Currency: East Caribbean dollar

Antigua and Barbuda

Area: 442 km²
Population: 66,000
Capital: St John's (*pop:* 22,342)
Religions: Protestant, Roman Catholic
Languages: English, Creole
Political system: Constitutional monarchy
Economy: Tourism, fishing
GNP per capita: US$7,380
Currency: East Caribbean dollar

Dominica

Area: 751 km²
Population: 71,000
Capital: Roseau (*pop:* 16,243)
Religions: Roman Catholic, Protestant
Languages: English, Creole
Political system: Republic
Economy: Bananas, tourism
GNP per capita: US$3,120
Currency: East Caribbean dollar

St Lucia

Area: 622 km²
Population: 145,000
Capital: Castries (*pop:* 56,000)
Religions: Roman Catholic, others
Languages: English, Creole
Political system: Constitutional monarchy
Economy: Agriculture
GNP per capita: US$3,620
Currency: East Caribbean dollar

St Vincent and the Grenadines

Area: 338 km²
Population: 111,000
Capital: Kingstown (*pop:* 33,694)
Religions: Protestant, Roman Catholic
Languages: English, Creole
Political system: Constitutional monarchy
Economy: Agriculture
GNP per capita: US$2,500
Currency: East Caribbean dollar

Barbados

Area: 430 km²
Population: 264,000
Capital: Bridgetown (*pop:* 108,000)
Religions: Protestant, Roman Catholic
Languages: English, Creole
Political system: Constitutional monarchy
Economy: Sugar, tourism
GNP per capita: US$6,560
Currency: Barbados dollar

Trinidad and Tobago

Area: 5,130 km²
Population: 1,306,000
Capital: Port of Spain (*pop:* 50,878)
Religions: Christian, Hindu, Muslim
Main language: English
Political system: Republic
Economy: Oil, gas
GNP per capita: US$4,230
Currency: Trinidad and Tobago dollar

Grenada

Area: 344 km²
Population: 92,000
Capital: St George's (*pop:* 4,788)
Religions: Roman Catholic, Protestant
Languages: English, Creole
Political system: Constitutional monarchy
Economy: Spices, cocoa
GNP per capita: US$3000
Currency: East Caribbean dollar

SOUTH AMERICA
Colombia

Area: 1,138,914 km²
Population: 35,099,000
Capital: Bogotá (*pop:* 8,000,000)
Religions: Roman Catholic, others
Languages: Spanish, Indian languages
Political system: Republic
Economy: Coffee, coal
GNP per capita: US$2,280
Currency: Colombian peso

Venezuela

Area: 912,050 km²
Population: 21,644,000
Capital: Caracas (*pop:* 2.784,042)
Religions: Roman Catholic, Protestant
Languages: Spanish, Indian languages
Political system: Republic
Economy: Oil, coal, bauxite
GNP per capita: US$3,450
Currency: Bolívar

Guyana

Area: 214,967 km²
Population: 835,000
Capital: Georgetown (*pop:* 250,000)
Religions: Christian, Hindu, Muslim
Languages: English, Creole
Political system: Republic
Economy: Bauxite, gold
GNP per capita: US$800
Currency: Guyana dollar

Surinam

Area: 163,265 km²
Population: 423,000
Capital: Paramaribo (*pop:* 200,970)
Religions: Christian, Hindu, Muslim
Languages: Dutch, Sranang Tongo, Hindi
Political system: Republic
Economy: Aluminium, bauxite
GNP per capita: US$1,240
Currency: Surinam guilder

See page 121 for an index to flags

Ecuador

Area: 283,561 km²
Population: 11,460,000
Capital: Quito (*pop:* 1,387,887)
Religions: Roman Catholic, others
Languages: Spanish, Quechua
Political system: Republic
Economy: Bananas, oil
GNP per capita: US$1,590
Currency: Sucre

Bolivia

Area: 1,098,581 km²
Population: 7,414,000
Capital: La Paz (*pop:* 784,976)
Religions: Roman Catholic, others
Languages: Spanish, Quechua, Aymará
Political system: Republic
Economy: Mining, oil
GNP per capita: US$950
Currency: Boliviano

Peru

Area: 1,285,216 km²
Population: 23,532,000
Capital: Lima (*pop:* 6,483,901)
Religions: Roman Catholic, others
Languages: Spanish, Quechua, Aymará
Political system: Republic
Economy: Minerals, fishing
GNP per capita: US$2,460
Currency: New Sol

Paraguay

Area: 406,752 km²
Population: 4,828,000
Capital: Asuncion (*pop:* 718,690)
Religions: Roman Catholic, other
Languages: Spanish, Guaraní
Political system: Republic
Economy: Agriculture, electricity
GNP per capita: US$2,010
Currency: Guaraní

Brazil

Area: 8,547,403 km²
Population: 155,822,000
Capital: Brasilia (*pop:* 1,601,094)
Religion: Christian
Main language: Portuguese
Political system: Republic
Economy: Mining industry
GNP per capita: US$4,720
Currency: Real

Uruguay

Area: 177,414 km²
Population: 3,186,000
Capital: Montevideo (*pop:* 1,383,660)
Religions: Roman Catholic, Protestant, Jewish
Main language: Spanish
Political system: Republic
Economy: Agriculture, livestock
GNP per capita: US$6,020
Currency: New Uruguayan peso

Chile

Area: 756,626 km²
Population: 14,210,000
Capital: Santiago (*pop:* 5,257,937)
Religions: Roman Catholic, Protestant
Languages: Spanish, Indian languages
Political system: Republic
Economy: Copper, wine
GNP per capita: US$5,020
Currency: Chilean peso

Argentina

Area: 2,780,400 km²
Population: 34,587,000
Capital: Buenos Aires (*pop:* 10,686,163)
Religions: Roman Catholic, Jewish, others
Languages: Spanish, English
Political system: Republic
Economy: Beef, wheat
GNP per capita: US$8,570
Currency: Peso

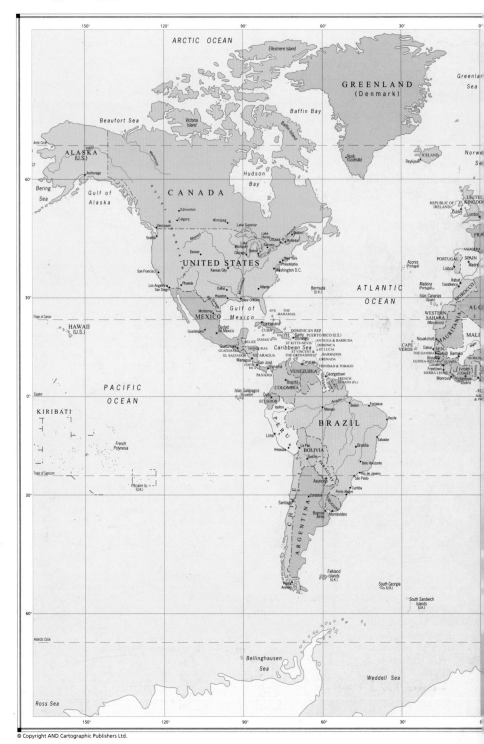

World

Equatorial Scale 1 : 154 000 000

0   1000   2000   3000   4000 km
0   1000   2000 miles

ARCTIC OCEAN

Ellesmere Island

GREENLAND
(Denmark)

Greenland
Sea

Baffin Bay

Beaufort Sea

Victoria
Island

Baffin Island

Nuuk
(Godthåb)

ICELAND

Norwe
Se

Arctic Circle

ALASKA
(U.S.)

Anchorage

Reykjavík

Hudson
Bay

UNITED
KINGDO

Bering
Sea

Gulf of
Alaska

CANADA

Edmonton
Calgary

REPUBLIC OF
IRELAND

London

60°

Vancouver
Seattle

Winnipeg

Ottawa   Montreal

Lake Superior

Lake
Huron

FRA

Denver

Missouri

Lake
Michigan

Chicago   Detroit

Toronto

New York
Philadelphia
Washington D.C.

Açores
(Portugal)

PORTUGAL   SPAIN

ANDORRA

San Francisco

UNITED STATES

Kansas City

Atlanta

Bermuda
(U.K.)

ATLANTIC

Lisboa

Madrid

Los Angeles
San Diego

Phoenix

Houston
Dallas

New Orleans

OCEAN

Madeira
(Portugal)

Casablanca

Rabat

MOROCCO

30°

Tropic of Cancer

HAWAII
(U.S.)

Monterrey

Ciudad
de Mexico

MEXICO

Gulf of
Mexico

THE
BAHAMAS

La Habana

CUBA

Islas Canarias
(Spain)

WESTERN
SAHARA
(Morocco)

ALC
S

Guadalajara

BELIZE

DOMINICAN REP.
Santo
Domingo   PUERTO RICO (U.S.)

HAITI

JAMAICA

ST KITTS-NEVIS

ANTIGUA & BARBUDA
DOMINICA
ST LUCIA

Nouakchott

CAPE
VERDE

Dakar

MAURITANIA

MALI

SEN

GUATEMALA   HONDURAS

Caribbean Sea

BARBADOS

THE GAMBIA

Banjul

BURKIN

EL SALVADOR

NICARAGUA

ST VINCENT &
THE GRENADINES

GRENADA

GUINEA-BISSAU

Conakry

GUINEA

Bissau

San José

Managua

TRINIDAD & TOBAGO

Freetown

IVORY
COAST

PACIFIC

COSTA
RICA

PANAMA

VENEZUELA

Caracas

Georgetown

FRENCH
GUIANA (Fr.)

SIERRA LEONE

Monrovia

Yamoussoukro

EQ
GH

KIRIBATI

OCEAN

Bogotá

COLOMBIA

Islas Galápagos
(Ecuador)

0°

Equator

ECUADOR

Iquitos

Manaus

Belém

Fortaleza

French
Polynesia

PERU

Lima

BRAZIL

Recife

Tropic of Capricorn

La Paz

BOLIVIA

Arequipa

Sucre

Brasília

Salvador

Belo Horizonte

Pitcairn Is.
(U.K.)

Asunción

PARAGUAY

Rio de Janeiro

São Paulo

Curitiba

30°

Córdoba

Santiago

URUGUAY

Porto Alegre

CHILE

ARGENTINA

Buenos
Aires

Montevideo

Falkland
Islands
(U.K.)

South Georgia
(U.K.)

Punta
Arenas

South Sandwich
Islands
(U.K.)

60°

Antarctic Circle

Bellinghausen
Sea

Weddell Sea

Ross Sea

150°   120°   90°   60°   30°

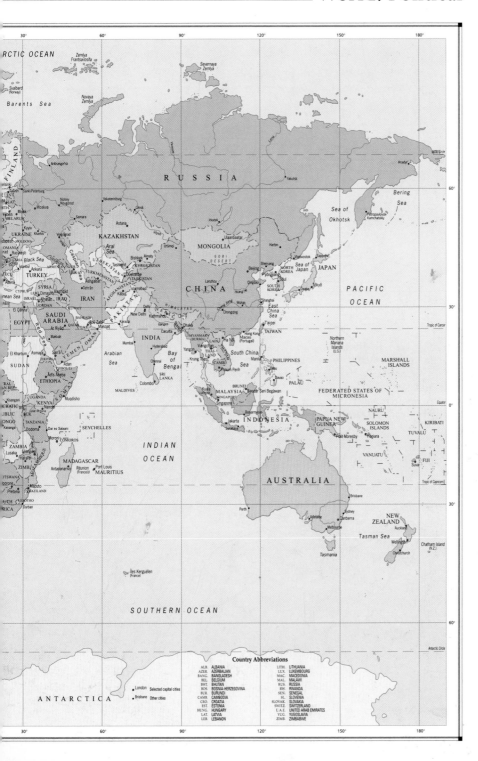

Country Abbreviations

ALB.	ALBANIA	LITH.	LITHUANIA
AZER.	AZERBAIJAN	LUX.	LUXEMBOURG
BANG.	BANGLADESH	MAC.	MACEDONIA
BEL.	BELGIUM	MAL.	MALAWI
BHT.	BHUTAN	RUS.	RUSSIA
BOS.	BOSNIA-HERZEGOVINA	RW.	RWANDA
BUR.	BURUNDI	SEN.	SENEGAL
CAMB.	CAMBODIA	SL.	SLOVENIA
CRO.	CROATIA	SLOVAK.	SLOVAKIA
EST.	ESTONIA	SWITZ.	SWITZERLAND
HUNG.	HUNGARY	U.A.E.	UNITED ARAB EMIRATES
LAT.	LATVIA	YUG.	YUGOSLAVIA
LEB.	LEBANON	ZIMB.	ZIMBABWE

London ● Selected capital cities

Brisbane ● Other cities

Scale 1 : 27 700 000

| 0 | 250 | 500 | 750 | 1000 km |

| 0 | 100 | 200 | 300 | 400 | 500 miles |

© Copyright AND Cartographic Publishers Ltd.

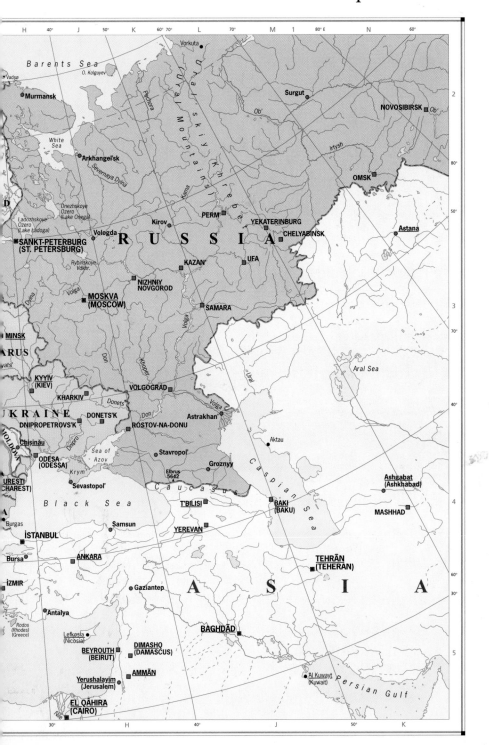

Barents Sea

Vorkuta

O. Kolguyev

Vadsø

Murmansk

Surgut

NOVOSIBIRSK

Ob'

Ob'

White
Sea

Arkhangel'sk

Severnaya Dvina

Irtysh

OMSK

D

Onezhskoye
Ozero
(Lake Onega)

Kirov

PERM'

YEKATERINBURG

Astana

Ladozhskoye
Ozero
(Lake Ladoga)

Vologda

R U S S I A

CHELYABINSK

SANKT-PETERBURG
(ST. PETERSBURG)

Rybinskoye
Vdkhr.

KAZAN'

UFA

Pechora

Kama

NIZHNIY
NOVGOROD

Volga

MINSK

MOSKVA
(MOSCOW)

SAMARA

Volga

ARUS

Don

Khoper

Aral Sea

vats'

KYYIV
(KIEV)

VOLGOGRAD

Ural

KHARKIV

Donets

Dnipro

Volga

KRAINE

DONETS'K

Don

Astrakhan'

DNIPROPETROVS'K

ROSTOV-NA-DONU

MOLDOVA

Chişinău

Krym

Sea of
Azov

Stavropol'

Aktau

ODESA
(ODESSA)

Ashgabat
(Ashkhabad)

URESTI
HAREST)

Sevastopol'

Elbrus
5642

Grozny

Caspian Sea

A

Burgas

Black Sea

Caucasus

T'BILISI

BAKI
(BAKU)

MASHHAD

İSTANBUL

Samsun

YEREVAN

Bursa

ANKARA

İZMİR

Gaziantep

A S I A

TEHRĀN
(TEHERAN)

Antalya

Rodos
(Rhodes)
(Greece)

Lefkoşia
(Nicosia)

BAGHDĀD

BEYROUTH
(BEIRUT)

DIMASHQ
(DAMASCUS)

AMMĀN

Yerushalayim
(Jerusalem)

Al Kuwayt
(Kuwait)

Persian Gulf

EL QÁHIRA
(CAIRO)

Nile

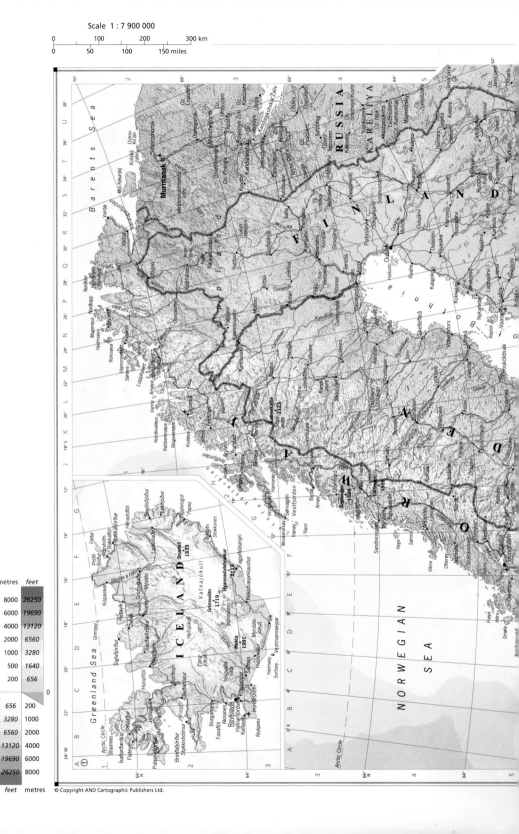

Scale 1 : 7 900 000

| 0 | 100 | 200 | 300 km |

| 0 | 50 | 100 | 150 miles |

metres	feet
8000	26250
6000	19690
4000	13120
2000	6560
1000	3280
500	1640
200	656
0	0
656	200
3280	1000
6560	2000
13120	4000
19690	6000
26250	8000

feet   metres

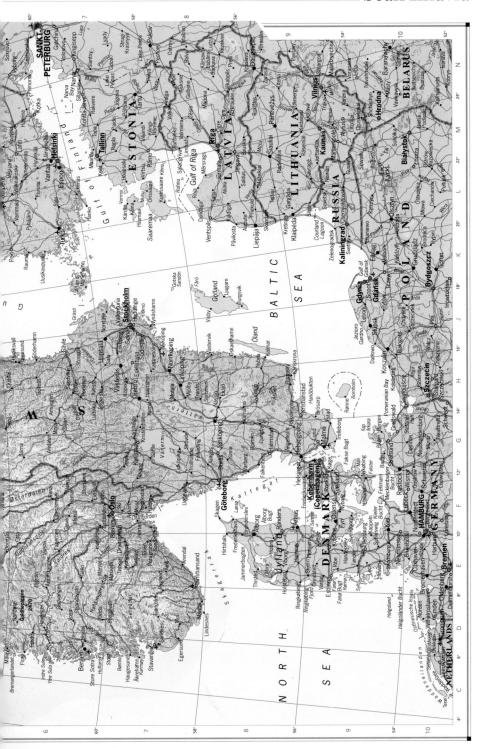

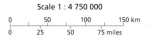

Scale 1 : 4 750 000

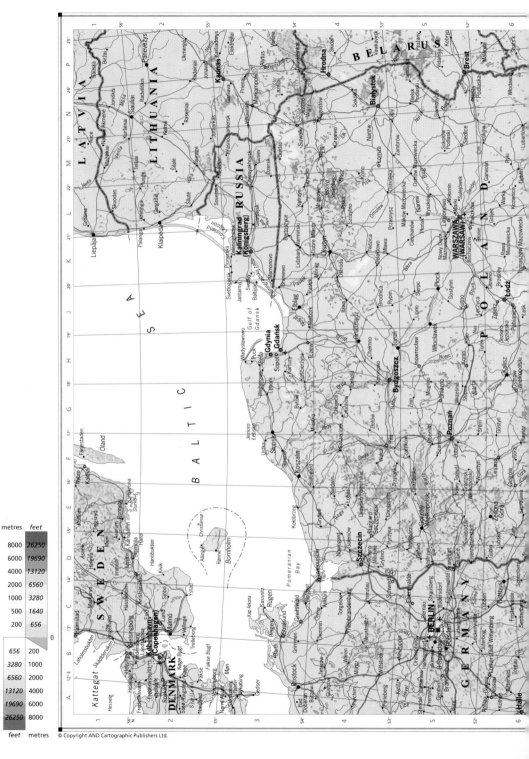

© Copyright AND Cartographic Publishers Ltd.

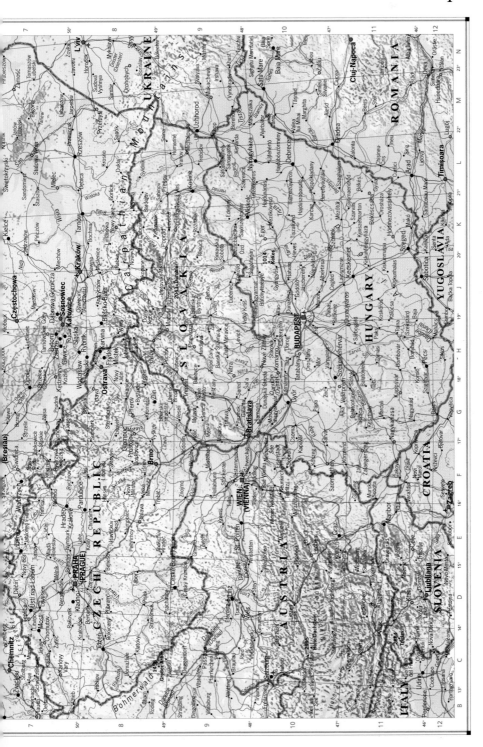

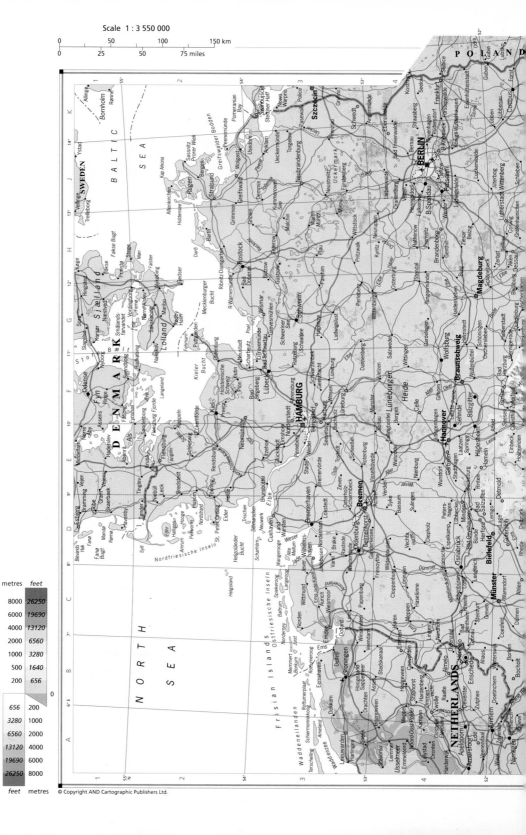

Europe

Scale 1 : 3 550 000

© Copyright AND Cartographic Publishers Ltd.

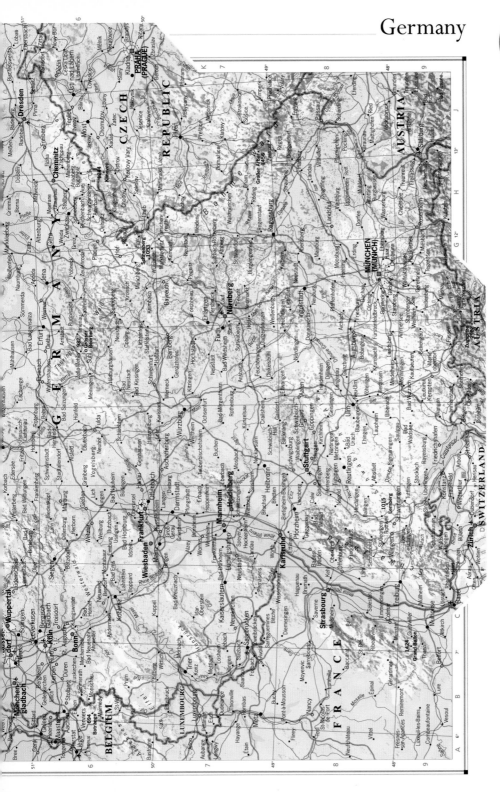

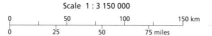

© Copyright AND Cartographic Publishers Ltd.

Benelux

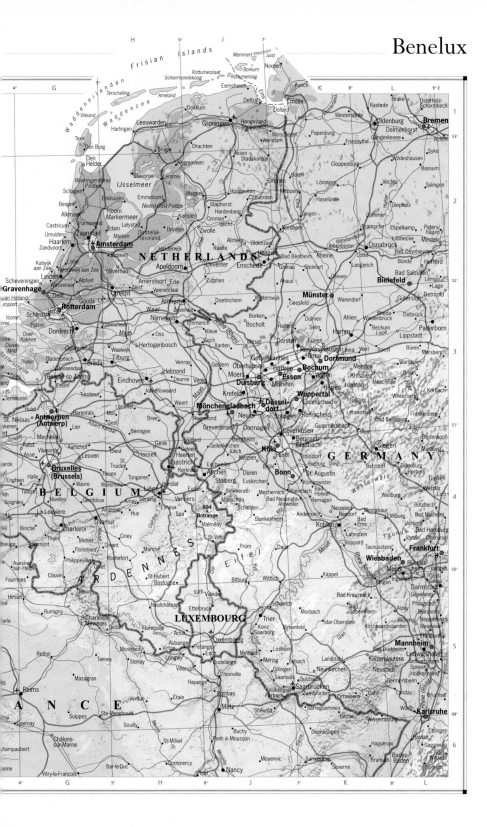

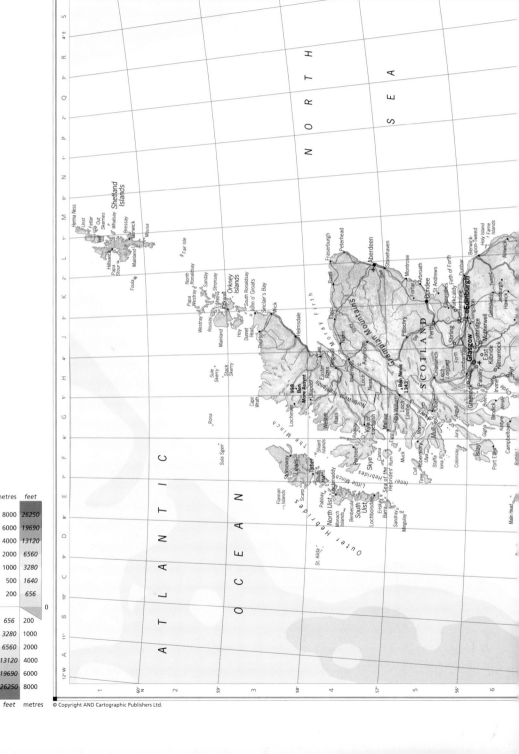

Europe

Scale 1 : 4 750 000

0 — 50 — 100 — 150 km

0 — 25 — 50 — 75 miles

metres	feet
8000	26250
6000	19690
4000	13120
2000	6560
1000	3280
500	1640
200	656
0	0
656	200
3280	1000
6560	2000
13120	4000
19690	6000
26250	8000

feet   metres

NORTH SEA

ATLANTIC OCEAN

The Minch

SCOTLAND

Grampian Mountains

Shetland Islands

Orkney Islands

Outer Hebrides

Inner Hebrides

Edinburgh
Glasgow
Aberdeen
Dundee

Ben Nevis 1343

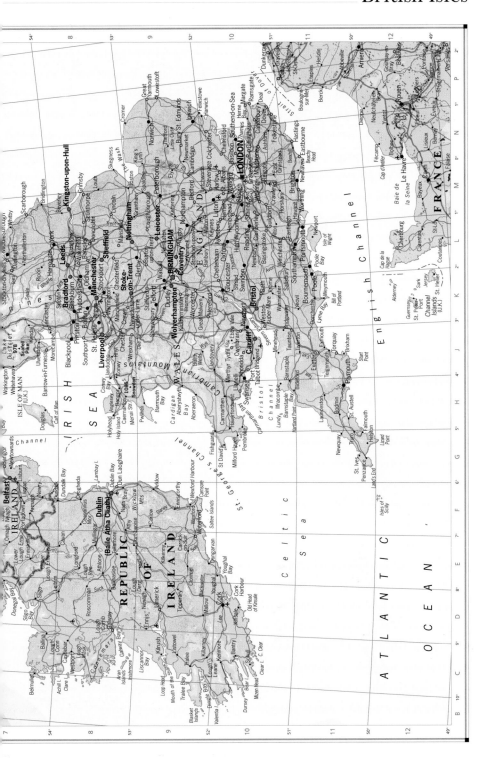

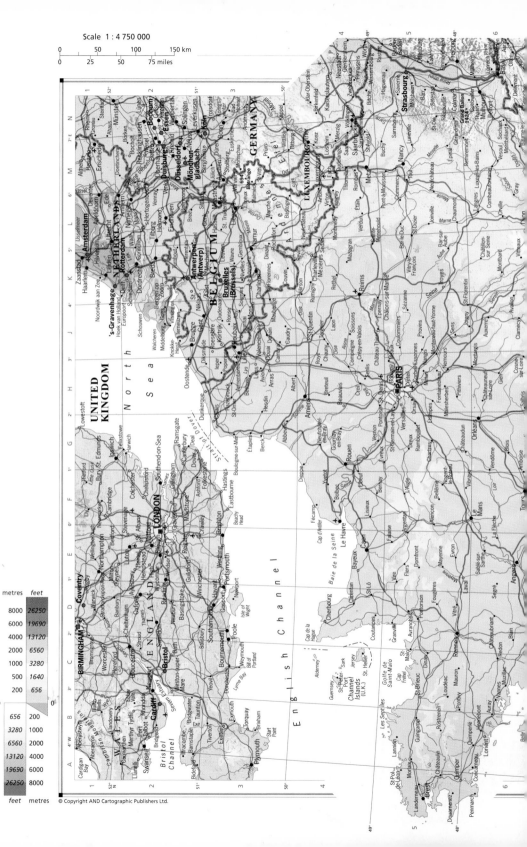

Europe

Scale 1 : 4 750 000

metres	feet
8000	26250
6000	19690
4000	13120
2000	6560
1000	3280
500	1640
200	656
0	
656	200
3280	1000
6560	2000
13120	4000
19690	6000
26250	8000
feet	metres

© Copyright AND Cartographic Publishers Ltd.

France

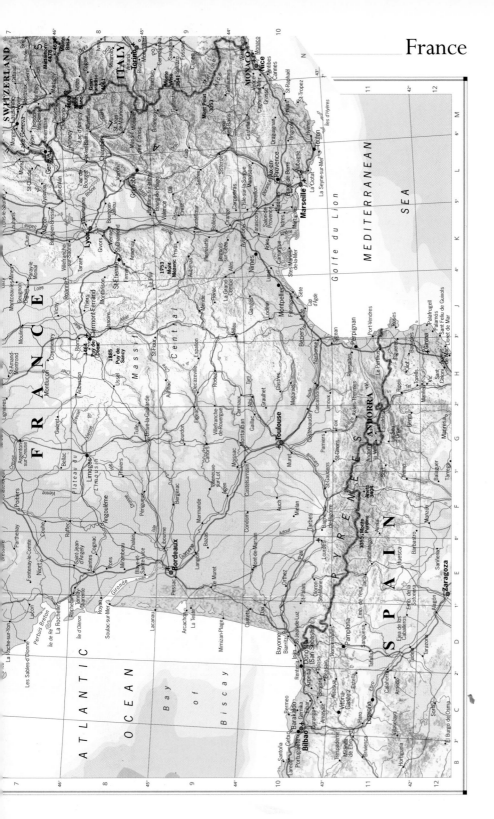

Europe

Scale 1 : 4 750 000

0   50   100 km
0   25   50 miles

© Copyright AND Cartographic Publishers Ltd.

metres / *feet*

metres	feet
8000	*26250*
6000	*19690*
4000	*13120*
2000	*6560*
1000	*3280*
500	*1640*
200	*656*
0	0
656	200
3280	1000
6560	2000
13120	4000
19690	6000
26250	8000

feet metres

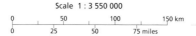

Scale 1 : 3 550 000

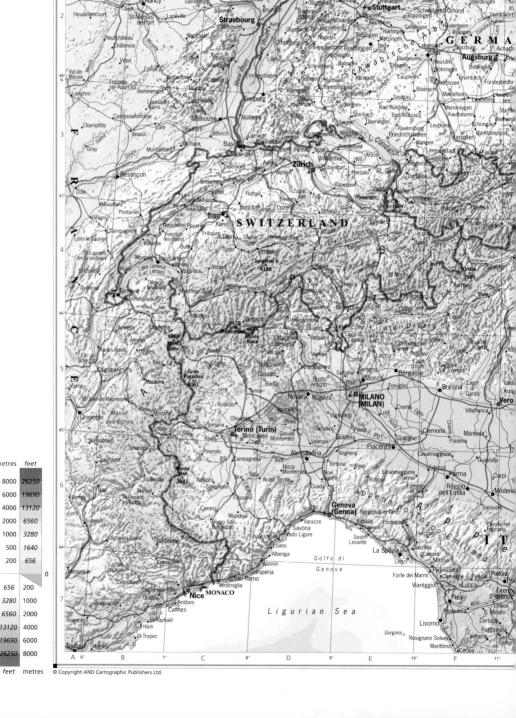

© Copyright AND Cartographic Publishers Ltd.

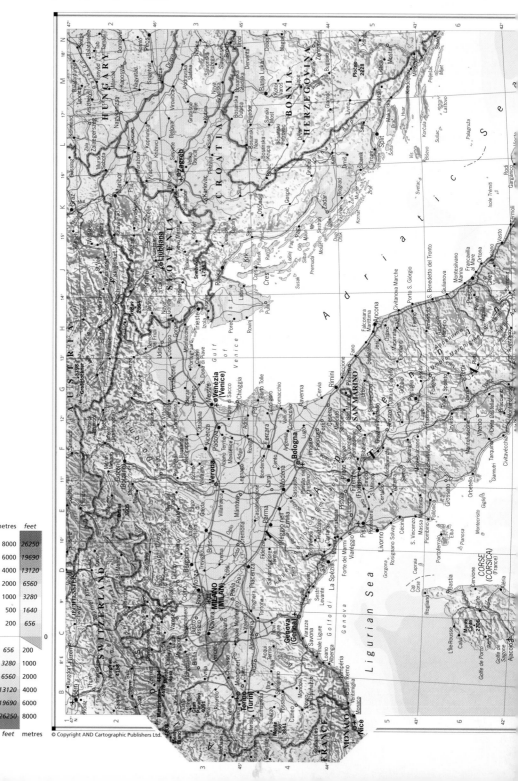

Scale 1 : 4 750 000

metres	feet
8000	26250
6000	19690
4000	13120
2000	6560
1000	3280
500	1640
200	656
0	0
656	200
3280	1000
6560	2000
13120	4000
19690	6000
26250	8000
feet	*metres*

© Copyright AND Cartographic Publishers Ltd.

Italy

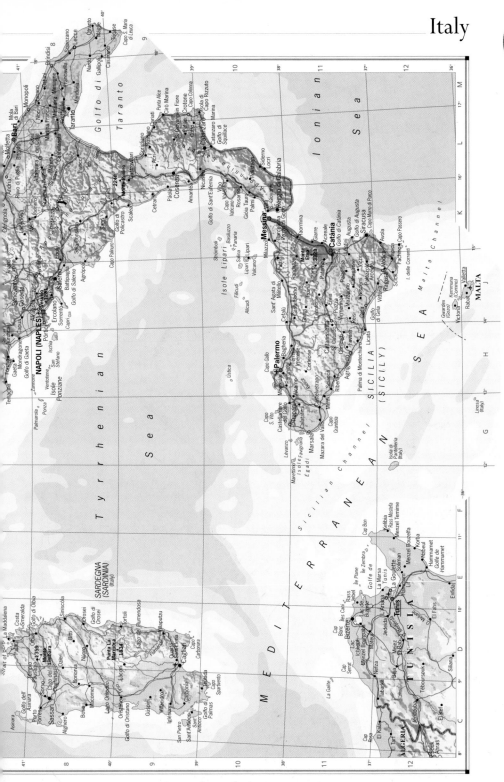

Europe

© Copyright AND Cartographic Publishers Ltd.

Scale 1 : 4 750 000

0   50   100   150 km
0   25   50   75 miles

Europe

metres	feet
8000	26250
6000	19690
4000	13120
2000	6560
1000	3280
500	1640
200	656
0	0
656	200
3280	1000
6560	2000
13120	4000
19690	6000
26250	8000
feet	metres

© Copyright AND Cartographic Publishers Ltd.

54

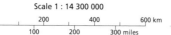

Europe

Scale 1 : 14 300 000

56

© Copyright AND Cartographic Publishers Ltd.

metres	feet
8000	26250
6000	19690
4000	13120
2000	6560
1000	3280
500	1640
200	656
0	0

feet	metres
656	200
3280	1000
6560	2000
13120	4000
19690	6000
26250	8000

feet   metres

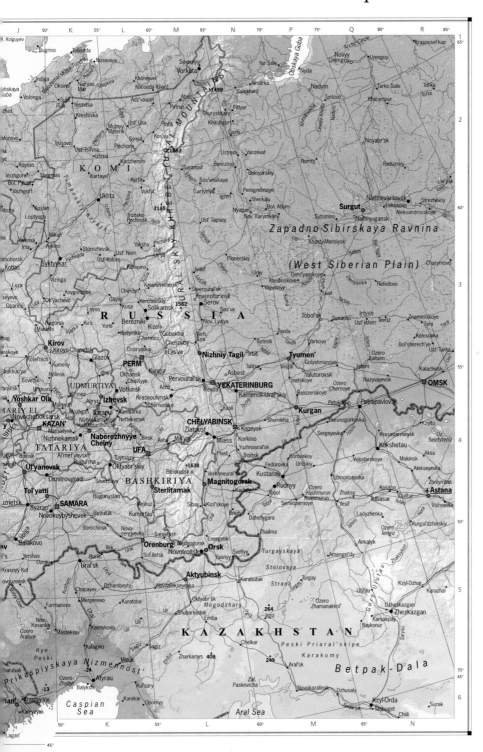

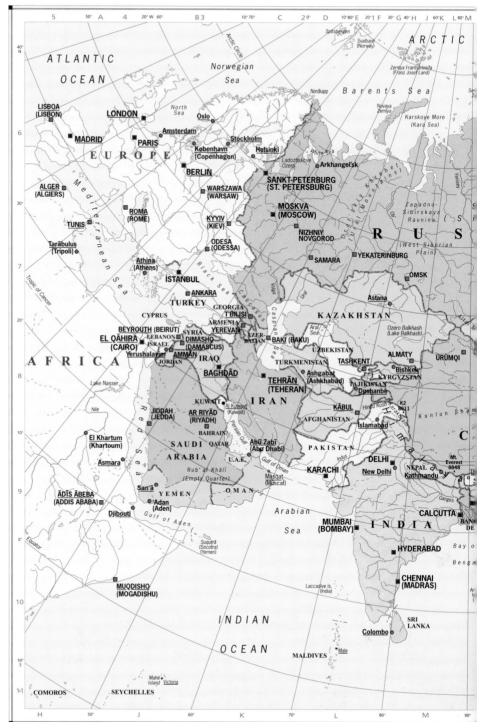

Asia

Scale 1 : 45 100 000

0   500   1000   1500   2000 km
0   500   1000 miles

© Copyright AND Cartographic Publishers Ltd.

58

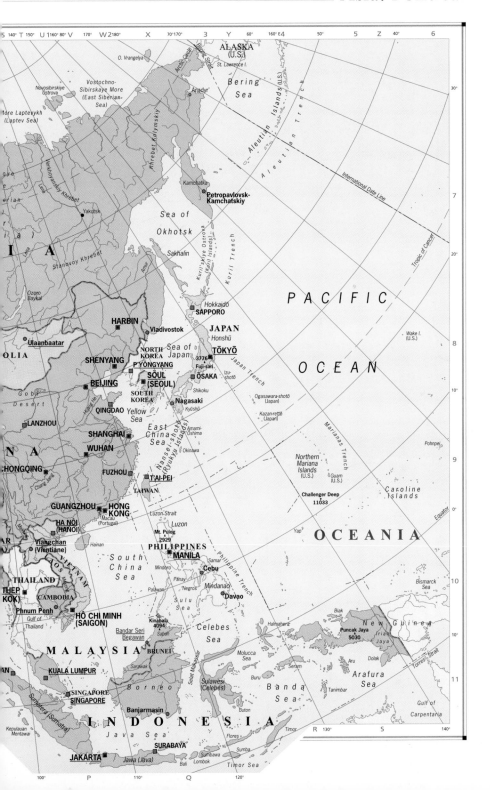

ALASKA
(U.S.)

St. Lawrence I.

O. Vrangelya

Novosibirskiye
Ostrova

Vostochno-
Sibirskoye More
(East Siberian
Sea)

Bering
Sea

Anadyr'

More Laptevykh
(Laptev Sea)

Arctic Circle

Bering Strait

Khrebet Kulymskiy

Aleutian Trench

30°

International Date Line

Verkhoyanskiy Khrebet

Lena

Kamchatka

7

Yakutsk

Petropavlovsk-
Kamchatskiy

Sea of
Okhotsk

Tropic of Cancer

20°

I A

Stanovoy Khrebet

Amur

Sakhalin

Kuril Trench

Ozero
Baykal

Kuril'skiye Ostrova
(Kuril Islands)

HARBIN

Vladivostok

Hokkaidō
SAPPORO

JAPAN
Honshū

Wake I.
(U.S.)

8

Ulaanbaatar

OLIA

SHENYANG

NORTH
KOREA
P'YŎNGYANG

Sea of
Japan

3776
TŌKYŌ
Fuji-san

Japan Trench

BEIJING

SŎUL
(SEOUL)

ŌSAKA

Izu-
shotō

10°

SOUTH
KOREA

Shikoku

Gobi
Desert

QINGDAO

Nagasaki

Kyūshū

Ogasawara-shotō
(Japan)

LANZHOU

Yellow
Sea

Amami-
Ōshima

Kazan-rettō
(Japan)

SHANGHAI

East
China
Sea

N A

WUHAN

Okinawa

Marianas Trench

Pohnpei

9

CHONGQING

FUZHOU

Nansei-shotō
(Ryukyu Islands)

Northern
Mariana
Islands
(U.S.)

Caroline
Islands

Chang Jiang

T'AI-PEI

Guam
(U.S.)

TAIWAN

GUANGZHOU

HONG
KONG

Challenger Deep
11033

Equator

0°

Macau
(Portugal)

Luzon Strait

HA NỘI
(HANOI)

Luzon

Yap

OCEANIA

AR

Viangchan
(Vientiane)

Hainan

Mt. Pulog
2929

Philippine Trench

VIETNAM

South
China
Sea

PHILIPPINES
MANILA

Samar

Bismarck
Sea

THAILAND

THEP
KOK)

LAOS

Cebu

Mindoro

Panay

Negros

Mindanao

10°

CAMBODIA

Davao

Phnum Penh

Gulf of
Thailand

HỒ CHI MINH
(SAIGON)

Palawan

Sulu
Sea

Biak

New Guinea

G.
Kinabalu
4094

Celebes
Sea

Halmahera

Puncak Jaya
5030

Irian
Jaya

MALAYSIA

Bandar Seri
Begawan

BRUNEI

Sabah

Aru

Dolak

Torres Strait

10°

KUALA LUMPUR

Sarawak

Molucca
Sea

Seram

Buru

Arafura
Sea

AN

Borneo

SINGAPORE
SINGAPORE

Selat Makassar

Sulawesi
(Celebes)

Banda
Sea

Tanimbar

Gulf of
Carpentaria

Sumatera (Sumatra)

Banjarmasin

Buton

11

Kepulauan
Mentawai

I N D O N E S I A

Java Sea

Timor

Flores

Sumbawa

Sumba

Timor Sea

140°

JAKARTA

SURABAYA

Jawa (Java)

Bali

Lombok

PACIFIC

OCEAN

59

Asia

Scale 1 : 18 900 000

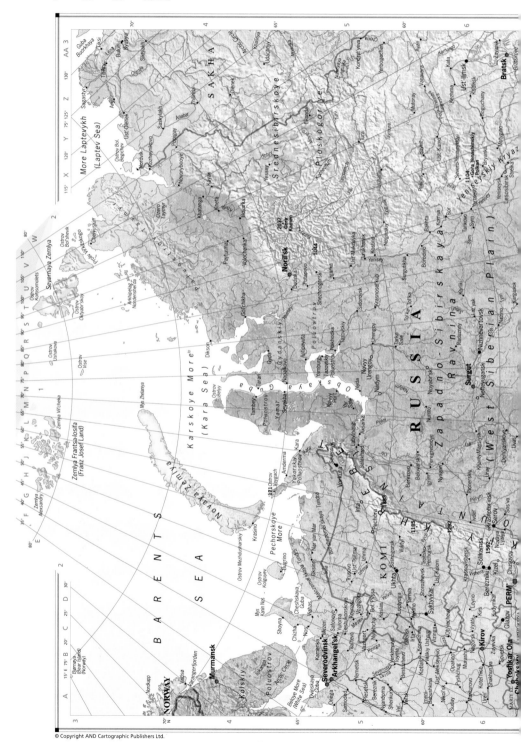

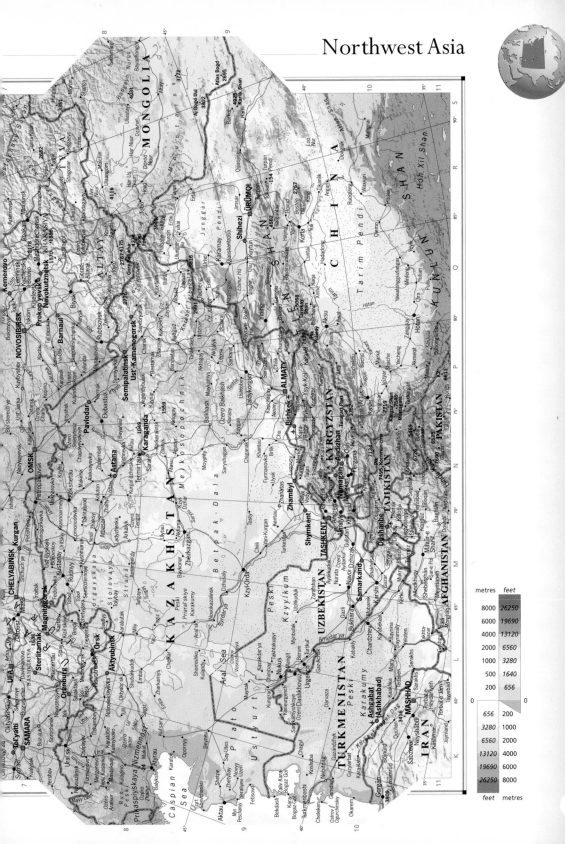

61

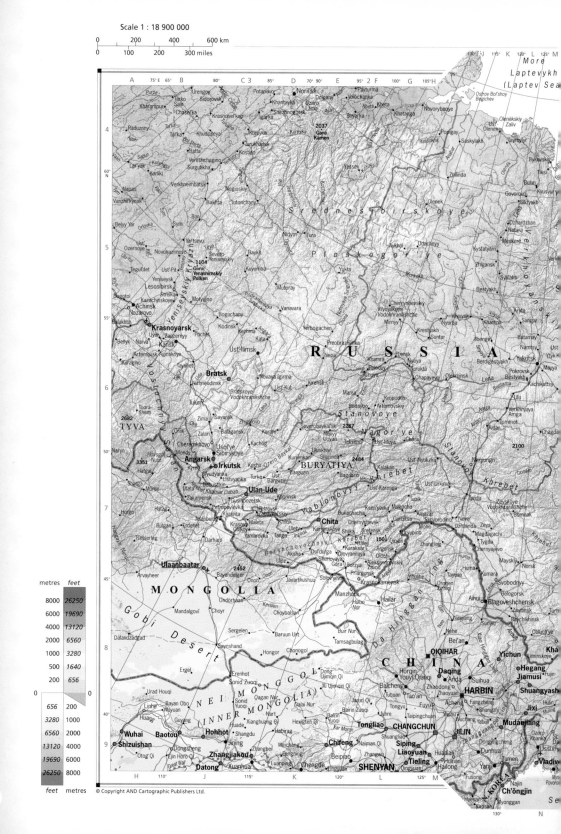

Asia

Scale 1 : 18 900 000

0	200	400	600 km
0	100	200	300 miles

metres / feet

metres	feet
8000	26250
6000	19690
4000	13120
2000	6560
1000	3280
500	1640
200	656
0	0
656	200
3280	1000
6560	2000
13120	4000
19690	6000
26250	8000
feet	metres

62

Scale 1 : 15 900 000

0   200   400   600 km

0   100   200   300 miles

metres	feet
8000	26250
6000	19690
4000	13120
2000	6560
1000	3280
500	1640
200	656
0	0
656	200
3280	1000
6560	2000
13120	4000
19690	6000
26250	8000
feet	*metres*

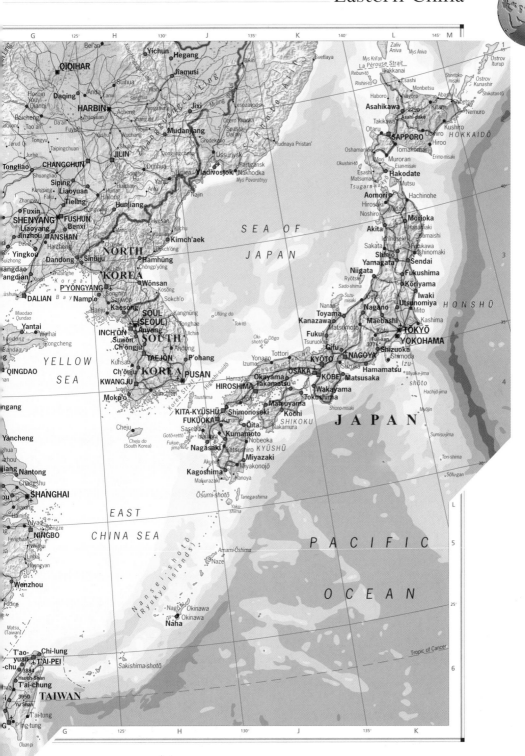

Asia

Scale 1 : 7 900 000

© Copyright AND Cartographic Publishers Ltd.

Asia

Scale 1 : 15 900 000

```
0        200       400       600 km
0    100      200       300 miles
```

metres	feet
8000	26250
6000	19690
4000	13120
2000	6560
1000	3280
500	1640
200	656
0	0
656	200
3280	1000
6560	2000
13120	4000
19690	6000
26250	8000

feet | metres

© Copyright AND Cartographic Publishers Ltd.

BHUTAN

INDIA

BANGLADESH
CHITTAGONG

MYANMAR
(BURMA)

MANDALAY

Bay of
Bengal

Mt. Victoria 3053

YANGON
(RANGOON)

Gulf of
Martaban

Andaman
Islands
(India)

Andaman
Sea

Nicobar Islands
(India)

Ten Degree Channel

INDIAN
OCEAN

SUMATERA
(SUMATRA)
Gunung Leuser 3145

MEDAN

KUALA LUMPUR

INDONESIA

SINGAPORE
SINGAPORE

Johor Bahru

CHINA

KUNMING

GUIYANG

Nanning

Pingxiang

HA NỘI
(HANOI)

HAI PHONG

LAOS

Viangchan
(Vientiane)

THAILAND

KRUNG THEP
(BANGKOK)

Gulf
of
Thailand

VIETNAM

Huế

Da Nẵng

CAMBODIA

Buôn Mê
Thuột

Nha

Phnum Penh

HỒ CHI MINH
(SAIGON)

Mouths of
the Mekong

MALA

Malay
Peninsula

Strait of Malacca

Kepulauan
Anambas
(Indonesia)

Kepulauan
Natuna

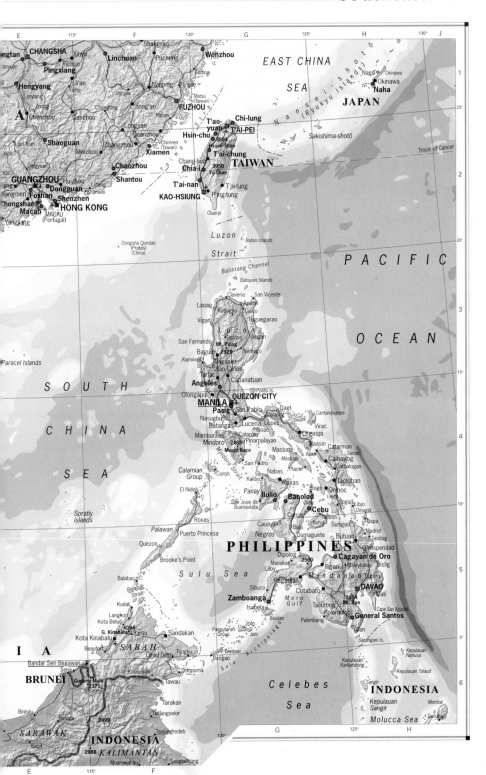

EAST CHINA

SEA

JAPAN

Nansei-shotō (Ryukyu Islands)

Naga   Okinawa

Naha

CHANGSHA   Xinyu   **Wenzhou**

anyuan   **Linchuan**   Pucheng   Shangrao

Pingxiang   Nanping   Yinde   Fuding

Hengyang   Ji'an   Jiangle

Leiyang   Changting   Yong'an   Putian   Matsu (Taiwan)

Zixing   **FUZHOU**   T'ao-   Chi-lung

A   Chenzhou   Ganzhou   Longyan   Quanzhou   Hsin-chu   yuan   **T'AI-PEI**

3884

Shaoguan   Meizhou   Zhangzhou   Xiamen   Chinmen (Taiwan)   Hsueh-Shan

Lian Xian   Qingyuan   T'ai-chung

Xian   Chang-hua   **TAIWAN**

GUANGZHOU   Huizhou   **Chaozhou**   Chia-i   3950   Yu Shan

jiangmen   Jieyang   Shanwei   **Shantou**   **TAIWAN**

Foshan   **Dongguan**   T'ai-nan   T'ai-tung

hongshan   **Shenzhen**   **KAO-HSIUNG**   P'ing-tung

Macau   **HONG KONG**   Oluanpi

MACAU (Portugal)

Yangjiang

Luzon   Batan Islands

Dongsha Qundao (Pratas) (China)   Strait

Balintang Channel

Babuyan Islands

Claveria   San Vicente

PACIFIC

Parcel Islands   Laoag   Kabugao   Aparri   Lasito

Vigan   Tuguegarao

San Fernando   Bontoc   Ilagan

S   Baguio   Mt. Pulog   Santiago   OCEAN

O   Alaminos   2929

U   Agupan   San Carlos

T   Tarlac   Cabanatuan

H   **Angeles**   Polillo Is.

Olongapo   **QUEZON CITY**

C   **MANILA**   San Pablo   Daet   Cantanduanes

Pasig   Calauag

H   Nasugbu   Lucena   Lopez   Virac

I   Batangas   Boac   **Legaspi**

N   Mamburao   Calapan   Pinamalayan   Maasin   Catarman

A   Mindoro   2488   Masbate   Allen   Samar

Mount Baco   San Pedro   Masbate   Caibayog

Calamian   Nabas   Catbalogan

S   Group   Coron   Kalibo   Place   Tacloban

E   El Nido   Roxas   Bogo   Ormoc

A   **Panay**   **Iloilo**   Leyte   Sogod   Libjo

San Jose de   **Bacolod**   Cebu   Dinagat

Roxas   Buenavista   **Cebu**   Talibon   Dapa

Carcar   Bohol   Surigao   Madrid

Spratly   Palawan   Cauayan   Bais   Tandag

Islands   Puerto Princesa   **Negros**   Dumaguete   Butuan   Prosperidad

Quezon   **PHILIPPINES**   Bislig

Dipolog   2560   **Cagayan de Oro**

Brooke's Point   Manukan   Iligan   Malaybalay   Bislig

S u l u S e a   Liloy   M i n d a n a o   Tagum

Pagadian   **DAVAO**

Sibuco   Cotabato   2954   **DAVAO**

Balabac   Kudat   Isabela   Tacurong   Mt. Apo

Balabac   Langkon   M o r o   Polomolok

Strait   **Zamboanga**   G u l f   **General Santos**

Kota Belud   4094   Isabela   Palimbang

G. Kinabalu   Basilan   Gian   Cape San Agustin

Kota Kinabalu   Ranau   Sandakan   Jolo   Pangutaran   Sarangani Is.

Beaufort   **S A B A H**   Tungku   Group   Bongao   Enniwitawi   Sangir   Kepulauan

I   A   Lahad Datu   Jolo   S u l u A r c h i p e l a g o   Nanusa

Bandar Seri Begawan   Kalabakan   Kepulauan

Seria   Semporna   Karkaralong

BRUNEI   Gunung Mulu   Tawau   Kepulauan Talaud

2371   Bareo   Tarakan   **INDONESIA**

Bintulu   C e l e b e s   Sangir

Belaga   2499   Tanjungredeb   S e a   Kepulauan   Morotai

S A R A W A K   Tanjungselor   Sangir   Daruba

INDONESIA   Molucca Sea

2988   **KALIMANTAN**   Sangkulirang

Muarawahau

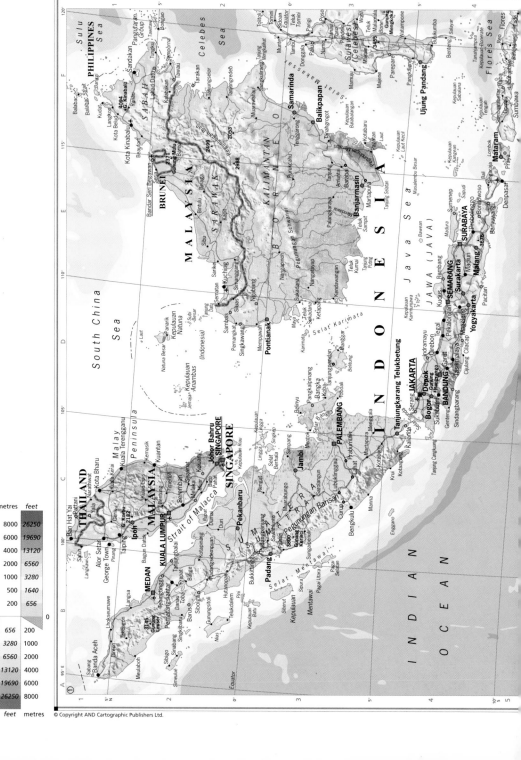

Scale 1 : 15 900 000

metres	feet
8000	26250
6000	19690
4000	13120
2000	6560
1000	3280
500	1640
200	656
0	0
656	200
3280	1000
6560	2000
13120	4000
19690	6000
26250	8000

feet metres

© Copyright AND Cartographic Publishers Ltd.

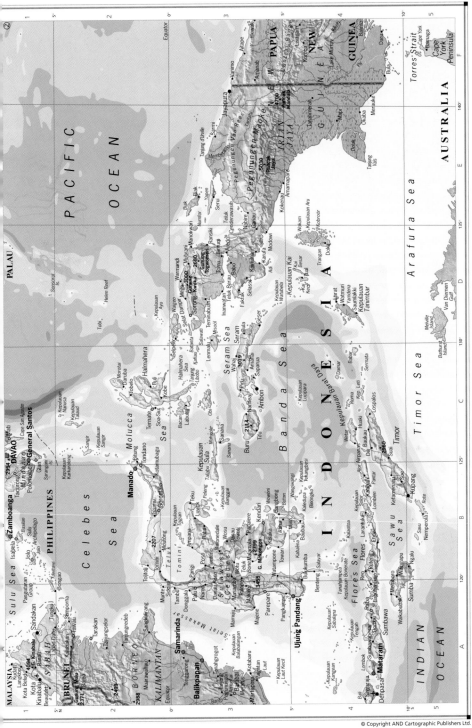

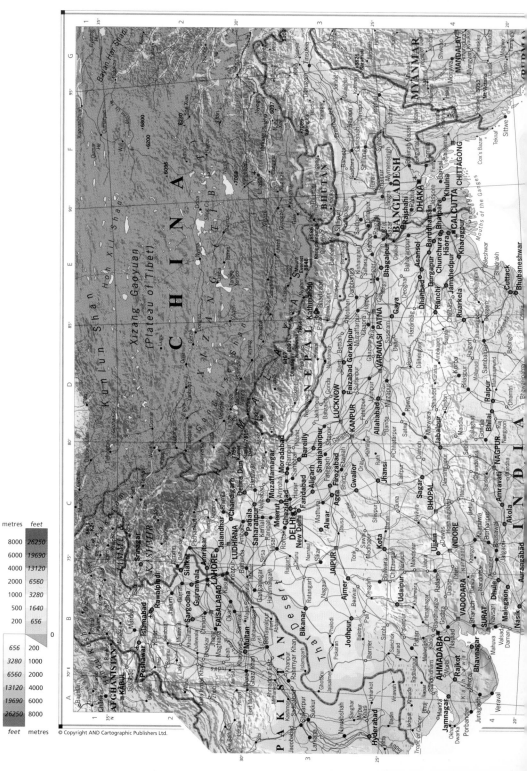

Asia

Scale 1 : 15 900 000

| 0 | 200 | 400 | 600 km |
| 0 | 100 | 200 | 300 miles |

metres	feet
8000	26250
6000	19690
4000	13120
2000	6560
1000	3280
500	1640
200	656
0	0

feet	metres
656	200
3280	1000
6560	2000
13120	4000
19690	6000
26250	8000

feet   metres

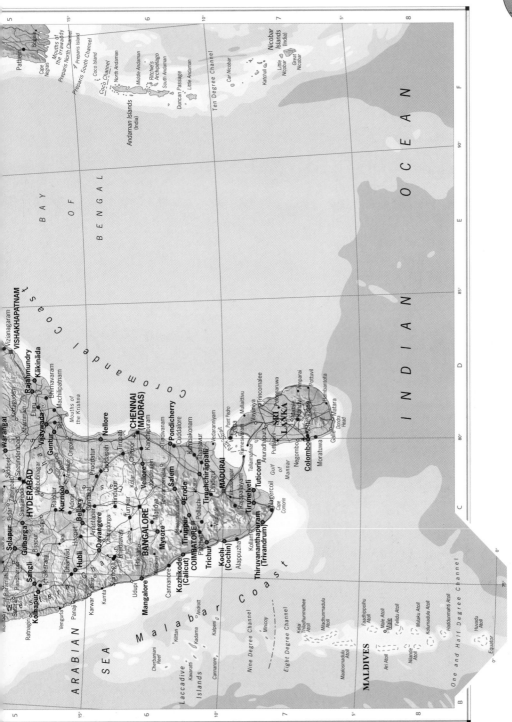

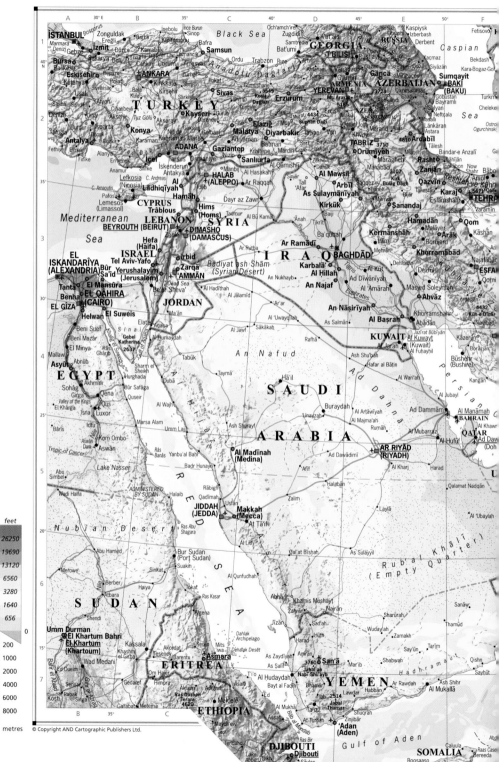

Asia

Scale   1 : 17 400 000

| 0 | 200 | 400 | 600 km |
| 0 | 100 | 200 | 300 miles |

metres	feet
8000	26250
6000	19690
4000	13120
2000	6560
1000	3280
500	1640
200	656
0	0
656	200
3280	1000
6560	2000
13120	4000
19690	6000
26250	8000

feet   metres

© Copyright AND Cartographic Publishers Ltd.

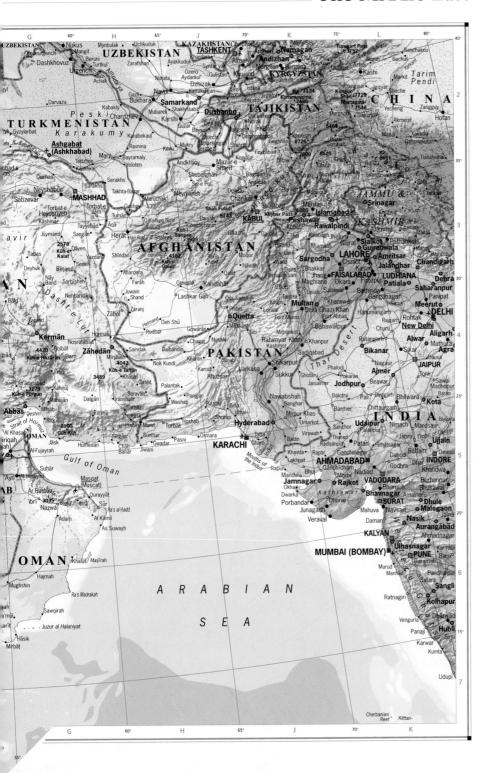

Scale 1 : 7 900 000

0		100		200		300 km
0	50		100		150 km	

metres	feet
8000	26250
6000	19690
4000	13120
2000	6560
1000	3280
500	1640
200	656
0	0
656	200
3280	1000
6560	2000
13120	4000
19690	6000
26250	8000
feet	metres

Krasnodar • Ust'-Labinsk • Svetlograd • Blagodarnyy • KALMYKIYA • Neftekumsk • Yuzhno-Sukhokumsk • Kutan
rymsk • Adygeysk • Armavir • Stavropol' • Budennovsk • Kizlyarskiy Zaliv
Goryachiy Klyuch • Belorechensk • Nevinnomyssk • Zelenokumsk • Kochubey • Kraynovka • Os. Chechen
Khadyzhensk • Maykop • Pshada • ADYGEYA • Cherkessk • Mineral'nyye Vody • Pyatigorsk • Prokhladnyy • Mozdok • Kargalinskaya • Babayurt • Agrakhanskiy Poluostrov
khaylovskiy • Tuapse • KARACHAYEVO- • Kislovodsk • Terek • CHECHNYA • DAGESTAN • Kaspiysk
Sochi • Karachayevsk • CHERKESIYA • KABARDINO- • Nal'chik • Groznyy • Khasavyurt • Makhachkala • CASPIAN
Adler • Teberda • BALKARIYA • Uros Martan • Gudermes • Buynaksk
Gagra • Gudauta • 5642 Elbrus • 5203 • SEVERNAYA • Vladikaykaz • Gunib • Levashi • Izberbash • SEA
Sokhumi • Och'amch'ira • OSETIYA • 5047 Kazbek • 4424 1276 • Dikloasta • Kumukh • Derbent
Zugdidi • Lajanurpekhi • Tskhinvali • U • Kasumkent
P'ot'i • K'ut'aisi • GEORGIA • Gori • 4131 • S • Xaçmaz
Bat'umi • Khashuri • Kaspi • T'BILISI • Telavi • Zaqatala • Aktáy • 4466 • Davaçi
Ozurgeti • Borjomi • Rust'avi • Dedoplis • Gora Bazardyuzi • Quba • Siyäzän
Hopa • Akhalts'ikhe • Bolnisi • Qazax • Mingäçevir Su Anbari • Gilazi
Pazar • Akhalkalaki • Tashir • Mtavari • Tovuz • Sämkir • Mingäçevir • Ismayilli • Sämaxi • Sumqayit
Trabzon • Rize • Ardahan • Dilijan • Ganca • AZERBAIJAN • BAKI (BAKU)
Giresun • Artvin • 3937 • Göle • Vanadzor • Qazax • 3724 • Barda • Kürdämir • Qazimämmäd
Gümüshane • Kars • Gyumri • 4090 • Hrazdan • Sevana Lich • AZERBAIJAN • Agdam • Imisli • Salyan
Oltu • Sarkamis • ARMENIA • YEREVAN • Vardenis • Xankändi • Saatli • Neftçala
Bayburt • Tortum • Ejmiadzin • Ararat • Sisian • Goris • Horadiz • Masali • Länkäran
Erzurum • Agri • Mt. Ararat 5165 • Sarbuz • AZER. • 3829 • Khoda-Afärin • Astara
Erzincan • Patnos • Ercis • Mäkü • Naxçivan • Mincän • Ardäbil
Varto • Muradiye • Paröh • Jolfa • Äharı • 4810 • Hashtpar • Tälesh
Bingöl • 4434 Süphan Dagi • Van • Qoint • Marand • Khvoy • Khrvés • Bandar-e Anzali
Elazig • Mus • Ercek • Van Gölü • Salmas • TABRIZ • Sarab • Rasht • Rüdsar
Malatya • Ergani • Silvan • Bitlis • Gevas • Baskale • Daryächeh-ye Orümiyeh • Bastänäbäd • Äzärän • MÄreh • Lähijän
Siverek • Diyarbakir • Batman • Sirt • Yüksekova • 3710 Kuh-e Sahand • Abhar
Hilva • Mardin • Cizre • Hakkäri • Bonäb • Maragheh • Miändowäb • Zanjan • Yangi Kand
Viransehir • Kiziltepe • Simak • Amadiyeh • Zeban • Bowkän • Kirk Bulag D. 3107
Sanlıurfa • Al Qämishlī • Zäkho • Dahük • Ravandiz • Sandaj • Divandarreh • Bijar
Akcakale • Tall 'Uwaynät • Mahäbäd • IRAN • Zägheh-ye Bälä
'Ayn 'Isä • Al Hasakah • Tall 'Afar • Ranya • Saqqez • Mariwän • Kermänshäh • Harsin
abulus • Al Mawsil • Säqqez • Päveh • Sanandaj • Eslämäbäd-e Gharb
Buhayrat al Asad • Ar Raqqah • Sinjär • Arbīl • As Sulaymäniyah • Halabjah • Ravänsar • Gilän Garb
Ar Rusäfah • Shadädah • Kirkük • Tuz Khurmätü • Kifri • Qorveh • Ilam
As Sukhnah • Dayr az Zawr • MESOPOTAMIA • Baiji • IRAQ • Kälär • Mehrän • Mälavi
Tadmur • Al Bū Kamäl • 'Anah • Tikrit • Samarra • Jalawlä • Muqdädiyah • Ba'qübah • Kühdasht
Äl Bü Kamäl • Al Hadithah • Buhayrat ath Tharthär • Khän al Baghdädi • BAGHDAD • Dehlorän
iyat ash Shäm (yrian Desert) • Ar Ramädi • Habbäniyah • Ar Rutba • Bar al Milh
RIA • As Sukhnah • SIRAQ

Scale 1 : 3 900 000

0   50   100   150 km

0   25   50   75 miles

metres	feet
8000	26250
6000	19690
4000	13120
2000	6560
1000	3280
500	1640
200	656
0	0
656	200
3280	1000
6560	2000
13120	4000
19690	6000
26250	8000
feet	metres

© Copyright AND Cartographic Publishers Ltd.

Scale 1 : 7 900 000

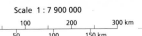

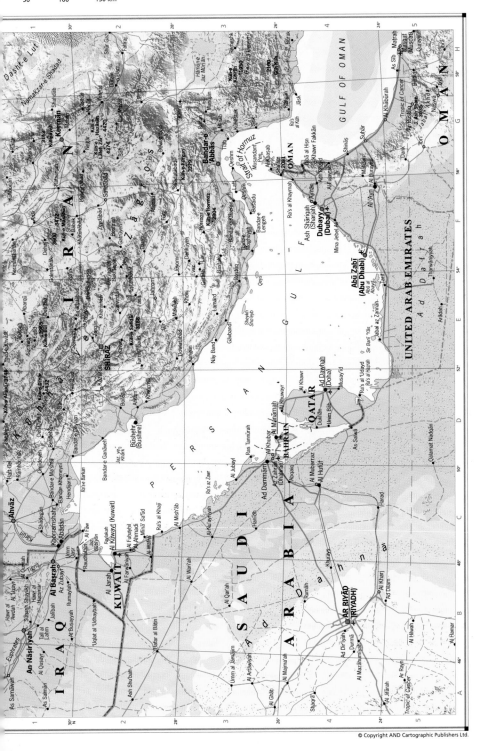

© Copyright AND Cartographic Publishers Ltd.

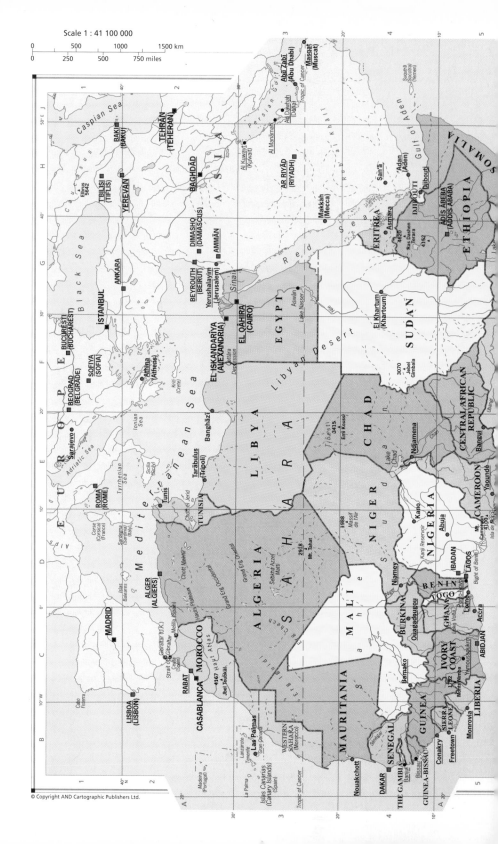

Africa

Scale 1 : 41 100 000

0   500   1000   1500 km
0   250   500   750 miles

© Copyright AND Cartographic Publishers Ltd.

Africa: Political

SEYCHELLES

Seychelles Is.

Coëtivy I.

Amirante Is.

Aldabra Is.
(Seychelles)

Agalega Is.
(Mauritius)

Cosmoledo Group

Glorieuses
(France) Tagnga
Bobaomby

Îles Crozet
(France)

Mayotte
(France)

ANTANANARIVO

COMOROS

MADAGASCAR

Nacala

Tropic of Capricorn

Tagnga
Volohmena

Prince Edward Island
(South Africa)

O C E A N

Mombasa

Pemba I.

Zanzibar I.

Mt. Kilimanjaro

Dodoma

DAR ES SALAAM

Juan de Nova
(France)

Mozambique Channel

TANZANIA

BURUNDI

Bujumbura

Lake
Tanganyika

Lake Nyasa

Mt Mulanje
3002

Lilongwe

MALAWI

Beira

HARARE

MAPUTO

Mocambique

DURBAN

SWAZILAND

Lake Mweru

Lubumbashi

Kananga

Lake
Mweru

Ndola

ZAMBIA

Lusaka

Lake
Kariba

Cahora Bassa

Zambezi

Bulawayo

ZIMBABWE

Limpopo

Mbabane

Drakensberg

Port Elizabeth

REPUBLIC

KINSHASA

OF CONGO

ANGOLA

Brazzaville

Kasai

Kwango

Cuanza

CABINDA
(Angola)

LUANDA

Cunene

Okavango
Delta

Makgadikgadi

Okavango

Etosha Pan

Windhoek

NAMIBIA

Brandberg
2574

Walvis Bay

Namib Desert

K a l a h a r i
D e s e r t

BOTSWANA

Gaborone

Pretoria

Johannesburg

Orange

LESOTHO

Maseru
2430

SOUTH AFRICA

St.
Helena
Bay

CAPE TOWN

Cape of Good Hope

Cape Agulhas

(Equatorial Guinea)

A T L A N T I C

O C E A N

St. Helena
(U.K.)

Ascension
(U.K.)

Tristan da Cunha
(U.K.)

Gough I.
(U.K.)

Tropic of Capricorn

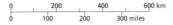

Scale 1 : 15 900 000

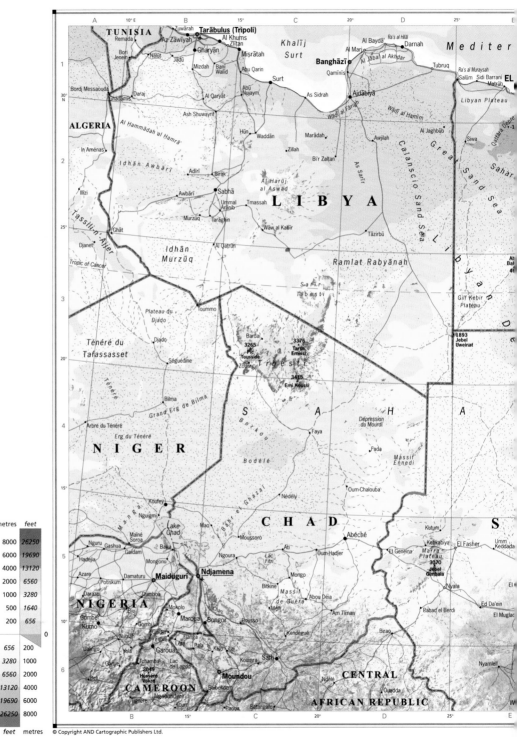

TUNISIA

Az Zāwīyah Zuwārah Tarābulus (Tripoli)
Remada   Al Khums
Bori   Nālūt   Zlitan
Jeneit   Gharyān Misrātah
Bordj Messaouda   Mizdah Banī   Abu Qarin
Daraj   Jādū   Walid
Ghadāmis   Abū   Surt
                      Al Qaryāt Nujaym
ALGERIA   Ash Shuwayrif

Al Hammādah al Hamrā'   Hūn   Waddān   Marādah

In Aménas   Zillah
                Adīrī   Birāk
Illizi   Al Harūj
Tassili-n-Ajjer   Awbārī Sabhā   al Aswad
        Ghāt   Umm al   Tmassah
                Arānib
Djanet   Murzuq Tarāghin
        Tropic of Cancer   Wāw al Kabīr
            Al Qatrūn

Idhān Awbārī

L I B Y A

Khalīj
Surt

Banghāzī

Al Bayḍā' Ra's al Hilāl
Al Marj   Al Jabal al Akhdar Darnah
            Tubruq
Qamīnis   Ra's al Muraysah
            Salūm Sidi Barrani Matrūh
As Sidrah Ajdābiyā   EL

Wādī al Farīgh
        Wādī al Hamīm
Al Jaghbūb   Libyan Plateau
        Siwa
Awjilah

Bi'r Zaltan   As Sarīr

Tāzirbū   Calanscio Sand Sea   Great Sand Sea   Sahar

Ramlat Rabyānah   Libya

Idhān Murzūq

Toummo   Sarīr   Gilf Kebir
        Tibesti   Plateau

Plateau du Djado   Bardaï   3376   1893
                Tarso Jebel
Ténéré du   Djado   3265 Emissi Uweinat
Tafassasset   Pic
    Séguédine   Zouar Toussidé   3415
                Tibesti Emi Koussi

S   A   H   A   R   A

Grand Erg de Bilma   Borkou   Dépression
Bilma   du Mourdi
Arbre du Ténéré   Faya
Erg du Ténéré   Fada
                Massif
N I G E R   Bodélé   Ennedi

Oum-Chalouba

Manga   Koufey   Nédély   Kutum   Kebkabiya El Fasher
    Nguigmi   C   H   A   D   Abéché   Umm
Maïné   Mao   El Geneina Marra Keddada
Soroa   Lake   Moussoro   Plateau
Nguru Gashua   Chad   Ati   Oum-Hadjer   3070 Nyala
Geidam Baga   Jebel
Hadejia Mongonu Ngoura   Lac   Mongo   Gimbala   El
Azare Potiskum   Fitri   Rahad el Berdi Ed Da'ein
        Damaturu   Bitkine   El Muglad
Darazo   Maiduguri Ndjamena   Massif   Abou Déia   Birao
NIGERIA Dumbtoa   de Guéra Melfi   Am Timan
Gombe   Biu Mokolo   Bongor   Kendégué
Kumo Gombi Maropa   Bousso   CENTRAL
Numan Guider Figuil   Kélo Koumra Sarh   Nyamlell
Jalingo Yola Flanga Léré Pala Laï   AFRICAN REPUBLIC
Ganye   Tchamba Lac   2049   Ndélé Ouadda
    Béli   de Lagdo Hossere   Moundou
    CAMEROON Vokré   Baïbokoum   Paoua
        Ngaoundéré Kourri   Batangafo

Mediter

ALGERIA

0   200   400   600 km
0   100   200   300 miles

metres	feet
8000	26250
6000	19690
4000	13120
2000	6560
1000	3280
500	1640
200	656
0	0
656	200
3280	1000
6560	2000
13120	4000
19690	6000
26250	8000
feet	metres

© Copyright AND Cartographic Publishers Ltd.

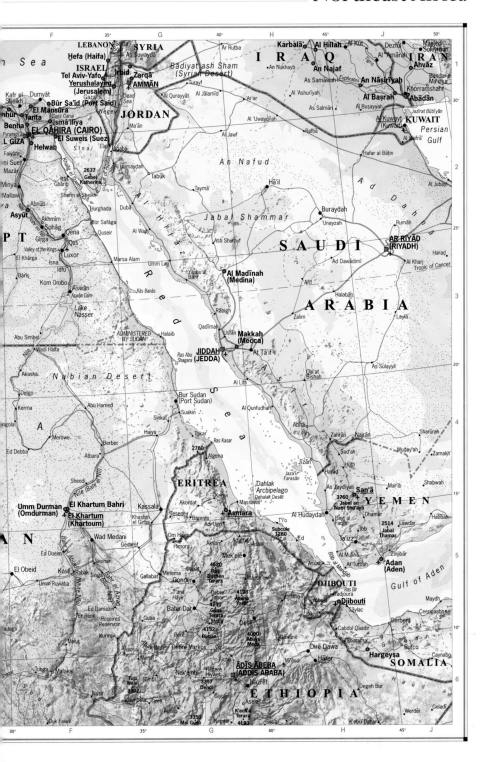

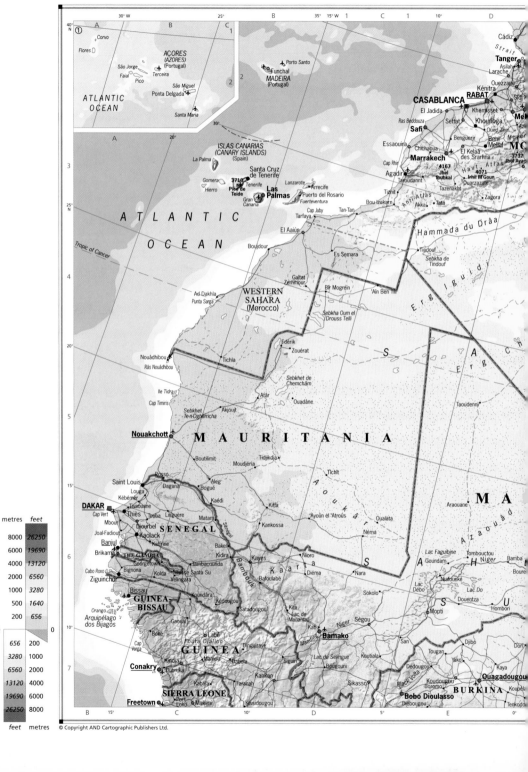

Africa

Scale 1 : 15 900 000

metres	feet
8000	26250
6000	19690
4000	13120
2000	6560
1000	3280
500	1640
200	656
0	0
656	200
3280	1000
6560	2000
13120	4000
19690	6000
26250	8000

feet   metres

84

© Copyright AND Cartographic Publishers Ltd.

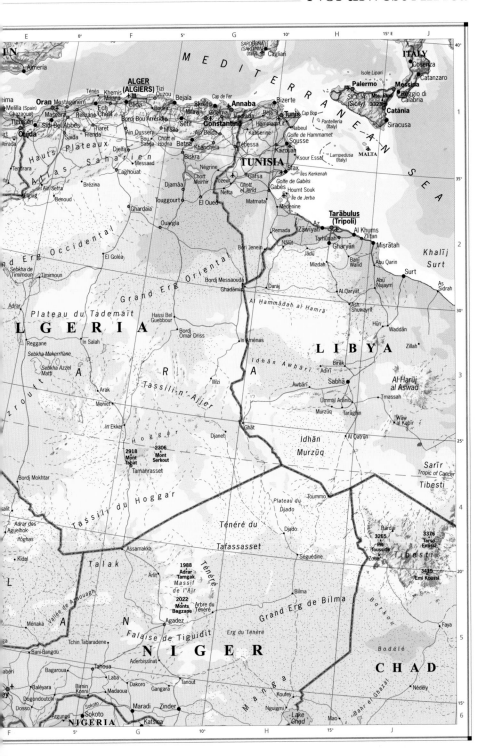

MEDITERRANEAN SEA

SARDEGNA
(SARDINIA)
(Italy)
Cagliari

ITALY
Cosenza
Catanzaro

Isole Lipari

Almería

Palermo
Messina
Reggio di
Calabria

Mte. Etna
3323

SICILIA
(Sicily)
Catánia
Siracusa

Melilla (Spain)
Ghazaouet
Oran Mostaganem
Tlemcen
Sidi Bel Abbès
Oujda

ALGER
(ALGIERS)
Tizi
Ouzou
Blida
Bouira
Miliana
Ténès Khemis

Bejaïa
Skikda
Mila
Jijel
Cap de Fer
Annaba
Bizerte
Beja
Tunis
Cap Bon

Relizane Ech Chéliff
Bordj Bou Arréridj
M'Sila
Sétif
Constantine
Aïn Beïda
Guelma
Souk Ahras
Nabeul
Hammam Lif
Golfe de Hammamet
Sousse
Kairouan

Frenda
Tiaret
Aïn Oussera
Bou
Saada
Batna
Khenchela
Tébessa
Kasserine

Saïda
Djelfa
Chott el
Hodna
Biskra
Négrine
Sidi Bou Zid
Sfax
Îles Kerkenah

Pantelleria
(Italy)

MALTA
Lampedusa
(Italy)

Laghouat
Messaad
Brézina
Chott
Melrhir
Tozeur
Nefta
Gafsa
Chott
el Jérid
TUNISIA
Golfe de Gabès
Gabès Houmt Souk
Île de Jerba

Ghardaïa
Touggourt
El Oued
Matmata
Medenine

Tarābulus
(Tripoli)
Az
Zāwiyah
Al Khums
Zlītan

Remada
Tarhūnah
Naḻūt
Gharyān
Mișrātah

Khalīj
Surt

Bordj Messaouda
Bori Jeneïn
Jādū
Banī
Walīd
Abu Qarin

Ghadāmis
Daraj
Abū
Nujaym
Surt
As
Sidrah

Al Hammādah al Ḥamrā'
Al Qaryāt
Ash
Shuwayrif

Plateau du Tademaït
Hassi Bel
Guebbour
Hūn
Waddān

Bordj
Omar Driss
In Aménas
LIBYA
Zillah

In Salah
Idhān Awbārī
Adīrī
Birāk

Reggane
Illizi
Awbārī
Sabhā
Al Harūj
al Aswad

Sebkha Mekerrhane
Ummal Aranib
Tmassah

Sebkha Azzel
Matti
Murzūq
Tarāghin
Wāw
al Kabīr

Arak
Djanet
Ghāt
Al Qatrūn

Meniet
Idhān
Murzūq

In Ekker
Sarīr
Tropic of Cancer
Tibesti

2918
Mont
Tahat
2306
Mont
Serkout

ALGERIA
SAHARA

Tamanrasset

Bordj Mokhtar
Toummo
Zillah

Adrar des
Aguelhok
Ifoghas
Plateau du
Djado
Bardaï
3265
Pic
Youssidé
Zouar
3376
Tarso
Emissi

Assamakka
Ténéré du
Tafassasset
Djado
Séguédine
Tibesti
3415
Emi Koussi

Kidal
Talak
1988
Adrar
Tamgak
Massif
de l'Aïr

Ârlit
Bilma

2022
Monts
Bagzane
Arbre du
Ténéré
Grand Erg de Bilma

Agadez
Erg du Ténéré
Borkou

Ménaka
Falaise de Tiguidit
Faya

Tchin Tabaradene
NIGER
Bodélé

Bani-Bangou
Tahoua
Laba
Aderbissinat
Bilma

Dogondoutchi
Bagaroua
Madaoua
Dakoro
Gangara
Tanout
Koufey
CHAD
Nédély

Dosso
Argungu
Maradi
Zinder
Nguigmi
Lake
Chad
Mao

NIGERIA
Sokoto
Katsina
Bahr el Ghazal

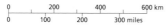

Africa

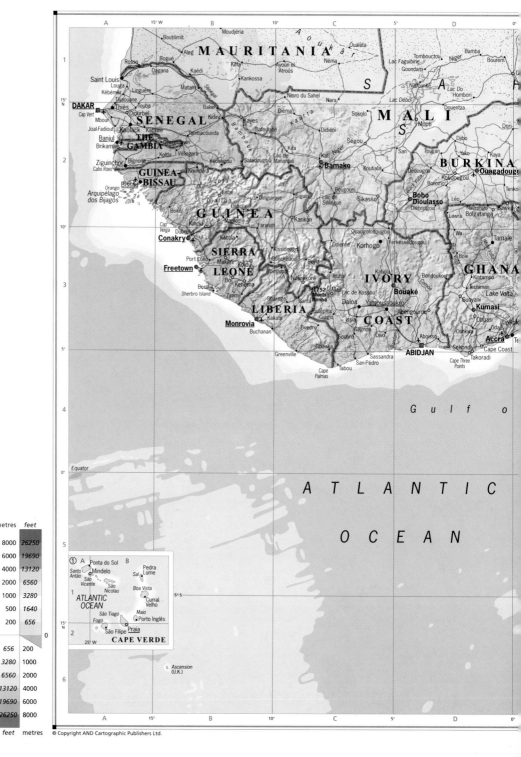

Scale 1 : 15 900 000

metres	feet
8000	26250
6000	19690
4000	13120
2000	6560
1000	3280
500	1640
200	656

656	200
3280	1000
6560	2000
13120	4000
19690	6000
26250	8000

feet   metres

© Copyright AND Cartographic Publishers Ltd.

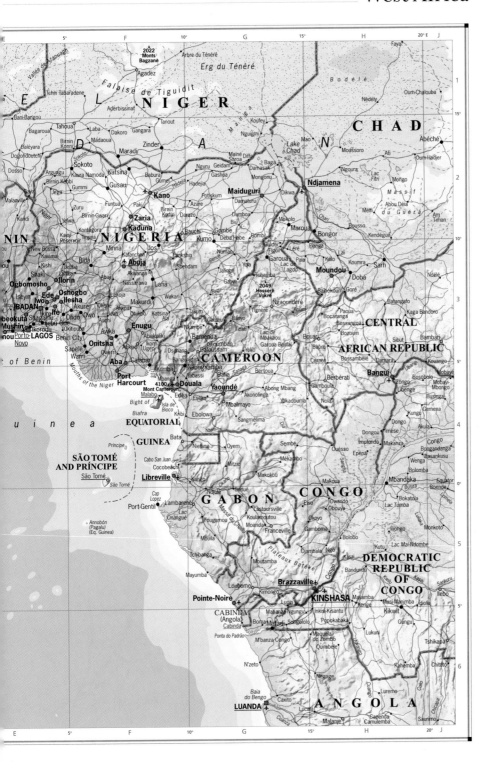

West Africa

5° F 10° G 15° H 20° E J

NIGER

2022
Monts
Bagzane

Erg du Ténéré

Arbre du Ténéré

Agadez

Falaise de Tiguidit

Bodélé

Faya

Vallée de l'Azaouagh

Tchin Tabaradene

Adérbissinat

Nédely

Oum-Chalouba

CHAD

Bani-Bangou

Tahoua

Laba

Dakoro

Gangara

Tanout

Koufey

Mao

Moussoro

Ati

Abéché

Bagaroua

Madaoua

Zinder

Nguigmi

Lake
Chad

Oum-Hadjer

Dogondoutchi

Birnin
Konni

Maradi

Mainé Soroa

Diffa

Damasak

Baga

Mongonu

Ngoura

Lac
Fitri

Mongo

Massif

Dosso

Argungu

Katsina

Nguru

Geidam

Gashoa

Dikwa

Ndjamena

Méfi

Abou Déia
du Guéra

Am
Timan

Kandi

Kaura Namoda

Gumel

Hadejia

Potiskum

Maiduguri

Damaturu

Azare

Chari

Bousso

Kendégué

Malanville

Birnin Kebbi

Gummi

Zuru

Paki

Darazo

Dimboa

Mokolo

Maroua

Bongor

Tega

Kano

Birnin
Kudu

Bauchi

Gombe

Biu

Guider

Léré

Fianga

Koumra

Sarh

Ndélé

NIGERIA

Zaria

Kaduna

Minna

Jos

Kumo

Deba Habe

Bombi

Figuil

Pala

Lac de
Lagdo

Dobá

Moundou

Baibokoum

Goré

Batangafo

Kaga Bandoro

BENIN

New Bussa

Kaiama

Kainji
Reservoir

Kontagora

Kafanchan

Pankshin

Numan

Yola

Garoua

CENTRAL

Kishi

Jebba

Bida

Nassarawa

Lafia

Shendam

Jalingo

Tchamba

Ngaoundéré

Kouri

Paoua

Bocaranga

Bossangoa

Bozoum

Kaga Bandoro
Bambari

Ogbomosho

Ilorin

Abaji

Makurdi

Wukari

Beli

Tignère

Sibut
Kaga Bandoro

Sambari

Iseyin
Iwo

Oshogbo

Ilesha

Akure

Okene

Lokoja

Otukpo

Katsina Ala

Takum

Banyo

Lac de
Mbakaou

Gatoua Boulaï

Bouar

Damara

Ibafa
Kouango

Bosobolo

IBADAN

Ife

Owo

Ondo

Auchi

African Republic

Mushin
Porto-
Novo

Shagamu
Ijebu-Ode

Okitipupa

Nkambe

Foumban

Yoko

Bafia

Bertoua

Berbérati

Gamboula

Bangui

Zongo

Mobayi

Libenge

LAGOS

Ikorodu

Benin City

Awka

Abakaliki

Bamenda

Pafoussam

Dschang

Nkongsamba

Abong Mbang

Nola

Bossambélé

Businga

Onitsha

Owerri

Ikom

Ugep

Nkongsamba

Kabass

CAMEROON

Yokadouma

Libenge

Gemena

Aba

Calabar

Kumba

Mbanga

Douala

Yaoundé

Akonolinga

Dongo

Akula

**Port
Harcourt**

Mont Cameroun
4100

Edéa

Mbalmayo

Sangmélima

Imése

Congo

Bongandanga

Basankusu

Malabo

Isla de
Bioco

Ebolowa

Dja

Dongou

Impfondo

Makanza

Wenga

Bolomba

Bight of
Biafra

EQUATORIAL

Ntem

Niefang

Oyem

Sembé

Mékambo

Ouésso

Epéna

Kungu

Bumba

**São Tomé
and Príncipe**

GUINEA

Bata

Mitzic

Makokou

Makoua

Mbandaka

Equator
Boende

São Tomé

São Tomé

Cabo San Juan
Cocobeach

Kango

Libreville

Baoué

Booué

Ewo

Owando

Obouye

Busira

Lac Tumba

Equator

Annobón
(Pagalu)
(Eq. Guinea)

Cap
Lopez

Port-Gentil

Lambaréné

GABON

Lastoursville

Koulamoutou

Moanda

Franceville

Okoyo

Okondja

Gamboma

Bolobo

Inongo

Lac Mai-Ndombe

Monkoto

Mouila

Massif du Chaillu

Fougamou

Kutu

Tchibanga

Lac Onangué

Djambala

Ngo

Bandundu

Iebo

Mayumba

Plateaux Batéké

Moutamba

**DEMOCRATIC
REPUBLIC
OF
CONGO**

Loubomo

Kimongo

Brazzaville

Mayama

Kenge

Masi-Manimba

Idiofa

Pointe-Noire

Lugzi

KINSHASA

Mabanza
Ngungu

Inkisi-Kisantu

Popokabaka

Kikwit

Gungu

**CABINDA
(Angola)**

Cabinda

Boma
Matadi

Songololo

Lukula

Tshikapa

Ponta do Padrão

M'banza Congo

Maquela
do Zombo

Quirebele

Kahémba

Chitato

N'zeto

Negage

Luremo

Caxito

Quimbele

ANGOLA

LUANDA

Baia
do Bengo

Cuanza

Malanje

Saurimo

Scale 1 : 15 900 000

0   200   400   600 km
0 100 200 300 miles

NIGERIA

C H A D

S U D A

CENTRAL
AFRICAN REPUBLIC

CAMEROON

CONGO

GABON

DEMOCRATIC
REPUBLIC OF CONGO

RWANDA

BURUNDI

ATLANTIC OCEAN

A N G O L A

ZAMBIA

metres	feet
8000	26250
6000	19690
4000	13120
2000	6560
1000	3280
500	1640
200	656
0	0

feet	metres
656	200
3280	1000
6560	2000
13120	4000
19690	6000
26250	8000

Mokolo • Maroua • Guider • Figuil • Lëré • Pala • Kélo • Lai • Koumra • Sarh • Moundou • Doba • Gore • Ngaoundéré • Baibokoum • Paoua • Batangafo • Kaga Bandoro • Bossangoa • Bangui • Zongo • Libenge • Berbérati • Gamboula • Nola • Yokadouma • Bocaranga • Bozoum • Bouar • Bossembélé • Damara • Carnot • Bertoua • Bambari • Sibut • Kouango • Alindao • Bangassou • Zémio • Obo • Tambura • Amadi • Djéma • Rafai • Mobaye • Yakoma • Monga • Bondo • Ango • Niangara • Faradje • Dungu • Isiro • Watsa • Arua • Mungbere • Bambesa • Poko • Buta • Akula • Lisala • Bumba • Banalia • Bomili • Nia-Nia • Beni • Butembo • Kisangani • Basoko • Yangambi • Bafwasende • Bumba

Brazzaville • KINSHASA • Matadi • Boma • Banana • N'zeto • LUANDA • Lobito • Benguela • Lucira

Kananga • Mbuji-Mayi • Kolwezi • Likasi • Lubumbashi • ZAMBIA • Ndola • Chingola • Kitwe • Mufulira • Luanshya

Lake Tanganyika • Kalemie • Lake Mweru • Great Rift Valley

© Copyright AND Cartographic Publishers Ltd.

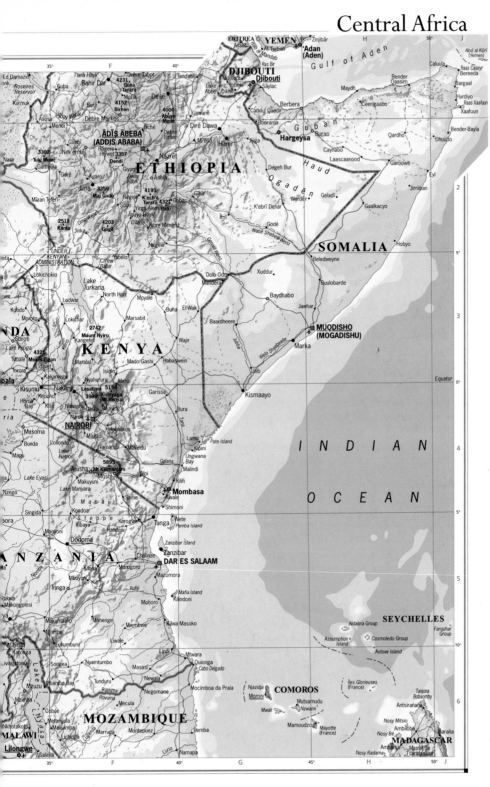

ERITREA YEMEN Zinjibār
Assab At Turbah
Bab al Mandab 'Adan
(Aden)
DJIBOUTI Djibouti Gulf of Aden Caluula
Obock Raas Caseyr
Bereeda
Maydh Bender Bargaal
Qaasim Hurdiyo
Saylac Berbera Ceerigaabo Raas Xaafuun
Xaafuun
Caddu Qaadd Burao Qardho Dhuudo
Booroma Bender-Bayla
Hargeysa Caynabo Laascaanood Garoowe Eyl
Jijiga
Haud Jirriiban
Degeh Bur Geladi
Werder Gaalkacyo
K'ebri Dehar

SOMALIA Hobyo

Gode
Wabē Shebelē Wenz Beledweyne

Dolo Odo Xuddur
Mandera Buulobarde
Baydhabo

Buna El Wak Jawhar
Baardheere
MUQDISHO
(MOGADISHU)

KENYA Marka

Uiib

INDIAN

Kismaayo Equator 0°

OCEAN

SEYCHELLES
Aldabra Group Farquhar
Group
Assumption Cosmoledo Group
Island Astove Island

COMOROS Îles Glorieuses
(France)
Njazidja Tanjona
Moroni Bobaomby
Mutsamudu Antsiranana
Mwali Nzwani Mayotte
Mamoudzou (France) Nosy Mitsio
MOZAMBIQUE Ambilobe
Nosy Bé
MADAGASCAR

Scale 1 : 15 900 000

0   200   400   600 km
0 100   200   300 miles

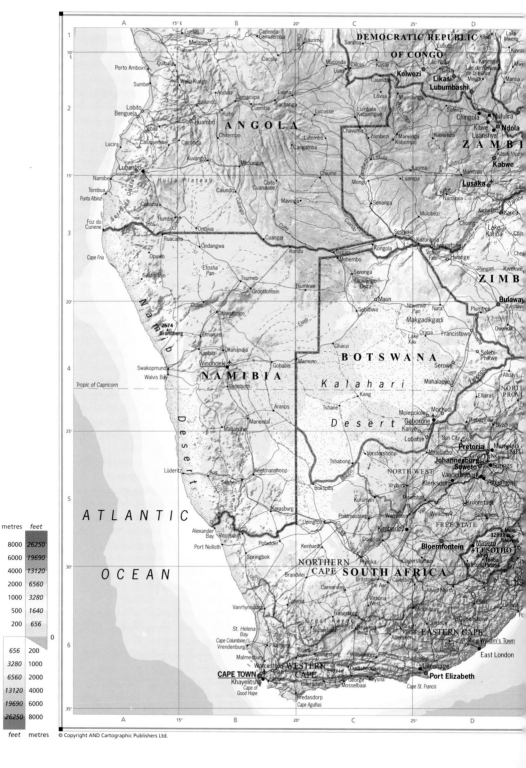

DEMOCRATIC REPUBLIC OF CONGO

Eugala · Melanje · Capenda Camulemba · Saurimo · Santoa · Kilwa · Lake Mweru

Porto Amboim · Quibala · Cacola · Muconda · Dilolo · Kasaji · Lac Nzilo · Lubudi · Kasenga · Les de Retenue de la Lufira · Mwe

Sumbe · Waku Kungo · Andulo · Camacupa · Luena · Sachanga · Lucusse · Lumbala Kaquengue · Luau · Kasai · **Kolwezi** · **Likasi** · Mansa

Lobito · Benguela · Lobito · Ubari · Huambo · Kuito · Cuemba · Lucusse · Lumbala Kaquengue · Lóvua · Kasempa · Chingola · Mufulira · **Ndola**

ANGOLA · Chitembo · Lutembo · Cangamba · Zambezi · Kabompo · Kaoma · Kitwe · Luanshya · **ZAMBI**

Lucira · Caluquembe · Caconda · Kuvango · Menongue · **Kabwe** · Kapiri Mposhi

Namibe · Huila Plateau · Caiundo · Cuito Cuanavale · Mavinga · Mongu · Luampa · Mumbwa · **Lusaka**

Tombua · Cahama · Humbe · Ondjiva · Cuangar · Senanga · Namwala · Mulobezi · Kariba Dam · Kariba

Punta Albina · Kunene · Ruacana · Ondangwa · Rundu · Bagani · Mohembo · Kazungula · Livingstone · Hwange · Che

Foz do Cunene · Opuwo · Etosha Pan · Tsumeb · Tsumkwe · Seronga · Okavango Delta · Victoria Falls · Shangani · Kwekwe

Cape Fria · Sesfontein · Grootfontein · Maun · Nxai Pan · Nata · Plumtree · Zvishave · **Bulaway**

Outjo · Otjiwarongo · Sehithwa · Makgadikgadi · Orapa · Francistown · Gwanda · **ZIMB**

2574 Brandberg · Omaruru · Eiseb · Lake Xau · Selebi-Phikwe · Alldays

Karibib · Okahandja · Mamuno · **BOTSWANA** · Serowe · **NORTH PROVI**

Swakopmund · **Windhoek** · Gobabis · *Kalahari* · Mahalapye · Ellisras

Walvis Bay · Rehoboth · *Tropic of Capricorn* · **NAMIBIA** · Kang · *Desert* · Molepolole · Mochudi · Nylstroom · Thabazimbi

Aranos · Tshane · **Gaborone** · Kanye · Sun City · **Pretoria** · Mamelodi · MPU

Mariental · Maltahöhe · Lobatse · Vorstershoop · Mmabatho · **Johannesburg** · Soweto · Springs

Keetmanshoop · Tshabong · **NORTH WEST** · Vanderbijlpark · Klerksdorp · Vereeniging

Lüderitz · Aus · Seeheim · Bokspits · Vryburg · Bloemhof · Vaal · Welkom · Kroonstad · Bethlehem

Karasburg · Kuruman · Warrenton · **FREE STATE** · Mont aux Sources 3299

ATLANTIC · Upington · Postmasburg · **Kimberley** · Douglas · Jagersfontein · **Maseru** · **LESOTHO** · Thaba Tseka · Maletsunyane

Alexander Bay · Vioolsdrif · Pofadder · Kenhardt · Prieska · **Bloemfontein** · Colesberg

Port Nolloth · Springbok · Brandvlei · **NORTHERN CAPE** · **SOUTH AFRICA** · Britstown · De Aar · Aliwal North · Queenstown · Umtata

OCEAN · Vanrhynsdorp · Calvinia · Carnarvon · Victoria West · Middelburg · **EASTERN CAPE** · King William's Town

St. Helena Bay · Fraserburg · Beaufort West · Graaff-Reinet · Cradock · East London

Cape Columbine · Vredenburg · Piketberg · Tulbagh · Laingsburg · Willowmore · Uitenhage

Malmesbury · Worcester · **WESTERN CAPE** · Oudtshoorn · **Port Elizabeth**

CAPE TOWN · Khayelitsha · George · Knysna · Mosselbaai · Cape St. Francis

Cape of Good Hope · Riversdale · Bredasdorp · Cape Agulhas

A   15° E   B   20°   C   25°   D

metres / *feet*

metres	feet
8000	26250
6000	19690
4000	13120
2000	6560
1000	3280
500	1640
200	656
0	0
656	200
3280	1000
6560	2000
13120	4000
19690	6000
26250	8000

feet / metres

Scale 1 : 55 500 000

0   500   1000   1500   2000 km
0   250   500   750   1000 miles

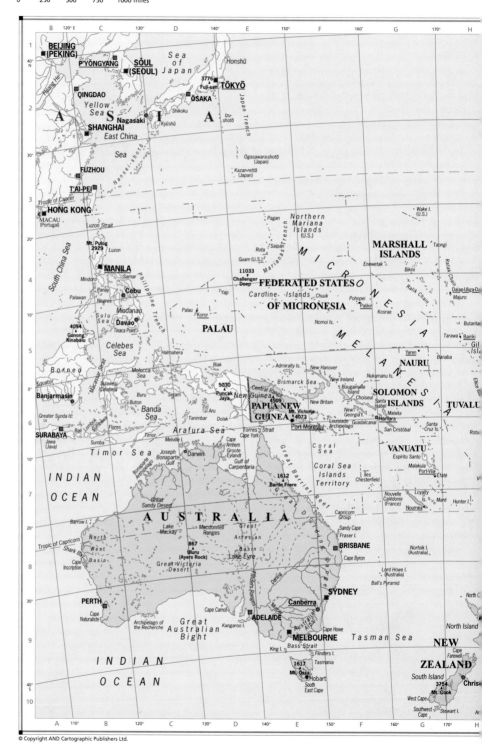

© Copyright AND Cartographic Publishers Ltd.

170°	K	160°	L	150°	M	140°	N	130°	P	120° W	Q

NORTH AMERICA

■ LOS ANGELES

■ SAN DIEGO

P A C I F I C

Guadalupe
(Mexico)

Tropic of Cancer

Hawaiian Islands

Laysan I.

Necker I.

HAWAII
(U.S.)

Kauai
Oahu
Honolulu ● Maui
Hawaii

Johnston I.
(U.S.)

N. W. Christmas Island Ridge

Line Islands

Palmyra I.
(U.S.)

Tabuaeran
Kiritimati

Jarvis I.
(U.S.)

...nd (U.S.)
...er (U.S.)

Is. Revillagigedo
(Mexico)

O C E A N

...ix Islands
...rnie
Rawaki
Manra

KIRIBATI

Malden I.

Starbuck I.

Equator

Atafu
...kunonu Tokelau
(New Zealand)

Tongareva

Marquesas Islands

Nuku Hiva

Hiva Oa

O L Y N E S I A

Swains I.

Danger Is.
Nassau
Manihiki

Vostok I.
Caroline I.

Flint I.

SAMOA American
Samoa
Savaii
Apia
Upolu Tutuila
Tafahi
Rose I.

Cook Islands
(New Zealand)

Suvorov I.

Motu One

Iles Palliser

Iles
Désappointement

Pukapuka

Raroia

Archipel des Tuamotu

ONGA

Niue
(New Zealand)

Palmerston I.
Aitutaki

Arch.
de la Société

Tahiti

Hao

Iles Duc de
Gloucester

French
Polynesia

Groupe Actéon

Rarotonga

Mangaia
Iles
Maria
Rurutu

Tubuai

Raevavae

Mururoa

Morane

Gambier
Is.

Mangareva

Tonga Trench

...ta
...zon Depth
0882

Tubuai Islands

Rapa

Marotiri

Oeno

Henderson I.

Pitcairn Is. Ducie I.
(U.K.)

Tropic of Capricorn

Easter I.
(Chile)

S o u t h   W e s t

P a c i f i c

B a s i n

170°	K	160°	L	150°	M	140°	N	130°	P	120°	Q	110°	R

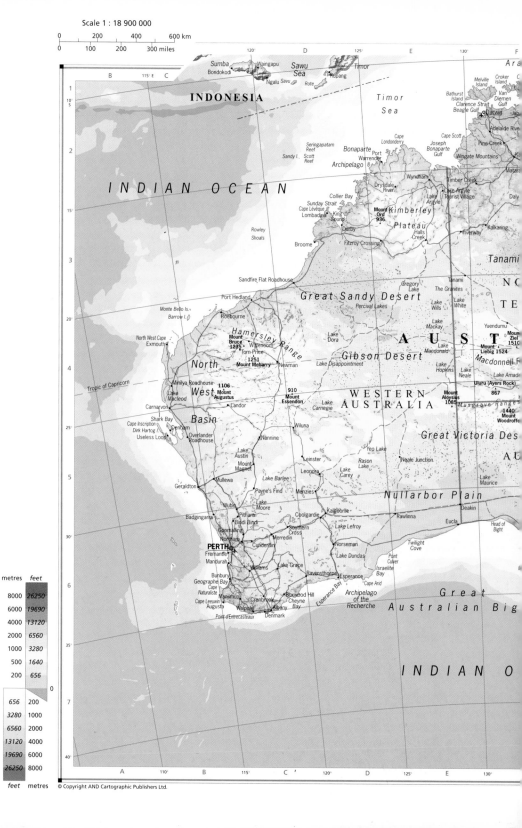

Oceania

Scale 1 : 18 900 000

metres	feet
8000	26250
6000	19690
4000	13120
2000	6560
1000	3280
500	1640
200	656
0	0
656	200
3280	1000
6560	2000
13120	4000
19690	6000
26250	8000
feet	metres

© Copyright AND Cartographic Publishers Ltd.

Australia

G 140° H 145° J 150° K 155° L

Cape Wessel
Wessel Islands
Cape Arnhem
Nhulunbuy
Bickerton Island
Groote Eylandt
Numbulwar
Sir Edward Pellew Group
roloola
Cape Crawford

Mulgrave I. Moa (Banks Island)
Torres Strait
Prince of Wales Island
Somerset
Bamaga
Duifken Point Weipa
Albatross Bay
Aurukun
Cape York Peninsula
Cape Direction
Cape Grenville

Port Moresby
PAPUA NEW GUINEA
D'Entrecasteaux Islands
Louisiade Archipelago

1 10°

Gulf of Carpentaria
Wellesley Islands
Mornington I.
Bertinck I.
Karumba
Normanton
Burketown
Lorraine
Carrooweal
Camooweal
Mount Isa

Kowanyama
Dunbar

Cape Flattery
Cooktown
Laura
Cape Melville
Silver Plains
Princess Charlotte Bay

Osprey Reef
Shark Reef
CORAL SEA ISLANDS

CORAL SEA

TERRITORY (Australia)

Bougainville Reef
Holmes Reefs
Diane Bank

2

Mareeba
Cairns
Port Douglas
Mount Garnet
1622 Mount Bartle Frere
Innisfail
Ingham
Halifax Bay
Greenvale
Mutarnee
Townsville
Ayr

Herald Cays
Willis Group
Magdalene Cays
Diamond Islets
Flinders Reefs
Malay Reef
Turtle I.
Tregosse Islets

PACIFIC

OCEAN

15°

ckly Tableland
Lake Nash
Mount Isa
McKinlay
Richmond
Hughenden
Tobermorey
Boulia
Winton
QUEENSLAND
Muttaburra

Charters Towers
Bowen
The Whitsundays
Proserpine
Repulse Bay
Mackay
Sarina
Nebo
Mount Douglas
Clermont
Emerald
Broad Sound
Clairview
Townshend I.
Swain Reefs

3 20°

GREAT DIVIDING RANGE
Jericho
Springsure
Yeppoon
Rockhampton
Curtis I.
Gladstone
Capricorn Group
Cato I.
Tropic of Capricorn

4

Simpson Desert
Great
Artesian
Basin
Birdsville
Jundah
Windorah
Batoota
Lake Yamma Yamma
Tambo
Augathella
Banana
Taroom
Bundaberg
Sandy Cape
Hervey Bay
Fraser I.

Lake Eyre Basin
Sturt Stony Desert
Tirari Desert
Lake Eyre North
Lake Eyre South
Grey Range
Charleville
Muckadilla
Roma
Miles
Goondiwindi
Dalby
Kingaroy
Gayndah
Maryborough
Gympie
Caloundra

5 25°

Marree
Leigh Creek
Glendambo
Pimba
Lake Blanche
Lake Callabonna
Tibooburra
Wanaaring
Hungerford
Thargomindah
Cunnamulla
Dirranbandi
Bollon
Bonogula
St George
Moonie
Toowoomba
Beenleigh
Moreton I.
North Stradbroke I.
BRISBANE
Mount Roberts 1387
Surfers Paradise
Gold Coast
Cape Byron

Lake Frome
Marree
White Cliffs
Louth
Bourke
Brewarrina
Walgett
Moree
Enngonia
Casino
Tenterfield
Ballina
Grafton

6 30°

Broken Hill
Wilcannia
Cobar
Coonabarabran
Narrabri
Gunnedah
Tamworth
Round Mountain 1608
Armidale
Black Sugarloaf 1494
Coffs Harbour
Lord Howe I.
Ball's Pyramid

NEW SOUTH WALES
Nyngan
Dubbo
Gilgandra
Quirindi
Singleton
Taree
Port Macquarie

Murray River
Ivanhoe
Condobolin
Roto
Orange
Cessnock
Newcastle
SYDNEY

Mount Gambier
Portland
Warrnambool
MELBOURNE
Geelong
Ballarat
Sale
Bairnsdale
Eden
Cape Howe

7 35°

A.C.T. = Australian Capital Territory

TASMAN SEA

TASMANIA

8 40°

G 140° H 145° J 150° L 155° M 160°

95

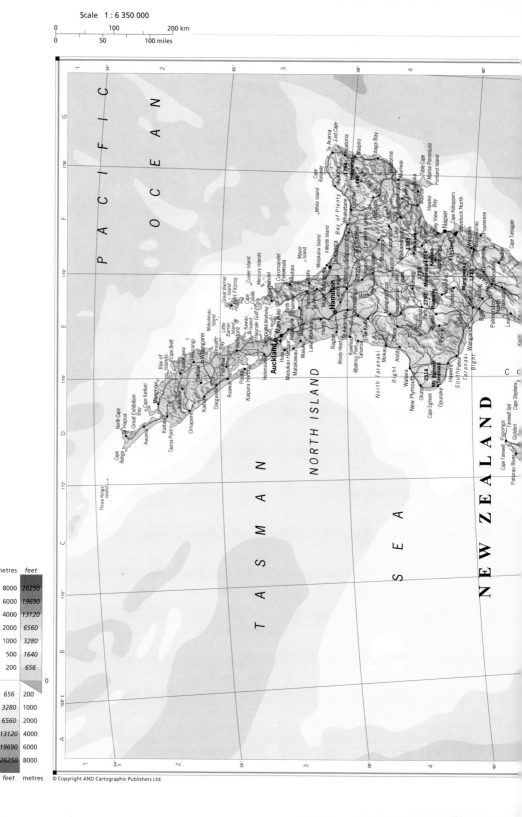

Oceania

Scale 1 : 6 350 000

PACIFIC OCEAN

TASMAN SEA

NORTH ISLAND

NEW ZEALAND

metres	feet
8000	26250
6000	19690
4000	13120
2000	6560
1000	3280
500	1640
200	656

656 | 200
3280 | 1000
6560 | 2000
13120 | 4000
19690 | 6000
26250 | 8000

feet metres

New Zealand

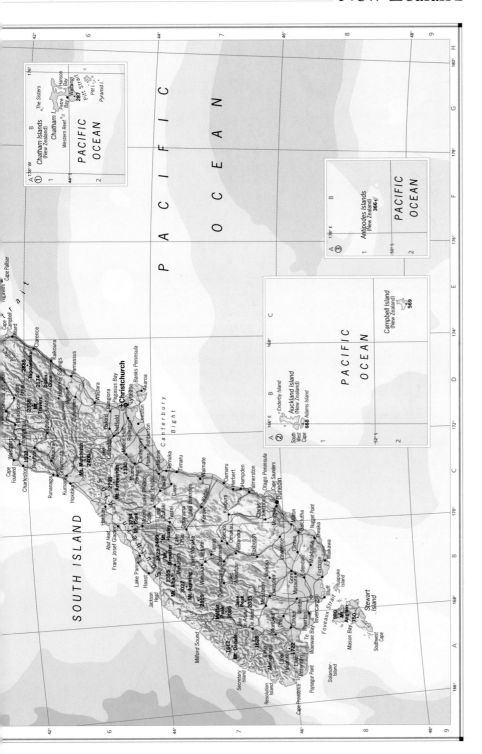

Chatham Islands
(New Zealand)

The Sisters
Hanson Bay
Waitangi
Petre Bay
287
Chatham I.
Pitt Strait
Pitt I.
Western Reef
Pyramid I.

PACIFIC OCEAN

Antipodes Islands
(New Zealand)
366

PACIFIC OCEAN

Campbell Island
(New Zealand)
569

Enderby Island
Auckland Island
(New Zealand)
Adams Island
South West Cape

PACIFIC OCEAN

PACIFIC OCEAN

PACIFIC OCEAN

SOUTH ISLAND

Christchurch

Cape Palliser
Cape Campbell
Ward
Clarence
Kaikoura
Kaikoura Ranges
Hanmer Springs
Waiau
Culverden
Waipara
Pegasus Bay
Banks Peninsula
Akaroa
Rakaia
Darfield
Leeston
Rolleston
Ashburton
Methven
Geraldine
Temuka
Timaru
Waimate
Oamaru
Herbert
Palmerston
Hampden
Cape Saunders
Otago Peninsula
Dunedin
Mosgiel
Milton
Balclutha
Kaitangata
Owaka
Nugget Point
Canterbury Bight
Fairlie
Pleasant Point

Westport
Reefton
Inangahua
1592
Mt. Murchison
2400
Springs Junction
Murchison
Maruia
2685
Tapuaenuku
2174
Mt. Travers
2338
Hokitika
Kumara
Greymouth
Runanga
Mt. Arrowsmith
2795
Cape Foulwind
Charleston
Mount Hutt
Mount Somers

Abut Head
Franz Josef Glacier
Haast
Jackson Head
Lake Paringa
Mt. Cook
3754
2495
Mt. Aspiring
3027
Mount Cook
2469
Lake Pukaki
Lake Tekapo
3754
Lake Ohau
Twizel
Lake Benmore
Fairlie
Kurow
Pukeuri
Ranfurly
Clyde
Alexandra
Clyde
Roxburgh
Lawrence
Tapanui
Clinton
Gore
Mataura
Edendale
Wyndham
Invercargill
Bluff
Foveaux Strait
Stewart Island
Ruapuke Island
Mason Bay
Southwest Cape
Winton
Riverton
Otautau
Tuatapere
Te Waewae Bay
Waewae Bay
Solander Island
Poysegur Point
Cape Providence
Resolution Island
Secretary Island
Milford Sound
Mt. Tutoko
2723
1612
Mt. Donald
1626
Lake Te Anau
Lake Manapouri
Lake Hauroko
Lake Monowai
Te Anau
Manapouri
Mossburn
Lumsden
Balfour
Kingston
Garston
Athol
Lake Wakatipu
Queenstown
Arrowtown
Cromwell
Wanaka
Lake Wanaka
Lake Hawea
Mt. Aspiring
3027
Makarora
Mt. Earnslaw
2819
Mt. Alta
2355
Mt. Aspiring
2035
Mt. Anglem
980
Mt. Peak
2065

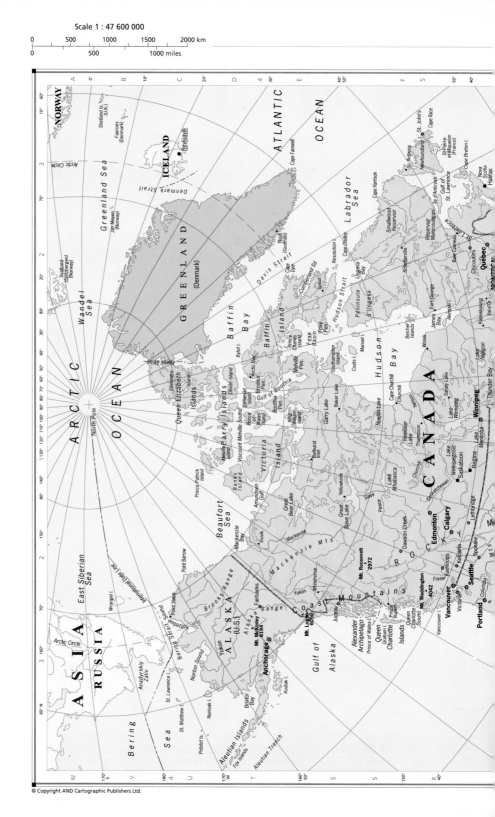

Scale 1 : 47 600 000

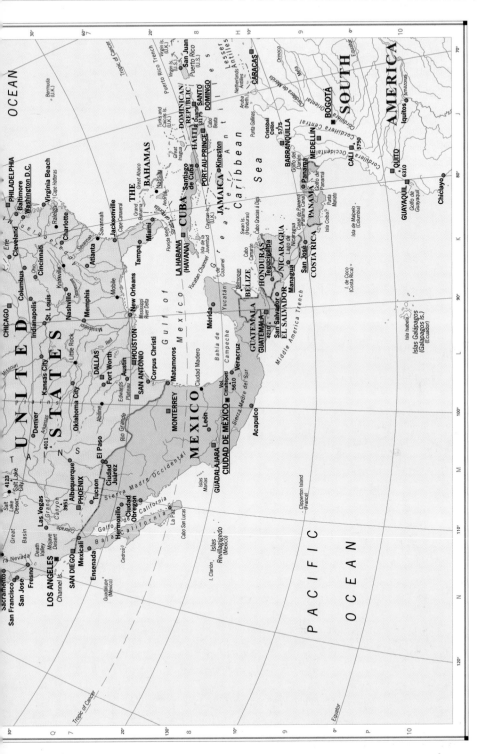

North America

Scale 1 : 18 900 000

0   200   400   600 km
0   100   200   300 miles

metres	feet
8000	26250
6000	19690
4000	13120
2000	6560
1000	3280
500	1640
200	656
0	0
656	200
3280	1000
6560	2000
13120	4000
19690	6000
26250	8000
feet	metres

100

© Copyright AND Cartographic Publishers Ltd.

Scale 1 : 21 200 000

| 0 | 200 | 400 | 600 km |
| 0 | 100 | 200 | 300 miles |

metres	feet
8000	26250
6000	19690
4000	13120
2000	6560
1000	3280
500	1640
200	656
0	0
656	200
3280	1000
6560	2000
13120	4000
19690	6000
26250	8000
feet	*metres*

© Copyright AND Cartographic Publishers Ltd.

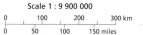

North America

Scale 1 : 9 900 000

| 0 | 100 | 200 | 300 km |
| 0 | 50 | 100 | 150 miles |

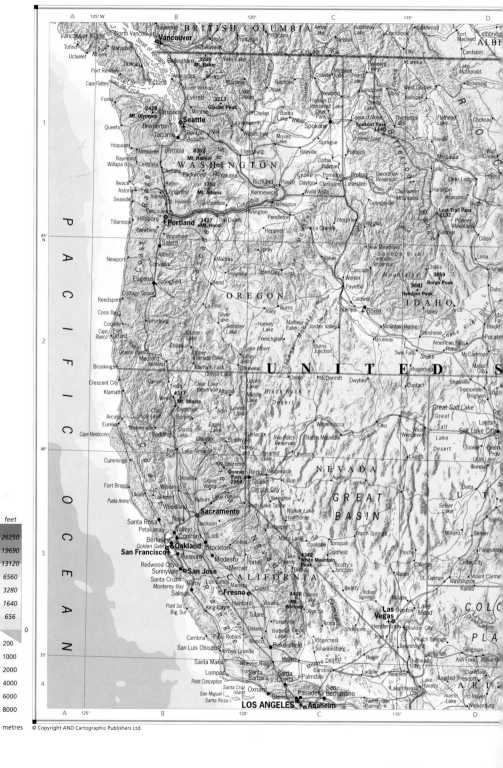

metres	feet
8000	26250
6000	19690
4000	13120
2000	6560
1000	3280
500	1640
200	656
0	0
656	200
3280	1000
6560	2000
13120	4000
19690	6000
26250	8000
feet	metres

© Copyright AND Cartographic Publishers Ltd.

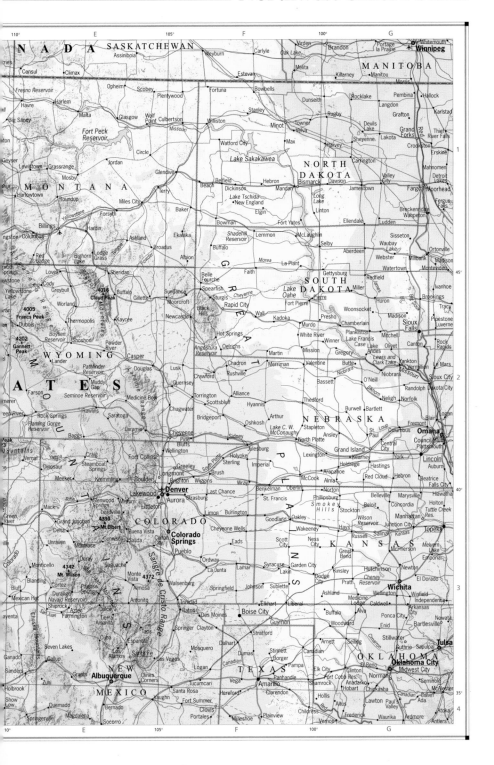

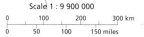

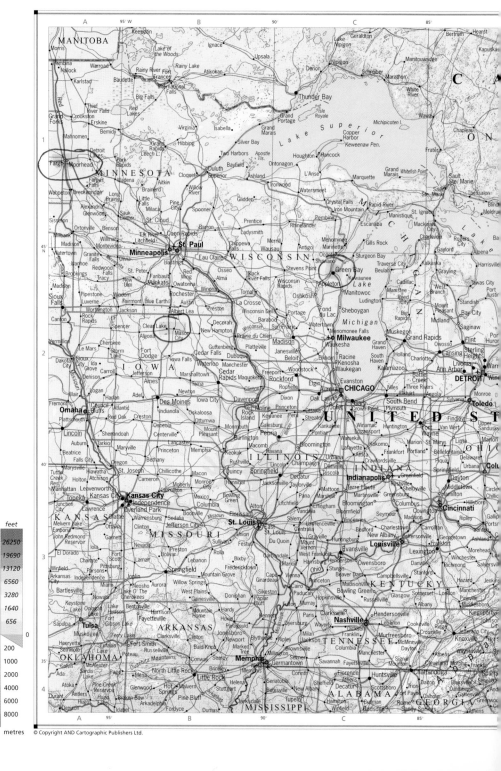

© Copyright AND Cartographic Publishers Ltd.

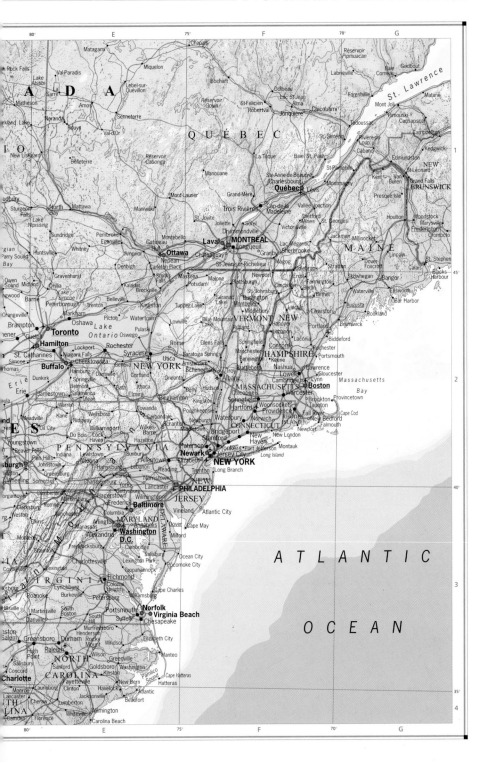

Scale 1 : 9 900 000

0   100   200   300 km

0   50   100   150 miles

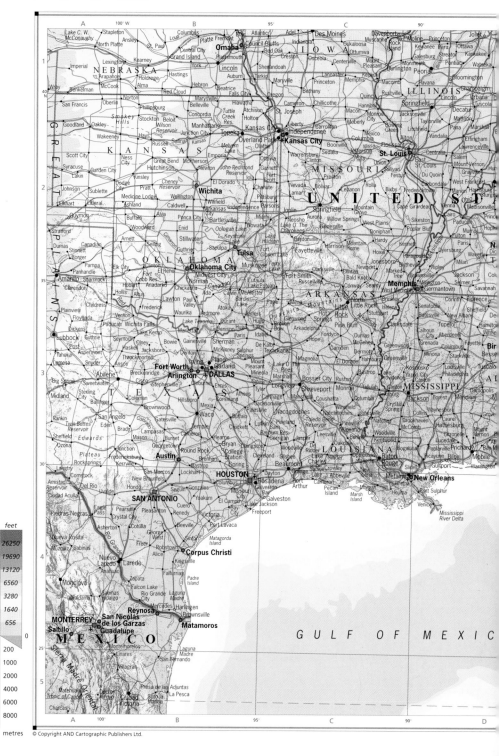

North America

metres	*feet*
8000	*26250*
6000	*19690*
4000	*13120*
2000	*6560*
1000	*3280*
500	*1640*
200	*656*
0	0
656	200
3280	1000
6560	2000
13120	4000
19690	6000
26250	8000
feet	metres

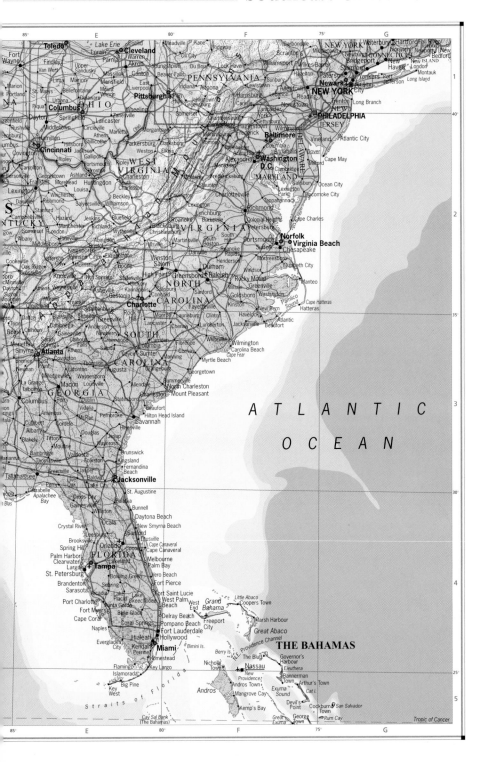

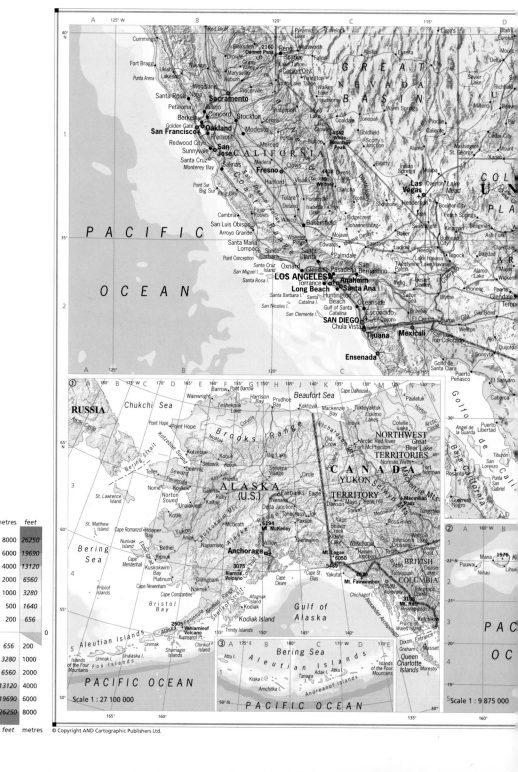

North America

Scale 1 : 9 900 000

metres	feet
8000	26250
6000	19690
4000	13120
2000	6560
1000	3280
500	1640
200	656
0	0
656	200
3280	1000
6560	2000
13120	4000
19690	6000
26250	8000

feet *metres*

Scale 1 : 27 100 000

Scale 1 : 9 875 000

© Copyright AND Cartographic Publishers Ltd.

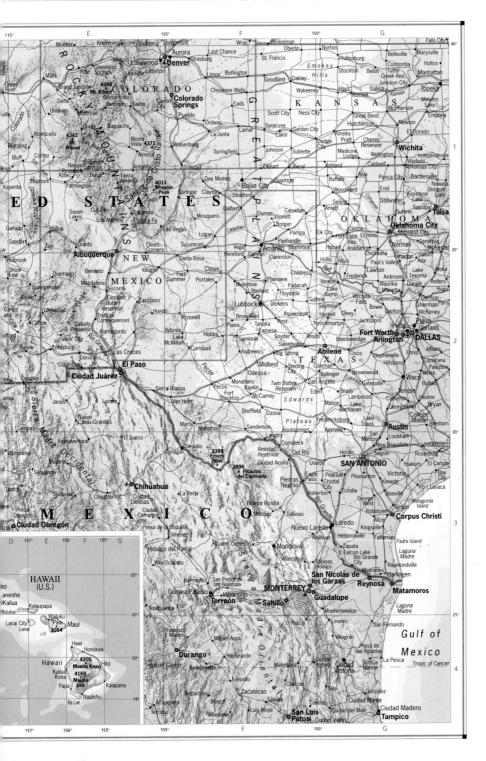

Scale 1 : 22 100 000

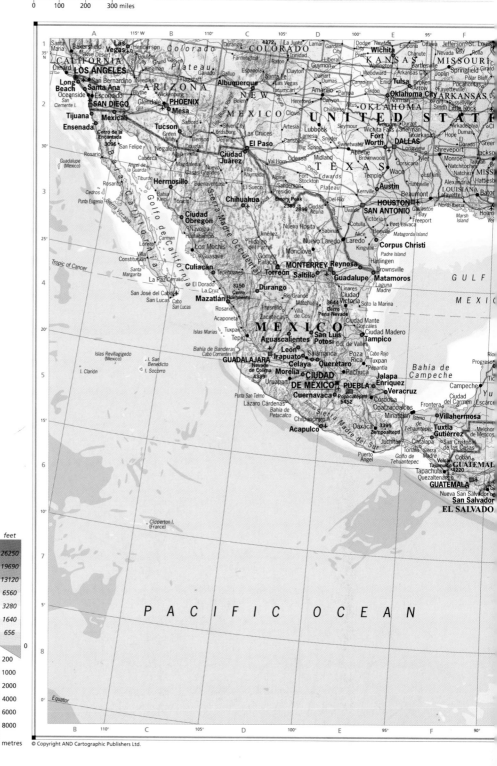

metres	feet
8000	26250
6000	19690
4000	13120
2000	6560
1000	3280
500	1640
200	656
0	0
656	200
3280	1000
6560	2000
13120	4000
19690	6000
26250	8000
feet	metres

Central America and the Caribbean

ATLANTIC

OCEAN

Bermuda (U.K.)
Hamilton

Tropic of Cancer

THE
BAHAMAS

Little Abaco
Grand
Bahama
Marsh Harbour
Great Abaco
Freeport
Bimini
New
Providence
Nassau
Andros
Eleuthera
Cat I.
San Salvador
Rum Cay
Long
I.
Crooked I.
Great
Exuma
Mayaguana
Turks and Caicos Is. (U.K.)
Acklins I.
Turks Is.
Little Inagua
Great
Inagua

DOMINICAN
REPUBLIC

Leeward Islands

Virgin
Islands
(U.K.)
Anguilla
St. Maarten (Netherlands)
St. Barthélemy (France)
Barbuda
Virgin
Islands
(U.S.)
ANTIGUA
AND BARBUDA
Antigua
St. Kitts-
Nevis
Montserrat
(U.K.)
Guadeloupe (France)
Basse Terre
Marie Galante

La Romana
Santiago
La Vega
Puerto
Rico
(U.S.)
San Juan
Caguas
Ponce
Mayagüez

DOMINICA
Roseau
Martinique (France)

HAITI
PORT-AU-PRINCE
SANTO
DOMINGO
Jacmel
Cabo
Beata

Fort-de-France
ST. LUCIA
Castries

Hispaniola

Pico
Duarte
3175

BARBADOS
Bridgetown

ST. VINCENT &
THE GRENADINES
Kingstown

GRENADA
St. George's

Windward Islands

Lesser Antilles

CUBA

HAVANA
LA HABANA
(HAVANA)
Matanzas
Pinar del Río
Guane
Golfo de
Batabanó
Güines
Santa Clara
Sagua
la Grande
Cienfuegos
Sancti
Spíritus
1156
San
Juan
Ciego
de Ávila
Victoria de las Tunas
Camagüey
Holguín
Manzanillo
Bayamo
Guantánamo
Santiago
de Cuba
Cabo Cruz

Isla de la
Juventud
Cayman Islands
(U.K.)

JAMAICA
Montego
Bay
Kingston

Swan Islands
(Honduras)

Greater
Antilles

Cap
Haïtien
Île de
la Gonâve

Windward Passage

Great Bahama Bank

Straits of Florida

Key West

CARIBBEAN SEA

Islas de
la Bahía
Cabo Camarón
Laguna de
Caratasca

Cabo Gracias à Dios
Cayos Miskitos

Isla de Providencia (Colombia)

Isla de San Andrés (Colombia)

Netherlands
Antilles
Aruba
(Neth.)
Willemstad

Punta Gallinas
Península de
Guajira
Golfo de
Venezuela

Coro

Islas Los
Roques
Isla La
Tortuga
Isla de
Margarita
Porlamar

Los Testigos

TRINIDAD AND
TOBAGO
Port of Spain
Trinidad

Tobago

Güiria
Carúpano
Cumaná
San Juan de
los Cayos
CARACAS
Los Teques
Barcelona
Maturín

Maracay
Valencia
Barquisimeto

Maracaibo
Cabimas
Valera
Acarigua
Guanare
Barinas
San Fernando
de Apure

San Cristóbal
Cúcuta
Pamplona
Bucaramanga
Bello
MEDELLÍN
Manizales
Pereira
Ibagué
Armenia
CALI
Buenaventura
Popayán

Santa Marta
BARRANQUILLA
Cartagena

Riohacha

Valledupar

Sincelejo
Montería

Achaguas
El Banco
Ocaña
Magangué

Puerto
Carreño

Puerto
Nuevo

Puerto Ayacucho

Cerro Yaví
2441

Ciudad Bolívar
Ciudad
Guayana
El Callao
El Dorado

VENEZUELA

La Gran
Sabana

Cerro
Marahuaca
2579

Cuao

RORAIMA

Orinoco

Puerto
Inírida

Mitú

Pico da
Neblina
3014

BRAZIL

AMAZONAS

Equator

COLOMBIA

Tumaco
Pasto
Florencia

Mocoa

Neiva

4686
5750
4560
Villavicencio
San José
del Ocune
Calamar
Mesa de
Yambí
Miraflores

Ibagué
BOGOTÁ

PANAMA
Panamá

COSTA
RICA
San José
Chirripó
3820
David
Volcán
Barú
3475
Chitré

NICARAGUA
Granada
Rama
San
Juan
Lago de
Nicaragua
Bluefields
Puerto Cabezas
Limón

South America

Scale 1 : 38 400 000

0 · · · 500 · · · 1000 · · · 1500 km

0 · · · 250 · · · 500 · · · 750 miles

Tropic of Cancer

ATLANTIC

OCEAN

Mid-Atlantic Ridge

I. Fernando de Noronha

Natal
João Pessoa
RECIFE
FORTALEZA
Maceió
Aracaju
SALVADOR

Barragem de Sobradinho

Chapada Diamantina

São Luís
Teresina

BELÉM
Mouths of the Amazon

Cayenne
Paramaribo
FRENCH GUIANA
SURINAM
Georgetown
GUYANA

Macapá

MANAUS

BRAZIL

Planalto do Mato Grosso

Pôrto Velho

Rio Branco

Boa Vista

3014 Pico da Neblina

VENEZUELA
Embalse de Guri
Orinoco
Meta
CARACAS
Boca Grande
Port of Spain
TRINIDAD AND TOBAGO
Isla La Tortuga
Isla de Margarita
GRENADA
ST. VINCENT & THE GRENADINES
BARBADOS
ST. LUCIA
Martinique (France)
DOMINICA
Guadeloupe (France)
Antigua
ANTIGUA AND BARBUDA
Barbuda
Montserrat (U.K.)
ST. KITTS-NEVIS
Virgin Is. (U.K.)
Anguilla (U.K.)
Virgin Is. (U.S.)
Puerto Rico (U.S.)
San Juan
8742
Puerto Rico Trench
Lesser Antilles
Netherlands Antilles
Aruba (Neth.)
Golfo de Venezuela
Lago de Maracaibo
Punta Gallinas

COLOMBIA
BOGOTÁ
5775 P. Cristóbal Colón
MEDELLÍN
CALI
5750
6310
QUITO
ECUADOR
GUAYAQUIL
Golfo de Guayaquil

Caquetá
Iquitos
PERÚ
Marañón

Cordillera Occidental
Cordillera Central
Cordillera Oriental

Negro
Amazonas (Amazon)
Madeira
Purus
Juruá
Ucayali

Guiana Highlands

Cordillera Oriental
Cusco
A
LIMA
Callao
Chimbote
Chiclayo
Trujillo

Islas Galápagos (Galápagos Is.) (Ecuador)

Isla de Malpelo (Colombia)

Isla del Coco (Costa Rica)

Equator

NORTH AMERICA
Managua
Tegucigalpa
San José
Golfo del Darién
Panamá
Isla de Providencia (Colombia)
Isla de San Andrés (Colombia)

THE BAHAMAS
Nassau
Cat I.
San Salvador
Long I.
Great Exuma
Acklins I.
Mayaguana
Great Inagua
Turks and Caicos Is. (U.K.)
DOMINICAN REP.
SANTO DOMINGO
3175 Duarte
PORT-AU-PRINCE
HAITI
Santiago de Cuba
Turquino 2005
Kingston
JAMAICA
Cayman Is. (U.K.)
CUBA
LA HABANA (HAVANA)
Isla de la Juventud
Swan Is. (Honduras)
Andros
Florida Keys
Straits of Florida
Yucatan Channel
I. de Cozumel

Caribbean Sea

Greater Antilles

Tropic of Cancer

80° W
70°
60°
50°
40°
20°
10°
0°
Equator
10°
20° N

© Copyright AND Cartographic Publishers Ltd.

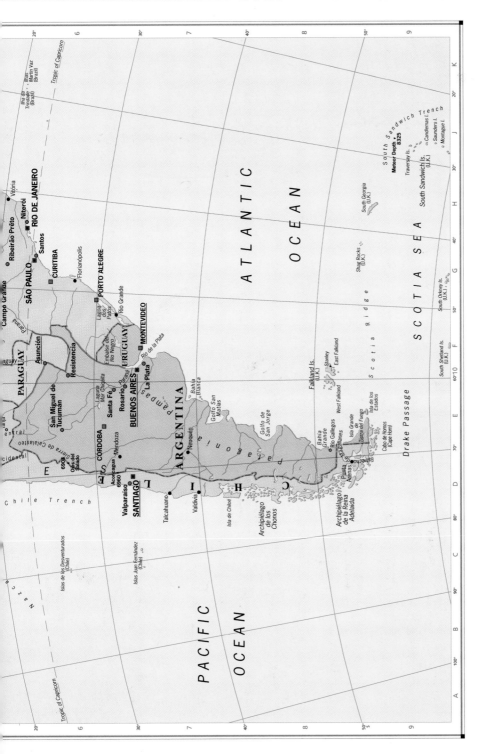

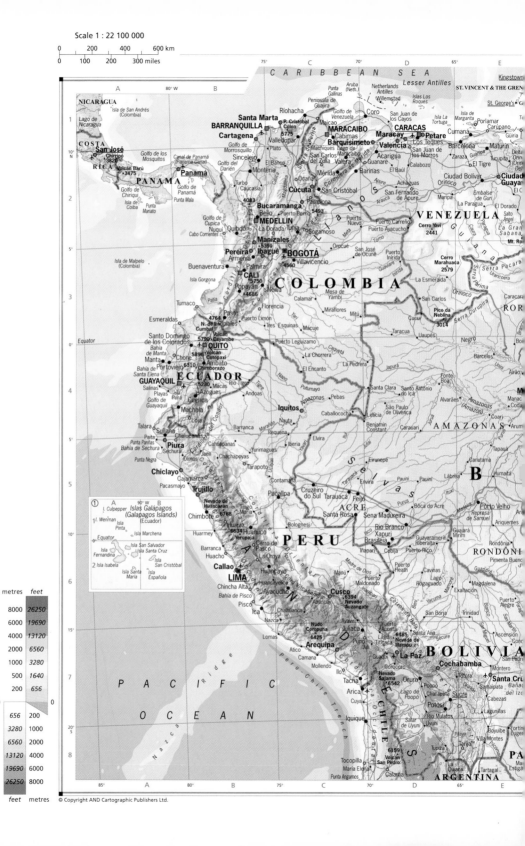

Scale 1 : 22 100 000

0   200   400   600 km

0   100   200   300 miles

metres feet

8000	26250
6000	19690
4000	13120
2000	6560
1000	3280
500	1640
200	656

0   0

656	200
3280	1000
6560	2000
13120	4000
19690	6000
26250	8000

feet   metres

© Copyright AND Cartographic Publishers Ltd.

CARIBBEAN SEA

Lesser Antilles

NICARAGUA

COSTA RICA

PANAMA

COLOMBIA

VENEZUELA

ECUADOR

PERU

BOLIVIA

CHILE

ARGENTINA

PACIFIC OCEAN

Islas Galápagos (Galapagos Islands) (Ecuador)

Scale 1 : 22 100 000

0   200   400   600 km
0   100   200   300 miles

metres *feet*

8000	*26250*
6000	*19690*
4000	*13120*
2000	*6560*
1000	*3280*
500	*1640*
200	*656*

0 — 0

656	200
3280	1000
6560	2000
13120	4000
19690	6000
26250	8000

feet metres

PERU

BOLIVIA

Cochabamba   Santa Cruz

La Paz

Sucre

Potosí

PA

Arequipa

Iquique

Antofagasta

Salta

San Miguel
de Tucumán

CHILE

Copiapó

Córdoba

CÓRDOBA   Rosa

La Serena
Coquimbo

San Juan

Cerro Aconcagua
6959

Viña del Mar
Valparaíso   SANTIAGO   Mendoza

ARGENTINA

PACIFIC

OCEAN

Concepción

Temuco

Valdivia

Osorno

Puerto Montt

Neuquén

Gen. Roca

Islas de los Desventurados
(Chile)
San Félix   San Ambrosio

Tropic of Capricorn

Isla
Robinson Crusoe

Islas Juan Fernández
(Chile)
Isla
Alejandro Selkirk

Archipiélago
de los

Chonos

Golfo de
San Jorge

Puerto Santa Cruz

Bahía
Grande

Río Gallegos

Archipiélago de
la Reina Adelaida

Punta Arenas

Tierra del Fuego

Drake Passag

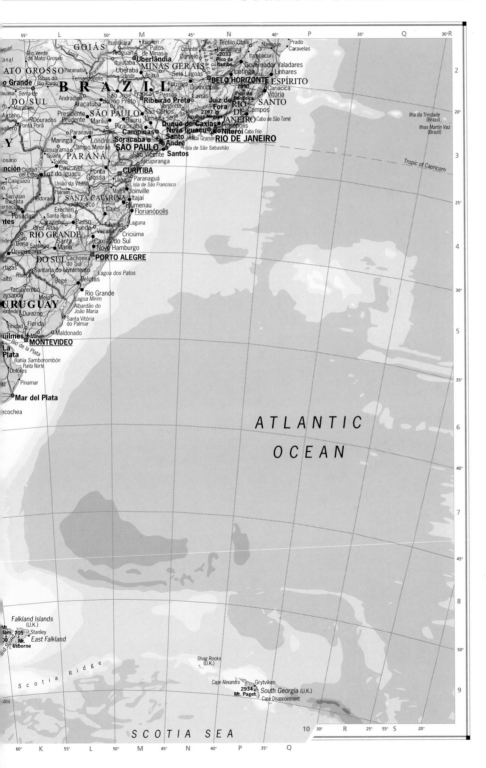

ATLANTIC

OCEAN

BRAZIL

MINAS GERAIS

BELO HORIZONTE ESPÍRITO

SÃO PAULO

RIO DE JANEIRO

CURITIBA

SANTA CATARINA

Florianópolis

RIO GRANDE

DO SUL

PORTO ALEGRE

URUGUAY

MONTEVIDEO

Mar del Plata

Tropic of Capricorn

Falkland Islands
(U.K.)
Stanley
East Falkland

Scotia Ridge

South Georgia (U.K.)

SCOTIA SEA

Arctic Ocean and Antarctica

Scale 1 : 69 500 000

0	500	1000	1500	2000
0	250	500	750	1000 miles

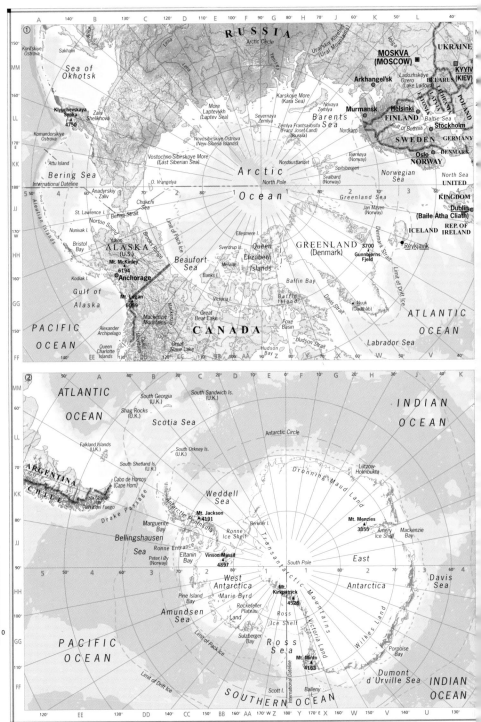

metres	feet
8000	26250
6000	19690
4000	13120
2000	6560
1000	3280
500	1640
200	656
0	0
656	200
3280	1000
6560	2000
13120	4000
19690	6000
26250	8000
feet	metres

© Copyright AND Cartographic Publishers Ltd.

is an alphabetical listing of the countries featured in the
▌d flags and statistics section which begins on page six of
tlas. Within the section the countries and flags are
▌ged within each continent in a north to south direction
▌ing easy comparision of any country with its neighbours.

Index

How to use the index

This is an alphabetically arranged index of the places and features that can be found on the maps in this atlas. Each name is generally indexed to the largest scale map on which it appears. If that map covers a double page, the name will always be indexed by the left-hand page number.

Names composed of two or more words are alphabetised as if they were one word.

All names appear in full in the index, except for 'St.' and 'Ste.', which although abbreviated, are indexed as though spelled in full.

Where two or more places have the same name, they can be distinguished from each other by the country or province name which immediately follows the entry. These names are indexed in the alphabetical order of the country or province.

Alternative names, such as English translations, can also be found in the index and are cross-referenced to the map form by the '=' sign. In these cases the names also appear in brackets on the maps.

Settlements are indexed to the position of the symbol, all other features are indexed to the position of the name on the map.

Abbreviations used in this index are explained in the list opposite.

Finding a name on the map

Each index entry contains the name, followed by a symbol indicating the feature type (for example, settlement, river), a page reference and a grid reference:

The grid reference locates a place or feature within a rectangle formed by the network of lines of longitude and latitude. A name can be found by referring to the red letters and numbers placed around the maps. First find the letter, which appears along the top and bottom of the map, and then the number, down the sides. The name will be found within the rectangle uniquely defined by that letter and number. A number in brackets preceding the grid reference indicates that the name is to be found within an inset map.

Abbreviations

Symbols

X	Continent name	↗	River, canal
A	Country name	◣	Lake, salt lake
a	State or province name	◤	Gulf, strait, bay
■	Country capital	◢	Sea, ocean
◫	State or province capital	▷	Cape, point
●	Settlement	⬚	Island or island group, rocky or coral reef
▲	Mountain, volcano, peak		
⛰	Mountain range	✳	Place of interest
⬚	Physical region or feature	⌘	Historical or cultural reg

X

Y